The Making of
Adolf Hitler

The Making of Adolf Hitler

The Birth and Rise of Nazism

Eugene Davidson

UNIVERSITY OF MISSOURI PRESS

COLUMBIA AND LONDON

Grateful acknowledgment is made to the Macmillan Publishing Company for permission to quote from Reck-Malleczewen's *Diary of a Man in Despair* and to S. Fischer Verlag to quote from the German edition of his *Tagebuch eines Verzweifelten*.

Library of Congress Cataloging-in-Publication Data

Davidson, Eugene, 1902–
    The making of Adolf Hitler: the birth and rise of Nazism / by
Eugene Davidson.
        p. cm.
    Originally published: New York : Macmillan, c1977.
    Includes bibliographical references and index.
    ISBN 0-8262-1117-8 (alk. paper)
    1. Hitler, Adolf, 1889–1945. 2. Heads of state—Germany—
Biography. 3. Germany—Politics and government—1918–1933.
4. Germany—Politics and government—1933–1945. 5. National
socialism—Germany. I. Title.
DD247.H5D38 1997
943.086'092—dc21
[B]   96-37316
                                                                CIP

♾ ™ This paper meets the requirements of the
American National Standard for Permanence of Paper
for Printed Library Materials, Z39.48, 1984.

Cover Designer: Kristie Lee
Typesetter: BOOKCOMP
Printer and binder: Thomson-Shore, Inc.
Typefaces: Friz Quadrata, Caledonia

For
SUZETTE MORTON DAVIDSON

Contents

Acknowledgments

It is a pleasure to express my gratitude to Fritz T. Epstein who despite the most adverse circumstances read the typescript of *The Making of Adolf Hitler*. Professor Epstein's knowledge of the time with which this book is concerned is that not only of a scholar but of one who experienced it at first hand and his criticisms have been invaluable.

I am indebted to my secretary, Maria Abbadi, for transcribing the complexities of the original manuscript and to Richard Meier of the University of Chicago for his careful checking of the references and notes. Fred Honig and the copy editors at Macmillan have been most helpful as have the staffs of the Regenstein Library at the University of Chicago and of the Institut für Zeitgeschichte in Munich.

The Making of
Adolf Hitler

CHAPTER 1

Austria

"In 1920 I MET HIM, a strange oddball, at the home of my friend Clemens zu Franckenstein, who was then living in the Lenbach villa. According to the butler, Anton, the man simply would not go away and had been waiting for an hour. And there he was! He had gotten into Clé's house (Clé, up to the time of the Revolution, had been general manager of the Royal Theater) by saying he was interested in operatic scene designing, which he apparently thought was related to his former profession of decorator and paperhanger. A still completely unknown outsider, he had arrived, so to speak, *en pleine carmagnole*, dressed up for his visit to the home of a man he had never met in riding leggings, a riding whip, and a slouch hat and accompanied by a shepherd dog. He looked, as a result, among the Gobelins and cool marble walls, very much like a cowboy who had thought it proper to appear in leather pants, enormous spurs, and a Colt to take a seat on the steps of a baroque altar. So, looking haggard and even a little starved, he sat there with the face of a stigmatized head-waiter, as delighted as he was inhibited to be in the presence of a real live *Herr Baron*, so awed he dared to sit uneasily on only half of his ascetic backside, snapping at the kindly but cool, incidental remarks of the host the way a starving cur goes at a piece of meat thrown to him. After some random talk he took over the conversation and began to preach like a division chaplain. Without any kind of argument from us, apparently in unconscious memory of the acoustics of the *Zirkus Krone*, he attained such a volume of bellowing that finally Franckenstein's household personnel, fearing a scene between host and guest, converged on the room to protect my friend. After he left, we sat together silently, helplessly, in no way amused but with the painful feeling one might have when the sole fellow traveller in a railroad compartment has turned out to be insane. We sat there a long time before we began to talk again. Finally, Clé stood up, opened one of the huge windows, and let in the foehn-warm spring air. I won't say that the dreary guest was unclean and in the country fashion of Bavaria had fouled the air. All the same, after a few deep breaths we were free of our depressing impressions. It was not an unclean body that had been in the room but rather the unclean spirit of a monster."[1]

This was the harsh and not entirely accurate judgment (Hitler had never been a decorator or paperhanger) of one contemporary of Adolf Hitler's, but many others who saw and heard him in those early days of his political life had a similar revulsion. Men of letters, soldiers, and politicians of both the Left and the Right expressed it, as did almost all the newspapers of the Reich with the exception of a few papers regarded by most Germans to be as crackpot as the National Socialist party paper, the *Völkischer Beobachter*. Even in 1928, after Hitler had been preaching his gospel of hate and salvation for nine years, the German electorate gave his party less than three percent (2.63 percent) of the total vote in the elections for the Reichstag. How then did this man who looked, as one observer said, like a beach photographer at some shabby resort, with little formal education and slim financial resources, come within a few years to be the mightiest man in Germany and, for a time, in the world? The answers to this question cannot be found in the character of the man alone or in some perverse kind of German miracle, and despite all that has been written, they are worth continuing investigation, because the riddle remains unexplained.

Adolf Hitler was born in one of the most provincial parts of a Germanic community that was itself a congeries of provinces. In writing of his father in *Mein Kampf*, Hitler described him as a man of the world, but the Austrian customs officer who had risen to middle-class officialdom from the shoemaker's trade was as far from that as were most of his neighbors. They were insular country people who lived in tight ethnic enclaves in the midst of a polyglot state and who looked with instant suspicion on anything or anyone who differed from them. They rejected not only Jews but all outsiders—Protestant Germans along with the Catholic Italians who shared Austria's high Tyrolean mountains, as well as the other regrettable nationalities who made up part of the Austro-Hungarian Empire: Poles, Czechs, Ladins, Slovenes, Croats, Serbs, Slovakians, Ruthenians, Walachians, and the rest.

The Dual Monarchy was made up essentially of a loose association of tribes, each inwardly territorial, bristling at any sign of another nationality's pretensions to power, which could only come about at the expense of one's own integrity and self-esteem. The peoples of Austria-

Hungary lived in an atmosphere of fierce tribal loyalties and conflicts, in a monarchy called Kaiserliche and Koenigliche; both an empire and a kingdom, since the emperor of Austria was also the king of Hungary, as well as the king of Bohemia, Dalmatia, Croatia, Slovenia, Jerusalem, and many other territories and the sovereign of over a dozen resident ethnic and religious minorities.

Austria had a long history of mixed peoples. Four hundred years before the birth of Christ, Celts had migrated there from Spain; Romans, Germans, a Tartar people called the Avars, and Slavs had all settled there and had left their imprint on the country and its later population even when they moved on. The German name for the Roman invaders was *Walsch*, or *Welsch*, and names like Walgau, Walchensee, and Seewalchen are related to what were Roman settlements. Slavic names are preserved in Feistritz (from *Bistrica* "fast water"), Fladnitz (from *Blatnica* "swamp water"), Liesing (from *Lesnica* "wood brook"), Görach (from *Gora* "mountain"), and Görtschak (from *Gorcia* "hill"). A Roman name like Anula became Anif; Lentia became Linz; Janiculum, Gnigl; and Cucullae, Kuchl. Salzburg was still known in the eighth century by its Latin name Juvavia as well as by its Germanic name. Vienna was called by the Romans Vindobona, from a similar Celtic name, and by the ninth century it was called Wenia, or Venia.

The villages in Lower Austria that the Hitlers, or Hiedlers, or Hüttlers (this name, too, had a number of variants) came from, along with the Schicklgrubers (meaning hedge diggers) and Pölzls on Hitler's maternal side, were, like most of the Austrian settlements, outwardly homogeneous: although non-Germanic elements were present, they were neither numerous nor conspicuous in comparison with the overwhelmingly German-speaking majority. But in these provinces, too, non-Germanic peoples had either intermarried with the Germans or, in a few cases, remained as undigested foreign bodies.

In Upper Austria, riots had occurred in Innsbruck when Adolf Hitler was fifteen years old. An Italian faculty had been approved for the law school of the University of Innsbruck (until the end of the eighteenth century, when it was replaced by German, Latin had been the language of instruction in Austrian universities); Italian students had met at an inn to celebrate the occasion; and in the course of counterdemonstrations, many of the Italians had been arrested and forty revolvers had been taken from them.[2] The German Austrians were always convinced of the need to defend their language and culture against the aliens around them even though they were often related to them.[*]

---

[*] The *Salzburger Lokal Anzeiger*, for example, on July 7, 1902, reported on "a devilish plan" to establish a Czech university in Brünn in Bohemia and on the Czechs' attempts to slavify the Alpine provinces. The *Deutsche Tiroler Stimmen* on March 27, 1907, published some verses of "The Song of the Germans in Austria":

Adolf Hitler had a great-uncle, who was perhaps a grandfather on both his maternal and paternal sides, named Nepomuk,* and the name Hitler is possibly of Czech origin, Germanized from Hidlar or Hidlarček. And although Adolf Hitler and thousands of his countrymen would always cherish the image of the tall, blond, blue-eyed German as the archetype of the Teutonic family to which they belonged, not very many of them resembled this reverenced figure. Hitler was what the anthropologists of his time described as an Alpine type, of obviously mixed blood, with brown hair and of medium stature; only his blue eyes matched the idealized *Urbild.*

Hitler's father, Alois, had come a long way up the social and economic scale by the time his children were born. Alois Hitler was the illegitimate son of Maria Anna Schicklgruber, a native of the tiny village of Strones, who bore him when she was forty-two years old. She was a hardworking woman who supported herself by doing domestic work. Neither she nor her husband, Johann Georg Hiedler, whom she married when she was forty-seven years old, ever lived in a house of their own, although Maria Anna was not impecunious. At the time of Alois's birth, her small inheritance from her mother came to 168 gulden, a little less than half the money it took to buy a small farm, and her parents' farmstead was worth the considerable sum of 3,000 gulden. Johann Georg Hiedler, a millworker, however, was impoverished all his life. Why he married Maria Anna five years after she bore her (and perhaps his) child, whom he never legally acknowledged or cared for in his lifetime, leads to interesting speculation. At any rate, Alois remained illegitimate during the lifetime of Johann Georg Hiedler and long after his alleged father's death; and although illegitimacy in Austria and southern Germany, as in other parts of the Roman Catholic world, did not have the stigma attached to it in more puritanical regions (40 percent of the children born in Lower Austria at the time were illegitimate and were usually legitimatized at a later date), it was a condition that seldom of itself led to communal preferment.† Alois Hitler, or Schicklgruber, as he remained until his fortieth year, had a long, hard road to take before he became a respected official of the Customs Service of the Kaiserliche and Koenigliche monarchy. At nineteen he had managed, with only an elementary school education, to leave a shoemaker's apprenticeship that

"We brought morality to this land / Against Welsch, Czechs, Poles we remain on guard."

* A name taken by many Germans of the region.

† Alois himself was the father of an illegitimate son, born to Franziska Matzelsberger in 1882. He married her a year later, and she died a year after that, in August 1884. Adolf Hitler's mother, Klara Pölzl, a relation of Alois's who had joined the household during Franziska's illness to help with the chores, was probably also pregnant by Alois before they were married in 1885.

he had entered on when he was only fourteen and to join the Customs Service, where he stayed until his early retirement at the age of fifty-nine. He had risen steadily in the Customs Service and had done as well as any of his colleagues who had earned their *Abitur* at a *Gymnasium*, which he could not have dreamed of attending. He had been assigned to a number of posts in Upper Austria; in Saalfelden near Salzburg, in Linz, and in Braunau am Inn, where he had been controller of the customs and where Adolf was born.

Alois Hitler was intensely proud of his career (he had once written to a relative of his mother's, "Since you last saw me 16 years ago . . . I have risen very high,"[3]) and of his place in village society, where he was esteemed as a progressive thinker and a reliable patron of the taverns, although he drank only beer and wine in moderate amounts. As an outward symbol of his worthiness, he wore the same kind of beard his kaiser, Franz Josef, did, and on occasions such as the emperor's birthday he appeared in the full uniform he was entitled to wear as an official in the imperial service.

Who Alois's father was is not known. The most bizarre story is that related by Hans Frank, a devoted follower of Adolf Hitler, legal advisor to the National Socialist party in the course of its violent rise to power, and later governor-general of Poland. In 1930 Frank was commissioned by Adolf Hitler to investigate the mystery of Alois Hitler's birth because of the ugly rumors of a non-Aryan stain on Hitler's family tree. Frank wrote in Nuremberg, before his execution, that stories spread by a "stepbrother" of Adolf Hitler's to the effect that the Führer had Jewish blood in his veins were being published around 1930 in various papers.[*]

In his investigations, Frank discovered, or thought he had discovered, that Fräulein Schicklgruber had worked in the household of Jews named Frankenberger in Graz, in Lower Austria, and that the father of the child she bore could have been the young son of the family she worked for. Frank wrote that the Frankenbergers had paid Fräulein Schicklgruber an *aliment*, that is, support for her child, until he was fourteen years old, and that after she left their employ she had continued a friendly correspondence with the family for many years.

But this story does not stand up under scrutiny. Frankenberger, it has been pointed out, is not a Jewish name, and the only people bearing it

---

[*] The "stepbrother" Frank refers to was Patrick Hitler, a son of Adolf Hitler's half brother, who, like their father, was named Alois. Patrick, whose mother was British, was an impecunious young man, chronically out of funds and alert to opportunities to raise money, whether from his uncle or anyone else. Adolf Hitler would have little to do with him. Patrick did write an account of his renowned uncle in the *Paris Soir* in 1939, and he had also been interviewed on the subject by various English papers, but no evidence has come to light that he wrote any article for any newspaper in which he said that Hitler had a Jewish grandfather. What he did say in *Paris Soir* was that Adolf Hitler's niece, Geli Raubal, with whom Adolf Hitler was deeply in love, was pregnant by him in 1932. (Werner Maser, *Adolf Hitler*, p. 36.)

in Graz were Catholic. Moreover, they had no son who could have fathered Alois. The Frankenbergers' son was younger than Alois.

Where Frank got this account and why he published it in his book *In the Shadow of the Gallows* are not known either. Frank, the man who at Nuremberg said, "A thousand years shall pass and this guilt of Germany shall not have been erased," had been one of the most fanatical anti-Semites among all the Nazis, and although in Nuremberg he had fully acknowledged his guilt for his and the party's grievous past, it may be that he wanted to implicate the Jews to some degree in their own genocide. It is also possible that he believed the story told him. There were a number of rumors of Adolf Hitler's Jewish ancestry in circulation, and no matter how preposterous they were, a good many people who heard them wanted to believe they were true. One man, Josef Greiner, who claimed he knew and who certainly disliked Hitler, said the name came from *Hut* ("hat" or "guard") and was therefore, like all Jewish names, a construct.

An article appeared on October 14, 1933, in the London *Daily Mirror* accompanied by a picture of a gravestone in a Jewish cemetery in Bucharest with a Hebrew inscription and the name Adolf Hittler on it, supposedly that of a grandfather of the Führer. This Hitler, however, before he was buried at the expense of a Jewish philanthropic society, had changed his name from Avraham Eliyohn and was therefore not the best of evidence for a Jewish Hitler. Nevertheless, there were in fact Jews who bore that name in eastern Europe, although no records are known to exist of any having migrated to Austria, or, if they did, of their having any connection with the Hiedlers or Hüttlers.

A much more plausible conjecture is that, not Johann Georg, but his brother Johann Nepomuk was the father of Alois Hitler. Johann Nepomuk was a prosperous farmer in whose house Alois was brought up until he was sixteen years old. It was through Nepomuk that Alois was legitimatized in June 1876, nineteen years after Johann Georg's death, by the testimony of three witnesses, none of whom could read or write and who therefore made crosses on the depositions the priest had written for them.* They testified that Johann Georg had recognized his paternity before his death in 1857 in their presence and so enabled the priest in Döllersheim, with the approval of his ecclesiastical superiors and the civil authorities, to grant the legitimation under the name of Hitler. Apparently the priest misunderstood the pronunciation of the name Hiedler, or more likely Hüttler, and wrote Hitler by mistake.

There are many indications that Nepomuk was the father of Alois. One of them is his solicitude for the boy, his readiness to have him as a member of his household, a step that must have been approved by Nepomuk's

---

* Compulsory education was introduced in Austria in May 1869.

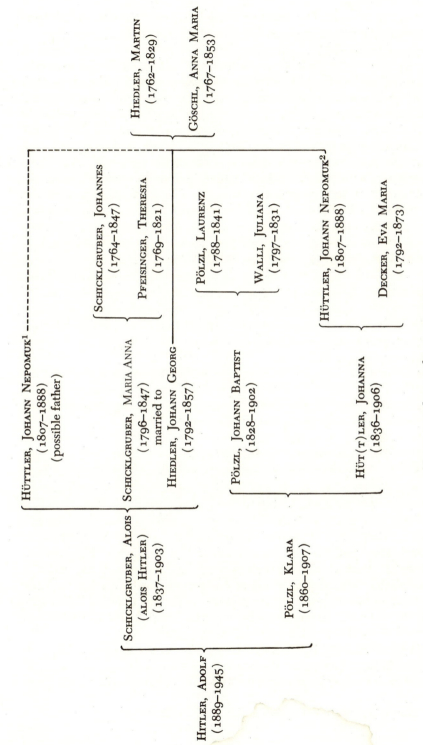

HÜTTLER, JOHANN NEPOMUK[1]
(1807–1888)
(possible father)

HIEDLER, MARTIN
(1762–1829)

GÖSCHL, ANNA MARIA
(1767–1853)

SCHICKLGRUBER, JOHANNES
(1764–1847)

PFEISINGER, THERESIA
(1769–1821)

SCHICKLGRUBER, MARIA ANNA
(1796–1847)
married to
HIEDLER, JOHANN GEORG
(1792–1857)

PÖLZL, LAURENZ
(1788–1841)

WALLI, JULIANA
(1797–1831)

HÜTTLER, JOHANN NEPOMUK[2]
(1807–1888)

DECKER, EVA MARIA
(1792–1873)

SCHICKLGRUBER, ALOIS
(ALOIS HITLER)
(1837–1903)

PÖLZL, JOHANN BAPTIST
(1828–1902)

HÜT(T)LER, JOHANNA
(1836–1906)

PÖLZL, KLARA
(1860–1907)

HITLER, ADOLF
(1889–1945)

NOTE: 1 and 2 are the same person

wife, a strong-minded woman fifteen years older than he, who might well have had a violent reaction had Nepomuk openly acknowledged Alois as his son. Another piece of circumstantial evidence is the fact that Johann Georg, when he did marry Maria Anna Schicklgruber five years after the birth of her son, did not then or later recognize him as his own child. Why should he have married a forty-seven-year-old woman and yet not have adopted their child if it was indeed his own? Further, Alois's mother had not named Johann Georg as the father either when Alois was baptized or when she was married, although following the local mores she would ordinarily have done both. In addition, in 1888, the year Nepomuk died, Alois Hitler bought a sizeable house and property near Spital worth 4,000 gulden. Nepomuk bequeathed nothing to his expectant heirs, and up to that time Alois had made no purchases on such a scale, nor would he have readily done so on his customs official's salary. It seems not unlikely that Nepomuk had convinced his impecunious brother to marry Maria Anna and thus enable Nepomuk to bring up the boy in his own house and eventually to have him legitimatized. But this, too, is conjecture.

What is certain is that there was incest in Adolf Hitler's parentage. Alois Hitler married Klara Pölzl, whose maternal grandfather was Johann Nepomuk Hüttler, so that if Nepomuk was Alois's father, he was Adolf Hitler's paternal grandfather and maternal great-grandfather. And even though, not Nepomuk, but Johann Georg was legally named as the father of Alois, when Alois and Klara married, they had to obtain a special dispensation from Rome because of their close familial relationship.

It is small wonder that Alois Hitler, brought up among unlettered people and owing his middle-class position in society mainly to his own strenuous efforts to educate himself and get ahead, spurred his sons to continue on his path of upward mobility. Three of his children, two sons and a daughter, died in infancy, and another son died at six years of age. Four children survived: Adolf; his sister, Paula; a half sister, Angela; and a half brother, Alois. The father was so ambitious for his sons, so insistent that they maintain the family's middle-class status, that he drove Alois from home when the boy was fourteen. Young Alois thereupon set out on a career of sporadic employment as a waiter and itinerant worker. He was twice arrested for theft. He later lived in Paris and Ireland, where he married and where his son Patrick was born. He was again imprisoned, this time in Hamburg for bigamy. And finally, after his half brother became chancellor, he opened up a restaurant called Alois in Berlin.

Hitler's father did not have much more luck in making Adolf a respectable student than he had had with Alois. Adolf was too much like his father to be a compliant son and do what his elders expected of him;

he, too, was stubborn and single-minded, but in a direction opposite from his father's. He wrote in *Mein Kampf* that he knew as a schoolboy what he wanted to be—a painter—and he knew even more clearly what he did not want, which was to follow in his father's footsteps. Adolf had done very well in the *Volkschule*, which he attended for five years; it was only when he arrived unwillingly at the *Realschule* in Linz and then in Steyr—schools he resisted as obstinately as his father urged him on—that he did badly in his studies. Adolf had to repeat his first year at the Linz *Realschule*; in his third year he failed French and had to take a make-up examination before he could start his fourth year in another *Realschule* in Steyr. In Steyr, at midterm in February 1905, Hitler failed German, French, mathematics, and stenography; years later he said that for the first and last time in his life, as the end of the semester was celebrated at a local inn, he got drunk, and in the course of the evening used his school report mistakenly for toilet paper. In any event, final marks for the school year 1904–1905 improved, but that was the last of his schooling.[4] In all, Adolf spent ten years in school, finishing nine classes and staggering through the last four.

Adolf saw little of his father before or after Alois's retirement. His father was away from home a good deal, at his customs post, pursuing his passion for beekeeping, or spending his evenings at the tavern, and when the two did meet they would readily quarrel over Adolf's deplorable marks at school. Hitler refers to his father dutifully in *Mein Kampf* as "the old gentleman" and as a "man of the world," and his father's position as a civil functionary was something he could reject and be proud of at the same time. Hitler's boyhood friend August Kubizek* reports that Adolf in their talks continually emphasized the importance of his father's status, and another memorialist, Josef Greiner, wrote that when Adolf was seeking admission to the Academy of Art, he thought his chances were good because the professors there were government officials like his father. But the idea of following a career like his father's was utterly abhorrent. Adolf dreamed of far greater things he would accomplish without the tiresome preliminaries.

Adolf was much closer to his mother, who, however, could no more than her husband persuade him of the need for doing well at the *Realschule*. Alois Hitler died when Adolf was thirteen years old, and Gustav Kubizek describes Adolf's bitter grief at the loss of his father. Nevertheless, his emotions must have been mixed with a welcome sense of relief from his father's nagging, and Hitler did, in the end, succeed in winning his battle against the *Realschule*. Two years after Alois's death, Hitler's mother permitted him to leave school. He had fallen ill of a providential illness that kept him at home for weeks. What his sickness was is not

---

* Kubizek wrote that Hitler disliked the name August and called him either Gustav (which he sometimes spelled with a *v* and sometimes with *ph*) or Gustl.

known precisely; Hitler calls it a pulmonary disease, and one doctor who never saw him thinks it may have been encephalitis.[5] At any rate the illness sprung him from the obnoxious school, and he was able to do nothing in the way of useful work—bread-and-butter work as he called it—for two years.

Klara Pölzl was an indulgent mother; she demanded little of Adolf, and in return he seems to have been as devoted to her as it was possible for him to be. In 1906 she allowed him first to visit Vienna for two months and later to live there, until she became too ill to manage her household and take care of her daughter Paula. That Hitler reciprocated her affection is evidenced from the fact that, if Kubizek is to be believed, when he came back to Linz he took over all the household chores (Angela had married in 1903), washing, cooking, cleaning, and scrubbing the floor, as well as supervising Paula's schoolwork. This story, too, may be apocryphal, for Klara Pölzl's sister Johanna was available to help with the housework, as was Angela.

He had cool but friendly relationships with his sister and half sister; a few years later, after their mother's death, he renounced in Paula's favor his share of the government allowance paid them when they became orphans. Although he would not live with Angela and her family because of his intense dislike of her husband, he would one day call on her to manage his establishment at Berchtesgaden; and it was her daughter Geli who was to become the great love of his life.

What Hitler did learn while he was at the *Realschule* that became a far more lasting part of his intellectual baggage than the French course he had to repeat or any other of the subjects taught him were the fundamentals of his lifelong anti-Semitism. In *Mein Kampf* Hitler wrote that before he first went to Vienna he had had no particular feelings of animosity toward the Jews, and that he had never heard the word *Jew* before he was fourteen or fifteen years old; up to that time he had simply regarded them as Germans. It was in Vienna, he wrote, that the sight of the *Handelee*, the Jewish pedlar from eastern Europe with his long side-locks, caftan, and wide-brimmed hat, so distressed him that he began to read anti-Semitic pamphlets, which set him on the road to the consuming passion of his political career, and in fact of his entire life—his hatred of the Jews.

The story is apocryphal. Hitler was anti-Semitic long before he reached Vienna. Most of the teachers and many of the students in the Linz *Realschule* were Pan-Germans, German Nationalists, followers, as was Alois Hitler, of Georg von Schönerer, a fanatical believer in a German Austria without the Habsburgs that would include the German Sudetenland, exclude Hungary, and be part of the German Reich. Schönerer, like Alois Hitler, came from Lower Austria; he was a leader in the mystical confederation known as the *völkisch* movement, whose followers believed the troubles of the industrial order—the harshness, the impersonality, the sharp dealing, the ruthless speculators—would only be exorcised by a return to Ur-Germanism, to the German community, the ancient Teutonic gods, and a Germanic society unsullied by inferior, foreign intrusions. Nations might endure such foreign elements, but a *Volk* was an organic unity with a common biological inheritance. *The* culture-bearing *Volk* of the world, incomparably superior among the races, was the German; therefore, the only proper function of a German state was to administer on behalf of the *Volk*; everything international was inferior and to be rejected. A sound economy would be based on agriculture rather than on industry with its international, especially Jewish influences; and in religion, a German God would have to replace the Jewish God.* Consequently, Schönerer and his followers were anti-Catholic, anti-Semitic, and often ludicrous. In the course of his crusade on behalf of Wotan, Schönerer shouted "Heil!" in the *Reichsrat*, and in words the Nazis would later echo, he denounced the Jew as the *Todfeind*—the deadly enemy. Among the slogans he adopted was *"Los von Rom"* ("Away from Rome"), but he nevertheless led what was called the United Christian party (*die Vereinigten Christen*) until 1888. In that year he was sentenced to jail for his wild behavior after he stormed into the offices of *Das Neue Wiener Tageblatt* to beat up the "Jewish" editors for prematurely publishing the death notice of the German emperor, Wilhelm I. After a four-month term in prison and the loss of his title of nobility, Schönerer became head of a small splinter group, the Pan-German (*Alldeutsche*) party.

Schönerer's ideas were widely shared in Linz, and the only teacher Adolf Hitler seems to have admired in the *Realschule* was Leopold Poetsch, a Schönerer disciple. Poetsch taught history, one of the three subjects, along with drawing and physical training, in which Hitler got above-average marks. Like almost all his colleagues Poetsch was a Great German† and a reader of the Schönerer illustrated monthly published in Innsbruck, *Der Scherer*. This was a satirical publication that regularly published anti-Catholic and anti-Semitic articles with drawings of fat priests and big-nosed Jews, the prototype of the Jewish image that would reappear in the National Socialist *Stürmer*.

A good many such anti-Semitic journals and newspapers were pub-

---

* In some *völkisch* versions Jesus was "Aryanized." Adolf Lanz, for example, called him *Frauja*.

† Up to 1866, to be a Great German in Austria was to favor Austrian leadership among the German states. After Prussia defeated Austria to become the dominant state in the Germanic region of Europe, the Great Germans believed Prussia to be the power ordained to lead the Pan-German movement. Their hero was Bismarck, and they were for the most part anticlerical and anti-Semitic and, in varying degrees, *völkisch*.

lished in Austria-Hungary, which was one of the minor but nevertheless important centers of anti-Semitism in Europe. *Völkisch* anti-Semitism was merely one variety that flourished among many forms, political, economic, religious, and social. The activist countries were tsarist Russia and Poland, where pogroms became endemic; but Austria, in a relatively modest and mainly nonviolent fashion, ranked high on the anti-Semitic scale. Anti-Jewish measures were not new. In December 1821, all the Jews in Karlsbad had been expelled from the city, and in Reichenberg, aside from temporarily exempted Jewish merchants, all Jews were ordered to clear out of the city. Those permitted to remain were not allowed to rent quarters to other Jews; on market days, all transients had to be sent to authorized inns, and after three days they, too, were required to leave the town. No private persons were permitted to lodge Jews.[6] Again in 1836, fourteen Jews were exiled from Karlsbad, and two years later ten more were told to leave the city within forty-eight hours.[7] In 1895 the anti-Semitic leader of the Christian Social party, Karl Lueger, was elected mayor of Vienna, an office he assumed, however, only in 1897, because the emperor, Franz Josef, twice vetoed his taking the position. Lueger's anti-Semitic and anti-Czech views appealed to a large section of Vienna's population, and since in addition he undertook an ambitious series of public works and reforms, he was steadily reelected until his death in 1910. The city government under Lueger took over the British-owned electric works, the gasworks, and the street car services; and one of the standard justifications for such measures that the voters found convincing was that the utilities were controlled by Jews, who shamelessly exploited the rest of the population. Lueger, although the higher clergy expressed reservations as to his purposes, was a professing Catholic, and he was thus able as a politician to combine socialist reforms with a stern orthodoxy in religious and ethnic questions. Schönerer with his *Los von Rom* principles was considered by his followers as more progressive than Lueger, but what the two had ineluctably in common was the belief that Jews were the chief source of the ills of Austria.

Hitler, whose mind had not been greatly occupied by his schoolwork, was certainly exposed to *Der Scherer,* which was on sale in Linz as it was all over Austria, and he was also an attentive reader of the *Linzer Fliegender Blätter,* another of the Pan-German, anti-Semitic papers available there. The first number of the *Scherer* appeared in May 1899, a month it called *Noreja* after the site of the victory of the Teutonic tribes over the Roman legions. *Noreja* was one of the words the *Scherer* and other *völkisch* papers would dig up to refurbish the heroic Teutonic heritage, although German words later came to be preferred over any others, even those commemorating great military victories. Every month had its Germanic name in the *völkisch* publications: in place of *Noreja* they substituted *Wonnemonat* ("month of delight") for May, and used *Gilbhart* ("hard yellow") for October, *Nebelung* ("mist") for November, and *Brachmond* ("fallow moon") for June. This was the positive, or quasi-religious, pole of the *völkisch* movement; at the negative, demonic pole, the *Scherer* supported violent revolution when, in its *völkisch* anxiety to get rid of anti-Germanic forces, it backed the anarchists, Marxists, and other left-wing revolutionaries against the tsar's government. *Der Scherer* supported old Catholicism against the new Catholicism's tolerance of the Jews, and the pantheon of the *Nibelungenlied* against the Judeo-Christian God; and for many Pan-Germans, it stood for absolute truth when it wrote: "We are the blond race of the north. We are the noble people of the world."[8]

Der Scherer attacked Jews and priests separately and together. One picture showed a Jew and a priest sitting heavily on a mound of protesting, squirming victims, who were the *Volk*. Another depicted a Jew and a priest being carried off by a noble knight, with the caption: "Must we always have to deal with these two?" Another showed the Devil with hellfire burning in the background and a sign saying, "Spa for Jews and Jesuits." The *Scherer* published a number of illustrations that were previews of the *Stürmer*'s later attacks on the supposed sexual habits of Jews. The first in one series of pictures (January 5, 1902) shows one Isaac Goldbaum hiring a Christian girl; in the next frame the girl is again in Goldbaum's office, this time holding a baby, and he says, "Ain't I a noble man? I haven't thrown you out and you have the bonus I promised you. Do you want another?"

The *Scherer* was read not only in Austria but also in France and England, so it was able to publish letters of approval from the editor of *Chrétien Français* and from *Le Siècle*, as well as from a cross section of devoted readers, including *Gymnasium* and middle (lower secondary) school students. One contributor signed himself Adolf, but he was almost certainly not the future author of *Mein Kampf*. The *Scherer* carried some of the decor and many slogans of the future National Socialists: it used a swastika as an arcane symbol of Germanism, and words and phrases like *Volksgenossen* ("Folk Comrades"), *Heil*, "Our People Awake," "Buy Only from Germans," and even "One Volk, One God, One Reich," which, with the change of one word, would be heard again when Hitler took power in Germany.

The *Scherer* was no voice crying in the wilderness. Daily papers, too, published blistering attacks on the Jews, which could have been published word for word decades later as Nazi party literature or Adolf Hitler's speeches. A letter in the *Vorarlberger Volksfreund* of February 4, 1905, used the identical phrase that would close the letters of many good National Socialists in the 1920s and the 1930s: "With German greeting." *Die Tiroler Stimmen, Die Tiroler Post, Die Linzer Post, Die Wiener*

Montags Post, and dozens of other newspapers* regularly attacked the Jews who were—everywhere, they said—gnawing at the roots of the economy and of the ancient Germanic virtues. Like the National Socialists to come, the Austrian anti-Semitic papers seldom left escape hatches for the Jews. Despite the formal position of the Church, many Catholics as well as Schönerers believed that baptized Jews were still Jews and often more dangerous than unbaptized ones. The *völkisch* anticlericals linked Jews with the reactionary Church, the clerical anti-Semites linked them with the *völkisch* heathens, and both sides joined in denouncing them for undercutting the living and quality of work of guild members, workers, and shopkeepers. Jews were, depending on the particular counterimage, either godless socialists or capitalist exploiters, proponents of Manchester liberalism, and the hidden, international rulers of financial and intellectual life. They operated everywhere; the murder of President McKinley in the United States was attributed by *Der Tiroler* to a Jewish anarchist (January 3, 1905).

The universal fear and dislike of the foreigner had been raised to a high pitch, in the case of the Jew, when Christianity conquered the heathen gods. The followers of the Prince of Peace brought not peace but a sword. The Church and the devout Christian in the Middle Ages saw in the Jew the Devil, who was in fact often drawn with the features of a Jew. This medieval tradition never completely faded away; *Die Tiroler Post*, a Christian Social paper, on March 7, 1903, told again the story of the murder of a Christian child by Jews in the fifteenth century while at the same time warning its readers against the "Jewification" (*Verjudung*) of the Tyrol. This Catholic paper wrote what Hitler himself would often repeat, that the goal of the Jew was world domination, that he was the carrier of the bacillus of destruction, and it quoted the *Linzer Post* approvingly for having written that anti-Semitism "is no more than the healthy egotism of people to permit their self-preservation."[9] The secular attacks could be more furious than these. The *völkisch Deutsche Tiroler Stimmen* told its readers on March 7, 1906, that Jews slaughtered not only animals but also members of the human race, and on May 30, 1906, it wrote that the Jewish race had to be exterminated. The paper wrote of the "bestial brutality" (*bestialische Grausamkeit*) of the race and of how Jews, "predatory beasts in human form always ready to throw themselves on the Aryan people," killed women and children. On May 11, 1907, the same paper explained that Jews could not be changed by baptism; in fact, when they did become Christians, and in some cases priests and even bishops, they did this only to subvert the true doctrine and confuse the faithful. Such spurious conversions and profes-

---

* *Der Kyffhäuser* (Linz), *Freie Deutsche Schule* (Vienna), *Der Hammer* (Eger), *Grazer Wochenblatt*, and *Neue Bahnen* (Vienna) are mentioned in a long list cited by André Banuls in the April 1970 *Vierteljahrshefte für Zeitgeschichte*.

sions to the priesthood had occurred, the paper said, in Spain, and they were obviously recurring in Austria, where in 1904 one Archbishop Kohn was accused of such malpractices as violating the confessional, engaging in shady financial deals, and making money while pursuing his religious vocation. Archbishop Kohn, the anti-Semitic papers reported, had been summoned to Rome to account for his sins, and the pope had absolved him from wrongdoing.*

Such accounts were used to confirm the anti-Semitism of the Christian Social papers defending Austrian Catholics, to confirm the malpractices of the economic liberals, and to fuel the anti-Semitism of the *völkisch* papers. On May 30, 1906, *Die Deutsche Tiroler Stimmen*, like the *Scherer*, linked the secret politics of the Jesuits and the Jews in a conspiracy for world domination. Lengthy case histories in Austrian newspapers told stories of crafty Jewish duplicity. In Innsbruck the Christian Social *Tiroler Post*, for example, on August 5, 1903, complained that a Jewish-owned store had had a window display of Croation folk costumes, and said that such effrontery would result in a short time in the disappearance of the Tyrolean costumes worn by Innsbruck women and girls. The Jewish owner of the store replied that he had neither Croation nor Tyrolean costumes for sale, but denials never had the slightest effect on the people who wrote the articles or on those who wanted to believe them. The cases were always cited as examples of the "Jewification" of Austrian life, and as soon as one was explained, another took its place. The Jews were regularly accused of underselling Austrian merchants, a charge that was often true, but the practice was obviously condoned by the people who bought the goods they wanted more cheaply than they would otherwise have done. Nevertheless, such stories documented the accusation that the Jews were undermining the standards of the Germanic guilds and crafts and that what the Jews wanted was a free market, which would put them at the head of the plunderers and destroyers of Austrian life. The Jew was gaining a sinister ascendancy, said the *Tiroler Post* on December 9, 1903, again reciting passages from the litany: he watered wine, he sold fuel at lower costs by exploiting the workers, and he seduced his female employees. It was not individuals who did these things, as in cases where Christians sinned, but the entire race, all Jews.

Stories of death and disaster were common then as now. The *Lienzer Zeitung* of January 7, 1905, ran the account of a woman who was having an affair with her brother-in-law and who had tried to kill her husband by mixing lead in his food. She had not succeeded in this, but she did

---

* Theodor Kohn, prince-archbishop of Olmütz from 1892–1904, had the rank of prince, and as such was entitled to sit in the upper chamber of the *Reichsrat*, which, on the English model, consisted of Houses of Lords and Commons. In 1904 he lost his office. (Hugo Hantsch, *Die Geschichte Oesterreichs*, vol. 2, p. 360.)

kill their child and burn down the family barn. For these crimes she
was sentenced to ten years' imprisonment.

The *Salzburger Tagblatt* of January 13, 1905, told how a Hungarian
count, Paul Čzapary, who had been president of the Park Club in Budapest, had absconded with funds belonging to the city. One of the richest
men of the aristocracy, the paper said, he had lost immense sums at
gambling, and his wife, who had 10 million marks in her own name, had
refused to pay his debts. Čzapary had fled to Paris and taken a job in
the *wagons-lits*. In no such accounts were any inferences drawn as to
the effect of race, class, or religion on the criminal. These were stories
of an individual's crimes and were left at that. But criminal or shady
transactions on the part of a Jew were recounted in the anti-Semitic
press as examples of the criminality of an entire people.*

Die Tiroler Post and other anti-Semitic papers gave a good deal of
space to the publication of the book *Die Grundlagen des 19 Jahrhunderts*
(*The Foundations of the Nineteenth Century*) by the English-born anti-
Semite Houston Stuart Chamberlain, who had demonstrated among other
things that Christ had been not a Jew but an Aryan.† Large sections of
Die Grundlagen were reprinted, along with favorable commentaries. All
the papers carried frequent reports on the pogroms occurring year after
year in Russia, and here too, in the articles in the anti-Semitic press, the
slaughtered Jews were depicted as the aggressors and killers. One report,
following pogroms at Homel and Kishinev, justified the action by declaring that Jews had shot at the tsar's soldiers from behind hedges and had
committed other cowardly deeds, which had brought on their well-de-
served punishment.[10]

Thus young Hitler had a number of choices as to which brand of anti-
Semitism he would adopt. He had a solid religious background, as well
as a Schönerer father. He had served at mass and sung in the choir connected with the ancient Benedictine abbey at Lambach near Linz when
he was nine years old, and for a time had thought of some day becoming
an abbot. But it was neither the theological nor the political anti-Semitism that would take possession of Adolf; rather, he would combine them,
as he combined much of what he read and thought, with the *völkisch*
view of the Jews, which considered them unredeemable no matter what
they did. The Jew became for him what Eric Voegelin has called the
counterimage, a projection of everything that is wrong with a man and
his society, a picture that will be the more cherished the more its holder

---

* The Jewish crime rate in Austria was on the whole relatively low, but their rate
of misdemeanors and malefactions linked to usury, illegal bankruptcy, and fraud was
high, in fact, twice that of the general population. (William A. Jenks, *Vienna and
the Young Hitler*.)

† Chamberlain lived in Vienna for twenty years and wrote his major books in
German.

is uncertain of his own powers and his ability to attain what he feels he is entitled to. The counterimage is the anti-ideal, the successful enemy who embodies vices intolerable to one's persona. Like the portrait of Dorian Gray, the counterimage can take on the lineaments of a man's own iniquities, leaving him unsullied by them. It is because of this enemy enshrined in the counterimage that the heart's desire remains unachieved; it is he who blocks the way to the worldly and spiritual comforts of those who, by their own singular virtues, deserve them. In Austria, in a time of massive economic and social change, when thousands of tradespeople were struggling for survival against the severe competition made possible by great concentrations of capital, it was the Jews, in the eyes of the small businessmen, who were the operators, the overbearing owners of the big department stores* and factories, the unfair competitors; just as it was the Jews, in the eyes of the rank and file of the anti-Semites, who were the speculators, bankers, plutocrats, radicals, aliens—in short, the source of the disillusionment of all those who saw a flourishing life out of their reach with no means of attaining it, and of those who had such a life and believed it in peril.

Young Hitler, like other adolescents who drop out of school, lost himself readily in such counterimages and in fantasies. When he bought a ticket for the state lottery, he assumed he had already won the main prize and made elaborate plans as to how he would spend the money. When the unbelievable happened and he won nothing, he told Kubizek that the State with its motley nationalities had manipulated the drawings.

August Kubizek, an upholsterer's apprentice nine months his senior, who was also a musician, was his one friend. Hitler would harangue Gustl for hours on end, and they went together to operas, concerts, and plays. They were spellbound by Wagner, but Verdi, with the exception of his *Aïda*, Hitler dismissed, saying once when they heard a street organ playing *"La donna è mobile,"* that a street organ was the appropriate instrument for such music. Great music for him was German: Beethoven's Ninth Symphony, *Lohengrin, Tristan, Tannhäuser, The Ring*. For two years, from the time he quit school in the autumn of 1905 at the age of sixteen until he left for Vienna in September 1907, Hitler spent his time daydreaming, reading, writing poetry, taking piano lessons, and going on long walks with Gustl. Hitler's passions were directed, not toward people or a career, but toward opera and redesigning Linz, the only city in Austria for which he would ever feel affection. More than thirty years later, he told Albert Speer that the situation of Linz was more beautiful than that of Budapest or Vienna and that he still had grandiose

* To protect the small specialty shops, department stores were prohibited until 1900. (William M. Johnston, *The Austrian Mind.*)

plans for it. Day after day, Hitler would show Kubizek what needed to be done: the railroad station had to be moved from the congestion of the center of the city to the countryside; the town and concert halls had to be rebuilt, as did a castle and a mountain hotel on the outskirts of the city. Houses had to be moved to enhance the beauty of the city square; the museum would be extended until its façade was the largest in Europe; a bridge across the Danube would be replaced by one that would be the most imposing in the world; and a huge hall of fame would dominate the city. These plans were not merely sketched; they were lived so intensely that nothing outside them mattered. Hitler presented Kubizek with a villa, that is, the design for one, but the gesture was as magnificent in this play world the two shared as if the actual building had existed. At the same time, Hitler, we are told, was reading anything he could lay his hands on. He had joined a lending library, and under the influence of the German nationalist Leopold Poetsch in Linz, and later on his own in Vienna and Germany, he read voraciously—Nietzsche, Treitschke, Martin Luther, Schiller, Karl May, who wrote books that fascinated generations of Austrians and Germans about the American West, although May had never been there; books on war and the army, Greek as well as German classics, books on German mythology, sociology, history, philosophy, literature—the works, or so at least his admirers, beginning with Kubizek, have written. But as Albert Speer reported, Hitler said he read mainly the last chapter of a book; that was where the important material was to be found, and with his retentive memory he could doubtless give the impression of more mastery of a subject than he actually had. Two books that made a great impression on him were Gustave Le Bons's *Psychologie der Massen* and William McDougall's *The Group Mind: A Sketch of the Principles of Collective Psychology*, although how much he actually read of McDougall's book is uncertain. *The Group Mind* was never translated into German, and Hitler's English was sketchy or nonexistent, so he may only have picked up the ideas in the book from German accounts of it.* He often referred in his conversations to Goethe and Schopenhauer, saying of *Faust* that it was more than the human mind could grasp. He unquestionably knew a good deal about the history of art and architecture. His memory was extraordinary. He retained a detailed knowledge of much that he had read that would continue to astonish his listeners, many of them specialists. One observer was to say of him when he was in his twenties that he had read more than most university professors.

But no direct evidence has survived that much of Hitler's reading in

---

* Lady Phipps, wife of the British ambassador to Berlin, observed that Hitler spoke only a few words of English. Speaking of Unity Mitford he had said falteringly: "Young lady, young English lady, Freeman, honourable lady. . . ." (David Pryce-Jones, *Unity Mitford: A Quest*, p. 100.)

Linz or in Vienna rubbed off on him in his youth. On the contrary, his postcards and letters to Kubizek betray a callow, pretentious, unlettered, and disorganized mind. In August 1908, Hitler wrote a letter to Gustl that makes plain his mediocre success in mastering the most elementary usages of German spelling and grammar, not to mention any coherent subject matter. The handwriting is childish, two words are scratched out and written over, other words are misspelled, punctuation is haphazard, and the style is rambling and disconnected. German spelling does not present the same kind of difficulty to the young student that English does. No vestigial spellings like *though, touch, read, colonel, psalm,* and such exist in German, which is spelled with dependable regularity. For young Hitler, however, the German language was mined with booby traps. The spelling in his letter is often erratic: *dann* becomes *dan, sofort* becomes *soffort, Katarrh* is spelled *chartar, dies* is spelled with two *s*'s, and so on. His use of capitals in this correspondence is also unpredictable.* Punctuation is omitted. In the August letter, as in others, he never used a question mark. He asks "Who really published the newspaper I sent you last time" without a question mark. In the sentence "Have you read the last decisions of the municipal council in connection with the new Teater," *Theater* is spelled without the *h*, which is part of the German as well as the English word, and again the sentence ends without a question mark. So does the following sentence: "Do you know any details." The pronoun *sie*, meaning either "they" or "she," is not capitalized in German usage, although *Sie*, the formal pronoun meaning "you," is. Hitler, however, capitalizes *sie* for "they" and for "she," just as he haphazardly capitalizes other pronouns that should be lowercased. Words are hopelessly run together—in one case seven of them, to make one long misspelled and inchoate formulation.

As to the content, the August letter rambles from one theme to another in what resembles free association. Hitler begs Kubizek's pardon for not having written sooner; he thanks him for sending his share of the rent money to their landlady; he thinks Kubizek's musical society is in a crisis. The weather is fine in Vienna; that is, it is raining, a gift from Heaven in what would otherwise have been bake-oven heat.

Hitler returns to his perennial theme of the new theater to be built in Linz and accuses the committee responsible for planning it of knowing no more about it than a hippopotamus does about playing a violin. He tells Kubizek that if his own copy of the architectural handbook were not so worn, he would like to send it to this (there follow the seven words in one characterizing the appalling committee).

---

* Hitler would in later years continue to prefer one *n* in words that should have two, like *denn, dennoch, wenn*, etc., sometimes even striking out what seemed to him to be the extra letter. ("Hitlers Handschrift und Masers Leserfehler" in *Vierteljahrshefte für Zeitgeschichte*, July 1973, pp. 332–35.)

So we have a picture, not of a *Wunderkind,* but of a boy whose allegedly wide reading, like his schoolwork, has slid off his skull. He writes a misspelled and ungrammatical letter to a friend he knows he can easily impress, with an attack on building plans he does not bother to criticize but says he could improve by sending the committee a book someone else has compiled.

Although he was in dire need of education, he was obviously programmed for something other than school, either toward being a dilettante bum who would talk on endlessly in the years to come if he got a sympathetic audience such as he had in Gustav Kubizek, or, if the breaks went his way, toward some as yet unformulated career where he might make use of his mixed and still embryonic talent. He had an opinion on every concert and opera he and Kubizek attended. The center of his daydreaming was building; the reconstruction of Linz and then of Vienna in a neoclassical and neo-Gothic but monumental style and the need for him to immerse himself in such grand-scale imaginings never left him. His own inner world was where he lived with excitement, and he would make the real world conform to it as far as he could. When he fell in love, he was convinced the girl was equally in love with him, although he was never to say a word to her. Her name was Stephanie, and Hitler and Kubizek saw her walking evenings on the *Landstrasse* and on her way to and from church. She became Adolf's great love when he was sixteen years old, and his ardors lasted for some two or three years, nourished on nothing whatever except an occasional smile or inclination of the young lady's head as she walked past on the arm of her mother. His love for Stephanie was matched only by his contempt for the young officers he sometimes saw walking with her. Adolf could not bring himself to speak to her, because he knew she would inevitably ask what he did for a living, and what could he say? When he left Linz for Vienna in 1906 for a two-month visit, he asked Kubizek to tell Stephanie he was a student at the art school, which is unquestionably what he greatly wanted to be. But here, too, his dream was to be unrealized. His application, made in the autumn of 1907 to the General Painting School of the Academy of Art of Vienna, was turned down, although he passed the preliminary examination in which he and the other aspirants were required to submit drawings on such biblical subjects as "Return of the Prodigal Son," "Expulsion from Paradise," and "Episode from the Flood" and such standard academic themes as "Morning," "Construction Laborers," "Music," "Prayer," and "Night." Of the 112 applicants, 33 failed this part of the examination, but when Hitler submitted his work for the second part, he was refused entrance to the school on the pedantic ground that he had too few heads among his drawings. This time he failed along with 51 other candidates. He was obviously not without a kind of artistic aptitude, and had he had more of it, the school might equally as well have turned him down, as academicians have other painters far better than he.

In November 1907, he was summoned back to his mortally ill mother in Linz, and when she died of cancer a month later, he was utterly crushed. Her Jewish doctor, Eduard Bloch, wrote that never in his forty years of practice had he seen a young man so broken up by grief and suffering as Adolf Hitler was.[11] Some clinical observers have seen in the loss of his mother and in Adolf's resentment of Dr. Bloch's medical intimacy with her a source of Hitler's violent anti-Semitism. An opposite interpretation may also be possible within the wide range of such specula- tions. Might not Hitler's anti-Semitism have come as well from an un- acknowledged debt of gratitude to Dr. Bloch, who was devoted to Frau Hitler, who charged very little for his services, and who was a member of a race that, as Hitler wrote in *Mein Kampf*, owed their special qualities (as Hitler himself did) to inbreeding? Probably not, but then there is no evidence for Hitler's sexual jealousy of Dr. Bloch either. Dr. Bloch was also Hitler's doctor, and either Hitler or his mother presented him with a number of Adolf's watercolors. Obviously the doctor had a deep sympathy for the boy in his sorrow, and what Hitler thought of him, aside from the evidence of the gift of the paintings, we simply do not know.* In any event, Dr. Bloch was one of a number of Jews with whom Hitler had amicable relations.

What was also true was that Hitler on Christmas 1907, partly by choice, was completely on his own, refusing to join Angela and her family, accountable to no one but himself and the perfunctory supervision of his official guardian, the mayor of Leonding. After the funeral, as soon as the financial arrangements for receiving his inheritance and orphan's pension were completed, he returned to Vienna. There he was joined by Kubizek, who came to study music at the conservatory, and the two lived together in a bug-infested room in the Mariahilf district. Hitler again threw himself into his self-imposed task of rebuilding sec- tions of the city whose polyglot population he hated.† He also continued his reading, borrowing books from the richly stocked *Hof-Bibliothek*, and he wrote an opera. Kubizek was polite about the opera's quality, but

---

* Dr. Bloch wrote many years later that at the time of Frau Hitler's death, a deeply moved Hitler told him he would be "forever grateful," and after Hitler came to power, Bloch believed he was in fact given special privileges. (Eduard Bloch, "My Patient Hitler," in *Collier's*, March 15 and 22, 1941.)

† Kubizek's accounts of Hitler's plans for slum clearance, housing development, and such are to be taken with more than a grain of salt. Hitler had already carried out such programs when Kubizek, in 1938, was writing his reminiscences of the young Hitler. While Kubizek was preparing his memoirs, he was in close touch with party functionaries who wanted the manuscripts for the party archives. Kubizek's account of Hitler's dislike of the Viennese and his admiration of much of the city's architecture are, however, borne out by the observations of many others, including Hitler himself. (Werner Maser, *Adolf Hitler*, p. 307.)

since he was a musician, he was not nearly so impressed with Hitler's musical gifts as he was with his architectural and literary performances. Kubizek returned to Linz in July of 1908 to spend a few months with his family before being drafted into the army, and when in November he came back to Vienna, Adolf was gone. Hitler had left no address; he had simply disappeared. From this point on, Hitler lived by himself, moving from one rooming house to another, no doubt to escape the fate suffered by his friend Gustl of being conscripted into the Army.

Hitler made another accommodation with the real world; to prepare for admission to the Academy of Art, he took lessons from a Viennese sculptor named Panzholzer, and in the autumn of 1908 he hopefully applied again for admission to the school. This time he was not even asked to submit his drawings. The Rektor told him that his work showed more promise for an architectural than for a painting career and that he should therefore apply to the Technical Institute for admission. The criticism, in the light of what has remained of Hitler's work, seems well taken; the work resembles architects' drawings much more than it conveys a painter's inner world. Nevertheless, Hitler had no way of entering the *Technische Hochschule*. Three years of secondary school were not enough for continuing study in a university or technical institute. They demanded an *Abitur*, the academic equivalent of a high school diploma in the United States, but actually a more solid intellectual achievement than the average American high school requires.

Hitler would write later that he had paid bitterly for having quit school, but he never considered returning to the *Realschule*, and he seems to have been incapable then or later of forcing himself to do disciplined work imposed on him by anyone else. He was one of those unresponsive youths who stubbornly go their own way regardless of threats or promises, an underachiever as educationalists say now. He was clearly intelligent—he had all 1's, the highest mark, in his *Volksschule* subjects —and his instructors in the *Realschule* could explain his poor grades only by his lack of interest. He was completely self-indulgent; he would do what he wanted to do and nothing else. It was the wide gap between what he felt he could accomplish if the world had as much insight into him as he did into it and the mediocre performances his elders actually witnessed that made his fantasies so compelling and so much easier to live with than the bleak realities.

In Vienna he read the work of the Viennese-born Dr. Jörg Lanz von Liebenfels, an anti-Semitic pamphleteer who published a journal ornamented with swastikas, *Ostara*. Lanz was not a doctor and the "von" was spurious, but in years to come he claimed Hitler as one of his foremost disciples, a claim that was watered down when Lanz added Lenin and

Lord Kitchener to the list of his followers. Lanz's *Ostara* claimed a circulation of 100,000 readers, to whom he preached the doctrine of the superiority of the noble, blond, blue-eyed race. On its behalf he founded an Order of the New Temple, which only blond, blue-eyed men who would promise to marry women of the same coloration could join. The other races Lanz dismissed as "Sodom's Apes." In the case of Adolf Hitler he was preaching to the converted, but Hitler would never object to repetitions on this subject.

It was not Lanz's biological anti-Semitism but his pseudomysticism, from which he emerged as a kind of pope of his monastic order, that irritated Hitler in the years to come, and when Austria became part of the Reich in 1938, Lanz was forbidden to publish.

Hitler later wrote of his five years in Vienna as a grim period that had taught him to be hard. "The Goddess of Misery," he wrote in *Mein Kampf*, clasped him to her bosom, but this, like much else he had to say of himself, is considerably exaggerated. His first serious biographer, Konrad Heiden, has told of Hitler's years of privation in Vienna—hungry a good deal of the time, without an overcoat in winter, sleeping in a flophouse or in doorways or on park benches—but the stories are based on what Hitler wanted his audience to believe and on the accounts of men who were dramatizing any relationship they may have had with a controversial figure suddenly projected into notoriety.*

Hitler was certainly not living a sybaritic life in Vienna, but he was probably doing a good deal better than many other young men of his age. After his mother was widowed, she, Paula, and Adolf had lived comfortably on some 120 crowns a month. When his mother died, he and Paula each received 25 crowns a month as orphans' pensions, plus 58 crowns a month which he inherited from the family estate, consisting mainly of the proceeds of the sale of the house that Alois had bought.

* The chief sources for the stories are Reinhold Hanisch, a street-wise tramp who had a partnership with Hitler for some months from the end of 1909 until the summer of 1910 selling postcards and other pictures Hitler painted, and Josef Greiner, who claimed he knew Hitler well during the period when Hitler was in rags and so dirty and lousy the manager of one refuge—the Maennerheim—wanted to throw him out. But both Hanisch and Greiner are doubtful witnesses. Hitler had Hanisch arrested in the summer of August 1910 for allegedly holding back the lion's share of the proceeds from the sale of one of Hitler's watercolors; Hanisch said he had received only 12 crowns for it, while Hitler declared the amount was 50 crowns. Although Hanisch may well have been paid only 12 crowns, he had, aside from Hitler's charge, other disabilities from the point of view of the police, having registered under a false name at the Maennerheim. He was sentenced to seven days in jail, and that was the end of any relationship with Hitler until after Hitler became chancellor and Hanisch tried to sell more pictures allegedly painted by Hitler. He was arrested after the invasion of Austria in 1938 and died in jail either from pneumonia or by his own hand. Greiner's account is filled with glaring misstatements and inaccuracies. (Reinhold Hanisch, "I Was Hitler's Buddy" in *New Republic*, 1939. Joseph Greiner, *Das Ende des Hitler-Mythos*.)

This was a sum he could live on the more easily since he neither drank nor smoked and his needs beyond food, lodging, opera, and theatergoing were small. Standing room cost 2 crowns, and since Kubizek reports that they went to the theater almost every day, this was the chief drain on his resources. When he moved to Vienna after his mother's death, his monthly income was about that earned by a young lawyer; or a teacher, who in his first five years of employment earned 66 crowns a month; or a post office employee, who earned 60 crowns a month.* Also, after 1911 Hitler had a small legacy from his aunt, his mother's sister, Johanna Pölzl, and as a consequence he seems to have been far better off than he would ever later admit to when he described the misery of his life in Vienna.† It is probably true that for some months in 1909–1910 after his monthly remittances from the family inheritance ran out he lived in a meager way, but he always had his orphan's pension of 25 crowns a month, until 1911 when he was sufficiently well off to be able to turn that over to his sister Paula. The pension would have been paid him until 1913 when he was twenty-four years old.

According to *Mein Kampf*, at some point in 1909—Hitler gave no dates —he took a job on a building project, an employment he did not hold for long. If there was such a job, it was the only time in his life that he worked for anyone other than himself, the party, or the state. He wrote in *Mein Kampf* that he was forced to leave his apprentice's job because his fellow workers were Social Democrats and his politics as a quasi Schönerer clashed with theirs. But there were reasons other than political that separated him from his colleagues. He was, after all, the son of an official, and these men were workers and the sons of workers. He could not look on them as either his social or intellectual equals. August Kubizek had been an upholsterer's apprentice, but he was also a music student and, even more important, an eager audience for Adolf's lectures and diatribes, something that Hitler's fellow workers were not.

In Vienna, Hitler was an outsider at every level of society. The schools would not accept him. He could only glimpse the dazzling life of the capital from the streets and the promenades of the opera and theater. The richly dressed men and women of the upper classes, the comfortable burghers, the bohemian artists and musicians—all were inaccessible to him. He fitted in nowhere, and he hated them all, especially the Jews, although with them he did business. When he added to his income by painting postcards and small pictures of the city's monuments and land-marks in watercolors and oils, one of the men who sold them was a Hun-

* Werner Maser, *Hitlers Briefe und Notizen*, p. 34.
† August Kubizek tells how Hitler subsisted mainly on bread and milk and canteen food, but Hitler never ate luxuriously even when he became chancellor of the Reich.

garian Jew named Neumann, and a number of art dealers and business-men who bought them were also Jews. Hitler met Neumann in a hostel he moved to in December 1909. This was a men's hostel, run by the city of Vienna, a well-kept lodging house where Hitler lived until 1913 along with retired army officers and young workers who paid the modest sum of 50 hellers—half a crown—a day, and where he could paint by day, which he had not been able to do in the shelter.

In addition to paintings of the parliament buildings in Vienna, theaters, churches, the *Rathaus*, and such, Hitler produced etchings, posters, and illustrations for advertising, among other things, cosmetics, shoes and shoe polishes, and women's underwear.

According to one doubtful account, while in Vienna Hitler experienced a hopeless love for a girl he met through an acquaintance (Greiner). Despite his raptures, she eventually decided to marry a half-Jew. Whether or not this story is true, Hitler's interest in women at this time seems to have been illusory, linked to his daydreaming; he had no boy-meets-girl relationships. In Vienna he lived alone, without women, in a man's environment, although female companionship was not difficult to find. Kubizek describes their walking through a red-light district. Hitler expressed his disgust at prostitution all during their walk, from one end of the district to the other and back again. On another occasion, when they were looking for a room, the prospective landlady, elegant but aging, according to Kubizek, undid her dressing gown so that they could see she wore nothing under it except her underpants. Hitler was so undone at the lady's brazenness that he fled from the house with his friend at his heels. Kubizek says that at the opera they took standing-room places in the promenade rather than in the gallery because Hitler could not tolerate the fluttering women who were allowed into the gallery. Hitler often spoke to Kubizek about keeping pure "the flame of life," and his relations with women, when he was young and it should have burned high, either were limited to the courtesy of *"Küss die Hand"* or were authoritarian, as they would be with his niece Geli and Eva Braun, both of whom he treated as sharers of his domesticity—on a somewhat higher level than his shepherd dogs. Hitler's sex drives seem to have been relatively weak; he was as abstemious about women as he was about food and drink; only on rare occasions could he wholeheart-edly indulge himself in what were then called physical appetites. Soviet doctors would report when they did a postmortem on what they believed to be Hitler's charred body in 1945 that they found only the right testicle. Assuming that the left testicle had not been taken off by a souvenir hunter and that it was actually Hitler's cadaver the Russians were dissect-ing, this medical finding would neither controvert nor affirm Hitler's sexual velleities. In any event, it is curious, if the Soviet report is correct, that no previous medical examination of Hitler reported that he was monorchid.

The Vienna Hitler lived in was one of the most glittering cities in Europe when seen from outside or from the top. Its geographical location between East and West, its mixture of races, and its opulence made it a center of extraordinary activity with a brilliant social and intellectual life. Vienna's medical school was one of the best in Europe, and the Law School, the Institute of Technology, and the various research centers all were staffed with top-ranking scientists and scholars. Notable philosophers produced out of Austria's racial mix included Ludwig Wittgenstein, Edmund Husserl, Martin Buber, and Ernst Mach, whose name has been preserved in designating supersonic velocity. Mach was of German parentage, Buber and Husserl were Jews, and Wittgenstein was of German-Jewish ancestry. Among Austrian writers were the charming and graceful Hugo von Hofmannsthal, gifted figures like Arthur Schnitzler and Robert Musil, and, later, Rainer Maria Rilke and the Prague-born Franz Kafka, along with a remarkable variety of feuilletonists who published opinions on everything. In Vienna, Sigmund Freud was working out his theories of the nature of the human psyche, Max Reinhardt was revolutionizing the theater, and Gustav Mahler was directing the opera. Johannes Brahms had settled in Vienna in preference to his native Germany, and there he was succeeded by Mahler, Richard Strauss, Oscar Straus, Karl Goldmark, and Arnold Schönberg. In literature, science, music, or a sophisticated life-style, there were few places in the world to match Vienna.

All the peoples of central and eastern Europe met there and somehow made a living, some of them, like the Magyar magnates, very easily from the earnings of their vast estates in Hungary; some of them so desperately that, half-starved and homeless, they barely kept alive. Over all of them presided a court of encrusted ritual, described by breathless foreign observers like Mrs. Trollope, who visited the city in 1837 when Metternich was still one of its chief ornaments, as the most magnificent they had ever seen. Adolf Hitler sometimes caught a glimpse of Emperor Franz Josef, who had maintained a precarious rule since midcentury, as he rode by in the imperial carriage, and everything Hitler saw only confirmed his contempt of the monarchy, as remote in his eyes as the leading figures in the operas he saw from the standing-room promenade, and as incompetent to rule on behalf of the Germans over the empire's mongrel peoples.

Despite its multifarious problems, Austria-Hungary was doing well according to most of the statistics by which European states measured growth and progress. Its population had risen from 35,812,000 in 1869 to 46,974,000 in 1900 and to 51,390,000 in 1910, after the annexation of Bosnia and Herzegovina. Vienna's population had gone from 431,000 in

1851 to 827,000 in 1890, and at the turn of the century it was 1,891,000.[12]
The Jews were a small proportion of this population—8.63 percent in
1910.

The years before World War I were times of enormous growth of
industrial production and commerce in the more or less free-trading area
the Habsburg empire provided for all its disparate peoples. With the
coal reserves of Bohemia, Moravia, and Silesia at hand, Austria had one
of the largest steel mills in Europe and was the foremost producer of
electricity, machinery, textiles, leather, glass, and beet sugar. A budget
deficit in Vienna in 1880 became a surplus by 1890. But the trouble was
that the well-being never spread throughout the society. Artisans and
peasants had flocked to the city from the countryside, as they were
doing all over Europe, and Vienna had the most serious housing shortage
of any city on the Continent—51 persons to every house, as against 45
in Budapest, 31 in Berlin, 30 in Paris, and 8 in London.

Thousands of the city's inhabitants lived in poverty; there were simply
too many of them for the jobs at hand. The children of indigent workers
in some quarters of the city were 80 percent of those on the school rolls,
and despite the free lunches provided by the city, they often went hungry
in order to take food home to their parents. Unemployment was high,
especially in winter when construction projects had to be stopped or
curtailed and workers were dependent on soup kitchens and their children's lunches to save them from starvation. Many of them slept in parks
and under bridges. A cartoon of the time shows two ragged men sitting
on a park bench; one of them, in a heavy Viennese dialect, says: "My
God, it's cold." The other answers: "Yeah, but not as cold as the people."

Laws protecting workers and their families were among the most
progressive in Europe, employment of women and children was limited,
child labor was forbidden in 1885,[13] shelters like the Obdachlosenasyl
and the Maennerheim where Hitler lived were maintained, accident insurance had to be taken out by employers, and health insurance was
provided for. But the worker's lot remained a hard one.

Although private and municipal charity provided help to the impoverished, the search for jobs when there often were none and the
frustrations of hopes that had brought thousands to the city for a better
life resulted in a potentially revolutionary movement in a country already coming apart at the seams with the drive of its minorities for
autonomy and independence. By 1907 the Marxist-oriented Social Democrats were the largest single party in Parliament, which was elected by
all males above the age of twenty-four. The Social Democrats elected
87 deputies as against 67 for the Christian Socials, 52 for the German
Nationals, 13 for the German Radicals, and only 3 for the Schönerers.
However, the voting bloc of the Christian Socials could count on the
support of 30 Catholic Conservatives, all of whom were German, while

the Social Democrats were made up of 50 Germans, 23 Czechs, 7 Poles, 2 Ruthenians, and 5 Italians, none of whom liked one another very well. In all there were 28 "fractions" representing not only political but nationalist divisions: Italians, Slovenes, Ukrainians, Croats, Rumanians, Serbs, and even Zionists. It was a democratic parliament but far from a democratic government. Ministers were appointed by and were responsible to the crown. Austro-Hungarian foreign policy was conservative in the sense that those in charge of it sought above all to keep the patchwork empire intact against the Pan-Slavs, the Pan-Germans, and the Magyar, Czech, and Italian nationalists who wanted to destroy it. Austria-Hungary was in no position to play a great role in world politics. Its sole scene of action was the Balkans, where it could hope, at best, to make the imperial position more secure by taking a prudent share of the Turkish Empire that was breaking up at its doorstep, and thus prevent Russia from increasing its already potent influence among the dissident minorities.

For Hitler the empire was an absurdity, Vienna its monstrous center, and the Jews the destructive termites within its shambles. The Jews of Vienna had always sought assimilation. There were more men than women among them, and intermarriages with Christians were frequent. But assimilation, not only for Hitler but for the Shönerers as for Mrs. Trollope, was utterly rejected. For the anti-Semites and Nationalists, Jews, from the rich cultivated ones who played a conspicuous part in the social life of the upper classes to the lowly *Handelee* Hitler described, had no place in a Germanic order. The Czechs, Poles, Slovenes, Magyars, and the other inferior races had none either, but they could conceivably be contained in their ethnic enclaves, whereas the Jew had simply to be gotten rid of.

That specific form of antiism was what men like Theodor Herzl, who had once believed in assimilation, came to identify as the major source of the widespread rejection of the Jews. Herzl had lived in Vienna for many years, but he was started on his crusade for Zionism by his experience in France during the bitter polemics of the Dreyfus affair. In a bizarre way, Herzl and Hitler came to the same conclusions: the Jews could never be an integral part of European life; assimilation did not work. Jews had to accept their separate identity no matter how fluently they spoke the idiom of their adopted country or how diligently they tried to become fully accredited citizens.

Hitler's conclusions, however, like those of the Schönerers and the Members of the New Temple, had more sinister implications than social and political rejection *per se*, the design to diminish the influence of the Jews in the economic and intellectual life of a country essentially foreign to them. The religious counterimage that in the Middle Ages had justified kings and local potentates in exiling Jews from their territories when plague or disaster struck was being secularized. The Jews had played an essential role in the drama of the Christian counterimage, the Devil was assimilated into Christian theology, and the Church had the ultimate duty of working for the Jews' redemption. But in the racial counterimage there was no room for redemption.

When Adolf Hitler left Vienna for Munich in 1913, he too was setting out for a Promised Land, where Germans ruled and where, incidentally, he would be more likely to escape military service under the Habsburgs. Vienna he would not see again until twenty-five years later, when Austria would welcome her returning son as a redeemer, and hundreds of thousands of Viennese would stand for hours deliriously cheering the leader they had never heard of—and very likely would not have cared to hear of—when he lived among them.

CHAPTER 2

Germany: The Promised Land

WHEN ADOLF HITLER ARRIVED in Munich on May 24, 1913, he came to a Germany at the height of its power. What had been little more than a linguistic agglomerate of dozens of territories in 1780, some of them independent states, others no more than a castle or village, had become at the end of the nineteenth century a nation, one of the mightiest in the world and one of the most impressive according to the values of the time. In higher learning, in almost every field of study in the sciences and humanities, in its industrial apparatus, and in its progressive social legislation on behalf of the working population it led Europe and, in fact, the world * "*Am deutschen Wesen soll die Welt genesen*"† seemed in many ways to be borne out, as ideas and techniques pioneered by German scholars, scientists, and technicians spread throughout the world along with the goods of the entrepreneurs who carried with them the material evidences of German efficiency and dependability. The reliable products of the Reich penetrated everywhere, to the countries of North and South America, the Orient, Africa, the Middle East, and all through Europe. No man of science went untouched by German proficiency in his subject; no textbook of any intellectual discipline but was filled with footnotes and references to the work of German researchers. R. W.

---

* In 1883 sickness insurance was introduced, paid for half by employers and half by employees; accident insurance was begun in 1884; and in 1889 old age and disability insurance, to which the state contributed at Bismarck's urging. (Bruno Gebhardt, *Handbuch der Deutschen Geschichte*, vol. 3, 9th ed., 1970, p. 306.)

† In German ways will the world be healed.

Bunsen in chemistry, Wilhelm Röntgen in radiation, Robert Koch in medicine, Rudolf Diesel in engineering, Alexander von Humboldt in geography, the brothers Jacob and Wilhelm Grimm in linguistics, Leopold von Ranke and Theodor Mommsen in history, Albert Einstein and Max Planck in physics—all were pushing back the frontiers of scientific and humanistic knowledge. German universities, like the University of Vienna, were centers of learning to which students of every nationality were drawn to find out more about their subjects than they could learn anywhere else.

The population had trebled since 1800 and more than doubled since 1875, cities like Berlin had ten times their former number of inhabitants, and the standard of living was the second highest in Europe, just behind that of Britain with its world empire and centuries of development as a nation. German industrial production had surpassed that of all the other countries of Europe including England. France had been overtaken in the 1870s, and by 1910 Germany was outproducing Britain by a considerable margin.[1] Foreign trade was led by Britain, whose exports and imports totaled 21 billion marks as against Germany's 17.8 billion marks, but Germany's foreign trade between 1891 and 1911 rose 143 percent as against Britain's 66 percent, France's 10.5 percent, and the United States's 70 percent. The German merchant marine, which in 1870 had been half the size of the French, by 1913 was twice as large.*

Along with the scientific and technological burgeoning, German philosophers (using that word in a broad sense) were overturning long-held ideas about the nature of man and his society. With Charles Darwin in England and Sigmund Freud in Vienna, they would reshape the contemporary *Weltanschauung* so it would never again be put together in the same way. Arthur Schopenhauer, Friedrich Nietzsche, and Georg Wilhelm Friedrich Hegel were among the movers and shakers of the nineteenth century, and to them must be added the names of Marx and Engels, who would mobilize the revolt of both workers and intellectuals against the enormous dynamism of the capitalist economy that had been mainly responsible for Germany's swift rise from a feudal to an industrial society.

In naked military power, too, Germany was formidable. The armies of Prussia had defeated Austria and then, joined by other German states, France, in two short, brilliant campaigns. The tinsel battalions of petty princes who had hired out their soldiers as mercenaries and the overage officer corps of the Prussia of 1806 that had been ignominiously defeated by Napoleon had been replaced with an imperial general staff, an officer

---

* In 1871 the German merchant fleet had 147 ships, totaling 81,994 gross tons. In 1913 it had 2,098 ships, with a total of 4,380,348 gross tons. (G. Stolper, et al, *The German Economy from 1870 to the Present*, p. 24.)

corps, and an army that had no equal anywhere. Men like Clausewitz and von der Goltz, who dealt not only with arsenals but with the reasonable purposes for which they were supposed to exist, were to be found mainly in Germany. Its highly trained general staff, designed to provide a substitute for the unpredictable military genius of a Napoleon, went about its business of analysis, calculation, and experiment for finding the solutions to military problems in much the same way that researchers in quieter, academic disciplines pursued their inquiries.* In addition, the German navy, one-quarter the size, to be sure, of the British, but superbly trained, was a potent striking force, from its dreadnoughts to its untried U-boats. The German officer both of the army and navy, but especially of the army, was held in higher esteem than in countries that were less in debt to their armed forces for their very existence. After the Battle of Jena, where the Prussian army had been disastrously defeated, the officer corps had been purged and reorganized to bring in younger and even in some cases extremely intelligent young men chosen not only for the moral qualities of courage, leadership, loyalty, and calm in the crises of life and death demanded of their calling, but because they had also gone to school, earned their *Abitur,*† and showed unusual intellectual promise. Prussia was by far the largest German state of the Reich, almost two-thirds of its territory and population, and the Prussian army was the backbone of the imperial army. The Prussian army, even after conscription was introduced, had never been a people's army; and like it, the imperial army continued to be the king's army, with officers and men swearing fealty to the person of the sovereign, who was commander in chief and, in time of war, *Oberstekriegsherr* ("commander in the field"). Prussia with its open boundaries, poor soil, and heterogeneous population of Germans, Poles, Lithuanians, and Danes had been held together as a state by its army, an *imperium in imperio*, as more than one foreign observer called it. The Prussian army existed to serve the king and his people, and its officers in turn held first place in his esteem and in the hierarchy of the state. In the time of Frederick the Great, 90 percent of the officers had been nobles; by 1913, with conscription and mass armies, 70 percent of Prussian officers and 48 percent of the colonels and generals came from the middle classes. Although the artillery and engineers were officered by sons of the middle class, and in the latter case often by artisans' sons, the officers of certain regiments, the Prussian guard and the cavalry among them, were almost all of noble birth. Every lieutenant

---

* The general staff, however, was considered a unity, with each member building on the work of his predecessor, a process that emphasized conformity rather than imaginative solutions.

† In 1890, 35 percent of the *Fahnenjunker* in the Prussian, Saxon, and Württemberg army had been awarded the *Abitur*; in 1912 the number was 65 percent. (Karl Demeter, *Das Deutsche Offizierkorps in Gesellschaft und Staat 1650–1945*, p. 89.)

in the Prussian army was *hoffaehig* ("eligible to be presented at court").*
In Bavaria only staff officers were *hoffaehig*, and Bavaria had a much
higher percentage of bourgeois officers than Prussia, although there, too,
certain regiments were the preserves of the aristocracy. While the highest
echelons of the army—the quartermaster general and his staff of five—
were all from the nobility, the Imperial General Staff by 1913 was about
equally divided between the aristocracy and bourgeoisie, although in
1906, 60 percent of its members had been nobles.† In the Prussian tradition every officer bore a privileged, personal relationship to the emperor,
because historically the officers of the king of Prussia had been lieges of
the king, owing obedience to him before all else, and it was, in fact, the
victories of the army that had made the king of Prussia emperor of
Germany.

Prussian officers and men in 1831 swore before God "the omniscient
and all-powerful" a "body" oath to serve the king in all circumstances, on
land and water, in war and peace, wherever they might be called on;
to serve him truly and honorably and to further whatever was most useful
and best for their all-highest sovereign.[2]

The troops of the German states in 1871, and again in 1878 with contingents from Alsace-Lorraine among them, swore almost the identical
oath to obey the kaiser similarly in all circumstances.‡ Higher officers
were administered the oath directly by the kaiser. Only Mennonites, by
virtue of their religious convictions, were exempted from taking the oath;
they were permitted to express their adherence to it with a handshake.[3]

The soldiery of the sixteenth and seventeenth centuries was little more
than a rabble, as Shakespeare, among others, observed, ready to steal
a shirt from every hedge.[4] They were men who had nothing to lose but
their lives and who were held in contempt and fear by the rest of the
population. In the eighteenth century, the discipline of the soldier was
still, until the outbreak of the French Revolution, dependent on the
standards imposed by the officers. When Prussian troops, retreating after
the Battle of Jena, bivouacked near a lumberyard, they took not a plank
for their campfires. Lumber was private property, not theirs to use, but

---

* Rarely, high rank could also be obtained even in the general staff by an exceptionally gifted man with meager credentials of birth and education. General Reyher,
chief of the Prussian General Staff under Prince Wilhelm, had begun his military
career as a company clerk, later became a sergeant-major, then by self-study passed
the officers' examination, qualified for the general staff, and in 1848 was named acting minister of war. (Herbert Rosinski, *The German Army*.)

† In 1914, of 113 general staff officers, 69 were of bourgeois origins. (Walter
Görlitz, *Der deutsche Generalstab*, p. 212.)

‡ The Bavarian army came under the command of the kaiser only on mobilization.
In peacetime, nevertheless, the kaiser had the right to inspect it. (Militärgeschichtliches Forschungsamt (eds.), *Die Generalstäbe in Deutschland, 1871–1945*, p. 15.)

Most of the armies of the German states were sworn to obey their respective constitutions after the Revolution of 1848. (Herbert Rosinski, *The German Army*, p. 86.)

it was their officers who demanded of them the observation of such proprieties.* The general belief was that the common soldier was capable of being taught his duty only by fear and coercion, and it is likely that every European commander would have agreed with Frederick the Great, who said that a soldier must fear the rod of the noncommissioned officer more than he does the bullets of the enemy.[5]

The French Revolution, however, set in motion enormous changes in the concepts of the Rights of Man, any man, and in the nineteenth century the common soldier had become an individual to be taken account of; corporal punishment was abolished in the Prussian army in 1808, and with the introduction of mass armies came the need for winning the allegiance of the rank and file as well as compelling it.

Soldiers were still highly disciplined, mainly by noncommissioned officers who saw to it that no button was loose, no gun barrel, belt buckle, or boot unshined. And while a grotesquely strict obedience, *"Kadavergerhorsam,"*† was often demanded, no one among either officers or men, in theory, was obliged to obey an illegal order of his superior. In the eighteenth century, one Prussian officer, Count Georg von der Marwitz, refused to obey an order of Frederick the Great to plunder a Saxon castle, because plunder conflicted with the code of honor of an officer, and rather than carry out the order he quit the service. He had carved on his tombstone the words "Chose disgrace (*Ungnade*) where obedience would have meant dishonor."[6] During World War I, every German soldier was instructed that he had to obey legal orders only, a state of affairs that would continue curiously enough after the National Socialists came to power and throughout World War II.[7] It was continued, that is, in theory, because innumerable illegal orders were in fact given and carried out. But while the army before World War I was the emperor's army, when Wilhelm II told his Prussian recruits in 1891 during a swearing-in ceremony that he expected them to carry out his orders even if they were told to shoot at their brothers and sisters or their fathers and mothers, he not only exposed his own megalomania but he also contravened army regulations that nevertheless remained in force.‡

Along with its industrial boom, Germany was one of the largest agricultural countries of Europe. A large proportion of its people lived on

---

* At Jena we find the Prussian army nearly perishing of cold close by huge stacks of felled wood and not daring to touch them, whilst after Auerstädt the troops went two days without provisions because to requisition from the peasants would have been a 'system of robbery . . . unknown in the Prussian army and repugnant to its spirit.'" (Major General J. F. C. Fuller, *War and Western Civilization 1832–1932*, p. 29.)

† Mechanical; literally, corpse obedience.

‡ The kaiser said: "With the present Socialist intrigues it could happen that I might order you to shoot at your own brothers and sisters, yes at your fathers and mothers. And then you must obey me without hesitation." (Hans Meier-Welcker and Wolfgang von Groote, *Handbuch zur deutschen Militärgeschichte*, vol. 5, p. 113.)

the land, 80 percent of which was owned by the farmers who cultivated it.* The great landowners whose opinions counted with the kaiser were mainly East Prussian nobles; the officers and chief functionaries of the Wilhelminian court were almost all from the same class. The rising bourgeoisie described in novels like Thomas Mann's *Buddenbrooks* might be far more cultivated, far more the chief support of the new German state based on industrial power than were East Elbean Junkers, but they were likely to cherish a reserve officer's commission as a sign of status far more than would their opposite numbers in any other country.† The class differences in German society were probably no more marked than they were in England or France, but there was less mobility among the social orders. The son of a worker was likely to remain in the same class as his father, because the path of upward mobility went through a system of education and preferment that cost money and demanded a psychological preparation which the son of a worker or peasant would be unlikely to have. Still, as happened in Austria in the case of Adolf Hitler's father, moving upward was possible in Germany, too, although the road was no easy one. Gerhard Scharnhorst, for example, founder of the National Army, was the son of a peasant who had been a cavalry sergeant in the Hanoverian army. For the middle classes, higher status was more accessible. Many of its members bought estates, built large houses, entertained lavishly, and lived in a grandeur far removed from the world of the early-nineteenth-century factory owner with his little house built near his plant. Members of the bourgeoisie might be ennobled, and some of them became the staunchest proponents of the special privileges of the class they had recently joined. A month after Hitler arrived in Munich, a debate took place in the Reichstag concerning the preferments enjoyed by the nobility with their preponderance in high military echelons and in certain fashionable regiments.

The controversy touched off deep-seated resentments of the outs against the ins. The nineteenth century had witnessed the rise of a class of intelligent, efficient, driving businessmen belonging to a bourgeoisie that had been proportionally much smaller in the German states than in France, England, and the Netherlands, but was growing rapidly. They were made fun of, as Molière had satirized the *bourgeois gentilhomme*

---

* In 1871 two-thirds of the population lived on the land; by 1913 city workers outnumbered farmers by almost two to one. In 1871, 36 percent of the population lived in cities; by 1913 the figure was 60 percent. (Bruno Gebhardt, *Handbuch der deutschen Geschichte,* 10th ed., 1970, vol. 3, p. 378.)

† Bethmann Hollweg, descendant of an old Frankfurt banking family that had been ennobled, wore his uniform as a major in the reserve when he first appeared in public in 1906 as *Reichskanzler.* By 1914 he was a lieutenant general in the reserve as well as chancellor of Germany. (Hans Meier-Welcker and Wolfgang von Groote, *Handbuch zur deutschen Militärgeschichte,* vol. 5, p. 87.)

of the seventeenth century. Writers said the newly rich had no standards of their own but could only ape the artistocracy or attempt to impress them with dreadful ostentation. In 1870 the king of Prussia travelled by regular railroad coach while the newly rich man of affairs often journeyed in his private train. He was also accused of living it up in a blatant, pre-Hollywood mindlessness, filling fish ponds with champagne, building enormous, lavishly furnished, tasteless villas, throwing his heavy weight around.[8] The Buddenbrookses, to be sure, had no part in this; they lived richly and modestly, surrounded by books and paintings, managing their shipping firms or industrial plants that made the country run. Yet they and their wives and children might be shut out from certain coveted preserves that were automatically accessible to Junkers—high rank in the state and army in the positions that influenced all foreign and much domestic policy. It was the emperor who made treaties, as well as peace and war, and the men whose advice he might take were rarely from the ranks of business or industry. But it was the entrepreneurs along with the lesser members of the middle class and the workers and peasants who were the chief source of the taxes that paid for everything—the glitter of the court, the great ships, the universities, and the elite regiments their sons could not join.

So the Reichstag debate of June 1913 was acrimonious. The chief representative of the nobility was one von Graefe, a man, his liberal opponents repeatedly pointed out, who was himself the son of a doctor who had been ennobled only a few years before. An opposing speaker called him a Talmi [Fake] Junker, and he was obviously neither the most elegant nor eloquent spokesman who might have been selected for his newly adopted class. He presented the case for privilege with an ardor and tactlessness that infuriated the opposition and alienated many of the people he wanted to speak for. Some of what he argued was half-true, for example, that in certain regiments the nobility had sacrificed their sons in higher proportions that had other classes. On March 14, 1814, he said, three-quarters of the Prussian Guard, one of the elite corps under attack for its one-sided representation of noble officers, had been killed before Paris; in 1866 it was the Guard that had broken the center of the Austrian army; at the battle of Vionville in 1870, one-third of its soldiers had been killed and more than three-quarters of the officers. It was true that much of the battle record of the elite corps was a heroic one; but in the years of their most glorious exploits, many of the great victories had been won and losses endured by formations that had middle-class as well as aristocratic officers, even though in later years the officers of such regiments might come entirely from the nobility.[9]

Graefe's chief opponent in the Reichstag debate, Müller-Meiningen, a member of the Progressive party, agreed with him on the notable feats of arms of the Prussian Guard but, after remarking that the speaker did not come from the class that had sacrificed their sons in those battles, pointed out that among Bismarck's chief opponents had been precisely those Junkers von Graefe was extolling. It was damaging to morale, Müller-Meiningen said, to have the army divided into classes in this fashion. In 1910, he said, of 44 lieutenant generals, 37 were members of the aristocracy and only 7 of the middle class; 75 major generals were of noble and 35 of bourgeois origins. It was not tradition, he said, that made an army but its *esprit de corps*, and its spirit was engendered, not by privilege, but by justice. Another opposition speaker, a National Liberal, said of course men of noble birth could be cited who had fought well, but so had countless others from the middle classes.

Von Graefe's arguments led him into still deeper waters; he added an anti-Semitic note when he said that no Moseses or Cohens had been among those who had taken part in the German colonial wars in Africa. A Socialist rose to ask him how many common soldiers had been killed in Africa along with the nobles and pointed out sourly that in those campaigns not one noncommissioned officer had been made an officer. And as for the Jews, he remarked, how many Prussian officers of noble lineage were looking for a "golden Rebecca" was evidenced in the marriage advertisements in German newspapers, and he asked how many others of their kind would have fared had they not succeeded in finding a bride among the daughters of the chosen people. Müller-Meiningen, too, attacked von Graefe on his anti-Semitism, telling him that real conservatives of the old school would turn in their graves if they could hear him. He named Jews who had served the Fatherland such as Elia Dusniz Abramovitch, who had recently been killed in an experimental zeppelin flight, and Emin Pasha, one of the greatest colonial heroes of Germany. The first man to die, he said, fighting against the Hereros in Africa was a Jew, Lieutenant Bendix, and Germany had built a monument to him. Graefe then returned to the battle to relate how well things were managed in England with its elitist political system, and there he fell into a trap of his own making, because his opponents could point out that the prime minister of Britain was a Jew by the name of Disraeli.

In attacking the Jews to further his cause, Graefe was using a tactic that many a demogogue after him would find useful. In pre–World War I Germany, two men above all would make anti-Semitism *salonfaehig*, that is, a discussible view that might be held by civilized, well-bred people as well as by crackpots. They were Heinrich von Treitschke, a fervent nationalist and eminent historian, and Adolf Stoecker, a Lutheran court preacher. Stoecker at first attacked Jews on religious grounds, using arguments not unlike those of the emperor, who told his troops that only a Christian could be a good officer. Stoecker for a time preached that only Christians, including converted Jews, could be good Germans; later, however, he attacked Jews on racial grounds, any Jews, as enemies of Germany, whether or not they were baptized Christians.

He had some success in his racial war. When he talked on the Old Testament or on subjects like "Is the Bible true?" his audiences were small, between two and three hundred, but when he denounced the Jews, his hearers grew to between two and three thousand. But while anti-Semitism could always gather a crowd, it never could recruit a substantial political following. Anti-Semitic parties, including the Christian Socials founded by Stoecker, elected 16 delegates to the Reichstag in 1893, 24 in 1894, and 25 in the elections of 1907. That was their high point, and they would not reach it again two decades later. At the moment of their greatest strength, it has been estimated that some 500,000 Germans in a nation of 65 million voted anti-Semitic.

In 1912, in a Reichstag numbering 397 deputies, it was the Social Democrats who won by far the largest number of seats. The Conservative party was down from 60 in 1907 to 43 in 1912; the Liberals and a mainly Catholic and middle-class Center dropped, too, the Liberals from 54 in 1907 to 45, the Center from 105 to 91; but the Social Democrats went up from 43 seats to 110. In this last election before the war, the anti-Semites won 4 seats. As for Treitschke, who coined the phrase the National Socialists would later adopt: "The Jews are our misfortune," his influence was exerted mainly on a relatively few intellectuals. One of his students, Heinrich Class, was a leader of the Pan-German movement. Class adopted Treitschke's anti-Semitism and joined in the attack on Jews as capitalists and materialists. But others, like the historian Theodor Mommsen, took an opposite position. Mommsen attacked Treitschke in an article called *"Auch ein Wort über Judentum"* ("Another word about Jewry"), which more nearly reflected the views of most German publicists and intellectuals in general. Nevertheless, some degree of anti-Semitism was to be found in all strata of the population; among religious leaders, the middle and upper classes, Catholics and Protestants, in the *völkisch* movement, and especially among peasants. The farmers were trying to survive, often on borrowed capital in a rapidly industrializing Germany, to stay solvent, and to compete as best they could with the ever-rising living standards of the city worker. Financing the operations of farms with a growing need for machinery and artificial fertilizers required loans, and Jews were readily identified with the slick, urban exploiters who made them. Anti-Semites appeared too among the members of the landed society, although a Junker like Bismarck was much too intelligent to share their opinions, much less join their ranks. The Reich had no Lueger to lead a mass political movement; the anti-Semites other than Treitschke and Stoecker (who eventually lost his post as court preacher) were relatively obscure men. There were a number of small fry, including one Dr. Buecker, who raised his standard of anti-Semitism among the peasants and founded two papers, the *Wucherpille* and the *Reichsherold*, which had a moderate circulation in rural communities. Arrayed, however, against the anti-Semitic campaigns was the full power of the workers' movement, the Social Democrats, the liberal intellectuals who were writing the books and plays and publishing the journals and newspapers that were highly regarded and widely read. One such journal was *Simplicissimus*, which delighted in satirizing the Catholic clergy, foppish army officers, the pseudo-elegant bourgeoisie, and the effete upper classes. It was a measure of its contempt for anti-Semitism that it did not hesitate to shaft both Jews and their enemies. In one drawing, a fashionable young lady is asking a count how he likes being the father-in-law of a Jewish firm and he answers: "Before I was regarded by people as the *clou* ["main attraction"], now I'm regarded as the clown." Another full-page drawing under the heading "Strictly according to orders" shows two dandified officers on the parade grounds. The senior officer is saying to his junior: "Herr Lieutenant, you shouldn't praise Private Cohen so often; he will realize he does better than all three of the officer candidates." To this the lieutenant replies: "I just didn't want to be unjust."

Anti-Semitism was mainly latent in Germany in the nineteenth and early twentieth centuries. Germany had no Dreyfus case to trigger Right and Left into furious warring camps and bring together, as Proust wrote, the French bourgeoisie and nobility on a common ground of chauvinism and anti-Semitism. Germany's anti-Semitism was nothing like as deadly as that of Russia and Middle Europe, where Jews were slaughtered by the scores in pogroms, some of them spontaneous, some organized. Nevertheless, as was the case in other European countries and in the United States, it was pervasive and taken for granted. The Jew, no matter how he strove to assimilate, remained identifiable in Germany as he did in the rest of Europe and in America; and his difference marked him off and down. This fashion of anti-Semitism, ranging from polite to outspoken rejection by individuals and communities, was generally accepted as a corollary to a civilized toleration of Jews, but blatant anti-Semitism was regarded by liberals, socialists, and the chief spokesmen for the dynamic Germany of the industrial era as a feudal relic to be razed. In the Good Friday liturgy of the Catholic Church appeared the phrase *"Oremus pro perfidis Judeis,"* which was translated into German as "Let us pray for the malevolent [*heimtückische*] Jews" or "Let us pray for the perfidious [*treulose*] Jews." Only, in fact, in the mid-twentieth century under Pope Pius XII were the words changed to "Let us pray for the unbelieving Jews."

The *bête noire* of the German Right, however, was not the Jew but the Social Democrats, and while the two were often linked, it was the economic and social heresies of the followers of Karl Marx and his disciples August Bebel and Wilhelm Liebknecht that seemed, not only to conservatives, but to the rest of the nonsocialist parties as well, a threat to the very substance of the Reich. The army's attempt to reeducate recruits, infected as the high command saw it with the cholera of Marxist ideology, made no use of anti-Semitism; it was based on the conviction that officers had only to explain to the troops the true meaning of loyalty and duty to the emperor, of obedience to their superiors, and of the need for accepting the divinely ordained division of upper and lower classes, haves and have-nots, and the scales of leftist, Marxist superstition would fall from their eyes. This transformation, of course, never took place; young Social Democrats, including noncommissioned officers, served their time in the army, did their duty and often did it well, listened to the army's strictures against the party and its leaders, and returned to both when their military service was over. This the army reports noted with candor as well as horror.

The Social Democrats, after the election of 1912, were the largest party in the Reichstag. Internationally minded, antimilitaristic, seeking social justice and the end of privilege, their adherents could not easily be persuaded that the status quo was the best of all possible worlds and that they should accept it as it was. Army officers reported that Social Democrats made admirable soldiers; one of them said that he was forced to acknowledge how well they served, and added that they were not unpatriotic either. And, as the next years would demonstrate, this was entirely true. The Social Democratic party, in a time of national peril, was as devoted to the Fatherland as any other, despite Marx's teaching that love of country was a bourgeois pitch designed to keep the workers in line. Although Social Democrats spoke of calling a general strike in the event of war, their leader, August Bebel, made an exception in the case of a defensive war, especially one with tsarist Russia, which was universally detested by all those left of center on the Continent and in England as well, and against which he said they would march as one man. Tsarist Russia was the abomination of the Social Democrats. In 1891 Bebel had told a party gathering at Erfurt that "German soil, the German Fatherland, belongs to us, the masses, as much or more than it does to any one else," and he added: "If Russia, that stronghold of brutality and barbarism, the enemy of all human culture, attacks Germany to fragment and destroy, and that could be the only aim of such a war... we would fight side by side with those who today are our opponents, not to rescue them and their state and social order, but to rescue Germany, that is, ourselves. . . ."[10] In 1913, in what was regarded as his political testament to the party, Bebel went further. He told the Reichstag during the debate on the budget that no one wanted to surrender a defenseless Germany to the onslaught of the enemy, that Germany had to reckon with the possibility of attack, and that with modern techniques such a conflict would be a world war and, for Germany, perhaps, a question of life or death. Everyone, Bebel said, wanted to avoid such a war, but if it should come, not only was the participation of every man justified, but it would also be indispensable. Bebel's words were echoed by Karl Liebknecht and other leading Social Democrats. What they believed in was a people's army and what they fought against was the idea of an elitist standing army. Bebel and his followers wanted a *Volkswehr*, a people's defense force where every citizen was a soldier and every soldier a citizen.[11]

They were caught in logical inconsistencies: the officer corps they regarded by definition as made up of class enemies, but at the same time the army could not function without it. The Social Democratic deputies consistently voted against bills to increase military expenses, yet a powerful army was essential; Germany had to be defended, and Social Democrats would fight shoulder to shoulder with their class enemies in the kaiser's army against any foreign foe. One of their chief purposes was to work for the destruction of privilege and the inner contradictions of a political and social system that made wars inevitable. So the party program rejected the voting system in Prussia and Saxony based on the taxes a citizen paid; it would change Germany, not by violence, but by parliamentary means, for despite its deep flaws the society had many virtues.*

A Marxist party, the Social Democrats expected to win power by a non-Marxist strategy. Bismarck believed social democracy to be the vanguard of the revolution that would overturn the monarchy; the emperor saw it optimistically as a passing phase; the upper classes, the bourgeoisie, and the peasantry agreed with Bismarck and also hoped the emperor was right, for they were convinced that the health and integrity of the state were rooted in them and the conflicting opinions they held. As for the army, the high command had read enough Marx to be convinced that the Social Democrats aimed at revolution and that when the time seemed ripe they would attempt to achieve it by violence. Thus no Social Democrat could be a career officer, nor could Jews.

* Bebel, the son of a noncommissioned officer, said in a party rally in Magdeburg in 1910: "There is no other state like Prussia, but if we ever once have this state in our power we will have everything . . . the South has no understanding of this Junker state in all its beauty." (Hans Meier-Welcker and Wolfgang von Groote, *Handbuch zur deutschen Militärgeschichte 1648–1939*, vol. 5, p. 21.)

The taboos against Jewish officers, both active and reserve in Prussia and Saxony (Bavaria had a few), were said to be religious, not racial;* the emperor himself declared that only a devout Christian could be a good officer,† and his and the army's idea of the good officer was a man of Christian virtue who would automatically reject any political heresy. Jews were not Christians; they often belonged to, or were tolerant of, the ideologies of the Left (no matter how many Jews might be bankers or businessmen who detested Marx and all his works); and it was best that they remain outside the officer corps.‡

The Prussian minister of war in 1908, Karl von Einem, said it was inadmissible (*unstatthaft*) to prevent one-year volunteers and reserve officer candidates from being promoted to officer status because of religious reasons, and in 1909 he repeated in a speech to the Reichstag that it was improper to keep a qualified young man from becoming a reserve officer because he was a Jew. His successor, Josias von Heeringen, however, told the Reichstag that such appointments sometimes met with disapproval, unjustified as this might be, and that this attitude, too had to be taken into consideration.

So Adolf Hitler found himself at home in Germany. His Austrian dialect was close to that of the Bavarians, and the people he encountered in Munich were likely to be Germans and not, as in Vienna, a motley assortment from all over Europe. He settled down in a room he rented from a Munich tailor, Josef Popp, continuing much the same kind of life he had led in Vienna. He painted pictures—the Hofbraühaus, the Town Hall, and such—and sold them, not through pedlars as he had in Vienna, but through regular Munich art dealers. He got along well with the Popps and their two children, a family that made no demands on him but provided him with a comfortable shelter and an audience. He had only one experience that might have had unpleasant consequences; the Austrian authorities caught up with him. They had asked the Munich police to locate him, accusing him of evading conscription. Hitler managed his escape from this dreadful threat to his refuge

* The problems of diet and of the observation of the Sabbath were considered to be among the barriers. In fact, a rabbi in Fulda, Dr. Cahn, declared in 1913 that any dispensation with regard to the religious laws was out of the question. (Karl Demeter, *Das Deutsche Offizierkorps in Gesellschaft und Staat 1650–1945*, p. 202.)

† Addressing recruits, he said: "You have sworn your fealty before God's altar and the open sky and on His crucifix as good Christians must. He who is not a good Christian is not a good human being." (*Münchener Neueste Nachrichten*, June 15, 1913.)

‡ The taboo might on occasion be broken. Before 1885 Jews had served as reserve officers in the Prussian army and in the 1860's, King Wilhelm I of Prussia seconded the son of a Jewish banker who had befriended him to a commission in one of the most exclusive cavalry regiments over the objections of its noble officers. The young man served in two wars with great distinction and was ennobled by Wilhelm II.

in Germany with the cool stratagems of a born confidence man. The Munich criminal police had his address; they found him on January 10, 1914, informed the Austrian police where he lived, and a week later they gave Hitler a summons to appear in Linz on January 20. On January 19 the Munich police took him to the Austrian Consulate in Munich, where Hitler was so persuasive that both the Munich police and the Austrian consular authorities, instead of sending him to Linz for his appearance on the following day, permitted him to remain in Munich and delay his arrival in Linz until February 5. Hitler thereupon sent a telegram to the Linz *Magistrat* asking them to permit him to appear in Salzburg, which is much nearer Munich than Linz, and when this request was refused, he wrote a letter to them, repentant, sorrowful, autobiographical, explaining everything and asking again whether he could not go to Salzburg instead of Linz for his examination.

He had matured considerably since he wrote his last letter to Gustav Kubizek in the summer of 1908. His letter to the *Magistrat* in Linz is a hoax, a bathetic appeal to the humane sentiments of any man of goodwill; a little drama in which he played the part of a poor, gifted, knightly Horatio Alger hero, a young man who has suffered much but has bravely sought to do his duty despite the heavy counts against him. Never, he wrote, had he sought to evade military service; an orphan making his way despite formidable obstacles, he had experienced hunger and hardship but he had remained an upright man of principle, a young artist, self-supporting and aspiring to an even higher vocation. The themes of the letter were *Leitmotive* that would often reappear in later writings, including *Mein Kampf*, and the sentimental appeal for understanding for the hard physical and moral struggle of a man of selfless, undeviating virtue who desired nothing more than to be permitted to do his duty, this theme, too, would reappear in years to come. It was the script he had written for himself and it would last him a long time.

He knew very well what would be likely to impress Austrian bureaucrats, men of some self-importance with a considerable feeling for middle-class status, who were paid to listen attentively to their clients, to deal justly with them, and then to stamp their papers. What else could they do but pay heed to the appeal of a young artist struggling to support himself, resisting illicit temptation, guilty perhaps of trivial sins of omission but basically sound, even admirable, whose father moreover had also been an Austrian official?

Hitler in his letter to the Linz *Magistrat* explained that he had received the summons to appear there on a Sunday, January 18, at four o'clock. But Sunday, he wrote, everything was closed, and on Monday government offices opened only at 10:00 A.M., so he would have had to travel on the afternoon of the nineteenth, which would have hardly given him time for the simplest physical hygiene, even for taking a bath. More important, he could not in that short space of time—six hours, he calcu-lated—raise funds for the trip.

He said the summons to appear had addressed him as a *Kunstmaler* (that is, an "art painter"), which indeed is what he had called himself for some years and was the same title he used in the letter, but, he wrote, although he was entitled to call himself that, the title was correct only in a limited sense. It is true, he wrote, "that I earn my living as an in-dependent artist, only, however, because I am entirely without re-sources (my father was a state official) and in order to permit me to pursue my further education. I can spend only part of my time earning a living, since I am studying to be an architectural artist." So his income, he told the officials, was very modest, large enough only to cover his basic needs. As proof he sent along his tax statement, which showed his income to be 1,200 marks—a sum, he said, rather too high than too low, and which did not signify that he earned 100 marks a month. "Oh, no," he wrote, "my monthly income is very uncertain and at the moment certainly very poor, because the art market in Munich at this time is hibernating, and 3,000 artists live, or want to live, here." As for saving any meaningful sums of money, that was out of the question, because his expenses were considerably greater than those of an equally well situated worker.

He therefore begged the authorities to be so kind as to understand why he had not been able with such a short time at his disposal—a half day—to obey the summons. He had gone to the consulate, he continued, on Monday to ask for advice, had sent a telegram seeking a delay, and had received the refusal on the twenty-first at 9:00 A.M. But he did admit to one fault: he had not reported (as was required under Austrian law) to the authorities in the autumn of 1909. Nevertheless, he had appeared in 1910 before the conscription authorities in Vienna and had paid a crown when he filled out an application asking if he could appear later for enlistment in Vienna. Then he had heard nothing further. He had had no idea of evading military service. . . . So he had been all the more confounded by this invitation to appear in Linz Which (his capital) came in the form of a summons, as though he had paid no attention to any of the other communications. And as for his having failed to appear for examination in 1909, this, he wrote, "was an endlessly bitter time for me. I was an inexperienced young man with no money and too proud to accept any assistance from anyone, to say nothing of asking for it. With no outside help of any kind, dependent only on myself, the few crowns, sometimes only heller, on hand from my savings hardly paid for a place to sleep." Then he wrote the very sentence that would appear almost word for word many years later: "I had no friend other than Sorrow and Want, no companion other than unappeasable hunger; I have never known the beautiful word *Youth*; today, five years later, I still have the remembrance in the form of chilblains on my fingers, hands, and feet. And yet, I can even so look back on this time not without a certain pleasure, because now I have risen above the worst. Despite the greatest deprivation, often in the midst of a dubious environment, I have always kept my name respectable [*unbescholten*] before the law and clean before my conscience up to the time of this unanswered military summons, which I never even knew about at the time. That is the only thing for which I feel myself answerable." And therefore, he hoped, a modest fine, which he would gladly pay, should be sufficient punishment. He wrote: "I send this letter independently from the form I filled out and signed at the consulate today. I also ask that you let further orders go through the consulate, and please be assured that I will not fail to carry out punctually these provisions." The officials at the consulate, he said, had been very kind and had expressed the hope that they might intercede so he could appear in Salzburg. Although he could hardly dare hope for this, still, he asked that the Linz authorities please not make matters more difficult for him.

The letter worked perfectly. He was permitted to go before the conscription officials in Salzburg, who rejected him for the army. "Too weak," they said.

The Austrian summons had spelled his name Hietler, and Hitler in turn continued either to use old forms or to misspell words with which he had formerly had difficulty. He still wrote *giebt* instead of *gibt*; as in his letter to Kubizek, he continued to capitalize the wrong pronouns; and syntax continued to cause him difficulty. But he had no difficulty whatever with the tone of the letter or its calculated effect. The letter was perfectly directed at its target, and it succeeded where many a more literate statement might have failed. How could well-nourished, well-intentioned bureaucrats reject the plea of the son of one of their own profession, a young man who admitted to only one transgression in his lifetime—that he had not showed up for his military examination in 1909? Everything else was plausibly explained, even though none of the explanation was true.

His penury was as imaginary as his chilblains, which developed for the first and last time in this letter. Far from being without means, he had been supported until his mother's death by his family, and when she died, by his inheritance plus the state subsidy and his earnings. As for his using his scant savings for instruction in architectural design, the closest he had come to furthering his education in the visual arts was to go to the theater or the opera almost every day in the week. Evading Austrian military service, in what he regarded as the contemptible Austrian army, had been one of the chief aims of his youth and was certainly a main reason for his having moved to Munich. The truest statement he made in the letter was that he had not reported for his military examination in 1909, and that would have already been well known to the Austrian authorities, who in their letter to the Munich police called him a draft evader. But his remarkable ability to play on the sympathies of an audience and to act out the role he had written for himself of a dauntless, tragic youth of stainless moral purity in a wicked world—these were successful ploys and not completely fake. He had not, as his contemporaries might have said, indulged in vice; he had not been seduced by women, alcohol or tobacco, or any kind of riotous living, although his abstinence had little to do with self-discipline. These were simply things that either did not interest him or repelled him.

Years later he called his months in Munich the happiest of his life, and here he was probably telling the truth. His long, detailed war letters addressed to Herr and Frau Popp, referring to their common acquaintances, and to a Munich assistant judge, *Justizassessor* Ernst Hepp, show that he was not altogether the sad loner in a city of strangers that he had been in Vienna. He had maintained contacts with these people and with other acquaintances, to whom he sent his greetings, as he had with art dealers, and he lived with some degree of content in a city and country far more congenial to him than Vienna and Austria. The German newspapers carried stories that could only confirm Hitler's belief in the greatness of Germany and the decadence of Austria-Hungary. A Colonel Redl, chief of staff of the Prague Army Corps, who had committed suicide when it was discovered he had provided Russia with important military information, was but another example to Hitler, Pan-Germans, and German nationalists of Austrian unreliability. For a time it had been rumored that Colonel Redl, who was a homosexual, had also revealed German mobilization plans to the Russians, but this was denied in Berlin, where officials said Redl had no access to such plans, thus demonstrating that Germany was able to defend itself not only against its ring of enemies but also against the treachery of an ally.

On the day before Hitler arrived in Munich, the king of England and the tsar of Russia, both of them cousins of the kaiser, were in Potsdam with their wives for the wedding of the Hohenzollern princess Victoria Luise with Prince Ernst August von Cumberland, Duke of Braunschweig and Lüneburg. A light rain had fallen during the morning, but the weather had cleared for the ceremony. In this an omen was seen by people earnestly looking for favorable auguries for brighter relations among the countries represented by these monarchs related to one another not only by blood but also by their high, when not divine, offices. The tsar, during his visit, received the secretary of state to the Ministry of Foreign Affairs, Gottlieb von Jagow, in a long audience that was viewed as another good sign, and newspapers expressed the hope that George V's stay in Berlin had also contributed to the relaxation of tensions between

England and Germany. A few days after the wedding, in the haze of amity and goodwill created by the festivities, the kaiser accompanied the tsar and the imperial party to the Anhalter railroad station in Berlin to see them off to St. Petersburg.

That it was a time of continuing danger to the peace of Europe, however, was evident to any reader of the press. War and preparations for war took up far more space than did any celebrations of international comity and mutual esteem. The New Year's issue of *Simplicissimus* had an illustration on its cover of a figure from the Apocalypse: Death riding before the portals of the European castle and the huddled, frightened people inside the gates praying that he be kept away. Another picture in *Simplicissimus* showed two disreputable-looking old generals of indeterminate nationality and, behind them, row on row of corpses. One general is saying: "We've killed a hundred thousand men; now we're a *Kulturvolk*."

The causes of war were perceived by the Left in the battle for markets of capitalist states, and the Social Democratic parties of Europe were, in principle, all deployed against it. European intellectuals in every country regarded war as the barbarous survival of a primitive past, and the men of business saw it as a threat to their enterprises. Large standing armies drained from farms and industry manpower needed for their development. Recruits seemed to be trained in idleness. The moral revulsion against war, however, was directed against a major European war, not against minor, limited conflicts like the coalition war in the Crimea, the wars of Prussia against Austria and France, the Russo-Japanese War, or the Boer War. The hundred years of peace enjoyed by Europe since the Napoleonic wars had been years of European tranquility, but they had not been years without war. Europe had never experienced such a time, and no one but millenerians thought she would be likely to in the foreseeable future. National states were, beyond everything else, Powers, whose ultimate recourse to preserve their borders and domestic peace was force. It was a statesman's manifest duty to strengthen the well-being, prestige, and security of his own country whenever and wherever he could and by any means that could be plausibly defended.

War in the Balkans flamed, sputtered out, and began again. The remaining European possessions of Turkey, torn by revolution, had been shown to be ripe for redistribution as Austria-Hungary formally annexed Bosnia and Herzegovina in 1908,* and Italy attacked Turkey in September 1911 to gain her share of Mediterranean territory where she had been competing without visible success against France and Austria. The

---

* Russia and Austria had agreed in a secret treaty of 1876 to a division of Turkish territory under which Austria would get Bosnia and Herzegovina in return for Austrian neutrality in Russia's forthcoming war with Turkey. The Congress of Berlin, after the Russo-Turkish War of 1877–1878, permitted Austria-Hungary to occupy the provinces that were still nominally Turkish.

Balkan League, formed under Russian auspices in the spring of 1912, took advantage of the Italo-Turkish War and, joined by Montenegro, rose against the rickety Ottoman Empire that had ruled them so long to free their compatriots and fellow Christians·in Macedonia, Thrace, and Albania. Thus at the expense of Turkey, Austria had obtained two more provinces mainly inhabited by Slavs. Italy, like Germany lately become a unified nation, was compensated with Tripolitania and Cyrenaica, and the Balkan countries divided the rest.

A general European war had been threatened in 1912 as Austrian Foreign Minister Berchtold and Chief of Staff Freiherr Conrad von Hötzendorff demanded armed intervention to prevent Serbia from acquiring more territory, including a harbor on the Adriatic, on Austria's uneasy borders. Russia supported Serbia, and France, Russia. But war was avoided, because both Germany and England made it clear they would not join their allies in a war so remote from their own central interests. In the summer of 1913 the Balkan war broke out again, this time waged by Serbia, Montenegro, and Greece, joined by Rumania against their ally of the year before, Bulgaria. It was a hopeless battle for Bulgaria, who lost most of the territory she had gained. Russia had supported Serbia against her, and as a result Bulgaria would turn for help in future encounters to the Germany-Austria alliance. Alliances then as now were arrangements of convenience, temporary structures that could be knocked down and reassembled overnight, and their most enduring cement was a common enemy. Napoleon's striving to unite Europe under French hegemony had brought Russia, Austria, Prussia, and Britain together with a fixed determination to bring him down and with him the French imperial design for dominating Europe that Napoleon had shared with Louis XIV. In 1871, the place that France had long occupied was taken by Germany. The rise of Germany as a major military and industrial power with a great army and powerful fleet upset all previous calculations on which security in Europe had been based. Old rivalries persisted, but the overwhelming fact, which affected every capital, was the power of Germany. England in 1902 had concluded an alliance with Japan, a move directed against Russia and her threat to British interests in Afghanistan, Persia, and Tibet. By 1907, however, Britain and Russia had succeeded in coming to an accommodation. Russia, having been disastrously and unexpectedly defeated by Japan in 1904, was in no position to challenge at the same time Britain in the East and Austria, which was supported by Germany, in the Balkans. In 1904, the Entente Cordiale between Britain and France put an end to centuries of bitter rivalry and wars that had been fought over much of the globe. France recognized the priority of British interests in Egypt and in return got a free hand in Morocco.

It was a unified Germany that was the cause of the realignments.

Britain's enemy had long been the most powerful nation on the European continent—France, Spain, even Holland. The island kingdom was dependent for its security on a preeminent sea power, bases all over the world that would help maintain it, and in addition a balance of power on the Continent that would further deter any nation from mounting an attack on her shores. Britain had to prevent, in other words, the attempt of any power to unify or dominate Europe; the national rivalries of European powers were her security, and her fleet kept the lifelines of supply open as well as keeping any foe from her shores. Germany, before she became unified, had never been an enemy; on the contrary, British subsidies had kept numerous armies of German states in uniforms and supplies, and it was Prussia, along with Britain and Russia, that had destroyed Napoleon.

Germany and France, too, had never been the traditional enemies publicists in both countries now declared them to have been. France's enemy in the sixteenth and seventeenth centuries was Austria, with its Habsburg allies in Spain, Italy, and Burgundy. After that the enemy was England. Not only Mme de Staël had admired the German ethos; generations of Frenchmen had been nourished on the work of Goethe, Schiller, and the German philosophers. Napoleon had counted Bavaria among his allies and Friedrich Wilhelm III of Prussia had sent half his army to march with Napoleon to Moscow. Germany, as long as it remained splintered, had been a source of both allies and intellectual stimulation to France before and after the Revolution. Maintaining the division of Germany had been one of the chief political goals of French foreign policy since Richelieu. A united Germany would add a new enemy to the long list of powers with which France contended on the continent—England, Spain, Austria, Russia—against all of whom France had fought long and inconclusive wars in her attempt to shore up her security and to dominate Europe. Thus it was the defeat of 1870 that France could not accept. When Napoleon had been defeated by the European coalition in 1815, the power struggle of dynamic nationalisms had been diverted for a time to other continents, where the competition for bases and colonies drained off a good deal of energy that had formerly gone into war at home. But the defeat of France in 1870 was something entirely new. A great power, much stronger than France, had appeared at her gates and had amputated two provinces, Alsace-Lorraine (historically no more French than German*), and these became the symbol of the catastrophe that had befallen her. Germany, with its hardworking population, its rising birthrate, and its industrial military

---

* Seventy-five percent of the mixed population of Alsace-Lorraine spoke German. Strongly Catholic, they resented French anticlericalism and they were even less enthusiastic about being transferred to Protestant Germany, which gave them an efficient administration but offended their sense of difference and self-esteem.

and organizational preeminence, had displaced France as the leading power of Europe, and its relative strength was increasing year by year. Russia with its anti-Austrian policy in the Balkans and its huge manpower and Britain with her navy and traditional opposition to the dominant European power were now France's natural allies, as they had been her natural enemies in her time of strength.

Every country felt itself threatened: Austria-Hungary by Russia and the Pan-Slaves; Britain by German pretensions to sea power combined with Germany's dominant position on the Continent; Germany by her encirclement by France, Russia, and Britain; France by the very existence of a unified German state; Russia by her political and military weakness, which had been exposed in the Japanese war, in incongruous contrast to her activist and expansionist policies. Any move by any country in one bloc or the other was a menace, the only answer to which was an increment in military strength.

The armament race was an expensive one. Britain in 1902 was spending more money on her fleet and army than any other country in the world. Calculated in German marks, British armament costs were 46.5 per capita per year, as against France's 24 and Germany's 16.6. By 1909 the figures were 28.1 for both France and Britain and 21.6 for Germany; and by 1913 the French were in first place with 33.5 marks per head and Britain second with 32.9, followed closely by Germany with 31.3.[12]

The long fuses leading to the European arsenals were laid, ready to be lighted no matter how many royal occasions were celebrated by the heads of state. Once Germany was united, the German genius would be applied to the organization of an army far more powerful than any France could hope to raise. With her smaller population and lower birthrate, France, to counter the weight of the German army, had to depend on the forces of allies, on contingents from her African colonies, on the protection of the British fleet, and on the presence on European soil of a British expeditionary force. What would help the British decide in favor of the Entente was not only German industrial competition and German military predominance on the Continent, but also the increasing size of the German fleet and the often intemperate harangues of the kaiser and his diplomats, few of whom had had much experience in the conduct of world affairs and the complexity of decisions involving a good deal more than the brandishing of guns. But Britain had fought against good and bad kings and even against armies led by a woman and a saint to prevent France from bestriding the Continent. The character of the rulers against whom she fought was of little consequence; what counted were the numbers and skill of the armed forces the leading Continental power had at its disposal across the Channel.

We speak of France, Germany, Russia, and Britain, but in each country counsels were divided on how to maintain and increase its security and well-being. There was a society for German-English understanding, there were the internationally minded socialist parties, there were peace societies, and in the various governments there were sporadic attempts to turn events from the great war that threatened. In 1897 Russia and Germany had collaborated in the Far East where Chinese territory was amicably divided between them, the Germans getting Kiaochow, the Russians Port Arthur. A year later, British Colonial Minister Joseph Chamberlain, concerned over Russian advances in China and French rivalry in West Africa, suggested to the German ambassador in London, Count von Hatzfeldt, the possibility of a radical shift in British policy on the Continent that would make Germany Britain's chief ally. He said, however, and with truth, that such a radical change in policy would have to be approved by Parliament. The German Foreign Office was hesitant. It feared that with strong anti-German sentiment in England and similar anti-British sentiment in Germany, a rejection of such a proposal would be all too likely, and that this would have disastrous results not only on relations between the two countries but on other powers as well—Russia in particular. And when the kaiser reported the British offer to the tsar, asking what Russia was prepared to do if Germany rejected the proposal, he was told the British had made the same suggestion to the tsar some months before, thus confirming Wilhelm and the Foreign Office in their skeptical views of the British approach. Discussions of an alliance were postponed, with the way left open for their resumption at a later date. Talks were in fact resumed in 1901, when the German counsel of embassy in London, Freiherr von Eckhartstein, himself a strong proponent of a "defensive alignment" between the two countries, reported to Berlin that the British were again prepared to discuss an alliance. But the prospect faded as both countries shied away from commitments they thought unduly advantageous to the other. The British proposal of a pact limited to the Mediterranean was rejected by the German Foreign Office in the belief that by accepting such an arrangement, Germany would only be defending British interests in the Mediterranean against France and Russia. The British, in turn, did not like the German suggestion that they join the three-nation treaty of alliance with Austria and Italy. Such short-lived and tentative explorations were not uncommon. Following the defeat of China by Japan in 1895, Russia, Germany, and France joined in a common front against further Japanese expansion in the Far East. In 1900, at the time of the Boxer Rebellion, France and Russia suggested a common French-Russian-German front against the expansion of British interests in China, and earlier, in March of the same year, the tsar had proposed the intervention of the three powers to bring about peace in the Boer War.

The counterforces of what statesmen took to be the laws governing national survival were far too powerful for such proposals of possible realignments to have much substance, and the great powers soon fell back to their original positions and all-out competition in the arms race.

In 1913, an increase in Russian peacetime troop strength from 1,200,000 to 1,420,000, financed with new French loans, rose out of the Balkan crisis and an increase in the forces of the relatively weak Austrian army.* The Russian measure† caused Germany to respond by adding 136,000 troops over a period of two years, and in turn the French government felt itself obliged to meet that additional threat to French security by introducing a longer period of military service for recruits. France was already calling up 82 of every 100 men, compared with Germany's 54 out of 100, and the only way to close the gap in manpower was to lengthen the period of service from two to three years.[13] The forces at the disposal of France and Russia were considerably larger than those of the Central Powers. The field armies of Russia and France numbered 5.3 million, as against 3.8 million for Germany and Austria. Germany, in the spring of 1914, would have 748,000 men in its standing army; the French, 750,000 with the three years' service, not counting colonial and native troops.

The debate in the Chambre des Députés in the summer of 1913 on the increase in the term of service was long and acrimonious and accompanied by scattered mutinies of French soldiers in Belfort, Toul, Châlons, Rouen, Bar-le-Duc, and Orléans. The mutinies led to house searches by the police to find the civilian instigators, and impassioned speeches in and out of the Chamber between the forces of Left and Right. The French minister of war, Etienne, citing alleged French inferiority in troop strength, told the Chamber the French decision to increase the term of service had hit Germany "like a clap of thunder" and asked the deputies, to shouts of "No, No," if they wanted to become German satellites.[14] "We will pursue our goal to the end," he told the Chamber. "We want a worthy peace, but if unhappily a war breaks out, then we have our unequalled officer corps which is the envy and marvel of all foreign armies . . . and they with our excellent corps of noncommissioned officers will win the victory."[15] In Vichy he told a meeting of French gymnasts they were to prepare "the victory of tomorrow."[16] A priest, Bishop Penon,

---

* The Austrian standing army numbering 385,000 men in 1912 was to be increased to 470,000 by 1914. It was technically, as well as in numbers, far behind the other European powers. (Bruno Gebhardt, *Handbuch der Deutschen Geschichte,* vol. 3, 1970, p. 373.)

The French loans were made for two specified purposes: (1) the building with the assistance of French general staff officers of strategic railroad lines going to the German border, and (2) an increase in the peacetime strength of the Russian army. (*Der Diplomatische Schriftwechsel Iswolskis 1911–1914,* Band 3, no. 936.)

† Russia also added to its military convention with France an agreement which provided for combined naval operations of both countries in the event of war. (Bruno Gebhardt, *Handbuch der Deutschen Geschichte,* vol. 3, 1970, p. 373.)

at the celebration in memory of Jeanne d'Arc at Orléans, told his audience: "As once Israel, now France is the nation chosen of God." He bade his audience remember that "God freed you by a miracle . . . [as] an immortal people destined to rule. . . . The great day is awaited, silently but with unfading hope, by the most faithful children of France."[17] In June 1913, speakers in the Chambre des Députés told of the French army's numerical weakness compared with the German forces and produced figures that were duly refuted in the German press. French Prime Minister Barthou said in the Chamber that the gap of numbers had to be closed, that the heroism of 1870 had not prevented the terrible amputation of the two lost provinces. Barthou, who was also minister of education, declared the teachers' syndicate left wing and antimilitary and said it had no right to join workers' unions in protests against the extension of military service. He threatened to dissolve all labor unions, saying that their agitation against the proposed law for three years' service was illegal, since they were permitted to demand economic reform only.[18] A former minister in a Briand cabinet, André Le Fèvre, told the Chamber that France had spent billions of francs less on armaments than had Germany in the last thirty years, and that while France was peaceful, she had not forgotten the humiliation of the loss of Alsace-Lorraine. Yet even, he said, if Strasbourg were still French, the new law would be needed; Russian mobilization would be slow, a German attack sudden. Those who had voted in 1867 against strengthening the army had brought on the war, which would probably not have occurred had France been strong. A socialist deputy, Guesde, replied to such arguments that it had been Napoleon III who had brought on that war, not French weakness, whereupon Le Fèvre told the deputies that if they, the defeated and the sons of the defeated, fell back into the same error as the generation of 1870, they too would be crushed. At this point another socialist deputy, Colly, called Le Fèvre a "comedy patriot."[19]

The recurring themes were 1870 and the humiliation. A spokesman for the army, Le Hérrissé, said he had experienced as a child the sad defeat and did not want to go through it again.[20] President Poincaré, speaking at Toulon, told his audience that for years they had had to bear a heavy burden of taxation, but that that was the price of security and of preventing any attempts at humiliating them. Should such an attempt be made, he said, "We want to be always strong, composed, and always ready."

Opposition speakers used a variety of arguments, economic, political, often impassioned. One deputy, Chautemps, said the proposal for three years' service hurt French repute abroad and was seen by foreign countries as a provocation. The increase in the size of the German army was not abnormal, and the Pan-Germans, whose extravagant speeches the government forces referred to, were without any serious influence. Whereupon a progovernment deputy, Pugliesi, replied that Chautemps talked like the German minister of war. Another opposition deputy said it was France's low birthrate that kept her from having an army equal to Germany's, and the socialist leader, Jaurès, said there was no possibility of the Germans' occupying the French border fortifications if they were in proper shape. Another deputy said it would damage France economically to send 200,000 more young men to barracks instead of to work. Socialists and others protested against the continuing house searches by police looking for printed material being used to subvert the troops and to bring about strikes and provide propaganda to defeat the bill, but despite everything the three-year service requirement was passed by the Chamber on July 19, 358 for and 204 against. With the approval of the French Senate, on August 7 the bill became law.

The chauvinism of the French and Russian governments was disquieting to their allies. In England, German papers reported, an article in the official *Westminster Gazette* asked whether France was becoming a Russian satrapy. Commenting on the French bill, the journal said it was no answer to France's manpower problem, but the longer period of service had been prescribed by Russian leaders in the course of Poincaré's visit to Moscow the summer before. Clemenceau, too, the *Gazette* wrote, had been taking part in the anti-German campaign, and he, in fact, had favored, not a three-year, but a five-year, term of service, a proposal that went beyond the limits of a normal society. France, the journal said, with her low birthrate and her inferior economic resources, was no match for Germany, and a relatively small sacrifice on the part of the German people could be fateful for her. The article warned that France should expect neither encouragement nor any kind of help from England if she made an aggressive move.[21]

The German papers gave a good deal of space to events in France and to the feverish state of French emotions. In early June, the *Frankfurter Zeitung* reported on a French story that a zeppelin with eleven officers on board had landed near Lunéville, causing tremendous excitement. According to the report, a crowd had demolished the dirigible and roughed up the German officers. Officials had been unable to get in touch with Paris and panic had spread; banks were stormed by depositors wanting to retrieve their savings. The whole story, it turned out, was a hoax, played by some pranksters on a news agency, but there was nothing exaggerated about French anti-German feeling. A dispatch that *was* true reported a warning by police that any display of a German uniform might cause trouble in a French theater. The prefect of police, therefore, wanted to know in advance of any scene in which an actor would be wearing a German military uniform in a concert hall or moving picture theater.[22]

In Germany, too, the conviction that the Fatherland was in danger was widespread and potent in all classes of the population. With England in control of the seas, Russia and its limitless hordes in the East, and France in the West, Germany, even in the eyes of the socialist workers, was encircled by a ring of enemies. The Austrian ally was considered a weak partner, its heterogeneous army of doubtful value, and even less reliance would be placed on the Italians, who had as many territorial quarrels with Austria as with any other of their neighbors and who at best would be neutral in any conflict not promising prompt and generous awards to Italy. It was a riddle to the kaiser and his advisors why so many statesmen in Europe mistrusted the Reich and its foreign policies. Germany, as its leaders saw it, was a state with no territorial ambitions in Europe, no gnawing appetite for revenge; it demanded only the same voice in the conduct of world affairs that was taken for granted among the other great powers. England's hostility they ascribed to jealousy, to Germany's industrial competition and to her claims to colonies or spheres of influence in parts of the world that were arrogantly considered by the British to be their preserves. France had never accepted the defeat of 1870 and the loss of Alsace-Lorraine, which in any event was no more French than German. France, German newspapers pointed out, carried on continuous anti-German propaganda in those provinces; thousands of anti-German pamphlets were regularly distributed, and this campaign was carried out in France as well.

The kaiser, who regarded the tsar as a weak cousin in constant need of his direction, wrote regularly to Nicholas, using the familiar form *Du,* as he did with the emperor of Austria and German princes, advising, admonishing, condescending. He believed the tsar to be surrounded, as indeed he was, with anti-German advisors who lost no opportunity to build up military forces in Russia, France, and the Balkans for a battle that would leave the tsar master of eastern Europe and the Dardanelles. The opposite numbers of these hypernationalists and Pan-Slavs were the members of the Pan-German Society, founded in 1891, and in England the believers in the Pax Britannica of Cecil Rhodes, Joseph Chamberlain, and Rudyard Kipling. The Pan-Germans were anti-English imperialists who wanted to make Germany, too, a world power on a level with her superior moral and intellectual qualities, whose weight, like Britain's, would be felt in every part of the globe.

Although Wilhelm II was not a Pan-German, he did succeed in making his voice heard on many occasions and often in a register that offended both Germans and foreigners. The kaiser was a volatile, neurotic ruler, a man of unusual ability, with an excellent command of English and French, a quick grasp of the essentials of complicated problems, and marked mood swings that went from deep depression to euphoria. What irked a good many people, from the editors of *Simplicissimus* to foreign chancelleries, were his bombastic utterances and his theatrical posturing

—evidences of the persona of a man who knew himself chosen by God for his high office but was uncertain of his relationship to other heads of state. At the kaiser maneuvers, he loved to lead the final, dashing cavalry charge that ended the war games, in which protocol decreed the troops under his command must be the victors. This impressive exploit, repeated annually, was the rococo climax of the maneuvers, and every staff officer knew it had no relationship at all to the realities of modern warfare. Wilhelm's diplomacy was of a similar kind, with heavy displays of iron will and not much account taken of the position of the other side. As one British observer said, the Germans entered negotiations as though every one of their demands was final and had only to be agreed to by the people across the table. And yet there could be no doubt that the emperor, for all his grandiloquence, was essentially a man of peace who had no intention of placing his country or his throne at risk by engaging in a general European war. Had he wanted war, 1900 would have been a good year for it, with Britain fighting the Boers, or 1904–1905, with the Russian debacle in the Far East and insurrection at home. In fact, neither England nor Germany had anything to gain from a general European war that would possibly match the terrible risks of fighting it.

Nevertheless, loud voices demanding war were heard in both countries. Lord Fisher, commanding the British fleet, wanted to "copenhagen"* the German navy in a preemptive attack and destroy it. General Friedrich von Bernhardi, a former German general staff officer, wrote a book, *Germany and the Next War*, published in 1912, that declared Germany must either become a world power or go under, and that to this end she must acquire colonies, defeat France even more decisively than in 1870, and organize a Middle European alliance under German leadership. Bernhardi's program was almost identical with that of the Pan-Germans under the chairmanship of Treitschke's student Heinrich Class. The movement, numbering some 25,000 members, demanded not only colonies but the establishment of a European economic bloc that would include Italy and Finland, as well as Middle Europe, under German leadership. Germany was to be a world power like England and at the same time impervious to a British blockade. Neither the views of Fisher nor those of Bernhardi and the Pan-Germans were widely shared in Britain and Germany.† But once war started, they gained converts in many quarters that up to 1914 had regarded them as crackpot.

* In September 1807, a combined British naval and military force bombarded Copenhagen, in neutral Denmark, on a report from British intelligence that Napoleon was on the point of invading the country.

† Nevertheless, war cries made good headlines. The *Daily Mail* in 1909 declared that Britain alone stood in the way of the German drive to world power, and an article in the *Saturday Review* said that if every Englishman were to be wiped out, the Germans would gain in proportion. Two growing nations were pressing against

The bellicose nations, that is, the nations whose long-range goals could be attained only by war, were Russia, France, and Austria, each for reasons that seemed overwhelmingly convincing to their policymakers and derisory to their opponents. Russia, her military and diplomatic leaders believed, had to expand her influence in the Balkans and reach out for the Straits. At the very least she had to prevent any third power from gaining control of the Dardanelles and in the long run she had to wrest their control from Turkey.* Russia had to support the Slav brothers and referee their acrimonies if she was to remain the dominant power in the Balkans, and as soon as the defeat by Japan had been partly digested, she proceeded to try to demonstrate her decisive power and influence there. To statesmen outside Russia, it seemed evident that the Balkans were no more than a peripheral interest to Russia while they were vital to Austria-Hungary. Without her Pan-Slav league and expansive aspirations, Russia would still be an *Imperium*; despite the military defeat and uprisings against the repressive rule of the tsar, she remained a great empire with its territory intact. The same thing could not be said of the rickety structure of multinational Austria-Hungary. Pan-Slav agitation, with Serbia as its spearhead, threatened not only its political stability but its very existence. Russia's fears had to do, not with its security, but with its aspirations and aims. Berlin's dispatch of a military mission to Turkey under General Liman von Sanders to reform (actually to command) the Turkish army was seen in St. Petersburg as an ominous threat to Russian ambitions to control the Straits. If Germany and Austria were again to demonstrate their strength and Russia's weakness in the Balkans, a dream of empire would go glimmering. And as for France, demoted as the leading nation in Europe because an upstart Prussia had unified Germany, losing economic and demographical ground each year to the new power she had long tried to prevent from emerging, her security could lie only in returning this Germany to the fragments that had been its origins.

When Britain and Germany avoided a major European war during the Balkan crisis of 1912, they had succeeded in meeting that one emergency only. The inflammable Balkans remained smouldering, with both Russia

---

each other "man to man all over the world. One or the other has to go, one or the other will go." (Joachim Remak, *The Origins of World War I*, p. 85.)

* The Russian foreign minister, Sazonov, reported to the tsar in late 1913 that Russia could not long endure the presence in the Black Sea of a Turkish fleet more powerful than hers. Turkish possession of the Straits, Sazonov wrote, had led to a deficit in the Russian budget when the Straits had been temporarily closed in 1912, and Sazonov asked rhetorically what would happen if the Straits were to fall into the hands of a country in a position to reject Russian demands. Russian efforts to control the Straits, Sazonov said, had not advanced a single step, and only in the light of the alliance with France and perhaps with England in the context of future European complications (*Verwicklungen*) could the goal of possessing the Straits be achieved. (*Der Diplomatische Schriftwechsel Iswolskis*, vol. 3, no. 1157.)

and Austria convinced that they could tolerate no recurrence of such insupportable belligerence on the part of the other. Germany and Britain had tilted the balance toward peace because Britain had no intention, as the *Westminster Gazette* pointed out, of fighting a major war at a time French or Russian chauvinists thought opportune, and Germany, too, found the Serb provocation insufficient to justify her backing her Austrian ally to the point of risking a major conflict.

The Germans, believing themselves the victims of the encirclement of jealous nations plotting their downfall, had little understanding of what other countries found objectionable or menacing in the German way of curing the ills of the world. The kaiser was convinced of a number of things, some true, some partly true, and some not true at all. He saw himself as a champion in shining armor crusading against the Yellow Peril and also as an apostle of peace in an intemperate world. Thus he had strongly supported Russia during the time of the Russo-Japanese War and he consequently expected the tsar to show some gratitude. Being a monarch himself, he held the profession of royalty in high esteem; in consequence he overprized the Russian officer corps with its mystical reverence for the tsar, an estimate shared by none of his own officers. Both the tsar and his regime seemed to them incapable of running a really competent government or army, and it seemed not at all unnatural that Russia would support the "burning and murdering" Serbs, as one German paper referred to them and their atrocities during the course of the war against Bulgaria.[23] The Germans could not understand either why foreigners were suddenly discovering in them unpleasant qualities that had escaped the observation of their nineteenth-century admirers like Carlyle and Queen Victoria. An American, Price Collier, wrote an article about the German character that was printed in the *Frankfurter Nachrichten,* and what he had to say more or less repeated what many other foreigners were writing about the Germans of the twentieth century. Collier wrote that Germany had too many thou-shalt-nots. More things, he wrote, were forbidden in Germany than were permitted. Citizens were warned not to throw paper on the sidewalk, not to walk on the grass; they were told when and where they could smoke, and they were given detailed rules for getting on and off trains. Germans, Collier wrote, seldom have an idea of how to behave unless they are instructed. Do you really, he asked, have to tell passengers after one hundred years of riding on railroads that it is dangerous to jump out of the train while it is in motion? Or that it is dangerous to throw out burning cigars? He also thought that women had an especially hard time in Germany and that in no other country was it more difficult for a woman to get along on her own. Collier noted that people in other countries were able to live without taking either uniforms or titles into private life. But Germans felt unhappy without either. Women, too, were affected by this title mania. The wife of a postmaster was called an *Oberpostmeistersgattin*, a resounding and taken-for-granted appellation that placed her honorifically in a stratified country. Germans would wait a half hour, uncomplainingly, for a streetcar; they would sit half a night in a beer hall, endlessly talking politics with terrible deliberation. Germany in a short time had moved from poverty to riches, but Germans were awkward in trying to work out what to do with their new wealth. What mattered to them was improvement in the standards of intellectual life and material comforts. No other city in the world had more places of amusement than Berlin. In the big German cities, families went out on Sundays and sat in beer gardens and restaurants; they brought along their children and consumed enormous amounts of food. They paid no attention to the simplest requirements of health until they again encountered a list of what was forbidden.[24]

These were views the German press printed and made no objection to. Other commentaries were more serious; writers complained that Germans were rude, brutal, grovellingly obedient to the demands of the *Obrigkeit*, incapable of acting without explicit directives. The list was long but it was also new. The *furor teutonicus* had been observed by the Romans, but the nation of thinkers and poets had been discovered and revered by most of Europe in the nineteenth century until the unification of the Reich and the resultant competition with the established powers of the Continent.

One of the Germans most difficult for foreigners to understand or like was the kaiser himself. He was a man deeply unsure of himself, who blustered his way into self-confidence at times when he was least convinced of the correctness of some simplistic or theatrical idea. He believed himself a ruler by divine right, but he could be as humble as he was arrogant. Once he was served sugar and cream in a cup of bouillon he and his hostess took to be coffee and he heroically drank it down without comment.[25] He saw himself as the romantic prince out of a heroic German past, in a splendid uniform, dashing on a charger, leading his devoted warriors to victory. When, after the assassination of the German ambassador to Peking, he sent the German expeditionary force to join the war against the Boxers, he spoke to them on June 27, 1900, from a high tribune built over the quay from which they were embarking. His words were never to be forgotten, either in Germany or in the countries outside. He said: "You are to take no prisoners, give no quarter. As the Huns under their King Attila made a name a thousand years ago that even now seems terrible in tradition and story, so shall the name of Germany be impressed by you in China so thoroughly that never again will a Chinese dare to look askance at a German."[26] The foreign minister, Prince von Bülow, who arrived a little late at the ceremony, was horrified when he first read the speech. He immediately revised the text and asked the newspapers to print it only with his changes. This they patriotically did, but the speech was bad enough even with the worst passages deleted, and fourteen years later the Entente would be at pains to remind the world by means of it of the Huns they had to fight against. Actually the German troops in China behaved in the same way as did the soldiers of the other powers in the coalition against the murderous Boxers, no better and no worse, but thanks to Wilhelm the world was prepared to see them as Huns instead of as representatives of the nation of thinkers and poets.

Despite the kaiser's love of uniforms, which he usually changed a number of times a day, when he visited Britain he was so impressed by British understatement that he took to wearing civilian clothes for a time. When he sent the German fleet to Kiaochow, he told its commander to sail in with "the mailed fist," although not much resistance could be expected from a nonexistent Chinese navy. His feudal concepts often clashed with the *Zeitgeist* of an industrial age, and this increased his self-doubts as he was forced to observe how out of step he was. He wanted as officials around him a "personal regiment" of men he could trust and influence. Thus the kaiser believed that he could master the mysteries of public finance in a few months and that the minister of finance could, after that, come to him for advice and the approval of the budget. Bismarck, too, was a victim of the kaiser's desire to be as many things to as many people as possible. Wilhelm had greatly admired Bismarck, but he could not tolerate a strong-minded rival for the conduct of policy. So Wilhelm often succeeded in pleasing nobody, not even himself. When he ascended the throne, he wrote letters to the German princes emphasizing his supremacy over them, although Germany under its constitution was a federation of sovereign or semisovereign states. For a long time he refused to negotiate a naval treaty with England that would have limited the size of the German navy and the proportions of both fleets,* but he also rejected the proposal of men like the then chief of staff, General von Schlieffen, and Baron von Holstein in the Foreign Office that he wage a preventive war against France while Russia was reeling from the effect of the Japanese defeat and civil disorders at home. He urged Austria to come to an accommodation with Serbia at the expense of Bulgaria, and a little over a year later told the Austrians Germany would support them even in demands that Serbia would be most unlikely to accept, believing the tsar would never back the murderers of royalty.

On October 28, 1908, he granted an audience to an Englishman, Colonel Stuart Wortley. Since the interview was designed to transform

---

* An agreement between Britain and Germany, however, setting the ratio for the building of new ships at 16–10, was made in 1914.

the unfriendly feelings of British public opinion, the kaiser permitted its text to be published in the *Daily Telegraph*. Explaining to Colonel Wortley that he was one of the few Germans friendly to England, the kaiser said that during the Boer War he had refused to receive the Boer delegates touring Europe to gain support, and he had also refused to join France and Russia in asking Britain to end the war. In addition he had sent his revered grandmother, Queen Victoria, a plan for defeating the Boers that contained precisely the same strategic plan that Britain later successfully used. He then went on to point out that the German fleet, of which Britain was so suspicious, was designed only to protect German commerce, and that Britain might one day, with Japan on the rise and China awakening, welcome its presence. It was a speech marvellously contrived to offend everybody—public opinion in Germany and abroad, the German Foreign Office, Britain, France, Russia, and Japan—and all to show Britain how well disposed he was. The kaiser had asked for and obtained the approval of the Foreign Office for publishing the interview, but the text had been read, not by the foreign secretary, Prince von Bülow, but by an underling who routinely approved it because he thought the emperor wanted it published. The British were incensed to be told that they owed their victory to the kaiser, the French and Russians were convinced Wilhelm's disclosures were made in an effort to destroy their alliance with Britain, Japan was insulted—in short, the interview was a masterpiece of ineptitude. The Germans were furious, and Prince von Bülow coldly placed all responsibility on the kaiser's shoulders, even though Wilhelm had followed protocol and obtained the Foreign Office's approval for publishing the speech. Wilhelm felt the earth tremble beneath his feet, and Bülow promised the Reichstag on his behalf that in the future, even in private conversations, the kaiser would "maintain the reserve indispensable to the interests of any consistent foreign policy...."[27] These assurances, however, were no more than a dressing over deep wounds, and the deepest were Wilhelm's. The whole episode so clearly displayed his weaknesses that it is doubtful that he ever fully recovered from it or from the shock of the violent public reaction against him. Even conservatives in Germany joined in talk about the desirability of his abdicating in favor of his son, and although the kaiser stayed on and his moments of blustering self-confidence returned, this was a trauma that could only confirm his deepest doubts and uncertainties.

Nevertheless the kaiser, for all his irresponsibility, played an important part not only in keeping the peace at critical times but also in the enactment of far-ranging social legislation forbidding Sunday work and limiting the work hours of women and children, and he had wanted to call an international conference for the purpose of extending such measures to other countries as well. Commentators have made much of his withered arm to explain why he rattled the sword so loudly and often, but Napoleon III was also a sword rattler and wielder, too, as were Clemenceau and Poincaré and Russians like Sazonov, all of whom assumed risks of war the kaiser shied away from and none of whom had withered arms. Sir Edward Grey, too, the British foreign secretary, was sound of body and confused in judgment. In 1906 he approved military and naval conversations between the French and British general staffs in which both countries exchanged secret military information and discussed in detail how they would operate in the event of war with Germany. In a private memorandum written in February 1906, Grey agonized over the decision, but he nevertheless came out for supporting France even though he wrote that the war would be horrible. France, he said, believed that Britain would support her in the event of war; and if Britain did not, the French would never forgive her, the United States would despise her, and Russia and Japan would pursue other courses. Grey would write later in his memoirs that he had doubtless made a mistake when, on January 31, 1906, he had told M. Paul Cambon, the French ambassador to London, of likely British backing amounting to a "defensive alliance" without consulting the cabinet. It was a commitment that Parliament and the British people would learn about only in August 1914.[28] Although he made no binding written agreements and explicitly told Cambon that a formal defensive alliance would need the approval of Parliament, what Grey did say and do led directly to the agreement in 1912 for the withdrawal of the French fleet from the Atlantic, which left the protection of the western coast to the British navy. These were fateful decisions, made in the light of Britain's traditional hostility to the dominant land power on the Continent and the buildup of the German fleet. They also had the effect of encouraging the war parties in France and Russia, whatever later admonitions might be made on behalf of prudence and whatever warnings might be published against unleashing a war on insufficient grounds.

Grey's secret diplomacy may well have been mistaken in both method and consequences, but given his estimate of the German strategic threat to Britain, he had few choices. For Germany a great fleet was an indulgence, a matter of prestige, not one of life and death, as it was for England. Although Germany had been building a fleet, in accord with the design of Admiral Tirpitz,* not to contest control of the seas with Britain but powerful enough to prevent Britain, in a crisis, from imposing its will on Germany, neither the German Admiralty nor the Foreign

---

* The building plans were designed for a German fleet operating on the defensive and utilizing harbor basins, canal locks, and shallow coastal waters; to this end, limits were placed on the length, beam, and depth of the ships. Offensive action, with the exception of sorties of task forces, was to be left to surface raiders and U-boats. (Karl Friedrich Nowak, *Chaos.*)

Office would ever be able to convince men like Grey or Churchill or Fisher that a great fleet combined with a great army was being put together solely for defensive purposes. British policy in response to German power on land and sea evolved into a moral commitment to France as binding as any treaty of alliance.

The war itself came, one lurch after another, as though some giant Rube Goldbergian device had been set in motion that might well stop or break down at any time before the last string that held the axe was cut. When Hitler heard of the assassination of the Archduke Franz Ferdinand and his wife in Sarajevo on June 28, 1914, he at first feared that the murderers might be German students who had decided to kill the pro-Slav heir to the throne, and he was later relieved to learn that this devoted friend of the Slavs had been the victim of Slav assassins.[29] Franz Ferdinand was well known for his espousing of Slav interests in Hungary against the attempt to "magyarize" the country. He had favored giving the Slavs a voice in the administration of the Austro-Hungarian monarchy on a par with the Germans and Hungarians, and later he advocated universal suffrage to increase Slav representation in the government.

The Austrian authorities were convinced from the start that the assassination was linked, at least indirectly, to the Serbian government. The perpetrators were Bosnian Serbs, the murder weapons, bombs, and Browning revolvers had come from Serbian army depots. Serb officials had permitted the conspirators to cross the border with their armament, and what the rest of Europe called the Sarajevo outrage was celebrated as a triumph in the Serbian press. In fact the assassination, as was learned later, was carried out by members of the Union of Death, or as it was more widely known, the Black Hand society, an underground terrorist organization led by a colonel on the Serbian General Staff, with some assistance from the network of *Narodna Odbrana* ("National Defense"), another Serbian propagandistic, anti-Austrian organization with close relations to the Serbian government.

There was sharp dissension in Serbia between leaders of the Radical party led by Nikola Pašić, who was prime minister, and the leaders of the Black Hand, Colonel Dimitrijević and other army officers, but their differences rose over the administration of territories conquered from Turkey and had nothing to do with policy toward Austria. Relations between the government-supported *Narodna Odbrana* and the Black Hand, in any event, were close enough to enable them to cooperate in the preparations for the assassination.

Had Austria, immediately after the crime, marched into Serbia, such a move might well have been accepted in most European capitals, including London, as an understandable measure taken against the perpetrators of a horrendous crime in which the Serbian government was at least indirectly involved. But instead the Austrian reprisal was preceded by moves and countermoves and a stiff ultimatum that set and kept in motion the fateful machinery of the alliances. The kaiser, believing as he did in the divine calling of all royalty, this time immediately promised the Austrians that he would support any demands they made on Serbia and then proceeded as planned to go on a North Sea cruise. The tsar, he was certain, could not possibly support Serbia and the murderers of an archduke and his wife. The Austrians, provided with this blank check and knowing their existence as a state was threatened by a terrorist attack that was certainly part of an organized attempt to destroy the Dual Monarchy, were determined to put an end to Serbia's provocations—the British historian Seton-Watson says the murders were the sixth outrage in less than four years—and Germany was fully prepared to back her ally. What Germany and Austria were ready to do was to risk a local war, no new thing in the Balkans or in Europe either, and they both believed that harsh demands on the country that had aided if not recruited the terrorists would be fully justified.

The attitude of the war parties in France and Russia was of a different nature. The president of France, Raymond Poincaré, was a foremost leader of the *réveil national,* a man accused by his opponents in France of having replaced, as his ambassadors, moderate men with chauvinists and puppets. Poincaré arrived in St. Petersburg on July 20 for a three-day stay, the trip having been arranged in the previous January. It was the second such visit in two years, and so doubtful was the French Left of Poincaré's purposes, that the Socialist leader in the Chambre des Députés, Jean Jaurès, tried to prevent funds for the trip being placed at Poincaré's disposal.* Much of what went on during Poincaré's stay in St. Petersburg is unknown because, contrary to custom, no résumé of the talks was ever made. The blank spots are the more curious because René Viviani, the French prime minister and minister for foreign affairs, who had written the minutes of the meetings in 1912, again accompanied the president.

From this visit, however, no notes of Poincaré's talks with high Russian officials have been found. The only telegrams between St. Petersburg and Paris turned up by a French commission seeking the minutes of Poincaré's discussions were concerned exclusively with domestic French affairs.[30]

But Poincaré had not gone to Russia to talk about French internal matters. He was discussing other problems with the tsar, with Minister for Foreign Affairs Sazonov, and with Russian military leaders, and the substance of some of these conversations is known. Sergei Sazonov was

---

* The money was voted on July 7 by the Chamber 428–106. (*Schulthess' Europäischer Geschichtskalender,* p. xii, 4.)

a man of vacillating mind who could not easily bring himself to tough decisions, but he did believe Sarajevo to be an expiation for the crime committed when Austria annexed Bosnia and Herzegovina, and he was under constant pressure to act from his predecessor as foreign minister, now Russian ambassador to Paris, Alexander Izvolsky. Izvolsky repeatedly told him that this time Russia could not evade the German challenge, and that for over a year France had been surprised at Russian passivity in matters that were crucial to her. He also told Sazonov that the alliance with France would be in mortal danger if this time Russia remained passive.[31] Maurice Paléologue, the violently anti-German French ambassador to St. Petersburg, told Sazonov the same thing, urging him to take a hard line against the Germanic powers and promising the full support of France. If he was not echoing Poincaré's words, he could certainly have said none of these things without his approval. Moreover, the Russian court had its full share of men commanding Russian armies or in high government positions like the grand duke and other notables who were oppressed by the domestic unrest (Petersburg was in the grip of a major strike during Poincaré's visit, one of the many portents of things to come) and who were anxious to retrieve Russian honor after the defeat at the hands of Japan.

At a dinner given for Poincaré by the Grand Duke Nicholas on July 22, Paléologue chatted with the Grand Duchess Anastasia and her sister, both Montenegrin princesses. Anastasia showed him a box she carried with her of "real Lorraine soil," and the table of honor was decorated with thistles, Lorraine thistles, she pointed out. She told the French ambassador there would be war, that she had heard this from her father, the king of Montenegro; France would get back Alsace and Lorraine, and Austria and Germany would be destroyed.[32] A day later at the march-past of Russian troops in honor of Poincaré's visit, a military band played the march "Sambre et Meuse" along with the march "Lorraine." This was the mood in St. Petersburg, and it was music to the ears of Poincaré, Paléologue, and many others sharing their views in France and Russia.

When war came, it was a war that neither Grey nor the kaiser wanted, although both had contributed to its outbreak. For hundreds of thousands of Germans and Frenchmen it came as a great relief. Germany would at long last break through the iron ring forged around her; France would rid herself of the German incubus. Hitler wrote years later that he fell on his knees to thank God for the opportunity of taking part in this war, and the blown-up photograph of him among the thousands hearing the news of the declaration of war, in the Odeonsplatz in Munich, shows his fervor. He stood enraptured, with a broad smile on his face, waving his hat as he learned that the day had come that would permit him to take his part in the great theater of history, rescue Germany, and, with luck, witness the end of the Austro-Hungarian Empire.

Wars in their beginnings are more often than not welcomed by the people who have been living under their threat for a long time, as well as by those living drably by comparison with their dreams of glory, and Hitler was no exception. It was the war that would make him, the war that, for the first time since he left school, would give him an estimable place in society. And Hitler did what millions of other German soldiers did in the course of the war—he served devotedly and courageously, joining up immediately and being sent to the front with little or no training. War was declared on August 1. Hitler immediately offered his services to the king of Bavaria, Ludwig III, and on the next day he was told he could report to a Bavarian regiment of his choice. He chose the Reserve Infantry Regiment No. 16, later called the List regiment after its colonel, who was killed at the end of October 1914, and sixty-five days later he was on his way to the front lines.

Those little more than two months were all he had of military training; like so many others, he was issued a uniform and sent to battle, sent from civilian life to a war that for Hitler was the beginning of a career and for millions of others, the end of one.

CHAPTER 3

The War and the Corporal

EVERY COUNTRY HAD PREPARED for the Great War, but no one was prepared for the course it took. As the German General Staff had foreseen, the Russians invaded East Prussia in the first days of the conflict while the bulk of the German army hurled itself west, into Belgium and then France. For two weeks the course of the war followed the lines the general staff had laid down; after that the generals followed the course of the war. The way the general staff had planned it, small German forces would fight a delaying action against the Russians with their huge but often incompetently led field armies; they would permit them temporarily to invade East Prussia while the mass of the German army rolled up the left wing of the French; it would capture Paris, and having fought the French army to its knees and driven the British expeditionary force to the Channel, would then turn its full weight against the tsar's forces.

Speed was the essential element in the German plan. Only Germany was faced with major enemies on two fronts and only a swift attack against one and then the other could counter their numerical superiority. In pursuit of a lightning victory, as the German strategists saw it, they were compelled to go through Belgium. It was an invasion imposed by military necessity, a measure that the Entente, too, had repeatedly considered and that its generals had urged on their governments. In 1906 staff talks had taken place between British and Belgian officers who discussed the landing of 100,000—later increased to 150,000—British troops on Belgian soil; and again in 1912 the British High Com-

mand worked on a plan to send an army into Belgium to forestall the
Germans. General Joffre had also wanted to invade Belgium with French
forces, but while Poincaré agreed in principle with the plan, when it
met Belgian opposition it was rejected on political grounds. The talks
between the British and Belgian general staffs had gone into all the
details of uniforms, supplies, and requisitioning required for a joint
operation, which was at least a technical violation, as the Belgian chief
of staff himself admitted, of international law.[1] The British plan had also
envisaged violating Dutch neutrality with a landing in the Scheldt
estuary.

The difference between the Entente and the German policymakers
lay in the decisive role played by the army high command in Germany
and the secondary one played by their opposite numbers in the Entente.
Thus the Entente, weighing political against military considerations,
never completed such plans, whereas the Germans, in a much more
precarious military situation, decided to carry them out.

German commanders like General Ludendorff were convinced that
Belgian neutrality, which had been guaranteed by the Great Powers,
was in any case a sham. Ludendorff pointed out, after the war, that all
the Belgian defenses had been arrayed against the German frontier and
few or none against the French. But like many people unshakably convinced of their own righteous purposes, he made no mention of the
long-prepared German plan of invasion of which the Belgians were well
aware.

In any event, the invasion of Belgium on August 4, 1914, was a clear
breach of a treaty Prussia had signed, and it enabled Sir Edward Grey,
who eight years before had assured France that Britain would go to
war to defend the Entente, to obtain the votes in the British Cabinet
of wavering members who might otherwise have left him and his assurances high and dry.* Paul Cambon on August 1 had reminded Sir Edward of the British obligation to come to the aid of France, an obligation that arose from the naval agreement of 1912 under which France
had withdrawn her fleet from the Atlantic to the Mediterranean and
Britain had moved its Mediterranean fleet to the Atlantic, thus undertaking the defense of the French Atlantic coast. On the night of August
1–2, England had mobilized its fleet, and on August 2, after opposition
Unionist party leaders Bonar Law and Lord Lansdowne affirmed that
England must stand by France and assured Prime Minister Asquith of
the support of their party, Grey was able to tell Cambon, with the ap-

---

* Sir Edward had never, until 1912, informed the cabinet of the British military
and naval conversations with France. Parliament and the public learned of them
only on August 3, 1914. (Sidney B. Fay, *The Origins of the World War*, vol. 1,
pp. 208–9.)

proval of the cabinet,* that the British navy would protect the French coast against any German attack. The German invasion of Belgium gave Sir Edward Grey, Winston Churchill, and the other adherents of Britain's traditional policy of hostility to the leading military power on the Continent the opening they may have needed to persuade the cabinet and Parliament to go to war, but the promises and measures of military and naval support for France preceded the invasion of Belgium and were unconnected with it.† [2]

The decisive act in the unleashing of a general European war was the Russian mobilization ordered on the evening of July 29, rescinded for a few hours by the vacillating tsar, and then irrevocably ordered on July 30. Up to that time a general European war might have been averted. The Austrian ultimatum to Serbia, sent on July 23, called a *"befristite démarche,"* a note with a time limit (to be answered within forty-eight hours), was stiff, but under the circumstances not unbearable‡ in the context of Austria's assurances that she had no territorial demands to make on Belgrade. Had Russia pressed Serbia to accept the conditions of the ultimatum, perhaps with minor alterations, peace might well have been preserved. And even after Austria had found Serbia's

* Two anti-war members, Lord Morley and John Burns, resigned their portfolios in protest.

† It is interesting to speculate on what would have happened had the German General Staff followed a proposal Helmuth von Moltke, chief of the general staff, made in 1910 to reverse the Schlieffen plan, stand on the defensive in the West, and conduct the major offensive against Russia. Such a strategy would have made it difficult for Grey to convince the cabinet to go to war on the side of France had she then attacked Germany, but given the range of the Russian space and the size of the tsar's armies, it would also have made a quick, decisive victory impossible. That, in short, is why the Schlieffen plan was adopted.

‡ The Austrian ultimatum, after reciting the evidences for Serbian toleration of and complicity in the crimes committed, demanded that Serbia condemn anti-Austrian propaganda, express its regret for the participation of Serbian officials in such propaganda, and repudiate any interference with the inhabitants of Austria-Hungary. In addition, it demanded (1) that Serbia suppress anti-Austrian publications; (2) dissolve the *Narodna Odbrana*; (3) eliminate anti-Austro-Hungarian instruction in the schools; (4) dismiss officers and functionaries engaging in anti-Austrian propaganda; (5) accept the collaboration in Serbia of representatives of the Austrian government for suppression of the anti-Austrian subversive movement [which would have been a violation of Serbian sovereignty]; (6) start judicial proceedings against accessories to the plot, permitting Austro-Hungarian delegates to take part in such investigations; (7) arrest two men named as being compromised by the inquiry; (8) stop the cooperation of Serbian authorities in illicit arms traffic across the border, and punish officers of the frontier service who had let the arms used in the Sarajevo murders cross the frontier; (9) explain why Serbian officials at home and abroad continued to express their hostility to Austria; and (10) notify the Austro-Hungarian government of the execution of such measures. A reply, the ultimatum said, was expected by six o'clock on July 25.

reply unsatisfactory* and had declared war, hostilities might have been limited to the kaiser's formula of a march to Belgrade† and no further, had it been strongly urged upon Serbia and Austria by their respective allies. In other words, had Russia not mobilized, and had sufficient leverage been applied by the Great Powers to resolve the latest Balkan clash, it might well have ended as had other Balkan crises, in a compromise that pleased no one but that nevertheless worked.

It was the Russian mobilization that made any compromise or further negotiation impossible. That mobilization was the equivalent of a declaration of war was clear to the tsar (which is the reason why he rescinded his first order on July 29) as well as to the Russian and French chiefs of staff and to the high commands of all the Great Powers. In 1892, during negotiations between the French General Boisdeffre and the Russian General Obruchev, it had been openly stated that mobilization meant war, and when General Boisdeffre had repeated these words to Tsar Alexander III, the tsar had replied, "That is exactly the way I understand it."[3] The precept was explicitly confirmed in 1912 when the Russian General Staff informed the general commanding the Warsaw district that "the telegram relative to mobilization is to be regarded at the same time as . . . the opening of hostilities against Austria and Germany."[4] The order was later revoked for technical and political reasons, but from the military point of view it remained a fact. The Russian chief of mobilization, General Doborolski, writing of the Russian mobilization in 1914, confirmed this. He wrote: "The whole plan of mobilization is worked out ahead to its end in all its details. When the moment has been chosen, one has only to press the button, and the whole state begins to function automatically with the precision of a clock's mechanism. . . . The choice of the moment is influenced by a complex of varied political causes. But once the moment has been fixed, everything is settled; there is no going back; it determines mechanically the beginning of war."[5] It was this crucial order that France made no attempt either to stop or to urge be rescinded, although the Russian mobilization was a breach of the Dual Alliance, since it had been issued without consulting France.

---

* The Serbian answer, as has been noted by Sidney B. Fay in *The Origins of the World War*, was evasive with regard to numbers 4, 5, and 9, and number 6 the Serbians flatly turned down.

† Bethmann Hollweg, in transmitting the kaiser's plan, told the German ambassador to Vienna to express himself to the Austrian foreign minister, Count Berchtold, "emphatically," but added: "You are carefully to avoid giving the impression that we wish to hold Austria back." (Quoted Sidney B. Fay, *The Origins of the World War*, vol. 2, p. 424.) Grey, like the kaiser, thought it possible to localize the war "if Austria, while saying that she must hold the occupied territory until she had complete satisfaction from Serbia, stated she would not advance further, pending an effort of the Powers to mediate between her and Russia." (Quoted Luigi Albertini, *The Origins of the War of 1914*, vol. 2, p. 513.)

Germany predictably reacted, as the Russian and French high commands knew she would, with a demand that Russia demobilize within twelve hours; if she did not, Germany would order mobilization. At the same time the German ambassador to Paris, Baron von Schoen, called on French Minister for Foreign Affairs Viviani to ask whether France would remain neutral in the event of a Russo-German war; the answer was to be given within eighteen hours. The next day Viviani merely told Schoen that France would act in accordance with her interests. That was the reply the German High Command and Foreign Office had expected, but had the French said they would be neutral, Baron von Schoen had been instructed to ask for the German occupation of the forts of Verdun and Toul for the duration of the war, to guarantee French neutrality and the German army from being attacked in the rear while it was deployed fighting the Russians in the East. The German demand was, however, never made, because France never considered remaining neutral with or without conditions. Twenty hours after the Russian mobilization, the Austro-Hungarian army mobilized all their forces (only partial mobilization had been ordered for the war against Serbia), and France and Germany sent out their calls for general mobilization almost simultaneously.

Reichschancellor Bethmann Hollweg, in his speech to the Reichstag on August 4 and in his conversation later that day with the British ambassador, Sir W. E. Goschen, made the case that would always be convincing to Germans but would provide the Entente with enough propaganda material to last throughout the war and beyond. Bethmann, on information doubtless furnished by the German High Command, accused France of having crossed the border to attack German forces with cavalry patrols and of bombing a German railroad station, neither of which was true, and then he proceeded to tell the Reichstag what he and all its members accepted as self-evident. Russia, he said, had put the torch against the house, and he asked: "Should we perhaps have patiently waited until the powers between which we are wedged chose the time to strike? To have exposed Germany to such a peril would have been a crime. That is why we demanded on July 31 that Russia demobilize, the one means by which we could have rescued the peace of Europe." Russia had not answered, and Germany therefore had been forced to mobilize on August 1. Bethmann said he had asked France whether she would remain neutral in the event of a German-Russian war and France had replied evasively that she would do what her interests demanded. Bethmann continued: "We are now in a state of self-defense (*Notwehr*) and necessity knows no law. (*Not kennt kein Gebot.*) Our troops have occupied Luxemburg and perhaps have already entered Belgian territory. Gentlemen, that is contrary to international law.... The injustice, I speak openly, the injustice that we thus commit we will make good, as soon as our military goals are accomplished.* Whoever is threatened as we are and battles for his highest possessions should only be thinking about how he is going to hack his way through."⁶

Bethmann on the evening of August 4 received the British ambassador to Berlin and in the course of their conversation, during which he expressed his distress over the collapse of his policy of understanding with England, made the remark that would provide Allied propagandists with one of their best tag lines. Bethmann had been convinced that neither Britain nor Germany wanted war and that by working together they could avert it. Now, with everything he had tried to build collapsing, he asked Sir Edward Goschen: "How just for a word, 'neutrality,' —a word which in wartime had so often been disregarded—just for a scrap of paper, Great Britain was going to war on a kindred nation who desired nothing better than to be friends with her?" So another damning phrase was coined, on a level with the kaiser's speech about Attila's Huns: for Germany a treaty was a "scrap of paper."⁷

Allied statesmen could be eloquent about such duplicity, although every word that Bethmann Hollweg said applied, in cases of necessity, to the acts of state of every official piously wringing his hands, even though none of them had ever been so indiscreet as to say so. The only moves toward a compromise settlement during the Balkan crises had been made by Germany and England. In 1914 Germany again had made an attempt to get Austria to accept half a loaf with the march to Belgrade; France had made no similar attempt to restrain Russia either before or after the Russian mobilization.

President Poincaré, resolved not to repeat the mistake Napoleon III had made in 1870 of attacking first, this time ordered French troops not to enter a zone ten kilometers from the German border, but it was the president and his emissaries who also urged the Russians to stand firm and who assured them of France's support in the event of war. With the help of blundering German speeches they had made Germany appear to be the aggressor, but it was a French paper, *Le Matin*, that pointed out on August 1 that the time would never be more propitious for war.

The Schlieffen plan that had dominated Germany military strategy since the turn of the century envisaged bringing greatly superior forces to bear from the German right flank; the ratio of German to British-French forces in that critical sector was to be seven to one, while the hilly terrain of Alsace-Lorraine, with its high escarpments, would be defended with relatively light forces. As for the French, their plan

---

* The German Foreign Office promised at the end of the war to restore full sovereignty over Belgian territory and to pay any damages that might be incurred during the occupation.

was to mount an offensive through Alsace-Lorraine and then eventually, if all went well, across the Rhine, after the Russian steamroller closed on Berlin from the other side. Schlieffen had foreseen only a defensive battle in the East, a methodical retreat, permitting the Russians to oc- cupy much of East Prussia for two months, after which, with the defeat of the French army, another overwhelming offensive would drive the Russians out.

But as Ludendorff would write later, this strategy took no account of the horror of the East Prussian population at being delivered over to the Cossacks, or of the streams of terrified refugees fleeing before the tsar's troops, or of the situation of the Austrian army attempting to mount simultaneous offensives on two fronts against Serbia and Russia, and doing well on neither. In the first weeks of the war, 300,000 men of the Austro-Hungarian army were killed, wounded, or taken prisoners, in- cluding the flower of its officer corps. The German and Austrian general staffs had made no joint operational preparations—Schlieffen, with good reason, as the Redl case showed, had feared security leaks through the Austrian General Staff—and each was in the dark as to the other's opera- tional plans. The alliance had been primarily a political one, and the Austrians devised their own military strategy, which in the event was not much more sensible than their critics had thought it likely to be. The Austrian offensive against both enemies at the same time immedi- ately ran into serious trouble, and its Russian front was in danger of collapse. The German High Command thus had to shift its strategy at the very start of the war, and the result was the great victory under the command of Hindenburg and Ludendorff at Tannenberg in late August, and the fatal check in the West in early September. At Tannen- berg, the brilliant operational plans of Colonel, later General, Hoffmann had enabled Hindenburg and Ludendorff with an army of 153,000 men to annihilate an invading Russian army of 190,000 men.[*]

Only two thousand Russian soldiers escaped; the rest were killed or captured. East Prussia and the Austrian armies were rescued, but the German thrust into France was fatally blunted. Hindenburg and Ludendorff had defeated the Russians with the sparse forces already at hand in the East, but the German High Command had felt itself obliged to detach two army corps from the West to reinforce the eastern army; and while the victory in the East was everything they could have hoped for, it led in the West to the failure of the crucial offensive. More- over, the bulk of the Russian army, despite the dimensions of the defeat

[*] Hindenburg wrote in his memoirs that the Russian army in East Prussia during August-September numbered no less than 800,000 men with 1,700 pieces of artillery against 210,000 Germans with 600 guns. The entire Russian force arrayed against Germany and Austria-Hungary, Hindenburg wrote, numbered 3 million men, the armies of the Central Powers only one-third of that. (General von Hindenburg, *Aus meinem Leben*, pp. 80, 96.)

at Tannenberg, remained intact and had still to be fought off with an Austro-Hungarian ally that would always be in need of bolstering. For in addition to Russia and Serbia, the Austrians would soon have to reckon with their late Italian ally, who at the start of the war proclaimed its neutrality but soon, with Allied subsidies and alluring offers of Austrian territory, would join forces against its partners of the Triple Alliance.

For his part in the battle of Tannenberg Ludendorff was awarded the Iron Cross, Second Class, a decoration, although he was certainly unaware of it, that he would soon share with a lance corporal in the Bavarian army by the name of Adolf Hitler, who received the same award some two months later. Hitler's regiment had been sent down the Rhine in mid-October, then to Belgium by way of Aachen, where they were greeted, as were the troops in all parts of the country, with a tumultuous crowd of thousands of people brought together, as never before in Germany, in a shouting comradeship of every class and condition. Their train passed through Liège, Leuven, Brussels, and Tournai (spelled Dournay in a letter Hitler wrote) and arrived at Lille on October 23.

On October 29 they were thrown into action at Ypres, suffering losses that were heavy enough but that Hitler exaggerated in a letter to Herr Popp. Hitler wrote that of 3,600 men only 611 had survived the battle, which lasted four days. Actually, on August 29, the day the battle started, 349 men were killed, and between October 30 and November 24, the number of dead rose by an additional 373. By the end of the war, the regiment's death toll of 3,745 was higher than its initial strength.[8]

It is the story in little of what became an endless war of attrition. The German offensive had slashed forward through the strongly defended Belgian forts and into northern France so swiftly that by early September German patrols were within twenty-five miles of Paris. But there they were stopped, at the Marne, by a British and French counteroffensive directed at the gap between the first and second armies. It was a gap that should not have been there, according to the Schlieffen plan, but the German forces, with the distributions later adopted, lacked the preponderant strength to turn the French flank that Schlieffen had called for. By mid-September the battle in the West had bogged down to the deadly trench warfare that would slaughter millions of men on both sides.

The German High Command had made damaging changes in the Schlieffen plan. Not only was the German right wing reduced from the foreseen seven-to-one superiority to three-to-one, but large forces were held at the front line and in reserve against the French troops on the relatively static Alsatian front while they were desperately needed further west.

On November 1, Hitler was made a lance corporal, a *Gefreiter*, and although he would serve with undoubted courage and be five times decorated, that is the rank he stayed at during the entire war; it was as far as he rose in the German army until he became commander in chief some twenty years later. On December 2, 1914, he was awarded the Iron Cross, Second Class, and a week later he was sent to regimental staff headquarters to serve as a messenger carrying orders to the front lines, a post he held during the entire war. Never, either in his letters or in the memory of his comrades, did he show any sign of doubt or hesitation about what he and his comrades were fighting for; he believed in the war from the day it started until its end and in the sacred mission he was carrying out of defending the German Fatherland, and when he was wounded, he was impatient only to return to the front.

It is hard to know why he was not promoted. The only clue comes from one of his superiors, adjutant of the Regiment List, Fritz Wiedemann, who said later that Hitler did not have the characteristics of a non-commissioned officer; he apparently lacked the military bearing, the outward signs of leadership, expected of such men. And then Wiedemann added, Hitler himself did not want the promotion.[9] In any event, he carried out dangerous missions and took part in over thirty battles, risking his life daily and with sufficient dash and derring-do to earn himself toward the end of the war, on August 4, 1918, the Iron Cross, First Class. It was a decoration given to thousands of soldiers who like Hitler served bravely, and it was also withheld from thousands of others who did the same thing but who for one reason or another, often trivial, went unrecognized. Some of Hitler's comrades reported that he was a loner in the army too, one of the few who received no food packages from friends or relatives and little mail. He was called the *Spinner*, that is, a man who tells unlikely stories, perhaps to himself. Photographs, however, show him with his comrades unsmiling but a *Landser*, one of the boys, and the testimony of those who served with him is that he was a good comrade doing his dangerous job as well as or better than the others, ready for any assignment and eager to carry it out.

Some of the testimony of men who knew him is derogatory. One of Hitler's former superiors, a noncommissioned officer named Hans Mend, declared that Hitler was awarded the Iron Cross in 1918 by a fluke, after he had brought in a group of battle-weary French prisoners and told a blown-up story of a heroic exploit to his captain, Michael Freiherr von Godin, who spontaneously awarded the decoration to him. In his account, Mend called Hitler a recruit who had served only a short time at the front.[10] Mend's story on the face of it is nonsense. Hitler was no recruit, he was a soldier in the midst of combat for four years, and he received two Iron Crosses; the Military Service Cross, Third Class with Swords; a Regimental Diploma for conspicuous bravery; and the Medal for

Wounded. He also received the unanimous praise of the officers of the regiment, including the first lieutenant in the reserve, who recommended him for the Iron Cross, First Class. The recommendation came, not from Captain von Godin, but from the regiment's adjutant, a Jew by the name of Hugo Gutmann, and this the Nationalist Socialist party in later years would take great pains to conceal. Many people who, like Mend, knew Hitler before his rise to power took pleasure in cutting him down to size, and much of what they wrote was purely malicious or what they thought their audience wanted to hear. In fact, there seems no doubt that Hitler was an excellent soldier and that the army gave him as much as he gave it. He had become a member of the Establishment for the first time in his life; he could write to the Popps in November 1914, when he received his first Iron Cross, and ask them to please cut out the piece of the newspaper listing him as one of the recipients for a remembrance of the event. His letters[11] were now modest. He played down his being decorated, said there were others who deserved it too, although many of them were dead, said he had luckily remained unwounded in the midst of so many casualties, and, despite the fact that he had been a faithful and lengthy correspondent, he apologized for not having written more often. In place of the tissue of lies and fantasies he had woven for Kubizek, for the Austrian military authorities, and no doubt for himself, he could now appear, in all truth, as a soldier of the Reich, a man of some distinction, decorated for heroism, one who fitted as well as any into the Germanic ideals of sacrifice, selflessness, and unreluctant risk of life for the Fatherland.

He found time to sketch scenes he witnessed—of marching soldiers, one carrying an umbrella; of the shed he and his squad lived in behind the lines; of a ruined town; of the wasteland front in Flanders—all in the same manner that he had drawn the *Sendlinger Tor* in Munich or a cathedral in Vienna. He made no portraits, no sketches like the caricature he drew of his teacher in the *Linzer Realschule*; what he drew were buildings, or anonymous groups or places; if he was close to anyone, neither his drawings nor his letters show any sign of it. He writes of the job at hand and of abstractions—Germany, the heroic battle for the Fatherland, the drive to victory.

The letters evidence a good eye for the details of battle and an ear for the sounds of combat. He describes the carcass of a dead horse in front of their bivouac, and the cold and the wet and the *Angst* they all feel, but the Germans are heroes; as one man they shout to a lieutenant, the only surviving officer, to lead them to storm the enemy who has killed their comrades. He does not pity himself or beat his chest. It is as though he had at long last reached a frontier where he felt secure, where it was enough to describe the real world of death and destruction and German heroism he was now part of. No evil Jews or degenerate Habsburgs inhabit this world. Although it is a Jew who will get him the Iron Cross, no comment of Hitler's is recorded. Even the enemy across the lines is described coolly; Hitler says the first Frenchmen he saw, who were in a prisoners of war camp, were surprised at how many German soldiers marched past them, but he never vilifies either the French or the British troops. Now that he could vent his spleen in combat and be decorated, he felt no need to explain what he was doing or why he did not do better.

The war that killed hundreds of thousands of men trying to move forward to gain a few bloody yards of ground made Adolf Hitler. He was to write later that the experience was worth thirty years of university study, and in terms of his psychic needs this may well be true. Otherwise the war would prove an unmitigated disaster to the people and nations of Europe. The losses for all the countries involved, including the dead and severely wounded, were staggering.* Because the dead were almost all young, it was the manpower of one generation and the seed of the future that were lost, and no one, even among the conquerors, would ever believe that any victories that had been won were worth the sacrifice that went into the winning. An earthquake had ravaged Europe, and the prewar landscape was never to be restored; the cracks, faults, and fissures were always evident beneath any new rebuilding. Austria-Hungary and tsarist Russia were overturned by the war. France was never to obtain the security she had fought for; although Alsace and Lorraine were returned to her, a united Germany remained on her border, and 1,300,000 of her young men had been killed to win what her leaders greatly feared would be at best a few years of respite before the next call to begin the bloodletting all over again. For Britain, the war led to the end of her dominance of the seas and the beginning of the end of her empire. For Germany, its result was not only the loss of millions of her youth but also the beginning of a period of despair, humiliation, and disorder that would end in a revolution of nihilism. For Italy, too, although the war would win her large portions of Austria,† it would lead to bitter disappointment, revolution, and more war. Europe as a whole would never fully recover from the calamitous effects of World War I, and World War II was but one of those effects.

---

* The losses of the Allies and associated powers were 5,150,000 dead, 12,800,000 wounded. The Central Powers lost 3,386,000 dead, 8,388,400 wounded.

† Italy, as her price for coming into the war, had been promised in the Treaty of London of 1915 the Trentino and the Tyrol up to the Brenner Pass, as well as Trieste, Istria, and Dalmatia. In addition, at the end of the war, she demanded Fiume. Her acquisitions included thousands of German-speaking Austrians in the Tyrol and 250,000 Slavs in Venezia Giulia and on the Istrian peninsula. She received only a small portion of what she wanted of Dalmatia, most of which went to Yugoslavia, and she did not get the territorial compensation she had demanded for the acquisition by France and Britain of the German African colonies.

The German armies proved themselves far tougher than the Entente had thought they could be. Outnumbered on every front, they nevertheless fought the Russian army to a standstill and then to overwhelming defeat, which brought down the whole complex of the tzar's state. Despite the Allies' blockade and their enormous material superiority, the German army would stop offensive after offensive on the western front,* until in 1917 one of the most disastrous attacks, under the command of General Nivelle, led large numbers of the French army to revolt. It was only the intervention of a non-European power, the United States, that made the decisive Allied victory of 1918 possible, and here again the results both for Europe and the United States would have long-range consequences that were gratifying to neither.

Up to the time massive American forces were at hand, it had seemed possible to achieve a negotiated peace, one of the many that had been made in the course of centuries of European warfare, a peace on the pattern perhaps of the Treaty of Vienna, which had lasted one hundred years. Both sides had suffered heavy losses, and voices of reason were to be heard on both sides, along with the heavy demands of militants for breaking the back of the enemy's capacity to wage the same kind of war again. The kaiser had said in his *Thronrede*, the speech from the throne made to the Reichstag on August 4, that Germany had no desire for conquest, and although powerful proponents for accumulating territory and political and economic advantages to the Reich argued their case until the end of the war, what the kaiser said was substantially true. Germany had no territorial demands in Europe to match the French obsession with reacquiring Alsace-Lorraine and diminishing German strength and territory; the status quo up to the time of the war had been advantageous enough for the Reich's swift climb to a summit of influence and prestige, and while the kaiser, and no doubt the country as a whole, wanted Germany to be a world power, this was a desire shared on their own behalf by every one of her chief enemies. A peace to restore the status quo would have been regarded as a defeat by the Entente, and they never wanted to consider it, although without American intervention they would have been forced to give it earnest consideration. Nevertheless, once the war started, even Bethmann Hollweg wanted as a minimum strategic boundaries that would put an end to the encirclement. He conceived of a Europe within a customs union under German leadership but with at least nominal equality for the whole European community. He pursued what he called a diagonal

---

* The pride, even of antimilitarist intellectuals, in the achievements of the German army may be observed in what Thomas Mann wrote during the war. He estimated that Germany had a front of 1,800 kilometers against 600 for the French and 250 for the British, which he pointed out was itself a commentary on the Allies' charge that Germany had deliberately precipitated the war. (Thomas Mann, "Betrachtungen eines Unpolitischen," p. 341.)

course between the Pan-German phantasmagoria and the sober thinking of men like the Social Democratic leader Philipp Scheidemann, who spoke out for a peace with no territorial acquisitions.

Appetite came with the eating and German victories. The Pan-Germans and important industrialists like Hugenberg and Stinnes had a plan to keep Belgium and the French coast to the mouth of the Somme under German domination, as well as for German forces to occupy French forts from Verdun to Belfort and to make of Toulon a German harbor. French and Belgian possessions in Africa were to become German along with the Baltic states and Russian Poland. General Hoffman, on the other hand, the most able member of the general staff, wanted not a foot of Belgian territory, no more than did the most pacifist of the Social Democrats.

And so it went, sights being raised and lowered with the fortunes of war and the political platform of the observer. Similarly exaggerated demands were made on behalf of the Allies. France aimed to annex part of Prussian Rhineland and the Palatinate; Schleswig-Holstein was to go to Denmark, southern Silesia and western Galicia to Russia, and Austria was to be divided into three parts, with Serbia getting Bosnia, Herzegovina, and northern Albania. In addition, the tzar suggested to Paléologue that Russia absorb part of East Prussia, and this, too, was approved by the Paris cabinet.[12]

The Austrian High Command also had far-reaching claims; they wanted to annex Serbia, Montenegro, Albania, and Russian Poland including Galicia, but there they met head-on the claims of Germans like Ludendorff, who was not at all anxious to see Austria in Poland and who favored an independent Poland under German governance.

But all such dazzling programs were little more than the uninhibited wishes of a wide variety of people who had one thing in common—the dream of creating the kind of mini–political paradise this side of heaven in which their inner composure would best thrive. Such daydreams are far from uncommon; they have arisen in every nation; Spaniards, Frenchmen, Englishmen, Arabs, and Israelis have had them, as have Americans and Tartars and the Crusaders, both Christian and Muslim. What had rudely awakened them all were the counterclaims of other peoples and the limits of their own resources.

The essential differences between the Allied and the German positions may be seen in matters such as the peace proposal made by Bethmann Hollweg in a speech to the Reichstag on behalf of the kaiser and the allies of Germany on December 12, 1916. Bethmann said that Germany was ready for a peace of reconciliation that would give every country the opportunity to develop in honor and freedom. Germany and her allies, he said, were able and willing to fight on, but they were also ready to make peace. The speech was delivered after the bloody failure of the Allied Somme offensive, the collapse of Rumania, and Russian defeats on the eastern front, but the Allies indignantly rejected it. They cloaked their refusal to negotiate with a fog of rhetoric: they were united for the defense of the freedom of nations, Germany had made no offer of peace, instead she had made a maneuver of war, Germany had started the war, Germany had declared that necessity knows no law and that treaties were scraps of paper—in short, the Allies would not deal with her.

In contrast to these lofty moral utterances, the Bolshevik government, eleven months later, in November 1917, would publish the text of the secret treaty of April 26, 1915, by which Italy had been brought into the war, signed by Grey and Paul Cambon as well as by Italian and Russian representatives, and giving purely Austrian territory to Italy, along with Dalmatia, Trieste, and the Dodecanese Islands, and generously permitting Italy to share with her new allies in a partition of Turkey. Italy was also to be compensated for Britain and France's acquisition of German colonies in Africa by obtaining additional territory in Eritrea, Somaliland, and Libya, and she was to be awarded her share of reparations in proportion to her sacrifices and exertions.[13]

The Italian agreement had been paralleled by a pact with Russia, which the Soviet government also released for publication. It had been made in March 1915, a month earlier than the Italian agreement. The tsar's foreign minister, Sergei Sazonov, with the approval of the British and French governments, had summarized Russian postwar territorial claims on Turkey, subject, they all agreed, to a successful conclusion of the war and the satisfaction of British and French claims. Constantinople and the west coast of the Bosphorus, the Sea of Marmora, the Dardanelles, and southern Thrace, along with other territories in the region, were to go to Russia without disturbing the special privileges of France and Britain; the neutral zone of Persia would fall into the British sphere of influence, with Russia getting compensation in the cities of Ispahan and Jesd.[14] In addition, the Bolshevik government published a note of February 1917 from the imperial Russian foreign minister, Pokrovski, to the French ambassador in Petersburg, Paléologue, that confirmed in turn that the tsar's government would support the French territorial demands for Alsace-Lorraine with extended strategic borders, that the Saar would become French, that the left bank of the Rhine would be entirely separated from Germany, and that the sector not acquired by France would become an autonomous and neutral state occupied by French troops until all the conditions of peace were met by Germany.[15] And on March 6, 1917, Britain, France, and Russia had completed arrangements begun in the spring of 1916 for dividing what remained of Turkish territory in Asia Minor.[16]

The Allies were in no position to make such agreements public or, in their hidden light, to restore the boundaries of Europe to what they had been as of August 1914. Although many people in the Allied camp, from pacifist groups to Sir Edward Grey, would, by the end of 1916, doubtless have been ready to negotiate a peace, men like Lloyd George, Winston Churchill, Clemenceau, and Poincaré would have nothing to do with negotiations. How could the secret treaties, or the plans being pushed by the Comité des Forges for the Saar and the left bank of the Rhine to go to France, Friesland to Holland, Schleswig-Holstein to Denmark, and Posen and the lower Vistula to Poland, be made public when the Allies were explaining to the world and especially President Wilson that they were fighting on behalf of the freedom and rights of all people?*

While the entry of the United States into the war in April 1917 and the promise of a huge, fresh American army dimmed any prospect of negotiations, the state of the Allies, without timely American intervention on a grand scale, was dismal. Paul Painlevé, the French minister of war, said on May 17, after the disastrous failure of the Nivelle offensive, that only two reliable French divisions were in action between Soissons and Paris, and in the French officer corps voices were raised asking whether this might not be the time to make a moderate peace. On June 8, General Henry Wilson told the British cabinet that Pétain was not in a position to go through a fourth winter without a great political or military victory. Lloyd George confirmed this by saying that the only real fighting spirit was being shown by British and German troops, and following a visit to France, he reported to the cabinet that the French army had practically ceased to fight.[17]

Matters would soon be even worse for the Entente. The last Russian offensive undertaken by the provisional government of Kerensky broke down in the summer of 1917, as did the British attempt at Ypres to break through in the West. In October, the Italians were badly defeated at the Isonzo, where German and Austrian forces took more than 250,000 prisoners. In England and Germany there were strikes, and unrest was evident among the sailors of the bottled-up German navy. People everywhere were sick unto death of the war, whose only reliable product was mass slaughter.

It was a time when peace might have well been made, although neither side could have dictated its terms. American troops were still one year and 3,000 miles away, and imperial Russia was finished. On June 26, 1917, the *nuncio* to Germany, Archbishop Pacelli, as a German diplomat, Kurt Riezler, would later reveal, had inquired of the German Foreign

* The texts of the secret treaties did become known, however, when they appeared as pamphlets and in the newspapers of many countries, including the United States, after the Soviet government released them in late 1917.

Office with "the fine pointed delicacy" that often marked Vatican diplomats, whether there was conceivably any possibility of Germany's making concessions that might be transmitted to the enemy powers and lead to negotiations toward peace. Bethmann Hollweg had told the *nuncio* there was such a possibility. Under what circumstances? asked Pacelli. Was Germany prepared to return, for example, territories France was convinced were inalienably French? Bethmann had answered that Germany was indeed prepared to negotiate on the basis of *"rectifications réciproques des frontières,"* meaning, as Archbishop Pacelli well understood, according to Riezler, a privy councillor and a close friend and advisor of Bethmann's, that Germany was ready to make territorial concessions with regard to Alsace-Lorraine in exchange, perhaps, for the ore and coal of Longwy and Briey. Pacelli asked whether Bethmann spoke with the authority of the kaiser and Bethmann assured him that he did, for, he said, he had discussed the matter with the emperor and His Majesty's words had been those he had quoted.* The Vatican's peace effort, however, came to nothing, because here again the Allies flatly refused to negotiate.

Lloyd George, the most influential man in the British cabinet, had told an American journalist that what Britain wanted was a "knockout blow," which is what the French hard-liners demanded too. Only it was not in the power of the Allied armies to deliver it; the one country in the world that could provide the strength for a decisive victory was the United States, whose president talked ambivalently about being "too proud to fight" a "peace without victory" and the need to fight for freedom and democracy.[18] If Mr. Wilson, though, supplied the muscle for the knockout blow, his rhetoric could be dealt with in due course. Whatever he might say to send a shuddering down the spine of Clemenceau or Poincaré, he bore with him the promise of achieving most of the ends of the secret treaties.

The political chessboard imposed far more complicated moves than the military one. Armies had the relatively easy-to-define job of winning a battle, a campaign, or a war, while peace involved reconciling deeply conflicting domestic claims, as well as those of allies, of the enemy, and even of neutrals. As early as September 1915, a meeting of French and German socialists had taken place in Switzerland. A joint statement of the two delegations declared: "This is not our war," and it denounced the invasion of Belgium, demanded that her independence be restored, and declared that the French and German socialists would never agree to their governments' plans for territorial acquisitions. The war, they said, had its origins in the imperialistic and colonial policies of both France and Germany, and both bore the responsibility for it. Their declared aims

---

* This story was told the author by Kurt Riezler in 1939. It does not appear in his *Tagebücher, Aufsätze, Dokumente.*

would be echoed in a few years by the Bolshevik government in Russia: a peace without annexations and the recognition of the inviolable right to self-determination of peoples.[19]

On June 12, four months after the outbreak of the Russian Revolution, the Socialist parties of Europe called a meeting in Stockholm, attended by the German Social Democrats, who were granted visas by their government, although the Allied governments refused travel permits to their delegations. The German Social Democrats repeated what the French and German socialists had demanded in 1915 in Switzerland, the formula that had again been advanced in March 1917 by the Petersburg Soldiers and Workers Council for a peace of reconciliation, without annexations or reparations, to be made on the basis of the self-determination of peoples. The Social Democrats also called for the restoration of the independence of Belgium, which was to be a vassal of neither Germany nor the Entente. On the question of Alsace-Lorraine, however, they pointed out that only 11.4 percent of the inhabitants spoke French as a native language, and they declared that the territory should remain part of the German Reich in full equality with the other German states.* [20]

Such views were in considerable contrast with what the German High Command had in mind if they could get it. On April 23, 1917, at the so-called Kreuznach Conference that took place some two weeks after the United States entered the war, Bethmann Hollweg signed, with representatives of the high command Hindenburg and Ludendorff, a memorandum on war aims. It provided for the Baltic territories of Courland and Lithuania to go to Germany; the Polish border was to be dependent on the future relations of Poland to Germany; if Germany secured military, political, and economic predominance, the frontiers would be more favorable to Poland, although Germany, in any event, would retain possession of militarily important border territories. In the West, Belgium would remain under German military control until it was ripe for a political and economic alliance with the Reich; Liège and the coast of Flanders would remain in German possession. Luxemburg was to become a German state; the ore and coal district of Briey-Longwy in France was to go to Germany. Other minor border changes with France were foreseen, and in return France would be offered a small part of Belgian territory at Marienbourg, which, the memorandum said, Napoleon III had wanted.[21]

It was a plan for peace that followed the prescriptions of the German army, but the government was forced to drop it only a few months later because it was patently unobtainable. Germany had won notable

* The left-wing Independent Social Democrats, in a separate statement, called for a plebiscite in Alsace-Lorraine, which they said had been annexed in 1871 against the will of the population.

military victories, but as Hindenburg himself observed, up to 1917 she had not succeeded in knocking out the armies of any of the countries arrayed against her with the exception of Montenegro.[22] Belgium had an army in the field, as did Serbia and Rumania; the encirclement, though wobbly, was still intact and the continuing need to bolster Austria, Turkey, and Bulgaria remained a heavy drain on strained German resources and manpower.

In mid-1917, although Russia was virtually eliminated from the conflict, the Central Powers (and the Entente as well) were showing unmistakable signs of war weariness bordering on exhaustion. Only a few months after the Kreuznach Conference, it was evident to German political leaders that a negotiated peace was the only hopeful solution for the Reich. On July 14, 1917, the Reichstag, echoing the declarations of the Social Democrats and the Petrograd Soviet, declared that Germany was ready for peace, a peace without indemnities or annexations, a peace of understanding and lasting reconciliation, the kind of peace Mr. Wilson, too, had said he advocated, with an international organization to uphold it, with freedom of the seas, and with the abolition of economic restrictions.

It was a time when negotiations still seemed possible, and in September a majority of the British cabinet declared they wanted to learn what the German peace proposals were. Lloyd George was another who believed Germany might be ready to make great concessions, but when Painlevé asked him to make a public pledge that Britain would continue to fight until the French won back Alsace-Lorraine, he wearily agreed, provided that Painlevé could give assurances that France would hold out. Any willingness to listen to terms was very short-lived. If there was any possibility of compelling her, Germany had to acknowledge defeat, and the symbol of the defeat was Alsace-Lorraine. In this vein, former Prime Minister Asquith told Parliament that the German occupation of Alsace-Lorraine was a crime, and since no one in Germany, from Left to Right, could accept such a premise (the utmost in concessions had been suggested by the Independent Social Democrats when they asked for a plebiscite), any attempt at negotiation fell flat. The spokesman for the German Foreign Office, *Staatssekretär* von Kühlmann, answered Asquith with a torrent of patriotic oratory quite different from what Bethmann had said to Archbishop Pacelli. Asquith, said Kühlmann, had put the French demand for Alsace-Lorraine on the same level as the restoration of Belgium. But it was not for the restoration of Belgium that the peoples of Europe were shedding their blood; it was for the future of Alsace-Lorraine. England had declared she would fight for the return of Alsace-Lorraine to France as long as France herself demanded it. So, Kühlmann said, he would make the German position clear. To the stormy applause of the entire Reichstag, he said that Germany would never give up Alsace-Lorraine, never while a German hand could grasp a gun; it was part of the glorious heritage handed down by their fathers, the symbol of Germany unity.[23]

The fundamental differences between the positions of the Entente and of the Central Powers thus remained fixed. Alsace-Lorraine, not Belgium, was the sticking point. Germany could accept a peace on the basis of the status quo, the Allies could not, thus throwing some doubt on their assertions that it was Germany who was bent on conquest. If the Allies could hold out, with the United States taking the place of Russia, not only the return of Alsace-Lorraine but the knockout blow became an even more promising likelihood than it had been when the tsar's armies had prepared to steamroller their way to Berlin. And the knockout was a far more glittering prospect to the formulators of the secret treaties than any compromise peace. Even in the darkest days of the war, the indomitable hard-liners in Paris, St. Petersburg, and London had been buoyed up by the well-founded hope that America would one way or another come into the war and enable the treaties to be fleshed out.

The pro-Allied views and measures of the American government were unmistakable from the start of the war, although America's grounds for entering it would seem less than cogent to some critics at the time and to many more in later generations. President Wilson had agreed at the outset, in mid-August 1914, with the Allies' view that they were fighting on behalf of civilization against a wicked enemy, and he was determined to help them;* but at the same time he saw himself as a man of peace, an arbiter between the warring camps, and the architect of a lofty edifice of international comity—first a League of American States, later a League of Nations.

So from the beginning of the war Mr. Wilson's evenhandedness, his neutrality, was fictive. He agreed with the British government that British merchantmen could be armed against submarine attack with what they and he called defensive weapons, and still be considered merchantmen, using American harbors as such, but similarly armed German merchantmen the British government and he considered warships. British ships in the British and American view were armed for self-protection, while German ships were armed for destroying commerce. Wilson accepted, with token protests, the British measures of

* In August 1914, twelve days after the war started, President Wilson told his friend Colonel House that "if Germany won it would change the course of our civilization and make the United States a military nation," and on May 1915 he told his cabinet that "the Allies were standing with their backs against the wall fighting wild beasts." (Charles Seymour, *The Intimate Papers of Colonel House*, vol. 1, p. 293; *New York Times*, January 29, 1925, quoted in Edwin Borchard and William Potter Lage, *Neutrality for the United States*, p. 35.)

blockade against Germany, although they contravened international law as codified at the Hague Conference and its extension in the London Agreement of 1909.*

The Declaration of London confirmed established international law which held that "a blockade must not extend beyond the port or coasts belonging to or occupied by the enemy," that a ship could not be captured if on her way to an unblockaded port no matter what her ultimate destination, and that blockading forces must not bar access to neutral ports or coasts. Under international law as well as under the declaration, contraband was material destined for the fighting forces of a belligerent power—arms, ammunition, powder, military clothing, armor plate warships, etc. Conditional contraband consisted of articles that might be used by the combatant forces—clothing that could be worn by the military, food destined for the army, gold or silver, balloons and flying machines, barbed wire, etc.

Traditional international law held that goods that had both military and nonmilitary uses were not confiscable unless the captor could prove they were destined for use by the enemy navy or army. Such goods were conditional contraband, but by 1916 the British had abolished the distinction; it was the owner of the cargo who had to prove that his goods would never go to Germany. The British decided that all goods shipped to neutral countries might, at some point, reach Germany, so anything a neutral imported was subject to British approval. In effect the British declared everything, including food, contraband, and as early as September 1914 the American State Department made it plain that the United States would raise no serious objection to the British position. Nor did the American government seriously object to the British blacklist of firms that could not be traded with, although the blacklist violated the rights of neutrals, including the United States. The list was intended to prevent an American firm from dealing with a company anywhere in the world that the British proscribed, which meant not only that an American firm could not deal, for example, with a German enterprise in Chile, but even with a Chilean firm it was on the blacklist. Canada, which was at war, refused to accept the British blacklist, but it was acquiesced in by a neutral Washington.[24]

As Sir Edward Grey said (and the White House agreed with him),

* The Declaration of London had summed up much of existing international law as it appeared in the Hague and other treaties. Although it was accepted by France and Germany, its ratification had been advised but not completed by 1914 by the United States Senate. It had been approved by the British House of Commons but rejected by the House of Lords, which disapproved of its limitations on British measures of blockade. Nevertheless, the American State Department asked the warring sides to adopt the declaration as a rule of law in the present conflict, which Germany and Austria agreed to do but the British rejected. As a result, the United States soon dropped its advocacy of the declaration, and based its arguments, not on traditional international law, but on President Wilson's principles.

"Of course many of the restrictions that we have laid down and which seriously interfere with your trade are unreasonable, but America must remember that we are fighting her fight as well as our own to save the civilization of the world."[25]

It was, however, the German use of the submarine and the American reaction to it that was the cause of the United States's entering the war. When the war started, the U-boat was an untried weapon, but despite their small number they soon proved themselves to be a formidable challenge to British shipping and even to her warships. The submarine was new, and new weapons are likely to appear in a horrendous light to those who can maintain their superiority with the older ones.* The U-boats could not follow the rules of cruiser warfare, because when they did, they were often sunk. Submarines were vulnerable to a single shot fired by a gun on any vessel, and in February 1915 the British Admiralty instructed its merchant ships to fire on a submarine at sight or, if they could not otherwise escape, to ram it. The difficulty, if not impossibility, of expecting a U-boat to follow rules designed for surface vessels was well described by an American official, the counselor to the State Department, later Secretary of State Robert Lansing, who as much as any other was promoting a one-sided neutrality. Lansing wrote in 1915: "You will recall the case of the *Baralong* where a German submarine was bombarding a vessel from which the crew had escaped in boats, when a tramp steamer approached flying the American flag. The submarine remained on the surface and awaited the steamer, which on nearing the submarine lowered the American flag, hoisted the British colors, and with a gun mounted on the stern (a defensive armament according to our early definition) opened fire and sank the German vessel, killing all the crew.†[26]

Despite this lucid description of what had actually happened when a submarine attempted to follow the rules of cruiser warfare, both

---

* The crossbow, when it was introduced, was considered a terrible and indiscriminate weapon, "hateful to God and unfit for Christians," because it could penetrate the armor of knights. In 1139, Innocent II banned its use except against infidels, but it continued to be a chief weapon in the medieval arsenal until it was supplanted by the superior English longbow. And Pierre Terrail Bayard, "le chevalier sans peur et sans reproche," as he lay dying in 1524 after he had been shot by a harquebus, was solaced by the thought that he had never given quarter to a musketeer. (Lynn White, Jr., "Technology from the Stance of a Medieval Historian," *The American Historical Review*, February 1974, vol. 79, no. 1, pp. 1–13; E. Davidson, *The Nuremberg Fallacy*, p. 284.)

† What had happened had departed even further from the rules of war than Lansing's report indicated. The *Baralong* had not only sunk the submarine but killed all the crew—five of them, including the captain, as they were swimming, some of them treading water with their hands up in surrender, and six "like dogs," as witnesses said, on the deserted ship *Nicosian*, where they had sought refuge. (Colin Simpson, *The Lusitania*, p. 247; Thomas A. Bailey and Paul B. Ryan, *The Lusitania Disaster*, p. 51.)

Messrs. Wilson and Lansing demanded that the U-boats continue to abide by them; that like a surface ship, a submarine must first send a boarding party to her victim to ascertain whether or not it carried contraband and, if it did, to put the passengers and crew in a place of safety before sinking it. It was a demand that ignored what Lansing had so clearly shown, that a submarine could be, and had been, sunk by a single gun mounted for so-called defensive purposes on a merchant ship. Thus not only did Mr. Wilson acquiesce in the arming of British merchant ships and agree with the British that they should be treated as peaceful ships, but at the same time he denied the right of the German government to take the only effective countermeasures they could to break the British blockade, which was in fact no more legal than the conduct of the German submarines. The loss of life among the German civilian population arising from the lack of food and medicaments as a result of the blockade did not occur as dramatically as when a British ship went down, but the blockade nevertheless killed a good many more civilians than did submarine warfare. Mr. Wilson went, in fact, much further. He invented a principle of international law, maintaining that United States citizens could travel anywhere they wished, even into war zones, and that when they travelled on a British boat either as passengers or as members of the crew, they bestowed upon it immunity against attack. It was a novel doctrine and had no relation to international law, which held that the nationality of a ship is determined by her registry and the flag she flies and that passengers and crew on a foreign vessel are on foreign territory.

Thus when the *Lusitania* was sunk off the Irish coast on May 7, 1915, it made no difference from Mr. Wilson's point of view that both she and her sister ship, the *Mauretania*, were considered to be auxiliary cruisers as well as passenger ships° or that a large part of the *Lusitania's* cargo consisted of war material. Mr. Wilson was both a man of peace and a stern upholder of a one-sided international morality that can all too readily lead to war. His protests to the German government were both eloquent and threatening, but at the same time that he was preparing his first note to Berlin, he made a speech to recently naturalized American citizens on May 10, 1915, which perhaps, because he was not altogether certain of the course he was following, emphasized his veneration of peace. He said: "The example of America must be the example not merely of peace because it will not fight, but of peace because peace is the healing and elevating influence of the world and strife is not. There is such a thing as being too proud to fight."[27] Three days later, however, in his note to the German government, Mr. Wilson declared that the destruction of unarmed merchant ships without visit

---

° The British *Naval Pocket Book* for 1914 listed them as "Armed Merchantmen"; Brassey's *Naval Annual,* 1914, as "Royal Naval Reserved Merchant Cruisers."

and search was unjustifiable; and rejecting the protest of the German government that the sinking was vindicable because the *Lusitania* was armed and carried munitions, he said, repeating a phrase he had used a few months earlier in February, that in the event of any repetition of the sinking, the United States would hold Germany to "strict accountability." In a second note, he told Germany that "nothing but actual forcible resistance or continued efforts to escape by flight when ordered to stop has ever been held to forfeit the lives of her passengers and crew."* [28]

The sinking of the *Lusitania* may have been a political blunder, but it could well have been justified from the military point of view. The vessel's use in wartime, as envisaged by British naval authorities, may be seen from the fact that a silhouette of the *Lusitania* appeared in *Jane's Fighting Ships* for 1914 and, as has been noted, it was listed in Brassey's *Naval Annual* of 1914 as a merchant cruiser and in the *British Naval Pocket Book* as an armed merchantman. Even if she carried no armament, like all other British ships, merchant or passenger, as the German admiralty knew from captured documents, she had orders to ram any submarines on sight. A British journalist, Colin Simpson, has stated categorically that in early August 1914 the *Lusitania* went in drydock to be fitted with guns and on September 17 it was listed in the Admiralty fleet register and the Cunard ledger as an armed auxiliary cruiser, a statement that has been sharply controverted.[29] Emplacements for twelve naval guns were, however, provided for in the blueprints for her construction, and according to Simpson, both she and her sister ship, the *Mauretania*, were rated as being capable of mounting a heavier broadside than the E-class cruisers defending the British Channel.[30] As the most valuable of her cargo, the *Lusitania* carried 4,200 cases of rifle ammunition with a total of 4,200,000 cartridges containing 10½ tons of powder and 1,248 crates of shell casings.

Both the British and American governments denied that the *Lusitania* was armed, and this may well be true. Nevertheless, more than half a century later the denial and the background of the torpedoing are still controversial. Despite the lack of credible, contemporary eyewitness evidence of the presence of naval guns, two deep-sea divers who made repeated descents to the hull of the *Lusitania* in the early 1960s have helped to keep the story of armament alive. One of them, John Bright, an American, said that he had seen in the half-light of the deep waters the outline of what might have been a gun, and his companion was more certain of his identification. They also reported seeing a cut-out rectan-

---

* The contention undoubtedly held for the traditional rules of surface warfare when raiders intercepted enemy or neutral vessels, but it had little or no relevancy to U-boats operating against armed merchant ships with Admiralty orders to sink or ram submarines.

gular hole amidships, where the *Lusitania's* blueprints called for a gun. As Bailey and Ryan in their careful investigation point out, however, such weapons were most useful mounted either in the bow or in the stern, and amidships would be an unlikely place for one or two guns, which were in short supply.

But whether the *Lusitania* was armed or not, the sinking was a major human tragedy: 1,138 passengers, among them 138 Americans, were drowned, many of them women and children. Although the German government, despite the official warning it had caused to be published in American newspapers against travelling on the vessel, offered to and did pay damages to the families of those who had died, the horror and shock of the American public and government were not to be assuaged by expressions of regret or cash payments. According to Mr. Wilson's doctrine, the Americans had not been travelling on this belligerent ship at their own risk, although they could have taken an American vessel sailing from New York on the same day as the *Lusitania* that was neither armed nor carrying munitions. Mr. Wilson held that the Americans had been on the *Lusitania* by right and that their presence had precluded the Germans from sinking it.

His views of the matter were rejected by a good many people, among them Secretary of State William Jennings Bryan, who resigned his office because he was convinced Mr. Wilson's course would inevitably lead to war with Germany, as well as Secretary of the Navy Josephus Daniels, Senator La Follette of Wisconsin, and others who agreed with Bryan that ships of a belligerent nation carrying contraband could not be protected by the presence on board of Americans. Curiously enough, British Admiral of the Fleet at the time the *Lusitania* was sunk, Lord Fisher, who after he had retired to private life was conducting a friendly and secret correspondence with his former opposite number, German Admiral Alfred von Tirpitz, also disagreed with the president. Fisher wrote to Tirpitz on March 29, 1916: "I don't blame you for the submarine business, I'd have done exactly the same thing myself."[31] Twenty years later, the Earl of Cork and Orrery held much the same view. In a speech before the United Service Institution in 1936 he said: "If you look back at the late war, you will remember that the great advantage which the allies had over the enemy . . . lay in the British Merchant Marine; yet we held up our hands in horror when the Germans sank our ships. . . . Very often we condemned this action of the enemy on the ground that there were noncombatants and women and children in the ships. . . . If women and children choose to travel in ships in a war area, they must take what they get. It is a very cowardly thing for us to try to defend our merchant ships by this plea."[32]

Up to the time the United States broke diplomatic relations with Germany, only three Americans had lost their lives on an American ship, and that ship—the *Gulflight*—was sailing under British convoy. Two members of the crew jumped overboard when she was torpedoed and were drowned, and the captain died of a heart attack.[33]

Nevertheless, President Wilson held that the United States was being attacked and its citizens were being killed by a ruthless enemy of civilization, and it was this stubbornly held view that brought the United States to a point where war was certain unless Germany renounced the only weapon that would take the pressure off her hard-pressed armies and break the blockade that was starving her civilian population. The Germans did not have a wide choice; either accept Mr. Wilson's demands, and with them defeat, or risk war with the United States with some chance of victory.* The decision was to take the risk of war; only by an all-out blockade could Germany defeat Britain or bring her to the negotiating table; if German submarines were successful when unhampered by restrictions, American aid, which was pouring out to the Allies in any case, would be diminished or cut off; and it they were not, the Reich would have a new and powerful enemy in the place of Russia and the war would be lost. The German declaration of unrestricted submarine warfare in the waters around the British Isles was an illegal measure designed to counter an equally illegal blockade in which the United States acquiesced. When, as a result, American ships were sunk and American lives were lost, Mr. Wilson's demand for a declaration of war could only be approved by Congress.

In the later revulsion against American involvement in the European war, many theories were advanced to explain how it came about. The open and covert activities of munition makers, the economic alliance that resulted from American manufacturers supplying the Allies with millions of dollars' worth of war equipment, the industrial boom emerging from Allied war purchases, the circumstance that before the United States entered the war the firm of J. P. Morgan had British notes on hand for 400 million dollars that Britain was in no position to pay—all these were considered to have played an important role in America's becoming a belligerent. Colonel House† and Robert Lansing, however,

---

* The chances of victory by means of the submarine counterblockade were greatly overestimated by the German High Command. At the start of the war Germany had some 10 U-boats that could put to sea against England; they had 21 submarines in all, of which 12 used gasoline instead of diesel oil, and no more than half the fleet could be at sea at the same time. Toward the end of 1915 only eight U-boats were in action; the high command, however, believed they would have between 40 and 50 at hand for unrestricted submarine warfare. (Gerhard Ritter, *Staatskunst und Kriegshandwerk*, vol. 3, p. 147.)

† The title had nothing to do with any military career; it became attached to his name when he was appointed to the staff of Texas Governor James S. Hogg. House was invariably addressed as Colonel by his correspondents who appear in Charles Seymour's edition of *The Intimate Papers of Colonel House*, and the title is also used to head his own prefatory note to that volume.

were not much interested in economic alliances. Like the anglophile American ambassador to London, Walter Hines Page, it was the moral issue, they were devoutly convinced, that was decisive. Page helped the British Foreign Office answer American notes; he sent the State Department long accounts of alleged German atrocities furnished by the British and almost all untrue. He believed that "it will be a great good fortune for the U.S. if we go to war with Germany," for it would bring, among other benefits, "emancipation from femininity and fads."[34] Page was a man with peculiar notions of what the United States was in need of: he wanted to keep Negroes, Jews, and Germans out of the country; Negroes and Jews he considered racially unassimilable and the Germans politically unassimilable.[35] Both Messrs. Page and Wilson were convinced of American moral superiority over all the peoples of the earth, and Page agreed with Wilson that the United States must place itself at the service of humanity if the world was to be saved.

To this end Mr. Wilson, a few months after the *Lusitania* was sunk, had sent Colonel House to Europe on a mission that expressed his own mixed purposes. House was to induce the warring nations to permit the American president to act as mediator in the conflict, and to persuade the British to accept his mediation in principle with the expectation that the Germans would turn the plan down and the United States might then enter the war on the side of the Allies. In a letter Colonel House wrote in October 1915, before he departed on this peace mission, he told Sir Edward Grey, in explaining his purposes, that if the Central Powers were obdurate, it would probably be necessary for the United States to join the war on the side of the Allies "and force the issue."[36] Early in 1916, at a conference with British leaders, Ambassador Page asked Mr. House what the United States wished Britain to do. House replied, to the gratification of all those present: "The United States would like Great Britain to do those things which would enable the United States to help Great Britain win the war."[37] The trip came to nothing; under the circumstances neither the French nor the British saw any advantage in joining in peace negotiations and the French said so clearly. Mr. Wilson might talk of the glories of peace, but his rhetoric on such occasions bore little relation to much of what he said and did in his day-by-day, practical decisions.

Far more important than the economic alliance was the set of American opinion as it was expressed by men in high places in the American government and in what would be called today the media. The deep, often violent suspicion of the British that had begun with the American Revolution and continued through the Civil War had faded in the minds of the country's opinion makers (despite its persistence among many Irish and German-Americans) as a century had gone by without warfare with the former mother country. The common language and cultural heritage had made both communication and susceptibility to British propaganda far easier than for other, European countries. The bloody atrocity stories printed in the British and American press and attested to by eminent scholars in both countries were almost all false, it would later be found, but they were the stories large sections of the American public and key figures in the administration read and believed, and German denials were as straws in the gale of official and popular indignation against such alleged German barbarities. It was an age not only of American innocence in such matters; many Britains and Europeans, too, believed the lurid tales. The very idea of highly organized propaganda as an arm of combat was novel, although the technique had been described by the Chinese strategist Sun Tsu over 2,400 years before World War I and used, although in a relatively haphazard way, ever since. Neither the American people, however, nor their government had much of a notion about how large-scale psychological warfare could be waged; nor did the Germans, despite the fact that they, too, tried to use it. The German propaganda apparatus was run by the army, and in comparison with the work of the brilliant civilian operators in charge of the British effort, it was clumsy and unconvincing. Nevertheless by 1914, with the use of mass conscript armies and the mobilization of the resources of the home front, a propaganda apparatus had become indispensable, and a lance corporal in the German army would learn a great deal from the lessons the Allies taught him.

What propaganda techniques can achieve can themselves be greatly overblown by propaganda, but skillfully used they provide a formidable weapon. Propaganda, to be successful, must be plausible, must bear a relation to what people think may be true. It can withhold or distort or embellish facts, but if it merely seems preposterous, it is self-defeating, even in cases where it may not be propaganda but the unvarnished truth. It may be that it convinces people only of what they want to believe; it is doubtful that either it or any other kind of advertising ever successfully sold what the public rejected out of hand* or was not ready to accept.

With some categories of propaganda, however, the Germans themselves were of considerable help to the Allies, for example, the scrap-of-paper remark of Bethmann Hollweg, the Hun speech of the kaiser, the execution of the British nurse Edith Cavell, the sinking of the *Lusitania*, the execution of hostages, and the deportation of Belgian and French

---

* Examples may be seen in the failure of promotions of commodities like the Edsel car and of political candidates whose overfinanced campaigns far outran their appeal to the voters.

workers to Germany. Almost all these acts would later be justified or re-interpreted by many Allied and neutral observers, but with the heated emotions of wartime they did serve to dramatize differences in the manner of waging the war and perhaps in national character. The En-glish nurse Edith Cavell, to take one instance, was certainly guilty of an offense punishable by death; as the matron of a training school for nurses in Brussels, she had aided the escape of some 200 young men from occupied Belgium and thus enabled many of them to fight again in the Allied armies. During her trial she readily admitted what she had done, and said she knew that some of those she had helped smuggle out of the country had rejoined the Allied forces. Nevertheless, it was a major error in the tactics of psychological warfare to execute her, and one the British did not themselves commit when they arrested German women agents, even after the shooting of Miss Cavell.*

The execution was approved not only by the German general who confirmed the death sentence but also by Thomas Mann, who wrote that Miss Cavell had misused her nurse's uniform and that if she was a heroine, it was not because of her pure patriotism, since she was En-glish and the soldiers she had helped escape were Belgian, but because what she had done was a political act for which she was prepared to take the consequences.[38] Both the German General Staff and the man of letters would no doubt have regarded it as an unworthy reaction to Entente hyprocrisy were they to indulge themselves, in time of war, in such sentiments as were expressed in the verses "Between the stirrup and the ground / He mercy sought and mercy found," nor could they accept as applying either to her case or theirs Miss Cavell's own words when she said, as she faced the firing squad: "Standing before God and eternity, I realize that patriotism is not enough. I must be free from hate or bitterness."

With such aid from the Germans, the Allies could invent the most outrageous accounts of gruesome behavior and over a period of time recruit impassioned believers, even in the highest places, among their own citizens and Americans as well. Not much attention was paid in the United States, except among German-Americans, none of whom held important posts in the government, about the alleged atrocities of Russian soldiers in East Prussia, which was the only part of Germany, with the exception of French penetrations into Alsace-Lorraine, a foreign foe occupied. But since the German armies had invaded France, Belgium, Poland, and Russia, a flood of atrocity stories that could not be easily checked could be circulated, and the denials never caught up with the rate of production. Thus the American and Allied presses were soon running accounts of children whose hands had been cut off by German

---

* Mata Hari, shot by a French firing squad, was a professional spy and therefore not a symbol, as was Miss Cavell, of selfless, humanitarian virtues.

bayonets,* of women whose breasts had been amputated, of the manufacture in Germany of soap made from rendered human fat, of crucified
Allied soldiers and babies—all of them attested to most solemnly in
official reports based, so it was said, on affidavits by eyewitnesses.† A
Rumanian paper reported that German women wore necklaces made of
eyes gouged out of French wounded; Belgian accounts told of a farmer
who had had his arm sliced with three longitudinal cuts and then had
been hung upside down and burned to death. In Antwerp, it was reported, priests had been tied to church bells and used as clappers. Young
boys were said to have been forced to run about a field naked while
German soldiers used them as targets, a man had had his ears cut off
before he was thrown into a burning house to be consumed with it. The
atrocity stories ran on and on: pregnant women had had their bellies slit
open, wells had been poisoned, German bayonets had been made jagged
with saw teeth so they would be more likely to inflict a mortal wound.
The bayonets were supplemented with bullets that had been scraped
to soften the tips, so that when they entered the body of a victim they
would spread. And then came the ultimate, dastardly weapon, which was
not a propaganda invention—poison gas, first introduced by the Germans and later adopted by the Allies. The Germans, Allied propaganda
proved over and over, had no interest in the laws of God or men: they
sank merchant and hospital ships and shot up the survivors, they bombed
hospitals, and they encouraged their allies the Turks to commit mass
murders against the Armenians. It was a long list of accusations and it
lasted for the entire war.

Attempts to counteract the atrocity stories were not very successful.
During the first week of September 1914, a number of American news-
papermen—Irvin S. Cobb of the *Philadelphia Public Ledger*, Harry
Hansen of the *Chicago Daily News*, and James Bennett and John Mc-
Cutcheon of the *Chicago Tribune*—who were with the German army
in Belgium declared they had not been able to substantiate a single
wanton brutality, and similar testimony came from other neutral observers, which would be borne out in great part by postwar investigations, including those of Allied commissions. Excerpts from thirty-seven
diaries had been compiled, and 500 depositions were printed from among
the 1200 said to have been relied on in the famous Bryce Report, published in 1915, on German atrocities in Belgium, and many years later

---

* One sympathetic and rich American wanted to adopt these children, but not a
single case was ever found. (James Morgan Read, *Atrocity Propaganda 1914–1919*,
p. 36.)

† A British professor of law wrote that the slightest failure to comply with German soldiers' demands resulted in instant death: when a young mother at Bailleul
was unable to provide twenty-three German soldiers with coffee, one of them seized
her baby and dipped its head in scalding water. (J. H. Morgan, *German Atrocities—
An Official Investigation*, p. 77.)

an American scholar stated that "not one clear-cut case of confessed 'atrociousness' was in any one of them although many tell of the execution of alleged *francs-tireurs* and more, of plunderings." In addition he noted that the official Belgian reports of 1922 "failed utterly" to substantiate the Bryce Report's charges.[39]

Nevertheless, atrocities were committed and by both sides. It is not possible to fight a long war with millions of men engaged in mutual slaughter without violations of the customs and usages of war. And in addition there were the brutalities that, according to technical definitions, were not war crimes. In Belgium the Germans were to kill, in the course of the war, some 5,000 civilians, some of them as hostages, some of them as alleged *francs-tireurs*, that is, civilians without uniforms or insignia plainly identifying them as combatants who were accused of firing on German soldiers. Among the civilians were women and children, killed, the Germans said, by inadvertence when they had been caught between battle lines or in houses from which snipers were shooting and which therefore had been set on fire. But the main case against the Germans was their shooting of hostages. To Germans brought up to regard a uniform as an honorable, if not sacred, vestment, shooting at unsuspecting troops by people dressed in civilian clothes was a major crime. It was one thing to shoot, and be shot at, by a man who could be readily identified as an enemy soldier, but when, for example, a German company marched into a Belgian town and a lieutenant was killed and four men wounded by gunmen in civilian clothes, hidden behind the walls of seemingly peaceful dwellings, that was murder and had to be dealt with as such.

Since the murderers often could not be found, the cruel but traditional measures against such hit-and-run tactics were resorted to; hostages were taken from among the civilian population and their lives held forfeit against future killings in the neighborhood by *francs-tireurs*. When the French occupied part of Alsace-Lorraine in 1914, they also took hostages, as did the Russians in East Prussia. The execution of hostages, usually innocent people, was an extreme procedure intended to prevent a recurrence of illegal acts that could not be stopped in any other way. It was a harsh measure, but like the shooting of Miss Cavell, it was not illegal, and it would continue in many occupation armies long after World War I.°

° The execution of hostages was regarded by the military law of almost all countries as a legitimate reprisal against an illegal act—against a violation of international law. Hostages were taken by the Romans, by the British in India, and by the French in North Africa. In the American Civil War, General Sherman had fifty-four prisoners of war executed as a reprisal for the murder of twenty-seven of his own soldiers. *The British Manual of Military Law* declared such reprisals "indispensable as a last resort." (August von Knieriem, *The Nuremberg Trials*, pp. 380, 385.)

The Belgians held that many of those executed by the Germans had been fighting according to the rules of international law and that hundreds of hostages had simply been massacred. The Germans, on the other hand, considered all resistance during the occupation illegal, a view that would later be adopted by Americans when they occupied parts of Germany in World War II. Although the question of the *francs-tireurs* and the reprisals against them was a sensitive one for both the Germans and the Belgians, the Belgian commission investigating war crimes, reporting after the war, dropped the word *atrocity* from their description of the countermeasures the Germans had taken and substituted the word *attentat*, that is, violation or outrage. And as passions cooled, the behavior of the Germans began to have its defenders among neutrals as well as among Allied generals and diplomats. As early as 1918 General Pershing denied that some of the most bizarre of the atrocities had ever been committed; Admiral William Sims declared that German submarines in general had been used in a humane manner, and that U-boat crews had on more than one occasion provided the survivors of ships they had sunk with food and water; a British naval commander, J. M. Kenworthy, called the submarine campaign "legal and logical"; and a British diplomat, Harold Nicolson, confessed, "We lied damnably during the war" and said he was sorry they had.[40]

Although atrocities were undoubtedly committed by both sides during the war—the Germans, too, had compiled a long list of those allegedly committed by the Allies—it was only those committed by the Germans that received any serious attention and that had serious consequences for the entire population. The most onerous provisions of the Treaty of Versailles were justified by a moral indictment, Germany was held solely responsible for starting the war, and the kaiser was to be tried for "a supreme offense against international morality and the sanctity of treaties." It was only Germans who were to be tried for committing acts in violation of the customs and usages of war, and the reparations to be paid by Germany as compensation for any damage done to civilian life and property in the Allied countries were owing as a result of the aggression of Germany by land, sea, and air. It was because Germany was declared solely responsible for the war that the treaty saddled it with a debt that no country in the world could possibly pay, and in addition it severed German territory from the Reich, divided East Prussia with a Polish corridor, and left the Reich almost defenseless with an army of 100,000 men without armor or air force. A guiding principle of self-determination, enunciated both by the Soviet Union and Mr. Wilson, was made to apply to everyone but Germans.* Large tracts of land

---

* Mr. Wilson's Fourteen Points, enunciated to a joint session of Congress on January 8, 1918, made no mention of self-determination. The fourteen points, which both

in eastern Germany, in Silesia, and, under the Treaty of St. Germain, in the Sudetenland were turned over to countries run by non-German governments who demanded for themselves the right to self-determination that they were not disposed to grant Germans either inside or outside their borders.

The front-line soldiers, Adolf Hitler among them, had no notion that they had behaved in any way worse than the troops in the opposite trenches. Nor would they or the civilian population at home ever believe that the German government had been solely responsible for the war that had kept them fighting desperately for more than four years—

---

the German government and the Allies accept as a basis for peace negotiations, provided for:

1. "Open covenants of peace, openly arrived at. . . ."
2. "Absolute freedom of navigation upon the seas. . . ."
3. "The removal, as far as possible, of all economic barriers among all the nations."
4. "Adequate guarantees given and taken that national armaments will be reduced to the lowest point consistent with domestic safety."
5. "A free, open-minded and absolutely impartial adjustment of all colonial claims. . . ."
6. "The evacuation of all Russian territory" and the opportunity to be given her for the independent determination of her own political development and national policies.
7. The evacuation of Belgium and the restoration of its sovereignty.
8. The evacuation of occupied French territory and "the wrong done to France by Prussia in 1871 in the matter of Alsace-Lorraine" to be righted.
9. A readjustment of Italian frontiers "along clearly recognizable lines of nationality."
10. "The peoples of Austria-Hungary, whose place among the nations we wish to see safeguarded and assured, should be accorded the freest opportunity for autonomous development."
11. Rumania, Serbia, and Montenegro to be evacuated; Serbia to be given "free and secure access to the sea."
12. The Turkish portions of the Ottoman Empire to be assured sovereignty but the other nationalities under Turkish rule to be assured security of life and "an absolutely unmolested opportunity for autonomous development," and the Dardanelles "permanently opened as a free passage to the ships and commerce of all nations."
13. An independent Poland to be erected and to include the "territories inhabited by indisputably Polish populations" with access to the sea.
14. "A general association of nations must be formed" to afford "mutual guarantees of political independence and territorial integrity. . . ."

A number of Mr. Wilson's later speeches dealt with the principle of self-determination, which had made an early appearance in the pronouncement of the French and German socialist parties and the Petrograd Soviet. On February 11, 1918, Mr. Wilson told Congress: "There shall be no annexations, no contributions, no punitive damages. People are not to be handed about from one sovereignty to another. . . . National aspirations must be respected; peoples may now be dominated and governed only by their own consent. 'Self determination' is not a mere phrase. It is an imperative principle of action, which statesmen will henceforth ignore at their peril." Lloyd George, too, spoke in favor of the doctrine, as did General Smuts, but any reference to it was excluded from the Covenant of the League of Nations. The terms of the Treaty of Versailles were too patently in conflict with it when Germany was concerned. (C. E. Carrington, "National Self Determination," *Modern Age*, vol. 11, no. 3, pp. 247–58; James Brown Scott, *President Wilson's Foreign Policy*, p. 368.)

an incredulity that would be shared by historians and publicists of every nation in the years to come. It was, however, the alleged guilt of Germany for deliberately starting the war and the belief of the Allied statesmen in their own propaganda about the inhuman manner in which the Germans had fought that provided the moral and even the legal* justification for the terms of the treaty that every German left, right, and center would regard as the infamous *Diktat* of Versailles.

Hitler had been twice wounded, the first time in the autumn of 1916 at Le Barqué, where he had been hit in the left thigh,† the second time in 1918, less than a month before the armistice, when he was gassed near Wervik. He had suffered a temporary blindness and heard in his hospital bed the news that revolution had broken out and Germany had been defeated. For him and thousands of others who had fought the war the news was shattering. They had given the battle everything they had, they had seen their comrades die by the thousands; but all the sacrifices, the pounding they had taken day and night, the hopeless positions somehow struggled for and held, all this was for nothing. Battle-worn troops who returned to the Fatherland from the occupied territory in Belgium, France, and Russia had none of that sense of defeat that comes from the knowledge that the forces of the enemy have been superior in the field. They had fought bitterly against great odds of men and material for those four years, and they had achieved, as even their enemies conceded, prodigies of valor up and down Europe and in Africa, where one German army held out even after the armistice and where, despite Mr. Wilson's promise in his Fourteen Points that impartial adjustment of colonial claims would be made, all the German colonies would be lost and parcelled out among the victors. Neither Hitler nor thousands of others who had fought in the front lines or stolidly endured the hardships of the homeland would ever be able to digest the defeat. It would always be incomprehensible to them, only to be explained by black treason, betrayal, the stab in the back, Communists, Jews.

The German victories in Russia had enabled the Reich to impose a peace, a *Diktat*, of its own making at Brest-Litovsk,‡ but it did not prepare the German people for the *Diktat* of Versailles. Although the terms of the Brest-Litovsk peace were harsh, they had not severed from

* Article 231 read: "The Allied and Associated Governments affirm, and Germany accepts, the responsibility of Germany and her allies for causing all the loss and damage to which the Allied and Associated Governments and their nationals have been subjected as a consequence of the war imposed upon them by the aggression of Germany and her allies."

† Hitler was invalided for five months, part of the time in a hospital at Beelitz, near Berlin, after which he was sent to a reserve battalion in Munich.

‡ Negotiations between the Russians and the Central Powers began in December 1917, and the peace treaty was signed on March 3, 1918.

the motherland purely Russian populations or territory, nor did they exact reparations on the Versailles scale.* The lands that were detached from the Soviet Union were non-Russian—Poland, Latvia, Lithuania, Finland, and the Ukraine, as well as the districts of Kars, Ardahan, and Batum, which went to Turkey.†

The loss of population and territory to the Soviet Union was very large—46 million inhabitants and some 386,000 square miles—but for millions of these people in Poland, the Baltic States, Finland, and the Ukraine, the Brest-Litovsk Treaty gave some hope of liberation from the suzerainty of what they had always regarded as a foreign government. Although the loss of the Ukraine would have dealt a serious blow to the Soviet economy, its inhabitants were for the most part whole-heartedly anti-Soviet and anti-Russian and would remain so for years to come.‡ Neither they nor the people of the other liberated states had any desire to exchange Russians for Germans and Austrians as masters, but as a result of the Russian defeat they had some chance for a national life even if the Germans planned, as they did, to dominate much of it. As for the revolutionaries in Russia, the war had given them an opportunity to get rid of the reactionary, feudal, tsarist regime and to start creating a new society. They could afford to trade territory and population for even a transitory peace, and time was on their side.

Or so they thought. The entire peace delegation at Brest-Litovsk would be liquidated, in due course, by the revolution they had helped to make. Joffe, the first leader of the delegation, would commit suicide; Trotsky, his successor, would be assassinated in his exile in Mexico; Admiral Altvater and General Samoilo would be killed during the reign of terror of 1918; two others, Sokolnikov and Radek, would be sent to Soviet concentration camps; and an additional two, Kamenev and Karakhan, would be executed in later purges.[41] But at the time the Brest-Litovsk Treaty was signed, revolutionary uprisings in the territories severed from Russia and all over Europe, as well as in the armies of the Entente and the Central Powers, were confidently expected by the Soviet leaders.

Despite any temporary loss of population and territory (the Red Army would soon reconquer the Ukraine and would attempt to reconquer

* The Brest-Litovsk Treaty excluded reparations in Article 9, but in a supplementary agreement of August 27, 1918, the Soviet government agreed to provide Germany with 25 percent of the Baku oil production and to pay "six billion marks for losses to Germany caused by Russian measures. . . ." (John W. Wheeler-Bennett, *The Forgotten Peace*, p. 440.)

† General Hoffmann pointed out that although the Allies denounced the terms of the Brest-Litovsk Treaty, they in their turn accepted its main provisions, which detached the Baltic countries and Poland from Russia. (General Max Hoffmann, *Der Krieg der versäumten Gelegenheiten.*)

‡ The Ukrainian delegation to the Brest-Litvosk conference refused to speak Russian and conducted their negotiations with General Hoffmann in Ukrainian.

Poland) and despite the civil war in Russia and the intervention of the
Allied powers, the Communist revolutionaries could look with optimism
to the future. As they saw it, history was following the inexorable laws
of Marxist doctrine, imperial Russia was finished, they had defeated
Kerensky and his puppet regime controlled by the Allies, and they could
endure the hunger and misery of postwar Russia and win the fight
against the remnants of the tsar's armies aided by the Allies because
they were the advance guard of the new order, not only for Russia, but
for the entire world. For the Marxist leaders of Soviet Russia, Brest-
Litovsk was no more than a temporary, removable roadblock, as indeed
it proved to be; it was obliterated in the terms of the November armistice.

The case of Germany was very different. The German revolution, like
the Russian, was imposed by military defeat, but it bore with it none
of the messianic fevers and the belief in historical imperatives that
characterized the Communist seizure of power. The German revolution
produced a republic, in large part because Mr. Wilson had declared he
would only negotiate with a democratic government,* and the republic's
establishment and the cease-fire were but preludes to continuing disaster.

The Allied blockade continued in force until June 12, 1919, two days
after Germany ratified the Treaty of Versailles, and Germans estimated
that it cost the lives of three-quarters of a million people; the bloody
armed risings that took place in many parts of the country were led by
imitators of the Russian Revolution and could be put down only by more
shooting on the part of dispirited men clinging to the tattered shreds of
what they had left behind them when they went to war, as hungry and
confused as their opponents.

No one, not Schlieffen or Poincaré or Lord Grey or the kaiser or President Wilson, had foreseen the consequences of World War I. Its most
important outcome was the triumph of the Russian Revolution, the
establishing of the Union of Soviet Republics, an event that would transform the domestic policies and power relationships of Europe and the
world far more than the founding of imperial Germany in 1871. As a
result of the war, England would be toppled as the leading commercial
and naval power of the world, France would have regained a shaky
hegemony over Europe but still be confronted with the huge shadow of a
unified Germany, and Clemenceau would write of the grandeur and
misery of victory. The United States would withdraw from Europe in a
violent reaction to the policies of Mr. Wilson, whose plan for a League of
Nations was so biliously regarded by French leaders as to cause them to
demand and obtain, as a price of their joining it, a military alliance with

---

* Mr. Wilson said that if the United States was to "deal with the military masters
and the monarchical autocrats of Germany . . . it must demand not peace negotiations
but surrender." (Quoted John Morton Blum, *Woodrow Wilson and the Politics of
Morality,* p. 150.)

both Britain and the United States. For Germany there was no grandeur, only misery; she was not only defeated, she was humiliated, left with little else than the legend of an incomparable army. The army she was permitted to have now was large enough, perhaps, to put down the risings of uprooted men in a civil war but unable to defend the shrunken borders of the Reich against any serious attack of Poland and France with their millions of troops, air force, and tanks. Nor was Germany to be permitted to take any part in the apparatus of peace promised by Mr. Wilson, which would make such frontiers less important than they had·been before the advent of the new internationalism of the League of Nations. She was a guilty nation thrust into a separate corner of the world made safe for democracy.

What Hilter and the millions of returning German soldiers witnessed and took part in was the beginning of a revolution of nihilism, imitating in small segments the tactics of the Russian Revolution and put down by the counterrevolution of men who had no program but to put it down. Hitler, when he left the hospital for Munich at the end of November, could readily fit this revolution into the framework of his simplistic view of what caused nations, especially Germanic nations, to rise and fall. The complicated construals of the Manns and Spenglers were not for him, nor were the Marxist ones. He had found a home and a refuge in the war and the army; the comradeship of the front lines marked the only time he had ever broken through the barriers that had separated him from the Viennese and the Müncheners and his own family. It was that that he would be seeking for many years to come, and the movement he helped to found would be based on it as much as on hate. Comradeship means exclusion; comrades are made by a common enemy, common danger; and in Munich, where the Workers, Soldiers and Peasants Council under the chairmanship of Kurt Eisner,* a romantic socialist and a Jew, proclaimed the Bavarian Republic on November 7, the enemy would soon be as easy to identify as he had been in Vienna and in the trenches.

* Eisner, a Berliner, was theater critic for the *Münchener Post* and an aspiring dramatist. Antimilitarist, anti-Prussian, anti-Bolshevik, he wanted to establish "a regime of goodness" and hoped to prepare Germany for entry into the League of Nations.

CHAPTER 4

The Desert of Defeat

ALL OVER GERMANY the old political order collapsed without much sound or fury. Revolutionary committees made up mainly of Social and Independent Democrats assumed power. They had no need to fight for it; their demands for a republic were accepted by the princes and kings, the *Obrigkeit* that had ruled for centuries, in almost every case as soon as they were made, sometimes before they were made.*

The only way open was to the Left. The one leader in the Allied camp who had spoken of a peace without victor or vanquished was Woodrow Wilson, and on October 24, 1918, he had told the Germans the American government would not negotiate with the government of William II; if "the military rulers and monarchist autocrats" remained in power, Germany would have to surrender. He said, too, he could propose to the Allies only an armistice that would make a renewal of hostilities on the part of Germany impossible. Neither of these statements seemed inconsistent with Wilson's previous declarations on the subject of peace.†

---

* The kaiser alone resisted abdicating. Early in November 1918, he left Berlin for the refuge of the high command's headquarters at Spa, where he talked of leading the troops back from the trenches to put down the insurrectionists. But Wilhelm could not indulge in such fantasies for long. When even Hindenburg told him he could no longer rely on the loyalty of the troops, the kaiser had no choice but to renounce his throne, both as emperor of Germany and king of Prussia.

† On July 4, 1918, Mr. Wilson added four more points to his peace program:

1. The destruction of every arbitrary power anywhere that can separately, secretly, and of its single choice disturb the peace of the world; . . .
2. The settlement of every question, whether of territory, of sovereignty, of economic arrangement, or of political relationship, upon the basis of the free

On October 26 Ludendorff was dismissed, and on November 9, one day after the proclamation of the Bavarian Republic, a Social Democratic leader, Philipp Scheidemann, proclaimed the German Republic from the Reichstag. Prince Max of Baden turned over the chancellorship to Friedrich Ebert, chairman of the Social Democratic party since 1913, a former saddler, and editor of the Social Democratic newspaper *Vorwärts.* Hindenburg and General Groener,* who had replaced Ludendorff, declared they would support the new government immediately after they had told the kaiser the army would no longer support him.

As in Russia, military defeat had set the revolution in motion, but the German army, unlike the Russian, fought on, resisting the enemy tenaciously on all fronts until it was ordered to return to the Reich. Only then did it march home. Three million men returned in disciplined order from France and Belgium in the space of three weeks. That was true of the front-line army; things were different in the rear, and in the ranks of the troops awaiting demobilization, who not infrequently demobilized themselves.

---

acceptance of that settlement by the people immediately concerned, and not upon the basis of the material interest or advantage of any other nation or people. . . .

3. The consent of all nations to be governed in their conduct toward each other by the same principles of honor and of respect for the common law of civilized society that govern the individual citizens . . . to the end that all promises and covenants may be sacredly observed, no private plots or conspiracies hatched, . . . and a mutual trust established upon the handsome foundation of a mutual respect for right.

4. The establishment of an organization of peace which shall make it certain that the combined power of free nations will check every invasion of right and serve to make peace and justice the more secure. . . .

And on September 27, 1918, five "particulars" were spelled out:

1. The impartial justice meted out must involve no discrimination between those to whom we wish to be just and those to whom we do not wish to be just. It must be a justice that plays no favorites, and knows no standards but the equal rights of the several peoples concerned.

2. No special or separate interest of any single nation or group of nations can be made the basis of any part of the settlement which is not consistent with the common interest of all.

3. There can be no leagues or alliances or special covenants or understandings within the general and common family of the League of Nations.

4. . . . there can be no special, selfish, economic combinations within the League, . . . no . . . economic boycott or exclusion except as the power of economic penalty by exclusion from the markets of the world may be vested in the League of Nations itself as a means of discipline and control.

5. All international agreements and treaties of every kind must be made known in their entirety to the rest of the world. (Harry Rudin, *Armistice 1918,* pp. 400–3.)

* Groener was the antithesis of Ludendorff. He was not a Prussian but a South German from Württemberg, and like other members of the new government, the son of an artisan family.

The front had bent but it had not broken. In mid-July, a few days after the last German offensive had failed to pierce the Allied lines, American and French troops, led by 600 tanks, had broken into the German flank at the Marne. A few weeks later, on August 8, in a thick fog, British divisions with 400 tanks had swept through the lines of the 2nd Army at Amiens, and the Germans had been pushed back, unable to hold their ground but on the whole retreating methodically, taking and inflicting heavy casualties as they went. The Germans no longer had either the reserves or the tanks to mount the counterattacks that up to then had blunted the Allied offensives, and if August 8 was, as Ludendorff said, "the black day in German history," even blacker days were ahead. In mid-August, the Austrian emperor, Karl, told the German government that Austria-Hungary was compelled to ask for an armistice, and by the end of September Bulgaria was out of the war and the Turks were about to follow suit. Ludendorff panicked. Fearing an allied breakthrough at any moment, he demanded, on September 29, that the German government seek an immediate armistice, and Hindenburg agreed with him.

The celebrated analytical qualities and clinical objectivity of the German High Command had worn thin. An August 13, only five days after Ludendorff had spoken of the black day in German history, he declared that Belgium and Poland must remain under German influence. As late as September 2, Hindenburg had promised that, despite the American troops on the western front, Germany would be strong enough to impose a peace in the West as it had in the East. Then, a few weeks later, he joined Ludendorff in an admission that not only was victory impossible but a military catastrophe impended.*1

Nor was this the end of the mood swings in the chiefs of the high command. Two days after Ludendorff had told the staff officers of the desperate situation on the western front, the German chancellor, Prince Max of Baden, on October 3 asked Hindenburg how long the German army could hold off the enemy from the German borders. Hindenburg replied that such questions could not be answered precisely because of many unpredictable factors, but the German army, he could hope, would keep the enemy out of Germany until spring. Although the troops must reckon with enemy penetrations, Hindenburg did not believe the front would collapse. To Prince Max's question as to whether the high command was aware that a move for peace under military pressure might lead to the loss of the German colonies, Alsace-Lorraine, and the

---

* On October 1, Ludendorff told the chiefs of the high command that the German army was finished, the war could not be won, in fact a final defeat was inevitable. An armistice must be concluded as quickly as possible. Colonel von Thaer wrote in his diary that these words had an indescribable effect on the officers who heard them. Sobs and groans could be heard, and most of the men present openly wept. (Herbert Michaelis, et al, *Ursachen und Folgen*, vol. 2, p. 323.)

purely Polish parts of the eastern territories, Hindenburg replied haughtily: "The high command, if necessary, takes into consideration the possibility of giving up small, non-German-speaking parts of Alsace-Lorraine, but the surrender of eastern territories is not to be considered."[2] And one week after that, on October 11, Ludendorff had so far recovered from his despair that he said that Germany could continue the war if she could secure a breathing space—which is what an armistice meant to him—a pause to regroup and fight again if need be.

Such extreme shifts in the judgments of the high command made no sense to the home front or to the rear echelons. The front-line officers and men stolidly kept on fighting, but the German people were completely unprepared for a lost war. For them the war had meant privation and suffering, but for a transcendent cause—the preservation of the Fatherland. Enemy after enemy had been defeated, Russia and Rumania had collapsed under the hammer blows of the German army, and a final victory had been promised with the last great offensive in the spring of 1918. Now suddenly they learned that everything was lost; that they had been led into disaster.

No signs of revolt appeared in the front lines, but behind the lines it was another matter.* On November 1, General Groener reported that the morale of the fighting troops was threatened by the depressed mood of soldiers returning from leave, and that one division of the *Landwehr*† that had fought in the East and included many Poles and Alsatians, had refused to move up to the front line. Soon such reports of the unreliability of other divisions in the rear areas would multiply. The mutiny on October 30 in ships of the German navy ordered to assemble at Wilhelmshaven had been the rising, not of U-boat crews who were in front-line service, but of men who in these last years of the war, since Jutland, had done no fighting.‡

---

* An army report of September 4, based on an examination of 53,781 letters sent back from the front, found that 886 contained complaints of various kinds. Some were purely factual, saying that the Allied artillery was greatly superior to the German; others showed signs of political disenchantment, saying that Junkers, capitalists, and landowners were faring too well, as were war profiteers and black marketers. Such views were sometimes coupled with remarks such as: "We won't go along with this any longer," "We won't come back from leave," and "Any more German successes can only prolong the war." Letters also described the meager rations; not only meat but potatoes were in short supply A relatively small percentage of the letters, however, were pessimistic and defeatist; the majority of the troops showed no outward signs of disaffection, and relations between officers and men continued to be good. (Herbert Michaelis, et al, *Ursachen und Folgen*, vol. 2, p. 300.)

† Reserve troops of older men.

‡ The battle of Jutland had taken place May 31–June 1, 1916. It was the only large scale naval action during World War I, and the German fleet lost 1 battleship, 1 battle cruiser, 4 cruisers, and 5 smaller ships. The British lost 3 battle cruisers, 3 cruisers, and 8 smaller vessels.

The plan of the German Admiralty to send out the fleet in a last desperate action against the British in the forlorn hope of relieving the pressure on the hard-fighting German army was met by the refusal of the German ratings to take part in such a hopeless enterprise.* The mutinous sailors, many of whom had fought well at Jutland and in minor encounters, were ready, some of them said, to defend the German coast with all their strength, but they would not attack the British fleet. In early November, in Kiel, a sailors' council was formed, and when a meeting was called to protest mass arrests following the Wilhelmshaven mutiny, the sailors were fired upon by troops who killed eight and wounded twenty-nine men. The commandant of the city was killed by a navy patrol.†

It was the first blood of the revolution that spread to Hamburg, Lübeck, and Bremen, and then from the seaports to the interior. It was an undirected, uncoordinated revolution, led mainly by Majority (SPD) and Independent (USPD) Socialists,‡ that is, by men who had pressed for the peace resolutions of the Reichstag and supported the war and the monarchy only *faute de mieux*, because they might both lead to the long-sought-after, higher stage of social justice within Germany and a socialist international order of which Germany would be a major part. Few of the Social Democrats had wanted the kaiser to quit until it became clear that he had lost the war and that if he remained on the throne not even Mr. Wilson's Fourteen Points would stand between them and a peace of vengeance.§

The German people had been living on the promise of victory and on short rations for a long time, and many of them were severely undernourished. The mortality rate between 1915 and 1918 went up by three-quarters of a million people, and a million fewer children were born.

---

* The orders for the ships to sail were sent out without knowledge of the government under Prince Max, which was trying to negotiate an armistice.

† The sailors of the German navy had been showing signs of disaffection for more than a year. In 1917 crews protesting bad rations and ill treatment by their officers had struck and refused to obey orders. Their protests were only partly satisfied, in the opinion of the sailors, when rations were increased and the quality of food improved, and the still unhappy crews were ready for further demonstrations at any time. One German captain pointed out that some of the men on his ship, who volunteered for four years service that should have ended in 1914, had been forced to remain in the service until 1918.

‡ The Independent Socialist party was formed in April 1917 by left-wing, pacifist members of the Social Democratic party

§ A leading Social Democrat, Gustav Noske, said on March 29, 1917, that the kaiser was no tsar, and the Social Democratic paper *Vorwärts* wrote a few days later, on April 3, that as long as the monarchy filled the needs of the people, republican agitation would have no support. Difficulties would have to be overcome, but this would be accomplished and in a short time, with no trace of violent upheaval and without the fall of the monarchy. (Herbert Michaelis, et al, *Ursachen und Folgen*, vol. 2, p. 545.)

Influenza, typhus, and dysentery took a high toll. Medicines were lacking, as was clothing, although everything could be had, for a price, on the black market, where those who knew their way around grew fat. Adolf Hitler, after he had been wounded in 1916, had seen some of this despair and high living when, late in the year, he was on leave in Berlin. He wrote later that he had been shocked by the disaffection, hunger, and resignation of the home front, by the slackers who were proud of their cleverness, by the hypocrisy and egotism of the war profiteers, and by the bickering of the political parties. Behind them all, he saw clearly, was the sinister figure of the Jew.[3] The winter of 1916–1917 was called the turnip winter, and the contrast between the well-nourished operators feeding off the black markets and the ordinary citizen living mainly on turnips after the failure of the potato harvest was as striking as that between the lot of the black marketers and the troops at the front.

The beached sailors were closer to the mood of the civilian population than were the fighting troops; they saw at first hand the ravages of the blockade on the people at home, and since they had nothing more to do than to drill and keep their ships in order, they also had time to ponder on the revolution that had taken over Russia and the means by which the Soviets of workers, soldiers, and sailors had ended the fighting. What had been minor grievances became major: the fact that married officers and men had trouble finding living quarters for their families in Wilhelmshaven; the wide gaps of privilege between ranks; the harsh punishment for minor misdemeanors; the close, uncomfortable quarters on the ships that lay idle;[4] the poor, inadequate rations; the routine broken only by spit and polish and drill—all these things were dispiriting, and without battle they became intolerable.

The German revolution, although it took a very different course, would always remain under the enormous shadow of the Russian Revolution. The sailors' council at Kiel was formed a year after the sailors at Kronstadt, along with detachments of Russian workers and soldiers of the Petrograd garrison, had stormed the Winter Palace. Lenin thought Germany the explosive core of the coming world revolution—an industrialized country, far more ready for a Communist takeover than had been feudal, agrarian Russia. In October 1918, he wrote to a member of the Central Committee in Moscow that within a week the international revolution had progressed so swiftly that they must reckon with developments within days. Russia must make no alliance of any kind with the government of Wilhelm II or with Wilhelm's government "plus Ebert and the other jerks" (in the German translation, *und andere Schurken*), but "we put our lives at stake to help the revolution begun by the German workers. . . ." Therefore, Lenin drew his conclusions: the Bolshevik government must increase tenfold its efforts to supply grain for itself and for the German workers and increase ten times the call-ups for the army, so that by spring Soviet Russia would have an army of three million men to support the international workers' revolution.[5]

The Russian embassy in Berlin, functioning since the signing of the Brest-Litovsk Treaty, was a center for Bolshevik propaganda and contacts with the German radical Left. When one of the most prominent among the German left-wing Socialists, the former SPD Reichstag deputy Karl Liebknecht, who had voted against war credits in 1914 and 1915, was released from prison where he had been sent in 1916 for leading an antiwar demonstration, three members of the Soviet Central Committee, Lenin, Swerdlov, and Stalin, telephoned their congratulations to him in its name through the Russian ambassador in Berlin.[6]

On October 18, 1918, Lenin sent a letter to the conference of the extreme-Left Spartacus League,* urging on their efforts to form workers' and soldiers' councils and sending his best wishes for the success of the movement, which he said would play the chief role in the rapidly ripening German revolution that he hoped would soon bring the decisive blow to world imperialism. He ended his letter with: "Best greetings and with the firm hope in the near future to be able to greet the proletarian revolution in Germany."[7] For the German radicals, the course the revolution must take was clear; it had to follow the immanent laws of revolution as laid down by Marx and also the directives as laid down by Moscow. Funds and propaganda leaflets were provided through the Soviet embassy in Berlin until it was closed by the Ebert government for its undercover activities and the staff was sent back to Russia.†

The Communist party was founded on December 30, 1918, by Spartacists and "intellectuals," with, as subsequent voting would demonstrate, little or no mass following among workers, soldiers, or peasants. Members included Karl Liebknecht, Rosa Luxemburg, and Wilhelm Pieck, who would many years later become president of the German Democratic Republic. But the influence the Communists had on events bore no relation to their numbers. On November 9, 1918, Friedrich Ebert, in announcing that he had become chancellor, called the new state "a

---

* The Spartacists were members of the Independent Socialist party until December 1918, when they founded the German Communist party.

† The German government was well aware of the embassy's clandestine activities. A case containing incriminating documents being sent from Moscow to Berlin had been broken into in the Friedrichstrasse station in Berlin, and subsequent searches of the Soviet embassy had revealed conclusive evidence of its subversive activities. Relations with the Soviets had also been put under a strain when the German ambassador to Moscow, Count von Mirbach, was shot and killed by a Social Revolutionary without, the German government believed, serious efforts being made by Soviet authorities to deal with the perpetrators. This, however, was at worst a crime of omission on the part of the Bolsheviks. The Social Revolutionaries, who rejected the Brest-Litovsk peace, had resigned from the government in protest and gone into opposition against both the Leninists and the Germans they regarded as Leninist allies.

People's Republic,"⁸ and the proclamation of this People's Republic by Philipp Scheidemann had preceded by only a few hours Karl Liebknecht's proclamation of the "Free Socialist Republic" and the world revolution, to both of which Liebknecht had the crowd listening to him swear an oath of allegiance.

Liebknecht's colleague, Polish-born Rosa Luxemburg, who like him had spent part of the war years in prison, was one of the most brilliant of the Marxist theoreticians and a formidable critic of Lenin. A fanatical believer in the virtues of the dictatorship of the proletariat, she had nothing but contempt for moderates or compromisers, whether Social or Independent Democrats. It was the hour for action, for declaring yourself, she told the Berlin workers; the parties should represent not all classes of the population, as Ebert and Scheidemann and other middle-of-the-road Socialists urged; the revolution must be made on behalf of the masses; it must establish in power the workers and the workers alone. Part of what she said was the simon-pure doctrine preached by Lenin both in Russia and Germany, and that it would inevitably lead to the slaying of thousands of people and a reign of terror was acknowledged and taken for granted by Lenin but not by Rosa Luxemburg. Terrorist tactics were deliberate in the Russian Revolution, and Lenin told the Germans to adopt them. Rosa Luxemburg opposed their use. She believed that the dictatorship of the proletariat would bring "the application of democracy, not its abolition," but nevertheless she preached the crusade on behalf of one class only; all the others were to be expropriated and made harmless.

The party program for Germany that she drew up followed the line she and Liebknecht had lived with for years. Published in the newspaper of the Independent Socialists, *Die Rote Fahne*, it demanded on behalf of the Spartacus League the disarming of the police, of nonproletarian soldiers, and of all members of the ruling classes. Workers were to be armed and formed into a workers' militia, and to these formations were to be added a proletarian Red Guard for the defense of the revolution. Officers and noncommissioned officers were to be stripped of their authority, and the officers were to be expelled from the soldiers' councils. All political organs and authorities of the former government were to be replaced by representatives of the workers' and soldiers' councils. Revolutionary tribunals were to try the "chief criminals responsible for the war and its prolongation, the two Hohenzollerns, Ludendorff, Tirpitz and their co-criminals as well as all conspirators of the counter revolution." Foodstuffs were to be confiscated to assure the sustenance of the people.⁹ Immediate coalitions with the brother parties in foreign countries were to be sought to deploy the revolution on an international front. The manifesto ended with the words: "Rise Proletarians! To battle!

There is a world to conquer and a world to fight against. In this last class war of world history on behalf of the highest goals of mankind our word to the enemy is: Thumb in eye and knee on chest [*Daumen aufs Auge und Knie auf die Brust*]."[10] It was a call to battle that could match Lenin's.

Every postwar German government until Adolf Hitler took power had to make its way between the forces that made such demands and tried to put them into practice and those of the Far Right that called for another kind of dictatorship and the death of the Communist leaders. Whatever numerical weaknesses the German Communist movement revealed in free elections, the right-wing parties always perceived behind it the menacing forces of the revolution unleashed in Russia. Neither Karl Liebknecht nor Rosa Luxemburg could get themselves elected to the Congress of Workers and Soldiers Councils of Germany where the SPD had an overwhelming majority, but that did not prevent them from organizing uprisings of workers in Berlin and attempting to seize power following the prescriptions of the party program, or from being arrested and killed by soldiers bent on putting down the revolt and preventing any recurrence of it.

Nor was the Far Right alone in estimating the prospects for a successful Communist revolution. The chief of the Communist International, Grigori Zinoviev, in March 1919 foresaw victory in Germany within the next few months, and by the end of the year in all Europe.[11] The likelihood of a Communist takeover was the one notion leaders of the Far Left and Right could agree on, and both sides were ready to use the most ruthless means either to win it or to prevent it. The elections of 1919 revealed an overwhelming majority of the country in favor of a moderate course of republican, parliamentary democracy, but any government had to operate under the constant threat of putsches from the extreme Right and Left. The extreme wings were paradoxically sustained by the foreign enemies of the Reich, who were most hostile to both of them. The struggle for the survival of the nascent republic was overwhelmingly complicated by the demands made on it by the Allies.

French leaders approached the armistice, the peace, and the postwar years to come with a passion for security that was to become an obsession. It was as if they themselves could not really believe they had won the war. When the German delegates to the armistice commission met with Marshal Foch in the railroad carriage in the forest of Compiègne, Foch asked Matthias Erzberger, the chief of the German delegation, what brought them there. "What do you wish of me?" Foch asked. Erzberger replied that he awaited proposals relative to the conclusion of an armistice on land, sea, and air, to which Foch replied stiffly that he had no proposals to make. Erzberger was finally able to frame his answer to Foch's question to the marshal's satisfaction, but Foch was intent on making clear from the start that it was the Germans who were asking for terms. The Boche had to admit defeat; French newspapers would keep telling their readers that for months to come, with quotes from high sources.

The conditions of the armistice, like those of the peace to come, were staggering, designed, it seemed to the Germans, as the obligations imposed on them mounted, to deprive them of the most primitive means of survival. Under the terms both of the armistice and of the peace could plainly be detected the bones, not of Wilson's Fourteen Points, but of the secret treaties. The armistice terms required of the Germans not only that they turn over to the Allies large quantities of their war materials, including 1,700 planes, the submarine fleet, 6 battle cruisers, 10 battleships, 8 light cruisers, and 50 destroyers, but also that within 31 days of the signing of the armistice they surrender 5,000 locomotives, 150,000 freight cars, and 5,000 trucks, and further, that they pay an unspecified sum of reparations. The military clauses included the provision that the German armies evacuate, in addition to the Allied territory they held and Alsace-Lorraine, the German districts on the left bank of the Rhine. Allied and American garrisons would hold the principal crossings at Mainz, Coblenz, and Cologne, together with bridgeheads at these points of a 30-kilometer radius on the right bank. A neutral zone on the right bank was to be reserved "between the river and a line drawn parallel to the bridgeheads and the river and 10 kilometers distant from them running between the Swiss border and Holland." All Allied prisoners of war were to be evacuated without reciprocity, and the blockade was to remain in force. This was only the beginning of the demands to be made on the Germans.

For each of the three extensions of the armistice a price tag was attached. For the first, extending the armistice from December 13, 1918, to January 17, 1919, the Allies were to be permitted to occupy the neutral zone on the right bank of the Rhine from Cologne to Holland. For the second, granted on January 16 for one month, because the Germans were unable to deliver 500 locomotives and 19,000 freight cars, they had to turn over 58,400 pieces of farm machinery as well as 5 to 10 kilometers of the right bank of the Rhine near Strasbourg, alone with other strong points. In addition the entire German merchant fleet was placed under Allied control. For the third renewal of February 16, 1919, Polish possession of large parts of Posen taken over by Polish partisan forces was confirmed, at least temporarily, by the provision that the Germans must stop all "offensive operations" in those areas, while no inhibitions were placed upon the Poles.[12]

The Allied demands grew. Under the terms of the peace treaty, huge consignments of raw materials° and livestock were due the Allies,[13] and a British white paper reported that although Berlin was getting less than a quarter of the milk consumed before the war, 150,000 milk cows had to be turned over to the Allies by a population not far from famine.† Food was filtered into Germany slowly and in carefully rationed quantities,‡ and the blockade was lifted only eight months after the armistice was signed and after the Germans had signed the peace treaty.

The armistice was the first of a series of increasingly harsh documents the Germans would be forced to accept, and they would always find it difficult to detect any point where a republican government had been able to secure terms better than would have been accorded the kaiser. An armistice is not intended to give the power seeking it advantages it would not otherwise have, and the Allies were not disposed to let General Ludendorff have his breathing space so he could fight again, nor were they disposed to negotiate a peace. The French leaders were determined to win much more than temporary advantages after Compiègne and Versailles. France, they knew, was weaker than Germany; that had been demonstrated during the entire course of the war, and the problem they faced was how to reweight the balance in France's favor.

An article in *L'Homme Libre* explained what was irreparable in the French position:[14] France, at the end of the war, had a population of 39 million people, and if the downward trend of the birthrate continued, she would, in fifty or a hundred years, be depopulated without any help from the Germans. At the time of the French Revolution, France had been the most populous nation in Europe, with 20 million people, while Prussia had 2 million, the Austro-Hungarian Empire 13 million, and Britain 7 million.

Poincaré, Clemenceau, and Foch could do nothing about this; all they could do was to cut Germany down to size; weave around her a tight net of alliances with the new states Poland, Czechoslovakia, Yugoslavia, and Rumania; diminish the size of the German army and its weapons; impose economic conditions that would impede industrial recovery, from which a military machine might again emerge; detach provinces from the body of the Reich and other German territory from the Rhineland, East Prussia, and Silesia; and sequester the sources of the iron and coal

---

° France was to get 7 million tons of coal to balance the difference between the prewar and current production in the mines of northern France and the Pas de Calais that had been wrecked during the war. Belgium was to get 8 million tons of coal for ten years, and Italy a sliding scale of deliveries up to 8½ million tons a year for ten years. (Herbert Michaelis, et al, *Ursachen und Folgen*, vol. 3, p. 408.)

† In September, German papers reported that one-third of the school children were badly undernourished. (*Augsburger Postzeitung*, September 10, 1919.)

‡ On March 15, 1919, the first food shipment of 270,000 tons of foodstuffs was sent to the Reich, paid for cash on the line with 100 million gold marks and 25 million marks in foreign securities. (*Die Entwicklung der Reparationsfrage*, 2nd edition, p. 8.)

of the Saar and of the Ruhr for the benefit of France. After that the state of things as of 1918–1919 would be frozen for an indefinite time by means of guarantees of the Versailles frontiers by the British and Americans, as well as by what the French regarded as the far less dependable collective security apparatus of the League of Nations. Any attempt to change such an order of things would be a breach of the peace and of "legality."

All this was, no doubt, understandable enough. It followed the prescriptions of the secret treaties, and it might readily make sense to men anxious to return home from the peace conference and accustomed to deal in terms of European power politics. The trouble, especially for the Germans, was that it bore little or no relation to President Wilson's Fourteen Points and his subsequent declarations, which were what the Germans had accepted and the Allies had agreed to. To the Germans, as the screws tightened, the terms of the armistice, of the interim demands for deliveries from current German production, and of the peace treaty and the interpretation that France put upon its fulfillment became one of the most monumental pieces of hypocrisy of all time. A republican, democratically elected German government had expected to negotiate a peace, but its representatives were merely summoned to sign a document drawn up entirely by their enemies. A drawing in *Simplicissimus* depicted the French *coq gaulois* with a bloody beak poised over a prostrate Germany chained to a rock. The rooster is saying: "Stop coming at my beak with your liver." Another cartoon showed Allied dignitaries telling one another that Bismarck was guilty of everything; if he hadn't constructed Germany, they wouldn't have to destroy it. In the real world, children were begging for scraps of food where the well-fed Allied soldiers were in occupation, and another cartoon in *Simplicissimus* showed a little boy being asked what he wants to be when he grows up. His answer is "*Satt,*" to be full, to have enough food for once. With the raising of the blockade, *Simplicissimus* depicted a parade of cooks marching into a cemetery and one of them saying: "Even if it comes too late, we'll be paid for it."[15]

The Allies were agreed on only one point, that Germany must be forced to pay "until the pips squeaked" for the ravages of the war. In the election campaign of 1919, Lloyd George promised the British voters that the kaiser would be hanged and that Germany would pay to the last farthing. But aside from that principle, enthusiastically concurred in by all the Allies, not much agreement was observable. The French wanted the Rhineland, the Saar, and the Ruhr for themselves, and neither the British nor the Americans were ready to go along with such demands, not only because they would be difficult to reconcile with Mr. Wilson's speeches, but also because France, weak though she was, was now again the dominant power in Europe, and Britain, especially, was unwilling to create a series of Alsace-Lorraines that would make the waging of another war certain and soon. While French leaders were single-mindedly intent on producing as accurate a replica as possible of the congeries of German states of the eighteenth century, the British saw little future for themselves or for anyone else outside of France in such a rearrangement of the demography of Europe. Nevertheless, in the first draft of the Treaty of Versailles, all Silesia was handed over to the Poles, and while this provision was one of the few subsequently modified to permit plebiscites to be held, the economically most important part of the territory was awarded to Poland, along with three-quarters of the coal production and two-thirds of the steel works, even though 60 percent of the population voted for Germany.

Memel, culturally a German city with a large German population and whose Lithuanian inhabitants had evidenced no desire to be separated from East Prussia, had been placed under the administration of the League of Nations. But it was awarded as compensation to Lithuania after Poland had forcibly annexed Vilna. Danzig, completely German, was detached from the Reich and made a free city under a high commissioner appointed by the League of Nations, with the Poles controlling its customs and with a corridor separating it from German territory.

The British and the Americans effectively resisted the French demands only at the Rhine. The German colonies in Africa, despite Mr. Wilson's promise that the question of the colonies would be equitably adjudicated, were divided among the Allies in the form of mandates awarded them by the League of Nations. Germans had been no worse than any of the other colonial masters of Africa, and certainly far more humane than the Belgians and Portuguese, as may be evidenced by the devotion with which the native troops of General von Lettow-Vorbeck fought for him and the Reich for four years against overwhelming odds. Lettow-Vorbeck's exploits were so remarkable that the British press praised him highly when he returned from East Africa, not only for his military skill but for the chivalry with which he had conducted his campaigns. The *Times* called him "a popular and legendary figure."[16] That made no difference. All Germany's African colonies were lost to her, with no discussions, no bargaining. The Treaty of Versailles was a package, and the Reich had to sign for it. Not much territory claimed by one of the Allies or regarded by any of them as strategically valuable would ever become part of Germany. The Austrian Constituent Assembly called its new state German Austria and voted unanimously to join the Reich, but this could hardly be permitted; it would have made Germany numerically stronger than she had been in 1914, and the war in the French view would have been far more lost than won. Both Austria and Germany were forced to agree, in signing their respective peace treaties, that they would not seek the merger of their countries. Wherever purely

German populations were to be found—in the Sudetenland given to Czechoslovakia or in the Tyrol given to Italy or in what was left of Austria—they had no voice whatever in determining their nationality. Salzburg voted 98 percent and the Tyrol 95 percent, to become part of Germany when plebiscites were held in April and May of 1921, but self-determination was not for Germans or Austrians, only for those who had fought against them, and territories that for centuries had been populated with Germans were turned over to Czechs, Italians, Yugoslavians—anyone but Germans.

Under the terms of the armistice, the Germans were to pay reparations only for damages done civilian populations and their property, not for the entire cost of the war. But the provisions of the treaty were again quite different. The Germans were to pay for everything, with all the objects of value that could be extracted from them.* The decision on the final amount of reparations was deferred until 1921, but provisional payments of 20 billion gold marks, as well as deliveries in kind, were to be paid at once to the Allies, and when the Germans failed to meet any of the payments or deliveries, sanctions followed—the occupation of cities and customs offices or of whole regions. Hjalmar Schacht later calculated that what the Allies demanded of Germany was twelve times the indemnity of 6 billion francs (later reduced to 5 billion) in gold the Germans had levied on France in 1871. France had paid reparations amounting to 110 marks per person, or 3.2 percent of her capital, but Germany was to pay 38 percent of her capital to the Allies—1,350 marks per person. The French reparations had come to 25 percent of France's income of 1869, while the German reparations were 229 percent of the German income of 1913. The reparations paid by France had amounted to 100 percent of the monetary metal of France, while the German reparations were 2,200 percent of that of the Reich.

The Germans were by no means the only ones appalled by the terms of the treaty. John Maynard Keynes, a noted economist and member of the British delegation, resigned in protest and wrote a book, *The Economic Consequences of the Peace*, demonstrating the irrationality of the punitive reparations and economic provisions of the treaty and attacking the men responsible for it, especially Wilson, whom he called "a blind and deaf Quijote, performing like a preacher of a dissident church, a theologian not an intellectual, full of phrases but with no plan at all for Europe, of which he knew very little."†[17] England, Keynes wrote, had

---

* One French writer, quoted in a German newspaper, declared that France claimed all French art in public or private German hands, even in cases where Germans like Frederick the Great had bought the paintings directly from the artist. (*Münchener Neueste Nachrichten*, February 6, 1919.)

† The Big Four at the peace conference communicated with one another through interpreters. As Keynes pointed out, neither Lloyd George nor Wilson knew any

destroyed a trade rival and the French had won a round in a centuries-old battle, but that round was certainly not the last one.[18] William Bullitt and five other members of the American delegation protested against the peace terms, and Bullitt resigned.[19] They were joined by Mr. Wilson's secretary of state, Robert Lansing, who called the peace provisions "immeasurably harsh," many of them "impossible of performance."[20] A German paper commenting on Lansing's view that Wilson had been no match for Clemenceau wrote that in effect Clemenceau had told Wilson: "Let me have the treaty that gives us power today; tomorrow we can erect the League, the servant girl of the people," to which Wilson responded: "Give me the League, the treaty doesn't disturb me."[21]

The treaty was denounced on all sides: by liberals and conservatives in the United States, by the morally outraged *Nation* and *New Republic*, and by the left-wing press in Europe, from *L'Humanité* in Paris to *Izvestia* in Moscow. General Smuts said he had signed it on behalf of South Africa, not because it was a satisfactory document, but because the war had to be ended;[22] Herbert Hoover was convinced that its consequences would "pull down all Europe and so injure the United States."[23]

The British diplomat Arthur Ponsonby said that this war for international justice was just the same as all previous wars, and he perceived with shame the aggressive policies of the Allies as their statesmen greedily fell on the booty. England, he wrote, had fought to win 3,250,000 square kilometers of land, eleven times the size of her own territory. Ponsonby saw neither statesmanlike nor peaceful solutions for the new Europe in the Treaty of Versailles, but rather the seeds of future wars. It remained, he said, for England to try to change treaties that had been made by men whose only motives were revenge and triumph.[24]

The American Congress came to join the critics. The Senate would only approve America's entering the League of Nations with reservations Mr. Wilson felt would destroy its internationalist purposes, and the treaty was therefore defeated, along with the proposal that the United States ally itself with France as Mr. Wilson had agreed it would do.

In Germany, both the extreme Right and Left had solutions for preventing this swift collapse of what had been the promise of a new order. For the Left, the solution would come by means of a Communist revolution in Germany, an alliance with the Soviet Union, and extension of the revolution to all Europe. To the Right, the way out was to crush the Left and the "November criminals," as Hitler and many others would call them; the defeat had been no defeat at the front but a stab in the back. As Hindenburg explained, the army had not been defeated; despite

---

French, and while Orlando spoke Italian and French, Clemenceau was the only one who spoke French and English.

the enemies' superiority in numbers and material, the unequal battle would have been brought to a successful conclusion if the homeland had acted in iron solidarity with the front and if it had not been for the secret, planned subversion by the revolutionary movement behind the lines. At the end, the fighting troops had had to bear the entire burden of the battle alone.[25]

The Reich was polarized between these two irreconcilable, ideological positions, and neither the Far Right nor the Far Left would ever be able to gain a majority of the votes in any free election. Germany, including the generals, would soon come to terms with Moscow, but no compromises would ever be worked out with its *Weltanschauung*.

The Russian Revolution was a vast complication for the Allies, too. Britain and the United States had sent some 15,000 troops into Russia in 1918, first to guard the supplies they had been sending by way of Archangel and Murmansk to the Russian ally and then to help the anti-Bolshevik counterrevolution. The French sent both a fleet to the Black Sea and an army to the Ukraine. The Allies' ill-defined goals varied from month to month: to protect the supplies from falling into the hands of the Germans; to guard the Trans-Siberian and Chinese Eastern railroads; to keep Russia in the war fighting the Germans; then, with the end of the war, to prevent the Germans from making use of the revolution to establish new centers of influence in the Baltic countries, where German Free Corps units were fighting with many of the same confused goals the Allies had. The Free Corps, too, were dedicated after the war had ended in the West to preventing the spread of Bolshevism. They aimed to build up the forces of the emerging Baltic countries against it and also to obtain individual grants of land promised them by the Latvian provisional government.

The Allies at first were not only in favor of the German soldiers' remaining in the Baltic countries to fight the Bolsheviki; they ordered the Free Corps to continue their military operations until their own forces could replace them—a time that never came. When, however, the Bolsheviks were thrown back and it seemed possible that the German formations, now quasi-independent units, might establish military centers in the Baltic, the Allies demanded their withdrawal.[26]

By 1919, the Allied armies in Russia were part of an amorphous anti-Bolshevik coalition aiding former imperial Russian officers like General Denikin, Admiral Kolchak, and General Yudenich in their attempts to overthrow the Soviet government. But Lenin had said that sending Allied troops to the Soviet Union was the equivalent of enrolling them in a Communist university, and so it was. With the aid of skillful Communist propaganda came widespread disaffection in the American and British troops; a revolt in the French fleet in the Black Sea that swept the battleships *France, Jean Bart, Justice,* and *Mirabeau* and the heavy cruisers *Vergniard* and *Waldek–Rousseau*;[27] the defeat of French forces in the Ukraine; and the refusal of French units in Bessarabia to carry out their orders. Other Allied troops, including the Americans, did not revolt, but they showed little enthusiasm for their assignments, and neither they nor their leaders would ever understand what they were doing in the dreary wastes of the Soviet north, thousands of miles from home, standing guard or fighting in an undeclared war. Only the Japanese, who sent 70,000 men to eastern Siberia and the maritime provinces, knew their purpose, which was, if possible, to detach portions of Siberia from the Soviet Union; but they, too, were forced to withdraw, much more by Allied and American pressure on them than by any acts of the Russians.

In Germany, the first of the extremist groups to strike was the Left. *Räte*, that is, Soviet, republics were at one time or another set up in chief cities of the Reich: Berlin, Hamburg, Gotha, Bremen, Leipzig, Braunschweig, Munich, and Nuremberg among them. It was characteristic of the period that Kurt Eisner was shot and killed by a young rightist, Count Anton Arco-Valley,* although the Eisner government had just lost the election held on January 12, 1919, where his Independent Socialists had polled less than 80,000 votes in an electorate of almost four million and had elected only 3 out of 156 deputies. The Bavarian People's party, the largest party in the Landtag, had received over a million votes, with the Social Democrats in second place with 963,000 votes, and Eisner was killed when he was on his way to the first meeting of the new Landtag to announce his resignation. On the day of his murder, one of Eisner's followers, a butcher by the name of Lindner, shot at one of the Social Democratic deputies, Erhart Auer, wounding him badly; and in the tumult that followed a member of the Bavarian People's party was also shot down.

These murders marked the beginning of a period of wild disorder in Bavaria. Although the Landtag was able to elect, in mid-March, a former elementary school teacher and Social Democrat, Johannes Hoffmann, minister-president, neither he nor the Landtag would be allowed to govern. In the confusion that followed the shootings, the tasks of government fell to the workers' councils or Soviets, and in these the leftist extremists were soon to emerge as leaders. By April 4 the Räte forbade the Landtag to meet, and three days later they assumed all

---

* Arco's own fate was also a commentary on the time. He was sentenced to death by a people's court but without "loss of honor," because, the court said, of his youth and because he had been moved, not by low motives, but by a fervent love for his people and the Fatherland. His sentence was later commuted to life imprisonment, and in 1927 he was pardoned. (Cuno Horkenbach, *Das Deutsche Reich von 1918 bis heute*, p. 95.)

governmental authority. From the early programs of the councils of economic and political reform—the eight-hour day, universal suffrage for men and women over the age of twenty, and the like—the demands rose under pressure from the Spartacists for making the true, the class, revolution and for driving out the reactionaries who were responsible for the deaths of Rosa Luxemburg, Karl Liebknecht, and Kurt Eisner. Eisner, like Luxemburg and Liebknecht, was a Jew, and his enemies tacked on Kosmanowski to his name to indicate that he was not only a Berliner, which he was, but an Eastern Jew, which he was not. The name was an invention and had no connection whatever with Eisner or his family, but it served to stamp him in Bavaria as an alien, one of those identified by the Hitlers as a beneficiary of the war and the misery of Germany, one of the black marketers, the stabbers in the back of the army, the makers of Versailles.

Toward the end of November 1918, Hitler had returned to Munich, where jobs, with the closing down of the war industries and the influx of thousands of returning soldiers, were few, and so he remained in the army, partly at least, because he had nowhere else to go. In early February he served as a guard in a prisoners-of-war camp near Traunstein on the Austrian border, where Russian and French soldiers were being slowly released, and he returned a month later to Munich, where on April 7 the Räte Republic was proclaimed.

For their part the Räte, or the pseudo-Räte as the Communists called them before they took over their control, under the leadership of, among others, two anarchists, Gustav Landauer and Erich Mühsam, and an Independent Socialist, Ernst Toller,* adopted much of the program of the Communists: the dictatorship of the proletariat, socialization of the press, the dissolution of the Landtag, the creation of a Red army, and the creation of revolutionary tribunals to try the enemies of the revolution. It was a movement run by left-wing romantics, poets, and intellectuals. The pseudo-Räte did not last long; on April 13, two Social Democratic deputies, joined by part of the Munich garrison, attempted a putsch. Several of the leaders of the pseudo-Räte were arrested, and for a few hours it looked as though the councils had been overthrown. But the Spartacus leaders with the aid of some soldiers and armed workers put down the revolt and took over the councils and the governance of Munich.

With their seizure of power, the terror began. Two of the Räte members, Dr. Rothenfelder and its foreign minister, Franz Lipp, had spent

---

* Toller was an Expressionist writer, the author of a well-known play, *The Wanderer*. He had studied under the world-famous sociologist Max Weber, who liked Toller and appeared as a character witness at his trial for high treason, saying it was God's wrath that had brought Toller into politics.

some time in an insane aslyum.* The councils' leaders had far more ability to coin slogans than to govern. The right to the streets, they announced, belonged solely to class-conscious workers, although everybody continued to use them, and when a train stopped at Pasing near Munich, the Red Guards posted at the station went up and down the platform requesting all "reactionaries" to please get off the train.[28] Proletarian workers were encouraged in placards and handbills to expropriate the bourgeoisie, and this meant not only the affluent but artisans, small businessmen, employees, and minor officials, all of whom came under the Spartacist category of "middle class." Munich was suffering from an acute housing shortage, and the Räte told the workers the houses were theirs and they should move in. As the Spartacists broke into dwellings to hunt down followers of Hoffmann, a wave of plunder accompanied them.[29] Banks were closed, streetcars no longer ran, food was confiscated, and merchants were warned that if they sold food or clothing at higher than the market price they would be brought before a military tribunal.[30] Automobiles were taken over by the revolutionaries, and arms in the hands of the bourgeoisie or anyone but workers had to be surrendered; only proletarians could legally bear weapons. To pick up leaflets dropped by government planes was punishable by death.[31]

The Red troops, under the command of Ernst Toller, won a complete victory at Dachau, where Hoffmann's forces either fled or were disarmed.[32] Chicherin, the Soviet foreign minister, congratulated the Munich councils in a telegram sent from Budapest, where another Räte government, under Bela Kun, was shakily in power, and Lenin urged the Munich councils to proceed ruthlessly to take hostages and to use terror. In a letter of April 27, he asked them to let him know what concrete measures they had taken against the "bourgeois hangmen, Scheidemann and Company."[33] Had they armed the workers and disarmed the bourgeoisie? Given the workers, especially the small farmers, clothing and other goods? Taken over factories and large farms, cancelled mortgages and land rents for small farmers, doubled or tripled the wages of workers? Had they taken over printing presses to print handbills to distribute to the masses? Introduced the six-hour day? Occupied banks and the houses of the rich, mobilized workers in the adjoining villages, and arrested hostages from the middle classes? It was necessary, Lenin told them, to improve immediately and at any price the lot of the workers, farmhands, and small farmers, and to levy extraordinary taxes

---

* In a letter to one of the other Räte ministers, Lipp said he had declared war on Württemberg and Switzerland because they would not send him locomotives and he was certain he would win because he had the blessing of the pope, with whom he was well acquainted. (Gustav Noske, *Von Kiel bis Kapp*, p. 136. Cited Craig, p. 44.)

on the middle classes. He was addressing men very nearly as experienced in the rhetoric of the revolution as he was, and the councils had already ordered that many of these measures be carried out.

The Räte's leaders were ideally suited to alienate the Müncheners. Not one of them was a Bavarian. Three of them, Paul Borissovitch Axelrod, Max Levien, and his brother-in-law Eugen Leviné-Niessen, had been born in Russia, which was one step worse than being from Berlin, and in addition they were Jews. After the Räte Republic was defeated, it was widely believed that it had been the result of a Bolshevik-Jewish uprising, but only half of that was true. Bolshevik it certainly was in the main, but the names of the sixteen men who were brought to trial in September for their part in the killing of the ten hostages were all non-Jewish and many were manifestly Bavarian.*

The Communists had little support even among the ranks of the revolutionaries. Not one Communist had been elected to the workers' and soldiers' councils in Bavaria. Only in Munich were anarchists and Communists members of the more parochial soldiers' council,[34] and in the radical industrial councils the Communists were a small minority, with 66 members as against 283 SPD and 152 USPD.[35] No Communist was elected to the Munich Räte, but Communist leaders nevertheless clung to the power they had seized on April 13 in the unshakable conviction that they alone spoke for the proletarian masses who would make the true revolution. The Munich Räte alienated everyone but a hard core of party members, and the converts among the intellectuals who saw their revolution threatened by the force of reaction gathered around Hoffmann, the minister-president of Bavaria who had fled to Bamberg with members of his government, and Noske, the defense minister of the Reich. It was not until April 23, however, ten days after the Communist takeover, that Noske ordered an attack on Munich by government troops, under General von Oven with a Prussian volunteer corps, to be joined by Bavarian and Württermbergian contingents.

Nor was the opposition within Munich wholly without resources. Members of the Thule Society, a right-wing, *völkisch*, anti-Semitic organization, had got hold of the stamp of the Communist military chief of Munich, the twenty-one-year-old deserter from the navy Rudolf Eglhofer, and used it to forge orders and requisitions. Ten of the members of the Thule Society were taken as hostages from a meeting at the Hotel Vier Jahreszeiten, and then, as the government forces converged on Munich, they were executed in the courtyard of the Luitpold gymnasium as a reprisal for the deaths of eight members of the Red Guard who had been killed at Dachau.[36] Among those shot to death was a

---

* The names were Seidel, Schicklhofer, Widl, Purzer, Kick, Gesell, Hesselmann, Lermer, Bemer, Riethmeyer, Hannes, Fehmer, Volkl, Huber, Petermeier, and Schnittele. (*Augsburger Postzeitung*, September 2, 1919.)

woman, Countess Hella von Westarp, and the execution so horrified Ernst Toller that he forgot his revolutionary ardor and denounced Levien for the act, calling him a "lousy [*lumpen*] Slaviner." But for other members of the revolutionary committee the killings were an ineluctable part of the revolution. Eglhofer said, "It hurts me every time I come to Munich and don't see an army officer or a capitalist hanging from a lamppost."[37] Levien called Toller a "young punk" (*grassgrünen Lausbuben*), and the *Berliner Tageblatt* reported that leaders of the Räte had said that since millions of proletarians had been killed in the course of the war, for the benefit of capitalism, it was of small importance if a few thousand bourgeois got their throats cut. Eglhofer declared that the Räte needed, not judges, but military tribunals made up of workers who would be governed by their proletarian sentiments. And he himself was shot out of hand when government troops recaptured Munich.*

The weeks of Räte rule left the people of Munich with an abiding fear and hatred of the Left; the killings were final proof that the stories of Bolshevik atrocities and terrorism were all too true. When Reichswehr troops recaptured Munich, they, too, took reprisals; they shot, among others, twenty-four young men they believed to be Spartacists but who were in fact anti-Communists, members of a Catholic group. For the mass of the Bavarians, the Räte Republic was a bad dream from which they had awakened and which must never return. The republic had first been proclaimed in Bavaria, but any leftist rising from this point on was a threat far more menacing than one coming from right-wing organizations.

It was during this period that Adolf Hitler made his entry into politics. One of the main assignments of the army was to protect the government against putsches of either Left or Right. It had first to make sure of the allegiance of its own troops, and therefore, in cities like Munich, where Reichswehr soldiers had been fighting on opposing sides, to keep track of the activities of some fifty political groups and organizations, from Communists and anarchists to the Bavarian Royal party. To this end the army organized courses of instruction for selected officers and men, some of whom, in turn, were to instruct the troops and report on any political activities in the city that might subvert them. Hitler later wrote that he became a *Bildungsoffizier*, that is, an officer assigned to the political education of the troops, but he was never

---

* Two other members of the Räte met similar fates: Sontheimer was court-martialed and shot when the government forces entered Munich, and Leviné-Niessen was captured later, tried, and executed. Landauer, who had quit politics, was sentenced to prison and killed there by soldiers. Axelrod and Toller escaped from Munich but were later arrested and sentenced to prison terms. In 1933 Toller emigrated to the United States where in 1939 he committed suicide.

an officer of any kind in the German army until he took command of it. What he did become was "a man of confidence" for the army, a *V-Mann*, or *Vertrauensmann*, as the army called them, assigned to take one of the instruction courses and later to lecture to returning prisoners of war and to report on political activities, which were among the few flourishing industries in Munich in 1919.

The name "Hittler" appears on a list of V-men for May–June 1919; he was assigned to attend the courses of approved speakers at the University of Munich, many of whom were well-known scholars but one of whom was a Pan-German, Gottfried Feder, who believed the curse of the modern world to be the charging of interest on loans. The one common denominator of all the lecturers was that they were nationalists, anti-Left and anticlerical, because these were the sentiments of the officer in charge of the courses, Captain Karl Mayr. Mayr was quickly impressed by the capabilities of Adolf Hitler. On September 10, 1919, he addressed him as *Sehr verehrter Herr Hitler*, a kind of "Dear Sir" salutation, which, as a German historian has pointed out, is unusual in the correspondence of a captain with a man one step above a private.[38] Hitler moved up from attendance at the instruction courses to become a member of the "Instruction Commando," and one of his assignments was to attend the meetings of an organization calling itself the German Workers party (*Deutsche Arbeiter Partei*). Up to this time, it is unclear whether Hitler had any serious interest in becoming politically active. One story that went around years later was that he had thought of joining the Social Democratic party, but that seems unlikely, because the pacifism and antinationalism of the Social Democrats could hardly have had much of an appeal for a man with the Great German views that had brought Hitler to Munich in 1913 and sent him reverently off to war to serve with undiminished fervor for four years. What is certain is that he had no coherent political philosophy at this time, because he never really had one. He could not subscribe to the principles of any existing party; he could only make a list of his own. What moved him were hostilities, a catalogue of rejections of men and things he could not abide, and, beyond everything else, of course, his hatred of the anti-Germans, the Jews. When the government troops entered Munich, Hitler was one of the soldiers they arrested on suspicion of collaboration with the Räte, but from this ludicrous situation he was rescued by an officer who recognized him and vouched for his anti-Red sentiments.

Hitler performed his duties as V-man as he had those of a front-line soldier, in a fashion that quickly won the approval of his superiors. On August 23, 1919, he appears on a list of the "Instruction Commando Beyschlag" (named after its leader, Rudolf Beyschlag) to give a talk to the returning troops in the Lechfeld transit camp on "The Conditions of Peace and Reconstruction."[39] Two days later he talked on "Social and

Economic-Political Slogans." The speeches were designed as refresher courses in German patriotism. Beyschlag spoke on "Goethe and Germany," "War Guilt," and "The Rise of Germany in the Nineteenth Century." Other speakers talked about "Our Airmen in Battle," "The Experiences of a German War Prisoner in Russia" and similar subjects aimed at restructuring the martial pride of the returning soldiers. Extracts from the reports of soldiers who heard the talks show that Hitler made a very favorable impression on his listeners. A number of them called his speeches "spirited" (*Temperamentvoll*); one man called him "a born popular speaker" (*Volksredner*).[40]

A Lieutenant Bendt, however, had misgivings. In his report, Bendt wrote that while talking on capitalism, Hitler had brought in the Jewish question, and that if that problem were to be discussed, Jews could readily characterize it as Jew-baiting. Bendt had therefore ordered that the question should be handled with the greatest care, and he said further that any specific reference to "the race that was foreign to the German people" should, if possible, be avoided.[41]

Captain Mayr, however, took a different view. Obviously convinced of Hitler's competence in matters relating to Jews, he passed on a letter sent him by a man named Adolf Gemlich, who wished to be told why, if the government knew the Jews were such a national danger, it could not do something about them, and who asked whether the government was perhaps too weak to take steps against this dangerous Jewry. Both Mayr and Hitler answered the letter. Mayr wrote in a perfunctory fashion, but Hitler's response, written on September 16, 1919, expounded the main tenets of his anti-Semitism, which had explained everything he disliked when he lived in Vienna and which would last him until the day of his death. He told Gemlich he did not believe in what he called "the anti-Semitism of feeling." Anti-Semitism as a political movement, he wrote, must be based on facts, and the facts were that Jews were a race and not a religious community. Jews never called themselves Jewish-Germans or Jewish-Poles or Jewish-Americans, but German Jews, Polish Jews, American Jews. Jews living in foreign countries adopted only the language of the country, and a Jew speaking German and living in Germany could become German as little as a German living in France and speaking French, or in Italy or in China, could become French or Italian or Chinese. Thousands of years of incest had marked the Jew in race and specific character. Their power was the power of money. Their effect on people was that of a racial tuberculosis. Religion, socialism, democracy were only means to an end, to gain wealth and to rule. The anti-Semitism of feeling led to pogroms (still having trouble with spelling, Hitler had the wrong German plural for the word), but the anti-Semitism of reason, on the other hand, permitted the planned and legal abrogation of the privileges (*Vorrechte*) of the Jews and the attainment of the final goal, which must be the exclusion of the Jews from German society. Only a government of national strength could do that, not a government of national powerlessness.[42]

It was during his assignment as a V-man that Hitler learned that he could talk and people would listen. No longer was he "the spinner," the teller of tall stories. Professor Alexander von Müller, a historian teaching one of the army courses at the University of Munich, remembered years later how he had seen a group gathered around a pale, thin young man speaking with a guttural voice and had noted how they hung on his words. Hitler, too, certainly noted this and was confirmed in his newly discovered talent when, on September 12, four days before he wrote to Gemlich, he was given the assignment to report on a meeting of the German Workers party (DAP).

One of the many organizations in Munich with a program for social and political uplift, the DAP had been founded in November 1919 by Karl Harrer, a journalist, and Anton Drexler, a toolmaker who worked for the railroad, with the financial aid of the Thule-Gesellschaft. Its twenty-five members aimed to produce a classless, anticapitalist, socialist Germanic society, and to this end they met once a week in the Sterneckerbräu beer hall to listen to *völkisch* speakers, among them Gottfried Feder. On September 12 Feder made his set speech about the nefariousness of interest, and Hitler was about to leave the gathering when another speaker got up, a Separatist, who talked about creating an independent Bavaria. Hitler was enraged by a proposal that would have brought to ruin the whole edifice of his Pan-Germanism, one of the main landmarks of a faith that had brought him from Vienna to the Reich. He indignantly rose to his feet to talk the Separatist down, and as far as the members of the DAP were concerned, he succeeded admirably. A united Germany, a powerful Germany, one people without alien races— these were the unshakable beliefs that had brought him to Munich six years before and had sustained him in the trenches throughout the war. How could anyone but a traitor, a provocateur, an agent of dark, inscrutable powers talk of dividing the Reich? The members of the DAP were enchanted at what they heard. "Man, does he have a lot going for him! That's someone we can use,"* said Drexler, and it was no overstatement.

Hitler had said what they were thinking, and they were enraptured with him. The members of the German Workers party, which soon after Hitler joined it changed its name to the National Socialist German Workers party (*National Sozialistische Deutsche Arbeiter Partei*, NSDAP), shared many items on the wide list of hatreds and animosities that moved Hitler. Every German knew that the Treaty of Versailles was

---

* *"Mensch, der hat a Gosch'n den kunnt ma braucha."* (Joachim C. Fest, *Hitler*, p. 171.)

unjust, hypocritical, a disaster, so when Hitler attacked it he was preaching to the converted. But he did more than recite its injustices; he identified those who were responsible for it—"the November criminals," the anti-Germans, the Jewish wire-pullers who had plotted Germany's defeat and ruin. His listeners knew the list before he repeated it for them; he was not the only one saying such things, but as his listeners testified, he said them with more pathos and temperament than the others. It was obvious to those whose world had collapsed and to those threatened with the loss of the fragments they had left that someone was to blame for their troubles. Hitler identified those responsible. He made them come to life.

He could choose from a large supply of candidates: for some people it was the kaiser and his militarists who had ruined Germany, or it was the capitalists and their lackeys; for others it was the French with their lust for revenge, or it was the British and their jealousy of the accomplishments of the German spirit. For still others the Reich had been sabotaged by the Left, the levellers, the anarchists; and for some—still a small, semicrackpot group in Germany—the cause of all their *malheurs* was the Jew. Russian émigrés escaping to the Reich from the Bolsheviki declared the Jews had caused the collapse of Russia; they had been behind the ill-advised decision to go to war in 1914 and the revolution of 1917. Newly established Poland celebrated its independence with pogrom after pogrom against the Jews within its territory, and the Poles were joined by the Ukrainians, who historically had been in the forefront of a savage anti-Semitism that had butchered thousands of victims.

German anti-Semitism, like all the Western varieties, had been far more decorous than the Slavic brand. A series of articles in the Catholic *Augsburger Postzeitung* and the *Münchner Neueste Nachrichten* carefully explained why some people in Germany were anti-Semitic. The *Postzeitung* writer said that it was a fact that almost all the leading spirits among the German left-wing revolutionaries were Jews: Eisner, Landauer, Mühsam, Toller, Levien, Leviné, and Axelrod; and that without them the Räte would have been impossible. It was true, the paper went on, that many Jews had given their lives for the Fatherland, but it was also true that many had evaded war service and that they were overrepresented in the professions, and therefore Germans had the right to defend themselves against becoming helots in their own country. Men like Eisner and Liebknecht had opposed the authority of religion, and if Germans behaved like true Christians and stood up for righteousness, then many Jews would not be led astray.[43] The *Münchner Neueste Nachrichten* said the Jews were not a race but their success in business and their predilection for radical causes stemmed from the same sectarian protest. Marx, who preached equality and freedom for everyone, was the new Messiah. Jews, if they were allowed to participate in a society, took over the most potent, spiritual characteristics of the people they lived among; witness Disraeli in England and D'Annunzio in Italy, where Jews were anti-Socialist and nationalist, as they had been in Russia. Only in Germany were they internationalists and socialists. Germans did not like the Eastern Jews, but they did not like the Christians who migrated from eastern Europe either, because such people were of a lower cultural level than Germans. The Eastern Jews could not remain in the Reich, which had enough black marketers and racketeers as it was. The Germans could not get rid of them because of the pogroms in the countries they had come from, so the problem required the help of the Entente, which called itself the protector of humanity.[44]

Along with such learned articles were the scurrilous pieces reported in reputable newspapers that denounced other papers for repeating the immemorial stories about the eternal Jew and his diabolic ways. A cartoon showed a Jew talking to a figure of death. The Jew is saying in Yiddish German: *"Herr Todleben* ["Deathlife"], everything is fine, we've got Germany all set up for you." And one German newspaper denounced the clumsy story printed in Berlin that two hundred children were missing from the city, killed, it was suspected, to make wurst.[45] It was a variation on a calumny going back to the Middle Ages, and when the theme reappeared in Berlin in 1919, it was ridiculed as a grotesque forgery; yet no doubt it was believed by a small audience beyond those who were actively spreading it.

Hitler's speeches, although they carried much the same message, were a touch more sophisticated than such tales, and they were aimed at a potentially wider public than that of the mere Jew-baiters. The enemies represented a cross section of the hostilities of the *völkisch* German community: Bolsheviks, capitalists, exploiters of the working people, black marketers, profiteers, and anti-German conspirators of all kinds and colors, from the vengeful French and their black troops on the Rhine to the jealous English and the profiteering Americans. Their victims were the trustful, high-minded, hardworking Germans, deceived and swindled on all sides. Hitler compared the Treaty of Brest-Litovsk with the Treaty of Versailles—the treaty condemned by the Entente for its ruthless brutality with the "just" treaty they had imposed on the Germans. He ticked off some of the enormities of Versailles, what Germany had had to sacrifice in territory and reparations and to suffer in humiliations, and he said that if the bells in Strasbourg had tolled for two hours to celebrate the French victory, he promised they would ring for three days when the last Frenchman left.[46]

What he told his audiences he had devoutly believed since the Vienna years and earlier. It was Schönerer and Lanz brought up to date, and not much new was added. Germany was still beset by enemies from within and without, still surrounded by malevolent powers bent on her destruction. The Allies took, said Hitler, 400,000 horses and twice as many cattle; they appropriated German ships and coal; and the cattle sent to Holland the Germans had to buy back with their own hard-earned money. "We National Socialists," he told his audience, "do not imagine we have the power to defeat our oppressors; that is what differentiates us from the Communists." Talking about right and justice, Hitler said, "There is no higher justice, only the right that man himself creates." "Is the peace treaty a just treaty?" "Is it, for example, just that the Entente lets foreign peoples bleed for them on Europe's battlefields, that England floods China and India with opium and the North Americans with brandy in order to crush them and be able to govern them more easily?" Where is the natural right for food when Clemenceau says there are 20 million Germans too many? Why is Germany, one of the leading cultural states of the world, not in the League of Nations?[47]

Hitler's themes were few and uncomplicated, and it made no difference if he contradicted a statement he had made the day before, because for him and his listeners his utterances were suffused with essential truths that could not be contaminated by troublesome hairsplittings. What he gave his audiences was their own diverse collection of incitements to self-pity, brought together with a passion that overwhelmed any criticism.

England, Hitler said, controlled world commerce, and while she had exported merchandise, Germany had had to export people, who became working slaves, "artificial fertilizer" for other countries.[48] A paradise had been lost to the anti-German conspiracy, and Hitler compared the flourishing Reich (despite its having had to export people) before the war with the ruined Germany of 1919. Politics was only a means to an end, and the end was that one's own people flourished and prospered. The form of government, whether monarchy or republic, was unimportant; the only question was what was best for the *Volk*. Over and over he compared prewar Germany with its order, cleanliness, and meticulousness with the disorderly, revolutionary Germany they now lived in, whose greatest defect lay in its lack of national feeling and policy.

Hitler compared Wilson with Erzberger. Although Wilson was a criminal and a clod, he might merit the respect of his countrymen because he had brought advantages to the United States, whereas Erzberger, who signed the armistice, had only betrayed his own people and Fatherland.[49] The day would come, though, when it would be possible to call out "Germans arise!" and then the storm would break. People talked about the proletariat on one side and the middle classes on the other, but what they should say was: "You Germans, close ranks, fight for your own freedom." The battle must be waged against the exploitation of international capitalism and loan capitalism. Germany was saddled with 300 billion marks of debt, which meant payments of

15 billion marks in interest that had to be ground out of the people.[50] Germans, whether they worked with their hands or their heads, had to come together, to love their neighbors as brothers, to love and be proud of the *Volk*.[51] Any simple German worker was superior to a millionaire. The millionaire had sat comfortably at home while the worker fought in the trenches for four and a half years.[52]

What Germany and the world needed was not the division of class against class but classless, national socialism. The solution to Germany's troubles should start with getting the Jew out of public life, putting an end to the slavery of interest and the profiteers. Germany belonged to the Germans and yet Jews were running the republic.[53] The hostages in the Luitpold gymnasium had not been shot because they were profiteers but because they were anti-Semites.[54] The northern races had been hardened by adversity, the southerners were rotten. The power of the middle class rules in international societies. Freemasonry is international and so is the power of Jews. Thus every German had to become an anti-Semite.[55]

Germany, Hitler said, had never been conquered from without but always from within. National Socialism rejected all monarchist propaganda (a few days before he had said the form of government was unimportant), it knew no classes, only Germanic comrades.[56] The nationalist Right lacks social thinking, the socialist Left, national thinking. So the true revolutionaries belonged in the camp of the National Socialists to fight for both nationalism and socialism.[57] Germans were ruled by international capital, but private property from natural sources must belong to everyone alike.[58] To be a German citizen was the highest honor a *Volks* comrade could have, and citizenship could only be extended to racial Germans, each one of whom had the same rights and duties. First and most important, he said, is freedom of the person.[59]

These were all scraps of conventional *völkisch* wisdom interlaced with attacks on the treaty and on the exactions of the Entente with which no German could disagree. The principles were incorporated in the party program that Hitler together with Anton Drexler and Gottfried Feder wrote out in twenty-five points and that Hitler presented to a meeting of February 24, 1920, in the Hofbräuhaus. They had appealed greatly to the party constituency even though they had no prospect whatever of being realized in any foreseeable future. The party's program enunciated among other things the right to self-determination for Germany, with equal treatment and land and colonies to feed the German people. The Treaties of Versailles and St. Germain were to be abrogated. Only racial Germans could be citizens, and racial Germans were men and women of German blood regardless of religion, so no Jew could be a *Volks* comrade. Battle would be waged against the corruption of the parliamentary system based on party considerations, which took no account of character and ability. Every citizen had the same rights and duties; the general need came before the individual need; only a man who worked was entitled to an income; war profits were to be confiscated, the serfdom of interest broken. Profiteers, common criminals, and black marketers were to be executed. Trusts already nationalized were to remain so. In the interest of a healthy middle class, the party platform declared that big department stores would be communalized. It demanded land reform and the abolition of speculation in land. Poor children were to be educated by the state, child labor was to be prohibited, and health services were to be provided for mothers and children and young people. A people's army was to replace mercenary troops, and a strong central authority was to be established with complete authority over the Reich and its organizations.

Hitler succeeded in bringing in more and more members to the National Socialist party* and to attract thousands to its meetings, but he was regarded by the vast majority of Müncheners as nothing more than one among many demagogues to be heard in the course of noisy, crackpot meetings. The newspapers paid little attention to him; what brought people to the beer halls where Hitler spoke were word of mouth and fiery red street placards. People came to the meetings to argue with him, too. A delegation of Jews, under the leadership of a Rabbi Barsteiner, attended one meeting to protest the false quotations from the Talmud that were often cited. One such allegedly said that the Jew should be the last on the field of battle so he could be first to run away in the retreat. Barsteiner declared that the quotations were spurious and that the Talmud could be read and checked by anyone in the Munich city library, but the audience howled him down and he and his delegation were escorted out of the meeting. Communists and other left-wingers sometimes came to argue, but they too were either hustled to the doors or thrown out, for many of the men coming to the meetings and joining the party were young and tough and spoiling for a fight.

The party meetings attracted more and more people, but they remained insignificant in the mass of the electorate. Both the extreme Left and Right had small appeal to the masses as long as a reasonable peace such as Wilson had promised and a tolerable domestic order seemed possible.† The extremists could meet and shout and turn cities upside

---

* Of the 193 members of the party recorded in 1920, 51 were workers or artisans, 30 were university teachers and members of the intellectual callings, 29 were businessmen, 22 were professional soldiers, 16 were employees, and the rest were housewives, artists, and government officials. (Joachim C. Fest, *Hitler*, pp. 189, 1063.)

† In the voting for the National Assembly on January 19, 1919, only one party, the German National People's party, was promonarchy. With its allies it got 10.3 percent of the votes, electing 44 delegates. No extreme group was represented; neither the Communists nor insignificant splinter groups like the German Workers party were on the ballot. The SPD was the strongest party, with 11,509,000 votes, or 37.9 percent

down, but for a long time they could not gather a following large enough to enable them to rival the parties that accepted the parliamentary system. They could only turn to force, to uprisings, to putsches.

In March 1920 an East Prussian official, Wolfgang Kapp, formed a makeshift coalition with a Reichswehr general, Walther von Lüttwitz, who early in 1919 had recaptured Berlin from the left-wing rebels, to overpower the government on behalf of the Right. The uprising was better organized militarily than the Communist uprising in Munich; it relied on the military support of the Ehrhardt Brigade, one of the hundreds of rough, tough, well-trained volunteer *Freikorps* forces that emerged after the armistice.* They were made up of former soldiers and officers recruited to combat the extreme Left and to restore order in the cities, as well as to fight the Bolsheviks in the Baltic states and the Polish bands that with the help of the Polish and French governments were invading East Prussia and Silesia to occupy territory claimed by Poland. Hermann Ehrhardt had been a *Korvettenkapitän* ("a commander in the German navy"), and his navy brigade, like most of the Freikorps, was highly disciplined and well armed. Its only allegiance was to its commander, who told them what to do and when and with whom to fight. The Ehrhardt Brigade, like many of the other Free Corps formations and like Hitler, ran on a catalogue of rejections, on political sentiments with only *ad hoc* or romantic notions of ultimate objectives. All of them were violently anti-Spartacist, some of them were antirepublic, but the wide range of membership in the well-paid and well-fed Free Corps included socialists and perhaps as many pro- as anti-Republicans. Although they operated on their own authority and as individual units, they were an indispensable support to the government not only in the East against the foreign enemy but in the Reich against the repeated Spartacist attempts to seize power, and Free Corps units in Bavaria had been called on to join the government troops in the battles to recapture Munich from the Räte. They were invariably better

---

of those cast. The USPD polled 2,317,300 votes, or 7.6 percent; the German Democratic Party, 5,641,800 votes, or 18.5 percent; and the Center, 5,980,200, or 19.7 percent. The first cabinet elected on February 13 under Philipp Scheidemann, SPD, was made up of 7 Social Democrats, 3 Democrats, and 2 Centrists. It may be noted that no party identified itself as "Conservative" or "Right," although the German National People's party was an amalgam of former right-wing, conservative parties. (Herbert Michaelis, et al, *Ursachen und Folgen*, vol. 3, p. 245 from *Statistisches Jahrbuch für das Deutsche Reich*, bd. 27, 1928.)

* The first Free Corps unit had been established by General Maercker on December 14, 1918, only a month after the signing of the armistice. It was recruited from his former 214th Infantry Division and was composed of mixed units in the place of separate formations of infantry, artillery, etc. Unlike the local volunteer formations (*Einwohnerwehr*), the Free Corps could be used anywhere. (Waldemar Erfurth, *Die Geschichte des deutschen Generalstabes von 1918–1945*, p. 23.)

equipped, trained, and disciplined than such left-wing volunteer units as the Security Forces, People's Defense Corps, Red Guards, and other workers' formations that sprang up as the army demobilized.

The army formally accepted the republic; Field Marshal Hindenburg and General Groener had promptly assured Ebert of their support, and despite the soldiers' councils and their design to take over the command authority, the army had marched back from the trenches in good order under the leadership of the officers who had led them in battle. A provisional Reichswehr was voted in March 1919, with only the Independent Socialists dissenting, and it, too, depended on volunteers to fill its ranks and often on the help of the Free Corps to put down outbreaks and retake cities seized by the Spartacists.*

With heavy war casualties, the social complexion of the officer corps had changed. Officers could be selected in the provisional Reichswehr from the ranks of noncommissioned officers if, as had often been the case, they had served well at the front and performed the duties of an officer for six months. They more nearly represented a cross section of the population than had the former officer corps, and while most of the generals and higher echelons remained monarchists, few among the officers of any grade favored a restoration of the Hohenzollerns. Ehrhardt said he would be as much in favor of a strong republic as of any other form of government. But the entire officer corps was uncompromisingly opposed to the Far Left. Their list of grievances was mainly directed at actions tolerated, sponsored, or committed by left-wing groups. The demands in the soldiers' councils for diminishing the traditional command authority, the widespread Spartacist uprisings, the recurrent strikes, and the episodes where officers had had their insignia of rank ripped from their shoulders were glaring examples of subversive, Bolshevik influences. Linked with them were reduction of the army —four-fifths of its strength of 450,000 men in 1919 had to be cut—and the so-called "shame paragraphs" declaring Germany responsible for the war and requiring the Reich to deliver up to the Allies the kaiser and a long list of officers as alleged war criminals. All these had confirmed any number of officers in their conviction that only a strong, centralized nationalist government could restore security and sovereignty to the Fatherland. But despite the discontent and frustration, the early attempts at organizing any kind of revolt remained in the talking stage.

One of the most serious conspiracies centered on Minister of Defense

---

* In some cities, police had disappeared from the streets. In Berlin, in January 1919, the People's Navy Division had occupied the Berlin castle, and the government troops under General Lequis had been forced to withdraw from the city as a horde of revolutionists joined the sailors. Only in mid-January were progovernment—mainly Free Corps troops under General Lüttwitz—able to reoccupy Berlin, and they soon were ordered, with the exception of one regiment, to various suburbs where they would be relatively secure from attempts to convert them to the Spartacist revolution.

Gustav Noske, a Social Democrat. After the sailors' mutiny, Noske had been elected governor of Kiel by the soldiers' council and had won the confidence of the army by his resolute handling of that uprising and of the Spartacist revolts in Berlin and other cities. Noske was repeatedly approached by high-ranking officers, including Ludendorff's successor General Groener, to head a government that would once and for all master the street riots, the strikes, and the constant disorders in the cities.* Groener wanted Ebert to appoint Noske chancellor in the place of his fellow Social Democrat Scheidemann, and in this he was seconded by General Hoffmann, along with other influential officers, among them General Lüttwitz. What they wanted was a strong man wielding iron, legal authority at the top. A Social Democrat like Noske would do probably as well as anyone from the right wing.

The plan fell through because neither Ebert nor Noske would accept the roles assigned them. Ebert felt he could not appoint Noske to the post of chancellor because Noske's countermeasures against the Spartacists had earned him the hatred of many Independent Socialists as well as of other left-wing groups, and Noske did not see himself in a position to lead a movement against a government headed by members of his own party.† Despite the appeals to his patriotism and his own belief that stronger governance was essential to keep Germany united and functioning, Noske backed away from the plot. Any attempt, he wrote later, to rule against the will of the masses could only lead to a catastrophe,[60] and there was no evidence that the electorate wanted a dictatorship. He agreed with the generals that stern measures had to be taken, but like them he was not sure what they should be. The Fatherland had to be rescued from threatened chaos. Nothing was working properly in either the economy or political life. Germany was open to constant attacks in the East and was defenseless in the West, where, it was feared, a French invasion of Bavaria that could not be resisted by the Reichswehr might force Bavaria's separation from the Reich. But the rescue had to be effected by acceptable means, within the framework of the constitution and legality.

The putsch was triggered after the peace treaty was signed, and Noske was forced, under increasing pressure from the Allies, to order

---

* From January 9, 1919, up to the time of the Kapp putsch, there were more than forty major public disturbances—uprisings, street fighting, general strikes, and attempts at political assassinations. (Herbert Michaelis, et al, *Ursachen und Folgen*, vol. 3, pp. 559–61.)

† Noske had called himself a bloodhound when he accepted the assignment of putting down the Berlin revolt. Somebody, he said, had to do the job. The name stuck, and the Spartacists regarded him as a symbol of bloody reaction and SPD treason to the revolution. George Grosz depicted him in one cartoon carrying a bayonet with a child impaled on it and corpses strewn around him. (Gustav Noske, *Von Kiel bis Kapp*, p. 68.)

the disbanding of the Free Corps units. In a year's fighting in the Baltic States, the Free Corps under General von der Goltz had succeeded in driving out the Bolsheviks, and from the Allies' point of view that was enough. The Latvian government had promised the Free Corps volunteers citizenship and land when they enlisted to fight the Bolsheviks, but now it, too, was meeting opposition from its own nationals against handing out land to foreign troops. The volunteers had fought well, too well probably, and as far as the Allies were concerned, their job was finished and they were not to be permitted to augment German armed forces that had to be reduced to seven infantry and three cavalry divisions, a total force of 100,000. For four-fifths of the officers and men in an army numbering 450,000, the future was bleak. The *Chef des Truppenamts* ("chief of the troops office") General von Seeckt was convinced Germany needed an army of at least 300,000 men for its defense, but the Allies decided on one-third of that number, and within a short time thousands of men, many of them professional soldiers, would be without jobs and with nowhere to go.* Ehrhardt was one of these.

For Wolfgang Kapp, an official in the East Prussian Ministry of Agriculture, the war had never ended. He was a Pan-German and a cofounder in 1917 of the German Fatherland party, and after the signing of the Treaty of Versailles he had wanted the Reich to make war against Poland to recover the province of Posen. Like Hitler, he was not German by birth. Kapp was born in New York City, where his family had migrated after the unsuccessful revolution of 1848. His mother was a Jewess, a "very talented" woman one historian has called her;[61] his father, Friedrich Kapp, had returned to Germany in 1870 and was elected as a National Liberal to the Reichstag. Wolfgang Kapp wholeheartedly rejected the liberal tradition of his family. Although he had made a considerable reputation before the war in restructuring the terms of farm loans in East Prussia, few Germans had heard of him until during the war, when he became one of the founders of the Fatherland party. He was one of the most fanatical among the extreme nationalists, violently attacking Bethmann Hollweg and his policies while Bethmann was chancellor, and after the defeat he continued to hold the same unshakable Pan-German beliefs in the Reich's imperial destiny, which would yet be achieved despite the traitors' conspiring against it. For him the defeat and the republic were synonymous, and he accepted neither. His coconspirator, Lieutenant General von Lüttwitz, was a

---

* The economy was stagnating, but crime was not. Crimes committed by youths were double what they had been when the war started, and these did not include the political mayhem, plunder, and rioting in the streets. Few jobs were available for returning soldiers, and one officer's daughter advertised for a household position either as housekeeper or companion. (*General Anzeiger*, Jaunary 5, 1920. *Münchener Neueste Nachrichten*, March 6–7, 1920.)

Prussian officer of traditional mold, an aristocrat who obeyed orders to the letter unless they violated his conscience or his notions of propriety.

General von Lüttwitz, who commanded the army troops in and around Berlin, had been one of the generals urging Noske to become chancellor with dictatorial powers, and he could, however grudgingly, accept the authority of the republican government until Noske ordered him to disband the Ehrhardt Brigade. Lüttwitz reacted with fury. To dissolve the Ehrhardt Brigade, which was under his command, as well as the other Free Corps formations, would mean leaving the Reich virtually unprotected against a Bolshevik-Spartacist attack from the East and within the Reich's borders. Lüttwitz was convinced that Soviet Russia would overrun Poland within a year and that Germany would be confronted with large numbers of Bolshevik troops at its borders that it could not resist with an army of 100,000 men. He presented Ebert with an ultimatum: a new presidential election was to be held immediately, the National Assembly dissolved, General Reinhardt dismissed as Prussian war minister and chief of the Army High Command and a supreme commander named, the order for the dissolution of the Ehrhardt Brigade rescinded, and the rations and living conditions of the troops improved.* Ebert said he was ready to try to improve the food and housing of the troops, but the rest of the demands he refused. Noske, who was present at the meeting, irately informed Lüttwitz that the command of the Ehrhardt Brigade had already been taken from him and that he was to obey orders. As a preparation for his forced retirement, Lüttwitz was sent on leave, and Seeckt and Noske ordered the arrest of the chief conspirators—Kapp, Ludendorff's advisor Colonel Max Bauer, and Captain Pabst, general staff officer of the Prussian Guard Cavalry Division and Free Corps leader, who had been active in trying to recruit officers for the revolt. Also to be arrested were Karl Schnitzler, a dentist turned journalist, and Friedrich Grabowski, a Jew, who was acting as chief propagandist for the rebellion.†

The chances of success of a right-wing coup did not seem unpropitious. Ludendorff, who had returned from his brief exile in Sweden, was among those urging Kapp to act to clean out the Augean parliamentary stables. Ludendorff had ordered Colonel Bauer to sound out the British on their attitude to an army coup. Bauer had raised the question with

---

* Ebert had been elected president by the National Assembly. With the Weimar Constitution, which the Assembly had written, in force, the president would in the future be elected by popular vote, and many of the generals hoped Hindenburg would replace Ebert. A supreme commander of the army would be unacceptable to the Allies, who had proscribed the general staff and wanted to abolish anything resembling the high command of the imperial army.

† Grabowski had been head of the propaganda section of the Guard Cavalry Division, where Pabst had come to know and regard him highly.

the British military governor of Cologne, Colonel Ryan, who sent the inquiry on to British State Secretary Balfour. The British, apparently more concerned with the possible spread of Bolshevism in Germany than with the inveterate fears of their French ally, replied that they would not intervene directly or indirectly if a temporary military dictatorship should result from suppressing an attempt at revolution providing that it would lead to the establishment of a constitutional government, which might be a constitutional monarchy.[62]

Also to be taken into account were the uncharismatic personalities in the government. From the very beginning of the revolution, the republic was often made to appear not only weak but ridiculous. On the day Ebert was inaugurated as president, in a ceremony far less glittering than those of imperial days, a picture magazine, the *Berliner Illustrierte*, published a photograph of Ebert and Noske in bathing suits looking more like seedy *sportlers* than statesmen. And a trial involving Matthias Erzberger, one of the men most cordially detested by the extreme Right and Left, brought to a focus the hatreds and recriminations of the opposing camps.

Erzberger, in November 1918, had been assigned the ungrateful role of leading the German armistice delegation to Compiègne. In the view of the ultranationalists, he was one of the chief "November criminals" for having signed the shameful terms of the armistice and then urging the acceptance of the unacceptable peace. In the view of the Communists he was, along with Noske, Scheidemann, and Ebert, one of the chief enemies of the revolution. A devout Catholic with influential connections in the Vatican, Erzberger, during the war, had attempted to mobilize the influence of the Church on the side of the Central Powers, and from having been an annexationist in the early part of the war, he had shifted to become one of the leading proponents of a peace of reconciliation. His enemies laid the long list of humiliations that Germany had had to endure at his doorstep. Germany's powerlessness was the work of him and his likes. The surrender of the German fleet at Scapa Flow had been partly expiated, not by the politicians, but by the officers and men who had retrieved some kind of victory by sinking their ships as they lay at anchor in the Scottish harbor. In February 1920, the crews of the Scapa Flow ships returned in the midst of the Erzberger trial, and 1,000 sailors were addressed in a public gathering by Admiral von Trotha, who on the steps of the monument of Frederick the Great on Unter den Linden extolled their heroism; nine of their number had been killed and sixteen wounded in an action waged without arms but with honor.[*]

---

[*] The Right had to content itself with such moral victories. The French flags captured in 1870, which were to be returned to France under the terms of the peace treaty, were instead publicly burned in Berlin.

As a left-wing member of the Centrist party, Erzberger had opposed the decision for all-out submarine warfare, and he was a powerful advocate of the peace resolution adopted by the Reichstag in July 1917. In 1919 he became minister of finance in the cabinet of Chancellor Bauer, where he instituted a unified tax system with a capital levy of 50 percent on 3 million marks or more and high imposts on both personal income and corporate income, designed to enable the Reich to bear the enormous burdens incurred as a result of the war. Erzberger was convinced that capital and property should be subject to conscription in the national interest as well as "living bodies."[63] One of his innumerable enemies was Carl Helfferich,* who had been state secretary for finance during the war and who, like Kapp, was an uncompromising opponent of the policy of fulfillment of the peace terms that Erzberger and the republican government had reluctantly adopted. Helfferich unleashed a violent campaign of slander against Erzberger in a series of newspaper articles and in a pamphlet entitled "Away with Erzberger" (*Fort mit Erzberger!*) in an effort to goad Erzberger to sue him for libel. The tactic was successful; Erzberger brought suit and the trial became a cause célèbre engaging the passions of both Left and Right, who saw in it a morality play of the struggle for and against the republican government. A day before the start of the Kapp putsch, the verdict came down, in favor, technically, of Erzberger but in its effect a resounding defeat for him. The court decreed that Helfferich was to pay trifling damages of 300 marks and to bear the considerable costs of the trial, but a large section of the public was left convinced that Erzberger had not succeeded in refuting the accusations made against him. His opponents had charged him with malfeasance in office—of adopting confiscatory tax policies designed to dispossess the middle classes while at the same time evading the payment of his own taxes—and public opinion found him guilty. Erzberger's political career was destroyed. A right-wing newspaper had published his tax returns in an attempt to prove that he had defrauded the government, and while a court of inquiry declared the charges unfounded, Erzberger was never able to catch up with the accusations made against him.

Midway in the trial he was shot and wounded in the shoulder and chest by a twenty-year-old high school student,† and although he recovered from the wounds, he never recovered from the trial. He was

* Another was Albrecht von Graefe, who had been called a "Talmi Junker" during the 1913 Reichstag debates. Graefe accused Erzberger of being in the pay of the French and Austrians. (Harry Graf Kessler, *In the Twenties.*)

† The would-be killer, a former officer-candidate, a *Faehnrich*, Oltwig von Hirschfeld, was tried on the charge of "causing bodily injury" instead of on the more serious count of attempted murder, and because of "mitigating circumstances" (i.e., Hirschfeld's patriotic motives) he was sentenced to a year and a half of imprisonment.

killed a year later by two former members of the Ehrhardt Brigade.*

Erzberger was forever tainted with having been head of the armistice delegation, a post he had never sought but had had thrust upon him, and thus for being one of those who had brought the great troubles upon Germany. The case against him made by Helfferich and his astute lawyer evidenced for many patriotic Germans the duplicity and venality of the weak-kneed parliamentarians responsible for bringing the war and the eminence of the Reich to an untimely end.

Although Erzberger's trial undoubtedly confirmed for many army officers their low opinion of the character of much of the republican leadership, Kapp and Lüttwitz succeeded in rounding up relatively few of them to join the revolt. The conspirators did succeed in recruiting a number of generals,† as well as the commander of the Hamburg garrison, Colonel von Wangenheim, and the former police president of Berlin, Traugott von Jagow, but they had to be content with the prospect of many more from the army leadership joining them once the revolt got under way.

One of them was General von der Goltz, who had been relieved of his command of the Baltic Free Corps formations. Another was General Maercker, who had been responsible for the security of the National Assembly and who had promised to resign if the peace treaty were signed. Colonel Bischoff, the commander of the Iron Division, who had served under General von der Goltz, had flatly refused to order the division back to Germany.[64] Bischoff wrote a letter reminding the Berlin authorities that the Latvian government had made promises to the German volunteers and that the Reich had annulled the agreement; he demanded that at least 30 percent of the Iron Guard be accepted in the provisional Reichswehr and in the police, and that meanwhile the division be kept in position protecting the eastern frontiers. Then Bischoff had a talk with the commander of the Defense Sector of East Prussia, General von Estorff, who said: "Now my dear Bischoff, I know you want to march on Berlin and I can't stop you, because half of my people would go over to you and the rest wouldn't shoot. But don't do it. There's no point in it."[65] It was sound advice, but Estorff himself

---

* The brigade had continued after its dissolution in the form of a secret, anti-Semitic, anti-Jesuit, terrorist group under the name of Organization Consul, so called because Consul was Ehrhardt's cover name. The organization was one of those responsible for the series of so-called *Feme* (named after the German medieval "honor" courts), murders of men like Erzberger regarded as left-wing traitors. (Gotthard Jasper, "Aus den Prozessen gegen die Erzberger Mörder," *Vierteljahrshfte für Zeitgischichte*, October 1962, pp. 430–53.)

† Among them were some well-known figures: General von Estorff, commandant of Defense Sector # 1 (East Prussia); General von Bernuth, commanding Defense Sector # 2 (Pomerania, Schleswig-Holstein, Mecklenburg); General von Hülsen, commanding a Free Corps brigade.

did not follow it; when the putsch began, he and the Social Democrat August Winnig, the governor (*Oberpräsident*) of East Prussia, supported it.

The overwhelming majority of officers of all ranks and formations, however, did not join. Any number of generals, including Hoffmann, Oven, Maercker, and Seeckt, might yearn for a dictatorship, but it was a very big step from urging the need to establish one and actually taking part in a revolution that would impose it by armed force. Every Reichswehr soldier had taken an oath of allegiance to the Weimar constitution and its instrumentalities and to the president of the Reich. That did not mean, however, that a government could not be legally changed and given authoritarian powers that would still be consistent with the provisions of the constitution. Under the constitution, the Reichspräsident, who appointed the chancellor, could legally dissolve the Reichstag, and under Article 48, when the security of the Reich was in danger, he could call on the armed forces to restore order. For Ebert to have appointed Noske chancellor with power to rule by decree in an emergency would have been constitutional. The great majority of army officers would certainly have supported such a move, but to revolt against the lawful government, to attempt a putsch was out of the question for them, while for Lüttwitz and others like him such a desperate move was the last means to rescue the Fatherland.

The dismissal of Lüttwitz and the orders for the arrest of Kapp and company set the revolt prematurely in motion. Ehrhardt, who was quartered in Döberitz with his brigade of between 4,000 and 5,000 men, many of them former officers and noncommissioned officers in the Reichswehr, set out for Berlin. They were elite troops; before the putsch began, Ehrhardt, with Admiral von Trotha at his side, had taken his salute as they marched past, and a reporter who was present saw the brigade as a reincarnation of the incomparable swing and élan of the old imperial army. Now they marched off to Berlin in high spirits, singing, sure of themselves, with full field packs, rifles, and grenades, bearing the red, black, and white banners they had carried in the war in the place of the detested red, gold, and black of the republic. They wore swastikas on their helmets, the swastika being an ancient, mystical, Indo-Germanic sign highly regarded by members of organizations like the Thule Society as somehow connected with the northern mana.*

Not a shot was fired either at or by the brigade. On March 13 they marched under the Brandenburg Gate singing "Deutschland, Deutschland über alles" to the cheers of a crowd that included General Luden-

* A cartoon drawn in 1918 by George Grosz titled "The White General" depicted a fierce, bemedalled officer with a sword in his hand and a swastika on his helmet. (Harry Graf Kessler, *In the Twenties*, p. 87.)

dorff. Lüttwitz and his staff occupied the buildings of the Defense Ministry, Kapp the Reichschancellery. No one attempted to stop them. The government had prudently fled to Dresden, and Berlin was occupied by the rebels—the Ehrhardt Brigade, joined by other Free Corps units and the Potsdam garrison. All that remained now was to set up an administration.

It was at this point of apparent victory that the first hitches developed. So far the government had been unable to organize a defense. Noske and Reinhardt had wanted to call out the Reichswehr to defend the capital, but Seeckt had refused. He would not unleash a civil war with the army on opposite sides, nor was he ready to prevent one with the use of the Reichswehr. Seeckt said there would be no shooting with live ammunition at the Brandenburg Gate; his overriding duty, as he saw it, was to preserve the unity of the army. To preserve the republic was secondary. Seeckt was not alone in his estimate of patriotic duty and the officer's oath.

He had met with Noske in the Defense Ministry on March 13, 1920, as the news came that Ehrhardt was marching, and among those present were Generals Reinhardt, Oldershausen, and Oven along with Admiral von Trotha.° When Noske told the officers present that the Free Corps advance on Berlin had to be met by force, only his chief of staff Major Gilsa and General Reinhardt agreed with him. The others, as Noske reported later, shared Seeckt's unshakable principle that Reichswehr did not shoot at Reichswehr and his opinion that in any case the Berlin garrison was too weak to defend the city against Ehrhardt. The bloodbath would be fearful and the success of the rebels certain. Seeckt received permission to go on leave, changed to civilian clothes, and retired to the sidelines to await events.† Noske could only see to it that the members of the government fled the city, because he was certain that the majority of the generals outside Berlin would remain loyal, and this in fact they did.

In Berlin the sentiment was divided. A number of officers like General Reinhardt declared openly for the legitimate government, while most of them, like Seeckt, adopted a wait-and-see attitude. Both the military and civilian officials at the Defense Ministry adopted a resolution declaring they would continue to pursue their duties but would not take sides in the struggle. They were ready to help maintain peace and order while the negotiations were in progress that would lead to the formation of a

° What was left of the navy was on the side of the revolt. For one thing the Ehrhardt Brigade was a naval formation, for another the navy officers were very conscious that the mutiny against the kaiser's government had started in the navy. The future chief of counterintelligence, Admiral Canaris, then a lieutenant-captain on Noske's staff, was one of those on the side of putschists.

† He fell ill, apparently with an attack of malaria, and recovered when the revolt was over. (Erfurth, citing Blomberg, *Lebens-Erinnerungen*, p. 76).

government, as they said, backed by a majority of the population.[66] Since the legal government refused to negotiate with Kapp and Lüttwitz, the administrators in the Defense Ministry were carefully carrying water on both shoulders. It was in this prudent spirit that the officers in the ministry told Lüttwitz that they would continue to fulfill their assignments but that they did not recognize his command authority.

Outside Berlin, scattered commanders declared for the new regime. In Breslau, General von Schmettow and a Free Corps brigade under Wilfried von Loewenfeld took over control of the city on behalf of the revolt. In Mecklenburg-Schwerin, the hero of the East African campaign, General von Lettow-Vorbeck, supported the putsch as did General Hagenberg, the military commander in Weimar, whose local government he dismissed. In Magdeburg the commandant of Reichswehr Brigade #4, General von Groddeck, came out for the revolt but ran into the resistance of his subordinate, Colonel von Hahnke, who refused to obey his superior's orders and took over the command.[67]

It was mainly in eastern and northwestern Germany that Kapp and Lüttwitz were able to get the backing of military and civilian leaders; in the rest of the country they met either with active resistance or with neutrality, or at any rate a refusal to take arms against the government. Bavaria gave no support to Kapp despite its aversion to the Berlin government, and in other parts of the Reich battles erupted between left-wing, allied with progovernment, forces and the putschists. In the Ruhr, however, the radical wing of the Independent Socialists, making common cause with the Communists, took the opportunity to call again for the proletarian revolution as they resolved to take arms against both Kapp and the government forces.

As the developing resistance to the putschists would soon show, both the army and the civil population were overwhelmingly opposed to the mutiny. No sign of popular revolt appeared, and it was not doubt of the allegiance of the rank and file of the army or of the civil population that decided the cabinet to move from Berlin to Dresden and then to Stuttgart. Saxony, too, was progovernment, but the cabinet was unimpressed with the resoluteness of the local officials in Dresden, as well as with General Maercker's loyalty. Maercker told Reichsminister for Reconstruction Otto Gessler that although he supported General von Lüttwitz, he would defend the Social Democratic government of Saxony, an ambiguous position far more comfortable for him than for the cabinet, who therefore made their way to Stuttgart, where the Württemberg civil authorities and General von Bergmann assured them of their protection.

The cabinet had a difficult journey from Dresden to Stuttgart. They travelled in separate automobiles to avoid being arrested in a body. The car carrying President Ebert, Gessler, and Foreign Minister Hermann Müller-Franken ran out of gasoline, and with the general strike in force they could get no more fuel. Trains were running infrequently and were often under the control of Red Guards, who were as much a danger as the Kapp-Lüttwitz men. Awaiting a train late at night in Chemnitz, Ebert's small party spent some hours in an inn near the railroad station. The president, who had run out of cigars as well as gasoline, asked the innkeeper to let him see his cigars, and after carefully choosing one from a box, asked the price. When the innkeeper told him it cost 5 marks, Ebert put the cigar back in the box with the single word *Thanks*. He told his companions it would ruin his career if it were ever discovered that he had paid 5 marks for one cigar.* The next morning the cabinet met in Stuttgart, and from there it continued the nonviolent campaign with which it won the war.

Neither Kapp nor Lüttwitz had any trace of political skill. Lacking both a well-defined program and eloquence, their manifestoes addressed to the public sounded like bureaucratic memoranda. The first announcement that the former government had ceased to exist, declaring Kapp Reichschancellor and minister president of Prussia and Lüttwitz commander in chief of the army and minister of defense, identified Kapp as the functionary he was; it was signed by him as *Generallandschaftsdirektor*, that is, general agricultural director, and by Lüttwitz as general of infantry. Kapp then proceeded to produce a windy program explaining that theirs was not a monarchical putsch nor an attempt to start the war all over again, but a new government that would carry out the terms of the peace treaty while maintaining the honor of the German people and its means to existence.

He had his eye mainly on landowners and on the middle classes, although he was formally solicitous of the welfare of workers too. He promised his government would repay the war loans and see to it that property was taxed fairly. After every catastrophe, he said, it is landed property that is expected to bear the burden of sacrifice demanded for reconstruction, and he would restore economic freedom to property owners and at the same time see to it that food was available at reasonable prices. He also said vaguely that the new regime would enact laws to make possible for every German access to land and property, would protect government workers, and would consider as its most holy duty the welfare of the war wounded and of the war widows and orphans. It would protect the volunteer troops and their dependents, maintain the unity of the Reich, and treat any separatist moves as high treason. The new government would favor neither Left nor Right, but would recognize only German citizens. It would take the most severe measures against strikes and sabotage, protect workers against international capi-

---

* At the time the value of the mark was 100 to the dollar. (Otto Gessler, *Reichswehrpolitik in der Weimarer Zeit*, pp. 123–25.)

tal, and restore the old colors of black, white, and red. In his turn, Lüttwitz told the army the new regime would pay 1,000 marks to anyone wounded on its behalf and 2,000 marks each for any additional wounds. Further, he told the soldiers their pay would be raised 7 marks a day, and he promised that no one would be discharged from the army whose future was not assured.[68]

Not many Germans were impressed by the program. Landowners and people of property were doubtless gratified at the prospect of lower taxes, but few soldiers or workers would be won over for seven extra marks a day, or by an undefined chance to be able to obtain a piece of land and freedom from the exploitation of foreign capital.

Although the singing Freikorps with its imperial colors had been cheered as it swung down *Unter den Linden*, once the march was over it became immediately apparent that the rebels had no broad political or popular base. The putschists had the support of the security police, of the Ehrhardt Brigade, of the Potsdam garrison, and of a scattered, unorganized political following, and that was all. The bureaucrats at work in the government offices were polite but firm with Kapp and Lüttwitz. Although they, too, had little love for the republic, they had sworn an oath to serve it, and they declined to collaborate with the rebels or to obey their orders. When "Reichschancellor" Kapp sent an emissary to Reichsbank President Havenstein asking him to turn over 10 million marks to the new government, Havenstein said he had no right to do so, and he gave the same answer when "Reich Defense Minister" von Lüttwitz sent an officer demanding immediate payment of the money. Havenstein reminded his visitor that to take the funds by force would be illegal, a view that was seconded by his vice-president, who took part in the discussion. The next morning two officers in civilian clothes presented five checks for 2 million marks each, properly filled out and with signatures authorized for military expenditures. They were, however, made out, not to "Bearer," as was usual, but to the order of "Reichsminister of Defense von Lüttwitz or Bearer." These checks Herr Havenstein refused to cash, because a minister of defense by the name of Lüttwitz, entitled to receive such funds, was unknown to him. The officers departed to obtain new checks made out to "Bearer" only, but came back to say the Main Military Disbursing Office refused to issue any more checks and they would return to it the ones they had.[69] When Ehrhardt, in his turn, was ordered to get the money, he refused, saying an officer could not appear as a safecracker.[70]

The officials in the Prussian Ministry of the Interior told Traugott von Jagow, who appeared to take over his duties as minister, that they would continue to work on behalf of the public weal, but they would not recognize the new regime or follow von Jagow's orders. One man, Director in the Ministry Meister, was arrested and later suspended for refusing to collaborate with the new government, but on the whole the rebels were unwilling to use force against government functionaries. So while no strike of officials took place, nothing was done on behalf of the new regime either.

The German Volksparty, which had received a little less than 4½ percent of the votes in the election for the National Assembly, made a lukewarm pronouncement on behalf of the putschists.* But that was all the visible political support the rebels received, and it was of no practical use whatever.

Against the putschists was massed the overwhelming power of the workers called off their jobs in the proclamation of a general strike issued by Ebert, Bauer, Noske, and other Social Democratic leaders. Behind them were the vast majority of the people of Berlin, who had voted for the socialist and democratic parties. With the summons to a general strike, everything stopped in the Reich. Kapp and Lüttwitz found themselves isolated. Nothing moved in or to or from Berlin. Supplies were cut off, as were water, light, and gas. No newspapers were printed. By March 16, three days after the march through the Brandenburg Gate, workers and demonstrators filled the streets, and the revolutionaries were left with only the offices they had commandeered, the security police, and the Ehrhardt Brigade, which had no further assignments it could carry out.

The attempts of Kapp and Lüttwitz to win over the allies they had counted on came to nothing. Hindenburg privately sent his best wishes, but that was all the help the putschists were given by him. The old field marshal had appeared at a hearing of the Parliamentary Committee on Inquiry into the Causes of the War and the Collapse, and the public acclaim, when crowds caught a glimpse of him, showed again how deeply not only the army but the civil population esteemed him.† A word from him might well have had a decisive effect on public opinion and would certainly have been powerful with the officer corps. But Hindenburg was silent, as far as the public knew. At his appearance before the committee he had helped buttress the story, which he now undoubtedly himself believed, that the army had been betrayed. Despite the numerical and material superiority of the enemy, he said, reading from a memorandum prepared by Ludendorff, the army could have

* It declared that the "former government" had been unable to secure the confidence of a majority of the population; called on the new regime to maintain order, property rights, and the freedom to work; and said new elections should be held to establish a constitutional government.

† His appeal to all classes was extraordinary. In 1917, when a group of Social Democrats came to congratulate him on his birthday, Hindenburg, in thanking them, said he seemed quite popular with the comrades and would soon have to acquire a red beret. Later, when he was elected president, an observer said there were more red flags flying at a demonstration in the Lustgarten in Berlin than flags of the republic. (Harry Graf Kessler, *In the Twenties*, p. 413.)

ended the war favorably had it not been for the disintegration in the rear, and he quoted an unnamed British general as saying (and with truth, Hindenburg added) that the German army had been stabbed in the back.* [71] But Hindenburg no more than Seeckt could embrace a revolt against the legitimate government.

His thoughts on the events leading up to the revolution were now in perfect order. He called himself an unreconstructed monarchist; he had fulfilled his duty to his liege lord the emperor until the subverted home front had failed them both; the army had done its duty, had accomplished everything that could conceivably be demanded of it, but had been foully stabbed in the back; and his duty now, as before, lay in defending the Fatherland he and it existed to serve. He might privately send his best wishes to patriots revolting against the forces of dissolution and the legal government, but he would go no further than that. He would not dream of dividing the Reichswehr or bringing on a civil war in which it would have to fight on opposite sides.

So his good wishes were of no help to Kapp and Lüttwitz. Commander after commander announced they would support the Ebert government; Ludendorff told Kapp to hold out, but the commander of the Berlin security police, Colonel von Schönstadt, informed Kapp that he had to quit, and when the commandant of the Berlin Reichswehr said the same thing, Ludendorff had to agree. [72] Kapp's dictatorship had lasted one hundred hours.

Lüttwitz, for a short time, clung to the idea that he himself might become the ordained military dictator, but when a procession of Reichswehr generals, as well as Colonel von Schönstadt, informed him that he no longer had any support and that he and the other mutineers would have to leave Berlin so that law and order could be maintained in the capital, he too had no choice but to get out. Lüttwitz, though, was able to impose conditions. Before he would end the revolt, he met with representatives of the government parties, who agreed to hold general elections to the Reichstag as well as a presidential election by popular vote and to reshape the cabinet with experts in the place of politicians. He was also promised an amnesty for the rebels who had followed him and Kapp.† Lüttwitz then departed, but not before Ebert had promised he would not forfeit his pension. [73]

Both Kapp and Lüttwitz fled from Berlin, but they went on their

---

* Hindenburg did not name the general, who was rumored to be Sir Frederick Maurier. Maurier had written articles for the London *Daily News* that were translated in the *Neue Zürcher Zeitung*, and in these the word *Dolchstoss* "stab in the back" appeared.

† The government in Stuttgart did not know of these conditions, which were agreed to in Berlin by representatives of the coalition parties anxious to reach a settlement and end the general strike. The promised amnesty was never granted, and warrants were issued for the arrest of Kapp and Lüttwitz.

separate ways in relative peace. Lüttwitz was able to return to Berlin at the end of a week to spend the night in his apartment before he departed the city again, to stay with a Free Corps leader in Breslau. The following years, before he was amnestied, he spent abroad or hidden by friends on estates in Silesia. Kapp, too, remained in and near Berlin, where he was detained in protective custody by the security police and housed in an army barracks until the police arranged for him to take a plane from Tempelhof Airport for Sweden. News photographers for an illustrated magazine took pictures of him as he prepared to depart. He returned to Germany in 1922 to face trial, but he was mortally ill and died before any court could deal with him. Of the chief conspirators only three, von Jagow, von Wangenheim, and Schiele,* stood trial, and of these only Jagow was convicted of a crime. He was sentenced to five years of *Festungsarrest*, that is, imprisonment in a minimum-security place of detention.†

The fate of the others reflected the confusion in the German soul. General von Seeckt praised Captain Ehrhardt for his devotion to the Fatherland and permitted him to retain command of his brigade until it was disbanded in May. A warrant issued for Ehrhardt's arrest was never served. Some of the members of his brigade were inducted into the navy, from which they had come and which apparently was pleased to have patriotic mutineers after its experience with the other kind. High officers who had joined the revolt, Seeckt implacably dismissed, and he made no objection to their being interrogated by civilian commissars appointed for this purpose. In Seeckt's view, the generals and colonels who had broken their oaths had abrogated their sworn duty and deserved no protection from him. Seeckt's sole criterion for punishment of the lower ranks of officers was not whether they had remained loyal to their oath of allegiance, but whether they had obeyed the orders of their superiors, even of those who were being dismissed. Officers who had followed orders, including orders to mutiny, were not punished. In all, 63 officers were transferred and 172 were dismissed from the service, among them 12 generals. No officer was imprisoned.[74]

Noske was forced to resign because of pressure from both the Left and the Right. The Left, more suspicious than ever of the army, charged him with being too close to the officer corps and with failing in his duty to provide the government with military support in the crisis; the Right demanded he quit because his name was among those calling the general strike. General Reinhardt, who had sided with Noske and had wanted

* Georg-Wilhelm Schiele, a member with Kapp and Ludendorff of the National Union that succeeded the Fatherland party, was economics minister in the Kapp government.

† He served three years of his sentence under the mildest of conditions and was even permitted to pay visits to friends who lived in the neighborhood of his prison.

Seeckt to resist the rebels with the Reichswehr, resigned in solidarity with Noske. Seeckt, who had been austerely neutral in this struggle for the survival of the republic, was given the post, formerly held by Reinhardt, of chief of the Army High Command. Thus, as chief of staff and commander of the army, he now had the decisive voice in military matters, and since no government could function without the support of the Reichswehr, his opinion would be attentively listened to in political affairs as well.

The government was still caught between the forces of the Right and the Left. The Left and the general strike had defeated the revolt. The Communist party, which regarded the Social Democrats and the government with the same hostility it bore the putchists, took no part in the general strike until two days had gone by, and only then, believing the situation to be ripe, did it, too, order its members to join the strike. It saw an opportunity to reactivate the Marxist revolution that had subsided in Germany, and joined by left-wing members of the Independent Socialist party, it went to work again to bring down the bourgeois order, such as it was. For many die-hard nationalists in the Reich, the Kapp revolt had promised great opportunities. Adolf Hitler, when he heard the news of the rising, set off for Berlin by private plane* with his admirer Dietrich Eckardt, a well-known Bavarian writer, who had early been impressed by Hitler's gifts of oratory. They had planned to observe the revolution to discover if it might not provide an opportunity for a rising in Bavaria, but by the time they arrived in Berlin it was over.

Kapp and Lüttwitz had failed, and Seeckt, who believed in their purposes, had won. The unity of the army was preserved and the republic survived, despite little help from the armed forces that existed to protect it. For Seeckt and many like him, it was the army far more than the republic that mattered; the republic was, to be sure, the legal civil authority, but it was to be served only insofar as it served something that transcended any form of government—the Fatherland. The Fatherland could not be preserved if the army were splintered in a civil war; the Reichswehr could not fight against the republic to which it had sworn allegiance. When in 1921 Seeckt was asked why he had not joined the putsch, he replied, "A general doesn't break his oath." But he and the Reichswehr could stand aside to let the republic fight its own domestic battles rather than risk something far more important than the tenure of some socialists in office. What could not be placed at risk was the integrity of the army, the buckler and shield of the Fatherland itself. Seeckt's reasoning was complex and contradictory. He testified in 1921 that most of the army officers had remained loyal to the regime once the situation became clear, that is, when they learned the government

---

* It was Hitler's first flight. He flew with two others, including the pilot, in a two-seater plane.

had not abdicated but simply moved out of Berlin. That was true, but he himself was not one of them; he had not seen fit to defend the government and fulfill his oath of allegiance when he did know what the situation was. Pragmatically, it may be that he was right and not Reinhardt, who had wanted the Berlin garrison to resist the Ehrhardt Brigade. As a result of Seeckt's refusal to call out the Reichswehr, no blood was shed, the army maintained its unity, and the state struggled on with its tepid support and without civil war. Reinhardt's solution, which would have had the Reichswehr fire on other Reichswehr formations, could scarcely have had more felicitous results for the republic in either the short or long run.

When the government returned to Berlin, it was faced with a new enemy, this one made up of leftist extremists. The putsch from the Right had been put down, but the general strike was still in force in the capital and the Communists were recruiting a Red army in the industrial areas of the Reich.

CHAPTER 5

"The Enemy Is on the Right"

P HILIPP SCHEIDEMANN SAID in October 1919 in a phrase that would be often repeated: "The enemy is on the Right,"[*] but the enemy the government faced after the Kapp putsch was in fact on the Left. In the Ruhr, in Saxony and Westphalia, thousands of workers had been recruited to defend the revolution against the reaction, and since the chief activists organizing the defense of the revolution in the industrial areas were likely to be Communists, the enemy on the Right included President Ebert and the succession of Social Democratic chancellors. The Red army was formidable not only in numbers, but also in equipment and morale. Its arms, including heavy weapons, had been seized from the police, from army stores, and from the *Einwohnerwehr*, or local defense forces. While for Lüttwitz and Kapp a revolution was needed to restore the order and system that Germany had lost along with the war, for the Spartacists, the Communists, and the syndicalists, the revolution was intended to extend a new world to Germany, to overthrow the bourgeoisie and the capitalist system that had been responsible for the war and the Kapp putsch, and to erect in their place the dictatorship of the proletariat, of workers who shoulder to shoulder with their brothers in Soviet Russia would sweep away not only the Kapps and the Eberts but the Allied puppets of imperialism as well.

The Kapp putsch had brought the Marxist revolution to the surface again; with the mobilization of the general strike, new energy was lent

[*] The phrase had also been used during the Berlin street fighting of 1918 by the Independent Socialists to characterize the SPD. (Lewis Hertzmann, *DNVP*, p. 93.)

[150]

the movement that for short periods had taken over dozens of German cities—Berlin, Bremen, Munich, and others—only to be put down and forced to take cover until such time as its leaders thought they could make another bid for power.

The revolt of thousands of armed, determined men could be dealt with only by strong military forces, but main uprisings were taking place in and near the Ruhr, much of which under the terms of the peace treaty was a neutral zone to which the government was forbidden under any circumstances to send troops. What was the government to do? The French continued to demand the stipulated deliveries from the Ruhr, which could only be made if workers were in the mines and factories and not in the streets making a revolution; but if order were restored with military force, the treaty would be violated and the French given another pretext to take reprisals. The Red army was a redoubtable force made up largely of veterans who had fought in the trenches, and it succeeded, despite the stubborn defense of the security police, in occupying Dortmund and Essen in a westward sweep accompanied by plunder, murder, and beatings. Again the cry was raised: "All power to the workers"; again the Red army confiscated food, automobiles, and anything else it needed, as had the Räte government in Munich.

Many moderate workers were as bitterly opposed as were the Communists to the commander of the Reichswehr troops in the area adjacent to the Ruhr, General von Watter. Watter's attitude toward the Kapp putsch had been ambivalent, and much of the population of the Ruhr regarded him more as a suspicious character than as the appointed restorer of peace and order. The Berlin government found itself again caught in a predicament for which there was no solution without severe side effects. Not only would the Allies not approve the use of Reichswehr in the neutral zone, but a large section of the population wanted no part of its commanding general. Before Watter and his troops were ordered to march into the disaffected areas, the government delegated Carl Severing, a Social Democrat, to attempt to arrange a peaceful settlement with the workers, and it was owing to Severing's efforts that the non-Communists were split off from the hard-core Spartacists and syndicalists. Severing succeeded in bringing together in the town of Bielefeld a meeting of representatives of the unions and Social Democrats along with Independent Socialists and Communists. The Bielefeld Agreement of March 23, 1920, was a liberal if not utopian document designed to meet the chief demands of the revolutionists and at the same time to preserve the Weimar Constitution and the mixed economic system of capitalist enterprise and state intervention of the republican Reich. It provided for the dissolution[1] of counterrevolutionary, including Free Corps, formations; punishment of those who had taken part in the Kapp putsch; the socialization of industries ripe for the transition, including coal mines and potash production; administrative reforms; the passage of laws favoring social and economic equality for workers, employees, and government officials; the dismissal from the government of counterrevolutionaries, especially those in leading positions; and the surrender of arms by the workers' military formations. If the agreement were "loyally" carried out, the army would not intervene. The Bielefeld Agreement, signed by two Communists as well as by the moderate parties, left the segment of the revolters who wanted an immediate revolution on the Russian pattern isolated, as a band of marauders. But under the leadership of one Gottfried Karrusseit, who threatened death and destruction to anyone who blocked his path, they continued to occupy and terrorize sizeable areas in the Ruhr. Although Karrusseit was denounced even by dyed-in-the-wool Communists like Wilhelm Pieck, who called him "an irresponsible fool,"[2] Berlin had no recourse but to order the Reichswehr into the forbidden zone.

After hard fighting, government troops succeeded in defeating the Red army. But in putting down the revolt in the Ruhr, Berlin had been unable to secure the permission of the Allies to enter the neutral zone, despite Seeckt's promise that the troops would be withdrawn after three weeks. The former socialist Millerand was now prime minister of France, but his government's policies vis-à-vis Germany could scarcely be distinguished from those of any of his hard-line predecessors. Without consulting the British and Americans, French and Belgian troops occupied Frankfurt, Darmstadt, Homburg, Hanau, and Dieburg in reprisal for the Reichswehr's Ruhr "invasion," while at the same time France was demanding the full deliveries of Ruhr coal (2,400,000 tons a month), which could not have been made with a revolution in progress. The British protested the French occupation of the cities, but they had little more effect on such decisions by Paris than did the Germans.*

It was in Bavaria that the Kapp putsch and the Leftist risings had both immediate and long-range effects. The memories of the Räte republic were still vivid in that agrarian, Catholic state, and when the general strike was called, it aroused prompt reactions on the part of Bavarian conservatives. Leaders of the Free Corps, along with a civil servant and ardent supporter of the Wittelsbach monarchy, Gustav von Kahr; the police president of Munich, Ernst Pöhner; and another police official, Wilhelm Frick, were among those who urged the commander of the Bavarian Reichswehr, General von Möhl, to assume governmental authority in the emergency. Möhl agreed and told the Bavarian premier, Hoffmann, he could not be responsible for maintaining law and order unless he were delegated full emergency powers. Although Hoffmann at first refused, the other members of his cabinet, including the Social

---

* While Millerand promised France would not again undertake such unilateral actions, he added a broad escape clause: unless France's vital interests were affected.

Democrats, agreed to Möhl's demands, and Hoffmann was left without a cabinet. So the Social Democratic government in Bavaria stepped down and out, never to return. Kahr became the new minister-president, heading a coalition government dominated by the Bavarian Volksparty, a group that had broken off from the Center party and that placed Bavarian interests above those of the Reich or of any other secular state. Munich had been rescued from the Räte by Reichswehr troops, but von Kahr wanted the Bavarian contingents stationed in Berlin to return home to Bavaria, fearing that in the Reich's capital they would be bolshevized. The new minister of defense, Otto Gessler, however, was able on the occasion of Kahr's visit to Berlin to produce a march-past of the Bavarian troops stationed there that showed them so spirited and well disciplined that Kahr relented and permitted them to remain in the spiritually dangerous terrain of the Reich's capital.

Neither Kahr nor his party colleagues, however, would at any time modify their basic political philosophy based on Bavarian particularism, which held Catholic Bavaria to have a special mission and purpose different from those of the unstable North, especially from those of the alien Prussians. What the leaders of the chief Bavarian parties stood for was a quasi-autonomous state where Bavarian interests were paramount, to be upheld at all costs in any dispute with the central government. The left wing for Kahr, his colleagues, his rivals, and his supporters began with the Social Democrats and ended with Communists, and they wanted no part of any of them.

The national election for the new Reichstag held in June 1920 evidenced the beginnings of the polarization of the German electorate that would dominate the entire life and time of the Weimar Republic. The moderate, prorepublic, government coalition of Social Democratic, Center, and German Democratic parties lost more than ten million votes from their previous totals in the voting for the Constituent Assembly in 1919. Although the Social Democrats remained the largest party, with 102 seats in the Reichstag, their vote was cut almost in half, going down from 11,509,000 to 6,100,000. The vote for the more radical Independent Socialists more than doubled, going up from 2,317,000 to 5,046,000, and the party became the second largest in the Reichstag, winning 84 seats as against 22 in the Constituent Assembly. The Center party lost over two million votes and almost a third of the seats it had won in 1919. The German Democratic party, which, after the Center, had been the largest of the nonsocialist parties and had had six ministers in the coalition cabinet, lost almost half the seats it had won in 1919, dropping from 75 deputies to 39, and the percentage of its vote went down from 18.5 to 8.2. The German Volksparty, founded in 1919 by a former National Liberal, Gustav Stresemann, had turned sharply anti-Left with the slogan: "From the red chains, to make yourselves free / There is only the German Volksparty!" and its percentage of the vote went up from 4.4 to 13.9 and its seats from 19 to 65. The German National Volksparty, to which extreme Nationalists like Helfferich and von Graefe belonged, went up from 44 to 71 seats and from 10.3 percent of the vote to 15 percent.

The rising inflation, the unrelenting demands of the Allies, and the continuing wave of strikes and disorders drove thousands of middle-class voters from the Democratic and Center parties to those with more radical programs. In the same way, the moderate socialists drifted right and left; not only did the Independent Socialists more than double their vote, but the Communists received almost 600,000 votes, electing four delegates to the Reichstag. Within the parties the same polarization occurred. The antirepublican German National People's party that had cautiously backed the Kapp putsch had an influential anti-Semitic wing, but it also had a good many anti-anti-Semites, including Jewish members, especially in Posen and Silesia, and when the Berlin party center printed anti-Semitic leaflets, including one called "The Jews—Germany's Vampires," the party leaders in Silesia and Posen refused to accept them and sent them back.

As a result of the election, the socialist parties were not represented in the new coalition government. The Social Democrats for tactical reasons were not willing to enter the government without the collaboration of the brother socialist party, the Independent Socialists, and they, in turn, refused to join any government that was not entirely socialist. The new government therefore had to be made up of members of parties that had polled fewer votes than the Social Democrats, and the elderly Centrist leader Constantin Fehrenbach, a Catholic who had been president of the Reichstag in 1918, as well as president of the Constituent Assembly, was chosen as chancellor. Otto Gessler, a member of the German Democratic party, became minister of defense; Walther Simons of the German Volksparty, a lawyer who had served in the Foreign Office and had been a member of the German peace delegation at Versailles, became foreign minister; another Centrist, a lawyer and former mayor of Nuremberg, Joseph Wirth, remained finance minister; and General Groener became transport minister. In all, five ministers from the Centrist party, three from the German Volksparty, two from the German Democratic party, and two—Groener and Simons—who belonged to no party made up the Fehrenbach cabinet. It was a weak government, a coalition representing little more than one-third of the Reichstag, which could only remain in power as long as it had the support of sizeable blocs of the opposition.

On the eastern frontier the situation was precarious. Poland attacked Russia in the summer of 1920, and its armies penetrated as far as Kiev. Thousands of deserters from both countries, along with refugees from the war-stricken territories, flocked into East Prussia; 45,000 Poles and Russians were interned there between August and September, and the Poles threatened to invade. When the tide turned and the Russians drove the Poles back to the outskirts of Warsaw, the Reich was confronted with a new threat—the prospect of the armies of the Soviet Union on its borders with far larger forces than the Poles could muster and a revolutionary message and power that would bring the massive reinforcements the Räte had been lacking.

In addition, the Berlin government was faced with problems that could not be met either with the sword or with exhortations. The new minister of economics, Joseph Wirth, calculated the budget deficit for 1921 at over 50 billion marks, a sum that could only mean utter fiscal ruin for the Reich. Nor were any measures or economies available that would make much difference. Erzberger's tax reforms were designed to squeeze income for the government from whatever sources could be found. Among them were income and capital gains taxes and a war profits tax that went up to 70 percent for individuals and 80 percent for corporations, in addition to the indirect turnover and luxury taxes, tariffs, and the like. The capital gains tax was steep, rising to 100 percent on capital that had increased over 172,000 marks. But the government's obligations remained monumental; the national debt had risen from 5 billion marks in 1913 to 153 billion in 1919, with large increases too in the debts of the Länder and local communities. No sensible fiscal policies could be worked out with the constant turmoil in the streets, the diminished productivity of war-worn railroads and industry, and the reparations that alone amounted to more than the entire wealth of the Reich. Nor were reparations negotiable; they might be discussed at various conferences, but essentially the same bill always came back to the Germans.

Early in July 1920, the first postwar conference that included Germans as participants was held in Belgium, at Spa, the wartime headquarters of the German High Command. Again, however, the Germans appeared before the victorious powers as the representatives of a nation hauled before the bar of justice. This time there was no barbed wire around the German quarters, but the delegation that included Minister of Defense Otto Gessler, General von Seeckt, Minister of Finance Joseph Wirth, Chancellor Constantin Fehrenbach, and the Foreign Minister Walther Simons was still kept isolated from the Allied representatives and was jeered at by the Belgians, who came to see them go by in the automobiles provided for them.

A new face appeared in the French delegation. Poincaré's presidency ended early in 1920. Clemenceau ran for election as president but was defeated by Paul Deschanel, who held the Treaty of Versailles to be too lenient. Alexandre Millerand, a former left-wing socialist turned rightist, became premier in Clemenceau's place, and the implacable Poincaré was elected a senator. But French foreign policy remained precisely the same as it had been. The change in the French regime and the appearance of Millerand at Spa made no more difference than had Germany's becoming a democracy.

The Allies had decided what would be discussed and what was out of the question for Germans to be consulted about. The German delegates to the conference could not do much that would gain the approval of the victors. The Allies had wanted General von Seeckt as well as Reich Defense Minister Otto Gessler to be present to talk about the timetable for the reduction of the German army. Seeckt was determined to win, if he could, approval for an army of 200,000 instead of 100,000 men, a figure that General Foch had once thought acceptable. But the Allied decision was for 100,000 men, and the only concessions the Germans were able to obtain were permission to lengthen the time of the reduction by six months—until January 1921—and to cut the coal tonnage to be delivered from 2,400,000 tons a month to 2,000,000. The German local defense units were to be disarmed immediately,* the security police were to be limited to light-caliber weapons to prevent their being used as military formations, and all arms held by civilians were to be surrendered. If the Germans failed to meet any of these provisions, the Allies threatened to occupy more German territory, including the Ruhr.

Although some members of the Allied delegation were impressed with the decorum with which General von Seeckt conducted himself,† he aroused the ire of Lloyd George by his starched military bearing and by wearing his uniform with war decorations, including the Iron Cross. The Germans were handed papers to sign and again they signed. They were still pariahs.

Heinrich Friedrich Albert, a state secretary who attended the conference, told a Reichstag committee that what the German delegation had experienced was no more than a repetition of the *Diktat* of Ver-

---

* The local defense—civil guard—units like the Free Corps had proved essential in putting down bloody revolts like that of the Communist rising under Max Hölz in Saxony in April 1920. Hölz, in a proclamation, had threatened to burn down any city his army occupied and to slaughter all the bourgeoisie regardless of age or sex if the army or police moved against them. But in Bavaria the civil guard had also played a part in forcing the resignation of the government of Premier Hoffmann, and many Germans as well as the Entente leaders regarded them as politically dangerous elements. (Herbert Michaelis, et al, *Ursachen und Folgen*, vol. 4, p. 128.)

† Lord D'Abernon said he thought Seeckt carried through a difficult part like an officer and a gentleman. As Seeckt left the council chamber at the end of the conference that had put an end to the great German army, D'Abernon wrote that he could only admire him as he stood alone, waiting for his automobile, impassive, calmly looking at the audience, the only sign of "the emotion which certainly raged within him ... the spasmodic way in which he chewed the stump of a cigar." (Viscount D'Abernon, *Versailles to Rapallo*, pp. 66, 68.)

sailles.[3] Once, while the Allies were discussing matters among themselves, the Germans were kept waiting in a small anteroom where a cold buffet was to be served. When the Allied representatives returned to the room, they had tea together without offering the Germans any refreshments, and the next day the Germans refused to give them an opportunity to repeat the affront by declining to meet in the same room. Officially, no Allied representatives were supposed to visit the Germans in their hotel, and when one English representative, Lord Malcolm, broke the quarantine and went to the German quarters, it was, as he carefully explained, an exception.[4]

As was often the case in these conflicts of interest and principle, much could be said for the hard-line positions of both sides. The French demanded the coal, they said, because of the destruction of French coal mines during the war by the Germans. The Germans replied that the mines had been destroyed because of military necessity; war, like industry, in the early twentieth century ran on coal and iron, and destroying or inhibiting the enemy's capacity to wage war, while fighting was in progress, followed the accepted customs and usages of all European armies. From the French point of view, however, the Germans were responsible for the drop in coal production, and they were determined that it would be the Germans who suffered from the shortage, not themselves.

The representative of the German coal industry who appeared at the Spa conference, Hugo Stinnes, was not one well chosen to assuage French doubts of German goodwill or their fears of a vengeful, unrepentant Germany. Stinnes, who looked, with his sharp features and pointed beard, as one German historian wrote, like an Assyrian king who should have been riding a chariot, was a remarkable man. He had enormous holdings in German coal processing, mines, and industries, as well as in hotels, shipping, and newspapers, and when, dressed in a deliberately shabby fashion, he introduced himself as "a businessman from Mannheim," he irritated more people than he impressed with his ostentatious modesty. At the conference he made his debut in international politics by telling the representatives of the Entente, "I rise in order to look the members of the enemy delegation in the eye," and then he proceeded to speak of such matters as the "insanity of the victors." It took all the skill of the professional diplomats in the German delegation to placate the anger of the French and the Belgians and to prevent the immediate disruption of the conference, with Foch and the commander of the British army, General Wilson, ready to undertake a march into the Ruhr. The behavior of Stinnes was not calculated to build up confidence in the existence of a new, nonmilitaristic, cooperative Germany. Moreover, Stinnes was celebrated in the German press as a hero, a champion who had at long last appeared to speak up to their oppressors. It was something more than the professional diplomats or the army commanders had been ready to do for a long time.

Even Stresemann, who was a member of one of the government parties, thanked Stinnes for the way he had conducted himself at the conference. And following the Stinnes incident, on July 14, a young man in Berlin proceeded to haul down the tricolor flying over the French embassy to mark the national holiday celebrating the anniversary of the storming of the Bastille. As a result, the German government had to make a formal apology and to order a company of the Reichswehr to march to the embassy and to raise the flag that had been insulted. The Reichswehr company formally did what it was told to do, but entered the grounds of the French embassy in fatigue uniforms and caps (the parade uniforms having been abolished), failed to present arms since that act of militarism had been abolished too, and left the ceremony singing "Deutschland, Deutschland über alles," all in all behaving in such a cavalier fashion that the French were again insulted and demanded reprisals. The German captain was thereupon transferred to a garrison of his own choosing, and a German judge sentenced the man who had hauled down the flag to a fine of 500 marks, which amounted to about 50 gold marks, or some $13.*

No matter which course the government took, there were always those on the Right or Left to condemn it. When the Reichswehr company was on its way to the embassy to hoist the French flag, it was booed; when it returned singing "Deutschland, Deutschland über alles," it was cheered. When the German fleet was sunk at Scapa Flow by its own crews, the German Right applauded what they saw as the heroic deed of the crews, while a Reichstag deputy denounced it as an "unprecedented injustice." The provisions for disarmament demanded at the Spa conference were approved by the Reichstag by an overwhelming majority of the deputies, joined even by the nationalists, not because they liked disarmament, but because they had no alternative, whatever Hugo Stinnes and others like him might dream of in the way of German resistance.

In the years to come, the division between Left and Right would be further complicated by the division of German leaders into those who believed that the policy of fulfillment, of meeting as far as possible the demands of the Allies, was the only practicable one for Germany and

---

* Six weeks later France demanded another apology, this time for an attack on the French and Polish consulates in Breslau by German refugees who had fled from Upper Silesia. Paris wanted 100,000 marks in damages as well as the apology that was delivered by the German Foreign Minister Simons and Carl Severing, Prussian minister of the interior. The French ambassador in Berlin, Charles Laurent, took a relaxed view of the occasion and invited Simons and Severing to have a glass of wine with him, an invitation they accepted. (Carl Severing, *Mein Lebensweg,* vol. 1, pp. 302–3.

those of the opposition both Right and Left who believed that Germany could survive only by actively resisting the never-ending exactions.

The three persons who in their different approaches bore the brunt of these conflicting policies were two civilians, Walther Rathenau and Gustav Stresemann, and a soldier, Hans von Seeckt. All of them were uncompromising patriots. Stresemann had been a Pan-German, an annexationist, a believer in victory until the very end. Rathenau, too, had written in 1914, "We must win, we must"; and in 1918 he called for a desperate *"levée en masse"* of the German people against the Allied armies. By the time of the Spa conference, which Rathenau like Stinnes attended as an expert advisor, he saw no way out for Germany but by way of building bridges to the East and West, to France and the Soviet Union. Although he had had forebodings of a tragic outcome for Germany, he had never doubted the necessity for victory in the war and did his best to organize it. Seeckt the professional soldier was the very glass of fashion of the Prussian officer. He wore a monacle, he was outwardly self-effacing, personifying the general staff maxim of being more than seeming, and he had a fixed purpose when he became head of the Reichswehr in 1920: to use it not only as the ultimate defense of the Reich but to school it for the future, to prepare it for serving as the nucleus of the German army that one day would emerge again as the equal —at least the equal—of any potential opponent.

In their different ways, all three of these men led the Reich, as far as lay in their power, in the direction they believed its salvation lay. Germany was bankrupt and powerless; very well, they must guide it through a bitter time that would not last forever, and while each favored a different course, they were all moving toward the same destination, where Germany would be equal among the powers and as safe and secure as any of them. For each of these three men the Soviet Union would play an important role in the rehabilitation of Germany, although none of them approved of the Soviet government or had any illusions about the kind of cooperation that could be expected from its leaders. But it was inevitable, they believed, that the two pariah nations, both of them relatively passive objects of Entente policy, should find some means of concerting their efforts to throw off the chains the Entente had forged for them.

When in the summer of 1920 the Poles and the Russians were fighting a full-scale war, the problem became acute for the German government. It refused an Entente demand that it permit Allied military supplies for Poland to pass through Germany, not because it supported the Bolsheviki, but because neutrality was clearly in the German interest, as well as one of the few aspects of foreign policy it could control. In the same way, the German government refused to join the Russians, as

Communist leaders suggested it might, in a war against the Poles and thus solve the problems of the eastern frontiers and the Polish territorial demands once and for all. That could have consequences far too dangerous to risk; it would undoubtedly bring France to the defense of Poland and start a new war that could not be fought with any hope of success.

Any German government had to content itself with small victories won only when circumstances were overwhelmingly in favor of the Reich. Some of the disputed German territories holding plebiscites under the terms of the peace treaty not only voted for incorporation in the Reich, but were actually returned to it. One day after the start of the Kapp putsch, on March 14, 1920, 27,000 votes in Schleswig-Holstein were cast in favor of the Reich and only 9,000 for Denmark. On July 11, 96,889 voters in West Prussia opted for Germany as against 7,977 for Poland, and in the plebiscites in East Prussia 353,655 votes favored Germany and only 7,400 Poland. Accordingly, these territories remained German, with only minor modifications. In East Prussia, as Carl Severing noted, despite the overwhelming pro-German vote, the demonstration held to celebrate the outcome of the plebiscite was muted when it was discovered that the Allies had turned over to the Poles six villages on the east bank of the Vistula that had formerly been German. This action foreshadowed what was to happen eight months later when the plebiscite in Upper Silesia was held. Although 707,000 votes were cast for Germany as against 478,000 for Poland, by far the most valuable part of the territory would be awarded by the Allies to Poland.

Walther Rathenau, who for a short time would become one of the two or three most important men in Germany, regarded such events as of minor importance compared with the great design of history he saw unfolding. "The God of War in our day," he had written, "is economic power," and for him the God of Peace was economic cooperation within enterprises and between nations. The industrialized countries, he believed, found themselves in an era of technological change that would not only disenfranchise but dehumanize half their populations if they did not take measures to increase the upward mobility of the workers and thus enable them to achieve the possibility of equality with those who used their labor. What Rathenau foresaw as his version of utopia was a classless, *völkisch* society, or at least an open-ended one, which he called an *Euplutismus*, a plutocracy whose industries were headed by virtuous, conscientious, capable men, whose judges, army leaders, and heads of government were brave and wise, where workers as well as government officials would participate in the decisions of management.

One of the most brilliant and most controversial figures in the postwar Reich, Walther Rathenau was the son of a wealthy industrialist,

Emil Rathenau, an engineer who had founded the General Electric Company of Germany with a modest capital of 5 million marks in 1883. By 1914 he had made it one of the leading companies of the world, with a capital of over 400 million marks, manufacturing everything electric from light bulbs to turbines and locomotives, building railways and street-car lines, with branches in the Orient, South America, and Africa as well as in Europe.

Walther Rathenau was born before his father founded the electrical trust, while the family still lived in a far from pretentious house on Chaussee Street in a workers' quarter of Berlin. The family living space was part of the building where the father and a friend, who was his partner, owned a small manufacturing business turning out steam engines for the gas and water works of the city as well as apparatuses for the Royal Theater and Royal Opera. One of their constructions was a magnificent ship that sailed across the stage in Meyerbeer's opera *Die Afrikanerin*. Walther was the eldest of three children. He had a brother, Erich, on whom their father doted, and a sister, Edith, fifteen years younger than Walther. Erich died at the age of twenty-two while on a trip to Egypt with his father, who never fully recovered from the blow of his younger son's death.

Their mother, Mathilde, born Nachmann, was the daughter of a well-to-do Frankfurt banking family. Brought up in a household visited by the business and intellectual notables of the day, Franz Liszt, Ferdinand Lassalle, and the novelist Bettina von Arnim among them, Frau Rathenau was related to the painter Max Liebermann and was herself a lady of great elegance and cultivation, a puritan, somewhat unapproachable but tranquil and dignified, having what Rathenau's biographer described as "almost the healthy nerves of a peasant." Soon after Walther's birth, Emil Rathenau had sold out his small but profitable business, and before embarking on new industrial ventures, he had visited the exhibitions of the developing wonders of the new era in Vienna, Philadelphia, and Paris, where he had seen the electric light lately invented by Thomas Edison. Emil Rathenau had promptly grasped the enormous possibilities of its use if it were mass-produced, and this he set about doing when he acquired the patent from Edison. He was a man of business, focussed on concrete entities, to be produced if possible in huge quantities. A banker said of him: "He understands and deals with any sum up to 300 marks; after that there is a wide gap in which he is financially blind. Only with 300 million marks does his understanding begin again."[5]

Walther's interests were far more wide-ranging than his father's, and the two were not very close until the death of Erich. It was his mother to whom Walther turned for affection and understanding and who shared his passion for music and the arts. He studied mathematical physics with Helmholtz, chemistry with von Hofmann, and philosophy with Dilthey, and his dissertation was written on "The Absorption of Light by Metals."*

He was as much drawn to letters as to science, to painting as to business, and to metaphysics as to politics. When he was nineteen years old he wrote a remarkable play, *Blanche Trocard*, which was never produced or even shown to his friends, but which was far closer in its commentary on society and its characterization to Ibsen and Wilde than to the run of German plays before Hauptmann. Emil Ludwig wrote of Walther Rathenau that he knew how to paint portraits, design a house, build turbines and factories, write poetry, draw up treaties, and play the Waldstein Sonata.[6] Thomas Edison once said of him, "He knows things I have no idea of,"[7] by which he may have been referring to Rathenau's mystical side as well as to his knowledge of science.†
His contemporaries called him many things, many of them uncomplimentary—"the universal dilettante," because of the dazzling variety of his skills and interests, and "Jesus in a frock coat," because he preached to the German people like an Old Testament prophet while he was holding down the presidency of the electric company as well as membership in some hundred-odd boards of directors of German firms. He was the author of a long list of pamphlets and books, and he wrote regularly for a number of German newspapers and periodicals. He counted among his friends the chief writers of the time, including Gerhart Hauptmann and Hofmannsthal, and he was a frequent guest in circles of the high nobility usually closed to mere financiers, men of business, and unconverted Jews—all of which Rathenau was.

He was also a man of extraordinary perceptions and contradictions. Dark-haired and Semitic in appearance, he revered the blond, blue-eyed northern race of the *Germanen*. They, he wrote, were the *Mut-Menschen*, the race of courage, of derring-do, of depth of soul, as opposed to the *Furcht-Menschen*, the more intelligent people of fear who were the dark-haired races of the South. But it was the *Furcht-Menschen* who were the artists and thinkers of the world—the classical Greeks, as well as Moses and Christ, Luther, Goethe, Beethoven, Rembrandt,

---

* Hermann von Helmholtz was the author of a classical work on the conservation of energy. August von Hofmann's researches into aniline were one of the chief foundations of the dye industry. Wilhelm Dilthey wrote *Critique of Historical Reason*, designed to parallel Kant's path-breaking inquiry into the nature of the natural sciences.

† Rathenau was the original of Robert Musil's portrait of the ultimate cosmopolitan in the novel *Der Mann ohne Eigenschaften*. Musil's character, named Arnheim, is an enormously intelligent, rich, cultivated Jew, who is received everywhere in European society in the days just before World War I. He is one of the dominant figures in a celebrated salon in Vienna to which everyone comes, where the conversation is always brilliant, but where nothing much gets done. Like Rathenau, Arnheim is a man of many parts, a head of great enterprises, author of books celebrated by the *avant-garde*, a philosopher, musician, physicist, and mystic, a prototype of the great man of the future who may lead mankind to a higher level.

Marx, Shakespeare, even the mythological figures of Lucifer and Prometheus.

His *Mut-* and *Furcht-Menschen* were projections of the two souls struggling in his own breast. It was the *Germanen* Rathenau most admired, the northerners, the men of valor, of Prussian virtue, who symbolized a kind of integrity the South had learned about only from them. But it was the *Furcht-Menschen* who had brought the world its religions and culture as well as its decadence, and they had been victorious over the men of courage. The northerners had provided the soldiers and government servants. The southerners were the entrepreneurs, the businessmen operating on their own, and in Germany they had successfully adapted themselves, like Darwin's surviving animals, to the northern culture, where Jews became Germans while remaining Jews. Such views were not very original in Europe at the time; similar ones were held by Nietzsche, Gobineau, and Houston Stewart Chamberlain, among many others, and Rathenau's early opinions on the ambiguous place of Jews in German society were so close to those later adopted by Adolf Hitler that they would be quoted by Nazi writers as evidence that the Jews themselves recognized their essential differences from Germans. Rathenau, in an article called "Hear, O Israel" (Deuteronomy 6:4), had written as a young man that the Jews were a foreign body in the Reich, an oriental people in the midst of the *Germanen*, with alien ways of thinking and acting, and only years later did he revise this view to include the German Jews among the Germanic tribes, something, he wrote, between the Saxons and Swabians. He declared himself German to the core. "I have no blood," he wrote, "other than German, no other tribe and no other people."[8] At the same time, he was uncompromising in identifying himself as a Jew. Although he believed in the Christian revelation and—no doubt to the consternation of many of those present—quoted a text from the words of Jesus at his father's funeral, he refused to convert to Christianity. In a letter to Lili Deutsch, his friend of many years,* writing of Spain and the Sephardim, he told her they must one day visit Seville, "our home."

He was a man of many contradictions, but not where Germany was concerned; the Reich was the center of his universe, and it was this love affair with Germany that haunted him all his life. When Frau von Hindenburg urged him in 1922 to accept the post of foreign minister, he wrote in response that he and his forefathers had served Germany as best they could, but as she knew, like every Jew, he was a second-class citizen. "I could not be a political official," he wrote, "or in peacetime even a lieutenant. If I had changed religion, I could have been freed

---

* Lili Deutsch, Rathenau's great love if such he had, was the sister of the American banker Otto Kahn and the wife of Felix Deutsch, one of the chiefs of the German General Electric Company.

of these disabilities, but I would also, as I see it, have thereby aided the criminality of the ruling classes."[9] Like his friend the shipping magnate Albert Ballin, who was also a Jew and a friend of the kaiser's and who took an overdose of sleeping tablets[*] rather than survive the German defeat in 1918, Rathenau completely identified himself with his German Fatherland. Germany was much more his mistress than Lili Deutsch. For this reason he rejected Zionism; Germany, not a Jewish state in Palestine, was his homeland.

He discovered the genius of Ludendorff early in the war, Ludendorff the *Mut-Mensch*, and through him he hoped to be able to reach the ear of the high command with his ideas of a civilized peace of accommodation for Germany and for Europe. Rathenau was convinced of the ineluctable interdependence of peoples and nations; in the twentieth century, no country could prosper separately from the others, no economy could thrive if the others were failing. After the war, when French policy, it became clear, was directed to keeping Germany impoverished as well as powerless, Rathenau was convinced that this was as great a calamity for France as it was for Germany and, indeed, the entire industrialized world. Therefore, at Spa, together with his friend the Minister of Finance Joseph Wirth, he took the first steps toward the policy of fulfillment, which would enrage men like Stinnes along with those far more dangerous to Rathenau and the ideas he cherished than Stinnes would ever be. Stinnes wanted no part of fulfillment, and at Spa he called Rathenau a *"fremdrassige Seele"* ("a soul of foreign race"). Stinnes could on occasion look favorably on some of Rathenau's views, but it was the "foreign soul" that served most readily to explain their basic differences on the course Germany should take.

"Fremdrassige Seele" was an epithet that would stick.[†] Rathenau might feel himself as thorough a German as any Ur-Prussian, or the member of any Germanic tribe, but he would never be able to convince his detractors of this or perhaps himself either, which may explain his talking about "home" in Seville. When he ran for office a deputy in the Constituent Assembly, he was given an unpromising place on the ticket and was soundly defeated in an election that was not without anti-Semitic overtones. Whatever he attempted to achieve on behalf of the Reich he loved so well, he was always met with a chorus of derision and the epithet *"Fremdrassiger"* by the right-wing opposition whose mores he regarded so highly. Once he was even proposed as president of the republic in a telegram sent by some Germans living outside the

---

[*] Ballin was in ill health and suffered from insomnia. He left no suicide note, but he had written: "Better an end with dread than endless dread" (*Lieber ein Ende mit Schrecken als Schrecken ohne Ende*). (Lamar Cecil, *Albert Ballin*, p. 347.)

[†] General von Rabenau for one, later to be killed by the Nazis, used it to characterize Rathenau in his biography of Seeckt, *Seeckt—Aus Seinem Leben*.

Reich, and the nomination was greeted with hoots and shouts of laughter in the National Assembly. These were affronts he deeply resented but to which he could reply only in articles, in letters to friends, and in the continuing emendation of his evolving metaphysics.

His only direct political experience would come by way of appointment. Before the war, in 1907 and 1908, he twice accompanied State Secretary Bernhard Dernburg to German East and Southwest Africa and wrote a report on the colonies' economic and political importance to the Reich that impressed the then chancellor of the Reich, Prince von Bülow, as well as the kaiser. Rathenau, who moved in the society of court circles, had been presented to the kaiser in 1901, and he continued thereafter to see and admire him. The two men had much in common in their veneration of Germanic virtues as well as in personal charm, conversational gifts, and kaleidoscopic interests. Also, Wilhelm, like Rathenau, was a *Furcht-Mensch*, and Rathenau perceived that the kaiser had to struggle with the same kind of conflicts in his nature that Rathenau himself knew all too well. Wilhelm might be admirable, "a true prince," as Rathenau wrote, but Rathenau was sure he was not the man to lead Germany to victory.[10]

Although Rathenau remained devoted to the kaiser and to the monarchy, his relationship to Wilhelm, too, was ambivalent. He wrote a piece, "The Kaiser," in 1919, repeating what he had said at the start of the conflict, that Germany could not hope to win the war under the leadership of 1914. He wrote: "The moment will never come when the kaiser, as world conqueror, will ride through the Brandenburg Gate with his paladins on white horses. On that day world history would have lost its meaning. No! Not one of the great ones who went into this war will outlast the war."[11] What he wrote was true enough, but it would also turn into his own death warrant.

Rathenau approached politics as he did business, in the perspective of an all-embracing philosophy that brought not only refractory objective contradictions but also his own inconsistencies into some kind of order. A man of great wealth and erudition, he could reconcile himself to his advantages only in a wide social context. By what right, he asked rhetorically, did men like himself lay claim to their advantages at the expense of a proletarian caste condemned to drudgery, working without a spark of creativity and with no hope of escaping from their galleys, since the possibility of both education and wealth was denied them? The highest human values, he thought, could be achieved only by working without self-serving, material goals; what was godlike in man was selfless, a spiritual realm where man was able to develop a soul that transcended his ego, where through love and self-abnegation he became part of a higher order. "We are not here," he wrote, "for possessions, but for the glorification of the godly in the human spirit."[12]

The conflict in the industrial order he saw repeated in political and social struggles. It was not armaments that produced a great power, it was the economic, intellectual, and spiritual energies of a people. Political boundaries could be maintained only if the people were up to them; while the blockade was a most deadly weapon of war, it was far less so than the intellectual and moral isolation of a nation. Although Rathenau had written at the start of the war, "Germany must win, it must," he had added, "and [it] has no pure, eternal claim on victory." That had not been the case, he thought, in the other wars fought in the nineteenth century—in the German struggle for existence against Napoleonic France, in the war against Austria in 1866, or in the war for German unity in 1870. The World War he saw as contaminated, but he nevertheless did everything he could to help win a German victory. He was appointed by Minister of War von Falkenhayn to organize the provisioning of raw materials, which were short in Germany at the start of the war, some of them so short that Rathenau was told by an officer in September 1914 that the army could fight for only a few months longer unless some way was found to obtain nitrogen, which was cut off by blockade. He was an innovator in structuring a planned economy; the rationalized use of raw materials a wartime measure that would soon be universally adopted.

Rathenau never faltered in his belief in a German victory, but he was critical of a number of major policies adopted by the high command, among them the decision in 1917 to wage unrestricted submarine warfare. His reverence for Ludendorff declined when Ludendorff demanded the all-out U-boat war that Rathenau was certain would bring the United States into the conflict. But at the end, instead of asking for an armistice, a move that he thought ill-timed, he wanted to call for a *levée en masse*, a summoning to the colors of every German either to serve at the front or behind the lines in industry or agriculture. With Russia out of the war, Rathenau was convinced Germany could avoid a Wilsonian peace that would destroy her. The stiff-necked position, too, was a count against him for enemies he could never appease, for whom Rathenau was not only a *Fremdrassiger* but one of those who wanted to continue the slaughter, a *Kriegsverlaengerer* ("war prolonger"). Ludendorff thought no better of Rathenau's suggestion for a *levée en masse* than Rathenau did of Ludendorff's U-boat war, saying a mass rising would produce more confusion than manpower. But Rathenau no more than Ludendorff or Hindenburg could accept the German defeat when it came.

His plan for reconstructing the Reich after the collapse was basically simple. Since not material but moral qualities were the dominant factors in shaping the greatness of a country, Germany's first task must be to depollute the poisoned atmosphere of the war; it must reestablish relations with the East, with the Soviet Union, and at the same time it must find ways of reconciliation with France. The Reich could help rebuild the Soviet Union with German technology and trade, and at the same time it must convince France that it was in her own interest to have a responsible, productive Germany on her borders, prepared to pay reparations to the best of her ability and to join with France in solving their common problems.

With this in mind, Rathenau proposed that the sum of German reparations be fixed; otherwise industrial leaders could make no plans for the future, and Germany would be forced to respond to Allied claims instead of taking the initiative in setting reparation figures. Many German industrialists, however, objected; if the Allies set a lump sum, they could also raise it as Germany's economic situation improved, and at Spa Stinnes was ready to see Germany bolshevized and the Rhineland and Ruhr occupied rather than submit to the Allied blackmail on the amount of coal to be delivered. That his own rich domain in the coal fields would thereby remain unimpaired was noted by Rathenau and others who favored a policy of fulfillment and negotiation, but it is not clear that Stinnes was thinking only of his own economic interest. If Germany were bolshevized, Stinnes believed, that would bring the Russian Revolution to France's own doorstep, and she would be compelled to take a more reasonable view of the limits to which the Reich could be driven. A Communist Germany in alliance with the Soviet Union would also become a military and propaganda force to be reckoned with, and the French would have to take such a potential buildup into consideration too.

For Rathenau there could be no question of surrendering Germany to Bolshevism. He saw the Russian Revolution as a façade covering the power politics of the oligarchy ruling an agrarian people, and while he had read Marx and rejected his materialistic interpretation of the dynamics of history, he nevertheless took a benevolent view of the revolution made in his name.[13] Rathenau told a friend that he himself was Bolshevik by night but not by day, or not yet by day, when he saw workers and company officials dutifully at their jobs in the factories. He was the founder with some friends of a Study Commission on the Soviet Union, which sought to find a way to aid Russia to become a truly agrarian republic with a thriving trade with Germany. His solutions of the reconcilement of French claims with the realities of Germany's ability to pay were hardheaded and unideological. More than eight million acres of French land had been ruined, temporarily at least, in the course of the war; 300,000 houses had been destroyed and 60,000 more damaged. Rathenau proposed that half a million highly skilled German workers, whose wages would be paid by the Reich, be sent to France to repair the damage and to restore the land to production. That would help diminish German unemployment and French suspicions of the Reich's intentions at the same time. After he became minister of reconstruction, he worked out with Louis Loucheur, who was Rathenau's opposite number in the French government and like Rathenau a successful industrialist, an arrangement by which the German and French businessmen would deal directly with one another; German deliveries would be made to French firms without going through their respective government agencies. German firms were to deliver what the French ordered (up to 7 billion marks) and be paid by the German government. This, Rathenau believed, either would be practicable and a step toward satisfaction of French claims or would surfeit the French market with German goods it could not absorb. It was in fact the latter that proved to be true; French industrialists at the end of a year had ordered only 19 million marks' worth of goods, a far cry from the demands for hundreds of billions.

The main obstacle to Rathenau's hope to appease France lay in the fact that, for Poincaré, Millerand, and the French High Command, reparations were not designed for economic ends, but were intended to bleed Germany white, to make it impossible for the German people, including the twenty million Clemenceau said were too many, to gain more than a subsistence living. Since the reparations figures were always unrealistic in terms of what could actually be paid, they were also designed as a device, a springboard from which the French could take off to occupy the Ruhr and Rhineland when the Reich was unable to pay. French claims were so enormous that they appalled many reasonable people in the Allied camp, politicians as well as economic experts, and they were mainly claims on billions of gold marks the Germans did not have. In January 1921, the French minister of finance had suddenly fixed the total bill of reparations at 212 billion gold marks, with interest, plus 12 billion to be paid annually to amortize the balance. During the first twelve years the Reich was to pay from 2 to 5 billion marks a year interest, and after that, 6 billion a year for thirty-one years. The German Expert Commission of which Rathenau was a member suggested to their government that it offer as a counterproposal to take over the debts owed the United States by the Allies. The Fehrenbach cabinet rejected the idea, and instead, Foreign Minister Simons made a counteroffer to pay a total of 53 billion gold marks. Calculating that 20 billion had already been paid, Simons proposed to pay an additional 30 billion marks, 8 to 10 billion to be raised through loans, the remainder to be paid over a period of five years.

The German foreign minister was not only talking to the Allies, but had to talk a language acceptable to the Germans, too, and when he did that he had to deny that Germany was solely responsible for the war, a denial that could only confirm the built-in French doubts of German contrition. Simons's offer the Allies regarded as an affront, and as a result French troops were ordered to occupy the cities of Düsseldorf, Duisburg, and Ruhrort. Simons then made another proposal that fell on deaf ears: he suggested to the United States that the Reich place itself unreservedly under American tutelage to accept whatever sum the United States determined, the amount to rise as the German economy improved. Washington declined and declared itself ready only to forward any German offer to the Allies. The Allied Supreme Council then changed the figures. Meeting in London, it lowered the total of 212 billion gold marks to 132 billion and the yearly rate of payment to 2 billion gold marks plus a contribution of 25 percent of German exports. This again was presented to the Reich in the form of an ultimatum, to be met within six days.

The terms of the London ultimatum made no economic sense to Rathenau, and he was convinced they made no sense for France and the Allies either. Their acceptance, he calculated, would mean a reduction of 40 percent in the real wages of every German worker; 2 marks an hour would be taken out of their pay for every eight-hour day. No German government could carry out such terms, and if it attempted to, the workers could hardly be expected to spend almost half their time working, not for themselves and their families, but for a foreign country. Nevertheless, the Reich had no alternative but to accept the ultimatum if it was to stave off an Allied occupation of the Ruhr. The Reichstag approved the London terms by a small majority, but as a result the Fehrenbach cabinet had to resign. Wirth became chancellor. He appointed four members of the SPD to his cabinet and asked Rathenau, the German Democrat, to become minister of reconstruction.

It was a difficult decision for Rathenau. If he accepted the post, he would not only have to bear the personal attacks of men like Stinnes, to say nothing of the hard-line right-wing and anti-Semitic press, but also, because of the conflict-of-interest doctrine to which he held himself, he would have to resign from all his industrial jobs. If he turned down the post, he could pursue his multifarious business affairs and his writing, as he had in the past, or he could retire to a country estate and bring his ideas on the future of Germany and Europe into focus. His mother begged him not to accept the minister's portfolio, and at one point he did actually refuse it, but on reflection he finally decided to accept. He resigned his presidency of the electric company and his membership on the various boards of directors as well. He was entering, he told the Reichstag, a cabinet of fulfillment, in a government, he believed, that could find the means of laying the foundations for an era of European reconciliation and cooperation.

The reconciliation was, however, far easier to blueprint than to realize. Rathenau was minister of reconstruction for only three months. When the Council of the League of Nations decided on October 20, 1921, that the results of the plebiscite in Upper Silesia, where almost two-thirds of the population, including thousands of Jews, had voted to remain part of Germany, had to be reconstrued and the richest and most populous part of the territory awarded Poland, the German Democratic party in protest withdrew its ministers, Rathenau among them, from the Wirth cabinet.

The decision of the League Council was another hard blow against which the Weimar Republic could do nothing but protest. The Polish partisan leader Korfanty, a former Reichstag deputy, had led his bands, with the full support of the Polish government, into the disputed territory in May 1921, two months after the plebiscite had been held, in the weeks when the reparations dispute was at its height. If Berlin sent in Reichswehr detachments against him, France threatened to occupy the Ruhr, and French troops that were supposedly patrolling Upper Silesia to insure law and order until the results of the plebiscite determined its status took no action to control Korfanty. The Italians, however, who by 1921 had lost much of their wartime fervor, especially in areas where Italy had no interest, made some effort to keep the peace, and Lloyd George in the House of Commons called for "fair play," saying that it was unfair that Germany be forbidden to dispatch troops into Upper Silesia to restore order.[14] As it turned out, the *Einwohnerwehr* under General Karl Hoefer were able to defeat the Polish irregulars after hard fighting that lasted from May 21 to June 6, but this had no effect on the interpretation of the plebiscite that had been held on March 21. Since with the English-French-Italian split, the Allied Supreme Council was unable to decide on what course to take, the problem was turned over to the League Council, which accepted the French and Polish view that most of the disputed territory must go to Poland.*

Wirth was forced to dissolve his cabinet, but he was able after four days to form a new one in which he himself took over the portfolio of minister of foreign affairs until such time as Rathenau might be in a position to accept it. Wirth had need of Rathenau. Not only did he have the highest respect for Rathenau's judgment, but Rathenau also had developed good personal relationships with a number of important figures in the Allied camp, among them Loucheur, the French minister of reconstruction, and D'Abernon, the British ambassador to Berlin. Another was André Gide, who on reading Rathenau's book on Raphael, had written to him suggesting that they meet. They spent two days

* The League of Nations assumed jurisdiction of the dispute under the provision of its charter that interpreted the situation in Upper Silesia as a threat to peace and international comity. A commission of four countries—Belgium, Brazil, China, and Spain—made the recommendations that were then accepted by the League Council and the Allied Supreme Council.

together on the estate of a friend of Gide's in Luxemburg, and Gide noted in his journals what an extraordinary man he had encountered. Rathenau had talked, not of politics or business affairs, but of religion and art and man's relationship to the higher powers. Wirth had sent him to London to seek a loan, because the Reich could not meet the reparation payments it had just agreed to; and while Rathenau tried in vain to convince Lloyd George, the governor of the Bank of England, and financial leaders in the City to make the loan, he nevertheless succeeded in persuading Lloyd George that the reparations payments due in 1922 should be reduced by half a billion marks. At the same time he was working on far-reaching plans for the reconstruction of Russia through a consortium of the Western powers together with Germany, and for a peace pact with Belgium and France that would guarantee the security of France on the Rhine—the forerunner of Locarno. Wirth also sent him to Cannes to meet with the Reparations Commission and the Allied Supreme Council, a meeting that was brought to an abrupt end by the fall of the Briand cabinet* but not before Rathenau had addressed it eloquently in both French and German on behalf of solutions that he was convinced would be sensible for the Allies as well as for the Reich.

Four months after Rathenau quit as minister of reconstruction, Wirth asked him to accept the portfolio of the Foreign Ministry. Again Rathenau had to struggle not only with himself but with his mother, who begged him to decline the post. He eventually accepted and told his mother, "I had to because they haven't found anyone else."[15]

Albert Einstein, when he heard the news, said that Rathenau would accept the papacy if it were offered to him, and added that technically he would very likely do a good job, too.[16] It was the kind of comment that Rathenau would often hear; even many of those who admired him thought him ambitious and—behind a cloud of high rhetoric—self-seeking. An acquaintance, Wilhelm Herzog, described the celebration of Rathenau's fiftieth birthday in the Hotel Adlon in 1917, where Rathenau addressed his guests for an hour on the subject of his own achievements. Rathenau, Herzog wrote, had brought his secretary along to take down the speech, and two weeks later it appeared as a brochure under the imprint of Fischer to be presented to those who had attended the birthday party.[17]

Whatever his motives for accepting the post, once he did he single-mindedly set out on his policy of German and European reconstruction by way of rebuilding Germany's lines of communication with East and West. He had no easy task; there were the great goals to pursue and endless minor irritations to endure; in the course of two months, he told the Reichstag, he had to answer a hundred notes, demands, or com-

* Aristide Briand had become French Prime Minister in January 1921 and resigned in January 1922.

plaints from the Allied Military Commission. Germany and the Soviet Union had been outcasts too long for the health of Europe; France and England were far from thriving; and in England, increasing resentment over France's self-serving decisions had been made clear in Lloyd George's remarks about "fair play." Not only was an "economic conference" needed, but a European economic conference that would include as active participants both the Reich and the Soviet Union.

The greatest gathering of European statesmen since the Congress of Vienna was called to meet in Genoa in April 1922 to resolve some of the problems confronting them all. Invitations went to twenty-eight countries including the Soviet Union and the Reich, hitherto both held at arm's length by the Allies. Lloyd George led the British delegation, Barthou represented France, Chicherin the Soviet Union, and Wirth and Rathenau Germany. Poincaré, who was again prime minister, did not attend, but he prevailed upon Lloyd George to agree in advance that no discussion of the Treaty of Versailles, German reparations payments, or disarmament—precisely the questions most important to the Germans and in the long run to the peace of Europe—would be placed on the agenda.

As for the Soviet Union, it had stubbornly refused to go away: the counterrevolutionary movements had failed; it had just turned back a dangerous Polish attack; and voices were heard in Berlin, Paris, and London that spoke in favor of closer economic ties with Russia. Not only had Rathenau's study group been at work to discover how relations with the Soviet Union might be improved, but since January 1922 a Russian delegation had been in Berlin to discuss a trade treaty with Germany. The negotiations had been broken off, but on their way to Genoa the Russian delegation headed by Chicherin had stopped off in Berlin and again made it plain that they would be pleased to work out a treaty with the Reich. Rathenau, however, did not wish to present the Genoa conference with a *fait accompli*, and the treaty was again set aside. As for Russia, Rathenau believed it was not so much a matter of supplying her with what she needed, since the Soviet Union needed everything; the question was much more what German firms could afford to deliver and, parenthetically, what the Soviet Union could pay them and how.

Rathenau was not the only one in the Reich thinking about collaboration with the Soviet Union. Seeckt, too, who had no high regard for communism, nevertheless agreed with Russian military leaders that both countries could greatly benefit from closer relations. Since mid-1921 sporadic talks between officers of the German and Russian armies had been held. Seeckt had met Karl Radek in December 1921 and had succeeded a month later in getting Chancellor Wirth's approval for continuing negotiations on some form of military collaboration. Not only did the two countries complement one another in their productive capacities, but they were also both faced with heavily armed coalitions that threatened to destroy them. Working together, they might well reweight the balances.

This is what the Allies saw too. A German-Russian alliance was one of Poincaré's recurrent nightmares. He had opposite plans for the Soviet Union—to use it as an additional means of keeping the Reich in its powerless place. But French policy was inhibited by the nature of its postwar alliances. France had a pact with Poland, whose independence had been one of the keystones of the anti-German and anti-Soviet coalition, and France had not only done everything in its power to ensure the acquisition by Poland of the richest part of Upper Silesia, but she had also provided military aid for the Poles against the Russians in the war that had just ended. It would have been impossible to work out a pro-Polish and a pro-Soviet policy at the same time, and Poincaré did not attempt to do this. But what he did attempt was to make use of the Soviet Union against Germany. At Genoa the Allies revived the right of Russia—but a non-Bolshevik Russia had been in mind—under the Treaty of Versailles to receive reparations from Germany; reparations that would be used for the repayment to the Allies of the tsar's loans, which had been mainly raised in France and had gone down the drain when the Bolsheviki had announced they would not pay them. But the Soviet Union, with the passage of time, seemed to have become more flexible. The loans, Moscow had said, could not be recognized so long as the Great Powers did not recognize the Soviet Union, and in Genoa the Allied representatives thought something might be worked out.

Thus Moscow found herself for the first time in many years in a position where she could choose between two suitors, neither of which was greatly in love with her. But in a speech delivered in French so heavily accented that many present thought him to be speaking Russian, Georgi Chicherin cast a heavy curtain of gloom over the hopes of the Allies. He spoke in favor of disarmament, the taboo subject. Russia, he said, would dismantle its armed forces provided other countries did the same. And having read his speech in French, Chicherin proceeded to give it again, this time in his version of English.

It was a speech packed with dynamite, and it blew up, as Chicherin no doubt intended it would, any French pretensions of serious interest in the subject of disarmament except as it applied to Germany. Barthou made an emotional but feeble reply to the Russian heresy, protesting against any discussion of disarmament in his name, in the name of the French delegation, and in the name of France. Chicherin rose to his feet again to remind Barthou that not long before in Washington, Briand had cited as one of the chief obstacles to France's cutting down on its armaments the existence of a large Red army, and now here were the

Russians offering to disband their armed forces provided other countries did the same.[18]

Barthou, four years after the end of the war, no longer had a united Allied front to support him. The chairman of the conference was Italian Premier Luigi Facta, representing a country that had been deeply aggrieved by French failure to live up to the secret agreements with Italy, and Facta sternly told Barthou, who still had much to say, that he could not speak again, that the subject was finished. The affront to French high politics did not, however, prevent the Allied delegations from meeting with the Russians to urge again that the Soviet Union claim its share of the reparations from Germany which, under Article 116 of the Versailles Treaty, it was entitled to while the Germans were precluded from making any counterclaims.

Rathenau, though, true to his principles of reconciliation with East and West, tried to reach the French. On the first day of the conference he asked Graf Kessler and Carl Bergmann of the foreign office to meet with Jacques Seydoux of the economic section of the French Foreign Office to discover under what conditions Germany might be able to obtain a loan of four billion marks to help meet the reparations costs. Seydoux agreed with the Germans that this might be accomplished; but the plan had to be shelved after the shock of the announcement of the signing of the Rapallo Treaty by the Reich and the Soviet Union, a document that would overshadow everything that happened at Genoa.

Before Rapallo, Wirth and Rathenau had been confronted with a new, dire possibility, that the Russians would join the Allies in their demands for funds the Reich did not have and that Germany would find itself more isolated than ever, with the Russians again, as in 1914, in the camp of the opposition. The Soviet delegation, however, had no intention of playing the game according to rules laid down by Poincaré, and the Soviet negotiations with the Allies may well have been designed mainly as a show to apply pressure on the Germans. The Russians had come to Genoa to get economic aid and political recognition and to use the conference as a propaganda platform for the Communist cause. From the beginning, Lenin had been one of the chief deriders of the Versailles Treaty. His own regime had had to fight for its existence against armies for which the Allies had supplied money, equipment, and manpower, and he had fewer illusions about the good intentions of the Allies than did Rathenau.

As the Genoa conference opened, Barthou had proposed that the five "inviting powers," France, Poland, Belgium, Italy, and Britain, were alone to sit on all four subcommittees, while the "minor" powers, including the Soviet Union and Germany, should be invited to attend only specified ones. This proposal was voted down, but the Russians could not misinterpret the French attitude toward them.[19] When Chicherin invited the Germans to come to the villa in Rapallo where the Soviet delegation was staying to resume discussions of the treaty that had been ready for signature in Berlin before the delegations left for Genoa, Rathenau and Wirth had little choice but to accept. Chicherin had informed Baron von Maltzan, *Staatssekretär* in the Foreign Office who strongly advocated a Russo-German pact that an agreement with the Entente was imminent. The Soviet Union would either be ranged on the side of the Reich or in the French camp, and the Allies' negotiations with the Russians threatened to isolate the Reich more strictly than ever before. Wirth, more than Rathenau, was in favor of making the treaty with Russia. Rathenau's great design required a bridge to both East and West, not to the Soviet Union alone and not at the price of further alienating France. But under the circumstances he had no alternative, and he signed the treaty.

The Rapallo Treaty was essentially a peace treaty; after Brest-Litovsk and Versailles, the first to be made that was not imposed by one side on the other. It renounced for both countries all war claims, both private and public; it reestablished diplomatic and consular relationships; and it provided for trade and economic development on most-favored-nation terms. Both countries were to take into benevolent consideration the economic needs of the other, and Germany agreed to provide the Soviet Union with goods and services through private enterprise aided by the Reich government.

The American ambassador to Italy, Richard Washburn Childs (the United States was not represented at the conference), said the pact would shake the world, and so it did. Many of those present at Genoa were convinced it contained secret military clauses, although a military agreement would have been farthest from Rathenau's purposes. It was he who had prevented the signing of a trade treaty with the Soviet Union before Genoa, because it would have affronted the Allies and side-tracked the European consortium he had in mind from collaborating in the reconstruction of Russia. But the treaty was a dreadful portent, and the French were furious. Barthou called Wirth a liar, Poincaré was convinced that Russia had agreed to lend military aid to Germany, and Lloyd George told Wirth that the Germans had damaged the very principle underlying the conference.

The French delegation set about immediately and ostentatiously to pack their bags and prepare for leaving. Some of the German delegates were so distressed by the reaction that they asked that the treaty be declared null and void, but Rathenau and Wirth held firm, as did the Soviet delegation. Wirth maintained that the treaty in no way damaged German relations with any third state, that on the contrary it symbolized the goal of the conference to put aside the spirit of the past and to take the steps that would lead to a common, peaceful reconstruction of

Europe.[20] Lloyd George was a very good actor and his show of anger may well have been exaggerated, since he was far from enthusiastic about much the French were doing and to see Poincaré checked for once could not have been very painful.* As for Rathenau, in his closing speech to the conference, and the last he would hold before an international audience, he said, "The history of Italy is older than that of most European nations. More than once world movements have developed on this soil. Again, and hopefully not in vain, the people of the earth have raised their hearts and eyes to Italy in the deep conviction to which Petrarch has given deathless expression: 'I go through the world and cry: Peace, Peace, Peace!' "

Italian Foreign Minister Schanzer succeeded in keeping what remained of the conference alive. Rathenau agreed that Germany would renounce its right to sit in the subcommittee meetings when it discussed relations with the Russians, although the Reich would participate in all its other meetings. Poincaré made a speech at Bar-le-Duc on April 24 threatening military sanctions against Germany, with or without the support of France's allies. Lloyd George replied that if England had to choose between the Entente and peace, it would have to revise its attitude to the Entente, whereupon the French press broke out in a rage of vilification; even the moderate French journalist Philippe Milliet wrote that Europe would have peace only "when it vomited Lloyd George."[21]

Although the Genoa conference made little or no progress toward solving Europe's economic and political dilemmas following World War I, the Treaty of Rapallo was another matter. It produced what looked like a mutation in the European body politic, presaging basic shifts in the postwar imbalance of power. Germany and the Soviet Union had broken through the *cordon sanitaire* erected by the victors. They remained relatively weak, but the treaty nevertheless cast the shadow of an emerging force that would undoubtedly have to be reckoned with. Although no secret treaties were signed at Rapallo, the published document in itself was a statement of collaboration that ran directly counter to the overriding aims of France and, to a degree, of Britain, too. If Germany and the Soviet Union concerted their economic and political forces, the Treaty of Versailles and France's elaborate postwar network of security were doomed.

The reverberations of the treaty caused a rising Italian politician, a former socialist, Benito Mussolini, to pay a visit to Rathenau in Berlin. Mussolini had been elected a member of the Italian Parliament in 1921 with forty other members of his Fascist party, and he wanted to discover

---

* On the subject of French postwar policies, Lloyd George had said: "Poincaré knows everything and understands nothing, Briand understands everything and knows nothing." (Erich Eyck, *Geschichte der Weimarer Republik*, p. 269.)

at first hand what the meaning was of this dangerous treaty with Moscow. He assured the German foreign minister that he would defeat communism in Italy and that the fascism he was preaching, unlike communism, was not for export across the Italian border.[22]

The Rapallo Treaty was clearly a beginning; it had no military clauses, but it would soon lead to a considerable degree of military collaboration. It was a landmark for the Reich, but it met with mixed reception in Germany. President Ebert, for one, was unpleasantly surprised by it. He had not been consulted and he made plain his displeasure to Wirth and Rathenau. He and the majority Socialist governments under him had long borne the brunt of Communist attacks, and his party paper the SPD *Vorwärts* declared that as a result of Rapallo the Reich was completely isolated. Ebert called the treaty imprudent and unconstitutional, and he wanted to dismiss Baron von Maltzan from the Foreign Office for his conspicuous part in negotiating it. And while the Reichstag approved the treaty, it was anathema to many members of the Nationalist Right, though not to men like Seeckt or Stinnes or representatives of German industry, who promptly understood its implications for the future. Five hundred members of leading German firms in a meeting of the German-East European Economic Association (*Deutsch-Osteuropäischer Wirtschafts-verband*) expressed their approval of Rapallo, the one way, they said, of rebuilding Germany and Russia, not to mention their own firms, and the Leipzig Chamber of Commerce sent a telegram to Chancellor Wirth calling the treaty "a long-wished-for act of great political and economic importance." In Berlin a vast demonstration of German workers, including Socialists as well as Communists, demonstrated in favor of the treaty that they believed promised jobs and wages with no deductions for reparations.

But Rapallo also touched off an outburst of anti-Semitism that rocked Germany. The June issue of *Die Konservative Monatschrift* called Rathenau a representative of international Jewry and added that the honor of the Reich should not be an article of commerce "for international Jewish hands."[23] The sources of this rabid anti-Semitism were to be found in relatively small, fanatical, "patriotic" groups that invariably had many enemies besides Jews. More than 300 political murders had been committed in the first four years of the Weimar Republic, one of the most sensational being that of Erzberger in August 1921. Erzberger was not a Jew, but he was anathema to the same "patriotic" organizations that were denouncing Rathenau for making the sinister treaty with the power that had been behind the Räte governments and the attempts to subvert the entire Reich. Murder or attempts at it had become a part of the political process in the Weimar Republic, and the terrorists might strike anywhere, anytime. Only a little more than two weeks before Rathenau was killed, an attempt was made on the life of the SPD leader Philipp Scheidemann by some would-be killers who threw prussic acid at him. Scheidemann was not a Jew either, but he was a politician whose principles distressed his would-be assassins. Fortunately, however, they did little damage to their intended victim and were caught and sentenced to ten years' imprisonment.

Ernst von Salomon, who was a member of the *Organisation Consul* and who took a minor part in the plot to assassinate Rathenau, tried later to describe what the superpatriots were trying to accomplish. He said it was true that many of those who were slated for assassination were Jews, but that the real enemies were those who favored the policy of fulfillment, those who wanted to continue to carry out the policies of defeat. Rathenau, he said, was on the list because he was one of them, not because he was a Jew. The *Consul*, Salomon wrote, was, to be sure, anti-Semitic, and he had received letters from the German writer Ernst Jünger, as well as from people he did not name in Palestine, asking why he did not admit that Rathenau had been killed because he was a Jew. Salomon said he did not admit it because it was not true; one could almost say Rathenau was killed despite the fact that he was a Jew, because like Erzberger he favored the detested policy of fulfillment. Salomon wrote that Captain Ehrhardt was enraged when he heard of the assassination, saying it had demolished his entire political line.[24] But while the victims of assassins might be Jew or Christian or heathen, the epithet "Jew" summed up the rancors of the ultranationalists in a handy fashion. In Upper Silesia, the Self-Defense Corps sang a song: "Knock off this Walther Rathenau / The god-forsaken Jewish sow."[25]

Helfferich, who had been the chief opponent of Erzberger in the Reichstag, had turned his venom on Rathenau. Helfferich was not an anti-Semite, but he had an ecumenical detestation of all those who differed with his brand of 100-percent patriotism. Rathenau, in addressing the deputies, had praised the Saarländer for their steadfastness despite the continuing separatist pressures from the French occupiers of the Saar. He told the Reichstag that as Germans they could be proud of the Saarländer for holding fast to what was most precious to them—their Germanism—and Helfferich, one of the most uncompromising enemies of fulfillment, answered Rathenau by saying that the Saarländer had been betrayed and forsaken by their government. It was men like Rathenau who had brought deprivation and misery to countless people and had driven countless others to despair and suicide: they had surrendered large and valuable segments of the national capital to foreign countries and destroyed the foundations of the economic and social order.[26] Rathenau was shaken by the speech, and his supporters would link it to his murder. Actually, though, it had no direct effect on the plot; the speech was made on the day before Rathenau was killed and after plans for his assassination had been completed.

The wave of hate and resentment against Rathenau and the Rapallo Treaty was, however, engulfed in the tide of approval that surged through Germany. Huge crowds estimated at 150,000 people demonstrated in favor of the treaty in Berlin, and similar demonstrations occurred in other cities. But many important political decisions in the Germany of the bleak years after World War I were not determined by majorities or coalitions in the Reichstag, which also approved the treaty. Much of the country was too shaken, too divided, too frustrated to be content with parliamentary procedures. Rathenau, like many, very likely most, politicians, from the time he had taken office had received threatening letters, and now they came in greater numbers to be read in the context of political murder as a means of making and preventing policies. Wirth heard from a Catholic priest who visited him in the Reichschancellory that Rathenau's life was threatened. Impressed with the earnestness of the priest, Wirth warned Rathenau, who visibly paled as Wirth told him what he had heard. But Rathenau soon regained his composure, put his hands on Wirth's shoulders, and said, "Dear friend, that's nothing. Who would really want to do anything to me?"[27]

The night before he was murdered Rathenau spent at a dinner at the American embassy in Berlin given by Ambassador Alanson Houghton and then in a talk that lasted until four o'clock in the morning with Hugo Stinnes, who disagreed often enough with him but at the same time admired many things he stood for.

The actual instigators of the killing were boys. The plans began with a seventeen-year-old youth, Hans Stubenrauch, who was enormously impressed by the opinions of men like Ludendorff and Helfferich and who may have had some connection with them. Stubenrauch was a schoolboy, the son of a general, and at the precocious age of seventeen a member of a conspiratorial group, the Society of the Just (*Der Bund der Aufrechten*). He and a friend, another student, Wilhelm Günther, a young man with marked psychotic traits who had been previously convicted of desertion, started to make plans for the murder. Stubenrauch said he wanted to kill Rathenau because of Ludendorff's criticism of his pamphlet on the kaiser. Günther was in contact with a man by the name of Erwin Kern, a former naval officer and a member of the *Organisation Consul*, and with a friend of Kern's, Hermann Fischer. Both twenty-five years old, both blond and blue-eyed, Kern and Fischer took over the plot. They added to it, not the boys who had first planned the assassination, but Ernst Techow, twenty-one years old and a fellow member of the *Consul*. Techow was the son of a Berlin magistrate and, like Kapp, the grandson of a forty-eighter who had battled on behalf of the revolution against an autocratic Germany. Techow brought into the conspiracy his younger brother Gerd, sixteen years old, who had joined the *Consul* a year before, when he was fifteen. Kern, Fischer, and Techow were the assassins, and Salomon, together with a number of other members of the *Consul*, were to help them escape.

They gunned down Rathenau in gangster style as he sat in the back seat of his open car on a curve of the Königsallee where the chauffeur had to slow down. Kern pumped bullets into Rathenau from an automatic pistol, and then Fischer threw a hand grenade into the rear seat. A young woman, a nurse, witnessed the attack and rushed to Rathenau's side, but he died soon after they arrived at the police station 300 meters away.

Rathenau on occasion had carried a gun, but he had dismissed three policemen assigned to guard him. He had seen no point in such ostentatious protection, and also he had a strong mystical bent. Death, he had written, is an appearance; we experience it only because we have our eyes on the limb, not on the whole living structure. The leaves die but the tree lives, the tree dies but the forest lives, the forest dies but the earth that nourishes and consumes its children is green. If the planet dies, then a thousand similar ones bloom under the rays of new suns.[28] In the whole visible world we know no death. Nothing essential on earth dies. Only appearances change . . . Further, he had had a premonition that he himself had come to the end of the line. He had written a few weeks before his death, "There is really not much left of me, the flame burns down."[29]

Rathenau's death caused a volcano of emotion to engulf the Reich. He was killed on June 24, a Saturday, and on Sunday something like a million people filled the Lustgarten in Berlin and marched solemnly in columns through the West End from early morning to late afternoon under black, red, and gold banners of the republic. Similar demonstrations took place in Hamburg, Leipzig, and other German cities, where hundreds of thousands of people assembled to express their grief. The Reichstag met on Sunday in a tumultuous session. Shouts of "Murderer!" and "Throw the murderer out!" greeted Helfferich when he appeared, and while the president dutifully admonished the delegates, saying that every deputy had the right to be present, he was answered with catcalls and with shouts of "Not murderers!" Order was restored for only a short time, when Chancellor Wirth, a Catholic and Centrist, rose to pay tribute to his dead foreign minister. At the end of his speech, Wirth repeated the well-known phrase, "There is the enemy, where Mephistopheles strews his poison in the wounds of a people. There is the enemy—and let there be no doubt—this enemy is on the Right."[30] The tumult began again and continued until Helfferich was forced to leave the building.

Two days later, on Tuesday, June 27, Rathenau's body lay in state in the Reichstag, and all over Germany work was stopped as the unions called out their members for twenty-four hours. Frau Rathenau sat unflinchingly during the ceremonies, her face, as one observer said, like one carved in stone. The next day she wrote a letter to the mother of the man who had driven the car from which the shots that killed her son had been fired. She wrote: "In unspeakable pain I stretch out my hand to you, most unhappy of women. Tell your son that in the name and spirit of the murdered one, I forgive him, as may God forgive him, if he makes a full confession before an earthly court and repents before God. Had he known my son, the noblest person on earth, he would have aimed the murder weapon at himself rather than at him. May these words give your soul peace. Mathilde Rathenau."[31]

Techow, arrested on June 29, was the sole survivor among the assassins. Kern and Fischer were unsuccessful in escaping to Sweden. Three weeks after the murder, Kern was killed by the police, who surrounded their hiding place, and Fischer committed suicide. Of the three, only Techow stood before a court. Convicted and sentenced to fifteen years in prison as an accessory to the crime, he was released after he had served a little over four years.*

Of the accomplices, Techow's brother Gerd was sentenced to four years one month, Willi Günther to eight years, Waldemar Niedrig to five years, Salomon and two others to two months, one Karl Tillessen to three years, and three others to various sentences of two years to two months. Two were found not guilty.

It was a violent time. Governments and courts took a lenient view of political crimes, including murder. One judge spoke of the mitigating circumstances and of the laudable national sentiments of Arco when he killed Eisner, and when Erzberger's two assassins escaped to Hungary, which refused to extradite them, a former naval officer accused of helping them was freed by a German court.[32] A plausible explanation of such judicial behavior is to be found in the circumstance that the judges, like other German officials, were almost to a man to be found on the anti-Left side. They were paragraph men, men of order, and they, too, were appalled by the excesses of the Räte, the brutality that accompanied the Spartacist uprisings, and the disturbances that accompanied the general strikes. As a class they sympathized with those who were trying to undo the defeat and to break through the provisions of an unjust treaty, and while they deplored violence and murder, the motives of those who were violent had to be taken into account in accord with German and European law. It was one thing to kill in order to turn the Reich into an un-German Soviet republic, another to kill those who wanted to restore it to its former eminence. Thus the courts would deal leniently during

---

* The German historian Erich Eyck wrote that according to reliable reports, Techow did come to repent his part in the crime. After his release from prison, he joined the French Foreign Legion and later attempted to help Jewish victims of the National Socialist persecutions. (Erich Eyck, *Geschichte der Weimarer Republik,* p. 297.)

the lifetime of the Weimar Republic with what the political government called the enemy on the Right, Adolf Hitler among them.

As a result of the Rathenau murder, the Reichstag, much closer to the mood of the people than were the courts, passed a law "For the Protection of the Republic." It came under Article 48 of the constitution and provided that the government could prohibit gatherings and demonstrations that could unlawfully threaten the republic or a state, or threaten violence to a citizen. Fines and imprisonment were provided for anyone who openly advocated overthrow of the republican form of government or who calumniated its officials or the republic or the Reich colors. A special court was constituted to try such cases, the State Court for the Protection of the Republic. In addition, sentence of death or life imprisonment could be imposed on any participant in a gathering that aimed to do away with members of the republican government of the Reich or of a state, and anyone who knew of such a gathering and did not report it could be sent to prison. As a result, a number of right-wing organizations, including the Stahlhelm and the Pan-German Association, were temporarily dissolved.

Bavarian Minister of the Interior Franz Schweyer, however, did not want to use the new law against Adolf Hitler and his National Socialists. Bavaria, Schweyer said, was strong enough to deal with Hitler, whose movement was needed against the Marxists, who were still powerful in Bavaria and threatening revolution in neighboring Thuringia and Saxony. So while the National Socialists were proscribed as dangerous to the republic and Hitler was forbidden to make political speeches in Prussia, Baden, Saxony, and other states, the party continued to flourish in Bavaria. Its numbers had grown to more than 55,000 as Hitler hammered on his themes of anti-Marxism and anti-Semitism before audiences that saw no difference between them.

The National Socialists were but one of many ultranationalist, activist, splinter groups in Bavaria and elsewhere in the Reich calling for punishment of the "November criminals" and for a march on Berlin to overthrow the cowardly, incompetent republican government. Kapp had wanted to do that, as had the murderers of Erzberger and Rathenau and of 300-odd other political figures who had been assassinated. The National Socialists, however, had one striking advantage over their rivals in the right-wing movement—Hitler's gift of oratory, which he and his hearers had suddenly discovered when he addressed military audiences and the meeting of the German Workers party early in 1919. "The spinner" of the war years had at long last found his calling in a narrow circle of dedicated antirepublican, anticapitalist, anti-Marxist anti-Semites. To the vast majority of Germans he was, where he was known at all, still a ranting, absurd figure, a drummer for a political sideshow. But for a relatively small group of people he had a mighty compelling message.

His fury and his hatreds, repeated as *leit-motive*—what much later the world would call his oratorical charisma—were aimed at people very much like himself, "the terrible simplifiers" who exchanged with one another easy answers to hard questions. It was a politically, culturally, and socially unsophisticated audience. The complicated analysis of establishment politicians, economists, and political scientists or of the cloudy, "intellectual" Marxists was not for them; they were *völkisch*, racist *Germanen*, and they subsisted on half-truths, shreds of learning, and an unshakable belief in a world conspiracy against them and against the Fatherland made in their image.[*]

In 1923, 53 percent of the National Socialists came from the countryside and less than one-quarter from big cities. They were mainly recruited from among craftsmen, technicians, employees, and blue-collar workers whose skills were threatened by the mass production of big business. Less than 10 percent of the members in this National Socialist Workers party identified themselves as "workers." What they did have in common were youth and what much later would be called *machismo*. Only a little more than half—52.2 percent—were over twenty-three years old, and only a little more than 4 percent were women.

For these party comrades, Hitler could never talk too long or repeat himself often enough. Other anti-Semitic, antirepublican, and anti-the-slavery-of-interest speakers might address their audiences with endless harangues on the same subjects, but Hitler brought his hearers to their feet with his overwhelming, hysterical passion, shouting the same message they had heard over and over again, that they had been done in by traitors, by conspirators against the German *Volk*, by Communists, plutocrats, and Jews. He was preaching to the converted or to those ready to be converted, to men who had never been able to swallow the defeat on top of the vast complications of a malfunctioning industrial society and who were looking for revenge against the plotters who had brought such deep trouble on them and on the Reich. Fringe people like them had been around for a long time, and Hitler's newly discovered mission of rescue was greatly aided by the inability of Europe to get on with the job of reconstruction and, above all, by the French design to return Germany to the negligible political position it had held in the days of Richelieu.

When late in 1922 the Reich failed to deliver half of the 200,000 telegraph poles owed France under the reparations agreements, Poincaré

---

[*] The figures show that 81 percent of party members lived in southern Germany as against 18.4 percent in the North, but since the party was proscribed in Prussia and Braunschweig in 1922 and 1923, many of its northern members were registered in Munich. (Michael H. Kater, "Zur Soziographie der frühen NSDAP," in *Vierteljahrshefte für Zeitgeschichte*, April 1971, pp. 124–59.)

gave the long-planned, long-awaited order for French troops to march into the Ruhr. On January 10, 1923, the French and Belgian governments announced that they were sending engineers into the Ruhr to oversee the production of the German coal syndicates and that a contingent of troops would accompany the engineers to guarantee their safety. It was not, the French said, a military operation or occupation but merely a security measure on behalf of the reparations owed them.

It turned out to be a good deal more than that. Five French and one Belgian division marched into the Ruhr on January 11, 1923, first occupying Essen and Gelsenkirchen and then fanning out until the whole territory of more than 3,300 square kilometers and three million inhabitants was placed under French rule. They moved in with full military equipment, including heavy artillery and tanks, and when they entered a city like Essen, they would set up machine gun posts at strategic points— at the railroad station and on the roofs of houses overlooking squares— as though an enemy counterattack were imminent. Mines and supplies of coal and coke were requisitioned; the customs was taken over, as well as the railroads, ships, and every other means of transport; hundreds of German officials were put in jail; and when demands for supplies were not promptly filled, private individuals—Fritz Thyssen was one of them —were held responsible and even arrested.

The whole nation, Left, Right, and Center, gave voice to its indignation; observers said no such unity had been witnessed since August 1914, but the German government could do little to channel the emotions of solidarity that rose from what every section of the country felt to be an intolerable outrage. Military resistance was unthinkable. The government saw its only weapon in passive resistance, a resistance where miners would refuse to mine, railroads would not run, and nothing the French wanted would be delivered. The population of the unoccupied parts of the Reich was called on to contribute to the support of the people of the Ruhr. These measures provided some outlet for the universal revulsion to the invasion, but Adolf Hitler, the greatest, as people would say one day, of the *völkisch* psychologists, would have none of them. He refused to support passive resistance in the Ruhr, and articles appeared in Bavarian newspapers charging that he, like many Germans at the time, was on the French payroll. But for Hitler the most dangerous enemies were to be found, not in Paris, but in Berlin. For him, the despicable Reich government of parliamentarians and of the Left was the source of Germany's misfortunes. It had to be dealt with first; after that the foreign enemies would have their turn.

The German mark, which on December 31, a little more than a week before the occupation of the Ruhr, had stood at some 7,300 to the dollar, plunged, recovered, and then reached new lows almost daily. On January 31 it was 49,000 marks to the dollar, in June it was 74,000, in July

160,000, in August over a million, in September almost 10 million, in mid-October a quarter of a billion, and by the end of October it was over 130 billion. What had been a bad inflation became a frightening, devastating avalanche that flattened economic life. Workers, when they were paid their wages, threw the stacks of bills out of the factory windows into the waiting hands of their wives, who would rush with the bundles of marks to the markets before the price of bread or coal or whatever went up again. The government overprinted new figures on the mark notes already in circulation as prices doubled, trebled, quadrupled, and then went out of sight.

Millions of people on fixed incomes or working for wages who could not keep up with the skyrocketing prices faced starvation and ruin. In December, a Bavarian paper gave one example. A doctor, the paper said, earned 32 million marks for a consultation, paid for by the German health insurance system. That 32 million marks would buy one piece of coal the size of a hen's egg. Since twenty pounds of coal a day were needed to heat one room, no doctor could afford it even if he had 200 consultations a day. Bread cost almost 2 billion marks a pound, and a bar of soap cost twice what the doctor earned in a week. People, the paper went on, who had food often could not afford to cook it, what with the price of cooking gas in the billions; many were reduced to eating raw cabbage leaves. Children could not leave their homes because they had neither shoes nor stockings, and the rooms they lived in were unheated. Bed linen, shirts, and underwear wore out and could not be replaced. Families pulling wagons made trips to obtain wood in nearby forest areas, and they often had to sell it to get food instead of burning it. Newspapers and local governments appealed for help, and help poured in. People brought old clothes and even new ones to collection centers to give away, but disease, especially TB, rose sharply as temperatures went down and nourishment declined.[33]

Stefan Zweig wrote a short story called "The Invisible Collection" (*Die unsichtbare Sammlung*) in which a retired, blind official of the Forestry Service with a notable collection of rare prints—Rembrandts, Dürers, and such—proudly asks his daughter to show his treasures to a visiting bookseller. Actually nothing but empty mats and miscellaneous papers remain in the folders where the prints had been stored. The wife and daughter have been forced to sell the priceless collection to keep the family alive, for the pension the old man is paid is not enough to buy more than a slice of bread. They have sold the prints for sums that would ordinarily have supported them for years, but now everything is gone, the money in a few weeks, the prints forever. The old man, however, still thinks his treasures are safe and a certain bulwark against the future.

The effects of the inflation were felt everywhere. When Minister of

Defense Otto Gessler went to supper at the house of the new chancellor, Wilhelm Cuno, they were served a little bread and some hard wurst along with a good wine. That was all, Cuno's housekeeper told Gessler, they had in the house.[34] In October a lunch in a simple restaurant cost a billion marks; a few weeks later it would cost several billion. Savings were wiped out—the entire hard-earned resources of a frugal people who had counted on them for the rainy day that was now at hand. The economy had not done badly during the early months of the inflation. Business was thriving and unemployment was low, but the Ruhr invasion put intolerable strains on the Reich. If passive resistance was to work, the resisters and their families had to be supported, and nothing much was coming out of the Ruhr either for France or for Germany. After six months of occupation, the tonnage of coal and coke delivered to France (478,000 tons of coal and 500,000 tons of coke) was scarcely more than twice what the Ruhr had produced in the first eleven days of January before the French occupation.[35]

The Ruhr invasion may have been a harsh and brutal operation, but it worked well for Poincaré. British leaders* were critical of it as they had been of the other French invasions; the British member of the Reparations Commission said, referring to the missing telegraph poles, that no more damaging use of wood had occurred since the Trojan Horse.[36] The United States, tired of the endless European power struggle that had seemed so simple in its rights and wrongs in 1917, withdrew its troops from the Rhine bridgeheads they had held. But the only result of such protests was that the French took over the American bridgeheads while the British remained where they were, in enclaves of peace and order most welcome to the Germans.

The French were hard masters. In Essen French troops fired on Krupp workers, killing thirteen of them and wounding scores more. A few months later a French court tried, not the perpetrators of the shooting, but some of the chief members of the Krupp firm for having incited the workers to violence. The head of the firm, Krupp von Bohlen und Halbach, was sentenced to fifteen years in prison and a 10-million-mark fine. Two other directors got twenty-year sentences and the same fine; others got lesser sentences. Although unarmed workers had been shot down, the official French view upheld by the military court was that it was

* Lloyd George had been replaced as prime minister by Bonar Law in October 1922, when the Conservatives withdrew their support from his government because of what they regarded as his imprudent backing of the Greeks against the Turks. Here, too, in the Greco-Turkish conflict, the British and French had considerable difficulty composing their differences, and when in February 1923 Lloyd George denounced the Ruhr invasion, he was violently attacked in the French press. "England," wrote *L'Homme Libre*, "begins to understand that Lloyd George is a traitor," adding: "The leader of England during the time when he was opposing German hegemony was no more than a German agent charged with watering down the victory." (*L'Homme Libre*, February 11, 1923.)

the French troops who were being attacked. In the same vein, Poincaré asked rhetorically in a speech justifying the Ruhr invasion: "Can England be surprised if we defend our borders against a new rape?"[37]

Nor was the German resistance always passive. Some of the same stripe of young gunmen who were active in combatting the republic put their talents to work against the French and the Belgians in the Ruhr. Acts of sabotage were committed, sentries were shot, and troops were stoned. Reprisals followed. When a Duisburg bridge was blown up and nine people in a Belgian compartment of a train were killed, seven Germans were tried before a French military court in Mainz and executed for the act. In an Essen hotel, a young German businessman, Albert Leo Schlageter, was arrested for planning sabotage; he was tried before a French military court and sentenced to be shot. Despite Hitler's opposition to the Ruhr resistance, Schlageter was adopted by the National Socialists as the party's martyr, and in 1931 they raised a monument to him in the Schwarzwald. Schlageter had to share his posthumous glory with the Russian heroes of the revolution, for Karl Radek, too, extolled him as a "good soldier of the counterrevolution who deserved to be honored by the Communist soldiers of the Revolution."

German papers reported regularly on French and Belgian activities. They carried accounts of civilians who were beaten, shot, or raped by occupation troops, many of whom were black colonials; of banks and stores plundered; and of thousands of Germans arrested, hundreds of whom were sent into exile and some of whom were shot as hostages.* The Germans accused the French of being trigger-happy. One German describing what he saw, or wanted to see, said that the French never walked alone on the streets. When they marched, they marched apprehensively in the middle of the road with their heads down. A reporter for the *Manchester Guardian* writing from Trier told how the French soldiers commandeered the hotels and brought their families, including distant relatives, with them to live off the country. Black troops in red cloaks and turbans were among the occupiers, and one had to rub his eyes, the correspondent wrote, to be sure in a city where the churches were 1,700 years old he was really seeing Muslims pushing its inhabitants from the sidewalk.[38]

The German passive resistance was heroic and long-suffering, but the cards were stacked against it. The Berlin government could not support the policy of no deliveries from one of the richest parts of the Reich,

---

* In the first six months of the occupation, the Reich government reported that 92 Germans were killed and 71,000 were expelled from their homes in the Ruhr. (Otto Gessler, *Reichswehrpolitik in der Weimarer Zeit*, pp. 246–47.) By September, when passive resistance was abandoned, 132 people were dead, 150,000 had been expelled, and economic damage to the German economy was estimated as running between 3½ and 4 billion gold marks. (Cuno Horkenbach, *Das Deutsche Reich von 1918 bis heute*, p. 175.)

and Poincaré, who cared nothing about invectives or about resistance that was merely passive, had only to hang on, which is what he did. The Reich now had to buy coal from abroad with gold marks or foreign currency, and it still had bills to pay; more than 200 million gold marks were due Belgium between March and June for reparations. The Reich could not pay such sums from its gold stores and shore up the crumbling mark at the same time, nor could it defend itself or its borders except by such means as passive resistance. As the crisis deepened, it could not support even passive resistance. So in their different ways both Hitler and Poincaré were undoubtedly right. Poincaré could enforce his own terms for assuring Ruhr deliveries, although he could not deliver either the territory itself or the Rhineland, the Palatinate, or Bavaria to a separatist movement. And Hitler could concentrate his fire on the domestic enemies, since they were the only ones who were vulnerable to his kind of attack.

Three separate German governments tried to deal with the crisis. The first was that of Wilhelm Cuno, who succeeded Wirth in November 1922. Cuno had no political experience and no party affiliation. He had been Albert Ballin's successor as head of the Hamburg-America Line as well as a leading treasury official during the war. He had a considerable reputation in business and financial circles, and his lack of political experience was the chief reason for President Ebert's appointing him to head a government that Ebert hoped could meet the overwhelming economic problems without the political commitments of the party leaders. But Cuno broke under the strain. He lasted ten months before the Social Democrats in the Reichstag forced a vote of no confidence against him. Completely exhausted, he had to give up his post.

No one among the men of business, the politicians, or the generals could deal with the battered state of the Reich in 1923. There were too many irreconcilable conflicts. The country could neither live in peace nor wage war, and the parties turned wearily from one chancellor to the next without any effect on either foreign or domestic troubles. Cuno was succeeded in August by the leader of the German Volksparty, Gustav Stresemann. The world would soon come to regard Stresemann as one of the major European statesmen of the 1920s, but his two cabinets would last only three months before he was replaced by the Centrist Wilhelm Marx. As for the role of the generals against the foreign and domestic enemies, it was on the whole moderate and sensible, if arrogant. Seeckt's biographer, General Friedrich von Rabenau, says that the commanding general of the Reichswehr had considered ordering armed resistance against the French in the Ruhr. Rabenau's book was published, however, in 1940, during World War II; it had to be tailored to National Socialist tastes, and the assertion seems unlikely. The Poles in 1923 were threatening an invasion of Upper Silesia, and the 100,000-man Reichswehr would have had no chance whatever of fighting successfully against both the French and the Poles.

Seeckt did say to the British ambassador that if the French attempted to march from Dortmund (which they had occupied) to Berlin, they would have to wade through a sea of blood, by which he doubtless meant that he intended to resist with all the means at his command any attempt by France to conquer the entire Reich. To this end he permitted the clandestine recruiting of volunteers to increase the army's manpower. This was the so-called Black Reichswehr, a force that could be organized the more readily since the Allied Control Council was no longer functioning, owing to the German resistance and the inter-Allied rancors that accompanied the Ruhr invasion. These short-term volunteers, together with the army and the patriotic formations, including, no doubt, those raised by the left-wing movements in Saxony and Thuringia, could all have been used against the Poles or in a life-and-death struggle against France. But there could be no notion of armed resistance against the overwhelming forces that France could deploy for anything less than a last-ditch stand on behalf of the survival of the Reich, and Seeckt is unlikely to have seriously entertained one to defend the Ruhr alone.

Seeckt succeeded in his paramount aim of keeping the troops aloof from the raging political dissension. When at a cabinet meeting he was asked by President Ebert where, with Germany sorely beset on all sides by the French, by the risings of the Separatists they subsidized,* and by the threats from the radical Left and Right, the Reichswehr really stood, Seeckt answered laconically, "The Reichswehr stands behind me." The statement may have been some consolation to the government in Berlin, but what Seeckt was offering was only negative support. The army would not stage a putsch against the republic, but how it would be used in an emergency, Seeckt's words made clear, depended on the military, not the political leadership.

It was the survival of the Reich that Seeckt was single-mindedly determined on, and it was the sole purpose of the Reichswehr to ensure it. Any talk of a putsch from either side left him cold. At another cabinet meeting, after he had sat silently for two hours listening to discussions of the perils ahead, he finally asked to be heard. He said, "Gentlemen, in Germany no one can make a putsch aside from myself. And I say to you I will not make one."[39] He was, however, in his own mind a candidate to become Reichschancellor, and he drew up a sixteen-page pro-

---

* Repeated attempts were made by Separatists in the Palatinate, the Rhineland (where they printed Rhinemarks), and other regions to seize power while the French troops were in occupation. In Bavaria, where the French also entertained hopes of a separate state, a Professor Georg Fuchs, who for fifteen years had been music critic for the *Münchener Neueste Nachrichten*, was arrested with a number of accomplices for high treason. At his trial Fuchs testified he had been paid more than 100 million marks (at the old rate) by the French to further his separatist activities.

gram intended for a cabinet that would hold the Reich together against separatist movements pushing outward and revolution threatening to destroy the center. It was a temperate program, acknowledging the need for paying reparations but upholding the necessity for maintaining passive resistance and German political independence against England and France. He also called for cooperation with the Soviet Union abroad and a strong anti-Marxist line at home.[40] Seeckt's allegiance was, as it had been at the time of the Kapp putsch, to an abstraction—the unity of the Reich and of the army. The government that happened to be in power was relatively unimportant; it could be overthrown, and if it was left-wing it probably should be, but the overthrow had to be accomplished by acceptable means; it had to be the work of patriotic men expressing the will of the German people, by which Seeckt meant the will of the German nationalists. It was an army officer's formula, and it excluded any power bloc of adventurers left or right. Seeckt himself had none of the drive for personal power that marked men like Ludendorff and Hitler or even Kapp, and he never worked to build a political base for himself. Seeckt's biographer says that at one point President Ebert considered naming him chancellor, and Seeckt was actually given plenary, dictatorial powers late in 1923 by Ebert and the Stresemann government, but he made not the slightest attempt to use them for his own political advantage. And while it was true that the Reichswehr stood behind Seeckt and that Seeckt would defend the civil government against any putsch, not all the high command of the army stood behind him or behind the Berlin government.

The chief of the Reichswehr divisions in Bavaria was General von Lossow, a Bavarian who was under strong pressure from his own inclinations as well as from his state government to represent Bavarian interests when they conflicted with those of Berlin. In Lossow's view, as well as that of the civil government, the nationalist formations in Bavaria, including the National Socialists, were useful, if not essential, for the preservation of Bavaria's anti-Marxist character. Other states might outlaw the National Socialists; Bavaria would not. Furthermore, Lossow told Seeckt on a visit to Berlin in April 1923 that the "patriotic" units had access to 51 percent of the weapons at hand. The millions of rifles, machine guns, and other weapons that had been produced in the course of the war had never been entirely destroyed or handed over to the Reichswehr for its uses or for delivery to the Allies. Enormous stores of them were still available throughout the Reich, many of them, to be sure, unusable from neglect and improper storage, but a good proportion still intact, still lethal, and accessible to left-wing radicals in Thuringia and Saxony and to right-wing radicals in Bavaria. Lossow was unwilling to take possession of the caches of such weapons by force; on the contrary, he thought they provided an arsenal for patriotic groups he could call on in an emergency.

When 5,000 of Adolf Hitler's National Socialists demonstrated on May 1—the day when the left-wing formations paraded their strength—they were armed by weapons secured under various pretexts from barracks of the Bavarian Reichswehr. The guns had been obtained through the Reichswehr connections of Captain Röhm, a political advisor on the staff of the Free Corps leader Colonel von Epp and one of the leaders of the paramilitary units in Bavaria. Röhm had explained they were needed for maneuvers and had obtained the ammunition from stores separate from the guns. When the army and the Bavarian police discovered that the National Socialists were armed to the teeth, they took the guns away from them to prevent a bloody clash between Left and Right. But the Bavarian government took no further steps against Hitler, and the party still had access to large stores of illegal weapons, although ammunition was often lacking or of the wrong caliber. Röhm, who would become one of Hitler's most trusted adjutants, was also a well-known homosexual who made no secret of his love life. Hitler would later excoriate him for his "vice," but he made no objection to it for some ten years.

In 1923, Röhm was one of the cadre of officers and former officers who lent their energies to building the armed formations of the Right. Also among their number was General Ludendorff. Ludendorff and his second wife were both rabidly anti-Semitic, and his normally ultranationalist sentiments had been greatly intensified by the leading role he had played in securing an armistice when he believed all was lost at the front. Although he never joined the National Socialist party—that would have been beneath his dignity—he believed in all its main principles, and he was as ready to cooperate with Hitler as he had been with Kapp and Lüttwitz. Ludendorff's influence in Reichswehr circles was, however, limited to a few higher officers like Lüttwitz and to a number of the younger Reichswehr soldiers for whom he was one of the archetypal war heroes. Otherwise he was held at arm's length. When the Ruhr invasion started, he had "offered" to General von Seeckt the assistance of the *Kampfverbände*—organized military formations of right-wing groups that included the SA (*Sturm Abteilung*), the Storm Troops of the National Socialists, *Bund Oberland, Bund Bayern und Reich*, and so on—an offer that Seeckt had flatly declined. Seeckt would have nothing to do with military formations outside the control of the Reichswehr. Neither he nor the other officers of the high command would ever rely on them, as the subsequent history of the SA would reveal. But it was through the *Kampfverbände* that Hitler and Ludendorff could cooperate, and although the high command of the Reichswehr was unimpressed with their military potential, the name of Ludendorff continued to exert a considerable influence on a number of individual officers and men of the Reichswehr and of the volunteer formations.

By the autumn of 1923, the Berlin government was faced with crises on every front. Separatist demonstrations with both open and covert French assistance took place in Aachen, Cologne, Wiesbaden, and Trier. Communist leaders in Saxony and Thuringia made common cause with the Social Democrats and entered the local governments, while directives went out from the Central Committee in Moscow for uprisings in the streets. In Küstrin in Pomerania, a major in the Black Reichswehr attempted a ring-wing coup planned to end with a march on Berlin, and in Bavaria the Reich was on a collision course with the *Land* authorities, including the commander of the Bavarian Reichswehr.

For the Bavarian government, Marxism was the chief enemy, and Berlin, in its view, was infiltrated with Marxists and similar godless people waiting to seize every opportunity to encroach on Bavarian prerogatives as a state in her own right and to liquidate her liberties. The Bavarian right wing, in its turn, was awaiting the call to march on Berlin and to sweep aside these un-German, un-Christian conspirators against public order. They wanted not the separate state that Poincaré envisaged so much as a semiautonomous Bavaria and a reliable—that is, a rightist, non–Social Democratic—government in Berlin. Although Bavarian Minister-President von Knilling agreed with Stresemann that passive resistance must be abandoned, on the day before the Reich was to announce it was being given up, the Bavarian government proclaimed a state of emergency and Gustav von Kahr was appointed general state commissar with semidictatorial powers. The Berlin government then had no alternative, when it learned of Bavaria's action on the night of September 25–26, but to declare a state of emergency for the entire Reich, giving plenary powers to a civilian, Minister of Defense Otto Gessler, rather than to Seeckt, whose appointment might have seemed a challenge both to the Allies and to Bavaria.

And there was no lack of emergencies. A few days later, the Küstrin revolt occurred. On September 30, a Major Buchrucker, who had been active in recruiting "Work Commandos"* (the cover name for Black Reichswehr formations), called out the garrison in Küstrin to rise and march on Berlin. Only a handful of followers heeded the summons. Buchrucker was arrested by the local Reichswehr commandant, sentenced to ten years' fortress confinement, and released long before his term was up. And as a result of the attempted coup, the Black Reichswehr was

---

* The Work Commandos were recruited as civilians but wore army uniforms and lived in military barracks. Their theoretical enemy was the foreign foe, but they were very likely to see him in the Prussian police, who served a socialist state and were nearer at hand than the French.

ordered disbanded. Then the left-wing radicals in Thuringia had their turn. A meeting of the Congress of Industrial Councils (Räte) called for the mobilization of workers, employees, and government officials in groups called "Hundreds" (*Hundertschaften*), against the "fascist reaction" they were convinced was preparing in Bavaria to take over the Reich. The Communist party at long last approved its members' joining forces with the Social Democrats in the Thuringian and Saxon governments, and on October 10 two Communists entered the government of Minister-President Erich Zeigner in Saxony. Zeigner said the Communists' participation in his government was needed to forestall the danger of a dictatorship of big capital.

The German Communist party had received its new directives from Moscow. As later disclosures would reveal, Soviet Foreign Minister Litvinov and the central executive committees of the Third International and of the German Communist party had seen the Ruhr invasion and the widespread disaffection in the Reich as another opportunity to spur on the revolution, and in mid-September had ordered that full advantage be taken of the unstable situation. Litvinov told the Moscow meeting that the developments in Germany were advanced enough so that an armed rising was only a matter of weeks away and that the party was to mobilize all its resources to compel a revolutionary solution.[41] The Central Committee in Moscow called on the Communist parties in Saxony, Thuringia, Hamburg, Anhalt, and Brunswick to work together with the Social Democrats to sharpen the German crisis and to provoke the Reich into marching troops into Saxony. Then the armed resistance in Saxony by workers' brigades would spread to the entire country.

In Bavaria, right-wing groups saw their chance to sanitize the Reich and rid it of its alien bodies. With the appointment of the Communist ministers, the Bavarian government broke off diplomatic relations with Saxony, thus giving additional evidence to Zeigner and the Communists that the Right was organizing a "fascist" invasion. Zeigner was convinced that the Berlin government was basically on the fascists' side, prone to harsh measures against the Left while at the same time it tolerated treasonable activities in Bavaria. Zeigner exaggerated the one-sidedness of the Central government, although there was truth in the accusation that the scales were often tilted by judges and government officials, who were likely to be as anti-Marxist as any other solid citizens.

Nevertheless, Stresemann's government was trying with every means at its command to maintain the republic against extremists of both camps, a strategy that, as Seeckt pointed out, the Reichswehr was not strong enough to carry out. It could not fight against both Left and Right at the same time, although this is what the political arm of the government soon had to do.

Reacting to the Reichswehr's hostility to the armed SA formations, the *Völkischer Beobachter*, the party paper of the National Socialists that had been bought in December 1920,* now made a vicious personal attack on General von Seeckt and on his wife, who, the paper said, was a Jewess, born Jacobsohn.

As a result the Berlin government ordered that the paper suspend publication, a punitive measure much used by the central and *Land* governments when they believed public order to be endangered. Left-wing publications had been, from time to time, banned in Bavaria ever since the time of the Räte control of the city, and von Kahr had also stopped publication of issues of the *Völkischer Beobachter,* and other right-wing papers when their articles seemed too inflammatory. Now, however, the Bavarian government flatly refused to carry out the order to ban the publication of the paper, whereupon Otto Gessler ordered the Bavarian military commander General von Lossow to close it down, if necessary with force. Lossow was caught between two fires. He was bound on the one hand to obey the orders of his duly constituted military superiors, and on the other hand the civilian authorities in the Bavarian government forbade him to carry out his assignment. Lossow chose to obey von Kahr, and Gessler relieved him of his command. In reply the Bavarian government appointed Lossow *Landeskommandant*, that is, chief of its armed forces, and swore in to Bavaria's allegiance the Seventh Reichswehr Division, which he commanded.

Thus the Berlin government was confronted with mutiny in Bavaria and revolution in Saxony and Thuringia. Since the Reichswehr could not fight a two-front war, Stresemann picked the easier target—Saxony. A showdown with Saxony postponed the showdown with Bavaria; it demonstrated to Munich that Berlin could deal energetically with communism, and a military invasion of the left-wing *Länder* promised a relatively easy success.

Stresemann, declaring that it was unconstitutional for a German state to permit Communists in its government, ordered Zeigner to resign and dissolve his cabinet. Zeigner refused. The Communists and their allies again took to the streets with plundering and violence that eventually spread as far as Hamburg, where fourteen people were killed before the police could restore order, and the Reichswehr marched into Saxony and Thuringia. The operation not only restored order, but it had a mollifying effect on Munich. Bavaria had its armed forces on the Saxon-Thuringian border, and if it called on them to invade the neighboring states, they would confront, not the *Hundertschaften* of the left-wing formations, but the Reichswehr.

To counter the Bavarian mutiny, Seeckt wrote three communications,

---

* The *Völkischer Beobachter*, formerly called the *Völkische Zeitung*, had been acquired with the help of funds provided by Dietrich Eckart, a notary in Augsburg, Gottfried Grandel, and through Colonel von Epp, from the Reichswehr.

two addressed to the Reichswehr and one to von Kahr. On October 22 he issued an order of the day telling the troops that the Bavarian action in swearing in the Reichswehr and naming the dismissed Lossow *Landes-kommandant* was unconstitutional and that any soldier accepting it breached his oath of allegiance to the Reich. On November 4, with Lossow and Bavaria unbudging, Seeckt exhorted the Reichswehr to obey its superiors, hold to its allegiances, and stand firm. He told the troops he had never believed the rescue of the Reich would come from either extreme, Right or Left, or from any revolution accomplished with foreign aid. Germany would be saved only by hard, modest work, done under the law and the constitution. Without that there would be civil war, from which only France would benefit. The Reichswehr had to prevent this civil war through inner discipline and complete confidence in its leadership. The latest developments, Seeckt wrote, had brought into doubt the unity and determination of the Reichswehr to accomplish its mission. The army had to remain aloof from party struggles that were tearing apart the rest of Germany; it had to remain above political parties. The honor of a soldier lay, not in his being a know-it-all or a want-it-all, but in obedience. So he warned the soldiers against any division in their ranks that sowed distrust of their superiors. A Reichs-wehr, he told them, that remains united and obedient is invincible and the strongest element in the state. A Reichswehr in which the "splitting fungus" of politics has emerged will fall apart in the moment of danger. Seeckt therefore asked the commanders to make clear that any member of the Reichswehr who wished to engage in political activity was to leave the service immediately.[42]

Seeckt's letter to Kahr was different from the homilies of a general addressing his subordinates. It was written on November 5, one day after his communication to the troops and three days before the Beer Hall Putsch, to a man he had to win over if he possibly could. What he wrote certainly did not misrepresent his own convictions,* although the points he emphasized were undoubtedly those he knew von Kahr wanted to hear. But now it was not a general, aloof from the political strife of parties who was writing; it was a thoroughly political general, who made clear that he, too, was fundamentally antirepublican, unenthusiastic over the Weimar Constitution, and unalterably opposed to the Social Democrats, who, he said, were markedly dangerous in the Prussian government. Seeckt was, however, he reminded Kahr, above all a German patriot who would accept only a legal path to the overthrow of

---

* What Seeckt wrote to Kahr is essentially what he told Hitler when they met in Munich in March 1923. Any change of government, Seeckt made clear, must come only by legal means, and Hitler would write later in *Mein Kampf* that when he talked to the "chief of the Wehrmacht" about giving the National Socialists "the possibility of coming to grips with Marxism," he was preaching to deaf ears. (Friedrich von Rabenau, *Seeckt* p. 347; Adolf Hitler, *Mein Kampf*, p. 774.)

a legitimate government. His duty was to support the authority of the Reich, not that of any particular regime, and he would therefore follow the forms of the constitution. But the constitution itself was not an unviolable document; it could be changed, and since he opposed its basic principles he understood why Kahr fought against it. Seeckt reminded Kahr that he had kept the Social Democrats and the other parties, too, out of the Reichswehr; Germany had to recover its means of defense; it must develop an honorable foreign policy, and in this the Reichswehr must play a decisive role.

He told Kahr that, as he had already explained to Stresemann and Ebert, the Stresemann cabinet could not last, and a civil war was inevitable without a major restructuring of the government. How that would come about he could not say, but it would be a catastrophe if it were not accomplished through the unity of all nationally oriented forces. Only through such unity would there be a chance of success. Stresemann could not remain in office without the full support of the Reichswehr and the forces behind it, so the Reichswehr must not be pushed into a position where it had to contend against people who shared its opinions on behalf of a regime it fundamentally opposed.

On the other hand—and here Seeckt threw his last cards on the table —he could not tolerate the activities of irresponsible groups aiming to overthrow the government by force. To attempt to defend the authority of the state on two fronts would be to play France's game. So he asked Kahr for his help in meeting the crisis in Saxony and Thuringia and he promised that the Reichswehr would master the situation there, that in fact orders to do so had already been issued. Carrying out these orders would only be made more difficult if attacks were made by intruders. And the letter closed: "I ask you, highly esteemed von Kahr, to accept my word as that of a man trying to rescue the Fatherland from the gravest danger...."[43]

It was an adroit appeal addressed to a man who wanted above all to return to the good old days, a reverent monarchist who, like his colleagues in the triumvirate, was far from a swashbuckling revolutionary. The three men governing Bavaria—Kahr, Lossow, and the commander of the *Land* police, Hans Ritter von Seisser—tolerated Hitler but they had no intention of becoming his satellites. They were ready to make use of his SA, commanded by the former air force hero Hermann Göring, against the left wing, but Kahr considered himself an official representative of the Bavarian royal house and he told the defense formations that he forbade any revolt to take place without his express orders, to which Lossow added that he would put down any putsch by force.[44] Ludendorff, too, supported Hitler only as a means to an end, to help rid the government of the "November criminals" who had burdened him with the weight of a defeat he would never be willing to bear. None of the

Bavarian patriots had a coherent program; all of them wanted to defend Bavarian liberties and to purge the Fatherland of the treasonous republican government. And they had armed forces at their command that, if joined by sizeable Reichswehr formations, could make a successful, orderly, sensible revolution, a development Seeckt had no intention of permitting to happen.

Kahr called a meeting in the Bürgerbräu Keller for November 8, at which he intended to unfold whatever program he had in mind. Hitler, in his turn, had planned a mobilization of his forces near Munich for the night of November 10–11, after which they would begin the revolution by marching on the city as a first step toward marching on Berlin. But Kahr's meeting of November 8 changed Hitler's plans. He gave hurried orders for the SA to be ready to seize power on the night of the eighth, and with a small group of aides and *Kampfbund* formations headed by the recently formed "*Stosstrupp* Adolf Hitler" (a special formation of the SA presaging the later SS), he appeared at the Bürgerbräu Keller.

If ever a putsch was to succeed, it seemed to him, as it did to many others, the time was now. A year before, in October 1922, Mussolini had marched on Rome with an army of Blackshirts who announced they were ready to die for the anti-Marxist, nationalist cause. In Germany, where the crisis seemed more acute than it had ever been in Italy, how could the Brown Shirts fail in a similar mission? How could the traitorous republic survive with the currency worthless, the foreign enemy within the gates, separatist risings, Communist-led outbreaks, and three German states and one German general refusing obedience to the orders of the central government? All that was needed was a determined putsch and the flimsy edifice built by the "November criminals" would topple. Only two weeks before, in October, the French commander in the Palatinate, where Separatists had announced that Bavaria no longer exercised sovereign power there, had proclaimed an independent state. The Reich was obviously falling apart. The chief question was who was to take over. The meeting at the beer hall on November 8 brought together the leadership of the moderate and of the extreme Right in Bavaria, a leadership that was mutually suspicious, divided into separate camps with a common enemy but no common purpose except to get rid of him.

Kahr was never to finish his rambling speech denouncing Marxism. As he was talking, Adolf Hitler, accompanied by a handful of followers, strode down the aisles between the tables until he came to the speaker's rostrum, where he fired his revolver into the ceiling to obtain quiet and to take over the action. Neither Kahr nor the other members of the Bavarian triumvirate were a match for Hitler. He made a series of pronouncements to the gathering, only a few of which were true. He told them that the revolution, the national revolution, had broken out, that the room was occupied by 600 heavily armed men, and that no one would be allowed to leave it. If quiet were not immediately restored, he would have a machine gun brought to the galleries. The Bavarian and Berlin regimes were dismissed from office, he announced, and a provisional government would be established. The barracks of the Reichswehr and of the *Land* police, Hitler said, were occupied (not a word of which was true) and the Reichswehr and the police were already moving toward the beer hall under the swastika banners.[45]

That was only Hitler's first speech in the Bürgerbräu that night, and after he made it he asked Lossow, Kahr, and Seisser to follow him into a neighboring room. Since Hitler was armed and obviously ready to shoot, they listened uneasily for some fifteen minutes to his arguments for joining a government under him. Hitler then returned to the main hall, where he demanded quiet and then told the audience that the Knilling government was being replaced.

He proposed von Kahr as regent (*Landesadministrator*) and Ernst Pöhner* as minister-president with dictatorial powers. He repeated that the Berlin government was dissolved. A new German national government would be proclaimed that very day in Munich, and he proposed that until accounts could be settled with the criminals who were leading Germany to dissolution, he should head the provisional government, with Ludendorff as chief of the national army, Lossow as Reichswehr minister, and von Seisser as minister of the Reich police. The task of the provisional government was to mobilize the entire resources of Bavaria and of the rest of the country to march on the "sinful babel" of Berlin and rescue the German people.

Hitler admitted that he had had a hard time persuading Kahr, Lossow, and Seisser to join the new government, but he said they had agreed, and he now asked the gathering whether they too accepted this solution of the German question. He had persuaded them. They yelled their approval. He was careful to promise the Bavarians what he knew they wanted and what he had no intention of granting them. What the revolutionists sought, he told them, was a federative state with Bavaria receiving her just due. He asked everyone to behave quietly, repeated that the room was sealed off by the *Kampfbund*, and ended by telling the meeting what he had told the triumvirate: that morning would find either a German national government or him and his comrades dead.

Hitler was followed on the podium by General Ludendorff, who had come late to the beer hall to avoid any unseemly encounters and who now appeared in full uniform wearing all his decorations. Ludendorff was certainly not anxious to play a role secondary to that of Lance

---

* Pöhner had been dismissed as police president by Schweyer for his National Socialist sympathies.•

Corporal Adolf Hitler, but this was another revolution, like Kapp's, that he might join. He announced that he was placing himself at the disposal of the national government. He said he aimed at restoring the honor to the black, white, and red cockade which the revolution had taken from it. This, he said, was a turning point in German history, and he was confident God would bless their enterprise. Then Kahr, who with Lossow and Seisser had been permitted to return to the main room, got up again to say apparently the only thing he could think of: that in this moment of dire need, he took over the leadership of Bavarian affairs as a representative of the monarchy that had been so shamefully brought down five years before. He added that he did this with a heavy heart and said, "I hope for the blessing of the Bavarian Homeland and of our dear German Fatherland."[46]

That was the high point of the Beer Hall Putsch. By the following day it was over. It was an ill-prepared, amateurish affair. Lossow, Kahr, and Seisser had been forced to join forces with the National Socialists, but as soon as they were freed they recanted, and the police were brought into action, not on the side of Hitler, but against him. Kahr had posters printed and stuck up all over Munich denouncing Hitler for having broken his word, and he announced the dissolution of the National Socialists as well as of the battle groups *Bund Oberland* and *Reichskriegsflagge*.[47] On the morning of November 9, columns of the SA and of other members of the *Kampfbund*, including *Oberland* and greatly outnumbering the police, marched to the center of Munich, but against them were arrayed the disciplined forces of the law and order of the city, of the *Land*, and, if necessary, of the Reichswehr. Seeckt on the night of November 8 had been given dictatorial powers by the Berlin government, and the Bavarian Reichswehr contingents, despite Lossow's earlier mutiny, had assured him of their support.

Lossow himself had no more intention of serving in a government under Hitler than did Kahr or Seisser. Only Ludendorff among the putschists of the night before appeared in the ranks of the marching National Socialists, and when the police fired, he marched steadily on, sure they would not aim their weapons at him, looking straight ahead, untouched by bullets or any hand until he arrived at the police lines, where he was arrested. But among the other marchers were fourteen dead and wounded. Hitler had a dislocated shoulder, suffered when he fell or was pushed to the pavement. Göring was wounded, taken to a Munich hospital, and then smuggled across the border to Austria.

A whiff of grapeshot and the putsch was finished. What had seemed to be the incandescent moment of revolt had dwindled to an illusion. The people had not risen. One Münchener who saw Hans Frank, the future governor general of Poland, then twenty-three years old, occupy with his SA platoon a bridge over the Isar asked him if his mother knew he was out. Other citizens on their way to work made similarly unflattering remarks. The putsch had very little either popular or military support.

One group of young men, officer candidates in the Infantry School in Munich, did march with the National Socialists, but they were the only Reichswehr unit that showed the slightest disposition to join the revolt. The Infantry School, which included engineers, was made up of classes that had just begun in September and October; its officers had been trained in an accelerated program designed to compensate for their lack of military experience. They had none of the cohesion and discipline of conventional Reichswehr formations and were readily influenced by Free Corps leaders, among them Gerhard Rossbach, and the general they reverenced—Ludendorff. Seeckt had had misgivings about the morale of the school and had ordered its dissolution before the putsch, but his order had been rescinded because of Chancellor Stresemann's opposition. One day after the putsch, Seeckt closed the school. A few days later he ordered it removed to a little town, Ohrdruf, in Thuringia, and still later to Dresden. The seditious atmosphere of Bavaria would not again pollute the officer candidates. None of the students was punished, although when Seeckt addressed them at Ohrdruf, his aide reported that he was bursting with anger. After he had made his speech, he would talk to no one and drove off in grim silence. Seeckt dealt with the young men of the Infantry School as he had with the younger officers at the time of the Kapp putsch. They were treated leniently while their elders were held fully accountable. Lossow was never permitted to return to duty; a general who disobeyed orders was beyond redemption.

Nothing much had been won or lost in Hitler's beer hall rising. The republic survived, the crisis continued, and the enemy remained, on the right and left and beyond the border.

CHAPTER 6

Silver Streaks on the Horizon

GUSTAV STRESEMANN WAS ONE of the most impressive figures in German politics from the time of his chancellorship in 1923 until his death in 1929. He was also in the course of those years to become one of the acknowledged leaders among European statesmen of the period, highly regarded by the Reich's former enemies as well by the rest of the world, and little or no dissent was to be heard in foreign capitals when, together with Aristide Briand, he received the Nobel Peace Prize in 1926. Although Germany was well represented in the awards in literature and science* from the time they had started in 1901, the peace prize had never previously gone to a German.

Despite his international repute, Stresemann was never to be chancellor of the Reich for longer than the hundred days between mid-August and late November of 1923. Like the other leaders of the democratic parties under the Weimar Republic, he was cordially detested by both the Far Right and Left; by the Right for having renounced passive resistance in the Ruhr and by the Left for the invasion of Saxony and for permitting Crown Prince Wilhelm to return to Germany from exile. Nevertheless, Stresemann's accomplishments, even during the short period of his chancellorship, were undeniable: the worthless mark was replaced by a stable currency, uprisings against the central government were put down, and the unity of Germany was preserved. Stresemann could soon quote, with a good deal of justification, a remark made by a German expert on reparations, State Secretary Bergmann, that a long last

---

* In 1901 Wilhelm Roentgen received the award in physics and Emil von Behring in medicine.

a streak of light was to be seen on the dark horizon. It was a phrase that would be derisively repeated by Stresemann's innumerable critics whenever anything went wrong with the affairs of state, but it was nevertheless true: the long night of the Reich was ending and the sun of a new day, that was to be all too short, was rising.

Stresemann, although he would not again be called on to head a government, was eminently well suited for his role of foreign minister to which the new chancellor, the Centrist Wilhelm Marx, called him. He was bourgeois to the core, in his moderation, his common sense, his cautious optimism, his economic principles, and his tastes—all evidence of reliable qualities middle-of-the-road Europeans valued highly after the upheavals of the war and the early years of uneasy peace. In a period of exuberant experimentation in the arts, including the theater, a favorite play of Stresemann's was a conventional, sentimental drama, *Father and Son*, about Frederick the Great, written by Joachim von der Goltz, which told the historical story in the fashion of a Nō drama celebrating Samurai discipline and fealty to duty. In Goltz's drama, as in history, the crown prince who played the flute and wrote poems in French is finally reconciled to his terrible martinet of a father after having been sentenced to death by him and being forced to witness the execution of his friend Katte. Katte and the crown prince had been guilty of trying to run away from the military drill and responsibilities of Potsdam, and in the end Frederick asks for and receives his father's forgiveness in a great flush of understanding of their opposite natures that overcomes them both. *Father and Son* was the play that captured Stresemann's imagination, not the plays of Brecht or Hofmannsthal or Hauptmann. They were the playwrights of the intellectuals, of the sophisticated Berliners, of the avant-garde of revolt against authority and the faded, simplistic notions of middle-and upper-class virtue. Von der Goltz, on the other hand, was a playwright of the old school; a competent craftsman, he could dramatize for Stresemann the necessary triumph of legitimate authority, which, to be legitimate, demands of the ruler obedience to higher moral laws so that he in turn may demand the obedience of his subjects to them and to him. In von der Goltz's play, if not in the Germany of the twenties, such qualities could win the respect and allegiance of youth. That Stresemann should choose such a play to admire was typical, first of all, of a German patriot and after that of a good European and a believer in parliaments. Stresemann, like Rathenau, was a monarchist; he sent a telegram of congratulations to the exiled kaiser on his sixtieth birthday, and he permitted the former Crown Prince Wilhelm to return to the Reich when he promised not to engage in politics. Stresemann took the risk because he liked the young man, because he was certain he would keep his word, and very likely because he felt himself honored by their friendship. A constitutional monarchy, he said in a speech in the Reichstag, was the best form of government for Germany, but neither he nor anyone else in the German Volksparty wanted to push for it.

During the war Stresemann, who had been found physically unfit to join the army because of heart trouble, had been a conspicuous member of the annexationist camp. He had advocated unlimited submarine warfare and had supported Ludendorff against Bethmann Hollweg. At the end of the war he had still felt the same way; he had opposed the armistice and Germany's signing the Treaty of Versailles. The 180-degree shift in his views on German foreign policy had come about in the space of three years, but it was a genuine change in the thinking of an intelligent, conscientious man who could adapt himself to historical developments while he retained his uncompromising patriotism, which remained as intense as it had been when he believed the security of the Reich could be obtained only by acquiring strategic territory. Now he was convinced it could be won only through a policy of reconciliation and cooperation with the former enemy. He was accused by his detractors of being an opportunist, but the path he chose was far from popular with many of his longtime friends and it was also far more dangerous to life and limb than holding to the nationalist line.

Stresemann was born on October 5, 1878, the son of a saloon keeper in Berlin. His father had brewed and sold white beer, the favorite drink of thousands of Berliners, and when Gustav wrote his doctoral dissertation in economics he nostalgically compared the solid Berlin burghers who had come into his father's *Bierstube* to drink the steins of white beer and smoke their pipes with the nervous Berliners who replaced them in the snack bars of a later day, gulping down a quick beer while dragging on a cigarette. Not only had the clientèle changed, but the beer was brewed and sold by the same trusts that had driven men like Herr Stresemann out of business.

Gustav was the only member of his family of four sisters and a brother who went to the *Gymnasium* and then to the university. He was a bright boy, fond of reading. His mother called him a dreamer, a *Traumjörg*, lost either in books or in his own thoughts, but she and Stresemann's father recognized his promise and sent him to the *Realgymnasium*, which the family could not easily afford. In school and when he first entered the University of Berlin, Stresemann showed more aptitude for history and literature than for subjects like economics. He was fascinated by the German classics, above all Goethe and Schiller, and he wrote poems that were published in the literary section of the *Vossische Zeitung*. His marks in the *Realgymnasium* were "superior" in history and German and "unsatisfactory" in mathematics, but business opportunities for a young economist were a good deal more promising than they were for a historian, and Stresemann had no wish to enter the academic world. He took up the study of economics at the University of Berlin and at Leipzig, where he spent the winter semester of 1898. At both universities he was an active member of a middle-class student corps that celebrated the revolution of 1848 with its black, red, and gold colors, which would also become those of the Weimar Republic. Stresemann was no *Wunderkind*, but he was a bright young man who received his doctorate at twenty-three and who at twenty-nine was elected to the Reichstag as a member of the National Liberal party.

He had a successful business career from the beginning. His first job was in Dresden, where he was able to organize the chocolate manufacturers, who, like the other small industrialists in Germany, saw themselves threatened by the power of the great trusts of the kind that had taken over the white beer business. The chocolate manufacturers had to pay high duties for the raw materials they imported and were dependent on the sugar cartel for one of the chief ingredients of their products. Stresemann helped them establish a sugar factory independent of the cartel and he served on its board of directors for more than twenty years. After organizing the chocolate manufacturers in Saxony, a part of Germany where industry was dominated by medium and small manufacturers, Stresemann soon organized similar groups in other fields of manufacture who felt themselves being ground between the crushing power of the great cartels of the Rhine and Ruhr on one side and the enormous power of the labor unions on the other. He was a champion of the middle, middle class, an old-fashioned liberal in economic and domestic policies who went around making speeches about the need for organizing if small and medium industry were to survive. He inevitably clashed with the representatives of the coal and iron cartels as he tried to organize the competition against them and as he pursued a policy of conciliation and arbitration with labor rather than attempting, as did the great trusts, to meet force with greater force in times of wage disputes and strikes.

He married Käte Kleefeld, the young sister of a corps brother and the daughter of a well-established Jewish family that had converted to Christianity. His wife was a lady of remarkable cultivation and charm. When on one occasion an effusive dinner partner tried to compliment Stresemann by telling him how beautiful his wife looked that evening, Stresemann replied stiffly, "She is always beautiful." Stresemann himself soon came to look like one of the Allied war cartoons of the Boche; thick-necked, bald, with stubby red hair where he had any, a broad fat face, and a resonant, nasal voice. He was not a memorable orator but he spoke with intense conviction, obviously persuaded of the truth and weight of what he was saying. His directness had its appeal to his audiences; however much they might disagree with him, people were aware of his willingness to stand up for an unpopular view even against his own party and of his civil courage, characteristics that were not over-abundant among German politicians.

Stresemann had been one of the founders of the German Volksparty, a middle-of-the-road group, conservative in its economics and mildly nationalist, that could collaborate with Social Democrats and Centrists, in fact with all the political constellations except those of the Far Left and Right. It was Stresemann's government that put an end to the run-away inflation by stopping the printing presses and then limiting their output. The mark could not be instantly revalued against gold that the Reich did not have; one proposal was to base its value on the gold price of rye, a commodity in much greater supply in Germany than the precious metal, but what was finally decided on by Stresemann's finance minister, Hans Luther, and a young banker, Hjalmar Schacht, called on for technical advice as currency commissar, was a mark based mainly on a psychological standard—the *Rentenmark*. The *Rentenmark*, which was to be fully exchangeable for *Rentenbriefe*, or bills bearing interest, was supposedly guaranteed by the land values of Germany and obligations of industry, business, and the banks up to 3.2 billion gold marks. Actually there was no practicable way land values or industrial paper could cover the mark in this fashion unless people accepted the fiction that they could, and this they did. With limits set on government borrowing, it was enough for millions of Germans, avid for any kind of stable currency, to fall upon the new marks, one of which could be had for 1,000 billion of the old ones. Workers were ready to accept relatively meager wages if the marks they received had a dependable purchasing power, and the country had never had a deficit in its willingness to work and its capacity to produce.

The remedies were semiclassical in that the new currency, which became available on November 15, seemed to be related to a stable standard, and they might have been applied long before 1923 except for the fact that the political-financial leadership had been lacking and more pressing problems confronted the government than a deteriorating currency. Rudolf Havenstein, the president of the Reichsbank, in whose hands the fiscal decision lay, was a reputable down-the-line bureaucrat, the man who had courageously refused Lüttwitz the funds he demanded for his revolt, but Havenstein's only solution for the spiralling inflation had been to print more banknotes. Stresemann and Luther were able to short-circuit his powers with the appointment of Schacht as currency commissar, and when Havenstein died on November 20, he was replaced as president of the Reichsbank by Schacht. The stabilization of the mark was a major accomplishment, and it was made possible, despite the fact that it confirmed the expropriation of the savings of thousands of people,* only because the Reichstag had passed an Enabling Act on October 13 permitting the government, for a limited time, to issue decrees with the force of law without having to go through the Parliament.† The need for concentrating power in an emergency so that the government could move swiftly in a crisis without the debates and divisions of the fragmented Reichstag was one of the few points on which that body could agree, and Seeckt, too, had been accorded for a short period dictatorial powers to put down the Hitler revolt.

Another major victory for the republic was won with the help of an act of terror in the Palatinate. There, on January 9, the "president" of the "autonomous government of the Palatinate" was murdered and four of his followers were mortally wounded by unknown assassins in the Hotel Wittelsbacher Hof in Speyer. The perpetrators were never caught despite a reward of 50,000 francs for their capture. The killings brought an end to the fiction of a separatist government and in fact to the movement itself in a province that had never given the Separatists any serious popular support. Any pretense in Paris and the French press that they had was dealt a mortal blow when the British consul general in Munich, Robert Clive, was ordered to the region by Lord Curzon, despite French objections, to report on the situation. Clive found that 75 percent of the Separatists had been transported to the Palatinate and that 90 percent of the population opposed a separate state.[1]

The assassinations also marked the end of Poincaré's direct attempts to divide the Reich. The fall of the Palatinate Separatists marked the collapse of everything he had hoped to accomplish by setting up French dependencies on German territory, and it was followed by his own fall in the French elections. In May 1924, Poincaré's National Bloc was soundly defeated, winning only 218 in place of its former 425 seats in the Chambre des Députés, and Edouard Herriot, the leader of the Radical party who succeeded him, was far from a Germanophobe. Both Herriot and Aristide Briand, whose opposition parties won 365 seats, were prepared to become admirers—within limits to be sure—of a peaceful Germany and of Stresemann, and those limits were far removed from

---

* The runaway inflation could only be stopped by means of laws that damaged great sections of the population. People caught with large sums of worthless paper marks, bonds, mortgages, or bank accounts had been effectively expropriated when the new currency was introduced. If a man had bought a house before the inflation with a mortgage on it of 50,000 marks, he could have amortized his indebtedness with inflated marks that wouldn't pay for the paperwork. With rent controls in force, a tenant could live almost rent-free as the mark lost its value, and rents could not keep pace with the other costs of living. Under the Enabling Act the government attempted to impose some equality of sacrifice by providing first for a 15-percent and later a 25-percent revaluation of old obligations in terms of the new currency. In addition, taxes were levied by cities and townships on increases in property values.

† The Enabling Act was in effect only until March 31, 1924.

the implacable hatreds that had governed the French ruling party for so long.

In England, too, anti-German sentiment had subsided as not only the Foreign Office but politicians and the public as well became convinced that it was not Germany that was endangering peace or recovery in Europe. When Schacht went to London to try to obtain credits to bolster the new mark, he was completely successful. By late 1923 it was evident to any City banker that it was in the British interest both economically and politically to assist in the recovery of the Reich, which had once been a chief trading partner, and Schacht was granted the first of the postwar loans that eventually totaled more than the reparations the Reich had to pay.

The British electorate, like the French, turned left in their elections of December 1923. The Labour party in a coalition with the Liberals had a majority in the new Parliament, and Ramsay MacDonald, a man on whom Scotland Yard had once had a dossier as a dangerous radical, became prime minister. British and French foreign policies were affected by these developments, and they were also affected by the psychological and economic stagnation of their respective countries after the rosy promises of a new, flourishing order with the end of the war. France in particular had not prospered, and despite the rooted notion that the Reich would pay for everything, few Frenchmen or Englishmen found themselves much, if any, better off than they had been when they received no reparations at all. What Stresemann had to offer French and British leaders was both the text of reconciliation and a readiness to make difficult sacrifices in return for concessions that might lead them all out of their cul-de-sac. Stresemann was firmly convinced that no country in the long run could prosper at the expense of another. The impoverishment of one great exporter and importer of goods must have its pernicious effects on those that traded with it, and France had not done well with its policies of keeping the Reich as indigent and powerless as possible. France, Stresemann told a Volksparty rally in Hannover, did not feel itself a happy victor as a result of the Ruhr invasion. And as for Germany, "It is the duty," he said, "of a German government to accept all bearable costs in order to win German freedom. If it comes to a question of deciding between getting rid of the burdens and unfreedom, or accepting the burdens and winning freedom, there can be no doubt of the decision of an honor-loving people."[2]

Stresemann's words had an echo in a France which continued to be tormented by the inadequacies of a victory whose fruits of security and prosperity remained elusive. Poincaré may have won the battle of the Ruhr, but he could not persuade a majority of his countrymen that his hard line had brought them anything more than new troubles for which he had no remedies. A different approach to reconstruction was plainly needed, and Stresemann was the man ideally chosen to represent the views of a Reich that not only presented no immediate threat to the peace of Europe but whose republican governments were determined to find peaceful solutions that would extend into the future. Stresemann, like his predecessors in the chancellorship and foreign ministry, was convinced of the merits of the policy of fulfillment, and he therefore made the same domestic enemies on the Right and on the Left that Rathenau, Wirth, and the others had made. But he had one advantage his predecessors had lacked; the time was becoming ripe to make demands on behalf of the Reich that would not have been listened to even a few months before. If Germany were willing to make sacrifices, Stresemann expected tangible concessions in return. Before he formally abandoned passive resistance, he tried to get assurances from Poincaré that French troops would, as a quid pro quo, withdraw from the Ruhr. Poincaré, however, would not budge, and Stresemann had no choice but to end passive resistance without receiving any promises of any kind. That, however, would be one of the few occasions when he could gain nothing at all. What he meant by fulfillment was an honest attempt to meet France's demands for restitution and for security as far as possible but in return to obtain for Germany, step by step, the means of regaining its independence and freedom of action within a European community. That would be in the interest of the Reich, of France, and of all Europe.

He was not playing power politics, because he represented a country that had very little left in the way of political or military leverage. Nevertheless, the France he was addressing was far more ready to negotiate than at any time since 1914; it was a France struggling against a rising inflation of its own and threatened with finding itself in the blind alley of isolation, the dead end most dreaded by every French government of whatever political complexion. Both Britain and Italy manifested their disenchantment with French policies; Mussolini's government, with its eye on recovering Tunis and Corsica, was even making inquiries in Berlin about the possibility of an Italo-German alliance in the event of a Franco-Italian war. Poincaré had alienated France's allies and fueled German ultranationalism, and now here was a German foreign minister saying that in spite of everything he was ready to cooperate. Poincaré had been highly successful in attaining one goal: he had managed out of the Ruhr invasion to get what he had demanded in the way of "productive pledges." The Ruhr industrialists had been forced, in order to get their property back from the French occupants, to agree that they would turn over 30 percent of the Ruhr iron and coal production to the Allies. The Reich was to repay the industries for these amounts, to be credited to the reparations account. The agreement had been made on November 23 with the *Mission Interalliée de Contrôle des Usines et des Mines,* called Micum, and it was the forerunner of the Dawes Plan, worked out in the following months under the aegis of the future vice-president of the United States, Charles Dawes. Both the agreement with Micum and the Dawes Plan, while providing for stiff payments, seemed capable of fulfillment, and so, with the subsequent loans made to Germany and the new climate of conciliation, they turned out to be.

General Dawes, like Colonel House, was no military man, but he had been made a general in the course of service during World War I, where he had been head of supply and procurement for the American army in France. He was an able banker, and like his colleagues in London, he got along well with Hjalmar Schacht. With the German inflation stopped and the reparations account brought into rough balance, the way was clear for the kind of political negotiations at which Stresemann would prove himself a master. The time was ripe for interim settlements. Under the Dawes Plan, France would get its productive pledges in the form of mortgages on German railroads and heavy industries, and Germany would get back its sovereignty over the customs and the control of its railroads in the Ruhr.

Stresemann journeyed to London in February 1924 for negotiations with the bankers at the same time Adolf Hitler was being tried before a Bavarian People's Court for his Beer Hall Putsch. Both of them were successful in their opposite ways; Hitler because the People's Court, which, following an agreement with the Reich, was to be dissolved in April, was still in session and was run with the wide latitude that enabled Hitler to use it as a political forum; Stresemann because he worked well in the climate of conciliation, and after the Ruhr invasion, which shook both countries, the French and Germans were ready to talk about practical measures proposed by financial experts without overwhelming political prejudices.

The trial of Adolf Hitler and nine of his followers, including Ludendorff, Pöhner, Frick, and Röhm, became a forum with far better acoustics than the beer halls or the Zircus Krone. For the first time, the newspapers of all Germany and of foreign countries as well reported the speeches of this man with the shock of hair falling toward one eye, and what he had to say could be read by thousands who had never heard of him before his putsch. While Stresemann was painfully making his way through the thorny realities of the German predicament, Hitler was free to appeal to the dream world of the ultranationalists and to the resentments of the dispossessed. He made the most of the opportunity, turning the bloody muddle of the putsch into a triumph of *völkisch* rhetoric and his own brand of showmanship.

Again he appeared in his favorite role of the indomitable, selfless hero, a latter-day Siegfried for whom no sacrifice on behalf of his people was too great. He accepted full responsibility for the rising, which was made only to rescue the Fatherland. He was guilty, he said, of the act, but not of the crime, of high treason. "There is no treason," he told the court, "in taking measures against the treason of 1918." Furthermore, high treason could not be confined to the time between the eighth and the ninth of November. It must have been going on during the weeks and months of preparations preceding the uprising, and if this was treason, why, he asked the court, were not Lossow, Seisser, and Kahr sitting at his side in the dock? "I must in any case," he said, "reject the charge as long as those gentlemen are not here with me who wanted the same deed as we, and discussed it and planned it to the smallest detail." And as for his own guilt, he said, "I feel myself, not as one who had committed high treason, but as a German who only wanted the best for his people."[3] Hitler would always know his audience. The presiding judge, Georg Neithardt, was a nationalist who reverenced Ludendorff and gave the impression that he would have gladly pinned another medal alongside those the general wore when he appeared in full uniform before the court. The lay judges plainly shared Neithardt's views and were equally solicitous of the defendants. The officers among the accused wore their uniforms and their medals, and Hitler, although in civilian clothes, pinned his Iron Cross, First Class, under his breast pocket.

Hitler not only assumed all the responsibility for the uprising, but he was elaborately modest when it came to comparing his position in it with Ludendorff's. It was Ludendorff who held first place, he told the court, while he, Adolf Hitler, only led the political battle. For him to pretend to first place in a common enterprise with Ludendorff at his side was "unthinkable."[4] On the whole Hitler was treated gently by the prosecutors and judges, and only Lossow attacked him violently, calling him among other things "narrow, boring, brutal, inferior, and on the make." But Lossow could not compete with Hitler in the shouting match his testimony provoked, and Hitler could readily explain Lossow's petty motives. Lossow, he said, anxious for the title of minister, might try to diminish Hitler's role to that of propagandist and alarm crier, but small men like Lossow could only think small, and it was unworthy of a great man to want to go down in history as a minister. "What was before my eyes from the first," he told the court, "was a thousand times more than being a minister. I wanted to be the destroyer of Marxism. I will accomplish this task, and when I do, then the title of minister will be laughable. As I stood for the first time at Wagner's grave, my heart swelled with pride that here lay a man who had forbidden the line to appear on his grave: 'Here lies Privy Councillor, Musical Director, Excellency, Baron von Wagner.'" It had been enough for Wagner, as it had for so many men in Germany history, to content themselves with leaving not their titles but their names to posterity. So it was not out of modesty, Hitler said, that he had wanted to be the "Drummer of the Revolution"; that was the only title he desired; the rest was trivial.

What counted was purity of purpose and a willingness to make every sacrifice for the high end—the salvation of the Fatherland. Political majorities were unimportant: "The question whether a people is to be ruled by nationalists or Marxists is not a problem of voting but a problem of morality and decency. If there were only a thousand nationalists in a state and 100,000 others, the thousand would have the moral right before God and the world to represent the nation. That is a moral problem, not a problem for the majority."[5] The German Fatherland had not been founded by a majority but by the decisions of single individuals.

The words poured forth and his followers were enraptured, as they always had been when he told them of his and their valor and selflessness. Attacks on the Jews were muted.* Hitler accused them of completely controlling the press, but his chief enemies were those the court would be able to identify too—the defeatists, the traitors, the "November criminals." It is unlikely that any other court in Germany would have permitted such a display of self-serving speechifying, but the People's Court of Bavaria was a special instance in more ways than one, and the conduct of the trial was severely criticized not only by the press but by the Bavarian State Council of Ministers.[6] As in the case of his letters to the Munich police and to the Austrian authorities in Linz, what Hitler had to say was skillfully designed to his ends. He was talking, as the Germans say, from his liver when he was expounding on his own patriotism and the duplicity of the scoundrels who opposed him. At the Munich trial he could act out his role before an audience of his followers and a friendly court, which was even more stimulating than his customary beer hall ambiance. He was brash and self-effacing by turns. He told the court he categorically refused to be modest; when one is "called," he said, he has the duty to do what his calling demands.[7] But he also explained that he would never think of placing himself ahead of Ludendorff; if he had, a good many people inside the courtroom and out might have resented it and agreed with Lossow as to his effrontery.

Hitler's final speech before the court on March 27, 1924, was as filled with quivering emotions and self-dramatization as any of his most expectant Brown Shirts could have wished. He had stood, he said, for four

---

* Hitler's obsessive hatred of the Jews was never far from the surface, but it was a subject he could fit into a context. Albert Speer, who spent many hours with him over a period of more than a decade, says he can't recall Hitler's indulging in anti-Semitic tirades in the course of their conversations. And yet in his political testament to the German people, written just before his suicide, Hitler blames the Jews for his and the Reich's downfall, and in the last paragraph he adjures the new German leadership to keep the racial laws and to continue the "merciless resistance against the world poisoner of every people, international Jewry."

years shoulder to shoulder together at the front with his comrades, and he asked the court whether it could believe he would ever have raised his gun against one of them. What the rising had sought, he said, was a directorate, and that was what all Germany had wanted. In the final analysis he was a republican, Pöhner was a monarchist (meaning pro-Wittelsbach), and Ludendorff was true to the house of Hohenzollern. That men of such differing beliefs had been able to come together was evidence of the power of an idea. "Germany's fate," he told the court, "lies not in being a republic or a monarchy. What I fight against is not the form of the State but its disgraceful content." He and the putschists had wanted to free Germany from the iron fist of the enemy, to create order, to take up the battle against the slavery of international markets, against the cartelization of the German economy, the politicizing of the unions, and above all to restore the duty to bear arms. "Is what we wanted high treason?" he asked, and continued in a long passionate period with mixed metaphors: "High treason? Finally we wanted to bring the German people to revolt against the threatening enslavement, wanted the time finally to come when we would no longer accept with sheeplike patience box after box on the ears." Kahr, Lossow, and Seisser had said that it was he, Hitler, who had brought them to their predicament, but it was they who were guilty of that. "Kahr should have said honorably, 'Herr Hitler, we mean something else by a coup d'état, we mean something else by a march on Berlin.'" Kahr had not done that, and the consequences were to be borne solely by those three men.

Then he turned to a subject that was of the deepest concern to him —the proposal in the indictment that he be exiled under the Law for the Protection of the Republic. He begged the court not to make use of the law. He reminded its members that they had studied history as boys and had been filled with shame when they learned how the best of "our people" had been sent into exile when ministers regarded them as troublesome. "For four years," he said, "I was away from the soil I must call my homeland. There with glowing love I counted the hours until I would be permitted to return to it from France. If it were necessary I would go again even as an exile. Take care that you do not repeat in the future this greatest shame of the German nation. It is the mark of an inferior people when it no longer has such mutual respect that it need not resort to exile. What has been done here in the last months, as Germans have been exiled who wanted nothing more than the happiness of the Fatherland, will be taken one day by hundreds of thousands of German boys as a bitter shame flung in their faces, and they will say: 'How disgraceful we are compared with other peoples.'" The prosecution demanded the defendants be punished because their undertaking failed. "But," Hitler said, "the deed of November eight did not fail. It would have failed if a mother had come to me and said: 'Herr Hitler, you have my child on your conscience.' But I can assure you no mother has come. On the contrary, thousands have come and joined our ranks. It will be said one day, I can assure you, of the young men who died in the uprising what the words on the Obelisk* say: 'They too died for the Fatherland.' That is the visual proof of the success of November eight, that in its wake youth rises like a raging flood and is united. That is the great success of the eighth of November: it has not led to depressed spirits but has brought the people to the highest pitch of enthusiasm. I believe that the hour will come when the masses who today bear our crusading flags on the streets will join with those on November eight shot at them." Hitler said he had learned with relief that it was the state police, not the Reichswehr, that had fired the shots; and the day would come when the Reichswehr too, officers and men, would stand at their side. "The army that we have fashioned grows from day to day, from hour to hour, faster and faster. In these very days I have the proud hope that the time will come when the outlawed companies will grow to battalions, the battalions to regiments, the regiments to divisions; that the old cockade will be picked up out of the dirt, the old flags will wave again, and then the reconciliation will come before God's last court, before which we are ready to appear. Then from our bones and from our graves will be heard the voice of the court that alone is called on to sit as a court above us. Then [addressing the court] not you gentlemen will speak the judgment upon us, but the eternal court of history will speak out on the accusation that is made against us. . . . That court will not ask us whether or not we have committed high treason. That court will judge us, judge the quartermaster general of the old army, the officers and soldiers who as Germans wanted all that is best for *Volk* and Fatherland; who wanted to fight and to die. You may find us guilty a thousand times over, but the goddess of the eternal court of history will smilingly tear up the motion of the state prosecutor and the judgment of the court; for it will exonerate us."[8]

This court did almost as well. It freed Ludendorff and it sentenced Hitler to five years of fortress arrest, where he would be eligible for parole in six months, imposed on him a fine of 200 marks and mercifully declined to order him deported. The other defendants got similarly mild sentences. The court, because its judges, both lay and professional, were solid nationalists, had listened attentively to Hitler and had obviously been impressed by what he had to say. And his concluding statement was genuine Hitler, the words of the spinner, the teller of tall tales. Hitler told the court how it seemed to him, how it should have been: "In Munich, Nuremberg, Bayreuth, there would have been boundless rejoicing; an enormous enthusiasm would have burst forth in the Reich,

---

* Hitler refers to the obelisk in the Karolinenplatz in Munich erected to the memory of 30,000 Bavarian soldiers who were sent to fight for Napoleon and died in Russia.

and when the first division of the national army had left the last square meter of Bavarian soil and for the first time marched on to Thuringia, we would have seen how the people there would have rejoiced. They would have had to recognize that German misery was at an end; redemption could only come about through a rising. The pacifist-defeatist, completely immoral regime in Berlin would have had to bend before the storm."[9]

The lost battle, from which, in fact, all the leading figures except Ludendorff had fled, had been, in Hitler's peroration, not lost, but won, and thousands of people had joined the party, which was actually proscribed throughout the Reich. Instead of flocking to it, the Müncheners had regarded the rising either as dangerous or absurd and had shown no enthusiasm whatever for it. But Hitler saw all Germany streaming toward his cause, as the Brown Shirts, in his mythical presentation, marched, not to the Feldherrnhalle where they were stopped by the police, but on to Berlin.

Relatively few Germans saw the same vision; Hitler's appeal was very limited. In the election in May 1924, the National Socialists with their allies of the *völkisch* parties received 1.9 million votes, 6.5 percent of the total, and that was the most they would get in any of the next three Reichstag elections. In the following election, held in December 1924, their vote dropped to under 2.9 percent, and there it would stay through the elections of 1928, when they received 810,100 votes—2.6 percent of the total cast.

But as Hitler had told the court, it was not majorities that determined history, and whether in prison, where he wrote *Mein Kampf*, or on the political circuit, where he could drum up only the same crowds on or just off the lunatic fringe, he pounded away at the work for which he knew himself to be chosen, awaiting the day with absolute certainty when the masses would be bound to flock to him. Meanwhile it was Stresemann and his like who had to meet the crises and make the hard, practical decisions that would slowly make possible the recovery of the Reich.

Reparations were the main issue in the election of May 4. The Dawes Committee of Experts had worked out a formula that was well removed from the illusory figures that had given rise to impossible expectations on the part of the Allies as well as to so much German bitterness, and the Marx-Stresemann government had accepted it. The experts found that in normal years the Reich could pay 2.5 billion gold marks as an annuity, but since these were not normal times, smaller amounts, to rise on a sliding scale, could be paid for four years, after which the full 2.5 billion marks would be due.* No total sum of reparations was fixed, and

* Under the plan as finally adopted this amount, too, would be subject to increase.

Germany was to regain its economic unity with control of the customs and of the Ruhr railroads. The experts' solutions were to prove workable, but they inspired no one; it was a burdensome but operable schedule, and in the May election a majority of the voters were unable to attach themselves to any single party or coalition that had a solution they found to their liking. Out of a total of nearly 30 million votes cast, 7.5 million went to the Right, including the nearly 2 million cast for the National Socialists and their allies, while the Communists rose from some half million votes to 3.7 million. The Social Democratic party, which had had 163 seats in the National Assembly and 102 in the first Reichstag elected in April 1920, fell to 100 seats in the May 1924 Reichstag, polling slightly over 6 million votes. The Independent Social Democratic party elected no delegates at all as their percentage of the total vote fell from 17.8 percent to less than 1 percent. A large share of the increase in the Communist vote came from the disaffected members of the two socialist parties, whose leadership and programs seemed to many of their members erratic and undefined compared with those of the Far Left. For similar reasons Stresemann's Volksparty lost ground to the right-wing parties, dropping from 65 to 45 seats in the Reichstag.

Stresemann's fulfillment policies had been under heavy attack from the Right. A Nationalist deputy, Freytagh-Loringhoven, accused him of acting in French interests because his stepfather was a chief stockholder in a Czech armament factory, a charge made also in the National Socialist *Völkischer Beobachter.* The accusation was groundless; no one in the Stresemann family, as Stresemann declared in the Reichstag, owned any shares at all in the Czech concern, and his stepfather had been dead for twenty years.[10] But another rumor went around that Frau Stresemann was a sister of Poincaré's wife, and as always the denials could not keep up with the smears.

Fulfillment meant sacrifice, always it seemed at the cost of the German workers, and it had very little public appeal. So again it was a patchwork government of Centrists and members of the other moderate parties that would try to deal with Germany's foreign and domestic troubles. But in foreign affairs it was talking with a patchwork Entente that showed signs of wear and tear. The London conference, convened on July 16, under pressure from the French government, was to confine itself to considering only problems arising from the Dawes Plan and to maintaining the inviolability of the Treaty of Versailles. Such questions as the withdrawal of French troops from the Ruhr were not to be discussed. But the French position had deteriorated since Poincaré had ordered the Ruhr invasion, and before the conference opened, Herriot had agreed to the establishing of a fact-finding committee under the chairmanship of an American that in the future would determine whether Germany had deliberately failed to meet its obligations. The deliberations of this committee would replace the unilateral decisions formerly made by Paris. Only after a unanimous vote could sanctions be applied. In addition, Herriot agreed that with Germany's acceptance of the Dawes Plan, German economic unity would be restored.

After these compromises were reached, the Germans could be invited to the London conference, and on August 5 the German delegation, including Marx, Stresemann, Schacht, and Luther, the finance minister, arrived in London to be presented, not with documents ready for them to sign, but with the prospect of negotiating. The prospect dimmed when, in his first speech, the mild-mannered Wilhelm Marx had a few words to say about the French leaving the Ruhr in return for Germany's accepting the Dawes scale of reparations. Marx spoke in German, and the interpreter the delegation had brought along, instead of translating the chancellor's temperate words, took off on his own virtuoso version of them, which sounded to many of those present more like Ludendorff than Marx. The matter was smoothed over with some difficulty, and a new interpreter, Paul Schmidt, was brought in. Schmidt would manage to keep his job throughout the days of the Weimar Republic and on through Hitler's Reich. Both the Germans and the French in London were struggling against sentiments at home that would not easily tolerate any appearance of yielding to the enemy, for what was left of Pan-Germanism in the Reich was paralleled by the hyperpatriotism of the *Camelots du Roi*, an organization one French paper called *"Les Fascistes du roi."*[11] Stresemann and Marx had been able to persuade a majority of the Reichstag to accept the burdens of the Dawes Plan only because they promised it would mean getting rid of the French in the Ruhr, and if Herriot agreed to that, he had good reason to fear the French Parliament would overthrow him.

Actually, however, compromises were reached, and in return for Germany's accepting the Dawes scale of reparations with the possibility of sanctions being invoked, Herriot agreed to order the evacuation of Dortmund immediately and of all the Ruhr within a year. Moreover he won his vote of confidence in the Chamber of Deputies and the Senate, despite the heavy guns brought to bear against him by Poincaré, who attacked him and the concessions he had made as violently as Stresemann was denounced in the Reichstag.

In France as in Germany, the opposing currents of reconciliation and hostility were strong. France had little fear of the Germany of the mid-twenties. The threat to French security lay in the future. And a large section of the French population saw across the Rhine an unregenerate Germany plotting day after day to avenge the defeat. *Le Petit Journal* reported in January 1924 on a meeting of German nationalists at the University of Berlin attended by General von Seeckt, where the kaiser was acclaimed by students and the rector of the university. The newspaper's correspondent in Germany, Henry de Kerab, reported that the German republic was having a thorough militaristic and monarchistic reaction, and that after only six years of existence the republic was dead. Despite alleged disarmament, the correspondent wrote, the German army had increased its numbers, which probably came to 450,000 men without adding the police forces. A German cabaret performer who, toward the end of the war, had asked in a popular song, "When will we have bean coffee again?" was now singing the same tune, but the words were "When will we have war again?"[12] French newspapers never tired of the theme.

The Communist newspaper *L'Humanité*, on the other hand, under the caption "The Abominable Venality of the French Press," printed a series of letters provided by the Soviet government from the tsar's archives* showing how the Russian government before the war had paid large sums to more than twenty French newspapers, including many of the leading ones like *Le Temps, Figaro, L'Aurore, Le Matin,* and *Echo de Paris,* to take a favorable view of tsarist Russia and of the Franco-Russian alliance. The sums were paid out mainly to Radical-Socialist newspapers that had not been overly well disposed to the tsarist government, and the letters involved Poincaré himself in making the payments. In one letter, *L'Humanité* pointed out, all the conditions for the world war that would occur five years later were precisely enumerated. The Paris representative of the Russian Ministry of Finance, Raffalovitch, had written to Russian Prime Minister Kokovtzov in 1909: "The French government aware of its obligations, when Russian honor is engaged in Serbia against Austria, will fulfill its obligations." A Russian mobilization is foreseen; then the Austrians will occupy Belgrade, and a guerilla war with Serbia will follow. The Russians will mobilize on the Austrian border; the Germans will do the same on the French border, and England will mobilize its fleet. "But," the writer asked, "will the French public see peace compromised for Serbia and war with Germany as a consequence?"

How, asked *L'Humanité*, could the French government deny the responsibility of France and Russia in the war in the light of such documents?† André Tardieu, one of the chief editors of *Le Temps*, met with the Russian ambassador, according to the evidence in the letters, every other day, and other leading French politicians and newspaper writers,

---

* The letters, mainly written by the Russian ambassador in Paris, Izvolsky, to Foreign Minister Sazonov in St. Petersburg, were declared genuine by former Prime Minister Kokovtzov when he appeared as a witness in a trial in Paris. (Friedrich Stieve, ed., *Der Diplomatische Schriftwechsel Iswolskis 1911–1914*, vol. 1, in Introduction.)

† Raffalovitch referred to the funds provided by the Russian government as "a war treasury." (Friedrich Stieve, ed., *Der Diplomatische Schriftwechsel Iswolskis 1911–1914*, vol. 2, Letter #649, p. 406.)

among them Clemenceau, Briand, Pichon,* and Poincaré, were also involved in the disbursing of Russian funds that ran into millions of francs.[13]

In Germany, the Right continued to excoriate Stresemann and his policy of reconciliation with France with a fervor that equalled that of the French nationalists. Ludendorff, who had been elected a deputy in the May election, made a speech in which he said that what he had won at Tannenberg ten years before had been lost by Stresemann in a Jewish Tannenberg, and Helfferich two weeks before his death in a railroad accident called the acceptance of the Dawes Plan and the results of the London conference "the second Versailles."[14] But Seeckt supported the Dawes solution, not only because he knew the alternatives were far worse but because he was afraid if it were rejected new elections might bring further gains to the Left. As a result, 48 Nationalist deputies voted with the government coalition in favor of the Dawes proposals, and in Germany as in France the way to some kind of reconciliation, however grudging, was open.

The large number of splinter parties in the Weimar Republic† has often been blamed for its downfall, since no party was able to form a government except by way of unstable coalitions. New elections had to be held on December 7, only seven months after the last one. This time the Communists and National Socialists lost a million votes. The Communist seats in the Reichstag fell from 62 to 45, and the National Socialists won only 14 seats as against their former 32. Again the moderate and relatively moderate parties gained at the expense of the extreme Right and Left; the SPD won 130 seats in place of 100, the German National Volksparty went from 50 to 102, and Stresemann's German Volksparty went from 44 to 51. No party came to power in its own right. Voters milled from the extremists towards the center, splitting there into two fairly equal divisions of anti- and prorepublican groups; the one Nationalist-*Völkisch* plus Communists; the other Liberal, Democratic, and Socialist. As a further complication, a group like Stresemann's middle-class Volksparty had in it many promonarchists who, like Stresemann himself, were devoted servants of the republic and wouldn't lift a finger to restore the Hohenzollerns. Although the arts and letters and sciences flourished as never before in German history, no political figures, whether pro- or antirepublic, emerged in the twenties who captured the public imagination. Not only did elected political leaders look unimpressive in bathing suits; they were just as nondescript when dressed. Even the reverenced hero of Tannenberg, the great-grandfather of all

* Stephen Pichon, French minister for foreign affairs 1906–1911.

† Owing to proportional representation, which had been adopted because it was considered the fairest and most democratic form of voting.

Sketch of sixteen-year-old Hitler made by a schoolmate in the Linz
Realschule in 1905. *(Süddeutscher Verlag)*

The Austro-Hungarian Emperor Franz Josef and Karl Lueger, mayor of Vienna.

(Ullstein)

The kaiser and Bethmann Hollweg. *(Süddeutscher Verlag)*

Tsar Nicholas II and French President Poincaré reviewing the naval honor guard, St. Petersburg, July 1914.

(Ullstein)

General mobilization proclaimed August 1, 1914. Adolf Hitler in the crowd on the Odeonsplatz in Munich. *(Süddeutscher Verlag)*

Hindenburg, the kaiser, and Ludendorff, 1917. *(Süddeutscher Verlag)*

ABOVE Karl Liebknecht and Rosa Luxemburg at a Social Democratic rally, 1909. *(Ullstein)* BELOW Karl Liebknecht addressing a May Day demonstration in Berlin. *(Süddeutscher Verlag)*

Revolutionary sailors at the Berlin Castle, November 1918. *(Ullstein)*

Arms inspection, Spartacist unit, Berlin, December 1918. *(Süddeutscher Verlag)*

Colonel von Epp, Gustav Noske, and Friedrich Ebert with Reichswehr and Bavarian troops after the defeat of the forces of the Räte Republic, Munich, August 1919. *(Süddeutscher Verlag)*

Free Corps troops. The Ehrhardt Brigade returning to Döberitz after the defeat of the Spartacists in Berlin, September 1919. They carry the old, imperial war flag. *(Süddeutscher Verlag)*

Free Corps troops, Munich, May 1919. *(Süddeutscher Verlag)*

Wilson and Poincaré, Paris, December 1918. *(Süddeutscher Verlag)*

Ebert and Noske on summer vacation. *(Süddeutscher Verlag)*

Wolfgang Kapp.
(Süddeutscher Verlag)

Adolf Hitler (center rear) with a Reichswehr unit in Munich in 1919, after the fall of the Räte Republic. *(Süddeutscher Verlag)*

The Ehrhardt Brigade during the Kapp putsch in Berlin, March 1920. *(Süddeutscher Verlag)*

Hitler (second from left with turned-down hat) on a propaganda tour at Tegernsee, Bavaria, 1922.
(Süddeutscher Verlag)

LEFT The fake Hitler membership card, No. 5, in the German Workers party. RIGHT The genuine Hitler card, No. 555.

Wash baskets and carts being loaded at the Reichsbank in Berlin with paper marks for wage payments, 1923. *(Ullstein)*

The inflation. Members of the impoverished middle class selling their valuables. *(Ullstein)*

Homeless men in line for a night's lodging at a municipal shelter in Berlin, autumn 1923. *(Süddeutscher Verlag)*

100 Milliarden Mk.   № 16492

NOT~AUSGABE.

Die Bezirkssparkasse Berneck zahlt gegen diese Platzanweisung

Einhundert Milliarden Mark

Berneck, den 15.

One-hundred-billion-mark note, November 1923. *(Preussischer Kulturbesitz)*

Unemployed, including discharged soldiers, waiting for the doors of a city employment office to open, 1923. *(Süddeutscher Verlag)*

patriotic Germans, was only moderately impressive in his frock coat and his principles, still firmly held out of a lost war and time. When Friedrich Ebert died and Hindenburg was reluctantly persuaded to run for the presidency, he received, in the run-off election of April 26, 1925, a million votes less than the combined vote of his two opponents, Wilhelm Marx the Centrist and Ernst Thälmann the Communist.*

Fearing that Jarres, the right-wing candidate in the first election, would lose to Marx, now the candidate of the Center and Socialists in the run-off election, the Nationalists turned to the seventy-eight-year-old Hindenburg. The delegations they sent to persuade him to run in Jarres's place had little luck. Hindenburg told them he wanted nothing but his rest, and it took two visits by Admiral von Tirpitz† to finally convince the elderly field marshal that duty again demanded that he rescue the Fatherland, this time by serving as president of a republic for which he had little or no enthusiasm.

His words when he took his oath of office on May 12 essentially repeated what he had told the electorate before they cast their votes. He said: "I swear that I will devote all my strength to the well-being of the German people, protect them from harm, maintain the constitution and laws, conscientiously fulfill my duty, and be just to all. So help me God." And in his answer to the greetings of Reichstag President Paul Löbe, Hindenburg said: "Reichstag and Reichspresident belong together because they both emerge from the direct vote of the German people. Both together manifest the embodiment of the people's sovereignty. . . . That is the deep sense of the constitution to which I have solemnly bound myself."[15]

Hindenburg's election was received calmly in England, where the *Daily Chronicle* declared that it was no breach of the peace treaty and it was England's task to judge Germany by its actions, not its votes. The *Times* said Germany had reestablished its balance, the voters had chosen the old soldier, the victor of Tannenberg, as the best and most typical representative of national life, and it was best for Germany and for Europe that at the head of the German state stood a man of honor and resolution. But the French predictably took a sour view. *Le Temps* wrote that Germany had chosen a former army leader and by that wished to deny its defeat. "From this standpoint," the paper editorialized,

---

* Hindenburg received 14,655,641 votes, Marx 13,751,605 and Thälmann 1,931,151. In the first vote for president on March 29, 1925, the candidate of a number of right-wing and moderate parties including Stresemann's German Volksparty, Carl Jarres, received 10.4 million votes; Otto Braun, the Social Democrat, 7.8 million; Marx, 3.8 million; Thälmann, 1.9 million; and Ludendorff, the proto-National Socialist, a mere 285,000.

† Tirpitz had been elected to the Reichstag in May 1924. He aspired to the chancellorship but never could recruit any serious support for his candidacy. He did, however, have considerable influence with his old comrade-in-arms Hindenburg.

"the result of the election must be seen as a challenge not only to the Allies but to Europe and America. Germany has thrown off the mask with which it sought to convince people of the genuineness of its democratic sentiments and now shows its old face, in which its warlike instincts, its drive to rule are manifest. The entire policy of reconciliation is thereby morally bankrupt. . . ."[16]

For Germans Hindenburg was a symbol, not of the republic, but of the Fatherland that had been rooted in the army. Ebert had had the respect of many men who opposed him politically, but he remained the former saddler, the upright but seedy caretaker of a bankrupt empire with no trace of the charisma of the mythopoeic founding fathers Hitler was orating about in his courtroom speeches. Ebert's prosaic, commonplace style was characteristic, too, of the chancellors and of the members of their governments, although since ministers were less vulnerable to political turbulence than the heads of government, men like Gessler and Stresemann might stay on for years in successive cabinets under different chancellors. Government would succeed government, each in its turn wrestling with the problems it had inherited, and the new ones that always turned up, each in its turn to be overthrown when the tenuous party alignments shifted. People joined parties not by way of ideologies but out of *malheurs*. At one point during the debate on currency reform, a short-lived party was formed around that one issue. It was all hand-to-mouth except for what Stresemann was able to accomplish in getting loans from the United States and Britain and in getting the French out of the Ruhr.

He could not raise with Britain and France such issues as the clause on war guilt; he tried to, but even his well-wishers among the Allies told him not to do it. The principle of solely German guilt for the war was written not only into the Versailles Treaty but into the very souls of the French, and no French statesman could stay in office who for a moment accepted the German protest against the injustice of the accusation. The charge had never been true, but that did not deter millions of Frenchmen from believing in it as a fundamental article of faith, and if at any time a German statesman tried to show that the documents the German government had just released from its Foreign Office files and published as *Die Grosse Politik* or the documents published in 1924 from the secret tsarist archives* did not bear out the accusation, he merely infuriated the men like Poincaré who wanted to hear nothing of the rebuttal. Stresemann had suggested an impartial tribunal to weigh the evidence, but as the writer in *La Nation* said: "History has dealt with the question and pronounced its verdict." The publication of *Die Grosse Politik* made a

---

* These were published in Russian under the auspices of the Soviet government and in *Le Livre Noir* by Marchand in Paris.

great impression on historians all over the world, and they were a powerful contribution to the revisionism on the causes of World War I that dominated the next generation of scholars in Europe and the United States. But politically the line in France never changed; the war guilt clause had its own mystique; it remained in the treaty and in the thinking and the souls of those who wanted it to be there no matter what the evidence against it.

Thus Germans and Frenchmen lived in a chronic state of frustration and dissatisfaction. No course followed by the Reich could unite its factions. The painful issues split philosophies and parties. The Dawes Plan was approved because many of the Nationalist deputies voted for it as a necessary evil despite the fact that most of their party members were opposed to it. Seeckt was in favor of accepting it, but Ludendorff and others called it a "Jewish Tannenberg"; it was continuing evidence of the tragedy of the lost war, which the kaiser in exile now said had been brought about by Freemasons, Jews, and the leaders of France and Italy —thus leaving out his former *bêtes noires*, his cousins in Britain and the new deceased tsar in Russia.

Nevertheless Stresemann succeeded in reorienting not only German but also French foreign policy. France could never through her own strength gain the security she sought; she had neither the population nor the industrial apparatus to compete successfully with Germany. If she pursued the traditional courses of French diplomacy, she could maintain her great power status only by means of jerry-built alliances and by invoking the moral slogans of the League of Nations, which might well fall apart at the first serious test. England refused to ratify a device called the Geneva Protocol, which would have bound her to come to the aid of France with her military forces in the event of a German aggression. The language of the protocol was of course not as plain or limited as that. Recommended unanimously by the League of Nations on October 2, 1924, to the various governments represented in its chambers, the protocol provided for what was called "the peaceful settlement of international disputes." Under its articles every country represented in the League of Nations would be guaranteed against an unjustified attack and would be obliged to come to the aid of an "attacked or threatened state."[17] The whole idea originated with an Englishman, Lord Robert Cecil, and was proposed to the league by Ramsay MacDonald. The protocol, however, was unacceptable to the British dominions, which were no longer convinced of the practical need or moral imperatives for them to send their young men to fight in any European war other countries might decide to wage. The newly elected Conservative government of Stanley Baldwin rejected it, and France was left with her alliances with Belgium, Czechoslovakia, Poland, and the other small and militarily not very impressive succession states of World War I.

It was at this point that Stresemann revived an idea first put forth in December 1922 by Chancellor Cuno but rejected out of hand by Poincaré. This was the modest proposal that Germany and France together with Britain and Italy and with the United States acting as a trustee guarantee the status quo on the Rhine by mutually agreeing with one another not to go to war for a generation. Poincaré, who still nourished other hopes for the Rhineland, said in reply that the plan would only weaken the position of France and that she would not walk into the trap.[18]

This time the proposal fell on more willing ears. Briand, far from rejecting it, called it a boon to mankind, and the Pact of Locarno that resulted became a model for the postwar spirit of reconciliation and peaceful solutions of age-old differences. The pact provided for a treaty of mutual guarantees of the French, German, and Belgian borders, to be signed by those countries and by Great Britain and Italy; for arbitration agreements between Poland, France, Belgium, Czechoslovakia, and Germany; and, as double insurance, for Franco-Polish and Franco-Czechoslovakian treaties of mutual assistance in the event of an unprovoked attack. Locarno was hailed rapturously, but in both France and Germany it was also received with considerable skepticism, not to say cynicism. On October 5, 1926, on the occasion of a speech Stresemann had made in Cologne, the correspondent in Germany of *La Nation* wrote: "A malicious observer could note that Stresemann talked in a hall draped with imperial flags and where most of the delegates wore the insignia of the Hohenzollerns in their lapels. Nowhere were to be seen the little ribbons of the Republic. It is thus that in Germany one expresses his attachment to the Republic. . . . Populist or Democrat, Junker or Socialist, every German remains a German. Stresemann is a friend of all the world. But it is clear that he does not possess the mystique of peace that animates Briand. He inclines toward peace because at the moment it seems to him the best way to obtain the recovery of Germany, but he would incline to war with a tranquil head and regular digestion if he thought Germany would gain by it. He has had the bad taste—but is he not a German?—to insist heavily on the origins of the war and on the nonguilt of Germany. He is ready to have an impartial tribunal examine the question of responsibility for the war. That is useless! History has dealt with the question and has pronounced its verdict."[19]

In the Reich, the four German Nationalists in Luther's* cabinet resigned in protest against Locarno, Hindenburg had no enthusiasm for

---

* Luther, the man who with Schacht had stabilized German currency, had no party affiliation. A former mayor of Essen and minister of finance, he became chancellor because it was hoped that he could rally the support of a moderate coalition more easily than a man representing any one party.

the pact, and it was denounced by Ludendorff, who called it a document of "shame and dishonor." Fearing it would bring Germany into the anti-Soviet camp, it was also attacked by the Communist party leaders in Germany and in Russia, where Stalin called it "only a continuation of Versailles," designed to uphold the status quo where Germany remained the conquered and the Entente the victors. Locarno, he said, gave legal sanction to new borders that were favorable to France and Poland, it confirmed the German loss of her colonies, and it bound the Reich hand and foot in a Procrustes bed. Seeckt, too, thought Locarno one-sided and of no practical use. Germany, he said, was too weak to be able to act with the other states as an equal; the Reich was a mere object of policy, at the most a pliant ally that could be dropped when she was no longer useful or when a better ally could be found. What Germany needed, he thought, was a free hand in the East.[20] For Seeckt the solution to Germany's problems lay in regaining her military strength; when that was accomplished everything else would fall into place. Once the shackles of Versailles were broken, the French could invade neither the Rhine nor the Ruhr, and what had been lost in the East and West might well be regained in the same way it had been won by the enemy. Seeckt wanted a prudent Eastern orientation, a Russo-German relationship that at least in its military potential would more than balance that of the French and their allies.

A Russian alliance remained a dazzling and not always theoretical possibility for many German nationalists. Even Stresemann told the British ambassador, D'Abernon, that had the Reich been pushed too far by the French she would have had to turn to the Soviet Union, and together they would have flooded over Europe. D'Abernon thought Stresemann was bluffing, that German civilian and military leaders would never have agreed to the bolshevization of the Reich, which would have been an inevitable consequence of opening the gates to the Russian army, Soviet propaganda, and the secret police. Nevertheless, the idea was always more than a mere dream or a nightmare. As early as 1921, just after the plebiscite in Upper Silesia, the first German military mission was sent to Moscow for preliminary explorations on the possibility of military collaboration. Lenin had been all in favor of Russian approaches to the Reichswehr, and in 1922 Seeckt met with Radek in Berlin for military discussions that helped pave the way to Rapallo.

These were the beginnings of a successful if small-scale collaboration that would continue until after Hitler took power a decade later. The Soviet leaders, eager to break out of the *cordon sanitaire* that had surrounded them since 1919, offered the Germans an air base in Lipetsk, some 300 kilometers southwest of Moscow, and in 1924 the Germans began building it. This was followed in 1927 with the establishment of a school for gas warfare near Saratov on the lower Volga, and in 1930 with a school for tank warfare at Kazan in the middle Volga. Artillery shells were manufactured for German use in the Urals. In return the Soviet Union was permitted to train technical cadres in Lipetsk and to send officers to Berlin, where they were schooled in the operational practices of the German General Staff (despite its theoretical abolition under the Versailles Treaty) and in addition were allowed to accompany the high command on troop maneuvers.[21]

The numbers of men involved were not large. Lipetsk, for example, had four escadrilles with an average of 60 men each and ground crews of from 100 to 200 men, but the operation had a considerable psychological effect on the German personnel who took part in it, and it served to make them and the German High Command feel they were abreast of military developments. It also served as some kind of token reinsurance against the overwhelming military power of France together with her allies, a force for which the Reich had been able to find no reply except passive resistance when the Ruhr was invaded. German fliers were first trained in Germany in sports and commercial aircraft, and they graduated to the military flying school at Lipetsk for their final training. One hundred Fokker fighter planes were ordered in Holland, paid for out of funds earmarked for the passive resistance in the Ruhr. Junkers built factories in Russia, one near Moscow, that produced 300 planes a year, 200 for the Reich and 100 for the Soviet Union. Funds were hard to come by, in part because of the essential secrecy of the enterprise. Although the Reichspräsident, the chancellor, and the defense minister were aware of the training of the fliers and tank crews, in the nature of things the operation could not be publicized or debated in the Reichstag, and the average sum available for the Germans being trained in Russia and the supply and maintenance of their equipment was only 10 million marks a year. Both funds and materials were in such short supply that the Fokkers had to be cannibalized to provide spare parts as machines wore out. The main benefit of the cooperation was psychological on the German side. Planes could not be flown over Poland but flew to the Soviet Union by way of Lithuania and Latvia, at high altitudes and without intermediate landings. Ships manned solely by officers, for security reasons, sailed back and forth to and from Soviet ports, and the corpses of German fliers who were killed during the training in Lipetsk were shipped back to the Reich in crates labelled "machine parts." Not even close relatives in Germany were told the whereabouts of the young men who were sent to Russia. The Russo-German staff cooperation tended to be one-sided. Although Russian officers were permitted to participate in the German war games, attend maneuvers, go on inspection trips, and take part in the German training programs for higher officers, the Russian army did not, as a general rule, reciprocate. In 1925, however, German officers disguised as members of a visiting Communist delegation were permitted to go along on the great Russian maneuvers of that year, and later similar observers were allowed to wear their uniforms. But the combined air maneuvers that had been planned were never carried out, and the Germans were permitted only a limited observation of Russian artillery exercises.

The German personnel in the bases were under the continual surveillance of the Soviet secret police, but in carrying out their air patrols they were completely free; they could fly wherever they wished, without hindrances of any kind. In addition, the Germans lived well on supplies furnished by the Soviet Union in a time when the Russian population was suffering acute deprivations. The Russians were hospitable, but personal relations were kept to a minimum; all invitations were for groups; there was no opportunity for establishing close personal ties. Nevertheless, the Russians from the beginning were obviously in favor of the collaboration, as was the Reichswehr. Even after Hitler came to power, the Germans were provided with the same Soviet work forces they had had before, and the Reichswehr, too, would have been glad to continue the relationship.

From the point of view of the German High Command, the best hope of protecting the country lay in evading the conditions of Versailles as far as they could without provoking reprisals the army was too weak to counter. Under the treaty, the Rhineland was to be evacuated in stages, but when on January 10, 1925, the Allies were due to evacuate Cologne, they refused. The Germans, they said, had not carried out their treaty obligations; the general staff was still in being, police formations were in reality military units, and Krupp was manufacturing munitions and other firms other kinds of war materials beyond the quotas. The Allied Military Control Commission did not mention the German bases in the Soviet Union, because it knew nothing about them. But the Germans, from Stresemann to the Far Right and Left, were indignant at the continued occupation of Cologne. Luther and Stresemann pointed out that the so-called violations were trivial; that the army had been reduced to 100,000 men, and the air force, the tanks, and the big guns had been destroyed. Stresemann said in a note replying to the Allied charges that an occupation lasting so long and involving so much territory had scarcely a parallel in past centuries, that such measures had never furthered peaceful cooperation, that they were out of all proportion to the alleged violations on the part of the Reich, and that they were a heavy blow to German efforts to forward reconciliation.*

* Luther quoted Herriot's own admission that 33,000 cannons, 23,000 gun carriages, 11,000 minethrowers, 87,000 machine guns, 4½ million rifles, and 10 million hand grenades among other weapons had been destroyed, and against such figures the Allies could only bring up the discovery of an extra 100,000 rifle barrels,

It all made hard going for Stresemann, but he doggedly trudged along and slowly made his way, inside the Reich as well as outside. One of the Nationalists who opposed the Locarno Pact as well as Germany's joining the League of Nations was Crown Prince Wilhelm, and in a letter to him in September 1925[22] Stresemann explained what he was trying to do by way of Locarno and the League of Nations. Stresemann said that one of Germany's great tasks was to correct the eastern borders, including Upper Silesia, and to win back Danzig and the Polish Corridor. In the background, he wrote, was the *Anschluss* with Austria, which would, however, bring not only advantages but also disadvantages to Germany. It would mean a rise in the Catholic population and an increase of Bavaria's importance compared with that of Prussia, as well as an increase in the influence of the Catholic hierarchy and of the Socialists in Austria. The renunciation of Alsace-Lorraine, in any event, was theoretical, since Germany had no means of waging a war against France. Entering the League of Nations would not affect Germany's choice between East and West; a country has no real choices when it is powerless, so Germany could not be England's dagger on the Continent or ally itself with Russia. To flirt with Bolshevism was utopian. If the Red flag waved over the *Berliner Schloss*, Russia would bolshevize Europe up to the Elbe, and the Soviet Union would leave the rest of Germany for the French to devour. Nevertheless, the Soviet Union was changing. It would develop, and there would be opportunities for understanding on another basis. The Reich's most important task was to free German soil from foreign occupation and to get the throttler off its throat. Therefore Germany, as in the time of Metternich when Napoleon dominated Europe, had to make use of finesse and to avoid the big decisions.

Stresemann did not sign the letter, but its contents and authorship soon became known, and he was accused of dealing from both ends of the deck. Nevertheless, he was able to convince both Chamberlain and Briand that the charge was false or at least exaggerated; that he had but one main goal and that was to set a course of conciliation for the Reich and for western Europe that would last for at least a generation. After all, his letter to the crown prince was written to one of the ardent Nationalists whose support he could well use on behalf of Locarno and Germany's entering the league. Nothing in the letter essentially contradicted this foreign policy. Finesse was not new in European diplomacy,

---

17,000 machine gun barrels, 10,000 pistol barrels, and 100 tool kits. (*Schulthess' Europäischer Geschichtskalender*, 1925, pp. 20–24.)

Gessler cited figures of German armaments destroyed that were a good deal higher than these, and in addition he said the Allied Control Commission, with Britain and France often disagreeing with one another, had ordered the destruction of more than 50 million gold marks' worth of material that was to be used for purely peaceful purposes like housing. (Otto Gessler, *Reichswehrpolitik in der Weimarer Zeit*, pp. 226–28.)

nor was the aim to be strong and to deal as an equal confined to the Reich. Germany could only make use of the Eastern orientation as a threat and of an alliance with the Soviet Union as a last resort. Stresemann was well aware of this, and he had not only the Soviet Union in mind when he met with Chicherin for a long conversation to explain the Reich's neutralist intentions before departing for the Locarno conference. An out-and-out alliance with the Soviet Union was impossible, as Stresemann had said in his letter; nevertheless its potential must be maintained if Germany was to deal with the Allies as any kind of equal, and in the Reich not only military men but also diplomats like Ago von Maltzan and Brockdorff-Rantzau pressed strongly for closer ties with Russia.

Locarno represented genuine concessions on the part of the Reich. Despite Germany's military helplessness, to recognize formally and voluntarily the final loss of Alsace-Lorraine was a giant step for a country that had always maintained the territory to be more German than French and that asked why, if the French were so sure of the sentiments of the inhabitants, they did not hold a plebiscite. To defuse the border of the Rhineland and to accept the Reich's territorial losses in the West as definitive in a treaty backed by three of its late enemies were no light undertaking, and the immediate advantages for the Reich did not promise to be overwhelming by comparison with the renunciations. But the advantages were soon apparent. The French did not want to leave Cologne but they did, a little more than a year later than the Germans had expected, on February 1, 1926; and Locarno helped them move with some plausible explanations to their own nationalists as to why they should leave.

To be sure, the guarantees of the Locarno signatories did not include Germany's eastern frontiers; the Reich could not enter into an Eastern Locarno covering territory every German believed had been wrenched from them in the face of the Allies' principles of self-determination and the plebiscites favoring the Reich. No German regarded the Polish borders as final. The most any government in the Reich could concede was that its claims for territorial revision would be made by peaceful means, and in this view the Reich was supported by Britain, who had no intention of going to war over a French guarantee of Poland's acquisition of territory on Germany's eastern border. Separate treaties of arbitration were signed with Poland and Czechoslovakia, but there was no Eastern Locarno. No German government of any coloration could recognize the borders of Upper Silesia, the Polish Corridor, or the status of the Free City of Danzig as definitive in the way it could agree to the loss of Alsace-Lorraine. Stresemann said one reason the Reich could accept Alsace-Lorraine's returning to France was that, in effect, its loss could not be prevented. But the case was different with regard to what he **and** his countrymen considered a backward, incompetent Poland with its preposterous claims on ancient German cities and territory whose inhabitants, as demonstrated in a plebiscite, overwhelmingly preferred to be part of the Reich as their ancestors had been for centuries.

Linked to Locarno was the issue of Germany's joining the League of Nations. The league, as many German spokesmen in and out of the Reichstag often pointed out, was an organization rooted in the Versailles Treaty, and all shades of German opinion, including Nationalists, Social Democrats, and Communists, had long seen in it nothing more than an instrument specifically designed to nail down the victory of the Entente and cover its naked power politics. The league used elaborate declarations of high purpose to say, in effect, that now that the Allies had achieved their goal of reducing Germany to impotence, any basic change in the configuration of Versailles was illegal and immoral. An SPD deputy in the Reichstag said that the League of Nations represented the capitalists of the world,[23] and the German Communists followed what had been the Moscow line from the time of Lenin, who viewed the League of Nations as an organization of predatory, imperialist states that would be glad to have Germany join with them in their anti-Soviet conspiracy. Chicherin, the Soviet commissar for foreign affairs, thought Britain, with the Tories in power, was recruiting a united front against the Soviet Union. He said that Germany would be required under Article 16 of the league charter to let foreign troops go through Reich territory in pursuit of an aggressor, and the Soviet Union saw in the application of that provision the aim of the Allies to add the strategic territory of the Reich to the *cordon sanitaire* encircling Russia. In the event of another war with Poland, in which the league declared Russia the aggressor, France could demand the right to send troops through Germany (which is what she had wanted to do only a few years before) to the rescue of her Polish ally. Chicherin assured the Germans the Soviet Union had no intention of ever knocking at the door of the League of Nations for admission; the league would have to wait a long time for that, said Chicherin; as far as he was concerned, forever.[24]

Nevertheless, bound up not only with Locarno but also with the spirit of reconciliation was inevitably the issue of Germany's joining the Great Powers in Geneva. This was a prudent step that men like Stresemann were convinced would be useful to the Reich as well as to the cause of European peace if Germany made her conditions clear. Few Germans were enamoured of the league, but some of those who opposed it came to think there might be advantages in being inside its walls instead of out. Outside the league, the Reich could only protest the treatment of the German minority in Poland, where Berlin had a long list of grievances: Germans who had opted for the Reich were being expelled and their businesses confiscated; German schools were prevented from teaching in German; and frequent acts of brutality were committed against ethnic Germans. Inside the league, the Reich could make such protests more effectively. And there were other cases where the league might be a useful forum for German demands for equality. Under the terms of the Versailles Treaty, its members were committed to disarmament, but so far it was only the defeated powers that were disarmed. The French, as the German government pointed out in a note, had 5,000 tanks, 1,500 airplanes, and all the heavy guns of a power armed to the teeth; and neither France nor her allies in the little Entente showed the slightest evidence of intending to reduce their forces. A German note in December 1924[25] catalogued the numbers in the armies of France's allies: one country (Belgium) with less than 8 million inhabitants had a standing army of 80,000 men; another (Czechoslovakia) with less than 14 million had an army of 150,000 men; a third (Yugoslavia) with less than 30 million had an army of 275,000; a fourth (Poland) with less than 40 million had more than 700,000 men under arms. In addition, they all had conscription, which meant they could have many more men in case of war. Germany, on the other hand, found itself completely powerless, and if war came as a result of league sanctions being invoked under Article 16, Germany would be unable to prevent an invasion of its territory; the defense of the Reich would be entirely dependent on other members of the league, who could not be required to engage their forces on her behalf. In most foreseeable cases, the Reich's note said, Germany would be the predestined battlefield in any European war in which the league engaged. The very existence of the league was inconsistent with one-sided disarmament. Those were the Reich's reservations, and the compromise formula reached with the six league powers represented at Locarno attempted to meet them. It declared that the obligations of a member of the league were to be "consonant with its military strength and its geographical situation," a reservation that Stresemann thought protected the Reich even though Germany remained disarmed.

For Stresemann and Luther, the league's advantages considerably outweighed its disadvantages: the Reich had defined the limits of its obligations in its interpretations of the charter, and it would enter the league as an equal of the Great Powers; it would sit on the council as one of five permanent members, joining France, Britain, Italy, and Japan; this, indeed, was a precondition of its joining the league.*

This arrangement, agreed on at Locarno by Briand, Chamberlain, Luther, and Stresemann, provoked strong opposition within the League

---

* Under the league charter, four members of the council, later increased to six, were chosen from among the smaller states and were to be rotated from time to time. Belgium, Brazil, and Spain had been elected to the council in 1920 and had remained on it.

of Nations. Poland—it was believed in some quarters on the instigation of French nationalists, and strongly supported by their press—made its own claim for a permanent seat on the council, as did Spain and Brazil. On this point, however, Stresemann was unyielding, and since Brazil cast a negative vote in the League Council, Germany's entrance had to be postponed for some months. During the intervening time, the difficulty was met by a compromise acceptable both to the Reich and to most of the league members: Germany was admitted to the council as one of the five permanent members and three new seats were added, their occupants to be elected by two-thirds of the assembly. This would make it possible for Spain and Brazil to become at least semipermanent members of the council, but it satisfied neither of them, and they both quit the league. It was a trade the other members of the league were ready to make.

But Germany's eastern door was kept open. Chicherin, pressing for a strengthening•of the Rapallo Treaty to preclude even the shadow of an anti-Soviet united front that included Germany, had gone to Berlin, and he urged now that a new pact be concluded before the Reich entered the league. And Stresemann, who believed it possible to have good relations with both East and West, had little choice if he was to pursue this evenhanded policy. So the Treaty of Berlin was signed on April 24, 1926, a few days before the Reich was invited to take part in the deliberations of the study committee of the league that was to draw up the compromise to enable Germany to join the council as a permanent member. Stresemann, therefore, whether by design or not, was put in a position where he could still play the Eastern card to obtain concessions the Entente, in any case, was ready to make.

The Treaty of Berlin was to run for five years, and like the Treaty of Rapallo, it contained no secret clauses. It stated that German-Russian relations were based on Rapallo, that if either state were attacked despite its peaceful posture the other would remain neutral, and that neither would join an economic or financial boycott or coalition against the other. Stresemann explained in an accompanying letter to the Russian ambassador in Berlin, Krestinski, that the treaty was designed to uphold the general peace and that it was consonant with Germany's entering the league and with Articles 16 and 17 of the covenant that provided for sanctions against an aggressor. To this the Soviet ambassador merely replied that he duly noted the point. Stresemann also said that if a charge of aggression under these articles were made against the Soviet Union, it could be binding on Germany only if she agreed, and she could not be compelled to take sanctions.

Although both Briand and Stresemann had short terms as prime ministers in the twenties, they remained as foreign secretaries for long periods —Briand from 1929 to 1932, Stresemann from 1923 to 1929. France's economic crisis resulted in Poincaré's again being called on to form a government in which he was premier and minister of economics, but he did not intervene in the policies Briand had undertaken. Luther had to resign as chancellor on a seemingly trivial but highly emotional issue—the flying of the old imperial colors alongside the Reich's flag. The Weimar Constitution, as a sop to Nationalist sentiments, authorized the German merchant fleet to fly the black, red, and white flag with the colors of the republic in its upper-left-hand corner. Hindenburg, who for most of his long life had served under the imperial colors, had issued an order authorizing raising the merchant marine flag alongside the republic's black, red, and gold on German consulates and embassies and in foreign harbors, where by extension, it could be argued, the merchant marine colors might well be flown. Luther, agreeing with him, countersigned the order, and the result was a furious conflict that evidenced the deep schism in German political life. The republican parties saw in the order an attack on the constitution and the very being of the republic, a reactionary gesture not far removed from another attempt at a coup. The Social Democrats and the Democrats supported a resolution of "no confidence" against Luther, which passed in the Reichstag because the Nationalists abstained from voting rather than support the detested Luther, and he had to resign as chancellor. The order on flying the two flags remained in force, but the issue had brought to a boiling point the passions that seethed in every German election and in every mass demonstration; only on this occasion the Nationalists were brought to a state of quivering inaction by being caught between their ardor for the old flag and their rage against Luther.

Marx replaced Luther but Stresemann remained at his post, and thus the way was prepared for the ceremonial entrance, in September 1926, of the Reich into the system of collective security of the League of Nations. Stresemann's appearance before the League Assembly at Geneva was met with a tremendous ovation. The occasion marked the return of the Reich to a recognized place among the nations, even though as a power factor its position remained negligible. The Allies agreed to reduce the number of the troops guarding the Rhine bridgeheads in zones two and three, which remained after the evacuation of Cologne in zone one. A German note had called the occupation one of the most onerous conditions of Versailles, and German papers printed articles on its excesses and its costs, all of which were being borne by the Reich. The *Augsburger Postzeitung* showed that a French lieutenant general received 4,038 marks a month and his English counterpart 6,773 marks a month, as against the pay of a German lieutenant general, which was 610 marks a month. And so it went, on down the line: a French colonel received 2,520 marks a month, an English colonel 3,417, and a German colonel only 387; a French major was paid 1,956 marks a month, an

English major, 1,866, and a German major 287.75; a French captain received 1,567 marks a month, an English captain 1,347, and a German captain 241.25.[26] In any event, all of the costs in the Rhine garrisons were paid for by the Germans, who did not want foreign troops on their soil in the first place. Not only this, but contrary to the German practice when they had occupied French territory in 1871, the French brought their families with them, including remote relatives, and their upkeep, too, was paid for by the Reich. Briand said, and with some justice, that the Germans kept making demands—a maximum of demands as against a minimum of fulfillment—but in fact the Allies had written a ticket that would be impossible for any government of any country to redeem, and the Germans would have to wait a long time—perhaps, if the French had their way, forever—before they achieved genuine equality with their conquerors, who had needed so much outside help to get them to the Rhine.

Stresemann's policies of reconciliation and renunciation pleased the British and, to some degree, the French, but for a sizeable section of the German population what he had accomplished was ambiguous, and for the Far Right and Left it was little short of high treason. The war guilt clause remained, as did the reparations payments, which accompanied an unemployment rate in the Reich that in December 1925 went over one million for the first time since the end of the war. Nationalist speakers and the nationalist press made constant attacks on Stresemann, and one such fell little short of calling for his assassination. It was a campaign of hatred reminiscent of the defamation of Rathenau, and the wild story that Rathenau's sister was married to Radek was paralleled by the rumor that Stresemann's sister-in-law was married to Poincaré. Any weapon of any kind fitted into the arsenals of the fanatics of patriotism.

Nevertheless, Germany was slowly emerging from its state of dependency, and the tumultuous ovation given Stresemann on the occasion of the Reich's joining the League of Nations was but one manifestation of the welcome awaiting its return to a place of influence in Europe. The neutrals of the Continent, Switzerland, Sweden, Norway, Holland, and Spain, had never been as susceptible to the Allied charges of German war guilt and war atrocities as the United States had been, and they, as well as large numbers of the peoples who had fought against Germany in the war, could now applaud the reappearance of the Reich in the councils of Europe. What the enthusiasm meant was not entirely clear, but revisionism among the historians was paralleled in countless articles in the English and American press. It was also evident in the reactions of British and especially American soldiers who had served in France and taken part in the occupation of Germany, where many of them were reported as saying their countries had fought on the wrong side. In addition, there was confident talk about a new order of peace in the world, expressing the hope that the millions of war dead had not died for empty promises and that mass mechanized slaughter had become too horrible for the human race to endure. Germany's appearance in Geneva strengthened these hopes, but it did not change the bleak reality that the victorious powers on the Continent were still bristling with arms, even though they were faced, not with the millions of soldiers of imperial Germany, but with a demilitarized, democratic Reich and a militarily impotent Austria. The only concession France made to the promise of disarmament in the treaty was to reduce the time of service of her conscripts to one year, while her annual military budget continued to rise.

France, like Germany, felt herself called upon to carry a heavier burden than she could bear. Her military establishment was as large as ever and cost more than before; she had incurred war debts to Britain and the United States beyond her power to repay; she had lost millions of francs in Russian war loans repudiated by the Soviet government; and not only had the Boche failed to pay for everything, but the reparations did not even match the current deficits. When Poincaré again became premier, the franc had fallen to one-tenth of its prewar value, in contrast to Germany's now solid mark. When, following Germany's ceremonial entrance into the league, Stresemann and Briand met for breakfast at an inn in the little town of Thoiry in the Jura Mountains, it was Briand who was seeking help for France's financial troubles and it was Stresemann who was in a position to make conditions for giving it. What was needed, he told Briand, was a general solution of French-German differences: the Rhineland should be evacuated by the end of September 1927, the Allied Military Control Commission abolished, and the Saar returned to Germany on the mutually acceptable price for the mines of 300 million gold marks. In return Germany would make the funds available from the mortgages held on its railroads to shore up the sagging franc.* France's share, he estimated, would come to 750 million gold marks. As it turned out, Poincaré was able to improve the value of the franc without the German funds, but the meeting at Thoiry demonstrated dramatically how swiftly the economic balance had shifted. Only three years before, when France occupied the Ruhr, the Reich's currency had been worthless.

Even the hitherto inflexible Poincaré had to take account of the change, although he continued to make speeches in the old vein, ham-

---

* One of the chief safeguards of the German mark was the provision under the Dawes Plan for Germany to transfer reparations indirectly to the creditor countries, by way of the Reparations Commission, which would transfer the funds piecemeal so as not to endanger the stability of the mark. To turn over the sums represented by the mortgages directly to France would eliminate this protection, and Stresemann told Briand the proposal was meeting stiff opposition in Germany.

mering his theme of the kaiser's war guilt and accusing the Germans—
but not all Germans, he made clear—of still harboring designs to regain
Alsace-Lorraine. In a speech at Lunéville in June 1927,[27] he said France
had spontaneously stretched out her hand to the conquered, but only
on condition that no attempt be made to place her victory in question.
France, he said, had never made any demands beyond the treaty. She
required only security for her borders and reparations payments. She had
demonstrated her peaceful intentions at Locarno and Geneva; and, he
asked, why then, only two weeks ago, had Germany ostentatiously sent
a warship named *Alsace* to Lisbon? Why did a German minister [Strese-
mann] say after Locarno that Germany's renunciation of force was
dictated by its lack of power? Why did he say that Germany in no way
had morally renounced German provinces and their German inhabitants,
and why did another German minister explicitly say he regarded Alsace
as a German province? Why did German financial authorities already
foresee that within two years the Reich would demand a revision of
the Dawes Plan? If Germany would say to France: " 'I have renounced
Alsace-Lorraine that I tore from you by force in 1871 and that unanimously protested the annexation, and I don't ever intend to take it back
from you either by force or subterfuge . . .'; if Germany would reorga-
nize its police, dissolve the military formations, give up its arsenals and
barracks maintained in contradiction to the provisions of Versailles, then
it would give the world pledges of peace. . . . People have taken me," he
said, "for a kind of monomaniac, the hair-raising personification of the
poor Lorrainian who cannot free himself from any designs save those of
revenge. But," he added, "our dead have thought that a war declared
on them would not end until France got back its provinces that had
been taken from her. Victory has crowned our efforts, and France wants
nothing more than peace and the observance of the treaties."

That was the old, loaded speech that had been endlessly repeated,
but it was followed by different ones. Little by little the tone changed. In
1928 Poincaré said it was he who had instigated the discussions at
Thoiry to settle the outstanding problems between France and Germany. Not only had he permitted Briand to pursue his policy of reconciliation, but he took credit for initiating it. In a speech in Carcas-
sonne on April 1, 1928, he denounced his political opponents who would
return to a policy of mistrust of Germany; he was determined to work
for a reconciliation of the spirit and of the heart, he said. And in an
interview with a German journalist he went so far as to admit that
Article 231 of the Versailles Treaty, making Germany solely responsible
for the war, had been "regrettable." When his interlocutor asked him
why, then, he kept needling the German people with his accusation of
war guilt, he denied that he had ever done that; it was only the kaiser's
regime, he said, that he had been attacking. He had no rancor toward

Germans, none toward the republic. But the Germans might be excused for seeing his activities in a different light; it was not against the kaiser's Reich that Poincaré had ordered the French army to invade the Ruhr and the Rhineland cities, nor were his efforts to set up separatist states directed against the kaiser, but against the republic. The attacks on the Weimar Republic for its alleged failures to disarm seemed specious in the face of the enormous French armament plus that of her allies. The violations discovered by the Allied Control Commission were very minor; nothing had been found that would contradict the essential fact that Germany had indeed disarmed and could not possibly resist the war machine at the disposal of Poincaré's, or of any other French, government.

Poincaré's problem, however, remained what it had always been. He of course knew that Germany was disarmed and no possible threat to French security in the 1920s or for perhaps a decade to come. But what was to happen over a period of twenty or thirty years? As he said, neither France's birthrate nor the state of her economy was favorable compared with Germany's, and if Alsace-Lorraine was to remain part of France, it would only be held through a combination of strategies: by maintaining France's military predominance, her system of alliances, the collective security of the League of Nations, and, last but not least, Germany's acquiesence in the loss of the disputed provinces. Locarno had done that, but Locarno, too, was a moment in history, and what was this talk of never renouncing German territory and this business of naming warships *Alsace* but the rumbling of a distant drum?

So the policies of reconciliation were victorious in both countries for the same reasons: no alternatives to them were at hand for the short run, and both Stresemann and Briand were determined to make the run as long as possible. When the Nobel Peace Prize was jointly awarded them in December 1926, a good many people believed a historical breakthrough had been made, that a bloody enmity had been laid to rest and that the sacrifice of millions of young lives had been given a significance beyond their heroism. In a telegram of congratulations to Stresemann on his receiving the Nobel award, Hjalmar Schacht wrote: "Another three years of foreign policy under your leadership and the silver streaks will become the rosy dawn." The Reich had reached a wonderful plateau of general goodwill in which many countries shared. The German recovery had been made possible with the help of more than three billion marks in loans, mainly from the United States, and they were made available not only because the republic seemed to be a good financial risk but also because it promised to achieve a new level of international cooperation in the voluntary renunciation of territory, in the strengthening of collective security in the League of Nations, and in agreements to arbitrate differences without recourse to slaughter. That the change could come about only three years after the Ruhr invasion and the collapse of the German currency was a tribute not only to the Reich but also to the countries that had aided in its recovery—not forgetting the France of Briand.

The question was whether a brave new spirit was animating Europe, immanent in Briand and Stresemann, or whether they had merely created a short-lived state of euphoria. From the point of view of the nationalists in both countries, Locarno was either a sham, or a surrender of just claims, or a cosmetic device to obscure basic *malaises* that would inevitably reappear in a more virulent form. In Germany, General von Seeckt was forced to resign when it was discovered that he had permitted Prince Wilhelm, the son of the crown prince, to attend the autumn maneuvers of the Reichswehr. Seeckt had acted on his own without consulting Defense Minister Gessler, the chancellor, or the president. Since Wilhelm was heir to the Hohenzollern throne, his presence at the maneuvers had created a great uproar in the Reichstag and in the press that would have been difficult for the government to deal with under any circumstances, but it became impossible when it was learned that Seeckt had acted entirely on his own initiative and showed no disposition to repent of his indiscretion or to explain his action. He had never disguised his slight esteem for Gessler, a civilian defense minister handing down commands to officers accustomed to giving and receiving orders only from one another, and he did not think himself called on to excuse his conduct in this affair either to Gessler or to the Reichstag.

When the furor threatened the survival of the Marx government, it had no choice but to demand Seeckt's resignation, and this Gessler did in a polite letter that spoke of their long collaboration and Gessler's reluctance to see Seeckt leave. Marx and Hindenburg approved the decision and Seeckt obeyed, although there was some talk among the officers of Seeckt's placing himself at the head of the army and leading a revolt against what Seeckt regarded as the subversive elements in the country, whose real aim was the destruction of the army. The revolt never got beyond the talking stage, though; it would have meant a rising not only against the Marx government but against Hindenburg and the republic the generals had sworn to defend, and neither they nor Seeckt could seriously plan such an undertaking. The generals had never taken a favorable view of putsches, whether led by Kapp or Buchrucker or Hitler or Ludendorff. In the case of Seeckt, too, they could only consider the possibility and reject it as he did. In an order of the day of October 13, 1926, Seeckt said farewell to the troops. He told them he had been able to do nothing better than to try to transmit to them the virtues of the old army. "Whether I have been able to accomplish that only you, my comrades, can prove. . . ."

Seeckt's was a complex personality. Intelligent, aloof, inscrutable—one nickname for him was the Sphinx—with more than a touch of arrogance, he was admired by many but loved, or even liked, by few. The *Revue Militaire Française*, echoing Seeckt's own words about the Reichswehr's loyalty, said the army was so blindly devoted to him that it had not hesitated to fire on a general—Ludendorff—who had so often led it to victory. This was an exaggeration. The army had never fired on Ludendorff, although there is little doubt that it would have if Seeckt had so ordered. Arrogant he was, but one man's arrogance is another's indomitability, and when the Allies had demanded that Seeckt wear civilian clothes at Versailles, he said he would be glad to if Marshal Foch did the same.[28]

Seeckt was no sabre rattler; war, he said, is always a misfortune; what justifies it is survival. The goal of foreign policy, he believed, should be to promote understanding and peace and living together. But he thought France wanted to destroy the Reich and he had little confidence in Stresemann's policies; the league was not a structure of peace but an organization designed to perpetuate the conditions imposed by Versailles. Where had the league and its peace-keeping machinery been when the Ruhr and the Rhineland were invaded, or when the Irish claimed the right to self-determination, or when the Egyptians claimed independence from Britain, or when the Poles had taken Vilna from Lithuania, or when the Lithuanians had taken Memel from Germany? If it could be turned to any possible account on the Reich's behalf, he would not oppose Germany's joining it, but it remained weak and pretentious. Hindenburg thought him conceited, a serious defect in the eyes of the old field marshal with his Prussian standards of Spartan, self-effacing service to the Fatherland. But Seeckt had made of the 100,000-man Reichswehr a precision instrument that despite its size would serve both as a defense force and as a training cadre for the far larger armies that would one day be at the disposal of the Reich. He had created an army of professional, highly trained officers and noncommissioned officers who had enlisted for twelve years and who from the privates on up could assume posts of leadership above their rank when the opportunity came.

His monocle, his bearing, the distance he put between himself and the rest of the world—all these contrasted with his letters to his wife. The Seeckts were often separated when he served on the western front during the early days of the war, then in the Balkans and Poland, and later in Turkey. He wrote his wife almost every day, warm, affectionate letters to his "*Dicke*," his "Fatty," as he called her. They are revealing letters both in what they say and in what they leave out. Seeckt never complains when things are going badly at the front; he finds no scapegoats for the defeats or Siegfrieds for the victories. His heroes are the rank and file, the men who daily throw themselves on the enemy or stand their ground with no thought of themselves. He is always solicitous of his *Dicke*, concerned about everything she does, troubled if he fails to hear from her even for a few days. He sends conventional but affectionate greetings on the anniversary of their engagement: "A beautiful, dear and true day of memories. May God protect you and keep you for me as you have been for 22 years." From the Rumanian front, in the course of a long letter about what he is doing in which he advises her not to buy more war bonds with her small capital, he says he has hurt his foot slightly but she is not to worry.[29] The facts, as Frau von Seeckt later discovered, were very different. Seeckt had been pinned with a broken leg under his "fine little horse," which had fallen on the ice, and it had taken an hour under enemy fire for him to extricate himself. Finally stretcher-bearers had brought him to the rear, where they could load him onto a litter lashed to a donkey. With his leg still unbandaged, he had been carried for four hours, then shifted to another animal, and then to a train that took him to an Austrian field hospital. When he arrived at the hospital, he had refused to report sick, and with his leg in a cast he had dictated the orders for the next operations. Four days later he wrote to his wife again, expressing the hope that she was not worried and telling her the injury was merely uncomfortable and a bore; he had been walking with the cast for two days and only going up and down stairs bothered him.

The cover for one of Seeckt's most cherished operations was blown early in December 1926 when the *Manchester Guardian* disclosed the secret collaboration of the Reichswehr and the Soviet Union. Ironically enough, the story had broken when the Junkers company, which had been unable to complete its production contracts in the Soviet Union, had demanded compensation from the German government. Owing to the secrecy of the undertaking, Junkers had not been in a position to sue in the courts, but in order to put pressure on the government, had written a detailed account of its unpaid activities to a Reichstag deputy, from whom it had come into the hands of an English newspaperman. In addition, dockworkers in Stettin who had been unloading Russian ships with cargoes of hand grenades told a Social Democratic deputy, despite their pledge of secrecy, what kind of work they were doing. The story was picked up by *Vorwärts* and was the subject of an impassioned speech by Philipp Scheidemann in the Reichstag. Scheidemann told about the Junker planes and the huge sums being spent—70 million marks a year, he said, and sometimes 100,000 to 300,000 gold marks a day. He named the Russian ships that had sailed from Leningrad to be unloaded in German harbors, while another whose name he had forgotten had sunk, and in addition he accused the Reichswehr of maintaining relations with the forbidden *Verbände* and criminal organizations like *Consul.*

The Reichstag debate caused another enormous *krach* in the Reichstag, with the Right, Center, and Communists defending or denying the collaboration and the Social Democrats and their allies demanding reforms and a new government. Chancellor Marx denied that the Reichswehr had relations with the *Verbände* or any forbidden political organizations; he said the procedures for the allocations of funds for private purposes were being tightened, that the Defense Ministry's program of expenditures for such purposes could henceforth be presented to the Reichstag, if it wished, and he assured the deputies that the Reichswehr was a reliable instrument of the republic. The former Centrist chancellor, Wirth, reminded the Reichstag how critical the situation had been when he was chancellor and had to deal with French pressure and separatist movements on the Rhine and at the same time defend the eastern border against the Poles. A Communist deputy declared the documents of dubious origin and demanded to know how those who made the charges dared say that it was not honorable and proper for Reichswehr officers to negotiate with the Soviet government, with Communists who had made a successful revolution that had lasted for nine years and had kept Russia free from imperialist influences.[30]

Curiously enough the disclosures had little or no effect in Britain or on the Briand-Stresemann course of rapprochement. The *Times* said the matter should be left to the free development of German opinion; the *Manchester Guardian,* in the same issue in which the disclosures of the secret armament were published, called for the dissolution of the Allied Military Control Commission. The tide of collaboration was in full flood, and it was too welcome a change to be affected by relative trivia. After all, the Soviet-German dealings were on a small scale, and no matter how disturbing they might be to those who had nightmares over the prospect of a German-Russian entente, the Reichswehr's few planes and tanks did not seriously affect the extent of German disarmament. Furthermore, the uproar in the Reichstag and the German press was evidence enough of the German disposition to keep its own house respectable. So little were the relations between the Reich and its former enemies affected that the Allied Military Control Commission was in fact abolished at the end of 1927 and replaced by an investigations commission of the League of Nations, which had no serious task other than to cover the disappearance of the now defunct Allied military commission.

The silver streaks were brightening. The republic had survived the assaults made on it from inside and outside the borders of the Reich; its chief military officer could be dismissed by civilians with no violent reactions from either Seeckt or the officer corps. Seeckt himself had, however reluctantly, accepted his dismissal, an example of the Reichs-wehr officer who yearned for a different form of state but who would not resort to arms or sabotage to get it, and of the moderation of the Nationalists, who believed in legality whatever their low opinion of the Weimar Constitution and state might be. Far out were the kooky fringe of National Socialists and the clandestine organizations like *Consul* that were still in business and still eager to bring before their own bar of justice of the Feme Courts,* or simply to assassinate out of hand, the traitors to the Fatherland. Among them were not only savage young delinquents like those who had murdered Rathenau but Prince Oskar of Prussia, who, when he learned of the arrest of a man who had been planning to murder Stresemann, sent the prisoner fifty cigarettes and a note of appreciation. It is true that when the nature of what he had done was called to his attention he excused himself by saying he had not realized that the man had planned to murder Stresemann; he had merely thought him involved in some kind of nationalist affair. But Oskar nevertheless was another example of how unstable the psychologi-cal state of the extremists continued to be. Oskar was also a prime ex-ample of royal ingratitude; it was his brother, the crown prince, who Stresemann had allowed to return to Germany from his exile. And ranged with Prince Oskar and his like were the National Socialists. After less than nine months of imprisonment in a fortress where he had all the privileges of a guest in a provincial hotel, Hitler had emerged from his deluxe confinement in the Landsberg jail, where he had had the leisure to dictate *Mein Kampf* to Rudolf Hess. Hitler himself had been forced to curtail the list of visitors who wanted to see him in order to prevent their interfering with his work.

After he regained his freedom, he immediately reestablished his con-trol over the party, although he had to face a revolt led by the Strasser brothers and joined for a time by Joseph Goebbels, all of whom thought he had leaned too far to the capitalist side and demanded that more emphasis be placed on the socialism in the National Socialist formula. But the far-out groups were mainly a potential danger to the republic. Their putsches and assassinations had been dealt with, if only with a relatively light hand, and they had not seriously threatened the stability of the state any more than had a leftist terrorist organization like the "German Cheka."†

* The so-called Feme Courts were named after their medieval prototypes, which had often met in secret and handed down death sentences. An SPD Reichstag deputy, Müller-Franken, declared in January 1926 that sixteen Feme murders had been disclosed only a few weeks before and that twenty-eight suspects, mainly former army officers who had joined the Black Reichswehr or the Rossbach Brigade, had committed the crimes. He accused Gessler, Seeckt, and the Reichswehr of having supported these organizations and said any collaboration between legal and clandestine bodies could only lead to such events.

† The German Cheka was a Communist, terrorist organization designed to over-

The Far Right, including the National Socialists, could bring to their rallies and their party rolls no more than the 2 or 3 percent of the electorate they had collected in 1924. With President Hindenburg as head of state and Stresemann conducting foreign policy, the Reich had reached not only an equilibrium but a place where it could hope to surmount the rest of its problems, domestic and foreign, without putsches or armed conflict. The country was more alive than it had ever been in its history with experiments, ideas, and surpassing performances in the world of art, the theater, the cinema, literature, and science; and while the political scene was drab by comparison, the republic was functioning adequately enough and earning a place in world esteem that the Reich had not had since Bismarck. Left and Right were bitterly divided, but the head of state was a preeminent nationalist who had nevertheless sworn to uphold the republic and he had no hesitation in dismissing the Reichswehr's commanding general for his poor judgment and for failure to consult the civilian authorities. Furthermore, the whole operation had been conducted with no serious threat on the part of the army. The French were leaving the Rhineland, slowly to be sure, but they were leaving. The mark was one of the stable currencies of Europe. And best of all, the Hun had disappeared from the stock characters of Germany's former enemies to be replaced by the hardworking, dependable Michael.

---

throw the state and establish the dictatorship of the proletariat. Seeckt and Hugo Stinnes were among those on its list to be assassinated. Its chief vicims, however, seem to have been former Communists suspected of being spies. (Herbert Michaelis, et al, *Ursachen und Folgen*, vol. 7, pp. 298–99.)

CHAPTER 7

"Over Graves—Forward!"

WHEN, AFTER HIS RESIGNATION, Seeckt made his farewell speech to the officers of the Reichswehr Ministry on October 9, 1926, he said: "Winter may spread its shroud over the young seedlings, but over graves—forward!"[1] He liked the sentiment, which was a quotation from Goethe, so well that he repeated it in his last order of the day to the troops on October 13. "Over graves—forward!" he told them, too. It was rhetoric to which the army responded, and not only the army but the old guard—the bureaucracy, the monarchists, the nationalists of all descriptions. It was a denial of the defeat, a proclamation of purpose and hope, a reaffirmation of the spirit that survives the ruins. The wounds of the lost war and the deep divisions of the German people had never healed, never been overcome. Too many people had died, too much had been lost to reconcile the survivors to the gray, tormented world they had to live in. It would take more than silver streaks on the horizon to keep the country working together; the landscape might be green again and the sun shining in the heavens, but the bedrock had shifted.

When Seeckt was forced to resign, the fact that he could not and did not attempt any kind of coup, and that the army accepted his dismissal, was evidence of the strength of the young republic and the principle of civilian supremacy. But even here, had it not been for Hindenburg's towering presence as head of state and his approval of the cabinet's decision, Seeckt might well have resisted the invitation to resign. It was not only the Reichstag that was governed and dissolved by shifting coalitions of minorities. The press reactions to Seeckt's resignation were as mixed as those of the parties. On the whole he was rated highly, but one right-wing paper, the *Deutsche Zeitung*, said that those who saw Seeckt as a statesman either did not know what a statesman was, or they suffered from defective vision. Over and over again, the paper wrote, Seeckt could have saved the Reich from the malefactions of international high finance and the Jews, but he had always failed to act. To be sure, he had served the state, but he had made the Reichswehr a passive instrument of the state authority instead of making it into an activist attack force of national ideas. That was the true voice of the far-out Right, including the National Socialists, who rejected the man who had not only failed to join the Hitler putsch but was ready to use the Reichswehr against it. But there were other voices. The nationalist *Kreuzzeitung* asked rhetorically, "Who is Seeckt?" and answered, "the man celebrated and admired and still hated by the foreign enemy." Seeckt, the paper said, had fashioned the Reichswehr, and it could well be asked whether a German Reich would exist if this officer of the kaiser's army had not stepped into the breach. The whole episode, in the paper's view, was reminiscent of a play from an insane asylum. The *Berlin Lokal-Anzeiger* contrasted the Social Democrat, Carl Severing, who because of ill health had been forced to resign as Prussian Minister of the Interior, with Seeckt, saying that for Seeckt the Fatherland was the party while for Severing the Social Democratic party was the Fatherland. The *Deutsche Allgemeine Zeitung* wrote: "This convinced monarchist, out of his sense of military duty, has rescued the Fatherland. This is not the first case in the history of democracy when a lonely, towering figure has been brought down." The *Schlesische Zeitung* wrote: "General Seeckt has left. It is hard to say whether the rejoicing is greater in Paris or in the parties of the German Left." The *Times* of London called the dismissal a victory for German pacifism.[2]

But in the Reich clear-cut victories were few, and when they occurred they tended to be short-lived. The Right was divided, the Left was divided, and the parties in between were divided too. Stresemann's German Volksparty often failed to support him, because even the solid middle class which he and they represented was uncertain of the choices that promised to preserve it as well as the Fatherland. Curiously enough, it was the Volksparty that Seeckt joined a few years after his retirement, and later, after Stresemann's death, it was as one of its deputies that he was elected to the Reichstag. Despite their many differences, Seeckt and Stresemann were both uncompromising patriots and they could tolerate and make use of one another. Seeckt, when he left his army post, became an advisor to the foreign minister at a salary of some 20,000 marks a year, although it is not clear that he either gave, or Stresemann took, much of his advice. Their notions of where the weal of the Reich lay were too divergent for them to work closely together, but Seeckt's very presence at Stresemann's side made it difficult for the critics of fulfillment to cry treason whenever Stresemann made a proposal. For his part, Seeckt had too active a mind; he was too involved in the issues bedevilling the Fatherland to leave them to others. In addition he could use more money than his pension came to, which was about the same amount as his advisor's salary. He liked to live on a fairly high scale and he liked even more to make his presence felt.*

It is only in retrospect that a period appears in soft focus, as a time of moderation and happiness, or as a bright space for a swinging generation. For their contemporaries such intervals are as filled with tribulations as any other, and in Germany the mid-twenties were no exception. Few people seemed to take much pleasure in it at the time, but the country was doing well on almost every front: real wages climbed back toward their prewar levels, and for thousands of skilled workers they doubled between 1924 and 1928; German merchant ships were sailing the seas again; a zeppelin crossed the Atlantic. Lufthansa, with planes of advanced design, was flying passengers on regularly scheduled flights to Prague and Vienna. German chemical, machine tool, and electrical factories were producing more than ever before with new equipment bought with capital provided by foreign loans. In philosophy and art and science, the performances were dazzling. Einstein, Heisenberg, and Planck were reinterpreting the physical cosmos; Husserl, Heidegger, Jaspers, and Cassirer were providing or promising to provide new *Weltanschauungen*; and Karl Barth, Martin Buber, and Paul Tillich were wrestling with the ancient tasks of theology as perceived in the post–World War twentieth century. German writing provided one of the richest sources of contemporary literature in the fiction of Thomas and Heinrich Mann, Lion Feuchtwanger, Arnold Zweig, and Hermann Hesse; in the poetry of Rainer Maria Rilke and Stefan Georges; and in the theater of Brecht, Hauptmann, Zuckmayer, and Max Reinhardt. In the visual arts, the revolutionary designs of Walter Gropius, Mies van der Rohe, and the Bauhaus brought a new architectural style to Europe, the Far East, and the United States. The French Post-Impressionists had a more enthusiastic audience in Germany than in France, and painters like Max Beckmann, Paul Klee, and Oskar Kokoschka were made professors in Berlin, Frankfurt, and Dresden, respectively, an unusual recognition of modernists among academics.

The cities of the Reich were stone cauldrons where talent and sometimes genius boiled up, and where satirists like Kurt Tucholsky and George Grosz saw past the iridescent colors of the witches' brew the dregs at the bottom of the pot where the poisons lay. It was a time when

---

* Seeckt reported that Hindenburg, when the two men were discussing his retirement, had asked him whether he would accept an ambassadorship to Tokyo, London, or Madrid, and Seeckt had said he would. Nothing, however, seems to have come of the suggestion.

values were readily turned inside out, when people played with the idea that, as Franz Werfel wrote, not the murderer but the victim was guilty, and a favorite theme of successful plays was parricide.

Berlin was very likely the most wide open city in the world. Well-patronized homosexual bars and cabarets flourished, together with the square wickedness portrayed by Marlene Dietrich in *The Blue Angel.* The Roaring Twenties were louder in Berlin than in any other city in Germany or anywhere else in Europe or America, but there were other sounds as well—the music of Hindemith, Schönberg, and Richard Strauss, along with Beethoven, Bach, and Brahms, conducted by a Furtwängler or a Klemperer. Almost everything human surfaced in the Berlin of the twenties, and every conceivable mutation of the human spirit had its chance at survival; the possibility that it was the victim who was guilty was not much more bizarre than were the deaths of millions of young men innocent of any crime. For whom or what had they died? For the fat-bellied *Schieber* of the black markets, the absurd, vicious philistines crowding Grosz's drawings? The novelists, the playwrights, as well as writers like Spengler struggled with the answers to such questions, and the political and everyday worlds of mere survival were drab and tedious by comparison. In the contemporary writing, no one riding the subways in Berlin or toiling at the factory benches or running industries more efficiently than Europe had ever seen before is shown as having thought of the time as a golden age. It would only be much later, after the whole structure had collapsed, that it would seem to have been one.

In fact the Reich of the mid-twenties had its continuing troubles. Only in 1928 did the wages of industrial workers equal those of the prewar year 1913–1914, and the buying power of the population in the period 1925–1929 was 696 marks as against 728 marks in the period 1911–1915.[3] It was an uneasy society with reparations still to pay, unbalanced budgets, and demands on the government outrunning means of fulfilling them. The income of the bureaucrats, of the *Beamtentum,* who kept the wheels of German administration turning in every city, town, and hamlet, had been greatly diminished since before the war. German administrators had never been highly paid, but many of them, like army officers, married wives whose incomes from shares or savings helped them to live in what they regarded as a suitably respectable, middle-class fashion until the inflation and devaluation took their toll. Now the Reichstag, more than a third of whose members were themselves bureaucrats as well as deputies, voted a handsome increase that raised their salaries by from 21 percent to 25 percent depending on their civil service category. The increases, piled on other postwar expenses incurred by the municipalities and states, made a large dent in the federal budget. The Reich in 1913 had had expenses of 2,378 billion marks; in 1925 it had to pay out more than three times as much—7,903.9 billion, and the figures kept rising, to 9,182.5 billion in 1926 and to over 10,000 billion in 1927. The pay raises were undoubtedly not far out of line with the increases, during the same period, in the wages of skilled industrial workers, but the Reich could not afford to do everything it was called on to do, and Hjalmar Schacht, fearing for the stability of the mark, objected to the precipitous rise in state and municipal expenditures for what he said were mainly nonessentials: "swimming pools, libraries and sports fields." The American banker Parker Gilbert, who was general agent for reparations payments, warned that the high expenditures of the federal government, which had risen 1,700 million marks in two years, threatened the reparations due under the Dawes Plan.[4] Stresemann said much the same thing in a letter to the mayor of Duisburg, Carl Jarres. Stresemann wrote that the Prussian state had spent 14 million marks for rebuilding the Berlin Opera House, and that the final sum would probably reach 20 million. Not one of the victorious powers had been as extravagant. Other examples abounded. The mayor of Cologne, Konrad Adenauer, prided himself on having built in the city's Municipal Center the biggest organ in the world. Frankfurt am Main had a deficit of 2½ million marks for a musical exhibition it had put on. Dresden had built, with the help of Reich funds, a museum of hygiene. Stresemann asked Jarres please to tell him what he could say to the representatives of foreign powers when such performances gave the impression Germany had won, not lost, the war.[5]

The pressures for government spending had become almost impossible to resist in the Reich of the mid-twenties. With the revolution of 1918 and the abolition of the three-class voting system in Prussia, German political power had shifted from the middle and upper classes of white- and blue-collar workers to the masses, who demanded much higher expenditures for social services compared with what prewar governments had considered prudent. The growth of government was paralleled by the growth of German industrial cartels, which had risen to more than 2,500, protected by agreements with one another from domestic competition and from foreign sources by tariffs.[6] Productivity was rising in the rationalized factories running on American models of belt-line efficiency, but industries were undercapitalized and heavily dependent on foreign loans, and any depression would inevitably bring serious setbacks to both the private and government sectors, with consequent political instability far greater than before the war. Agriculture, too, had received big foreign loans—a large part of the 7 billion marks of farm indebtedness was owed abroad—and agricultural products were protected from foreign competition by import duties. This of course kept the prices of food high, but despite the criticisms of economists, the farmers, like the industrialists, were able with their right-wing support to keep the protectionist measures in force.

Nevertheless, despite the shaky substructure, the mid-twenties witnessed a period of substantial industrial expansion and a return of domestic and foreign confidence in the future of the Reich and of the capitalist world. The Reich continued the policy of providing social security begun under Bismarck and regarded by progressives in every country as one of the most enlightened anywhere. Conciliation committees, with equal representation of labor and management, and labor courts arbitrated industrial disputes to prevent another wave of strikes such as those that had followed the lost war and had often threatened to bring production to a halt. Sickness and accident insurance covered very nearly the entire working population, and government expenditures for social measures, including unemployment insurance, rose every year.[7]

In foreign affairs the Reich continued its slow emergence from the defeat so many Germans were still unable to accept. The celebration held in September 1927 to inaugurate the Tannenberg National Memorial commemorating the great victory of August 1914 was a ceremony of paradoxes. On the one hand there was the celebration of the historical triumph of German arms and leadership won by an army vastly outnumbered in guns and men that could nevertheless encircle and destroy a hard-fighting enemy. On the other hand there was the defeat still overshadowing Germany, with foreign troops still on German soil and punitive reparations to pay because the victors and the treaty declared the Reich responsible for the war.

Victory has a thousand fathers, as the saying goes, defeat none, and who was the victor at Tannenberg was still in dispute. Ludendorff was convinced he, not Hindenburg, had won the battle; others said it was Hoffmann's strategy that was decisive. Hindenburg, however, summed up the matter on an occasion when the controversy was brought to his attention. "It is fine," he said, "Tannenberg was won. Now a good many people have won it. If the battle had been lost, though, I alone would have lost it."[8]

At the opening ceremony of the memorial's dedication, the feuds emerged with the generals. Ludendorff refused to ride with Hindenburg in the same automobile from which they were jointly to review the troops, and Hindenburg in a rumbling, and for him, impassioned speech, denounced the notion that Germany was responsible for the war. Hindenburg said what all his countrymen firmly believed and what every Frenchman just as firmly rejected; after paying tribute to the memory of those who had died in the battle, on behalf of them and of those who survived, he said he felt himself solemnly bound to declare: "We, the German people of every class, unanimously reject the charge that Germany is guilty of this, the greatest of all wars. Not envy, hate, or lust of conquest placed the weapons in our hands. The war was much more for us a last resort, demanding the heaviest sacrifices of the very means of existence of an entire people against a world of enemies. We took the field with clean hearts for the defense of the Fatherland, and with clean hands the German army wielded the sword. Germany is ready at any time to place its case before neutral judges. . . ."[9] His speech, delivered as it was, not only by the legendary hero of Tannenberg but by the president of the Reich, raised a storm of protest in France. Poincaré did not reply directly, but at Belfort he reminded an audience that France had been invaded three times within sixty years, that she was dedicated to upholding peace but that peace in Europe depended on more states than one, and that France sought security, which could not be guaranteed by the League of Nations, admirable as its intentions were, and so had to depend on her own efforts. It was a theme he continued with in a speech at Bar-le-Duc on September 26, and he was joined by the French minister of justice, Jean Louis Barthou, who linked the German invasion of 1914 with the Moroccan war in which France was then engaged. Barthou said that France had wanted neither war, that Wilhelm II and Abd-el-Krim had started them. "We are guiltless," said Barthou, "of the blood that a power-seeking people, a Wilhelm II and Abd-el-Krim have spilled."[10]

No neutral judges could conciliate this conflict. The verdict, not of the Court of History, but of many historians was leaning at the time toward Germany, as British and American scholars became increasingly impressed with the evidence that had come to light.* But the more their inquiries diminished the war guilt of the Reich, the more the Germans with their bleeding borders, lost provinces, debts, and military impotence felt themselves aggrieved and the more the French felt themselves threatened.

France was still searching for the holiest of grails, which continued to elude her—security—the desperately sought-for, ultimate redoubt that she had never been able to find on the bayonets of her armies in the Ruhr and Rhineland, or in the collective security system of the League of Nations and the Locarno Pacts, or in the failed Geneva Protocol, or in her system of alliances.

But such a search can never be ended any more than the ultimate goal can be attained and Briand came up with a new proposal, this one designed to replace the treaty of guarantee France had obtained from

---

* The English historian Gilbert Murray together with other scholars, clergymen, and writers presented a petition in December 1925 that asked for a change in the war guilt clauses of Versailles, Articles 231 and 227–230. They wrote: "We are of the opinion that the Articles are manifestly unjust and a serious hindrance to international understanding." (*Schulthess' Europäischer Geschichtskalender*, 1925, pp. 262–63.)

In the United States, Sidney B. Fay in 1928 published his monumental work *The Origins of the World War*, which, like many other "revisionist" books by American scholars, placed the war guilt at least as much on the Allies as on the Germans.

President Wilson in 1919 but that had been rejected by Congress. Briand addressed himself in a message of April 6, 1927, not to President Coolidge or to the American State Department, but to the American people, proposing that the two republics, allies since before the United States obtained its independence, conclude a bilateral treaty renouncing and outlawing* war between them.

Since the last time France and the United States had gone to war had been between 1798 and 1800 when they had engaged in naval warfare without a declaration of hostilities, it was not immediately evident what practical effect such a treaty would have. For Briand, however, the goals and effects were clear enough; the United States was the chief forcing house for the cultivation of world peace movements, and while they were divided as to which measures would be most productive to this end, practically all of them were agreed that the United States had made a fateful mistake in rejecting the League of Nations and were determined to remedy the error.

Dozens of peace groups flourished in the United States,† ranging from militantly pacifist organizations whose members totally rejected the notion of bearing arms in any war, to revolutionary groups convinced that only by overthrowing the existing political and economic order could universal peace be won. Briand, however, had no interest in the pacifists, antimilitarists, or revolutionists; he was concerned to enlist the support of the believers in collective security, the members of organizations like the Carnegie Endowment for International Peace, the World Peace Foundation, the Foreign Policy Association, the Woodrow Wilson Foundation, and the American Committee for the Outlawry of War.

The most influential of these was the Carnegie Endowment for International Peace, with weighty academic credentials and a budget of more than $600,000 a year derived from a capital of $10 million invested in United States Steel bonds, which had risen considerably in the course of World War I. It had not only large sums at its disposal but a good deal of influence in educational circles and with newspapers like the *New York Times*. The endowment's president, Nicholas Murray Butler,

---

* Like Swift's Big Endians and Little Endians, the most influential peace forces in the United States were divided into two hostile camps, the "Renunciationists," headed by Nicholas Murray Butler, president of Columbia University, and James T. Shotwell, director of the Carnegie Endowment's Division of Economics and History, on the one side; and the "Outlawrists," headed by a Chicago lawyer, Salmon O. Levinson, on the other. As Robert H. Ferrell in his astute book *Peace in Their Time* pointed out, Briand, in his proposal, taking no chances on the reception of his plan, used the code words of both sides.

† In Europe the labor movement and socialist parties were invariably antimilitaristic, and there were also smaller organizations like the *Bureau International de la Paix* with headquarters in Geneva, the British League of Nations Union, the German *Friedensgesellschaft* founded in 1893, and the *Ligue des Droits de l'Homme* in France.

was also president of Columbia University, and the executive director of its Division of Economics and History, James T. Shotwell, was a member of the Columbia faculty.

Almost without exception the peace organizations were staffed with zealous, idealistic men and women genuinely convinced that war was the most devastating plague afflicting humanity and that it had become too destructive and too costly for the human race to endure. Another conflict like the last, and not only the lights of Europe, as Sir Edward Grey had said in 1914, would go out one by one, but the whole structure of civilization would be likely to collapse. The aims of the peace groups were not in question; what disturbed their critics, in addition to the yawning gap between the rhetoric of peace and the actual behavior of foreign offices, were the likely consequences of many of the peace proposals, ranging from collective security to the refusal to bear arms, on the freedom of action and the well-being of the United States. Concrete measures that could diminish the chance of war, such as the Naval Disarmament Conference President Coolidge had proposed before Briand sent his note to the American people, received no support whatever from Briand. France had declined to attend the meeting at Geneva, which was to be held in the early summer of 1927.*

There were other cooling factors, among them the still unpaid loans the United States had made to Europe during and after the war, amounting to more than $10 billion; the Allied attempt to limit their funding to Germany's payments; and the American disenchantment with the power politics of postwar Europe. President Coolidge and the State Department were therefore less than enthusiastic over the Briand proposal. The chief of the State Department's Division of Western European Affairs, J. Theodore Marriner, wrote a memorandum on June 24 suggesting that the draft of the Franco-American treaty Briand had prepared was trying to draw attention away from the Naval Disarmament Conference which had opened on June 20. Marriner wrote that what Briand wanted was "to give the effect of a kind of perpetual alliance between the United States and France, which would certainly serve to disturb the other great European powers—England, Germany and Italy. This would be particularly true as it would make the neutral position of the United States during any European war in which France might be engaged extremely difficult, since France might deem it necessary to infringe upon our rights as a neutral under this guarantee of nonaggression. It might likewise be used internally in France to postpone the ratification of the Debt Settlement and to create a feeling that payment was unnecessary."[11]

What France was seeking, in the State Department's view, was a negative alliance, something that would take the place of the positive

---

* France had been affronted when the Washington Naval Disarmament Conference of 1921–1922 recognized the Italian claim to parity with the French fleet.

alliance Mr. Wilson had agreed to in Paris in 1919. A negative alliance would involve the United States in the French security system and would make it difficult, as Marriner pointed out, for America to be neutral in any European war involving France. This, of course, was precisely what Briand and his American friends had in mind; he wanted not neutrality but a *posse comitatus.*

The forces of peace had large sums to spend on many kinds of publications, ranging from bulletins and periodicals to books, many of which dealt directly or indirectly with the need for the United States to join the system of collective security. The Carnegie Endowment for International Peace also sponsored International Relations Clubs in high schools and colleges and International Mind Alcoves, where suitable books were provided, and it helped to finance smaller peace organizations as well as endowing university chairs of international relations.

All in all the organized peace advocates exerted a good deal of influence in circles convinced that a new world order was at hand if only the United States would join it. The *New York Times* declared in an editorial that while outlawing war universally was difficult, outlawing wars one at a time as Briand proposed, between France and the United States, was clearly a step forward. However, with the combination of mistrust and skepticism shared by Coolidge, Secretary of State Frank B. Kellogg, and their advisors, the whole matter might well have been permitted to die had it not been that on May 21 Charles A. Lindbergh had flown the Atlantic. The symbol of the interrelatedness of continents and the uproarious reception accorded Lindbergh in France had given further impetus to the campaign for collaboration between the two countries to abjure war. Neither the president nor the State Department, however, would consider making a pact such as Briand proposed with France alone; if any such treaty were to be made, it would have to be open to all the countries of the world, which was not at all what Briand had in mind. But the moving finger of the peace movement was writing for him, too. Some kind of treaty on behalf of world peace had to be made, whatever the politicians and experts in their foreign offices might think of it.

The Covenant of the League of Nations, of course, already had articles designed to prevent war. In Article 10 every member pledged itself to respect the integrity and independence of the others and to join in protecting them against aggression. Article 11 declared that any war was a concern to all the members. Article 16 provided for economic or military sanctions against any aggressor. One of the main reasons the United States had refused to join the league was that under the covenant it might be required to send troops or battleships into action because the League Council declared a nation with which the United States had no quarrel whatever an aggressor. The State Department was still wary of such devices of collective security. France, for example, in 1926 found herself at war, allied with Spain, against the Moroccan forces fighting for independence headed by Abd-el-Krim, who, according to Barthou, had started the bloody conflict. France and Spain seemed able to contain Abd-el-Krim's independence movement with their own resources, but suppose they could not? Suppose the Moroccans were declared the aggressor Barthou said they were. Would this mean that under a new document involving the United States in the league's collective security, the United States would be expected to join battle to reestablish the French and Spaniards in that part of Africa? Then, too, there was the problem of the so-called "gap" or gaps in the League of Nations Covenant that the peace forces were attempting to close. One appeared when the council could not come to a unanimous agreement as to who was the aggressor, the other when a war occurred that might fit the Moroccan description, that is, one that came under domestic jurisdiction—civil or colonial war. Would a treaty such as the peace groups were advocating to bridge this gap bring the United States into conflicts even beyond those the covenant had foreseen?

It was the American secretary of state who came up with a solution that was more or less acceptable to everyone, although it took a good deal of correspondence to explain what the words of the pact meant and implied. It was clear from the beginning that the United States would not join the league's system of collective security or make any kind of alliance, negative or positive, with France alone. The British foreign secretary, Sir Austen Chamberlain, also made it plain that Britain would accept such a treaty only with reservations. In a note to Kellogg he said the pact would not apply to "certain regions of the world the welfare and integrity of which constitute the special and vital interest for our peace and safety. His Majesty's Government have been at pains to make it clear in the past that interference with these regions cannot be suffered."[12] The regions were not defined but they meant, for example, Egypt, and while Kellogg did not approve of the reservation, Chamberlain could point out that the United States had similar reservations for the Western Hemisphere, where the Monroe Doctrine was still in force. Stresemann in his note of acceptance inserted three reservations: the right of self-defense, the provision that any breach of the treaty would release the Reich from its obligations, and universal adherence as the ultimate goal of the treaty. Thus, if Russia and Poland again went to war, the Reich would not be required to involve itself in the hostilities or the countermeasures of Poland's allies. Nor was France, with its large army and alliances as its main line of defense, and preparing to spend 200 million francs on the Maginot Line, about to compromise its security with any universal pact renouncing war. A peace pact must buttress, not corrode, its system of defenses, and Briand therefore said the pact must explicitly exempt the legitimate right of self-defense within the framework of existing treaties, meaning not only Locarno but also France's military agreements with Belgium, Poland, Czechoslovakia, Rumania, and Yugoslavia. In France's case, too, Briand inserted the reservation that any breach of the treaty would release a signatory from its obligations.

Kellogg in replying to the various reservations said the right of self-defense was "inherent in every sovereign state and is implicit in every treaty. Every nation is free at all times ... to defend its territory from attack or invasion and it alone is competent to decide whether circumstances require recourse to war in self-defense."[13] So the final document that Kellogg brought forth and that was signed or adhered to by sixty-three nations either meant everything or nothing, depending on what was read into it. Whether it was a beacon lighting the way to the harbors of world peace or a straw fire on the same old horizon of power politics depended on the eye of the beholder. Following a preamble that spoke of the solemn duty of the signatories to promote the welfare of man, the pact declared: (1) "The High Contracting Parties solemnly declare in the names of their respective peoples that they condemn recourse to war for the solution of international controversies, and renounce it as an instrument of national policy in their relations with one another." (2) "The High Contracting Parties agree that the settlement or solution of all disputes or conflicts of whatever nature or of whatever origin they may be, which may arise among them, shall never be sought except by pacific means."[14]

Since the right of self-defense was, as Mr. Kellogg said, inherent in every sovereign state and in every treaty, and since, as he also said, every nation alone is competent to decide what constitutes self-defense, American critics of the pact declared, as did the Soviet Union, that it was worthless. Senator Carter Glass of Virginia said: "I intend to vote for the peace pact, but I am not willing that anyone in Virginia shall think that it is worth a postage stamp in the direction of accomplishing permanent peace. ... But I am going to be simple enough, along with the balance of you, to vote for the ratification of this worthless, but perfectly harmless peace treaty."[15] Edwin M. Borchard, professor of international law in the Yale Law School, said the pact, with the provision that every country was competent to decide for itself whether or not it was going to war in self-defense, was impossible to violate. He wrote: "In view of the fact that the Treaty apparently leaves each country ... the judge of what is 'self-defense,' who could assert that any signatory, going to war under circumstances which it claims require 'self-defense,' is violating the Pact? Has any modern nation ever gone to war (and without any suggestion of bad faith) for any other motive? How then could this Pact ever be legally violated?"[16]

Mr. Kellogg, too, played down any commitments involved in the pact. During the hearings of the Senate Committee on Foreign Relations, he was asked the question "Supposing some nation does break this treaty, why should we interest ourselves in it?" Kellogg replied: "There is not a bit of reason." He said the nations knew from his notes to them that he was not willing to impose any obligations on the United States. "I knew that was out of the question."[17]

Stresemann, after stating his reservations, had no hesitation in signing on behalf of the Reich, and since Germany accepted the treaty before France did, the American ambassador to Germany, Jacob G. Schurmann, could say in a speech that must have brought small comfort to Briand that Germany and the United States were "marching together in a great and noble adventure in the cause of humane civilization."[18]

The Soviet Union, still the pariah if not the outlaw in the eyes of the Great Powers, was not allowed to attend the formal signing ceremonies in Paris, but it did sign, and Soviet War Commissar K. E. Voroshilov explained that the Soviet government had never considered the Kellogg Pact seriously and had adhered to it for purely practical purposes to prevent other powers from accusing it of "red imperialism."[19] Eminent international lawyers and members of the peace groups, however, were impressed with the significance of the pact. Some declared that it made war illegal, that neutrality no longer existed, and that from here on in the world was organized against an aggressor. A number of authorities maintained that the reservations expressed in notes to Washington and in Kellogg's replies were without force since they were not part of the pact; that at the most they were clarifications of its meaning, and its meaning had brought a new day to the world. Professor Hersch Lauterpacht, the editor of the most distinguished publication of its kind, *Oppenheim's International Law*, said the exceptions were small compared with the magnitude of the change effected by the pact in the system of international law. The proponents of the pact agreed that war was now outlawed, and that states, in the event of war, were no longer required to be impartial. They could now differentiate between an aggressor and his victim so that the aggression gave no legal title to his conquest, and high officers of governments that went to war in violation of the pact were criminally liable for what had hitherto been considered acts of state beyond the law.

Sixty-three countries signed or adhered to the treaty. Only a few South American states abstained, together with Morocco, Liechtenstein, and San Marino. Among those who subscribed to the pact were the Soviet Union, the Irish Free State, the Union of South Africa, New Zealand, India, Italy, Poland, and Japan. Japan signed last of all, because Article 1 declared the pact was signed in the names of the peoples concerned, and for the Japanese the emperor signed a treaty only in his own name. But they, too, eventually signed and Japanese Foreign Minister Baron Kijuro Shidehara declared the pact opened a new chapter in the history of international relations.

Stresemann seemingly had no doubt of the efficacy of the treaty and said it corresponded to the inmost yearnings of nations. Stresemann's doctors had urged him not to go to Paris for the signing ceremonies, because his health was much too precarious, but he nevertheless went. He was received with a great ovation from the assembled crowds, as tumultuous a reception as he had received in Geneva when Germany entered the League of Nations. The Parisians shouted and waved their hats in the air, roused to a pitch of enthusiasm they had not felt for any German for a long, long time.

The pact, worthless or not in what it might do to prevent war or to outlaw an aggressor who as always would be difficult to identify unless he chose to identify himself, obviously spoke to a world that was hungry for the good tidings it was thought to bring. People, whether in France, Germany, or the United States, needed no experts in international law to tell them that war was a horror. The announcement of the pact was like a bulletin from the Ministry of Health saying that disease was about to be banished if everyone worked together to this purpose. Statesmen who signed the pact knew that all they could expect from it was that it might help to keep their respective countries out of hostilities in which they had no major interest; or failing that, it might bring them in on the winning side, which would invoke the pact if it was a status quo power and deny its applicability if it was not.

Stresemann was aware—although no more than he was forced to be by virtue of his office—of the attempts of the Reichswehr to evade the conditions imposed on it by Versailles. So was the minister of defense, Otto Gessler, another man of high principles, and when in 1927, as the Briand proposals were being directed to the United States, a major scandal broke, fanned by the left-wing press in the Reich, it touched both men, although it affected Gessler much more than Stresemann. Costs had been rising for the maintenance of the Reich's armed forces, small as they were. The budget for the army went up from 476 million marks in 1925 to 553 million in 1927; for the navy, from 156 million marks to 215 million in the same period. Gessler's own Democratic party was among those demanding a reduction of at least 10 percent in the military budget. The Defense Ministry with Gessler's approval, in order to increase the funds at its disposal for armament that would not have to pass the scrutiny of the Entente, placed a Captain Lohmann, who was head of its sea transport, in charge of establishing or buying into various profitable business enterprises. Faked budgets were presented to the Reichstag to cover up the operation. The correct budgets went to the rapporteurs for the Budget Commission, or a member of the SPD, the other of the Center Party who were moved to go along with the deception as Stresemann's representative, Henry Bernard reported, by their patriotic sympathies.* Lohmann was thus able to help supply the German navy with fast motorboats armed with torpedoes and to school crews to man them. He also put funds into the Dornier airplane works at Friedrichshafen, which set up a branch in Switzerland to supply foreign orders and to help keep the Reich abreast of developments in airplane construction, especially of the oversized planes in which Dornier specialized. But Lohmann's most extraordinary undertaking was the financing with Wehrmacht funds of a motion picture company, Phoebus-Film, intended to produce motion pictures that not only would make money but would help to revive the German spirit at home and make its virtues known abroad. The enterprise soon went bankrupt, and in the court proceedings following failure the whole story, including Gessler's part in it, came to light. This was the kind of operation men like Stresemann and Gessler wanted to know as little about as possible, and in the case of Stresemann the presumption of ignorance worked successfully within the Reich if not entirely in the skeptical minds of foreigners. But the whole project was a political as well as a financial disaster as the Social Democrats used it to whip their old enemies the militarists and the Right. Gessler was forced to resign. The waves of protest, however, only lapped at Stresemann's toes, and he could continue with his work of fulfillment and the spirit of reconciliation.

So far, in fact, had the cause of the Reich advanced under his guidance that when the British discovered a large Soviet spy and propaganda ring in their midst and tensions between the Soviet Union and Britain became acute, it was to Stresemann that Chamberlain and Briand turned to prevent the crisis from getting out of hand. In May, in a search of the quarters of the All Russian Cooperative Society (ARCOS), the Soviet trading corporation in London, British police uncovered evidence that espionage and the dissemination of Communist propaganda were included among the society's business activities. As a consequence, Britain on May 26 broke off diplomatic relations with the Soviet Union. A few days later, on June 7, the Russian ambassador to Poland was murdered in the Warsaw railroad station by a White Russian student, and the Soviet Union linked these actions to an anti-Soviet plot. On the same day the ambassador was murdered, Chicherin told Stresemann when they met in Baden-Baden, where Stresemann was taking a cure, that Pilsudski

* The total amounts made available for Germany's secret armaments, according to the testimony of the Social Democrat, Severing, at Nuremberg, came to between 5½ and 6 million marks. (Erich Eyck, *Geschichte der Weimarer Republik*, vol. 2, pp. 188, 195.)

was nothing more than a *"romancier"* and *"aventurier"* who wanted to go to war to set up a federative system of Poland, Lithuania, White Russia, and the Ukraine.[20] Chicherin's words deeply disturbed Briand who always had the Polish alliance and the French commitments to Warsaw in mind, and they added to the disquiet of the British.

During the June 1927 meeting of the League of Nations, Chamberlain, Briand, and the other foreign ministers of the Locarno powers concentrated on the Russian situation, and Chamberlain on their behalf appealed to Herr Stresemann to make use of his good relations with Chicherin to prevent the peace of Europe from being endangered. It was an assignment Stresemann was pleased to undertake; he was unalterably opposed to any anti-Soviet crusade (which neither Chamberlain nor Briand wanted, whatever the Russian doubts of their intentions) and the mere fact that Stresemann's good offices were asked was a tribute to the mana he had brought to the Reich's cause in the space of a few years.

Despite the pacts and the high oratory that dealt with banishing war from the world, no one anywhere relied on them. They were designed to be invoked; not to take the place of armies, navies, or air forces, but to reinforce them. The old methods of preserving peace or of winning wars remained in full operation. France was reluctant to reduce her land forces, Britain her navy. The British traditionally had maintained a navy that could match the combined fleets of the Continental powers, and in an alliance with Japan, made in 1902, it could outgun the American fleet, too. At the Washington Naval Conference of 1921–1922, Britain had reluctantly agreed to naval parity with the United States. Both countries would retain more than 500,000 tons of capital ships, defined as vessels over 10,000 tons with 8-inch guns, against 300,000 tons for Japan. The 1927 Naval Disarmament Conference at Geneva, which the French had declined to attend, had foundered on the issue of limitations on cruisers and guns. The Americans pressed for an agreement permitting the construction of cruisers of over 8,000 tons with 8-inch guns, while the British insisted on smaller cruisers with 6-inch guns, an arrangement which, with British naval bases dotted around the globe, would have continued their maritime superiority over all other powers, including the United States.

While Kellogg and Briand were working out the terms of their pact, Britain and France concluded a disarmament agreement on their own designed to thwart the American naval plans. The agreement proposed limiting surface vessels of or below 10,000 tons mounted with guns of more than six inches and up to eight, and oceangoing submarines of over 600 tons. Thus Britain and France were attempting to pressure Washington into an agreement to accept the size and armament of ships they were convinced they needed—light cruisers and small submarines—and to stop the kind of building the United States wanted—heavy cruisers and large submarines. The British-French agreement so disturbed Kellogg that he told the president he was sorry he had to go to Paris to sign the pact he had written. Otherwise, the only result of the Anglo-French attempt to limit the size and firepower of American ships was the largest American naval bill since the war, one that not Britain or France or Japan was in a position to match.

In 1928 the Germans, too, joined the naval competition, although in a modest way, with blueprints for ships that had to come within the 10,000-ton limit imposed by the Treaty of Versailles. The ingenious designs of German naval engineers would provide the Reich with a kind of ship the treaty makers had not foreseen—a 10,000-ton, heavily plated crusier carrying 11-inch guns. These ships would have a speed of 26 knots, which would make them faster than battleships, and enough firepower to blow any other 10,000-ton vessels out of the water. The new defense minister, General Groener, was a strong proponent of the project and asked the Reichstag to approve a down payment of 9.3 million marks on the first keel.

The proposal to build the new Panzerkreuzer raised a storm of protest throughout the country and in the Reichstag, among Groener's own Democratic party as well as among Social Democrats and Communists. It also became an issue in the Reichstag elections. The Social Democrats campaigned against the plan with the slogan "No armored cruisers but children's meals," and they were joined by the Communists not only on social grounds but because they suspected the ships were designed to be used against the Soviet Union. Sentiment against the navy was widespread. It was Admiral Tirpitz who had been mainly responsible for the fateful decision to wage unrestricted submarine warfare, the Ehrhardt Brigade had been commanded by a naval officer, and the revolution had begun with a naval mutiny.

Despite the opposition, the funds were voted by the new Reichstag. In Wilhelm Groener as defense minister the Reich had a man who might conceivably reconcile such chronic divisions between the Right and Left while being wholly acceptable to neither side. Groener was chosen by Hindenburg directly rather than by way of nomination by the chancellor to the president.* The Groener appointment was made the other way round; Hindenburg proposed him to Marx, who agreed with the president's choice. Hindenburg believed it essential to have a soldier, not a civilian like Gessler, at the head of the Defense Ministry, and the man he chose was the same general he had selected in 1918 to replace Ludendorff.

Wilhelm Groener, like everyone else in the Reich, had mixed credentials in the eyes of the Far Right and Left. From the point of view of

---

* Hindenburg first checked with the kaiser—whose abdication Groener had thought essential—on the suitability of the appointment.

the Far Right, the only thing in his favor was that Hindenburg had chosen him; otherwise he was hopeless. He had advised the abdication of Wilhelm II and worse still he had said that in revolutionary times concepts like oaths of loyalty and supreme warlords were mere ideas. He had gone further: in a speech to the Reichstag he said something unparalleled for a German and unusual for a general of any nationality. Groener said: "Like most of those who took part in the war, I profess my belief in a healthy and sensible pacifism, but certainly not the kind that fits the mentality of slaves."[21] It was Groener, too, who had counselled the signing of the Treaty of Versailles, because as both he and Hindenburg knew, the Reich had no alternative. But Hindenburg had let Groener bear the burden of telling Ebert he must sign, and while they were talking over the telephone, Hindenburg had left the room. It was difficult for the moderate parties to fault Groener, although Socialist leaders complained of the hard line he had taken when armament workers struck in late January and early February of 1918. He was a convinced republican. After retiring from the army he had served as minister of communications from 1920 to 1923. And he was also a former lieutenant general in whom Hindenburg obviously had complete confidence.

It was a sign of the restoration of Germany's fortunes that the allotment of 80 million marks to a cruiser could be not only considered but voted. In 1925 it had been difficult to find funds for building small cruisers and destroyers to replace the overage ships the Entente had allowed the navy to keep. But in 1927, a year when Britain and France were calling on Stresemann to use his good offices with the Russians, and Briand and Kellogg were at work on their pact, the Reich could consider embarking on a course of modest naval rearmament that would enable it, as Groener told the Reichstag in a speech in March 1928, to reinforce its defenses against any Polish attack on East Prussia or Upper Silesia. It was the speech in which Groener said that Reichstag's approval of the cruisers had nothing to do with militarism and in which he avowed his own belief in a reasonable pacifism. The Reich could not easily afford the cruisers, but it could not afford to be without them either.

The tides were running in favor of the republic. So far had confidence in it returned that the prohibition against Adolf Hitler's making any more public speeches could be lifted early in 1927 in Bavaria and Saxony. The Far Right was in a poor way; although it continued in business, its leadership was acriminiously divided, and the infighting among the pretenders to its high command was bitter, in inverse proportion to the numbers of their followers.

After Hitler had been sentenced to Landsberg, he had formally given up his leadership of the party for the duration of his imprisonment, and he asked his followers please not to visit him in the future. The grounds for his decision, he told people who had come to see him, were that it was impossible for him to take any practical responsibility because he was overworked writing a voluminous book, and he wanted to be sure of having the essential free time for it. During his absence, he said, General Ludendorff had asked Gregor Strasser to take over the leadership of the party.

The NSDAP had been outlawed, but it continued under two other names, the Greater German Volks Society (*Grossdeutsche Volksgemeinschaft*), led by Alfred Rosenberg, Julius Streicher, and the journalist Hermann Esser, and the Volksbloc in Bavaria, which became for all Germany the National Socialist Freedom Movement, or party, under Ludendorff, Albrecht von Graefe, and Gregor Strasser. In the Bavarian elections of April 1924, the Volksbloc had been able to elect 23 of 129 deputies to the state legislature, and the National Socialist Freedom party won 6.5 percent of the vote in the national election of May 1924. But from there on its fortunes declined, and in the December 1924 elections it received less than 3 percent of the vote. The Far Right could not agree on much of anything for long, not even on who was the chief enemy. Graefe and Ludendorff both quit the National Socialist Freedom party in February 1925, only a little more than a year after it was founded. In the opinion of one of its Reichstag deputies, Reinhold Wulle, the Catholics, toward whom he thought Hitler like many of the Bavarians had too friendly sentiments, were a greater danger than the Jews, and Wulle told a gathering of the party in January 1925 that Hitler would never again regain his former authority, a sentiment echoed by others at the meeting. When the National Socialist Workers party, along with the Communist party,* was

---

* The two parties had much in common from the point of view of many conservatives. Both aimed at destroying the republic and its parliamentary system; both wanted to destroy "international capitalism" and its false values, which were eroding the substance of the people; both believed that the redemption of the masses, or *Volk*, could come about only by a ruthless full-scale revolution leading to a classless society. The differences seemed often verbal. The left wing of the National Socialist party was as bent on putting an end to the Weimar Republic and its capitalist overlords as were the Communists. Both parties would find a short way with dissenters; for both of them the law was what the party leadership said it was. The Communist party had an elaborate *Weltanschauung* based on Marx, Engels, and Lenin. On the other side, everything in the National Socialist ideology was borrowed: the principle of messianic leadership, the salute with outstretched arm, and the title of Führer were taken by Hitler in 1921 from Mussolini and his Fascists; the party's economics derived from the whole range of anticapitalist sources; its antiparliamentarianism came from the meeting of the Far Left and Right; its generic anti-Semitism came from the Middle Ages, and its racist version of it came from Gobineau, Chamberlain, and a host of others. Anti-Semitism and racism went hand in hand with anticlericalism, and it was not always easy, as Wulle pointed out, to know which was considered the greater evil, the Jew or the Church of Rome. Neither Communism nor National

again legalized in February 1925, the internal dissension in the NSDAP was so great on matters of basic policy that Joseph Goebbels was reported to have denounced Adolf Hitler as "a little bourgeois" who should be ousted from the party. Goebbels and Strasser took a far more benevolent view of Soviet Russia than did Adolf Hitler. Goebbels was impressed with the utopianism of the Russian leadership, and Strasser wanted an alliance with Moscow against French militarism, British imperialism, and Wall Street capitalism. A major split appeared on the question agitating the Reich in the first half of 1926—whether the property of the former princes should be confiscated without compensation.* Who the actual owners of much of the disputed land really were was not entirely clear. Large sections of it had been acquired as state property when the princes had governed, and the German Democratic party as well as socialists and Marxists believed it belonged more properly to the community at large than to the princely houses. The left wing of the NSDAP, including Gregor Strasser and Joseph Goebbels, were among those who wanted the lands taken over for public use. At a party meeting in northern Germany at which Goebbels was present, NSDAP leaders asked why there was no compensation for the little pensioner, for the people who had invested in war loans and lost their money, and for the other creditors of the state and local governments if the princes remained as rich as ever? It was a question Hitler, too, in the early days of the party, would have asked, but fearing to lose the support of newly made converts to his cause from among the right-wing supporters of the princes, he had reversed his and the party's position.† Goebbels was enraged, and when Hitler spoke in Bamberg in February 1926, Goebbels asked himself in his diary what manner of man this Hitler really was and whether he represented anything more than the Reaction. Goebbels wrote in his diary on February 14, 1926: "Then through Bamberg. Delightful city. Old, Jesuit. Hitler races by in his car. A handshake. Aha. Berlin lineup, Streicher, Esser, Feder. Then to work. Hitler talks. Two hours. I am beside myself. What kind of Hitler? A reactionary? Astonishingly awkward and uncertain. Russian question: completely misses the point. Italy and England natural allies. Ghastly! Our task is the destruction of Bolshevism. Bolshevism is Jewish sham! We must inherit Russia!

Socialism would tolerate an opposition. Woe betide in either state the class or racial foe, or any other designated enemy of the people.

* The Communist and Social Democratic parties drafted a bill in January 1926 for the confiscation of such property. A petition signed by more than 12½ million voters was presented in favor of a national referendum, but when the proposal came to a popular vote it was defeated, receiving only 15 million votes instead of the necessary 20 million.

† It has been charged that Hitler was then receiving 1,500 marks a month—two-thirds of his income—from the divorced Duchess of Sachsen-Anhalt. (F. A. Krummacher and Albert Wucher, eds., *Die Weimarer Republik*, pp. 271–72.)

180 million!!! Restitution to the princes! Right must remain right. Also for the princes. Question of not disturbing private property! Gruesome! The program is enough! Satisfied with it. Feder nods, Ley nods, Streicher nods, Esser nods. It hurts me to my soul when I see you in that company. Short discussion. Strasser speaks, haltingly, quaking, awkward, the good honest Strasser. O God how little we're up to those pigs down there. A half-hour discussion after a four-hour talk! Nonsense, thou art victorious. I can't say a word. It's as though I've been hit on the head. By car to the station. . . . Farewell to Strasser. We'll see one another day after tomorrow in Berlin. I could weep. . . . A sad journey home, I can hardly say a word. . . . A terrible night! Certainly one of the greatest disappointments of my life. I no longer believe completely in Hitler. That is the worst part of it; it's as though I've lost my inner support. I am cut in half."[22]

Goebbels received his economic views from men like Strasser, for whom he acted as secretary, men who were determined to break the privileges of the possessing classes, free the German worker from his bondage, and enable him to participate in profits, property, and management. This had been Hitler's view, too, and that was why the movement had been named National Socialism, a movement expressly designed to smash the old order and replace it with a sense of community where birth and money did not play the decisive role. "We are socialists," said Strasser, "deadly enemies of today's capitalist system with its exploitation of the economically weak, the injustice of its wage system, its immoral judging of people on their holdings of property and their money instead of on their responsibility and performance . . . what has to be overcome is the spirit of materialism."[23] Gregor Strasser and his brother Otto were the chief spokesmen of those struggling to hold Hitler to the socialist path of the early days of the party. The *Gauleiter* of Hamburg, Albert Krebs, called Gregor Strasser an *Urbayer*, an original Bavarian, outwardly and inwardly coarse, eager to do battle but prudent, steadfast, and cunning. Strasser had once told Krebs a story of his return from the war in 1918. Strasser had ridden back from the front with his artillery unit, and when the battery returned to Landshut from whence they had departed at the start of the war, Strasser was incensed to have to listen to a speaker from the soldiers' council denouncing the "blood-sucking generals," the war mongers, capitalists, and bourgeoisie. Why Strasser felt so strongly about the denunciations must be attributed to his regarding the orator as a Spartacist agitator, since what the man was saying was very close to what he himself was to repeat in later years as he campaigned for the NSDAP. But, Strasser had told Krebs: "I sat on my horse and kept pushing the fellow back, little by little, said nothing and collected a mouthful of spit. Finally he was finished and yelled: 'Give up your weapons, tear down the flags and cockades, vote Soldiers Council'; then I was ready and with my mouth full I spat in his face. I drove the creep away. And then I ordered 'Battery trot' and we came back to Landshut just as we had left it in 1914."[24]

Only Adolf Hitler could resolve the contradictions in the party and in his own mind. Without him there were a dozen versions of ultranationalism and a dozen more recipes for getting rid of the republic, making a revolution, and restoring greatness to the Reich. Hitler was a fanatic, but unlike many of his kind he could change course in what he regarded as minor matters; reverse himself without missing a step and without ever losing sight of his goal. An instance of this was evident in his shifting view of private property. The "unchangeable program" of the party that he had drafted declared in point 17 that land not put to productive use should be taken from its owners. But when in 1928 the NSDAP was wooing the Bavarian peasants, a platform of that kind was a heavy liability. So Hitler switched. Like the princes, the peasants could keep their land no matter how they saw fit to use it. Private property was restored to sanctity. Hitler said that point 17 in the National Socialist program was directed against Jewish speculators, and that the party firmly believed in the principles of private property. Cynical people might see a political expedient in this, but Hitler was unconcerned with what they saw. He could either win them over to his view as he did Goebbels or lose them as he did Gregor Strasser and his brother, but he went his own way, single-mindedly set to win power and to smite the enemy, who was anyone standing in his way. He would not compromise with any *völkisch* or other rivals, but he would shift on any issues that seemed trivial to him compared with the great goal from which nothing could divert him. He had learned from his failed putsch, despite the bravado of his account to the Munich court of what a success it had been. Hitler later reported that when he was not dictating his book, he had read a good deal while in Landsberg—Treitschke, Chamberlain, Marx, Bismarck, and memoirs of generals and statesmen. Certainly he had learned to be more cautious and to speak softly to authorities like the minister-president of Bavaria, Heinrich Held. Through an intermediary, Bavarian Minister of Justice Gürtner, he had managed to have a number of interviews with Held, and Hitler told Held, too, what the minister-president wanted to hear—that the putsch had been a mistake, and he promised in the future to conduct the party's affairs in a legal fashion.

One grave danger Hitler eluded by way of the providence he so often invoked, a providence that assumed the human form of the Austrian chancellor, Ignaz Seipel. The Bavarian government had planned to expel Hitler to Austria as an undesirable alien after his prison term was over. The Austrian *Land* authorities in Linz had agreed to accept him, but the central government in Vienna categorically refused to allow him to be returned to his native land. Seipel instructed the border police that Hitler was not to be permitted to enter Austrian territory, and with that any plan to deport him was dropped. On April 27, 1925, Hitler went to Linz to ask to be relieved of his Austrian citizenship, on the grounds that he had lived in Germany since 1912, had served four and a half years in the German army, and wished to become a German citizen. On April 30 the *Land* government in Linz granted his request, and Hitler became stateless, a category he remained in for some years before he could finally win the German citizenship he had so long aspired to.

Hitler had to be able to win recruits to the party, and for that the party needed a legal existence and he a legal right to speak. But it was not easy to keep his or his followers' revolutionary ardors under control and their messages within the bounds of decorum, as state and local authorities interpreted them. As a result of a disturbance at a Berlin meeting presided over by Goebbels, the party was banned in that city from May 1927 until March 1928, and a decree forbidding Hitler to speak in public in Prussia remained in force until the end of September 1928. Some of what he had to say fitted into any sober political context. In a speech in Hamburg made before a closed audience in February 1926, he said that Germany's 30 to 32 million voters were divided into three groups. One-third of them cared little or nothing about politics, one-third was international in its thinking, and the other third was nationalistic. It was to a fraction of the last third that he was making his pitch, and a closed audience and an analytical style were a considerable barrier to his reaching them. Other speeches were in the old vein his hearers were waiting for. In the Zirkus Krone in Munich in March 1927, when he was again allowed to speak in public in Bavaria, he told his cheering followers that what the people want is not the rule of the majority; they want leadership, they want a flag; and the Germany he was talking about had no flag and nothing that could be called a government. Just look at the Landtag, he said, as he was talking about the ineptitude of parliaments, and his audience roared with laughter. He likened the persecutions of the Nazi party to the persecutions of the early Christians. He deplored Germany's sad situation, the "slave treaty" of Locarno, the wretched army, the high rate of unemployment. Since the National Socialists had nothing like a mass following in the Reich, and did not seem likely to get one, Hitler told his audiences that Heaven bestowed the right to rule to the majority, not of numbers, but of energy. What he could not do was collect a sizeable following.*

---

* At the annual rally in Nuremberg in August 1927, the party claimed an attendance of 30,000 SA men and 100,000 in all, while the police estimated that no more than 9,000 SA, SS, and Hitler Youth were on hand. The party grew slowly; by the end of 1927 it counted 72,590 members, by the end of 1928, 108, 717; but it had no luck in the national elections on May 20, 1928, when it received 2.63 percent of the total vote, 810,000 votes, compared with the Social Democrats' more than 9 million. (Adam Buckreis, *Politik des 20. Jahrhunderts*, pp. 509, 510, 515.)

The domestic issues before the Reichstag were pressing and decisive but not a threat to the survival of the republic. One controversy arousing powerful emotions was focussed on the struggle over religious teaching in the elementary schools. Protestants, Catholics, and opponents of religious instruction were again locked in an old struggle. The Weimar Constitution had tried to compromise the religious differences by providing for a so-called "simultaneous" school common to both Catholics and Protestants. This was declared to be the usual type, although exceptions could be made in the case of elementary schools where parents or teachers preferred either a denominational or a nondenominational school. The knotty question was never settled to the lasting satisfaction of the religious and nonreligious factions, nor did it fade away as had been hoped. England and France, too, had had similar disputes, but the problem in Germany was complicated by the division of the country into a Protestant majority and a large Catholic minority, as well as by a rising secular movement that wanted no religion taught in the classroom. The Nationalist Minister of the Interior Walter von Keudell, a Protestant, proposed that the Reichstag approve three types of schools: denominational schools of either faith, the simultaneous schools where both Catholics and Protestants could give religious instruction to children of their respective faiths, and the secular schools where no religious instruction would be given. The parents of the children in each community were to decide which kind of school they wanted.

The proposal strongly appealed to the Catholics, and the Marx government, headed by a Centrist, decided to adopt it, although the two German Volksparty ministers, Stresemann and Curtius, the minister of economics, believing it would destroy the community simultaneous school, were not in favor of it. Stresemann favored the simultaneous school. He favored limiting the influence of both confessions in the schools as far as possible. So intense were the emotions that the Centrists threatened to oust Stresemann from his post as foreign minister if it came to an election and he opposed the draft of the new school law. The differences led to the breakup of the coalition of middle-class parties that had been in power since 1923; new elections had to be held and the Marx government had to resign.

Voters were scattered among thirty-one parties, only fourteen of which elected any deputies to the Reichstag. Thus, well over a million voters had no representatives whatever in Parliament. Some parties were splinters of splinters; they had names like the Volksbloc of Those Damaged by Inflation, the Reconstruction and Revaluation party, the Unpolitical List of War Victims, Party for the Protection of Law and Tenants, and the German House-and-Land-Owners party. They represented minuscule gradations of philosophical, political, or ideological differences that could easily be undetectable to an outsider and thus were one reason why the electorate had no sharp profile. On the larger issues like the survival of the parliamentary system and the foreign policy of reconciliation, a majority could be formed in the country and in the Reichstag,* but it represented an unstable, fair-weather alliance that would hold only if there were no major shocks to unsettle its precarious foundations.

In the May 1928 elections, the right-wing parties were down sharply. The German National Volksparty dropped from 6.2 million to 4.4 million, the National Socialists from 907,300 to 810,000. Most of the middle-class parties lost ground too. The German Democrats and the Center each lost 400,000 votes, the Democrats going down from 1.9 million to 1.5 million, the Center from 4,120,000 to 3.7 million. Stresemann's Volksparty, a number of whose members disapproved of his foreign policy, went down from 3 million to 2,680,000, but some of its voters turned to new and other middle-class parties like the Reichsparty of the German Middle Class, formerly called the Economy party, which went up 400,000 votes, from one million to 1.4 million; the Christian-National Farmers and Land People's party, which won 582,000 votes; and the German Farmers party, with 481,000 votes. The left-wing parties, including the Communists, went up: the Communists' vote rose from 2.7 million to 3.2 million, the Social Democrats' from 7,881,000 to 9,153,000.

On the whole it was another drift, this time to the left. The SPD had campaigned on its slogan of more housing and food for children instead of cruisers and it had appealed to thousands of voters who thought the building program too costly and unpromising compared with the pressing domestic needs. The new chancellor was a Social Democrat, Hermann Müller-Franken, who had been chancellor before, for two months, from March to June of 1920. Müller represented the largest party in the Reichstag, but again he had to govern with a coalition of Democrats, Centrists, and German Volksparty, a mixture of middle-class and labor parties that predictably would have a hard time maintaining a united front on social and economic questions. Nevertheless, it was to stay in power for almost two years, from June 1928 to March 1930, longer than any other postwar government until Hitler was made chancellor. It was characteristic of the parliamentary merry-go-round that the Müller-Franken government, called "the great coalition," was made up of almost

---

* The prorepublican parties—Social Democrats, Democrats, and Center—had 256 seats plus 31 seats belonging to their allies among the small middle ground, mainly middle-class parties. The right wing of German Nationals, National Socialists, and their allies of the right-wing middle-class parties, including Stresemann's Volksparty, which as often as not opposed his policies, had 150 seats. Thus the parties favoring the republic were in a clear majority, but the antirepublican parties, including the Communists, had a total of 204 seats; the prorepublicans, 287 seats. (F. A. Krummacher and Albert Wucher, eds., *Die Weimarer Republik*, p. 253.)

precisely the same parties, plus the SPD, that had been represented under Marx.*

Stresemann, despite his party's reluctance to join in a coalition with the. Social Democrats, remained at his post as foreign minister. In a telegram of June 23, 1928, to Müller-Franken, he said it was essential for members of parties, from the Social Democrats to the Volksparty, to work together as individuals, "personalities," rather than as mere extensions of their parties' positions. They should be ministers in a cabinet that would represent a combined purpose to the Reichstag and would stand or fall by their program. This, he said, corresponded to the spirit of the Weimar Constitution, which recognized the responsibility of ministers, not of political groups. It seemed to be one way of overcoming the defects of the patchwork party system and of Stresemann's own difficulties with his Volksparty, but how threadbare a solution it was soon became evident when the cruiser bill was brought to a vote in the Reichstag. The Müller cabinet, under the strong urging of Defense Minister General Groener, who threatened to resign on the issue, submitted the bill for the new cruisers, but the rank-and-file opposition of the Social Democrats was so intense that the chancellor and his SPD ministers, including Carl Severing, who had joined the cabinet as minister of the interior, voted against the measures. They acted either out of conviction, as in the case of Severing, or on party orders, as in the case of Müller-Franken. Severing opposed the bill in the Reichstag debate because of its cost and the damage he said it would do Germany's demand for general disarmament.

The cruiser bill passed the Reichstag 257–202, but the ineptitude of the Reich's parliamentary system, with members of a cabinet opposed to a measure they had presumably agreed on, remained as glaring as ever to its enemies of the Right and Left. However, there were minor successes. With the triumph of the Social Democrats at the polls, the matter of a new school law was shelved. The Center party was no longer in a position to push for a sectarian solution as it had been in its earlier coalition with the Nationalists. But on some questions, like that of the armored cruisers, there could be no real agreement within the coalition; the parties were too entrenched in their ideologies for that. Individuals with the larger issues in mind might reject their intransigence, and one Social Democrat, Julius Leber, said: "I didn't know how many armored cruisers I'd be ready to vote for if it meant that democracy and the republic would thereby be rescued." But the paradoxes of the Weimar party system defeated such brave professions. If the cabinet did not support the armored cruisers, then Defense Minister Groener, former army gen-

---

* The only one missing was the German National Volksparty, which had lost almost two million voters in the May 28 elections.

eral and the man who said he was a reasonable pacifist, who wanted to do away with all secret funds for the Reich's armament, would resign and the government would fall; if it did support them, the chancellor and the other representatives of the largest party in the coalition would be compelled to vote against the bill they had sponsored.

Such were the political imbalances. The social troubles went deeper. The middle class had been the hardest hit by the inflation and the devaluation. Its confusion may be seen in the proliferation of middle-ground parties that could not fix on any common program. Stresemann in the speech he gave in 1927 when he was receiving his Nobel Peace Prize declared it was not the loss of territory, colonies, state, or private property that had been most costly to the Reich. The greatest loss was the damage done to the intellectual and industrial middle class, the traditional bearer of the idea of the state. Its members had sacrified all they had in the war and had then been proletarianized by the worthless currency the state had issued. Their losses had never been made good.[25] And the economic situation of the Reich, even after the euphoria of his reception in Paris, Geneva, and Oslo, seemed to him most precarious. He told a press conference in November 1928 that they should keep in mind in appraising the economic situation that Germany had been living in the last years on borrowed money. If Germany ever suffered a financial crisis and the United States withdrew its short-term credits, the Reich would be bankrupt. The government was taking in every penny it could from taxes, and he did not know of any sources of additional funds. "The statistics show," he said, "how much the cities have needed, how much industry has needed, and how much foreign money we have used to keep afloat. We are not only militarily disarmed. We are also financially disarmed. We have no more resources of any kind."[26]

It was a prescient speech, but for the moment things seemed to be going well for the republic. Articles appeared in the press declaring the end of the *Völkisch*-National Socialist movement, which was divided in its leadership and seething with as bitter resentments among its competing allies as it had against the common enemy of the Left. The whole movement, it seemed to many competent observers, could be written off. The voting curve for the entire Far Right was down; the Nazis could elect only 12 delegates to the Reichstag and the German Nationals 73, as against 153 for the Social Democrats, 62 for the Center, and 54 for the Communists.

Aside from such recurrent domestic crises, the cause of the Reich, compared with the recent past, seemed to be prospering. To be sure there were the danger signs that Stresemann pointed out, and in addition agriculture, especially in East Prussia and Schleswig-Holstein, was doing poorly. Crops had been down for two successive years, in 1926 and 1927, and the debts of East Prussian landowners and farmers rose 80 million marks in 1927. Interest rates for bank loans ran between 8 percent and 15 percent, and in some cases, with fringe benefits for the banks, as high as 23 percent, and taxes were heavy. Hindenburg set out to do what he could to help, proposing long-term credit for farmlands, lower taxes, and cheaper shipping rates for farm products—measures which in a few years would have to be extended to the entire Reich. But for the time being, it was East Prussia with its coarse soils and strategic and psychological vulnerability, emphasized by the Polish Corridor, that was bearing the brunt of the agricultural troubles. Hindenburg's concern for the province where he and his father's father had been born and lived their lives was ascribed by Otto Braun, the Social Democratic minister-president of Prussia, to a Junker conspiracy of big landowners, who were being repaid for their contributions to the gift of the family estate in East Prussia, Neudeck, to the president.* Although Hindenburg pointed out that half the land in East Prussia consisted of medium-sized farms, one-quarter of small farms, and one-quarter of large estate-farms, it was a calumny he could never answer to the satisfaction of those like Braun who wanted to believe it, even when the same measures he proposed had to be adopted for the whole country.

Another soft spot in the economy was increasing unemployment. Only in 1925 had unemployment dropped below a million. In January 1926 and 1927, some 2.3 million unemployed were reported; in January 1928 the number had fallen to 1.8 million, only to rise again in the course of the year, until it reached 3 million in early 1929. But on the whole production had been rising steadily. Real wages for the first time reached their pre-

---

* On his eightieth birthday on October 2, 1927, Hindenburg had received two gifts from well-wishers. One was Neudeck, the family estate he cherished all his life and to which he had retired before he became president. It was bought with relatively small donations from the rank and file of soldier organizations—the Kyffhäuser Bund and the Stahlhelm—and larger gifts from Hindenburg's admirers among landowners, bankers, and shipping and insurance circles. Neudeck was placed in the name of Hindenburg's son, Oskar, with a lifetime interest for the field marshal. The other gift was a trust for the war wounded and the widows and orphans of the war dead. It was called the *Hindenburg-Spende* and was administered by members of all the chief political parties along with industrialists and bankers, among them, Franz von Mendelssohn-Bartholdy and Georg Emil von Strauss.

The gift of an estate was not new in German history. Bismarck had been made a similar gift on his seventieth birthday, and Neudeck had originally been given to an ancestor of the president, Colonel Friedrich von Hindenburg, by Frederick the Great, for his war services. German generals and landowners were seldom plutocrats, and after the war the Hindenburg family found themselves unable to keep up their estate with its high taxes and low income. Hindenburg's acceptance of the gift and its being placed in his son's name to avoid inheritance taxes would be often criticized, but war heroes in other countries besides Germany have accepted similar presents. In 1946 a number of Winston Churchill's friends bought the family estate of Chartwell for his and his family's use, tax-free during his lifetime. In addition a London hotelier presented Churchill with a mansion at Sevenoaks near Chartwell, which Churchill in turn gave to the British Legion to be used as a convalescent home for wounded soldiers. (Robert Lewis Taylor, *Winston Churchill*, p. 396.)

war level of 1913–1914 in 1928, and per capita income was the highest it had ever been. The number of strikes had plunged from 1,614 in 1924 to 691 in 1928, and lockouts by management from 398 to 72 in the same period. An uneasy peace, but still peace.

Yet economic shoals lay ahead, and Stresemann saw them more plainly than most.* His health, too, was increasingly uncertain. In the course of the 1928 elections he had campaigned up and down the Reich on behalf of his party's candidates and brought himself to a state of exhaustion. He developed a severe illness resembling paratyphus; his kidneys were affected, and he had to drop his political activities for a cure at Baden-Baden. He never completely recovered.

But the wildness of the immediate postwar period had subsided. Even though a band of hectoring National Socialists had been able to prevent Stresemann from speaking at a political rally by yelling and whistling until he had to leave the platform, their party seemed tamed. The entire extreme Right had lost ground and was no longer an imminent threat to the state. The borders of the Reich were relatively secure, the economy relatively stable.

That large segments of the electorate were far from satisfied could be seen in the increase in the Communist vote from 8.9 percent to 10.6 percent, but the other antirepublican parties had gone down substantially, and no putsch from either the Right or Left would have had any chance of success with *Verbände*, the army, or the population at large. Opposition to the republic was still powerful, but it seemed reconciled to achieving its ends by legal means. The Communists wanted a plebiscite on the cruiser issue, the Stahlhelm on the constitution as a whole. The Stahlhelm, the organization of former front-line soldiers, stung by the defeat of the Nationalists, published a manifesto in October 1928 that declared: "We hate with all our soul the present state structure, its form, its content, its development, its nature. We hate this state structure because in it, not the best Germans rule, but a parliamentarianism that makes any responsible leadership impossible." The manifesto went on to enumerate the republic's defects: class and party warfare and the inability to free Germany from its slavery and the war guilt clause, to win necessary living space in the East, and to protect German industry and agriculture from the enemy's economic warfare. "We want," the manifesto said, "a strong state in which responsible leadership emerges from the best, not from irresponsible bigshots [*Bonzen*] and big-mouthed heroes." It closed with a call for the churches to renounce their international bonds and said the battle for freedom could be won only when a fighting church

* Germany's foreign debts came to 25 billion marks; 12 billion in short-term loans, 7 billion in long-term loans, and 6 billion in other foreign obligations. To offset this, the Reich had a total of 10 billion marks in foreign balances; 5.5 billion in short-term credits and 4.5 in long-term credits. (Peter Rassow, *Deutsche Geschichte im Überblick*, p. 658.)

led the German people back to the great fundaments of God and Christianity.[27]

The Stahlhelm leaders asked, however, not for a revolution but for a plebiscite to change the constitution and give more power to the president. Hindenburg was an honorary member of the Stahlhelm, but he was also sworn to uphold the republic it openly detested. As a result of the manifesto, the Volksparty forbade its deputies in the Reichstag and the Prussian Landtag to remain in the Stahlhelm, and loud demands were made that Hindenburg resign from it too. How could the president of the republic belong to an organization whose members said they still felt themselves bound by their oath of loyalty to the kaiser and whose spokesmen said they hated the republic? It was a difficult question for the old gentleman, who dealt with all problems great and small with a set of principles that had become rooted in his nature and without which life would be unthinkable. Duty, devotion to the Fatherland, the sanctity of an oath and of the legal order—these virtues had grown out of the great German tradition; they made for the only unchanging landfalls in a complex and uncertain world from which God often hid his face. The conflict between what he himself might want and what he must accept, between the necessities of state and what he took to be his deepest obligations, was sometimes not entirely clear, not even in the light of the simplicities of Hindenburg's Prussian conscience. Devotion to the Fatherland and devotion to present-day Germany were not the same thing, said the Stahlhelm leaders, but Hindenburg had to reconcile them, as he had had to reconcile his oath of allegiance to the emperor and his telling Wilhelm he must go into exile in Holland. "Would God it were otherwise," was all he could say to his king.[28] He would always feel himself spiritually closer to the Stahlhelm and to the farmers large and small of East Prussia than to the Social Democrats, but he liked and trusted Müller-Franken and he could endure Stresemann's foreign policy, even when it meant renouncing German territory if it was the policy of the legal government of the Reich. So Hindenburg summoned to him the leaders of the Stahlhelm to ask them about the manifesto, and when they assured him that they wished to achieve its ends only by legal, constitutional methods, he said he would remain a member of the organization. He did not easily yield to pressure from anyone. When the Nationalists attacked him for accepting the Locarno Treaty, which Ludendorff called a "document of shame and dishonor," he paid no attention to them, even though it was a treaty for which he himself had no enthusiasm whatever.

Stresemann's foreign policy may have been more gratifying to foreign countries than to millions of Germans, but a majority in the Reichstag and probably of the electorate approved it, and there could be no doubt that it had greatly increased Germany's weight in the councils of Europe and had made impossible another invasion of the Rhine or Ruhr. The Fatherland was not yet rescued, but it was alive in the shape of the republic. Bristling problems remained, arising out of reparations, the still occupied Rhineland, the chronic disaffection of large sections of the population, and the economy's operating on foreign credits. No one saw this more clearly than Stresemann and, no doubt, Hindenburg, but for the moment the skies were clearer than at any time since the war. It was no longer the silver streaks on the horizon that observers in the Reich were looking at; it was the cloud no bigger than a man's hand that Stresemann saw when he spoke to the journalists in Berlin.

CHAPTER 8

The Time of the Crooked Cross

I̲T WAS NOT to be a long period of remission. It lasted a few months
—a matter of days in the life of a nation, of hours in the life of a
people. In early 1929, reparations had to be dealt with again. The Dawes
Plan was meant to be an interim solution, and its conditions—the payment
of 2½ billion gold marks a year—could not be borne indefinitely. In the
summer of 1928, Hjalmar Schacht and Parker Gilbert began the discussions that would lead in March 1930 to what was believed to be the final
solution of the reparations problem—the Young Plan. In many ways it
was a reasonable solution, worked out by financial experts of the Allies
and Germany under the chairmanship of an American business leader,
Owen D. Young. Meetings in Paris of the specialists' committees that
lasted from February to June were followed by two conferences in The
Hague, the first in August 1929, the second, which gave final approval
to the Young Plan, in January 1930. By the time the final agreement
was reached, the depression had gained momentum, Stresemann was
dead, and the economic problems confronting the industrial nations were
beyond the powers of any conferences to deal with.

What the Young Plan (also referred to as the New Plan) did succeed
in doing was to put a ceiling on the total sum of reparations—121 billion marks to be paid off in 59 annuities. Henceforth reparations could
only be diminished, not, as under the Dawes Plan, increased as the Reich
prospered. Arbitration was to replace any economic or political sanctions,
and the imposts on German railroads and customs were abolished, as
were the special taxes on German industrial obligations. More important, since the Reich's actual payments continued for only a short time,

Stresemann was able to persuade the Allies in the course of the first Hague conference, as a quid pro quo for accepting the reparations agreement, to evacuate the remaining Rhine bridgeheads.

The first conference ended on August 31, 1929, and the British garrison hauled down their flag at Wiesbaden on December 12. The French agreed to depart from their last bridgeheads eight months after the ratification of the Young Plan by France and Germany and in any event not later than June 30, 1930, four and a half years before the time provided for in the Versailles Treaty.

It was an enormous accomplishment, draining very nearly the last resources of strength of the sick man, but as a result Stresemann was covered with obloquy by the ultranationalist press, which called him a traitor and a chief enemy of his people. Stresemann had scarcely been able to drag himself to the meetings at The Hague, he was so ill, but what the negotiations were costing him was more evident to the foreigners who sat opposite him than to many of his countrymen. When it seemed that the deadlock with France could not be broken because Briand, too, had to deal with his generals, nationalists, and skeptics, who wanted the French army to stay on the Rhine until the last day, until Judgment Day if possible, Stresemann had written him in his formal, nineteenth-century style a letter that nevertheless betrayed his deep feelings. "During the many years," he wrote, "in which I have had the honor and the pleasure of conducting political negotiations with you, I have never written a letter to you to give you my conception of any particular political question. If I deviate from that today and feel myself constrained by my conscience to write to you, please see in this the significance I attach to the question I wish to discuss with you.... I have never, in advocating my policies, in any way put German prestige in the front rank.... It is far from my thought to pay any attention to personal inferences that I might draw from a specific political situation. It is not because the pressure of public opinion now weighs on me ... but simply because my conscience demands it that I am impelled to tell you, revered Mr. Minister, that I cannot, as Foreign Minister, bring before my Cabinet a proposal of the kind you made today for the ending of the evacuation. And if such a date were held to, I would also not be in a position to put my signature on the Young Plan, which seems to me to involve a merging of economic and political questions. I am not a Finance Minister who has studied the figures, but a Foreign Minister who has conducted all our negotiations from the standpoint of a major European event, as the last stage of a policy you and I have followed over the years of German-French understanding. I do not feel myself personally in a position to pursue this policy further, when a solution, which I know comports with your view as it does with mine, for preparing the end of the occupation of German territory would lead to such a palpable failure. I have told my ministerial colleagues nothing of the existence of this letter. I ask you to look upon it as a personal communication. I fear, though, that you yourself might reproach me if I did not tell you of the seriousness of the entire political situation which I perceive as a result of our discussion today."[1]

It was a letter better understood in all its implications by Briand than by many German leaders of public opinion. Stresemann had collapsed after one of the meetings at The Hague and had gasped, "I can go no further." Briand knew this to be true and, as he had done before, he made his decision on the side of conciliation. Eleven and a half years after the end of the war, Germany was again to be free of foreign troops within her borders.

Stresemann recovered from his collapse at The Hague long enough to make one more journey to Geneva, where he heard Briand speak eloquently on behalf of a united Europe. Then on September 9, Stresemann made his last speech in the same vein. He paid tribute to Briand, reminding his listeners how hard it was to win the youth of a nation for peace and reconciliation after all the glorification of the heroism of war. "There is no doubt," he said, "and we can be glad of it, that heroism, the devotion to a great ideal, can never die out in a people. But I think that those who live in the memory of the heroism of the youth of all countries over the centuries, and millennia, should bear in mind that the war of the future, even if one leaves out everything else, will have little place for personal heroism." The triumph of man over nature, Stresemann said, offered sufficient opportunity for heroism and sacrifice. The enormous territory of mankind in relation to the cosmos remained to be explored. "We in our sphere," he said, "have the modest task of bringing peoples closer to one another, of bridging differences, and let there be no doubt: they are not as close to one another as we should like; let there be no doubt, there are differences. It will take hard work to move forward to diminish these differences. . . . And this will be accomplished not by élan and hurrah alone, but will be part of the process of which a great German poet [Schiller] once wrote:

> That for the building of eternities,
> It needs but grain on grain of sand,
> Yet from the great reckoning of ages,
> Strikes minutes, days, years."

An eyewitness described him as he made his last speech, a shadow of his former self in a suit much too big for him, finding it hard to breathe, with coughing spells that often drowned out his words. Stresemann would not live to see the French troops leave the Rhine, nor would he witness the final approval of the Young Plan. He died of a stroke in Berlin on October 3, 1929, at the age of fifty-one.*

Although the French occupation of German soil had been cut by four and a half years, any proposal that the Reich continue to pay reparations that would demand sacrifices by generations yet unborn was bound to meet with bitter resistance. And the Young Plan, which provided a slice of the German pie for countries that had been as far from the war as Japan and Portugal, as well as for France, Belgium, Britain, Italy, and the Kingdom of the Slavs, Croats, and Slovenes, one of whose nationals had killed the Austrian archduke and his wife, was an easy target.† Even the Socialist minister of the Exchequer, Philip Snowden, had returned to London from The Hague with the promise of considerably higher payments than the original schedules had provided for, and he was given a hero's welcome by British financiers, who believed the French and Italians had hitherto done too well at Britain's expense. Snowden said he did not want the British share to be increased by raising the amounts the Reich was to pay, but whatever sums Britain obtained had to come from only one source.

The adoption of the Young Plan united all the enemies of the republic. The Communists joined with the Right in demanding that the infamous agreement be rejected. Twenty-two German admirals and generals of the old imperial army and navy, among them Field Marshal von Mackensen and Admiral von Tirpitz, turned to Hindenburg to put himself at the head of the movement called Resistance to Oppression for aid in fighting against its adoption. The opposition to the plan brought together not only Communists and Nationalists, but it made Adolf Hitler what the Germans call *salonfähig* ("capable of appearing in polite society") because Alfred Hugenberg, the new leader of the Nationalists, who controlled an important section of what a later generation would call the media‡ could make excellent use of the talents of the little man from the streets of Vienna who could bring his followers bouncing to their feet for hours at a time, and Hugenberg was delighted to have the flamboyant National Socialists as his allies in the campaign against the agreement.

---

* The leaders of the republic were not good long-term insurance risks: Rathenau and Ebert died at the age of fifty-four, Matthias Erzberger at forty-six, and Friedrich Naumann, leader of the Democratic party, at fifty-nine. Hermann Müller-Franken would survive the end of his chancellorship in 1930 by only a year; he died in March 1931 at the age of fifty-four.

† In a separate agreement of March 13, 1930, Germany agreed to pay the United States 40.8 million marks yearly until March 31, 1981. In addition, a table of repayments with varying annuities through 1965 provided for the liquidation of the debt the Reich owed for the American occupation of the Rhine bridgeheads. (Herbert Michaelis, et al, *Ursachen und Folgen*, vol. 7, pp. 632–34.)

‡ Hugenberg was the owner of the *Berlin Lokal-Anzeiger, Der Tag, Die Woche,* and other publications as well as of the German film studio UFA.

The Young Plan resulted in Adolf Hitler's becoming the most conspicuous figure in the campaign against it and the republic. He became the chief spokesman for a movement that could be united only by what it hated. Hugenberg, Franz Seldte, and Theodor Duesterberg, the leaders of the Stahlhelm, and Heinrich Class, the head of the Pan-German Association, had never before made common cause with Hitler and his National Socialists, but now it was Hitler who led their onslaught against the enemy, and in the Hugenberg press he emerged as one of the heroes in the battle. The pent-up emotions of the long-frustrated hyperpatriots were suddenly released on this single issue.

Heinrich Class declared the people of the Rhineland would endure another invasion rather than see the German people pay a single penny under the terms of the New Plan; Hugenberg said he would prefer to see Germany, and presumably himself, proletarianized rather than agree to its terms; and the disparate groups set about preventing any of this from happening. They formed a "Reichscommittee for a German Plebiscite" and drew up the outline of "A Law against the Enslavement of the German People." The proposed law demanded a recantation of the war guilt clause of the Versailles Treaty and its formal nullification. Its paragraph 3 declared that "no foreign burdens or obligations could be undertaken that were based on an acknowledgement of war guilt" and that the German chancellor and plenipotentiaries of the government could be criminally prosecuted for signing any document with a foreign power that accepted it.

Placards urging attendance at protest demonstrations told voters that under the New Plan they would be paying out 80 gold marks a second for sixty years and performing slave labor for three generations. Hugenberg and his allies succeeded in obtaining 4,135,000 signatures for a plebiscite, a little more than the necessary 10 percent of the electorate provided for in the constitution and very nearly the peak of the popular support they would succeed in drumming up despite the intensity of their campaign. Hugenberg and Hitler appeared on the same platform before a tumultuous audience of 7,000 people at the Zirkus Krone to begin recruiting a majority that would vote down the plan in the plebiscite to be held on December 22, 1929. The National Socialists' posters, unadorned with swastikas or anti-Semitic battle cries, told the voters that the adoption of the "Freedom Law," or "Law against the Enslavement of the German People," would mean the rejection of the Young Plan and that it would enable the next generations to live from the products of their own labor instead of working for sixty years for international high finance. This, the Nazi placards assured the German electorate, was the Christmas present they could give their children by voting yes on December 22.

The National Socialist propagandists were as virulent as anything

Hugenberg could have hoped for. Goebbels had a recording made in which he said: "The German people are a slave people. From the standpoint of international law they trail behind the last Negro colony in the Congo. All the rights of sovereignty have been taken from us, and now we're just good enough so that the stock exchange capitalists can fill their sacks of gold with interest, money, and percentages."[2]

Such was the campaign of the Far Right, but ranged with them and the Communists, who denounced the Young Plan as an SPD betrayal, were sensible, moderate men like Heinrich Brüning, who although he eventually voted for the settlement, called it a *Diktat*. Hjalmar Schacht, too, who had been one of the chief architects of the plan, turned against it after conditions he considered both too dangerous for the stability of the mark and too onerous for the German economy were added to it at The Hague, and he resigned as president of the Reichsbank. For millions of Germans the plan was a witness, not to Stresemann's success in freeing the Rhine without firing a shot, but to the weakness of the republican government and the emptiness of the moral pretenses of the Entente, which, under the guise of a new and better order for Europe, continued to demand reparations that had to be paid because Germany had allegedly started the war, when really her only crime had been to lose it. A moderate and prorepublican like Brüning could be as tired of what seemed to be the endless exactions as were extremists like Class and Hitler.

But in the end only 5.8 million people, 13.8 percent of the electorate, voted for the so-called "Freedom Law"—21 million voters would have been needed for its approval—and the Reichstag accepted the Young Plan by a vote of 266–193. Twenty-one Nationalist deputies, among them Count Westarp and former Minister of the Interior Walter von Keudell, deserted their party on the issue.* They characteristically founded a splinter conservative group, which never succeeded, however, in attracting much of a following.

The opponents of the Young Plan still did not surrender; they made a last appeal to Hindenburg not to sign the bill. He rejected their appeal and approved the bill, with, as he said, "a heavy but resolute heart."[3] His decision evoked a response beyond party and ideological lines; many deeply committed partisans of both Right and Left, Nationalists as well as Social Democrats, agreed with it. Hindenburg's credentials as a Nationalist were impeccable, as were those of the members of the Kyffhäuser Society and of Count Westarp and the others who resigned from the Nationalist party, but they accepted Stresemann and Müller-Frank-

---

* They and the members of the Kyffhäuserbund took a position opposite to that of the other soldiers' organization, the Stahlhelm, some of whose members wanted Hindenburg's honorary membership cancelled when he supported the Young Plan. The Kyffhäuserbund backed Hindenburg's decision.

en's view that the Young Plan with all its defects had to be signed. Moreover, Hindenburg was convinced that it had a short life expectancy; it would not last, he said, more than two years, and he was a better prophet than anyone could have known at the time.

In an address to the German people explaining why he had approved the law, Hindenburg told them he had weighed the matter carefully in his mind, having listened to the arguments of those for and against, and had come to the conclusion that despite the burdens it imposed on the German people, the Young Plan was an improvement, economically and politically, over the Dawes Plan and on the whole a step forward on the hard road to the freedom and rebuilding of Germany. The conflicts of the last months, he said, must now give place to the practical job of recuperating the finances, stimulating the economy, and ameliorating the crushing unemployment and the no less dismal situation of German agriculture. He pleaded with the German people to get to work, to stretch out their hands to one another in the common purpose without regard to political attachments.[4]

This was something Hindenburg could do; he could stretch out his hand to Ludendorff, who ignored it,* and to Müller-Franken, who warmly returned the gesture. But it was impossible for the fanatics of the Far Right and the Far Left. Almost six million people had voted against the Young Plan; for Hitler and for Hugenberg, they were the advance guard of the new Germany, the first columns of an intrepid host who would no longer be enslaved, who would say no to the enemy no matter what the cost, even if it meant another invasion, as Class thought it might.

Stresemann's accomplishment of freeing the Rhine without firing a shot or losing a single soldier was derisory to the Far Right. But they had no means at their disposal of accomplishing the same end; all they could do was rage against the injustice of accepting the principle of reparations for another sixty years and declare they would never pay them. But what actually were the alternatives? No one, not Stresemann or Hindenburg or Müller-Franken or any of his cabinet thought it just that the reparations account should extend into the 1980s; none of them accepted the war guilt clause; none of them accepted the one-sided disarmament of the Reich as a lasting condition of peace; but they were the men who bore the responsibility of governing, and the German people overwhelmingly went along with their decision to bite the bullet. The Young Plan may have imposed onerous conditions, but as Hindenburg said, it was nevertheless an improvement over the Dawes Plan, and Germany could probably live with it. It would not have to do so for very long; another

* Ludendorff wrote in the *Volkswarte*, which he edited, that Hindenburg had destroyed what he had fought for in the war, and according to the laws of the old army he had forfeited the right to wear the field grey uniform in his grave.

catastrophe as devastating in many ways as the war itself was preparing to burst upon the world, and the center of its fury would be the Reich.

The Black Friday of the Wall Street crash occurred on October 24, 1929, three weeks after Stresemann's death, but the depression had begun in Germany before then. During an unusually hard winter, unemployment in January 1929 came to 2,850,000 people; in February the number rose to more than 3 million, and a year later, in January 1930, 3,218,000 people were registered as looking for work, a figure that rose to over 4½ million if part-time workers seeking full-time jobs and unregistered unemployed were counted. It was a return of utter frustration and anxiety for millions of people, and the battle over the Young Plan, along with the growing depression and unemployment, brought a new face to German politics.

Koblenz was one of the cities occupied by the French and Belgians, and under the terms of the Treaty of Versailles* it was to be evacuated by early January 1930. Their imminent withdrawal made it all the easier for the ultranationalist forces to make their pitch to those who had become suddenly aware of how fed up they were with their dispirited world, occupied by foreign troops for whom they would not cease to pay even long after the soldiers left. When people feel they waited too long for the glorious day of liberation, the closer it comes, the higher the scale of their indignation. In the communal elections in Prussia in November 1929, the National Socialists polled 38.5 percent of the votes cast in Koblenz, which the French would be evacuating at the end of November, forty days ahead of the time stipulated in the Versailles Treaty. This was the best showing the National Socialists had made anywhere in Prussia.[5] It was a similar story in Thuringia, where Landtag elections were held on December 8.† None of the government parties gained as a result of Stresemann's success in freeing the occupied Rhineland. It was the National Socialists who reaped the laurels of freedom. In Thuringia they suddenly vaulted into third place among the political parties, getting over 90,000 votes and electing 6 of 53 deputies, up from 2 deputies and less than 28,000 votes in 1927. The National Socialists thus became members of the government coalition, and Wilhelm Frick, one of Hitler's most faithful lieutenants, was elected Thuringia's minister of the interior and schools by a vote of 28–22 of the provincial diet—the first National Socialist minister in any *Land* government.

The economy was worsening rapidly. Peasant farms were being fore-

* The treaty provided for the evacuation of Cologne five years after ratification, Koblenz ten years after, in 1930, Mainz and Kehl fifteen years after, in 1935.
† On the same day, in the little city of Coburg in Lower Bavaria, the National Socialists elected 13 out of 25 councilmen as well as the mayor and deputy mayor, and won outright control of the city government. (Adam Buckreis, *Politik des 20. Jahrhunderts*, p. 521.)

closed at an unprecedented rate, and many of them stood empty as their owners gave up the hopeless task of meeting their debts and taxes. Ever increasing numbers of blue- and white-collar workers were looking for jobs. The foreign short-term credits proved as dangerous as Stresemann had foreseen: hard-pressed American creditors called in their loans, an act that was as heavy a blow to German agriculture as it was to industry. With the mounting economic stresses, the underlying fissures beneath the Weimar structure quickly reappeared. The increased demand for un-employment benefits had to be met, and the Müller-Franken government had somehow to figure out how they could be paid. It had become in-creasingly difficult to raise money. An attempt to float a new government loan of 500 million marks at the high rate of 7 percent, to which incen-tives were added in income, property, and inheritance tax exemptions, succeeded in selling only 177 million marks' worth of the bonds. Every-thing in and out of sight was taxed—income, property, inheritance, and goods and commodities of every kind. The only taxable source temporar-ily above the battle was beer. When the government proposed to raise the beer tax, the Bavarian Volksparty would not hear of it. If it were adopted, they would leave the government coalition. Taxes on brandy or any other drink could be raised, because *Branntwein* was never the symbol of German happiness and *Gemütlichkeit* that beer was. And the Bavarians had their way: beer for the moment was untouched. A middle-class party like the Volksparty, representing mainly entrepreneurs, wanted the unemployment premiums they paid on workers' wages and the benefits to remain as low as possible; however, the SPD demanded that they be increased. And when in early October 1929 the measure proposed by the Müller-Franken cabinet, including Stresemann, to raise the premiums on wages and salaries by a modest ½ percent to 3½ percent, the Volksparty refused to vote for the proposal. The best Stresemann, the day before his death, had been able to do was prevent his party's deputies from voting against the increase. They abstained, and the measure was carried in the Reichstag by a vote of 238 to 155. It was the last act he was able to perform on behalf of the republic. The opposition again brought a strange clutch of bedfellows together—Communists, Nationalists, the Economy party, and National Socialists; an odd assortment of conservatives and a hard core of grim and determined men who aimed to bring down both the government and the republic. They lost, but the tax controversy was not ended, and it was to force the resignation of the Müller-Franken government.

In March 1930, in order to take care of the spurting unemployment, Paul Moldenhauer, minister of economics and a member of the German Volksparty, proposed that the tax on wages be raised to 4 percent, but again his own party was opposed to any increase. Heinrich Brüning, leader of the Center party, and Oscar Meyer of the Democratic party tried to work out a compromise. The government, they proposed, would guarantee the extra funds needed for the year, amounting it was estimated to 150 million marks, and if, as was all too likely, this amount proved insufficient, the employment tax on wages should be raised to 3.75 percent. The cabinet, including three SPD members, Müller-Franken, Severing, and Robert Schmidt, the minister of economics, agreed; only the Social Democratic minister of labor, Rudolf Wissel, refused to go along. But Wissel's view was shared by the Social Democratic members of the Reichstag, and they refused to accept the compromise despite the fact that the Social Democratic chancellor and his two Socialist colleagues had voted for it. The SPD had 150 deputies in the Reichstag, over a third of whom were trade union leaders, and they rejected a proposal that seemed to them to threaten the whole system of unemployment insurance and that would leave them vulnerable to the Communists' standing accusation that they were betraying the working class. What Brüning and Meyer were proposing would postpone any decision to raise the tax until the autumn, but then, the SPD deputies feared, there would be more pressure from the other parties for a decrease in the tax than for an increase. So again Müller-Franken and the Social Democrats in his government were forced to vote against a measure they supported, and as a result he and his cabinet had to resign. It was a relatively trivial issue on which the Social Democrats overthrew a government led by one of their own members and in which they had more ministers than any other party, and they would pay dearly for their obduracy. They would never again be represented in any Weimar government.

Hindenburg, on March 28, 1930, turned to the Center leader, Heinrich Brüning, to head a cabinet made up of representatives of the same parties that had served under Müller-Franken minus the SPD. Brüning was forty-five years old, a political scientist who had studied in England and at the University of Bonn, a man of irreproachable character, intelligent, conservative but with close ties to blue-collar workers, with whom he had worked for many years in the Christian Trade Union movement. He had volunteered early in the war and had served as a noncommissioned officer until he was wounded in the head and chest. After five weeks in hospital he had been sent to officers' school, where he received a lieutenant's commission. He had fought in the murderous battles on the west front in a mobile machine gun detachment. He was a Centrist in more than a political sense—a man of moderation and seasoned judgment who understood the necessity for political compromise, a monarchist who supported the republic, and a former soldier who could establish a cool but cordial relationship with his old commander in chief.

He looked more like an ascetic—François-Poncet said a Catholic or

Anglican prelate[6]—than a politician. Thin-lipped, close-shaven, reserved, with scrutinizing eyes behind unrimmed glasses, he could have been what he later became, a professor of political science, instead of the polite champion of the republic unevenly matched against Adolf Hitler and his brawling National Socialists.

Hindenburg had a few simple but rigorous standards for judging the men around him. He esteemed the hardworking, incorruptible Müller-Franken despite his socialist principles, and he could respect the other party leaders who possessed the patriotic devotion and moral reliability he thought essential to high office. What he would have liked above all would have been a chancellor with no political affiliations, and since that was impossible, Brüning was a reasonable second choice. A middle-of-the-road man with solid political experience who had distinguished himself in combat and won the Iron Cross, First Class, would be likely to make a competent chancellor.

Hindenburg's confidence in Brüning was greatly strengthened by the support his candidacy was given by General Groener and Groener's chief of ministry, the then Colonel von Schleicher. Both Hindenburg and Groener regarded Schleicher as a remarkably gifted political advisor; Groener called him "My cardinal *in politicis*," a type so rare among German officers as to be easily overrated. But in backing Brüning, Schleicher was far more perspicacious than he would be in his later political judgment. He saw and persuaded Groener and the president to see in Brüning a man who was close to the Reichswehr's idea of what Germany urgently needed: a principled, informed, dependable political leader who would head a "presidential cabinet" responsible to Hindenburg instead of to day-to-day parliamentary coalitions that fell apart on trivial issues.

The trouble was that the Brüning cabinet, without either the SPD or the right-wing parties behind it, would not have the backing of more than an occasional majority in the Reichstag. But Hindenburg had, in fact, few alternatives; with the SPD having forced the resignation of a cabinet headed by one of its own members, and the parties of the Far Left and Right in opposition not only to the government but to the republic, he could only turn to the same middle groups that had governed with moderate success in a coalition with the SPD. It would be a cabinet of minority parties that added up to a minority, but it would have to function in the place of a nonexistent majority coalition. A cabinet of this kind without dependable Reichstag support would force the president to make frequent use of the emergency powers granted him under Article 48 of the constitution. And if he relied on Article 48 for anything but an emergency, it would seem to controvert Article 54, which declared that the chancellor and his ministers must have the confidence of the Reichstag to carry out the duties of their offices and must resign when it was withheld. Both Hindenburg and Brüning, as they told one another, were determined to govern only by constitutional means, and yet the constitution was not designed for the kind of government they were compelled to conduct. The Reichstag, under the multiple party system, was at best a Rube Goldbergian apparatus, even when it worked as it was intended to—as a democratically chosen cross section of the electorate that could be only temporarily overridden by the use of the presidential powers under Article 48. In this fashion—Ebert, in the unruly early days of the republic had had to use Article 48 136 times—the parliamentary system had succeeded in weathering crisis after crisis. When, however, the Reichstag ran out of coalitions ready to agree on such minor matters as an increase of ½ percent of the rate of unemployment insurance to deal with the rising hurricane of the depression, Article 48 became a built-in part of the legislative process.*

Without a functioning Reichstag, the president could only turn to a middle-of-the-road government responsible to him and hope that in time it would unite a parliamentary majority behind it. Within three days Brüning was able to form his cabinet, and Hindenburg had approved it. Brüning appointed the German Democrat Hermann Dietrich as minister of economics; he kept on Julius Curtius, who had succeeded Stresemann as foreign minister, from the Müller-Franken government; and in an attempt to gain right-wing support, he chose a member of the Economy party, Johann Bredt, as minister of justice and two former German Nationals, Gottfried Treviranus as minister for occupied territories and Martin Schiele as minister of agriculture.

Brüning's opening speech to the Reichstag on April 1 made a reasonable case for the course he intended to pursue. He pointed out that he was bound to no coalition and that his government had the task of dealing with the essential problems of survival of the Reich as quickly as possible. It would be the last attempt, he warned the deputies, to arrive at such solutions with this Reichstag. He had to meet the economic and agrarian crisis head-on. He would not hesitate to use extraordinary measures. Help would immediately be provided the desperate landowners in the East by means of a decrease in interest and mortgage rates and the provision of credits.

The Communists and Social Democrats thereupon moved a vote of no confidence in the new government, which would have been easily carried with the opposition majority of 200 delegates, but agrarian aid had the support of many of the Nationalist deputies despite Hugenberg's

---

* After the first stormy years of the republic, emergency decrees were issued rarely. None was issued between 1925 and 1930; from December 1930 to April 1931, there were 2 as against 19 laws passed by the Reichstag; from April to December 1931, 40 emergency decrees were issued and no laws were passed by the Reichstag. In 1932, the score was 59 emergency decrees and 5 Reichstag laws. (Otto Meissner, *Staatssekretär unter Ebert, Hindenburg, Hitler,* p. 210.)

violent attacks on the Brüning government and its program, and the no-confidence motion was defeated 253–187.

It was a short-lived victory for Brüning. When early in July his finance minister Hermann Dietrich proposed to raise both direct and indirect taxes to cover the heavy deficit, the Reichstag was opposed, and Brüning had to ask Hindenburg to make use of Article 48. The president thereupon on July 26, 1930, issued the government's decree "For the Resolution of Financial, Economic and Social Needs," a series of measures raising taxes and decreasing expenditures that Dietrich and Brüning believed essential. The decree also provided East Prussia with 100 million marks for the benefit of its farmers and landowners and a moratorium of three months on forced sales.

The use of emergency decrees, however, could in effect be overridden if a majority of the Reichstag voted to cancel them and called for new elections. This is what happened when Communists, Social Democrats, Nationalists, and National Socialists combined against the government. A progovernment coalition might have been formed had Brüning been willing to compromise with the Social Democratic demands that one of the new taxes levied, the head tax, be graduated according to income— a measure that was actually adopted later on. But Brüning refused to make any such concession; since everyone participated in elections, everyone must contribute to the support of the state, and the budget had somehow to be brought into balance. Dietrich had called in vain on the Reichstag to show, as he said, whether "we Germans are a mass of interests or a nation [*Staatsvolk*]."[7] The answer was given by the combined vote of Communists, Socialists, and the Right: 236 deputies from the SPD,[*] the Communists, the German Nationals, and the National Socialists demanded an end to the emergency decrees, and with 221 supporting the government, new elections were scheduled for September 14.

Twenty-eight parties presented candidates for the Reichstag elections, and the results of the voting were earthshaking. The far-out party of the Munich Putsch, composed of hoodlum street fighters and anti-Semitic warriors for the rebirth of the Aryan Fatherland, had become the second largest in the Reich. National Socialist deputies elected to the Reichstag numbered 107, in place of the 12 elected in 1928. And 6.4 million men and women, in place of 810,000 in 1928, had voted for them. The Nazis had increased their share of the vote from the 2.6 percent of the total of 1928 to 18.3 percent. The German Nationals' vote was cut in half, from 14.2 percent to 7 percent; their deputies dropped from 73 to 41. The

---

[*] The Socialists' opposition to Brüning in the Reichstag was in marked contrast to their cooperation with the Centrist leader Josef Hess in the Prussian Landtag. There, the two parties formed a governing coalition made possible by the conciliatory tactics of SPD Minister-President Otto Braun and Hess.

German Volksparty, lacking Stresemann's leadership, went down almost as sharply, from 8.7 percent to 4.5 percent. The Center, behind Brüning and with the continued backing of the politically unseduceable Catholic women, polled 400,000 more votes than it had in 1928, although its percentage of the total vote decreased slightly, and it increased its number of deputies from 62 to 68. The Democratic party lost five seats, dropping from 25 to 20. The Social Democrats lost 600,000 votes and 10 deputies, down from 153 to 143 seats and from 28.7 percent of the vote to 24.5 percent, but they remained the largest party in the Reichstag. The Communists were up from 54 to 77 seats, from 10.6 percent of the vote to 13.1 percent.

Although the prorepublican democrats still held 60 percent of the Reichstag seats, almost 14 million people had voted against the republic. The extremes of Right and Left had become key political forces. They had won more than 30 percent of the vote, gains made mainly on the one side at the expense of the German Nationals and other right-wing-to-moderate parties, and on the other as a result of defections from the Social Democrats and the moderate-to-middle groups. A big increase in the National Socialist vote had come from disaffected farmers; more than 400,000 votes had been cast for the party in Schleswig-Holstein, long a center of agrarian revolt.* But in part it had also come, political observers thought, from young people who had not voted before. The number of eligible voters had risen by 1.7 million between 1928 and 1930, and more of those qualified—82 percent in 1930 as against 74 percent in 1928—cast their ballots. All together, 4 million more people voted in 1930 than in 1928.

It was plain that a sizeable part of the German electorate had come to feel itself outside the society. Unemployment had passed the 3-million mark in September, and almost as demoralizing as being without a job was the fear of being without one. To a large section of the population, the weakness of the republican government, reparations, and the Young Plan were responsible for the deteriorating political and industrial economy. And the results of the elections themselves immediately contributed to the depression. The Reichsbank lost one billion marks within a week as foreigners withdrew their balances.

The National Socialists and Communists had ready explanations for the German catastrophe: the Reich was a treasury looted by international capitalism; it would never free itself without a revolution that overturned its exploiters. A National Socialist election poster showed a hardworking German Michael carrying his yearly tribute of 2 billion marks being stopped by an arresting hand that wore a swastika band

---

* The forced sales of farmlands in Schleswig-Holstein had risen by between 200 and 300 percent compared with 1913. Three-fourths of these were peasant holdings. (Walter Görlitz, *Hindenburg*, p. 334.)

above the wrist. And along with the international enemy were the old phalanx of National Socialist demons—the Bolsheviks and the Jews, who with the capitalists were ready to give Germany the last thrust of the knife.

The password for election day, September 14, said Hitler, is "Strike down the political bankruptcy of the old parties! Destroy the corrupters of our national unity! Down with those responsible for our decay! Volks-comrades! Join up with the Brown Front of awakening Germany!"[8] It was not a new message, but it was delivered to an audience far readier to hear it than ever before.

Brüning spoke of sacrifice for the well-being of the nation, Hitler of action against the dark conspiracy that was destroying the Reich and that had to be itself destroyed if the nation was to live. On October 5 Hitler, together with Frick and Göring, was received by Chancellor Brüning, who had had similar meetings with leaders of other parties, to discuss the possibility of Hitler's entering the Brüning cabinet with two other National Socialists. Nothing came of the talk. Hitler was not the man to collaborate with anyone; if he entered any government it would be in order to take it over. The National Socialists were revolutionists; they could operate only as a party of the revolution either in or out of power.

Hitler had no serious idea of collaborating with Brüning or anyone else. When the 107 National Socialist deputies appeared in the Reichstag in October, they wore their forbidden SA uniforms, which they had smuggled into the building. Outside on the Leipzigerstrasse, bands of National Socialists beat up people who looked like Jews and broke the windows of Jewish shops. Even the roll call of Deputies in the Reichstag was turned into a scene from the beer halls as the National Socialists hooted and yelled at those they particularly disliked. Severing in his memoirs says that the Nazis were unaccustomed to political argumenta-tion. What they were practiced in were outbursts of "Heils" and "Pfuis" and, when the opportunity presented itself, bouts of knocking around their opponents. As the new Parliament met, they used the tactics they were familiar with. They set out to depose President of the Reichstag Paul Löbe, shouting down opposition speakers and threatening to beat them up. Löbe was nevertheless reelected, and Severing, unimpressed by the Brown Shirts, walked slowly and deliberately through their ranks. They cursed him heartily as he went by and shook their fists, but no one laid a hand on him.

It was in this atmosphere that Brüning made his opening speech to the new Reichstag on October 16 amid shouts from the Communists of "Down with the hunger chancellor!" Brüning made a sober, scholarly defense of his policies and warned the deputies against voting down the emergency decrees. The economy was in dire straits; the deficit would come to between 450 and 500 million marks, and if things did not improve it would reach a billion marks. Foreign countries had withdrawn their credit balances, and many Germans unhappily had done the same. Nevertheless, an American bank consortium had declared its willingness to make a loan of 125 million marks—on condition that the deficits be amortized—and Brüning asked the deputies to have the same confidence in their country that these foreigners had and to accept his cut-to-the-bone measures for a balanced budget.

His speech was a plea for some kind of collaboration if not of unity. It was intended to woo the sensible Right and it took a hard line on both foreign and domestic issues. Brüning defended himself against the charge that what he was trying to do would mean a long-range diminution of real wages, but in the short run, he said, wages had to come down for German goods to compete in the world market. No one, government officials or anyone else, would be untouched by the cuts. Agriculture and the unemployed had to be supported, and the subsidies had to be paid for.

He preached Hindenburg's doctrine of German unity above all, begging the parties, with the dire need of the German people in mind, not to tear one another apart. Great sacrifices were required, but they could lead to freedom and recovery for the entire Reich. And he had words to assuage the Right. The highest aim of German foreign and domestic policy, he told the deputies, was the achievement of moral and material equality with other nations. He referred to reparations, to the Allies' repudiation of Wilson's Fourteen Points, and to Germany's one-sided disarmament, which could not continue, he said, while other countries paid no attention to their obligations to disarm. He thus linked the domestic crisis with foreign policy; one country could not alone overcome what was in fact an international crisis. Everything he said was aimed at accommodation; he would pursue Stresemann's policies and do away with reparations and one-sided disarmament, two of the chief horrors of the Nationalist opposition.

In December, in an emergency decree, he produced the promised austerity measures. All officials' salaries were cut 6 percent, as were their pensions and those of their families. Similar cuts were made in the salaries of the president, the chancellor, and his ministers and in the pensions of their inheritors. Unemployment insurance went up to 6.5 percent, and the extraordinary taxes and surtaxes were continued.

None of these measures stopped or even slowed the depression. It was a worldwide epidemic, and the like of it had never been seen before. A good deal of talk was heard about the need for confidence, as though the depression were only a state of mind and would go away if only people took an optimistic view of it. But the inescapable fact was that normal life where people could work and plan for the future was disappearing for larger and larger segments of the population.

Along with the domestic troubles were the continuing evidences that, despite the talk of peace and reconciliation, the Treaty of Versailles was still in full effect. True, the last of the Rhineland bridgeheads was evacuated by the French in June 1930 and all Germany celebrated. The Stahlhelm marched and there were torchlight parades and innumerable speeches, in none of which was Stresemann mentioned, although it was he who had persuaded the French to leave four and a half years ahead of schedule. In any event the Saar was still separated from the Reich, and Poland still occupied what thousands of East and West Prussians were convinced was as much German territory as Königsberg or Berlin. In a meeting in Berlin in August 1930 of the East Organizations of those "true to the homeland," the minister for occupied territories, Gottfried Treviranus, a former naval officer, pleaded that the energies of the entire German people be mobilized to bind up "the unhealed wounds of the east flank," and he told the Poles that their future would never be assured if German-Polish relations remained exacerbated by unjust borders. Under pressure from Brüning and Foreign Minister Curtius, Treviranus had to back down and explain to the enraged Poles and to Poincaré that he had not had in mind the use of force. But for millions of Germans, what he had first said was the eternal truth and his disclaimers eyewash. Clearly the only way the lost lands would be returned to the Reich was by direct action or negotiation from a position of strength, which was what Treviranus seemed to have been talking about. Thus the restoration of the Rhineland ahead of schedule merely placed in greater contrast the situation of the eastern provinces, which it seemed unlikely would soon be returned in the same way.

The issue was kept alive by graphic accounts of Polish terrorism against the German minority in Poland. In January 1931, Curtius presented the German case before the League Council so convincingly that a report essentially substantiating the charges against the Poles was unanimously accepted by the council under its chairman, British Foreign Minister Arthur Henderson, who congratulated the council for having so decisively supported the protection of minorities. But the reports of Germans suffering under their Polish overlords did not stop with the acceptance of the report, and a meeting of the Stahlhelm in May 1931 in Breslau confirmed the continued and belligerent German interest in the plight of the German minority in Poland and the lost territories. Despite the depression, 100,000 people turned out for the occasion from all parts of the Reich. Among those participating were the former crown prince and his wife, General von Seeckt, Field Marshal von Mackensen, and General Heye, who had just retired as chief of the Reichswehr.

Dramatically pointing to the Polish border, the Stahlhelm leader, Franz Seldte, said: "Comrades, there is the German East; there lies Germany's future, Germany's fate."[9]

The Poles protested, but had Brüning taken any serious steps to curb such gatherings or to repudiate the passionate sentiments, he would have had to resign before a storm of public and Reichstag disapproval, which would no doubt have included the Communists, who were as anti-Polish as the Nationalists.

With the increasing distrust of orthodox solutions, the propagandists of the Right and Left had dazzling opportunities to make converts even in the army. In January 1930, General Groener, minister of defense, had written a "pastoral letter" to the Reichswehr, warning the troops of the grave danger to the army and the Reich of the Communists and National Socialists, who threatened, he said, civil war when the Reich had enemies enough outside the country. Theirs was the way, he said, to national destruction, but means were also at hand to develop and strengthen the "natural forces" of the Fatherland, and it was the solemn task of the Reichswehr to curb the spread of class and party differences that would lead to civil war. The Wehrmacht was the extension of the idea of the state; it had no interest, no assignment other than to serve it, and he asked its officers to work together to educate the troops in political affairs. A month later in the so-called "Watch Decree," Groener returned to his theme. The attempts being made, he said, by radical elements to penetrate the Reichswehr had to be resisted, and to this end he proposed to reward soldiers who reported on their machinations with a suitably engraved watch, or with special leaves, or even, in exceptional cases, with a promotion.

The "Watch Decree" was widely regarded as a comic interlude, but Groener was not seeing ghosts. Three lieutenants assigned to the fifth artillery regiment of the Ulm garrison, Hans Ludin, Richard Scheringer, and Friedrich Wendt, none of them over twenty-six years old, were tried in September 1930 on charges of high treason. They had joined the National Socialist party, and two of them, Ludin and Scheringer, had travelled around Germany attempting to recruit other officers, as they said, for the movement against the leftist course of the army leadership and the spreading of pacifist doctrines. In their trial they described themselves as "nationally minded" (*vaterländisch gesinnt*), and they were distressed that few of the leaders of political parties held the same views as they. Ludin spoke of the Versailles Treaty that had forced the acceptance of the Young Plan, which the German people rejected, and he spoke of how the genuine will of the country was suppressed. The officers had not wanted to revolt, he said, but to show that young men in the army could really act in a "thinking" (*sic*) manner. It had been painful for him to see in almost every theater in Berlin plays critical of army officers. He mentioned the dismissal of Seeckt, who was, he said, a symbol, the creator of the German army, and although Ludin readily admitted that he was not in a position to judge the high politics of the Reich, he was convinced, he told the court, that he knew what evil effects they had on officers and men. Scheringer said the dismissal of Seeckt had politicized the army. Ludin confirmed this and added that the Seeckt case had been a slap in the face of the officer corps. The Prussian prince's taking part in maneuvers had been no more than a pretext for Seeckt's dismissal.

The testimony of the young men was not very convincing, but their trial provided a dramatic setting for Hitler to make another courtroom appearance and to explain in his own grandiloquent terms what the young officers had attempted to do. They were found guilty and sentenced to eighteen months of fortress arrest,* in the course of which one of them, Lieutenant Scheringer, announced that he had been converted to the Communist party and renounced Hitler and all his works. Scheringer and Ludin were dismissed from the army. Wendt resigned his commission.

The sensation of the trial was the appearance on behalf of the defendants of Adolf Hitler. His presence as a witness was asked for by Hans Frank, one of the defense lawyers, who explained to the court he needed Hitler's testimony to show how the National Socialists wished to come to power only by legal, constitutional means. Frank, the future governor-general of Poland, with a long experience of springing young Nazis from the clutches of the law after street brawls, wrote in his autobiography that more than 40,000 such trials were held between 1925 and 1933 and he was the defense lawyer in scores of them. In the trial of the young officers, he succeeded in persuading the court to hear Hitler, who again made the most of his opportunity.

With one eye on Hindenburg and the other on the electorate, he swore again that the party would come to power only by constitutional means. He assured the court he had no desire to subvert the Reichswehr. Since 1925, he said, he had decided that the events of 1923 should be completely obliterated. He had ordered the absolute disarmament of the SA, which was never to have a military character, and which had never in any case been intended as a battle group against the state. It was created to be used solely for the defense of the National Socialist movement against the strong-arm squads of the Left. The unauthorized possession of weapons and the conducting of military exercises were grounds for expulsion from the SA. When he spoke of revolution, Hitler told the court, he meant a spiritual revolution. Never, he repeated, under any

---

* The court said a prison sentence was out of the question in view of the defendants' high motives in acting as they did.

circumstances had he wanted to attain his goals by illegal means. The party had only defended itself against the Red hordes; it had sought to prevent its members from being beaten up when its meetings were invaded.

The president of the court reminded Hitler that he had said that one day heads would roll, "either ours or the others'," and Hitler explained, in the vein of his peroration before the Court in 1924, what he had really meant. "If our movement triumphs," he said, "then a new court will convene, and before this court the criminals of November 1918 will atone for their sins. Then certainly heads will roll."[10] The courtroom, packed with National Socialists and their sympathizers, rocked with applause, and the president had no further questions.

Hitler repeated other sentiments he had uttered in 1924. The day would come, he said, when 35 million of the 40 million voters would be part of his movement, and then they would understand exactly what the National Socialists sought. Their 107 Reichstag deputies would become 250—would become an absolute majority. Two or three more elections and the National Socialists would be in power.

But this, he kept repeating, would be accomplished by legal means, and Hitler told the court he had expelled from the party many of its members who thought otherwise, including Otto Strasser, who had played with the idea of revolution.*

As for the extravagant statements that were often made on behalf of the party, Hitler pointed out that millions of young people took part in the movement, young men who wanted only the best for Germany. They were often beaten up by Red mobs. They were arrested and persecuted. So if they sometimes, in their youthful exuberance, said things that did not comport with the movement's views, it was understandable.

The speech, like Hitler's plea before the court in 1924, lacked the anti-Semitic verbiage that characterized his harangues to the party. Again it was a devoted acolyte of the Fatherland who was addressing the court on behalf of Germany's just grievances and the young men who wished nothing more than to have them assuaged. Again the oratory was laced with liberal doses of fiction. The SA was not the harmless defender of the party's weal that Hitler described; it was the same battle group that had taken part in the putsch of 1923. Hitler's oath of legality was a tactic; as Goebbels told Lieutenant Scheringer, "a chess move of genius."[11]

---

* Hitler had broken with Otto Strasser on Strasser's continued insistence that the party pursue a socialist course along with its nationalism. Gregor Strasser, however, sided with Hitler in the dispute against his brother and remained one of the leading National Socialist deputies in the Reichstag until the end of 1932, when he resigned his party posts. Two years later, at the time of the Röhm purge, he was one of the former party leaders who fell victim to Hitler's wrath.

On October 12, 1930, the opening day of the Reichstag session, Gregor Strasser, too, had made clear what the party had in mind. "We are now for the Constitution" he told the Reichstag; "we are for the Weimar democracy and for the law for the protection of the Republic as long as it suits us. We will demand and keep every position of power based on this democracy as long as we wish it. You, not we, have constructed all that, and if today we use it against you, then you can turn against its authors in your own ranks."[12] "We come to the Reichstag," Goebbels had written four years before, "not as friends, not as neutrals, but as enemies. The National Socialists," he said, "plan to use this arsenal of democracy to bring it down." "Under the Constitution," he told the Reichstag again on February 5, 1931, "we are committed to the legality of means, not of ends. We wish to come to power legally, but what we will one day do with this power when we have it is our business."[13]

A few days later, on February 10, Goebbels, Gregor Strasser, and the other National Socialist deputies marched out of the Parliament followed by forty-one deputies from the Nationalists and four from the right-wing of the small, agrarian party, the *Deutsches Landvolk*, swearing they would return only "to thwart the especially malicious tricks of the enemies of the people in the Reichstag."[14] They considered convening a new anti-Parliament of opposition parties in Weimar, but soon dropped the idea in favor of returning to the Reichstag.

So ominous had been the progress of the extremists, both Left and Right, that as early as June 1930 Prussia forbade its state officials to be members of either the Communist or the National Socialist party, and both Bavaria and Prussia banned the wearing of the Brown Shirt uniforms. As a result the Nazis wore white shirts and continued their parades and demonstrations. Brüning, in March 1931, issued an emergency decree for "combatting political disturbances." It forbade carrying weapons,* a measure Hitler had assured the Leipzig court he had already taken with regard to the SA and the SS. But how much his protestations to the court had been worth may be seen in the order he now gave the SA and the SS: he told them they must obey the Brüning decree under penalty of being expelled from the party. He consoled them, however, at the same time. The Brüning order, he said, showed that the enemies of Germany were losing their nerve; National Socialism would inevitably be victorious over them. He was playing his hand with unwonted prudence, and as it turned out none of the countermeasures had any effect in the rise in strength of his movement.

Through 1928 the National Socialists had had no better luck than their anti-Semitic predecessors of before the war in recruiting a significant

---

* The decree also forbade calumniating the state or its officials or any religious organization.

following. The pre-1914, anti-Semitic parties, after thirty years of campaigning, had succeeded in mustering only 130,000 members, and the politically organized movement simply disappeared. Of the handful of six delegates it had sent to the Reichstag in 1912, five were absorbed into the Conservative party, and that was seemingly the end of political anti-Semitism. As the chief source of a political *Weltanschauung*, anti-Semitism was too sterile a concept for the Reich. The parties that had based themselves on it could only assemble the same collection of fanatics, who repeated their slogans year after year as similar groups had repeated them for decades in Austria, France, Russia, Poland, and many other countries as well.

But the anti-Semitic parties in Germany had never had the kind of long-lived successful political leadership provided by Karl Lueger, for example, in Vienna. During the war years political anti-Semitism disappeared from the German scene, and when it reappeared with Hitler's small band of National Socialist revolutionaries, it had, for more than a decade, no luck at all in electing a sizeable number of delegates to either state or national legislatures.

In a matter of months the situation was different. A chemical change took place in the reception Hitler received as he explained in speech after speech, to audiences that grew from meeting to meeting, that the "November criminals," international finance, Bolshevism, and capitalism were all vectors of the same un-German disease, whose source was the Jews. But along with the ritual anti-Semitism were denunciations of the men and the system that had brought ever-increasing misery to a once happy land. The anti-Semitism a convert could take or leave. Albert Speer, for example, paid no attention to it; for men like him the movement promised a German renewal, an economic and spiritual recovery. Nothing was new in Hitler's message. What was new was the readiness of the audience to hear it.

In 1914 the German armies had invaded Poland with a proclamation to the Jews that they came as liberators. A combined declaration of the German and Austrian armies issued in Berlin at the start of the war told the eastern Jews that the armies of the Central Powers were not making war against peoples but only against Russian tyranny. The proclamation said: "Jews in Poland! We come to you as friends and deliverers. Our flags bring you justice and freedom, the full and equal rights of citizens, freedom of religion and person in all economic and cultural areas." The pronouncement reminded the Jews of the hollowness of the Russian promises of freedom and of the pogroms, mass expulsions, and banishments that had followed them in so many cities ruled by the tsar. It reminded them, too, of the lying accusations of ritual murder that had bedevilled the Russian Jews; of how they had been hunted down, men, women, and children, "like wild beasts." It asked them to remember the punitive laws that had applied to Jews; how many doors, including the door to education, had been closed as Jewish children had been driven from Russian schools, towns, and villages. And Jews, like prostitutes, had to carry yellow passes to be permitted to live in Russia.

The proclamation went on: "Jews in Poland, the hour of retribution is at hand. The brave armies of Germany and Austria-Hungary are in Poland and with God's help will make a reckoning with your oppressor." The Jews were asked to lend their help. They had nothing to fear from the invading armies, they were told; not a hair of their heads would be touched. The soldiers of the Central Powers would pay well and in cash for anything delivered to them. The proclamation closed: "Help to defeat the enemy and work for the victory of freedom and justice."[15]

The proclamation, of course, was a piece of propaganda designed to raise all the help possible for the armies of the Central Powers. It had little if anything more than a military purpose behind it. Nevertheless, it was the kind of pronouncement that the really anti-Semitic countries of Europe—like Russia and its territories of Poland, the Ukraine, Latvia, Lithuania, and Esthonia—could not possibly have made.

But by 1930 enclaves of political anti-Semitism were reappearing in parts of the Reich. In Thuringia, Wilhelm Frick, minister of the interior, overruled a vote of the faculty and appointed a Nazi racial theorist, Hans Günther, to the University of Jena. He made another party member, Paul Schultze-Naumburg, principal of the United Academy of Arts in Weimar. Frick also forbade the playing of "nigger jazz" in Thuringian beer halls and restaurants and ordered new prayers for the school system, which because of their anti-Semitic overtones the Leipzig Supreme Court declared unconstitutional. Frick had to quit his post in April 1931 when the National Socialist–German Volksparty coalition in Thuringia broke up—but that was a momentary setback.

In Braunschweig on September 14, 1930, the same day the Reichstag election was held, the NSDAP received 22 percent of the votes and gained 9 of 20 seats in the *Landtag*. A member of the party, Anton Franzen, was elected minister of the interior. In November, in Danzig, the National Socialists became the second-largest party, electing 12 delegates as against 19 Social Democrats, 11 Centrists, 10 German Nationals, and 7 Communists. In Bremen, in the same month, the National Socialists won 32 of 120 seats. In Schaumburg-Lippe on May 3, 1931, they won 26.9 percent of the vote, and on May 17 in Oldenburg they won 19 of 48 seats, for the first time becoming the largest party in a German Landtag.

It was not that the German people, or even 18 percent of them, had suddenly adopted the political anti-Semitism they had steadily rejected for decades. Rather, the exposed, vulnerable section of the population of an eroding society was voting against the parties that did not seem able to hold its world together. Unemployment passed the 5-million mark in the Reich at the end of 1930. In England the figure was 2¾ million, in Italy one million, and in the United States 11½ million. But no one in those countries was paying reparations, and also the percentage of unemployed in the Reich was higher than in any other country in the world. By the end of 1932, 33 percent of the work force in the Reich could not find jobs. Out of every thousand of the population capable of work, 275 were unemployed, as compared with 207 in the United States, 186 in England, 110 in Japan, and 61 in France.[16]

Brüning attempted, as did most of the Western political leaders, to meet the crisis with conventional economic wisdom. The budget had to be balanced. On June 5, 1931, he cut unemployment benefits by 5 percent. Again he lowered the salaries of top government officials, this time by 20 percent, and of the cabinet by 30 percent, and wherever he could he raised the tax rate. It was a draconian program, and even if it had been successful, it would have taken a long time to produce results.

What Brüning feared most was another inflation. Make-work programs threatened to spark huge government expenditures that could only end in a worse situation than the one the Reich found itself in. It was terrible, Brüning said, for modern man to be without the work that gave content and meaning to his life. It led to moral damage, *seelische Deklassierung*. But make-work programs would bring greater disasters upon the Reich. The German people could not endure a second inflation. What was needed was concerted international action against the common plague, and the return of confidence that would come through reasonable political solutions. The problem, Brüning said, was that there were the unhappy conquered, but no happy victors. He therefore pleaded for disarmament and international cooperation.

So much for the rhetoric. In the world of events, emergency unemployment relief far beyond anything foreseen in the Reich's insurance measures had to be provided and tens of thousands of acres of farmland had to be rescued. Schlange-Schoeningen, Reichscommissar for aid to the East, calculated that 1,500,000 acres of farmland in the East were mortgaged up to 150 percent of their value and almost 3 million acres were mortgaged for 100 percent of their value.[17] Without immediate assistance that could be provided only by the central government, large sections of the eastern territory would lie fallow, Schlange-Schoeningen pointed out, and always at hand were the land-hungry Poles with their own radicals, who would be glad to step in if they could find a way. The 100 million marks the Brüning government had provided for East Prussia in the July emergency decree was a plaster on deep wounds. At least

850 million marks, it was estimated, was needed, and where such additional funds could come from in a ravaged economy was a grim riddle.

One measure that had seemed promising both economically and politically to Müller-Franken and Staatsekretär Bernhard von Bülow, an old-line diplomat, was a project for a customs union with Austria. Brüning and Curtius, who wanted a wider range of customs unions involving the Balkan countries, reluctantly accepted the Austrian version, and on March 22, 1931, it was announced in Berlin and Vienna that the Reich and Austria had come to an agreement on the conditions. Austria, instead of being the center of what under the Habsburgs had been a free-trade empire, was little more than a countryside around the faded city of Vienna, and for both countries the project seemed a long step toward economic, political, and psychological recovery. For Bülow it was also a shrewd stroke against Adolf Hitler, an activist move by German diplomacy to blunt the ultranationalists' attack on the weakness of the Reich's foreign policy. Austrian Foreign Minister and Vice Chancellor Johann Schober, a member of the National Economy bloc, a former Pan-German party, saw it as a rescue operation for his own beleaguered country.

But for France and her allies, a German-Austrian customs union was a nightmare. It could be nothing less than the prelude to the *Anschluss* and to an unthinkable increase in Germany's strength. A German customs union, from the French point of view, had a menacing history. The *Zollverein*, led by Prussia in the early nineteenth century (directed at the time against Austrian hegemony), had been the first step in the unification of Germany. France declared the proposal a breach of the Treaty of Versailles, in which Germany had promised to respect the independence of Austria, and a breach of the Treaty of St. Germain, in which Austria had promised to maintain its independence. At the very least, it could be argued, the customs union threatened Austria's economic independence, and Paris foresaw far worse consequences than that. France withdrew her bank credits from Vienna, and then, as François-Poncet said, Germany and Austria were haled "like two criminals" before the League Council. After that they were delivered to judgment before the World Court at The Hague, where the customs union was voted down 8–7.[18]

The representatives of France, Poland, Rumania, Italy, Spain, Cuba, Colombia, and El Salvador voted against the customs union, and Japan, the United States, Britain, Holland, Belgium, China, and Germany voted for it. It was, of course, a political, not a juridical, decision that was handed down, and it very likely had little effect on the course of the depression in either Germany or Austria. But it was additional proof for a large number of Germans and Austrians that even if for purely political reasons France disapproved, an attempt to work out economic problems in some reasonable way was impossible, no matter what sound arguments could be made.*

Briand had what he regarded as an alternative to any customs union. Part of his grand design was a European union, a more limited version of collective security than that offered by the League of Nations, with a potential for levelling both economic and political barriers. It was a proposal on which Britain, with her overseas Commonwealth, looked with the same cool eye with which she had regarded the Geneva Protocol, and Brüning, who feared a European union would block any revision of the eastern frontiers, declared the Reich could not enter such a federation without British participation. Thus that plan had been dropped, but in any event, what economic effects its adoption might have led to lay too far in the future to affect the immediate crisis.

Some kind of prompt international action, as Brüning pointed out, was essential to avoid the Reich's economic collapse. Nations do not go bankrupt; individuals, financial institutions, businesses, even cities may declare themselves insolvent, but nations are able to print money, and while their currency may be inflated and their indebtedness arbitrarily deflated, they become only morally—never fiscally—bankrupt. Bankruptcy is reserved for their banks, their industries, and sometimes their cities. In May, the largest bank in Austria owned by the Rothschild family, the Vienna branch of the Austrian *Kreditanstalt*, could not meet its obligations and had to close its doors. Its failure affected almost all of Austria's chief industrial entreprises, and the Vienna government had to supply an emergency loan of 100 million schillings, which could only come from foreign sources. Germany was soon to face a similar crisis. In July the Darmstädter und National Bank, called the Danat Bank, one of the four largest in the Reich, had to close its doors. The Danat Bank failure was the largest in European history, and its reverberations shook the already precarious structure of the German economy to its foundations.

Brüning's emergency decree of June 5, 1931, for the "Security of the Economy and Finances," which made further cuts in salaries and unemployment and welfare payments, was another turn of the screw for millions of people already living at a bare subsistence level. Because the Reichstag was not in session and would not meet again until October, he could be attacked only by the press and spokesmen for the political parties. When he travelled to Cuxhaven on his way to England, the dockworkers shouted *"Hungerkanzler!"* ("Hunger-chancellor!") an epithet used

---

* The fact that Austria and the Reich had voluntarily renounced the plan on September 3, two days before the World Court's decision, was attributable to the strong political and economic pressure to renounce it and no doubt to foreknowledge of the court's decision. (Erich Eyck, *Geschichte der Weimarer Republik*, pp. 404–5.)

by Goebbels as well as by the Communists, who also demanded his dismissal. Like Stresemann, Brüning was held in far greater esteem by foreign countries than by the Reich. When he visited London, he was cordially received by the king; in Paris he went to Mass at Notre Dame, which pleased a considerable section of the French population, and he was well regarded by Briand and Pierre Laval, the newly elected French prime minister. They, like the British government, were acutely aware of the presence of Adolf Hitler in the wings and they tried to show, up to a point that did not include the customs union, their high regard for Brüning.

But Brüning and the Reich were in need of more than homage, and during his London visit Brüning told his British hosts that Germany could not long continue to meet its Young Plan obligations. The imbalance in receipts and outlays was catastrophic. On June 19 Hindenburg was forced to send a cable to President Hoover in which he said the distress of the German people compelled him to beseech America's help. Hindenburg's biographer says it was a difficult message for Hindenburg to send, one, in effect, that placed his country under the protection of a foreign power, but he had no alternative. Unless immediate steps for relief were taken, one-third of Germany's industrial workers would be out of jobs; the Reich had done all it could, but its means were exhausted. The United States, owed large sums by most of the countries of Europe, victors and vanquished, was the only country in the world, despite its own fiscal troubles, in a position to provide massive help.

President Hoover responded the same day he received Hindenburg's cable. He proposed a one-year moratorium on all payments of debts owed the United States and asked that the Reich pay no reparations until July 1932. Britain agreed to the plan immediately, the French after some delay. Paris was afraid that stopping the so-called "unprotected" annuity payments, which were exempted from a moratorium, would mean the end of all future reparations. Therefore, protracted negotiations had to be conducted until a device was found that would keep alive the fiction, at least, of the payments. The Reich formally agreed to deposit the sums due to the Bank of International Settlements, which would then return them to Berlin.

Despite the American rescue operation, the crisis persisted. When the doors of the Danat Bank closed on July 13, the government guaranteed its deposits, but that did not prevent a run on all the German banks, so Brüning had to issue a decree temporarily closing them, a forced bank holiday that lasted until August 5. Four billion Reichsmarks had been withdrawn from German banks since the September election, Dietrich declared, and German depositors had joined the foreigners in demonstrating a lack of confidence in the stability of the Reich and its financial institutions.

Brüning again turned to the creditor nations for a loan. He went to London by way of Paris, and in both cities he met not only with the representatives of the European creditors but also with American Secretary of the Treasury Andrew Mellon and Secretary of State Henry Stimson. France held the key to any loan. Briand and Laval set as a preliminary condition to the discussions that reparations were not to be on the agenda, and while they were ready to consider participating, together with representatives of the other powers, in making a loan of $500 million, they wanted political as well as fiscal collateral. Germany was to guarantee not to disturb the status quo for ten years, not to make claims for changes in the Polish Corridor or the Reich's eastern boundaries, and not to renew any attempt for an *Anschluss* with Austria. Brüning, with the utmost politeness, declined such conditions. Neither he nor any other chancellor would have the slightest possibility of remaining in office much longer than it took the president or the members of the Reichstag to read his signature on such stipulations. And on July 21, while the London conference was in progress, Hitler and Hugenberg sent an open telegram to Brüning warning him that they would not recognize any agreement that accepted French encroachments on German sovereignty and telling him that the Reich must rely, as had Frederick the Great after the Seven Years' War,* on its own resources. What was needed, Hitler said, was "character, self-confidence, and belief in God."[19]

The meetings produced no loan but they did result in a standstill agreement in which the creditor nations recommended that their nationals leave their deposits in Germany. The agreement, which was to last for six months and was renewable, succeeded in stanching the loss of foreign balances. In addition, two state visits followed the conferences, one by MacDonald and Henderson in late July, just after the London conference ended,† the other in late September when Laval and Briand journeyed to Berlin. Not much of a political or economic nature resulted from these meetings either, but Briand laid a wreath on Stresemann's grave, and he and Laval met with Hindenburg. Their request for a meeting had, in itself, some significance, since Hindenburg was still on the list of German war criminals and their desire to meet with him could be interpreted as a gesture that all was forgiven. It was a formal

---

* The success of Prussian autarchy under Frederick was one of Hitler's favorite themes.

† The Labour government was having its own unemployment and financial troubles. MacDonald, like Brüning, tried to solve Britain's difficulties by making deep cuts in the budget, including unemployment benefits. When a foreign exchange crisis struck, his measures, although supported by his chancellor of the exchequer, Philip Snowden, were opposed by Henderson and a majority of the cabinet, and the cabinet resigned on August 24. MacDonald unexpectedly remained as head of a coalition government in a cabinet of Tory, Liberal, and three Labour ministers.

occasion making no change whatever in the predicament of the Reich, but Hindenburg seemed pleased to meet his guests. He took aside the French ambassador who accompanied the ministers to observe solicitously of Briand that the long journey must have tired the old gentleman. Briand was then sixty-nine, Hindenburg eighty-four.

The withdrawals from the German banks had far exceeded the sum of unpaid reparations, and the Hoover moratorium had no visible effect on the Reich's empty purse. So again there was talk of the need for restoring confidence. But the French demand that the Reich renounce for ten years any attempt to revise the peace treaties as a precondition for a loan was also a demand, if he accepted it, for Brüning's political suicide. Not only were scholars critical of the treaties, but the German press could note with satisfaction that even the American Legion had adopted a resolution calling either for their revision or the conclusion of new treaties to supplant them. The only people who were steadily gaining confidence were those with a stake in the downfall of the republic—Hitler, the ultranationalists, and the Communists. Such an attempt as the French were making to freeze what seemed to every political faction in Germany an unacceptable status quo in the East strengthened the position of those who said the only way to change it was by regaining military power. If France still held that the eastern borders must not be brought into question in any conference, Adolf Hitler could gain far more advantage from her obduracy than Brüning could from Briand's placing a wreath on Stresemann's grave. Although the logic was tenuous, Hitler could ask what the policy of reconciliation had led to for the millions of destitute Germans living on hopelessly from day to day with no hope of climbing out of the pit they had not dug.

The main forces driving to organize the unemployed—almost six million people by the end of 1931—were the Communists and National Socialists. The violence and street brawls were increasing; Prussian Minister of the Interior Severing reported in 1931 that over 300 political murders had been committed in one year, and as he moved impartially against what he called the desperados of the Right and Left, they made common cause to get rid of him. Toward the end of May, Prussian police searching a garage in Breslau used by the Communists found a large cache of dynamite, enough to blow up every house for blocks around. National Socialists and Communists used any weapon they could pick up, on one another and on the police as well. A number of police were killed while attempting to make house searches or put down street riots. The Communist strategy, as captured documents revealed, was to keep the police off balance, to divide their forces, to create disturbances. They organized strikes and demonstrations, and their instructions were to use, along with knives, brass knuckles, and gasoline-soaked rags, hand grenades, axes, bricks, and boiling water as weapons against police in the streets of the working-class districts. "Hit the fascists wherever you meet them" was the watchword, and a fascist was liberally interpreted to mean anybody who was in their way. Severing forbade political demonstrations with provocative slogans in Prussia, and as a result both the Nazis and the Communists announced mass meetings in the form of sports events. The SA announced a "sports" rally at which Goebbels was to speak. The Communists announced what they called a *Spartakiade.* Severing stopped both of them, but the prohibitions could scarcely keep up with the stratagems. The Prussian Landtag, with its successful coalition and with men like Josef Hess, Braun, and Severing in the government, was a thorn in the flesh of the radical Right and Left. The Communist paper *Die Rote Fahne* declared that the Social Democrats were the pseudo-Marxist seducers of the proletariat, more sinister than the National Socialists; they were "the chief enemy of the proletariat," against which, the paper said, the party would wage the main attack in the class war.

To break up the democratic coalition in Prussia, another working alliance of the Far Right and the Far Left developed. The Stahlhelm organized a plebiscite demanding the dissolution of the Prussian Landtag, and with the help of the Nationalists and National Socialists collected almost 6 million signatures calling for a national referendum. They were soon joined by the Communists, and although the antiparliamentarian forces failed to get a majority, they did succeed in obtaining 9,740,000 votes, 37 percent of the electorate. It was the kind of defeat the right wing could interpret as a victory. Nearly 10 million people had voted against a bulwark of the republic; that was 4 million less than was needed to dissolve the Landtag, but it was nevertheless a vast, powerful, disruptive minority around a core of musclemen and hoodlums far more disposed to mayhem and terrorism than to the use of the ballot.

One of the options Brüning had, in theory, was to enlist the Social Democrats among his supporters by bringing men like Braun and Severing into his cabinet. Tucholsky called the Social Democrats the "Jein" party, the party that said *ja* and *nein*, yes and no, and that had informally agreed to tolerate the Brüning government despite what they considered its reactionary emergency decrees. Brüning had discussions with Braun and Severing, but the potential alliance got no further than the preliminary talks, because, according to Severing, Brüning, after having initiated the discussions, let the matter drop. The coalition undoubtedly foundered on the reluctance of Hindenburg to attempt again to conciliate the Social Democrats. The president was convinced, as he had been since he took office, that the salvation of the Fatherland lay in winning the support of the conservative Right, which no one represented better than he, to the standard of the Brüning government. But allies were hard to come by. With the collapse of the plan for the customs union, Julius Curtius had to quit his post as foreign minister. Curtius was a member of the German Volksparty, and with his resignation his party was inclined to ally itself with the right-wing opposition. They were joined by the deputies of two agrarian parties, the *Landbund* and *Landvolk*, that had hitherto supported Brüning, and he, too, with his diminished support, resigned with his entire cabinet.

Hindenburg, however, immediately asked him to form a new government, again one that would be above the parties, that is, without much parliamentary support. The only casualties from his former cabinet apart from Curtius were Joseph Wirth and Theodor von Guérard, the minister of transport and, like Wirth, a Centrist. Hindenburg had never had much enthusiasm for Wirth, who had declared at the time of the Rathenau murder, "The enemy is on the Right." The loss of two Centrists in a cabinet headed by a Centrist could be a further step in the direction of a purely presidential cabinet outside the parties and the shifting Reichstag coalitions, but it brought the government no visible parliamentary support. Groener became minister of the interior as well as defense minister, a double post that in view of the rise of the right-wing radicals seemed to be a prudent consolidation. Brüning, who could rely on the counsel of the experienced von Bülow, took over Curtius's portfolio as foreign minister. Treviranus succeeded von Guérard; Hermann Warmbold, a former member of the board of directors of I. G. Farben, became minister of economics; and Dietrich remained finance minister. These were mild attempts to gain right-wing allies, and Hindenburg would have preferred more decisive steps in that direction by appointing the career diplomat Konstantin von Neurath as foreign minister, along with the conservative mayor of Leipzig, Carl Goerdeler, and Otto Gessler, the former defense minister, to the new cabinet, but all three had declined.

The second Brüning cabinet would be further removed from the letter and spirit of a parliamentary government than was the first. The essential constitutional reforms that would have done away with proportional representation and with it the collection of minuscule splinter parties could not be carried out against the resistance of the *Länder*, especially Bavaria, and of the deputies and the officeholders who believed they owed their posts to the ramshackle system. More and more Brüning had to rely on emergency decrees. Between April and December of 1931, 40 were issued, while the Reichstag met 41 times in the year. In 1932 there would be 59 emergency decrees and 13 sessions of the Reichstag.[20]

The attempts to form a middle-of-the-road-to-right coalition that would stabilize a government under Hindenburg and Brüning failed mainly because the radical Right was now certain of victory and many influential members of the conservative parties feared the extremists' hopes were all too justified. Hitler, in 1924, had foreseen the thin ranks of the National Socialists swelling to thousands and then to millions, and in 1932 it was actually happening. Hitler had become much too powerful to be ignored by the government or the Reichswehr. General von Schleicher, who had had no high opinion of him, nevertheless had come to believe him to be "an interesting man with an extraordinary gift of oratory. In his plans," Schleicher wrote, "he climbs to higher regions. You have to pull him down by his lapels to the solid facts."[21] In the event of hostilities in the East, where Polish bands, Schleicher thought, might again cross the frontier, the SA would be indispensable as a defense force, so he kept in touch with both Hitler and Röhm, the SA chief of staff.

Hindenburg clung to the hope that every patriotic German, even Hitler, might be won to the cause of German unity, and while the Brüning cabinet was being reformed, the former field marshal and the lance corporal had their first meeting. The president was far from enthusiastic about Hitler and the National Socialists. Their press had printed scurrilous attacks on him, and Goebbels had called him an idiot—indirectly, to be sure, since Goebbels was quoting from a nineteenth-century characterization on Marshal MacMahon—but there was nothing subtle about Nazi journalism and Goebbels's intention was plain enough. Whether or not Hindenburg had read any of the attacks on him, he was certainly aware of the Nazi tactics, and Hitler got a cool reception. He appeared at the meeting with the president accompanied by Hermann Göring, who wore his war decoration, *Pour le Mérite*. Hindenburg, although what Hitler said was carefully pitched, was unimpressed with Hitler's unstanchable flow of rhetoric. When Hitler told him the country needed unified leadership and assured him he would use only legal methods in attaining it, Hindenburg pointed out that despite the talk of legality, the party had a record of violence, and he referred—in some excitement, Meissner reported—to the National Socialist attacks on Jews. Hitler replied that violence had occurred only in self-defense against Marxist assaults. Hindenburg's appeal to Hitler's patriotism, his so-often-affirmed love of the Fatherland, to tolerate or conceivably to cooperate with the Brüning government had no more effect on Hitler than Hitler had on Hindenburg, and the two parted as far apart as ever. Hindenburg told Brüning that Hitler had spoken pleasantly enough but that he could not be made a minister.

Nevertheless Hitler was riding high. On October 11 he travelled to the little town of Bad Harzburg in Braunschweig to a conference of the so-called "National Opposition" organized by Hugenberg. It was a loosely assorted gathering ranging from the leaders of the Far Right, Hugenberg, Seldte, Duesterberg, and Hitler, to more orthodox conservatives like General von Seeckt, now a German Volksparty deputy, and General von der Goltz. At the meeting, too, were industrialists like Ernst

Poensgen of the United Steel Works, bankers like Hjalmar Schacht, and two sons of the kaiser, Prince Eitel Friedrich and August-Wilhelm, who had lately joined the SA. It was the second time that Hugenberg set out to win Adolf Hitler for his campaign against the republic. Hitler, dressed in his Brown Shirt (which could legally be worn in Braunschweig) sat next to him at the opening ceremonies, where they both delivered speeches. Hugenberg announced that here at this gathering were the majority of the German people, and he warned the time-servers, the political big shots of the republic, and those others who were plundering the Fatherland that a new world was in the making. Hitler was not much impressed by the occasion, and in a routine speech he said Germany had the choice between national rebirth, that is, the National Socialist party, and communism.

Schacht presented himself as a troubled patriot with no party affiliations. He denounced the "system" of the man who had succeeded him as president of the Reichsbank, Hans Luther, and of Finance Minister Hermann Dietrich. What he saw was "deceit, uncertainty, the incapacity to conduct the Reich's business." Like Hitler, he said the country must return to the virtues of Frederick the Great and depend on itself, its character, self-confidence, and belief in God.[22] Schacht had never recovered from the shock of having been replaced as head of the Reichsbank.

Hitler took part reluctantly in any event at which he did not preside, and he appeared at Harzburg only for the publicity and the show of Nationalist strength. Harzburg was an occasion of spurious unity, ending with demands for the resignation of Brüning and Braun, for new elections in the Reich and Prussia, and for Hindenburg to form a truly national government. The speeches and resolutions were followed by a march-past of the SA, SS, Stahlhelm, and *Vaterländische Verbände*, but for all such demonstrations of togetherness, Hitler held himself aloof. He failed to attend the lunch with Hugenberg and the Stahlhelm leaders and remained only for the march-past of the SA and the SS; when the Stahlhelm formations that followed them paraded by, he had left.

Seldte and Duesterberg were indignant, and an acrimonious exchange of letters with Hitler followed. The Stahlhelm leaders sent him a list of complaints about his conduct: he had stationed himself fifty meters from the reviewing stand, he had not taken part in the ceremonies with the leaders of the other formations, he had left early, and so on. Hitler took very little pains to conceal his slight regard for Seldte and Duesterberg when he answered. He explained that he never took the salute of a march-past unless it was under his orders and—what was of course highly improbable—that he had not been aware of the Stahlhelm's intention to parade. In any case, he said, had he been present he would not have known in what form to salute the Stahlhelm formations or their banners. He said he had arrived late the day before the meeting because 44 SA homes had been shut down by the government,* 1,000 of his men had no place to stay, and 4,000 had been deprived of the meals provided by these SA "Service Centers." He said he had not appeared at the lunch at Harzburg because 80 percent of his SA were without work and had empty stomachs, and they could only have been aggrieved to see their Führer dining at such an opulent table. He reminded the Stahlhelm chiefs that he was the leader of the largest nationalist movement and said he thought that under the circumstances he had used only the mildest language. The National Socialists would continue the fight against the Weimar system but would tolerate no outside interference.

The Harzburger Front, as it was called to emphasize its unified, belligerent purposes, was obviously off to a shaky start, and it was in fact to have no staying power. Hugenberg might again seek an alliance with Hitler, the gifted "drummer of the masses," as he had at the time of the battle against the Young Plan, but Hitler had little short of contempt for him or, for that matter, the leader of any rival party. A few weeks after the meeting, Hugenberg complained of the continuing barbed attacks made on his party by the National Socialists. The Harzburg Front was never operational; like so much else on the Far Right, it represented a vaporous wish that could never be realized, because its leaders spent their energies at least as much in in-fighting as they did fighting the common enemy. Hindenburg's design to form around Brüning a government of nationalist unity—basically a conservative government that would bring together the forces of moderation from the Democrats to the Nationalists—was not much more substantial.

The president was showing unmistakable signs of old age. In the autumn of 1931, he came down with influenza, and during his illness Brüning thought he had suffered "a temporary blackout." As early as July 1930, when after the Rhineland celebrations Brüning met the president's train in Berlin, Hindenburg failed to recognize him or Treviranus, who accompanied Brüning. Hindenburg's son, Oskar, observing that his father seemed unaware of the identity of the two, tried to rouse his father, repeating: "Here is the Herr Reichs Chancellor and Minister Treviranus." But Hindenburg still failed to register.[23] Hindenburg's physician, Dr. Hugo Adams, on the other hand, reported that he was without traces of senility until 1934, the year of his death, and Hindenburg's state secretary, Meissner, and his military adjutant, Lieutenant von der Schulenburg, said the same thing. Brüning, however, was deeply disturbed at the decline in Hindenburg's faculties, and in later years he repeated that the president had often failed to recognize him.

* Brüning's emergency decree of October 6 "For the Security of the Economy and Finance and for the Struggle against Political Unrest" ordered the closing of all centers dangerous to the state.

The actual state of Hindenburg's intellectual sharpness depended, as it often does in old age, on the day or even the hour an observer had met with him. Like many old people, he had marked variations in his mental acuity; Brüning said he was at his worst toward the end of a long day. Those who were close to the president, like Meissner, Schulenburg, and his doctor, and who were accustomed to seeing him frequently might not as readily have detected, or wished to detect, the lapses that were more apparent to Brüning, who saw him only when state business brought them together. And Hindenburg had his good as well as his off days, when Brüning found him as mentally spry as ever. But there was no doubt of the overall decline in his intellectual powers. When Brüning gave the president his reasons for resigning in 1931, Hindenburg wrote them down, and when he attempted to repeat them to Brüning, he had them all wrong. So they tried again, with Hindenburg carefully writing the corrections between the lines he had first written. But what he read the second time was even more confused than what he had read the first, and Brüning had to let the matter drop. Hindenburg himself seems to have had some insight into his mental condition; his presidential term was to end in April 1932, and he did not wish to be a candidate again. It was to take a great deal of persuasion and many appeals to his duty to the Fatherland on the part of men as far removed from his political views as the Social Democrat Otto Braun to convince him that he had no choice but to run again. He was harder to persuade to be a candidate for a second term than he had been for his first term, although he had not wanted to be president then either.

But the dangers to the Fatherland were clear and present, and Hindenburg would have little choice. The Reichstag reconvened on October 13; on the fourteenth the National Opposition, the deputies of the Harzburger Front, which had been formed a few days before, declared they were ready to take over the government. The Nationalists and the National Socialists introduced a resolution of no confidence in the Brüning regime and demanded the dissolution of the Reichstag. Both proposals were defeated, the demand for Brüning's resignation 295 to 270, and that for the dissolution of the Reichstag 319 to 250. Again Brüning was rescued by the votes of the Centrists, the Social Democrats, the Economy party, and maverick members of the German Volksparty, along with a few defectors from other small parties that had hitherto supported him. But as a result of their defeat, the National Opposition once more marched out of the Reichstag, which was prorogued until February 23. It was a nonfunctioning legislature, and as the parliamentary parties declined, the National Socialists gained strength. On November 15 they became the largest party in Hesse in the Landtag elections, winning 27 of 70 seats, a considerable increase from the last election, when they had won only one seat.

But again there were evidences of inner disruption in the party. One of the Nazi deputies, Schäfer, turned over to the Frankfurt police a collection of documents outlining a war plan on which National Socialist leaders had agreed on November 25, 1931, at meetings in the Boxheimer Hof near Worms in Hesse. The documents contained directives the party was to follow after "the former state authority" was abolished and "after defeat of the Commune." All power, the directives said, was to be vested in the National Socialist organizations, the SA and such, and in most cases any opposition against a party decree or any resistance or sabotage was to be punishable by death. Anyone who failed to deliver a weapon in his possession to the SA within twenty-four hours was to be shot on the spot as an enemy of the people. Food supplies were to be turned over to National Socialist authorities, and Jews would get none. Any disobedience to orders was to be punished by death, and as a final triumph of the Socialist half of the National Socialist program, it was announced that until further notice private income was abolished. The author of this document was Werner Best, a lawyer and party leader in Hesse. Best would later be named Reichscommissar for occupied Denmark.

At the very least the Boxheimer documents were evidence that the Nazis were prepared to commit high treason. But the chief reaction to them came, not from Brüning or the courts, but from the Reichswehr, whose leaders demanded that the wearing of all uniforms by members of nongovernmental organizations be prohibited. Brüning, in principle, was in favor of such a decree, but he was also trying to promote a coalition between the Centrists and National Socialists in Hesse, and forbidding the Brown Shirts to wear uniforms would end that possibility. He feared too that Hindenburg would resist, as he had before, any interdiction of uniforms that included the Stahlhelm. In addition, Brüning pointed out that Communist formations for two years had been forbidden to wear uniforms but that that had in no way diminished their acts of terror. If the Reichswehr leaders, however, believed they required the measure for military reasons, he would issue another emergency decree— number 4. That is what happened at a meeting attended by General Groener, Minister of Justice Kurt Joël, General von Schleicher, Erich Zweigert from the Ministry of the Interior, and Hermann Pünder from the Reichschancellory; the recommendation was made that the uniforms be forbidden, Brüning agreed as did Hindenburg, and the decree was signed on December 8. Again, the order was issued as a decree for the "Security of the Economy and Finances and the Protection of Domestic Peace," which also had as one of its chief goals another reduction of prices. To this end a commissar for price control was appointed— the mayor of Leipzig, Carl Friedrich Goerdeler.

The uniform *Verbot* was a small matter compared with the vast centrifugal thrusts toward political extremes. The civil government and the army felt impelled to come to some kind of accommodation with Hitler, with or without SA uniforms. The Reichswehr had forbidden any Communist or National Socialist to be recruited, because both parties aimed to overthrow the republic, but on January 29, 1932, the implacable anti-Nazi General Groener issued new orders to the effect that such applications for enlistment should be rejected only when it could be proved that the applicant had taken part in impermissible activities designed to subvert the constitution. Lapses on the part of individual leaders would not be a reason for excluding members of their units. Groener defended his order by quoting Hitler's pledge to use only legal means to win power. Brüning, too, in his unremitting search for allies right and left, sounded out Hitler as well as Gregor Strasser and the left wing of the National Socialist party to win them to some kind of cooperation. He was himself too correct, however, too much a man of probity and conscience, to have much insight into Hitler's demonic will to power. Brüning met frequently, often secretly, with Göring and other Nazi leaders as well as with Hitler himself, under the impression that his appeals were having an effect on them and that they might be brought to see that his politics served the national purpose. He could not help but know from documents and from the press how dangerous the National Socialists were, but he never held them in the abhorrence he had for the Communists. He had been a witness to the left-wing disorders, the soldiers' councils, and the depredations of the Spartacists after the war. The Communist terror he had experienced at first hand, the Nazi terror he had only read about; he knew the character of their leaders from reports and relatively polite encounters, and he kept hoping he could win them over. Even the Boxheimer papers could be explained away, as they were by Nazi spokesmen, as a local matter, directives applicable only in the event of a Communist putsch. Brüning used the same tactics with Hitler that he used with Hugenberg or, for that matter, the Social Democrats, patiently explaining his policies in the hope that Hitler would see the light. It was a tactic that worked with old-line Social Democrats, moderates, and conservatives. He was able to secure the toleration and even the sporadic support of SPD leaders and of many Conservatives like Count Westarp.

Brüning's ultimate aim in the crisis was to gain time in order to prepare for a legal restoration of the monarchy—a goal that Hindenburg, too, had always believed in—if and when the German people were ready to approve it. But Brüning's grand design and his stratagems were useless with Hitler. As his troubles deepened, he saw clearly that everything depended on Hindenburg's continuing in office. If the old gentleman could be persuaded to run again, or if two-thirds of the Reichstag would vote to allow an extension of his presidential term, then the republic would survive, a way would be prepared for a constitutional monarchy, the threat of Hitler would be exorcised, and peace and order would be returned to the Reich. Brüning was convinced that his program of reasonable nationalism, which would continue the policy of reconciliation, end reparations, obtain a degree of arms equality, and expunge the war guilt clause, was making good progress in winning support in Britain, Italy, Scandinavia, Belgium, Holland, and the United States. His deflationary measures, which he planned to continue with a 20-percent devaluation of the mark and an additional 10-percent cut in industrial wages and salaries to make German goods more competitive in international markets, would be bound to turn the tide of the depression if he and the country would only hold out a little longer.*

The forces of the opposition, however, seen and unseen, were far more powerful than he imagined. More and more great and small concerns were either going bankrupt or facing collapse. The shipping firms Hapag and the North German Lloyd were hard hit, Brüning reported, as were two of the most important coal producers, Dahlbusch and King Ludwig. All the book-publishing houses with the exception of Ullstein were struggling desperately to survive, as were newspapers like the *Frankfurter Zeitung*, the *Kölnische Zeitung*, and the *Volkszeitung*. To Brüning's dismay—he thought the purchase an invasion of an independent press—the *Frankfurter Zeitung* had to be rescued by I. G. Farben. The threatened coal mines were bought by French interests, and government loans were required to shore up Hapag and the North German Lloyd. In January 1932, over 6 million people were registered at unemployment offices, but if those on short-term work and the unregistered unemployed were included, the number of people looking for jobs was calculated at over 9.6 million. Millions of them were from the middle class—shopkeepers, clerks, bookkeepers, actors, and salesmen, their white collars frayed and turning gray. A soberly dressed man was photographed on a Berlin street carrying a sign that said: "Employ me. I am looking for work of any kind and am used to good hard work. Speak fluent French, Dutch, Russian, Polish, German, and English. . . ." Public soup kitchens were opened in the cities, and in the frigid winter of 1931–1932, warming rooms were provided where people could come in out of the cold for a short time. There were youth centers, too, where young men could thaw out and play chess. All such government aid programs had one main requirement—they had to be cheap.

Hitler and the Communists made common cause in demanding increases in unemployment benefits and the end of wage cuts. They did

---

* That wheat prices in the Reich in 1931 were three times higher than those in the United States and four times those of the Argentine was a result of the high tariffs the Brüning government had adopted to help meet the agrarian crisis. Brüning would have nothing to do with the Keynesian formula of government spending, which he considered dangerously inflationary, but with his *dirigisme* and high tariffs he was far, too, from following the orthodox free-market economists.

much more than that: they formed a militant community daily on the march whose members were convinced they would one day soon smash their way to a promised land. Hitler, assuming he would actually keep his promises to operate within legal limits, had two ways of coming to power. He could either succeed Hindenburg as president or secure the election of enough National Socialist deputies to compel Hindenburg to appoint him chancellor. Although Hitler told Brüning the National Socialists in the Reichstag might vote for prolonging the term of Hindenburg's presidency, he did not tell him that one of his conditions for going along with the plan was that Hindenburg agree to dismiss Brüning. The other conditions called for new elections, in which Hitler was certain the Nazis would score an even more impressive victory than they had the last time, and the appointment of a right-wing government. But Hindenburg would accept no conditions, so Hitler decided for both alternatives. He would be a candidate for president and his party would win the Reichstag elections. To run for the presidency against Hindenburg was to accept unlikely odds. On the one side was the mythologized hero of the war and head of state, on the other the former lance corporal, Austrian-born, now stateless, who did not even have the right to vote in a German election. But Hitler told Meissner what he undoubtedly believed to be true, that he would run and he would win.[24]

CHAPTER 9

The Seizure of Power

HINDENBURG SET three preconditions for his candidacy in 1932. He wrote Brüning that he would run only if he were convinced that his continuing in office was essential to the welfare of the Fatherland, if his candidacy would not result in the solid opposition of the Right, and if it were certain he would win on the first ballot. As it turned out, only one of his conditions was fulfilled. But Hindenburg soon perceived the danger, if he did not run, of a radical right-wing candidate being elected, or even conceivably a Marxist candidate, agreed on by Communists and Social Democrats to block Hitler. And he soon had striking evidence that his personal appeal to millions of Germans was undiminished. Brüning organized a nonpartisan committee under the chairmanship of the mayor of Berlin, Heinrich Sahm, that in one day collected more than 100,000 signatures petitioning Hindenburg to run, and in two weeks the number of those signing came to more than 3½ million. Members of all parties from Social Democrats to Conservatives joined in urging him to be a candidate, and on February 16 Hindenburg announced his decision to run: "Conscious of my responsibility for the fate of our Fatherland." The fact that he had been asked to serve, not by political parties, but by a broad cross section of the people had led him to see where his duty lay. "For me," he wrote, "there is only one true national goal: the unity of the people in their struggle for existence, the full devotion of every German in the hard battle for the preservation of the nation."[1]

The Communists nominated their candidate, Ernst Thälmann in January. In February, the Harzburger Front crumbled when Hugenberg refused to back Hitler, who in the event of victory demanded the chief government posts for himself and his followers. The German Nationals and the Stahlhelm chose as their candidate the second in command of the Stahlhelm, Theodor Duesterberg, a retired lieutenant colonel. Then Goebbels exultantly announced that Hitler, too, would run. "Four weeks ago," he told a National Socialist gathering in the Berlin Sportspalast on February 22, "15,000 people spontaneously leapt to their feet and hailed the name of our Führer. I myself stood with them with palpitating heart and I dared not speak." Now he could bring them the glad tidings. "Hitler," he told the gathering, "will be our Reichspresident."[*] [2]

It was a prophecy that would not come true for a long time, but Hindenburg had an unexpectedly hard battle. Although he received 4 million more votes than he had won in 1925, the Right for the most part was ranged against him, and with three candidates in the field,[†] he failed to gain a majority by 0.4 percent—250,000 votes. Hindenburg received 18,650,730 votes (49.6 percent), Hitler 11,339,285 (30.1 percent), Thälmann 4,983,197 (13.2 percent), and Duesterberg 2,557,390 (6.8 percent). Thus Hindenburg had to bear the humiliation he had hoped to avoid—a runoff election against Adolf Hitler.

He had other unpleasant evidences of the changed temper of the electorate. It was not the Right with which he had been identified all his life that voted for him but the Left and Center. Brüning, during both campaigns, did all he could on behalf of the only man he believed could redeem the Fatherland. He raised funds and he made speeches up and down the Reich, in Breslau, Weimar, Berlin, and Düsseldorf, some of which the Nazis tried to break up. At one gathering he noted a sudden restlessness in the audience, and some people even left. He found out the cause later. The Nazis had brought to the hall boxes of white mice— one of their favorite and more fanciful devices[‡] for breaking up gatherings not to their liking—and had released the contents, which were scurrying up and down the aisles, causing, Brüning reported, part of the audience, particularly women, to hurry out of the auditorium. But Brüning had considerable success in unexpected quarters. At Weimar, where it was so cold that he had to wear an overcoat while delivering his speech, he had an enthusiastic response, and many in the audience, he noted, sat through the speech in the frigid hall without overcoats.

The Right, with some notable exceptions, deserted its former hero. The

[*] Hitler at long last had been made a German citizen when a National Socialist minister of the *Land* of Braunschweig, Dietrich Klagges, appointed him a state councillor of the Braunschweig legation in Berlin. Hitler's appointment gave him another opportunity to profess his commitment to legality. At the induction ceremony in Berlin, he swore to support the constitutions of Braunschweig and the Reich.

[†] A fourth candidate, a Saxon lawyer named Adolf Winter with no party affiliation, received a scattering of votes. He favored restoring the value of the old thousand-mark bank notes.

[‡] The National Socialists had also used white mice to disrupt showings of the pacifist film *All Quiet on the Western Front*, based on Erich Remarque's novel.

United Organizations of the Fatherland under General von der Goltz came out against Hindenburg. His old friend Elard von Oldenburg-Januschau, the man who had headed the group that made him a gift of Neudeck, came out for Duesterberg, as did many other East Prussian and Pomeranian landowners. One of Hindenburg's supporters, Baron von Berg, told the president he had been forced to resign as chairman of the Nobles' Society because of a letter he had published supporting Hindenburg's candidacy in the German *Adelsblatt*. The National Organization of German Officers told its members that while it could not make open war against the field marshal, personal considerations must be put aside; the overriding aim must be to prepare a way to end the system that had grown out of the events of November 1918.

Brüning had difficulty raising money. Although some 12 million marks were contributed by Hindenburg's old supporters in big industry, including Friedrich Flick, Gustav Krupp von Bohlen und Halbach, Robert Bosch, and many others, a considerable number of similar big donors supported Hitler. The United Steel Works, Brüning reported, gave 5,000 marks to Hindenburg and a half million to Adolf Hitler. Over 5 million marks were still owed on printers' bills and the like from Hindenburg's 1925 campaign, and Brüning had to use government as well as private funds to pay off the debts. The use of government money was justified by the scrupulous public officials involved, among them Minister of Finance Dietrich and Prussian Minister of the Interior Severing as well as Brüning, as a measure essential to the preservation of law and order, by which they meant defeating the Nazi leader. The funds were made available to parties and to organizations like the Reichsbanner, specifically for expenses incurred on behalf of the president's candidacy. Hitler, on his part, suddenly had direct access to funds he had never been able to touch before.

The entire social and political climate had changed; a large segment of the population, including conservative men of big business, had been radicalized. Hitler, up to the 1930 election, had had very little support from such sources. Fritz Thyssen, piano manufacturer Carl Bechmann, Director-General Emil Kirdorff of the Rhine-Westphalian coal syndicate, Munich publisher Hugo Bruckmann, the locomotive manufacturer Ernst von Borsig, and a scattering of others had given him substantial sums in the past, but by January 1932 Thyssen could arrange for Hitler to speak at the Düsseldorf Industry Club to a gathering of the Reich's chief industrial and financial leaders, who had hitherto kept their distance from him.

Hitler, as always, was masterful in adapting his strategy to his audience. He told them what they were already convinced of, that democracy did not work any better in the area of politics than it did in their business affairs. Democracy, Hitler said, meant replacing genius with a

Walther Rathenau, 1922. *(Ullstein)*

President Ebert proclaiming his policy of "passive resistance" to delegates from the French-occupied Ruhr, April 1923. *(Süddeutscher Verlag)*

Proklamation
an das deutsche Volk!

Die Regierung der November=
verbrecher in Berlin ist heute
für abgesetzt erklärt worden.

Eine provisorische deutsche
National-Regierung
ist gebildet worden.

Diese besteht aus

General Ludendorff, Adolf Hitler
General von Lossow, Oberst von Seisser

The proclamation of the pro-visional "National Govern-ment" of Hitler, Ludendorff, et al., Munich, 1923. *(Preussischer Kulturbesitz)*

The Hitler putsch. The arrest of the mayor of Munich with his city council by SA and Free Corps units, November 11, 1923. *(Preussischer Kulturbesitz)*

The Munich trial of Hitler, Ludendorff, and other leaders of the failed putsch, March 1924. The defendants are at the left. *(Süddeutscher Verlag)*

A page from *Simplicissimus*. Hitler, recruiting new followers after his release from prison, selling a book of his speeches and *Mein Kampf* in a beer hall. The captions read, above, "Yesterday still on a high horse." Below, in Bavarian dialect: "Twelve marks for this book? A little expensive, neighbor. You got any matches?" *(Süddeutscher Verlag)*

The National Socialists march on the "German Day" in Halle, March 1924. *(Süddeutscher Verlag)*

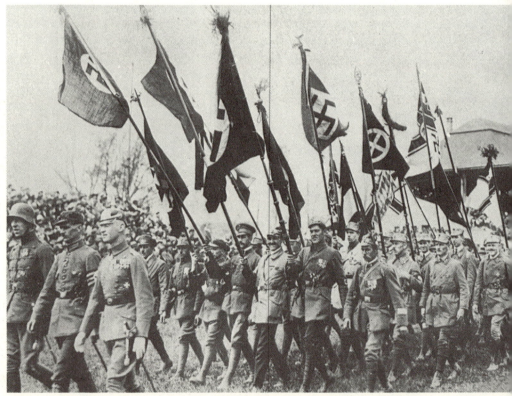

Hitler refounding the NSDAP in the back room of a Munich restaurant, 1925. Alfred Rosenberg is third from Hitler's right. To Hitler's left: Gregor Strasser, Heinrich Himmler, Karl Fiehler (a leader in the 1923 putsch), and Julius Streicher. *(Süddeutscher Verlag)*

Mock-ups of tanks made of wood and cardboard used by the Reichswehr for maneuvers. Under the Versailles Treaty the army was forbidden the possession of heavy weapons. *(Preussischer Kulturbesitz)*

The newly elected Reichspresident Paul von Hindenburg, Minister of Defense Otto Gessler, and General von Seeckt with a guard of honor, Berlin, 1925. *(Süddeutscher Verlag)*

Gustav Stresemann with the British foreign secretary, Sir Austen Chamberlain, and the French foreign minister, Aristide Briand, September 1926. *(Süddeutscher Verlag)*

Hitler at the National Socialist Party Day in Nuremberg. On the running board, the then leader of the SA, Captain Franz Pfeffer von Solomon; behind him, Rudolf Hess; far left, Julius Streicher. *(Süddeutscher Verlag)*

The depression, 1930. Unemployed in the coal-mining district of Upper Silesia. Unable to pay rent on the dole allotted them, they have moved to shacks at the edge of town. BELOW Rural unemployed in Thuringia receiving official beggars' permits. *(Süddeutscher Verlag)*

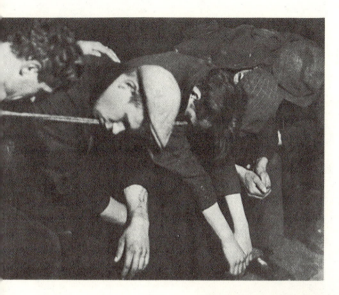

The depression. ABOVE "On the line." Unemployed paid pennies to sleep in this fashion for a few hours protected from the weather. RIGHT Unemployed living in a vacant lot in Berlin at the sign of the "Golden Corner Boarding House." BELOW A "warming room" in Berlin, winter 1929–1930. *(Süddeutscher Verlag)*

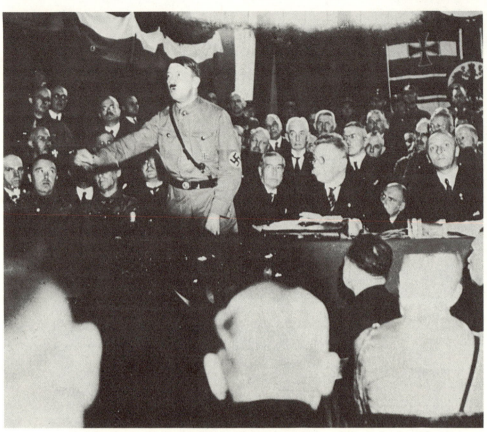

Hitler at the Harzburger Front meeting. Right, at the speaker's table, Hugen-berg; far right, Duesterberg. *(Süddeutscher Verlag)*

Brüning's visit to London, 1931. Left to right: Chancellor Brüning, Ramsay MacDonald, Konstantin von Neurath. *(Süddeutscher Verlag)*

Communists and National Socialists join forces supporting a rent strike in Berlin, September 1932. *(Preussischer Kulturbesitz)*

LEFT A Hitler election poster in Berlin, 1932. "We Want Work and Bread. Vote Hitler!" RIGHT SPD Poster, 1932. "The Worker in the Reich of the Swastika." *(Süddeutscher Verlag)*

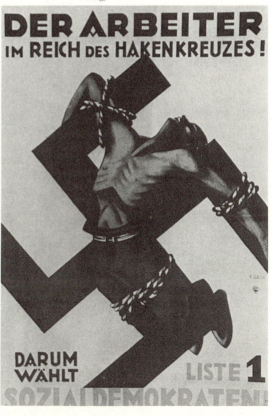

Hitler leaving the Defense Ministry after a meeting with Kurt von Schleicher, Papen's minister of defense, 1932. *(Süddeutscher Verlag)*

Hitler and Goebbels in Weimar, May 1932. *(Süddeutscher Verlag)*

Schleicher and Hammerstein, summer 1932. *(Preussischer Kulturbesitz)*

Left to right, facing camera: Franz von Papen, Wilhelm von Gayl, Paul von Hindenburg, Kurt von Schleicher. Back to camera: Otto Meissner. *(Süddeutscher Verlag)*

Hitler campaigning in Munich, 1932. *(Süddeutscher Verlag)*

Hitler campaigning, 1932. Left to right: Göring, Frick, Hitler, Gregor Strasser, and Goebbels. *(Süddeutscher Verlag)*

majority; it meant, not the rule of the people, but the rule of stupidity, mediocrity, weakness, and inadequacy. It was an absurdity, he said, to base economic life on the principle of performance, "that is, practically, on personal authority," and to deny this authority in politics and to replace it with the law of the greatest number, with democracy. The analogy of political democracy in economic affairs was communism. Only an authoritarian state could guarantee economic freedom, because behind it was the unified will of the nation.[3]

He talked for two hours, and at the end his listeners gave him a standing ovation. They did better than that; they gave him money, something that had hitherto been very hard for him to come by, and much of this money in the past would have gone to Hindenburg. Hitler's speech was skillful, but he had made similar speeches before this one and very few among the business and industrial leaders had been impressed by them. In 1932, these men of affairs were frightened, just as frightened as were their employees. Britain had gone off the gold standard, and everywhere in the Reich old and solid enterprises were folding. What Brüning was doing, however sound the German economists might find it, did not seem to be accomplishing much to prevent the downward spiral from becoming an unstoppable plunge. These *grands seigneurs* of industry had two obsessions: the threat of communism and socialism and the increasing power of the unions, which in their view would readily lead to one or the other. In his relentless resistance to the Left, Hitler spoke their language, word for word, but until 1931 what he had to say had had no more appeal to them than it had had to the workers or farmers or white-collar employees, who had also failed to vote National Socialist in election after election.

Soon after Duesterberg's candidacy was announced, the Nazis discovered that he had a Jewish grandfather, which converted him into a made-to-order target for the Nazi press and speakers. Duesterberg, a former lieutenant-colonel, had the Iron Cross, First and Second Class, and was second in command of the martial Stahlhelm, but that did not prevent Goebbels from calling him "racially inferior." He thus became one of the early victims of the party doctrine that even one Jewish grandparent made anyone ineligible to high office or even full citizenship in an Aryan state.

Hindenburg was attacked by Goebbels in a speech in the Reichstag on February 25 for the support he was getting from "the asphalt press" and from the SPD, "the party of the deserters." An SPD deputy, Kurt Schumacher, counterattacked, calling the National Socialist tactics "a standing appeal to the inner swinishness of man, the final mobilization of human stupidity." Schumacher was a formidable antagonist who had suffered severe wounds in the war, and he went on to say that the Nazis had spread the rumor that he had maimed himself, a canard that had resulted in the convictions of three members of the National Socialist party for slander. Behind his words was the knowledge of surely every deputy in the Reichstag that Goebbels, who spoke so easily of "the party of the deserters," had a clubfoot and had spent the war years, while men like Kurt Schumacher were at the front, far behind the lines in the safety of the Reich.

Alfred Rosenberg, too, in the course of a Reichstag debate, made a tactical error similar to Goebbels's when he called Brüning a traitor. Rosenberg was a Baltic German who spoke better Russian than German, and Brüning rose to his feet in the Reichstag to say that while Rosenberg was living in Paris uncertain of his nationality, Brüning had been returning from the trenches with the troops that aimed to put down the revolution. It was an adequate reply to Rosenberg, but it did not precisely endear Brüning to the Social Democrats, including Schumacher, who had been on the side of the revolution.

After the first balloting Duesterberg withdrew his candidacy, and in the runoff election the German Nationals, although the party called on them to abstain, voted heavily for Adolf Hitler, and they were joined apparently by considerable numbers of Communists. Hindenburg received 19,359,633 votes, 53 percent of the total; Thälmann lost a million votes, dropping to 3,706,655 (10.2 percent); and 13,418,051 (36.8 percent) voted for Hitler. Thus Hindenburg was elected to serve another seven years, but his support from the time of the first ballot had risen by less than a million votes while Hitler's, with the help of the Far Right and Far Left, went up two million. The results of the election were a grave disappointment to the field marshal, who felt himself deserted by the people he had relied on all his life. It was the Center and the Left that elected him, a significant change from 1925, when he had won the election with the massive support of the Right against the Center candidate Wilhelm Marx and the Communist Thälmann. The results of the election were also a grave disappointment to Adolf Hitler and his followers. They had been convinced he would win, and with his defeat the Strasser wing of the party became more critical of Hitler's strategy and his stubborn insistence on refusing to collaborate with any kind of coalition. The more than 53 percent of the vote that went to Hindenburg was no doubt a tribute to the abiding power of his legend as well as to the enduring middle-of-the-road preferences that had long characterized the German electorate. Still, the almost 47 percent of the vote that had been cast against him was evidence that a large, disenchanted minority of entrepreneurs, workers, shopkeepers, and farmers and an army of the unemployed demanded more radical solutions than Hindenburg and any parliamentary government would be likely to provide. The little man with the hoarse, strident voice who looked, as one observer said, like a marriage swindler and who for more than a decade had left the country hostile or unimpressed had taken on for millions of people the lineaments of a savior. But for many of them the Nazi solution for the trouble of the Reich was summed up in the hopeless saying "Better an end with horror than an endless horror."[4]

Few political leaders in the national and state governments could have any doubt of the dimensions of the Nazi threat. In March, police searches in Prussia and Bavaria had turned up evidence that the National Socialists planned, in the event that Hitler was elected president, to arm the SA and the SS from Reichswehr arsenals and take over the government. Hitler, in an election speech in Lauenburg in Pomerania, had promised the Brown Shirt formations on the east border that they would not be sacrificed for the "system"—the border would be defended only after the system was destroyed. In Bavaria police confiscated a cache of weapons near the Chiemsee, and the minister-president of Bavaria, Heinrich Held, in a speech to the Landtag said that Nazi outrages had become intolerable; they were making the lives of the people and state officials unendurable to the point where they could not perform their normal duties.

The ministers of the interior of all the large states—Prussia, Baden, Bavaria, Württemberg, Hesse, and Saxony—told General Groener the central government had to act to preserve public order, and if it did not they would. Groener needed little urging. After a discussion with the chiefs of the army and navy, who agreed on the need for taking active measures, he advised Brüning that he and Hindenburg should issue an emergency decree dissolving the SA and SS. Brüning himself was uncertain; he was afraid such a move might increase the National Socialist vote in the upcoming Prussian elections to be held on April 24, but if the Reichswehr thought it essential he was ready to recommend the decree to the president.

Schleicher, who was Groener's chief of ministry, had at first enthusiastically endorsed such a dissolution order, but on second thought had advised moving slowly. He had little liking for Hitler, but he thought the National Socialists had too easy a time of it in the opposition; that what was needed was to bring them into the government, where they would be as open to criticism as any other party that had to assume responsibility for difficult and unpopular decisions. Schleicher preferred to ignore the Führer's words to the Brown Shirts in Pomerania, and like the generals commanding the troops on the eastern borders and the young officers in the Reichswehr ministry in Berlin, he was convinced the National Socialist formations must play a decisive role in any hostilities on the Polish border. In place of an emergency decree, he urged, at a second meeting with Groener, that Hitler be given the opportunity to dissolve the SA and SS himself, and if he did not, then the government decree would follow. Schleicher, however, was overruled by a unanimous decision of Brüning and his cabinet, and Hindenburg signed the order after Groener had assured him that the *Länder* and the Reichswehr demanded it.

The decree went out on April 13 dissolving not only the SA and SS but the minor auxiliary organizations of the National Socialists as well: the Motor Corps, the Flying Corps, the cavalry, the naval formations, the Leadership Schools, the SA installations, and the rest. The order was felt as a body blow by the party leadership. Goebbels, who was often given to exaggeration, wrote in his diary that if it were not lifted the party was through. Severing, who as Prussian minister of the interior had conducted the police searches that turned up the evidence of the subversive activity of the National Socialists in Prussia, wrote in his memoirs that the only thing wrong with the emergency decree was that it had come so late.

Although this was the view of the staunch republicans, the decree blew up a storm of protest in other quarters. Hindenburg was immediately placed under great pressure to retract the dissolution order or at least in some way to balance it by banning the leftist private forces as well. The crown prince and former Reichswehr generals who, like Schleicher, were concerned with the vulnerability of the eastern frontier, were rigorously opposed to a further weakening of the available defense forces. They believed Polish incursions a far more imminent danger than a National Socialist seizure of power. Hindenburg was soon in a state of considerable confusion. People on whom he relied for advice, like Schleicher, Meissner, and his ungifted son Oskar, a colonel in the army and a dabbler in politics, did nothing to lessen it. Oskar, more than Schleicher and Meissner, was in a position to give Hindenburg an uninterrupted flow of advice, and while he undoubtedly had strong filial feelings, he had a good deal less appreciation of other people or of political events. In the army he was nicknamed 1:100,000 as an index of his stature compared with that of his illustrious father, and the nickname was at least an indication of what his brother officers thought of him. But by living in the same household, he had the ear of his father, and so to a lesser extent did Meissner, the state secretary, who had been appointed to his post by Ebert. Meissner was a former captain in the reserve. He was a cautious, reliable civil servant, and he managed to keep his job under the Social Democrat Ebert, then under Hindenburg, and finally under Hitler, which reveals more of his talents for tactfulness than for any strong convictions.

Schleicher had turned against the dissolution order, and Oskar feared its damaging effect on his father's already shaken position with the Right. Their views, which supported those of the numerous other critics of the order, added to the old gentleman's perplexities. Groener had assured him that all the *Länder* and the Reichswehr favored the decree, but Hindenburg soon learned that some of the smaller states where the Nazis were well entrenched opposed it, as did many younger Reichswehr officers. Groener had been talking about the older ones, who were suspicious of Hitler and who had no liking for private armies. General von Hammerstein, who had succeeded Heye as chief of the Reichswehr, had told a meeting of his generals that it might be necessary to use force against Hitler if, as Hammerstein said, the German people should be so insane as to vote such a fool into power, and the generals, including Schleicher, had agreed with him. But Schleicher had changed his mind about the decree, and the decision to issue it against his advice had deepened the chasm between him and Brüning. The disagreement confirmed Schleicher's growing conviction that neither Brüning nor Groener was up to his job. A month earlier, in March, at a dinner in the Russian embassy (Schleicher was a strong advocate of the military collaboration of the Reich with the Soviet Union), he had told Severing that "the good Heinrich" was through; Brüning, he said, was indecisive, and as a result of his policies more and more unemployed walked the streets.[5]

Since 1931 Schleicher had been convinced that the Nazis could be made use of in the government's search for right-wing support. Intelligent, cynical, ambitious, and entirely devoted to the Reichswehr, he was highly regarded by many of his fellow officers for his ability to unravel what seemed to them hopelessly tangled political skeins and for his talent for combining soldiering with politics, something they usually said they deplored but without which they were sure the Reichswehr would be further depleted. Others mistrusted and disliked him; he had not commanded field troops for years, and as one observer, Major General von Holtzendorff, wrote, in a time of political weakness and domestic discord the role of any political soldier in the Reichswehr could only be unpopular.

Schleicher, in a way that had never been true of Groener, was nevertheless a member of the in-group in the officer corps and in the estimation of Hindenburg. He had been a class behind Hammerstein in the Cadet School and a member of the Third Infantry Regiment of the Guards, the same regiment to which Hindenburg and his son Oskar belonged. He had served on the general staff from 1913 on and after the war had been a political advisor to General Groener and then to Seeckt. He was thought of as an exceptionally able young officer, worldly and adroit, but he overrated his ability to work both sides of the street; to keep Hitler in check and at the same time to manipulate the National Socialist party and the SA on behalf of the Reichswehr and against Brüning and Groener. Schleicher had come to believe that both of them were past their usefulness, by which he meant they no longer took his advice. He firmly believed he could tame Hitler and at the same time get rid of these incompetents with a strategy more subtle than Brüning's and as purposeful as Hitler's. He had never had a high opinion of the Führer, and at the same dinner at the Russian embassy where he had spoken disparagingly of Brüning, he had also said the Reichswehr would never permit the National Socialist to take power.[6] He saw the SA as a cadre of excellent manpower in need of the discipline and the kind of education for service to the Fatherland that the army could provide, and as for Hitler, he could be held in check through the contradictions within the ranks of the party and by forcing him to assume responsibility as one member of a right-wing government.

The pressure on Hindenburg had its effect, and two days after he signed the decree, he wrote a letter to Groener that was published in all the newspapers. With it was enclosed a dossier that had come to Hindenburg from sources in the Reichswehr—perhaps from Schleicher—with purported evidence on the danger to the state of the left-wing uniformed organizations like the Reichsbanner, the counterpart of the Stahlhelm, made up of former front-line soldiers, most of them affiliated with the SPD and the trade unions. Groener, the letter said, had assured the president that the anti-SA decree was essential to preserving the authority of the state, but after he had signed it, he had been given evidence that other parties had organizations similar to those he had banned. In carrying out the nonpartisan obligations of his office, he wrote, he felt that such organizations should be treated in the same manner. It was a bumbling letter, publicly rebuking the man who had served him loyally in anguished times; it was also an attack on those who had supported him and an appeasement of those who had done everything they could to oust him from the presidency. Moreover, no evidence appeared in the dossier to indicate that the Reichsbanner's purposes could be equated with those of the SA or any other National Socialist organization. The language of ostensible fairness and equal treatment was doubtless convincing to Hindenburg, but in this case it was nonsense. The Reichsbanner had been recruited to uphold the constitution and the republic; not a shred of evidence had been found to indicate that it had ever planned a revolt, while abundant material was at hand to show that that was precisely what the National Socialists had in mind.

Groener said he found nothing in the documents to justify dissolving the Reichsbanner or the Stahlhelm; he was right and Hindenburg was wrong, but Groener's days in office were numbered. He had never, in the aristocratically oriented officers' corps, been a model of a general. He had liberal political views, his father had been an army paymaster, and, after being long a widower, he had married a lady in 1930 whom the officers' corps and their wives considered unsuitable. The marriage ceremonies had been followed only five months later by the birth of a son, nicknamed, in the ribald officers' casinos, Nurmi, after the swift

Finnish runner, and neither of these events raised Groener's status in the eyes of Hindenburg.

When Groener rose in the Reichstag to answer the attack of Göring on behalf of the National Socialists, he made a poor showing. The Nazi deputies had yelled questions at him as he stumbled through a lackluster, unconvincing speech. He was in bad health, suffering from diabetes and a severe case of boils, one of them on his forehead, so he spoke with his head bandaged and with a high fever, and even to his well-wishers he did not seem up to defending himself against the Nazi onslaught. General von Hammerstein, who was as anti-Hitler as any, nevertheless joined Schleicher and the other generals in distancing himself from Groener. On May 12 he had to resign his post as defense minister and on May 29 as minister of the interior. Brüning, who had loyally supported him, thereupon proffered the president his own and his cabinet's resignation.

Far more important in their downfall than the stratagems of Schleicher were the election returns; the *Länder* elections that took place on April 24 had resulted in dramatic gains by the National Socialists, who became the leading party in every state except Bavaria, where they nevertheless won 43 seats—up from 9—in a Landtag of 128 members. In Prussia they won 162 seats out of 423 in place of the 6 they had won in 1928. In Württemberg, where they had only a single delegate, they won 23 out of 80 seats. In Anhalt it was the same story; they won 15 seats out of a total of 36, although in 1928 they had elected only one deputy. In Hamburg they won 51 of the 160 seats. A few weeks later, in Oldenburg, they won an outright majority, electing 24 of the 46 deputies in place of their former 3.

Their strength compared with that of the other parties was impressive. In Prussia, Hugenberg's German Nationals went down from 71 seats to 31 and the Social Democrats from 137 to 94. As a result the Social Democrats, no longer the largest party, had to surrender the presidency of the Landtag to the National Socialists. The Center did comparatively well; it lost only 4 of its former 71 seats. But the liberal parties were down sharply, the Volksparty to 7, the Staatsparty to 2, delegates. The Communists went up from 48 to 57 seats, and either the right-wing or the Left-Center coalition would need their votes to gain a majority.

The *Länder* elections were a heavy blow to the republic and to the Brüning government. The democratic bastion of the Prussian Landtag, where a coalition of Centrists and Social Democrats had maintained a majority for years and where the Prussian police had been under the control of the resolute anti-Nazi Severing, now had a majority of fanatical antirepublicans. With Reichstag elections ahead, the National Socialists had to be dealt with by more potent measures than banning the SA, whose dissolution had in no way diminished the party's political strength.

Brüning took much the same view as Schleicher, that the Nazi party had to be brought into the orbit of government, and he tried to work on the Strasser faction. He had elaborately secret talks with representatives of Gregor Strasser. On one occasion he took a series of taxicabs, getting out and skulking down side streets, then driving in the wrong direction before eventually meeting Strasser's emissary at a friend's house. But the talks led nowhere, and Brüning's one remaining card was his foreign policy. With two important conferences ahead on disarmament and reparations, Hindenburg was urged by his conservative friend Count Westarp to keep Brüning in office at least until those issues were resolved.

The disarmament conference had been in session in Geneva intermittently since February 2, but the results had been meager. French Prime Minister Tardieu had proposed a plan designed to maintain France's arms supremacy and the overall status quo; the Germans had proposed to abolish weapons they themselves lacked—heavy artillery, military planes, and poison gas—and neither country's proposal had much appeal to the others.*

During an absence in Geneva of Tardieu, who had pleaded illness, Brüning had, in late April, succeeded in winning Britain and the United States to accept the German view that the principle of arms equality finally had to be granted. As far back as October 1931 he had explained to the Italian foreign minister, Grandi, that his purpose was to substitute for the dictated peace of Versailles Wilson's Fourteen Points, which all Germans were convinced had been flagrantly violated by the Allies. It now seemed likely that when the full conference met, Brüning would succeed in bringing it to accept at a minimum, the German view of the inequality of the arms balance, and possibly even of the need for revising the eastern frontiers, where the principle of self-determination had been lost without a trace. At the April meeting without Tardieu, the American representative Norman Davis had said of Brüning's proposals: "It is very fair what the Chancellor is asking for, very fair indeed." Henderson and MacDonald had agreed.[7]

Brüning made a spirited speech to the Reichstag on May 11, telling the deputies his goal was to procure equality through general disarmament and to get rid of reparations once and for all, and when that was accomplished, peace might at long last come to the world. Even the National Socialists had listened to him in silence as he told the Reichstag they were only 100 meters from the goal. The deputies had given him an ovation and a vote of confidence at the same session where the Nazis had hooted at Groener and shouted him down.

* France had revived the notion of a European police force similar to that foreseen in the Geneva Protocol, and Britain and the Reich continued to reject any such idea.

With Hitler just offstage, Brüning's arguments seemed increasingly persuasive to the Americans and British. The Reich, he told Ramsay MacDonald and Henry Stimson, could not afford even the modest military outlays foreseen in the next five years; for the last two years the manufacture of munitions had been practically stopped. Four-fifths of Germany's military expenditure, he said, was determined by the compulsory twelve-year enlistment period with resulting high pensions. Enlistments, he said, should be cut to six years. The 100,000-man army should be increased, perhaps by forming a militia of the same size, and the armies of the other powers should be cut back.

Clearly what he was proposing was to arm the Reich for defense, to try to discourage anything like another Ruhr invasion, and to protect the Polish border. Under the terms of Versailles, Brüning pointed out, weapons and munitions could not be produced in the same factory, so freight and loading costs consumed 50 percent of the arms budget. Munitions workers and their machines could be used only two months of the year, although wages and interest on the investment had to be met for the remaining ten months when men and machines were idle. France and Poland had powerful attack forces, and the Polish cavalry could be in Berlin within twenty-four hours, cutting off Silesia from the Reich. For this reason the German garrisons had been withdrawn from the province, because Upper Silesia could not be defended. In Alsace, Brüning said, he and the American peace advocate, Norman Davis, had toured the countryside and seen the great fortifications France had built —most of them with German reparations payments.[8]

There was little doubt that Brüning would be able to obtain some kind of agreement in principle on armaments when the next meetings with France present took place. His path would be smoothed, he thought, as a result of the French elections, which again returned a left-wing government headed by Edouard Herriot, a leader of the Radical Socialists and a much easier man to deal with than André Tardieu, the old collaborator of Clemenceau. But Brüning never reaped the rewards of his high policy. What he was trying to do was prepare the way for a restoration of the monarchy, he told Schleicher, as he tried to persuade him to support his cabinet. Brüning promised Schleicher he would be his successor and said Schleicher could himself take the last steps that would lead to a Hohenzollern restoration. But Brüning had no luck. Schleicher was too wily to board a sinking ship. Brüning, he knew—no one would know it better—was finished.[9]

Hindenburg listened as Brüning explained to him what he had in mind—to hold out long enough to prepare the way for a constitutional monarchy. Hindenburg listened, but Brüning was not at all sure he understood what his chancellor was saying. The president told him he wanted to talk matters over with the party leaders, plain evidence to Brüning that Hindenburg was no longer relying on his chancellor.

Brüning's last meeting with the president was perfunctory and very short; it lasted three and a half minutes. Hindenburg had told Brüning the day before that he had become too unpopular to remain in office, and now, turning to his spare stock of political homilies, he said he had to ask Brüning to quit "because of my name and my honor."[10] He then asked him if he would not take over the post of foreign minister, and when Brüning declined the meeting was over.

As Brüning left the president's office, the navy band was playing in commemoration of the Battle of Skagerrak, and the venerable field marshal was about to take the salute as it marched to the garden under his window. He had not uttered a word of thanks to the chancellor who had served him as best he could for twenty-six months and to whom more than any other he owed his victory over Hitler. It may well be that he could not forgive Brüning for his unpopularity or for his major part in the victory won over the opposition of many right-wing conservatives with whom Hindenburg had been identified all his life. Hindenburg's legend had become something he himself accepted, and he felt himself betrayed and deserted by the very people he had always considered his own. To be beholden to Catholic Centrists and Social Democrats for his election was to find himself suddenly in the camp of the neutrals and the enemy, and it was that that he felt to be inconsistent with his name and his honor.

The man Hindenburg chose as Brüning's successor, Franz von Papen, was like Brüning a devout Catholic and unlike Brüning an apostate, right-wing member of the Center party. He was little known in the Reich. His future finance minister, Schwerin von Krosigk, when he heard the news of Papen's appointment, was attending an economic conference in Paris, and he reported that everyone at the meeting, including the German ambassador, had asked who Papen was. François-Poncet said that no one could believe it when Papen's appointment was announced, and that when it was confirmed people either smiled or laughed. Neither Papen's friends nor his enemies, François-Poncet said, took him seriously. He was thought of as superficial, vain, ambitious, and an intriguer; his only favorable quality was aplomb, audacity.[11]

Papen had been a deputy in the Prussian Landtag, where he had long opposed the Center's coalition with the SPD, and in an article in the *Ring*, published by the German Herren Club, he had lately written precisely what his friend Schleicher wanted to read. In his article Papen asked the rhetorical question whether, if the Center could pride itself on its historical mission in bringing Social Democrats into the state to make them bourgeois, it should not have the same historical duty to work together within "the Movement that today was flooding the political scene."[12]

Papen had pat answers for such questions, and he readily believed Hitler could be gentled and set to work at responsible projects. His article greatly appealed to Schleicher; they were old friends, had served together at the War College, and called one another Fränzchen and Kurtchen. Thus Papen became Schleicher's choice for the chancellorship. Schleicher knew that Papen was not very intelligent, but when a member of the Pomeranian Landtag objected that Papen was no head, Schleicher, agreeing, said he was at least a hat. And that was all Schleicher felt he needed at the moment. He himself did not wish to become chancellor; he disliked public appearances, preferring to direct the action from offstage. Papen had written a long letter to Schleicher airing his views on the political situation, and when the two met in Schleicher's office in Berlin on May 28, 1932, to discuss its angles, Schleicher informed Papen, to his professed astonishment, that he was the candidate he had in mind for chancellor and that his entire cabinet had been chosen for him. Papen has written that he was disinclined to take the post, but he seems only to have been grateful for Schleicher's thoughtfulness in providing him with a cabinet. Schleicher told him that the president wanted the new cabinet to be nonpartisan, a cabinet of experts but this time of right-wing experts, although what expertise Papen himself would represent might have been difficult for an outsider to discover.

He had served during World War I well enough on two fronts, in the West and in Palestine, but in other government service he had a record of extraordinary incompetence and bad luck. Nevertheless, Schleicher believed Papen could, with Hindenburg's support and Schleicher's tutelage, serve a useful purpose in the design to bracket Hitler and bring together a strong nationalist government. As evidence of progress in this direction, Schleicher told Papen that in conversations with Hitler and Röhm he had extracted a promise that Hitler would "tolerate" a Papen cabinet on condition that the prohibition of the SA and SS be lifted and that new elections be held. Hindenburg was won to Schleicher's solution by the promise of a right-wing, nonparty government of the kind he had hoped Brüning would successfully lead. Papen was persuaded by appeals to his patriotism and his soldierly sense of duty, and above all by his ambition, which far exceeded his political sophistication.

By nature Papen was an affable *charmeur* with a repertory of social graces. A former cavalryman, he rode well in amateur racing and he was a renowned gun at shooting preserves. After the war he had become a journalist when he acquired 47 percent of the stock of the Centrist paper *Germania* and was made chairman of its board of directors. The descendant of an old Catholic family that had lived in Westphalia since the fifteenth century, he had joined the Center party, although he might well have been more at home in one of the respectable right-wing parties. He had married the daughter of a rich industrialist of French descent, a circumstance that stimulated him, as he said, to learn French well and to become something of a Francophile. He seemed always to be at the beginning of a promising career that somehow never developed.

During the war he had been posted to Washington as military attaché of the German embassy, and his appointment had ended in a catastrophe for him and the Reich. He had set out to diminish, as far as possible, the flow of munitions from the United States to the Allies, arranging for the sabotage of American war production by, among other devices, persuading workers of German and Austrian origin to slow down production. He also gave one man, who was promptly captured when he crossed the border, $500 to blow up a Canadian bridge. His sole success was achieved when he bought, on behalf of Germany, a munitions factory in Bridgeport, an enterprise designed more to consume raw materials needed by the factories working for the Allies than to produce arms and ammunition for the Central Powers, which had no means of obtaining what the Bridgeport factory produced. One of Papen's assistants, a Dr. Heinrich Albert, left important and incriminating papers in his briefcase on a New York elevated train, and three days later the *New York World* published them. They gave the details of Papen's attempts to organize German and Austrian workers and of his sending information to Germany on arms shipments bound for the Allies.

That was only the beginning of Papen's misfortunes with secret documents. A few weeks later he entrusted a letter he had written to his wife to a journalist who was on his way to the Reich. It read in part: "Unluckily, they stole from the good Albert in the Elevated a whole thick portfolio. How splendid on the eastern front! I always say to these idiotic Yankees that they should shut their mouths or better still express their admiration for all that heroism."[13] The letter was intercepted when the journalist's luggage was searched at Falmouth, and it, too, was widely published a few days later. When Papen was declared *persona non grata* in the United States and sent back to Germany with a British safe-conduct on the Dutch ship *Nordam*, his luggage was searched at Falmouth and his personal papers were confiscated. They included cancelled checks for agents to blow up Canadian bridges, and they told of his efforts to build a German spy ring in the United States. These letters, were also published in the Allied press and in the United States.

Later in the war, while Papen was serving in Palestine, he went on leave from Nazareth to Germany. During his absence, the British captured the ancient city along with another batch of Papen's papers. These had to do with rebellion in Ireland and India and with sabotage in the United States, and as a result of them, according to testimony given by one of Papen's collaborators, Captain von Rintelen, a number of German agents were arrested in Britain and the United States and either imprisoned or executed.*[14]

After the war Papen had served for twelve years as a Centrist deputy in the Prussian Landtag, and there and in *Germania*, the paper he controlled, he tried to bring the party to his view of the need for a right-wing alliance in place of collaboration with the SPD. It was his conservative, largely Catholic constituency of farmers and landowners in Westphalia that kept electing him, mainly, no doubt, because of his advocacy of a program of agrarian aid beyond what the government was doing. He had regarded the Brüning program of farm resettlement with the same horror as did the East Prussian and Westphalian landowners, but he had no plans that went beyond Brüning's proposals to deal with the economic crisis. He proceeded with the same emergency decrees Brüning had asked the president to issue, with cuts in unemployment and welfare benefits to balance the government's loss of income. But he was in an even weaker political position than Brüning, who had had the support of at least one party.

One of the reasons that Schleicher had wanted Papen as Reichschancellor lay in his hope that Papen would bring with him the support of the Center, a party that Schleicher had always believed should make its alliances either left or right as the situation demanded. Now, in Schleicher's estimate, it was the turn of the Right, a turn that Papen had long been urging in the Prussian Landtag as he attempted to break up the coalition of Braun and Hess.

In the light of the election trends, it may well have been a plausible direction for the Center party, but the appointment of Papen was a disaster from the beginning. The Center was appalled by his acceptance of a post inherited from one of its leading members, and had he not resigned from the party, it would have expelled him. The promise that Schleicher thought he had extracted from Adolf Hitler to tolerate the Papen government was never fulfilled. Hitler gained what he had been demanding. On June 4 the Reichstag was dissolved and new elections announced for July 31, and on June 14 the prohibition of the SA and SS, the wearing of uniforms, and the holding of demonstrations was rescinded.† But there was no sign of Hitler's toleration, much less his support of Papen, and only a few days after the new government took office, Papen found himself isolated without the backing of any party in the Reichstag. The Center, incensed by his acceptance of the chancel-

---

* It is an ironical twist in Papen's story that one of the great coups of espionage during World War II was connected with him. It was through him, while he was ambassador in Ankara, that the spy "Cicero" provided the German intelligence service with the time and place of the Allied landings in Normandy during World War II, information that was wrongly evaluated in Berlin.

† Bavaria and Baden, however, issued new prohibitions of uniforms and demonstrations within those *Länder*.

lorship after the dismissal of its chief statesman, was unanimously opposed to him; his defection was all the more obnoxious because he had promised the head of the party, Monsignor Kaas, that he would not accept the post. It was a decision Kaas had gratefully reported to a meeting of Centrist deputies, where he had praised Papen's selflessness, only to learn a few hours later that Papen, after talking with the president, had indeed accepted.

The Papen cabinet, too, aroused no enthusiasm. With the exception of three members, Hermann Warmbold, held over from the Brüning cabinet as economics minister; Franz Gürtner, the former minister of justice for Bavaria, who now took over that ministry in the Reich; and Hugo Schäffer, a former Krupp director, who became minister of labor, every cabinet member had a *von* before his name. Papen attributed this circumstance to the fact that a number of ministerial posts had been offered to and declined by non-nobles, but in any event the cabinet as it stood was called, not a cabinet of experts, but a cabinet of barons, who had not much more appeal to any organized political constituency than did Papen himself. Von Neurath, who had been ambassador to England, where he was well liked, became foreign minister. Baron von Gayl, an East Prussian, became minister of the interior. Von Schleicher, who had first proposed another man, General Otto Hasse, for the job, had finally accepted the post of Reichswehr minister. The rest of the cabinet appeared to be made up of competent if uninspired reserve officers, members of the aristocracy. Like Papen, they evoked derision in the Far Right and Far Left and they gained no support for the government from the moderates. In later years most of them disappeared from public view, although five of them, including Papen himself, were to appear again in Hitler's first cabinet.

What Schleicher and Papen had in mind to do could not be done, although Schleicher at least had persuasive reasons for believing he had a sound, pragmatic solution for the political crisis. The important thing, as he saw it, was to bring Hitler away from the rewarding sidelines where he could criticize every move and onto the team where he must accept some responsibility for what happened. From Schleicher's point of view, the manpower of the National Socialist movement had to be recruited for the service of the Fatherland. Like all other Reichswehr officers, he abhorred private armies, and he was convinced that once Hitler took part in the government he would be confronted with the demands of the SA and SS to form the new core of the armed forces of the Reich. Since this would be impossible for any government to accept, the Nazi movement would be split. It had had its heretics before— Gregor Strasser, even Goebbels, not to mention the sizeable number who had left the movement—and it was still divided into left and right wings as well as on the future role of the SA and SS. Schleicher was no fool;

he often could analyze events with considerable shrewdness, and in theory his plan to bring in the National Socialists from their street brawls and riots to government offices where they would have to join in difficult and often unpopular decisions was a shrewd move. Or it would have been had he been dealing with someone other than Adolf Hitler.

Papen had no program of his own; he spoke readily of the need for Christian Conservatism, but what he had in mind concretely was nothing more than continuing what Brüning had been doing. Schleicher was much more sophisticated politically than Papen, but he, too, had no experience with a fanatic like Hitler.[15] He thought he had succeeded in persuading this Führer to adopt a more reasonable attitude toward the Jewish question—the kind of tactical shift he and Papen could easily convince themselves was an actual possibility. But in fact they were ideal opponents for Hitler—he with his iron will and utter indifference to conventional norms, fixed on one goal, and they with their boy scout devices for containing him.

Nevertheless, something had to be done about the National Socialists. The movement, Papen had written, was flooding the country. Actually, it was not doing that well; the election that took place in July 1932 gave them a resounding 37.7 percent of the vote, but it was far from a flood. And that was the highest percentage the National Socialists would ever achieve in a free election. It was large enough, however, to make governing without their participation almost impossible. In Mecklenburg-Schwerin on June 5, the National Socialists had won an absolute majority in the Landtag: 30 of 59 seats. They were the largest party not only in the Reichstag but in Prussia, Hesse, Thuringia, and other states as well. What was perhaps worse from the point of view of the republicans was that the antidemocratic parties, after the July elections, were in a majority in the Reichstag as well as in Prussia; the Nazis and Communists together had more than 51 percent of the Reichstag seats.

With the appointment of Papen, who had no perceptible support in the Reichstag, Hindenburg had in effect brought an end to the parliamentary system, and with the new election his decision was confirmed. No democratic parliament could function with a majority sworn to its destruction and legally able to throttle it. The Weimar Republic was falling to pieces, and it got little help from outside the Reich. The disarmament conference, which Brüning had been confident would grant the Reich arms equality, did nothing of the kind. In session from February 2 until it adjourned on July 23, it failed to meet the demand of the Reich for military equality, and on the day it adjourned the German delegate, Herr Nadolny, told its members that without the clear recognition of the equality of all states in matters of national security, the German government would not continue its collaboration with the work of the conference. It was not until December 11 that the other members agreed with the Reich that equality had to be granted Germany, and by that time Schleicher was chancellor and Hitler was treading on his heels, so the concession came too late to benefit anyone but Hitler.

The reparations conference at Lausanne had better results for Papen. It was clear to everyone, friend and foe alike, that the Reich was no longer able to pay reparations; the most that could be hoped for was some kind of final payment that would come due only when the Reich was in a position to make it. At Lausanne, too, Papen had made a characteristic blunder. The German delegation accompanying him, consisting of Neurath, Bülow, Schwerin-Krosigk, and Warmbold, had agreed among themselves that the Reich would agree to make a final lump-sum payment, but this decision was to be kept secret and used as a last trump card in the negotiations. Papen, however, interviewed by a French journalist during the first days of the conference, with his characteristic impulsiveness told him that the Reich was prepared to make this gesture, thus depriving the Germans of their chief bargaining counter. Not that it would matter much, for although the Lausanne conferences, after long discussion, agreed on a final payment by the Reich of 3 billion gold marks to be paid the Bank of International Settlements in the form of bonds to be marketed after three years, the deal never came to pass. By the time the three years were up, matters were in the hands of Adolf Hitler; neither the Reich nor the debtor nations expected him to pay a cent, and he never did. Lausanne, however, was a minor success for Papen, although he was past being able to benefit from such help as far as the Reichstag or the German electorate were concerned.[16]

It was a Papenesque success. Papen spoke fluent French, which made a good impression on Herriot and the French delegation, and he also came up with a breathtaking proposal. With the French obsession with security in mind, he proposed nothing less than a Franco-German military alliance, with members of both general staffs exchanging positions. Papen wrote later that the French were favorably impressed with his remarkable plan but that it failed because the British would not tolerate such a Continental imbalance. Actually, however, it was never taken very seriously by anyone. Papen himself told Ramsey MacDonald that it was of course "a preposterous idea whether in France or Germany,"[17] and he had no political backing in Germany to put it through the Reichstag even if the French had accepted it, which they showed no signs of doing. The proposal simply faded away, but Papen was always convinced he had nearly won the French to a revolutionary new course.

In his domestic policy, everything Papen touched seemed to turn to ashes. One bold move, however appealing it might have been to right-wing zealots at one time, now succeeded only in isolating him more than ever. Prussia had long been a thorn in the side of Adolf Hitler, and on July 20 Papen set out to remove the irritant. With the defeat of the Social Democrats in the Landtag election, former Prussian Minister-President Braun had stepped down from his post and the state's affairs had been run, as they had been in Bavaria and other *Länder,* by an administrative device whereby day-to-day business was conducted by a committee, of which Severing was a member. What the National Socialists wanted above all in Prussia was to get rid of Severing and his police president, Albert Greszinski, the men who were responsible for the house searches that had disclosed such uncomfortable information about the party and who had not hesitated to use force against the violent tactics of the SA and SS.

Papen simply took over the administration of Prussia. Armed with an emergency decree, he called three key members of the Prussian administration, Severing, Minister of Welfare Heinrich Hirtsiefer, and Minister of Finance Otto Klepper, to a meeting in the Reichschancellory on July 20, where, after greeting them courteously, he explained that they were no longer in office. A few days later a state of emergency was decreed for Berlin and all Brandenburg, and Schleicher placed the commandant of Defense Area III, General von Rundstedt, in charge. Thus the entire apparatus of Prussian administration and security was in the hands of Reichscommissar Papen and von Schleicher.

Papen had a number of plausible explanations to justify his action: one was the need for combatting the widespread disorders; another was that he had heard from Schleicher, who had the report from the Ministry of the Interior, that a "most threatening alliance" was in prospect between the two Marxist parties, the Social Democrats and Communists; and still another was the desire on his and Schleicher's part to keep the Prussian police out of the hands of the National Socialists.[18]

About the disorders there could be no doubt. In the course of one month after the SA was again legalized, permitted to wear uniforms, and demonstrate, 99 people were killed and 1,125 wounded. At Altona, near Hamburg, on Sunday, July 17, some two weeks before the Reichstag elections, 17 people were killed and 64 sent to hospitals after clashes between the National Socialists and Communists. The police president of Altona, Otto Eggerstedt, a Social Democrat, had given the National Socialists permission to conduct a preelection march. The Communists had protested, and when the permission was allowed to stand, the Communists announced that they would turn to "self-help." Seven thousand National Socialists, many from Hamburg, had assembled for the demonstration. They marched through the workers' quarters in Altona for two hours, without incident until the first shots were fired from windows and rooftops.

The rumor of an SPD-KPD alliance was a myth. Even as early as

1924, Grigori Zinoviev, president of the Communist International and a member of the Politburo, had denounced the SPD as "a wing of fascism ... an open battle organization of the counterrevolution."[19] The SPD and the Communists were further apart than the Communists and the National Socialists. Moscow was convinced that a "fascist" takeover in the Reich was a necessary prelude to a Communist victory, so the KPD cooperated far more with the Nazis than with the Social Democrats.

The parliamentary administration in Prussia was still functioning, however, under Severing and his Centrist allies, with some 85,000 police under their control, a situation that after the spring elections Adolf Hitler found intolerable. For Papen, getting rid of the Prussian government was not undesirable in itself and was certainly a small price to pay if it would win the support of Adolf Hitler for his chancellorship.

There was no resistance in Prussia; nothing like the general strike that had broken the Kapp putsch took place. How could a general strike be called in the face of six million unemployed, or the police be ordered to resist the Reichswehr? Severing said he would yield only to force, but when two policemen accompanied by the newly named Police President Franz Bracht, former lord mayor of Essen, appeared at Severing's office, that was force enough and he left.

Severing's civil courage cannot be justly faulted; he had time and again, against the threat of physical violence, stood up to the Nazis, but the force he yielded to this time was token. No disorders, no real resistance occurred. Instead the Prussian government, with Bavaria and Württemberg joining it, appealed the takeover to the State Court, which issued on October 25 what was widely called a Solomonic verdict. Whatever it was called, it settled nothing, except that the state of emergency with Papen in charge could legally continue. The court delivered itself of a heavy judgment, elaborately weighing considerations on one side and on the other which declared the action legal and illegal. It was legal in that the president could issue an emergency decree temporarily suspending the Prussian government if public order and safety were seriously disturbed or endangered. But at the same time the court rejected Papen's chief excuse for intervention, which he had based on Prussia's neglect of its obligation to preserve public order. Thus it appeared that the president did have the right to issue the decree he had signed on behalf of the maintenance of public order and safety at a time, as the court said, when political parties were prepared for open conflict. But Papen and the president had acted on insubstantial grounds, and the Prussian ministers, although they were out of office and without power to pursue their functions, remained ministers. After the elaborate legal reasoning had ended, what was really clear was that Prussia remained under Papen and Schleicher's control.

The decision was regarded in republican circles as a portentous evasion of the constitutional issue, and it is still difficult to see it as anything else. The Weimar Constitution was never intended to permit any president, not even Hindenburg, to exercise or confer such powers as Papen assumed on such flimsy grounds, although they were powers that Adolf Hitler would soon make commonplace.

Whatever Papen's intentions may have been, his intervention in Prussia proved to be another failure. It failed to appease the Nazis, it alienated everyone left of Hugenberg, and the street riots continued. On the night of the Reichstag elections, July 31, another bloody encounter erupted in Königsberg where National Socialists used bombs and guns against their political enemies and one Communist deputy was killed while he lay in bed.

The government took countermeasures; on August 9 a decree provided the death penalty for any attack that "out of anger and hate, in the passion of political battle" resulted in a deadly attack on an opponent.[20] In other words, a spontaneous political murder was subject to the same penalties as premeditated murder.

No sooner was the decree announced when on August 10, in the village of Potempa, in Upper Silesia, nine uniformed SA men broke into a dwelling where a Communist coal miner by the name of Konrad Pietrzuch lived with his brother and mother. The brother was struck over the head but survived, while Konrad, in the presence of his mother, was beaten and stomped for half an hour until he died.[21]

The perpetrators were quickly arrested and tried by a special court in the neighboring town of Beuthen. The trial was held in the presence of a noisy audience of storm troops, among them SA leader Heines with a murder of his own among his activist credits. On August 22, less than two weeks after the crime was committed, five of the band of nine were sentenced to death under the new decree for the punishment of political murders, and the next day Hitler sent a telegram of solace and encouragement to the convicted men. It read: "In the face of this monstrous verdict I feel myself bound to you in limitless devotion. From this moment on your freedom is a question of our honor. The battle against a regime under which this was possible, our duty."[22]

The brutality of the crime horrified the rest of the country, including many within the National Socialist party. From this point on, popular support for the movement declined markedly. The murder and Hitler's telegram revealed more clearly than any limning by opponents the true face of the movement that proclaimed its purpose was to regenerate the country, and not even the fact that the victim was a member of a party that had its own contingents of strong-arm men and murderers condoned the bestiality of the crime for millions of Germans.

Papen was attacked in the Nazi press in the swollen verbiage Hitler had made his own. He wrote in the *Völkischer Beobachter*: "Herr von Papen, now I know your bloody objectivity . . . We will free the idea of Nationalism from the embrace of an objectivity whose real inner purpose is revealed by the verdict of Beuthen against national Germany. With it Herr von Papen has inscribed his name in German history with the blood of nationalist fighters."[23]

The Potempa murder stopped the steady rise of the National Socialists. Most of the bloody incidents that had occurred in the past had resulted in charges and countercharges about who was responsible, but in this case there could be no possible doubt. This was no reprisal against a foul attack. It was murder and torture for the sake of a political ideology, and a wave of revulsion swept the country. Thousands of former supporters turned against the National Socialists. General von Hammerstein said now he could sleep quietly at night; the Reichswehr was outraged by the Nazis, and it would obey any order to shoot at them.

Hindenburg, too, pointed to the Nazi acts of terror and violence when Hitler presented himself before the president on August 13. Accompanied by Frick and Röhm, Hitler had met with Papen and Schleicher, neither of whom seems to have been affected by the murder, some hours before his audience with Hindenburg, and he had refused their offer to become vice-chancellor. Then he went on to the presidential palace, where Hindenburg together with Meissner and Papen received him. When Hitler told Hindenburg that he would take no post in the Papen cabinet but must be given full governmental responsibility, Hindenburg's answer was a flat no. He could not, he said, turn over control of the government to any party, especially one that would not tolerate people who disagreed with them. And he added that he was disturbed by the great disorders and by their effect on foreign countries. Hitler replied that he saw only the one solution. Hindenburg admonished him then to conduct his opposition chivalrously. He said he had no doubt of Hitler's love for the Fatherland, but he would react with utmost sharpness against any acts of terror and force by the SA. According to one report, his words were "Herr Hitler, I will shoot." Then with a characteristic appeal to a former front-line soldier, he said, "We are both old comrades and so we want to remain" and offered Hitler his hand. The twenty-minute interview was over.[24]

When the Reichstag reconvened on August 30, in accordance with Reichstag custom its oldest member, the Communist deputy Clara Zetkin, was in the chair. Predictions had been freely made that her life would be in danger, but she returned, nevertheless, from a visit to Moscow to preside over an unexpectedly peaceful session until the new president of the Reichstag was elected. Frau Zetkin was even able to deliver an uninterrupted speech in her fragile, old lady's voice about the need for a united front of workers against fascism and her hope to see a Räte Republic in a Soviet Germany of the future.[25] It was a speech that ordinarily would have been shouted down by the Nazis, but this time they listened in silence that continued even when a Communist delegate called for "three Red Front" cheers for Frau Zetkin. Hermann Göring as the leader of the largest party in the Reichstag was elected president. It was a position of considerable strategic importance, and Göring was to make the most of it. At a reception at the presidential palace for officers of the Reichstag, he asked Hindenburg to deny rumors that he intended to exclude the Reichstag from the governmental process (which explained the reason for the Nazis' unusual spell of decorum while Clara Zetkin was in the chair). The Reichstag, he said, had a working majority. It would defend itself against its exclusion, and he had the unanimous approval of the Reichstag to bring this to the president's attention.

Göring's statement was immediately contradicted by Walther Graef, a member of the German National People's party and vice-president of the Reichstag, who said the Reichstag's officers were not a political body and had no authority to give the president political advice. But Göring's words were a declaration of war against Hindenburg and Papen's government by decree, and although it was precisely what the Nazis had in mind for themselves, it was clear that Papen would have a hard time with the new Reichstag.

On September 2 Papen made one more gesture to appease the National Socialists; he commuted the Potempa death sentences to life imprisonment. He continued, however, to issue emergency decrees, one on September 4 for the "Restoration of the Economy" based on his conviction that the low point of the depression had been reached. Among other measures such as stepping up the make-work program, business was to be stimulated with tax certificates that could be used to pay off, at a 40-percent discount, certain taxes and provide credits for new enterprises. To increase employment, workers could be hired for such enterprises under the prevailing wage scales, a proposal that left the Social Democrats and Communists aghast and did nothing to win the support of the Nazis.

Thus on September 12 when the Reichstag reconvened, the National Socialists and the Communists joined forces to rescind the latest emergency decree and to put through a vote of no confidence in the Papen government. Papen had prepared a detailed speech for the Reichstag to explain his policies, but he was never to deliver it. Göring, as the session opened, immediately recognized the Communist deputy Ernst Torgler, who moved that the order of business be changed and who presented the anti-Papen resolutions. A half-hour recess followed, during which time Papen was able to obtain from Hindenburg another emergency order dissolving the Reichstag.* After the recess Papen held the dissolution order in his hand, enclosed in its conspicuous red cover, traditional since Bismarck's day. As Reichschancellor, he had the prescriptive right to address the Reichstag at any time, but he waved his red wallet in vain to get Göring to recognize him. Göring ignored the frantic Papen. He ordered that the voting proceed, and the two resolutions annulling the emergency decree and the no-confidence vote were adopted by an overwhelming vote of 512 to 42. Only after the vote was tallied did Göring pay any attention to Papen and his dissolution order, which, in light of the vote of no confidence, he declared invalid. It had been countersigned by Papen and the minister of the interior, von Gayl, and they, Göring explained, were no longer in office. He was resolved, Göring said further, to keep unsullied the prestige of the Reichstag, above all of the right of the representatives of the German people to perform their duties under the constitution.

Both sides proclaimed their passionate devotion to legality and both were on shaky ground. The emergency decrees were never intended to be regularly substituted for the Parliament's law-making prerogatives; they were to be used under special circumstances, not systematically over a long period of time as Hindenburg was using them. But on the other hand, voting the ouster of Papen and his cabinet from their posts when the presidential order was already at hand for the dissolution of the Reichstag was illegal, too. But in any event, the Reichstag was dissolved and new elections were called for November 6, which is what Hitler had been demanding.

Just before that happened, however, an event occurred that evidenced again the unlikely kinship of the Communists and National Socialists. In Berlin the transit authority, like all public agencies, had to cut costs, and it attempted through a new agreement with the Transit Workers' Union to lower hourly wages. A majority of the workers called a strike, without, however, securing the required three-quarters majority of the union membership. The "Communist Union Opposition" nevertheless declared its solidarity with the strike, which took place after an arbitrator had made his decision, which should have ended it. The strike was therefore shunned by the regular union but backed by both the Communists and the National Socialists. As one observer wrote, it was a strange sight to see these sworn enemies walking arm in arm down the silent streets or joining forces in trying to stop, by any means at hand, the attempts to set up emergency means of transport. Strikers attacked strikebreakers, rails were torn up, riots broke out, and blood

---

* The decree had already been prepared in Neudeck, but *Neudeck* had been crossed out and *Berlin* substituted. (Georg Usadel, *Zeitgeschichte in Wort und Bild*, p. 251.)

flowed again. But the strike was lost when the National Socialists, with the coming of the election and the lack of an immediate incentive for trying to win the workers' votes, abandoned the strikers. The walkout ended the day after the election.

The November election was a solid defeat for Adolf Hitler. The party lost almost 2 million votes, falling from 13,745,800 to 11,737,000, down from 37.2 percent to 33 percent of the total, while the Communists went up 700,000 votes, from 5,282,600 to 5,980,000, or from 14.2 percent to 16.8 percent of the ballots cast. The German Nationals and the German Volksparty, the group whose deputies provided Papen with his sole support on the no-confidence resolution, gained at the expense of the Nazis. The Nationals went up from 2,177,400 to 2,959,000, the German Volksparty from 436,000 to 661,800. The Social Democrats lost votes to the Communists and were down again from 7,959,700 to 7,248,000. The Center, too, went down slightly, from 4,589,300 to 4,230,600. In Berlin the Communists outdistanced the National Socialists by a wide margin. The National Socialists received 269,294 votes, the Communists 450,793.

The Nazi defeat was certainly not all due to Potempa. Unemployment figures had gone down in October by 123,000, and Papen had allocated 2,200,000 marks for public works jobs. However, the brawls and strikes and killing associated with the Nazis also played their part, as did Hindenburg's peremptory refusal to turn over the government to Adolf Hitler. Hitler's defeat should have been a Papen victory, somewhat dampened by the Communist rise to 100 deputies in the Reichstag. But the parties that might be regarded as likely to support him, the German Nationals and the German Volksparty, had not much more than one-tenth of the votes in the Reichstag. The National Socialists were still the largest party, with 196 deputies, and no sizeable coalition could possibly be assembled that would support Papen; nine-tenths of the Reichstag wanted to be rid of him. The only two parties that could produce a majority (and that a bare 50.4 percent) of the votes in the Chamber were the National Socialists with 196 out of 584 votes and the Communists with 100, but their only shared goal was the destruction of the Weimar Republic. They could collaborate against Papen and in aid of the Berlin transit strike, but that was as far as any common front could possibly go. Papen was left with only his desire to remain chancellor and the support of the president. On November 10 Hindenburg asked him to discuss with party leaders under what circumstances they would cooperate with him in a government of "national concentration" to forward his program of constitutional reform.*

* The plan Papen had worked out might have had some appeal to Hindenburg but very little to a mass following. Papen had developed a blueprint for what he called "an authoritarian government" to be established through a constitutional

Papen had no luck in his talks with the Centrist leaders, who would not forgive his treason, or with the Social Democrats, who detested him. His attempt to convince Hitler to join his cabinet was met with another refusal. Hitler's setback in the November election had no perceptible effect on his self-confidence. He saw no point, he wrote to Papen, in coming to Berlin to talk over the offer; they could deal with the issues by letter, and he had no wish to repeat his experience of August 13. He would not participate in any coalition, and he added that the situation of the Reich under Papen was deteriorating day by day.[26]

Papen had nowhere to turn. Schleicher had long ago decided he was useless; from Schleicher's point of view, he had not even been a hat Schleicher could use. Papen had followed his own inept, independent course, which could only lead to another chancellor. On November 17 at a cabinet meeting, Schleicher proposed that Papen and the entire cabinet resign to give the president an opportunity to form a new government. With no possible support in prospect from the political parties, the labor organizations, or the Reichswehr, Papen had no alternative but to hand in his own and the cabinet's resignations to the president. Hindenburg, however, asked them all to remain in office until a new government could be formed, and he still cherished the hope that Papen might be the man to lead it. Meanwhile he conducted his own search for a political solution. He received the Center and the right-wing party leaders on November 18, one after the other, and asked for their cooperation in his proposed government of "national concentration," but while they all agreed with Hindenburg's purposes, they politely left the decision over the chancellorship to him. However, Monsignor Kaas, chief of the Center party, told the president it must not be another Papen cabinet like the last one.[27]

Hindenburg's negotiations with Hitler, which began with a meeting on November 19 and continued with another conversation and an exchange of letters through November 24, were no more successful than Papen's. The discussions broke down on the same disagreements that had wrecked them before—Hitler's demand for the chancellorship in a presidential cabinet and Hindenburg's refusal to turn the government over to what he said would inevitably be a one-party dictatorship. Hitler would have to win a parliamentary majority for Hindenburg to name him chancellor; the president would not appoint him to head a presidential cabinet, which in Hindenburg's view had to be above the parties.[28]

On November 24 their talks came to an end, and to some observers that

---

amendment that would provide for a bicameral legislature, the Upper Chamber to be appointed by the president as a balance to an elected Reichstag. A system of weighted balloting would give the heads of families and war veterans more votes than the general electorate. (Hans Otto Meissner and Harry Wilde, *Die Machtergreifung*, pp. 106, 281.)

seemed to mark the end of Adolf Hitler. Hindenburg's rejection of him, his defeat at the polls, the financial crisis in the party, and the split in its ranks could well be fatal. Harold Laski, a leading ideologue of the British Labour party, wrote that the threat of National Socialism was over. Hitler, Laski said, would no doubt live out his days in a Bavarian village and during evening strolls in the park tell his cronies how he had one day nearly overthrown the Reich.[29] *Simplicissimus* published in its New Year's Poem some verses to the same effect:

One thing is sure for all of us,
And we're delighted every one,
Hitler gets it in the puss,
This "Führer's" time is done.

(*Eins nur lässt sich sicher sagen / Und das freut uns rund herum, / Hitler geht es an den Kragen, / Dieses "Führers" Zeit ist um.*)[30]

Hindenburg turned again to Kaas to see if he could perceive any way to form a majority cabinet. Kaas told Meissner, the president's inter-mediary, that it was a pity Hitler would not cooperate, but that it was impossible to return to Papen, and he suggested that perhaps Brüning might again be named chancellor. When on November 25 Hindenburg received Kaas in person, in his perplexity he asked if he, the president, might be an obstacle to a political solution, and Kaas replied reverently: "On the day when you, Mr. President, leave us, the last hope for consolidation of forces will disappear." Hindenburg replied sorrowfully that on one hand he was offered sugar bread and on the other a whip. He could not name Brüning again, and he would not name Hitler.

In fact, the alternatives Hindenburg had in mind were all unpromising. At a meeting on December 1, attended by Meissner, Schleicher, and Oskar von Hindenburg, Papen asked the president to declare a state of emergency, dissolve the Reichstag, and permit him to govern under Article 48 without new elections until he could win a following for his constitutional reform. Then, Papen said, either a plebiscite or a constitutional convention could decide whether or not to accept the new political blueprint. Such a course, Papen conceded, would be a breach of the constitution, but he thought that, under the circumstances, the lesser evil.

Schleicher rejected both Papen's plan and Papen. At this point he had one main objective—to get rid of him. With his own blueprint for the salvation of the Reich in hand, Schleicher had been sounding out Hitler and Strasser on the possibility of their entering a cabinet in which he would be chancellor. Hitler had rejected the idea, but Strasser was well disposed. It is doubtful that Schleicher himself much wanted to be chancellor. The British ambassador, Sir Horace Rumbold, and others doubted it. He knew himself to be a poor speaker in public; it was not in his character to enjoy the glare of publicity; and he had had other candidates in mind for the post—Schacht, for example, and Franz Bracht, whom he would later name minister of the interior. But one thing was sure: Papen had to go, and if necessary Schleicher himself would take his place.

Schleicher considered himself a man of broad-gauged, pragmatic political philosophy. In a radio address a few months before the meeting with Hindenburg, he had told the German people that it was not the task of the Reichswehr to support outmoded economic systems or property holdings. He had long been in touch with leftist as well as with right-wing forces in the Reich; he was one of the architects of German-Russian military cooperation; he had connections with trade unionists as well as with the Strasser wing of the National Socialist party. When he met with Hindenburg and Papen, however, he had no time for further maneuvers or parleys; he had to act quickly. He told the president he could be spared the necessity for breaching his oath of office and the constitution by naming him chancellor. Schleicher outlined a plan by which he said he could win a majority in the Reichstag by splitting the National Socialists with the help of Strasser and some sixty Nazi deputies who would join his government together with what he called "the trade-union axis"—the middle-class parties and the SPD. It was an unlikely coalition and Schleicher never succeeded in organizing anything like it. In any case, Hindenburg was not greatly impressed and chose Papen's solution over Schleicher's. But not for long.

Schleicher had a trump card Papen could not match, and the next day when the cabinet met he played it. He had given Colonel Ott of the Defense Ministry permission to work out a war game that would forecast, in theory, what might happen in the event of a general strike throughout the Reich, a strike which the Nazis, the SPD, and the Communists would support. A similar situation had already occurred during the Berlin transit strike, and Ott came up with the answer that the Reichswehr plus the police could not guarantee order in such an event; the Reichswehr could not control widespread internal disorders that would be bound to occur and at the same time defend the Reich's borders. In the Ruhr and Rhineland, separatist movements might well reappear; the police were weak in those regions and perhaps, in the event of a Communist uprising, unreliable; and the army would not even be permitted to enter the demilitarized zone. In the East matters were worse; there, Polish radical groups might well seize the opportunity presented by German civil struggles to invade territory they had long claimed. In addition, the National Socialists were well represented in the lower ranks of the army, and how they would respond to orders to shoot at their late comrades was problematical. Ott did not say that the presence of these young men recently of the Brown Shirts or the SS was largely owing to Schleicher's desire to make them eligible for army enlistment. That was a course Schleicher had helped persuade Groener to adopt. Nor did Ott point out that any chance of real cooperation among the National Socialists, SPD, and Communists was close to zero.

Only on the Polish front did he have a possible point. After Hitler was in power, Marshal Pilsudski, without the required permission from the League of Nations high commissioner, gave orders on March 6, 1933, for a Polish marine battalion to march into the Westerplatte situated at the entrance to Danzig harbor and reinforce the Polish garrison there. Pilsudski was taking the kind of risk Hitler would soon make a commonplace; it was widely interpreted as designed to provoke a German countermove and thus bring in French military support for the Poles, but in this case, after long discussions in the League Council, the dispute ended in a compromise when the Polish reinforcements were withdrawn.[31]

Ott's evaluation, however, was designed to predict what might happen under the worst circumstances—always one of the purposes of a general staff study. But whatever its substantive merits, it overthrew Papen. It would have been almost impossible for anyone in the cabinet, after hearing Ott's report, to vote for Papen's solution, and it was rejected. When on the next day Papen reported to Hindenburg the news of the cabinet's decision, the president had to reverse his decision of the day before. "I am an old man," he said, "and I cannot take the responsibility, at the end of my life, for a civil war."[32] With tears in his eyes, according to Papen, the president thereupon dismissed him and, as a parting gift, presented him with his photograph, on which the president wrote in a strong hand and heavy black ink the line from Uhland's poem on a soldier's death: "I had a comrade."

Schleicher became chancellor and made only two changes in the Papen cabinet. He appointed Franz Bracht as minister of the interior in the place of Baron von Gayl, who had supported Papen, and Günter Gereke, an agrarian expert, as commissar for eastern settlement. Neither brought with them much political support. Bracht, when he was Prussian Reichscommissar, had been the butt of many jokes as the author of a decree that prescribed strict regulations for the style of bathing suits that could be worn in public swimming pools, and Gereke had announced a plan for make-work programs that, while attractive to labor unions, won over none of the SPD leaders and was rejected as inflationary by industrialists.

What Schleicher had in mind was not unlike what Mussolini had done in Italy: he wanted to make of the Reich a super-Wehrmacht where the political parties and social strata would be represented and work together in a disciplined cooperative state which would overcome the depression and the Reich's military vulnerability. He sent Ott to talk with Hitler; he met with Strasser and with the trade union leaders

Theodor Leipart and Wilhelm Eggert; and like Gereke he proposed a wide-ranging plan for work projects, including a youth program and land resettlement, designed to appeal to labor and win the cooperation of the SPD with his government. His strategy came to nothing. The SPD leaders could not forgive him for his part in the takeover of Prussia, and the right wing was suspicious of his talk of outmoded economic systems and his land reform projects. For Hitler, Schleicher was an old enemy, and although Strasser would have liked to collaborate with him, Hitler forced him to reject Schleicher's offer to enter his cabinet.

Nevertheless, what Schleicher was trying to do did not seem impossible. Above all he had aimed to split the National Socialists, and the time seemed not at all unpropitious to do that. Röhm was openly critical of "Adolf Légalité" of what he regarded as Hitler's timeserving; and the entries in Goebbels's diaries tell of the despair of the party leaders facing an empty treasury and huge debts while public opinion turned against them. In Thuringia, Goebbels wrote, the party had lost almost 40 percent of its former vote in the communal elections on December 4, and he called the situation "catastrophic." On December 8, he wrote that the party leaders were all depressed and that money troubles made any kind of purposeful work impossible. "Rumors abound that Strasser is planning some kind of palace revolution . . . we are inwardly so stricken that we wish for nothing more ardently than to get away from it all for a few weeks. At midday the bomb exploded. Strasser has written the Führer a letter in which he told him he was laying down all his party offices." Hitler was at a low ebb, Goebbels wrote. At two in the morning Goebbels was summoned to the Kaiserhof, where Hitler, Röhm, and Himmler were gathered. They had the morning edition of the *Täglicher Rundschau* with an article telling of Strasser's quitting his posts and going on to say that nothing was left but for the party to choose Strasser over Hitler as leader of the movement. "Treason! Treason! Treason!" Goebbels wrote. Hitler strode up and down the hotel room for hours, Goebbels reported, and at last he stopped his pacing and spoke: "If the party ever falls to pieces, then I'll make an end to everything with a pistol in three minutes."

Goebbels had wan hopes for the future. On December 15 he wrote that there seemed not to be the slightest chance of the party's coming to power, and on December 21 he noted that the "money calamity" still continued.[33]

It looked as though it were now the Nazis who were faltering 100 meters from the finish line, but help was at hand from two incompatible sources—the Social Democrats and big business. The Social Democrats refused to deal with Schleicher despite his prolabor decrees, and in mid-November an impressive list of figures prominent in finance and industry announced their support of Hitler as Reichschancellor. Twenty of them including Hjalmar Schacht, Fritz Thyssen, Albert Vögler of the United Steel Works, and Baron von Schröder, the Cologne banker, signed a letter addressed to Hindenburg respectfully asking him to name Hitler chancellor. Some of them, like Thyssen, were old Nazi sympathizers, but others, like Schacht, had had little enthusiasm for Hitler or his party. The reasons given for their shift were various. Schacht explained that his cooperation was offered to prevent the kind of economic nonsense Gottfried Feder was preaching from dominating any future Hitler government. Thyssen said his financial help was given the National Socialists "for a single definite reason ... because I believed the Young Plan spelled catastrophe for Germany."* 34

But there were certainly other reasons that neither of them mentioned. Since 1931 Hitler's attitude toward big business had become more respectful, as was manifest in his Düsseldorf speech. What the bankers and industrialists wanted was a stable right-wing government that took a favorable view of capitalist enterprises and rejected left-wing socialism and all its works. The increase in the Communist vote in the November election was disconcerting, as were Schleicher's remarks about "outmoded economic systems," his "inflationary" program for works projects, and his "agrarian Bolshevik" program for land settlement. Hitler had told his Düsseldorf audience of entrepreneurs how highly he regarded them, and many of them believed him, mainly, no doubt, because they had so few alternatives.

At the moment their letter to the president had no effect. Hindenburg would not appoint Hitler chancellor, and the Nazi treasury remained empty. What Hitler needed in rescue funds† could come from only one source—the public purse—and toward that end the support of the twenty signers and others like them would soon be decisive.

The SA jangled their tin cans, soliciting contributions—one observer even saw them at a funeral—and they stood at street corners in Berlin calling out, "Winter help for the NSDAP." Some of the more roguish ones shouted, "Help for the wicked Nazis!" Their important help came from men like Baron von Schröder, Franz von Papen, and the bankers and industrialists who had hitherto avoided them but whose hearts were now more softened toward them than were those of most of the passersby. Papen said he had never in his life expected to be chancellor, and that may well be true, but what is also true is that once having held the office, he hated leaving it, and he turned on Schleicher, who had given him the job and then forced him to quit.

What took place between mid-December and the end of January has

---

* He had, however, given the party 100,000 gold marks in 1923, long before the Young Plan.

† Much of the party debt was owed small businessmen such as printers, who could not afford to wait long for their money.

been elaborately explained by Papen in his books, in his Nuremberg testimony, in interrogations, and at his German trial. He has denied that he sought out Hitler or did anything to torpedo Schleicher, although he seems in fact to have done both. At bottom neither Papen nor Schleicher had wanted Hitler to be Reichschancellor; both of them certainly distrusted him and believed he had to be held in check by men like themselves. Schleicher had said that the thing to do was "to put the fellow in the middle and hang weights on him," and then with himself and the Reichswehr on one side and Hindenburg and his authority on the other, "we will soon do Adolf in."[35] However, after Schleicher tried to split the party and failed, he realized it had come to all-out war with Hitler, and he was ready to use the police and even the Reichswehr against him and the SA.

Papen, on the other hand, out of office and with no political prospects, revived his earlier hope that Hitler could be made use of for his benefit and that of the Fatherland. Papen had just been the target of the kind of searing attacks in which the National Socialist press specialized because of what it saw as his malevolence toward the Potempa murderers, and he knew that as a first step he had to overcome Hitler's aversion to him. It was only through Hitler that he would again be in a position to play the part he believed he deserved in directing great events. Papen could easily persuade himself of his ability to overcome obstacles that might well daunt anyone possessed of more self-criticism. Moreover, his vanity had been bruised; Schleicher had unhorsed him, and the possibility of unhorsing Schleicher with the aid of Hitler had its own appeal.

On the night of December 16, Papen again gave a speech at the Herren Club, at a dinner attended by some 300 of the *Prominenten*: industrialists, landowners, and officials. He defended his chancellorship and his cabinet of barons, but he told his audience that the ruling elements in a society cannot come from one class alone; they must draw on the entire people. This was a *völkish* litany that could have been a direct quote from Hitler, but Papen became more precise. He said: "The tragic failure of the Brüning government seems to me to have been the failure to include the National Socialists in a National bloc . . . the people were torn in two halves. . . ."[36] Political life today, he said, is like a battle; if the man who carries the flag falls, then another must pick it up, raise it high, and carry it forward to the attack. Individuals are nothing; the cause is everything. Never was the principle of a Führer and his followers more alive and compelling than in these days, and again and again, he said, we have to lift the eyes of the nation to the man who incorporates in himself our best *völkisch* characteristics. He was referring to Hindenburg, but the message was not designed for him alone.

These quotations come from Papen's published version of his talk, but others who were present at the dinner have a different memory of the speech, the original text of which seems to have disappeared. One man who was there said it was not only an invitation to the Nazis to enter the government, but it was a stab in Schleicher's back, especially damaging because everyone at the dinner knew that Papen was a confidant of Hindenburg's. Another man, Erwin Planck, chief of the Reichschancellory, called it the swan song of a bad loser.[37]

As to what followed, again the stories vary. Papen said that Baron von Schröder, who had been present, telephoned him to propose that he meet with Hitler to discuss the possibility of Hitler's coming into the Schleicher cabinet. Papen said he agreed, although he was doubtful that Hitler would want to see him after their rancorous differences.

That story, too, is unlikely, and Schröder and Meissner say things didn't happen that way; they say it was Papen who wanted to have a talk with Hitler. In any event, after Papen's speech, a friend of Schröder's, Wilhelm Keppler, director of a factory making gelatin for photographic plates and an economic advisor to the National Socialists, wrote to Hitler telling him that Papen now realized that Hitler had to become chancellor and would support his candidacy. Papen, Keppler wrote, would like to meet Hitler secretly at Schröder's house in Cologne. Papen later explained that Keppler's letter was written only to overcome Hitler's dislike so that they could have their meeting and Papen could be given the opportunity to persuade Hitler to join Schleicher's cabinet as vice-chancellor. But Keppler's letter to Hitler also said that Papen had come to know the personality of Schleicher, who had always deluded and deceived his co-workers in order to further his own cause. Schleicher's position, moreover, was very weak; Hindenburg's opinion of him was now unfavorable, while Papen had the complete confidence of the old gentleman.

In the light of Keppler's letter, too, Papen's account falls apart. How, after Keppler's assurance to Hitler that Papen would back his candidacy for the chancellorship, could Papen propose that Hitler accept the post of vice-chancellor in, as Papen called it, a "duumvirate," with Schleicher as chancellor? Since Hitler had previously turned down any such offer, what would have been the point of Papen's merely repeating it on behalf of the "deceitful" Schleicher? The obvious answer is that he did nothing of the sort. He wanted to see Hitler to offer something other than a high post with Schleicher, and in fact that is what, later on when Hitler was chancellor, Papen himself would take credit for.

Two additional pieces of evidence confirm the unlikelihood of Papen's account. On January 5, a day after the meeting at Schröder's house, Goebbels wrote in his diary: "The discussion between the Führer and Herr von Papen in Cologne has taken place. It was supposed to be secret but through an indiscretion has reached the public. . . . People seem to suspect what went on here [*was hier gespielt wird*]. One thing the regime in office must know: there is a serious question of its downfall. If this coup is successful, then we are no longer far from the goal." And Hitler, describing the meeting a decade later, in 1942, said he had the impression at the time of his talk with Papen that everything was going well, and that no compromises would be necessary.[38]

From Hitler's point of view, despite his contempt for Papen, the invitation to a meeting with one of Hindenburg's most trusted advisors must have seemed an act of Providence. Hitler and his party were at the end of a long rope. He personally owed some 400,000 marks on his unpaid income tax,* and among other large running expenses that had to be met, he had his considerable bill at the Kaiserhof, where he entertained on a large scale. The party and the SA were also deeply in debt. The Nazi deputies in the Reichstag could not even join in a vote of no confidence in the Schleicher government, because the party could not finance another full-scale election campaign. The clock was ticking against Hitler.

The meeting was arranged for January 4 at Schröder's house with the most elaborate precautions to keep it secret. Hitler and his party took the train from Munich to Bonn, where in the early morning Julius Schreck, Hitler's chauffeur, was waiting for them at the station. They were driven to Bad Godesberg, where they had breakfast at one of Hitler's favorite hotels, the Dreesen. A sedan with curtained windows then drove up, and Hitler together with Keppler, Hess, and Himmler rode off. The rest of the party stayed behind. Dietrich, following careful instructions, took Hitler's usual place next to Schreck and put on the same kind of automobile cap Hitler was accustomed to wear. They drove three miles past Cologne on the road to Düsseldorf, where they waited two hours for Hitler and the others to return. Dietrich was never told the purpose of the trip or where Hitler and the others were going, so tight was the security.[39]

When Hitler and his party arrived at Schröder's house in the curtained sedan, they found a photographer from the *Tägliche Rundschau* ready to take their pictures, as well as Papen's when he got out of a taxicab. Schleicher had not been known as the *Kardinal in politicis* for nothing. From Reichswehr funds he had provided a subvention to keep the *Tägliche Rundschau* afloat and have available a mouthpiece in the German press. The editor of the *Tägliche Rundschau*, Hans Zehrer, had a man in his pay in Hitler's security service,† and through his informer

---

* This is the amount he still owed in 1934. (Oron James Hale, "Adolf Hitler: Taxpayer" in *The American Historical Review*, vol. 60, July 1955, pp. 830–42.)

† This *Sicherheitsdienst* had no relationship to the sinister organization that Hitler and Himmler developed after Hitler was in office. It was merely another security apparatus to help protect the Führer and high party officials.

Zehrer was in a position to know at any time what Hitler planned to do and where he planned to go.

Hitler and Papen for the first time in their respective careers could collaborate. And while Papen's account of what they talked about is fanciful, Schröder's is probably close to what actually happened.[40] Hitler, he says, complained to Papen about the sentences of the Potempa murderers, and Papen said that under the law they were inescapable. Hitler replied that at least Hindenburg could be asked to pardon them. Then he turned the conversation to Hindenburg's refusal to name him chancellor, which he thought was owing to Schleicher's influence. Whereupon Papen made his pitch for a coalition government of conservatives and Nationals with the National Socialists. It was then he suggested a duumvirate, not with Hitler and Schleicher, but with himself and Hitler sharing power. Hitler repeated what he had always said: he must be chancellor, but Papen and his Nationalist allies could be members of his cabinet. And, he added, no Jews, Social Democrats, or Communists could hold leading positions in the country. A hazy agreement on some kind of sharing of power seemed to have been reached for the moment by the two men, who greatly needed one another, and thus, says Schröder, they came to a basic understanding.

Although no reliable, detailed report of what was said at the meeting was ever available, the situation of Hitler and Papen is plain enough. What Hitler could offer Papen was a return to a seat of power and importance, and Papen in the euphoria of that prospect could easily brush aside any fear he might have of the result of such a collaboration. He could see himself outmaneuvering both Schleicher and Hitler and at the same time performing a glorious service to the Fatherland by bringing Hitler at long last into the government in a position where he would have to act responsibly because he would be under the control of Papen and his conservative friends. It was much the same plan Schleicher had proposed, but as Papen developed it for his purposes, it took two forms. In one he would be chancellor in a duumvirate with Hitler as vice-chancellor until such time as he could convince Hindenburg of the reliability of the new housebroken Hitler; then once the president got to know this remarkable man, he would be willing to appoint him chancellor. That was undoubtedly Papen's favorite proposal. The other foresaw Hitler as chancellor, again in a duumvirate, with Papen as vice-chancellor; they would have coequal powers, and Papen with his conservative allies would overbalance Hitler and the one or two National Socialists he would be permitted to name to the cabinet. This, too, would provide for the containment of these street fighters by prudent men on whom the president knew he could rely.

The Nazi leaders, if they could be believed, were providing abundant evidence of a remarkable change of heart. Göring assured Papen that the National Socialists did not demand control of the government; they were .willing to cooperate with other nationally minded parties and to make common cause with them. Hitler told the president he was not primarily a party leader, but simply a German who had founded and organized a movement to save Germany from Marxism. In a letter to Meissner, Hitler wrote: "I promise that I will sacrifice myself for the salvation of our Fatherland, utilizing fully the resources of my person and my movement." Anything he did, he told Meissner, would be based on the constitution; he would work with the Reichstag, but only under legal conditions, by which he may have meant that he wanted no more presidential decrees to sustain a non-Hitler cabinet.[41]

In their talk at Schröder's house, when Papen presented his proposal for a duumvirate, Hitler at first seems to have shied away from it. Then perceiving what Papen had in mind, he agreed, and the two parted with smiles and a handshake in front of Schröder's door, where they were again photographed.

The photographs and the stories of the Hitler-Papen meeting exploded a sensation in the German press and fury in Schleicher. Hitler and Papen could and did explain in a joint communiqué that they had discussed only the possibility of "creating a great, national, politically united front" and that no discussion of the present cabinet had been involved, but no one, least of all Schleicher, believed the story for a moment. Schleicher had, however, only a limited area of counteraction. Papen was much closer to Hindenburg than he in every sense; Papen lived near the president's temporary quarters in the Reichschancellory,* and unseen by reporters or anyone else he could enter Hindenburg's apartment by way of the gardens any time he thought useful. Papen says he informed both the president and Schleicher about the substance of his talk with Hitler and his attempt to persuade Hitler to enter the Schleicher cabinet. And in fact, after the meeting, having noted the photographer, he had immediately written to Schleicher to explain what had happened. But Schleicher had no difficulty in seeing through the ink cloud behind which Papen was conducting his operations, and he asked Hindenburg to forbid Papen any such unconstitutional activities in the future and not to receive him except in Schleicher's presence.

That was just about all he could do, appeal to Hindenburg. His grand design had failed. He had failed to persuade Hitler to tolerate him or to enter his cabinet, and he had failed to split the National Socialists or to enlist the support of the Social Democrats; he could only continue to rule through presidential decrees like Brüning and Papen before him

---

* The presidential palace, long in need of repair, was being remodeled. The thrifty Hindenburg had been unwilling to have the work done until he was told that the beams were so worm-eaten the building could soon collapse.

and with no more parliamentary support than Papen had had. Hindenburg had long been well disposed toward him; the president, sending his New Year's greetings, told him he had enjoyed the quietest Christmas in years and he thanked Schleicher for it.

But outside the presidential sanctuary the country remained in deep trouble. On December 5, the day the Reichstag convened, a news report said that civil war threatened. Communist documents had been discovered with plans for insurrection and instructions on how to fight.[42] In the Reichstag's opening session, the acting president, replacing Clara Zetkin, was a National Socialist, a retired general, Karl Litzmann, who was convinced he, too, had won the battle of Tannenberg for Hindenburg and who in his opening speech declared that Hindenburg was threatened with "the historical curse" of driving the German people to despair and to Bolshevism although a redeemer was at hand. His oration was frequently interrupted by Communist catcalls and yells of "Pfui," and a few days later a pitched battle was fought in the Reichstag between Communists and National Socialists, where heavy fixtures and telephones were ripped out of their fastenings, and cuspidors, chairs, bronze ashtrays, desks—anything that could be picked up was hurled at the enemy. Similar brawls with more conventional weapons such as guns took place on the outside, where Communists and Nazis continued to battle, and dead and wounded were counted on both sides. And the plight of the population showed little sign of improvement, although the economy was said to be better. One person out of three, a Munich paper asking for contributions on their behalf reminded its readers, was in deep distress, and the sad advertisements continued their own tale of woe. "Help me," one man wrote in an advertisement in the *Münchner Neueste Nachrichten.* "Who can give a married man in deepest need work of any kind? I am a young man of good family with good references." The same paper had pictures of two children going to school barefoot in mid-December in a frigid town in Bavaria.[43]

Then on January 15 one of those political happenings took place whose significance was almost entirely symbolic. Elections were held in the tiny *Land* of Lippe-Detmold with 163,000 inhabitants and about 100,000 voters. The National Socialists could afford to campaign in a state the size of Lippe, and they threw in all their forces. Hitler spoke sixteen times in various localities there, promising land for the farmers but not, as he said Schleicher proposed, providing it by driving farmers off the land.*

As a result the National Socialists got some 6,000 more votes than the 33,038 they had polled in the November election. They received 39,065

* Schleicher had proposed nothing of the sort; he wanted to divide bankrupt estates into small and, as he hoped, profitable farms.

votes, 39.6 percent of the total, not as many as they had polled in July, when they received over 42,000 votes, but enough to claim a great moral victory. An increase of 6,000 votes was not huge, but it was blown up as a mighty sign of the resurgence of the party and the yearning of the German people to see it in power. Added to everything else, it also marked the beginning of the end of Schleicher's chancellorship.*

After the Hitler-Papen meeting, Hindenburg might well have agreed with Schleicher that Papen had gone too far in his discussions with Hitler in Cologne, but he could not have welcomed Schleicher's asking him not to meet again with Papen except in his, Schleicher's, presence. That sounded too much as though the president needed a guardian. At any rate, Papen was able to persuade Hindenburg, despite Schleicher's protest, that the president's long-hoped-for consummation of a Nationalist coalition might be at hand, for the reformed Nazis were willing to govern with other right-wing parties as partners in a parliamentary regime. So Hindenburg told Papen he could continue to negotiate with Hitler, although he had no intention, as he repeatedly told visitors in the course of the next weeks, of appointing Hitler chancellor. Still Papen could continue in his soundings, and Hindenburg, too, would have talks on his own with party leaders.

The meetings that led nowhere continued. On January 11, the president saw Gregor Strasser, a man he liked a good deal better than he did Hitler. But Strasser told him that splitting the National Socialists was out of the question, and Hugenberg, with whom Hindenburg also had a talk, had no solution to offer. The elections in Lippe provided Papen with more ammunition for his campaign with the president. It was like an American or English bye-election, he explained to Hindenburg, a measure of the electorate's current sentiments, which could only be interpreted as pro-Hitler and anti-Schleicher.

The very situation that had allowed Schleicher to topple Papen was repeated in reverse. It was Schleicher who proposed to rule by emergency decree against the combined forces of Communists, National Socialists, and Social Democrats. The German Nationals rejected Schleicher's land reforms; the Center and the splinter parties were as likely to oppose as to support him. Hitler knew very well that it was now or never if he was to win the chancellorship. Hindenburg was the aging giant astride his path. He had already conquered Papen; if he could win over the president's son and Meissner, no one close to the president would be left to strengthen Hindenburg's resistance.

Hitler sent Joachim von Ribbentrop, the son-in-law of the owner of the

---

*The German Nationals were down, as were the Communists, but the Social Democrats increased their vote from 25,782 to 29,827. (Ernst Deuerlein, *Der Aufstieg der NSDAP 1919–1933 in Augenzeugenberichten*, p. 415; *Schulthess' Europäischer Geschichtskalender* 1933, p. 20.)

Henkell champagne vineyards firm, a not very well known but devoted party member, to Papen asking him to come to a meeting at the Ribbentrops' villa in Dahlem, a residential suburb of Berlin. Oskar von Hindenburg and Otto Meissner were also invited, and again the most elaborate precautions for secrecy were taken. Young Hindenburg and Meissner, while attending a performance at the State Opera, slipped out of their box in the darkness. They took a taxi to Dahlem, got out some distance from Ribbentrop's house, and walked the rest of the way in the snow. Hitler was already on hand, and while they were gratefully warming up with the help of Henkell champagne passed by liveried servants (Hitler drank only mineral water), Hitler suddenly rose and asked Oskar to accompany him to an adjacent room. The versions of what took place during their talk include the possibility that Hitler threatened to expose the "Neudeck scandal," the terms under which the president and then Oskar had been given the family property without payment of taxes. It is not a likely story; Hitler had much sharper weapons than threats to use on Oskar. Besides, there was nothing illegal or scandalous in the Neudeck story. The disclosures of fraud in East Prussian land grants involving the squandering of millions of marks by some large landowners never touched the Hindenburgs.*

Although little is known of what was said during the hour that Hitler and Oskar von Hindenburg spent alone, a good idea of the Hitlerian strategy may be gained from Meissner.[44] While Hitler and Oskar were closeted together, Meissner and Göring had a talk, during which a jovial, thigh-slapping Göring assured Meissner that the party had no idea of demanding full governmental powers. It had never asked for that, said Göring, and did not ask for it now. To rescue the Fatherland, he solemnly promised, the party would work together with the other Nationalist parties; the National Socialists would rigidly respect the constitution and would govern only according to law. Furthermore, they asked for only two ministries in a twelve-man cabinet—foreign affairs and defense. The modesty of the proposals took away Meissner's breath; he wasn't sure he had heard right. "Only two?" he asked. "Two," Göring repeated, thumping his chest for emphasis. Furthermore, the Führer was ready to accept any tenable conditions if only "the self-understood, justified and essential demand was met—the chancellorship."[45] And then,

---

* One friend of Hindenburg's, Elard von Oldenburg-Januschau, had been granted a loan of 610,000 marks, 400,000 marks of which he had already received. He had said, in making his claim, it was to be spent for the purpose of aiding his bee culture, but he actually used the 400,000 marks for acquiring more land. Other large landowners had used the government funds to bail out their bankrupt estates, for holiday trips to the Riviera, or for buying racehorses or automobiles. Many proprietors who did not indulge themselves in such luxuries nevertheless took the money as a providential windfall to enable them to maintain a comfortable standard of living without having to cut down on their expenses. (Friedrich Martin Fiederlein, *Der deutsche Osten und die Regierungen Brüning, Papen, Schleicher.*)

said Göring, the reforms the National Socialists had in mind would culminate in a restoration of the monarchy, which Hitler knew was close to the president's heart. But this goal, he made clear, could be reached only through the National Socialists.

It was therefore a prospectus for an orderly, cooperative, and transitional government under Adolf Hitler that was being offered. Meissner was thunderstruck by Göring's temperate proposals, but says he remained skeptical. As he drove back to Berlin with Oskar, he hoped the president's son would tell him what Hitler had said, but Oskar was long silent. Then he spoke only to say: "I'm afraid we won't be able to get around this Hitler. He's making so many concessions and gives so many promises that you no longer know on what grounds he could be turned down."[46] Meissner could only agree with him. This meeting, too, despite all the elaborate precautions, was not secret. Early the next morning Schleicher telephoned Meissner and asked him how the talks with Hitler had gone.

The president's last defenses were crumbling. His most trusted advisors, his son, his state secretary, Papen—all were either resigned to Hitler's chancellorship or, in the case of Papen, actively campaigning for it. And Schleicher himself did little to help. The Reichstag had been due to convene on January 24, but the Elders' Council had postponed the date until the thirty-first.* What Schleicher asked of Hindenburg because he had no reliable support in the Reichstag was once more full powers to govern by decree; and in addition, because little political support for him was in prospect among the electorate, he asked the president to postpone the Reichstag elections indefinitely. He needed time to put his plans for social reform and for the economy into practice, but above all he needed time to outmaneuver the Hitler-Papen coup. What he was asking of Hindenburg, however, would have been just as unconstitutional as it was when Papen had made the same demand of the president and had been refused.

The Reichstag could be dissolved by presidential order, but elections could not constitutionally be postponed indefinitely. Hitler knew either from Papen or from another source that Schleicher had not received the dissolution order from the president, and if Schleicher could not dissolve the Reichstag, all Hitler had to do was continue to hold his line until Papen, Meissner, the president's son, and the need to take action forced Hindenburg to accept his modest proposals.

Without the threat of a dissolution order, and with Schleicher isolated, there was no need for Hitler to make concessions or deals. There would be no new elections the party could not afford, and the chancellorship

---

* The Elders' Council was an intraparliamentary group with the authority to set the time of meetings of the Reichstag when it was not in session.

must fall into his lap. And yet two-thirds of the electorate had not voted for him, and even his part-time allies had few doubts about the true face of the National Socialists. In a statement issued on January 24, the leaders of the German Nationals addressing their organizations in the *Länder* clearly evidenced their lack of enthusiasm.

In the event of new elections, they instructed German National speakers, they should bear in mind the cases where the National Socialists had placed in office incompetents or men who acted only from narrow party interests; the cases in which their officials, especially *Länder* ministers, had used questionable methods either because of lack of knowledge or because of their one-sided views; the cases in which the National Socialists had made propagandistic proposals that it was known in advance could not be carried out or whose purpose was only to compete with Communists and Social Democrats to sharpen the class warfare; the cases where the National Socialists by their votes had acted contrary to their propagandistic positions or to what they had said they stood for in Parliament; the cases where National Socialist deputies or communal representatives had taken part in acts of violence with ashtrays, cuspidors, etc.; and finally the cases where Nazi representatives or leaders had participated within or outside their parliamentary tasks in dubious transactions including embezzlement.[47]

If the dishonesty and duplicity of the National Socialists was that patent to their allies, and the president refused to appoint Hitler chancellor, it seemed as though Schleicher might indeed, with an order of dissolution, force Hitler to some kind of compromise. Hitler had already modified his demands for complete power, or seemingly so, and he could not afford to have a new election unless he was already in office, with government funds at his disposal.

But in a series of separate talks Hindenburg had with Schleicher and Papen between January 26 and January 28, Hindenburg refused to do what either Schleicher or Papen wanted. He would not give Schleicher the presidential decree he asked for, and he would not name Hitler chancellor. Weary, not in the best of health, and sometimes confused, Hindenburg was at a loss how to proceed. Very likely he wanted Papen back as chancellor and kept hoping that might be worked out. Schleicher had cast a wide net to find support in Strasser, in Hugenberg and his German Nationals, in the unions, and in the Social Democrat party, and he had failed. Strasser could bring neither himself nor any National Socialists into his cabinet, Hugenberg regarded Schleicher as a socialist, Schleicher dismissed Hugenberg as a reactionary, and the Socialists and trade unionists refused to cooperate in what they considered a military dictatorship. Schleicher's only way out was to obtain full governing powers from Hindenburg and meet Papen and the National Socialists head-on. He had tried everything else; all that was left was to make a final assault on the enemy while accepting the risk of losing not only the battle but the war.

Hindenburg asked Meissner if he could, under the constitution, issue the dissolution order and postpone the elections. Meissner said that would be unconstitutional. Elections had to be held within sixty days of a dissolution order; otherwise a government would be able to rule indefinitely by decree. Hindenburg said that was what he had thought, and the stage was set for the showdown.

On the morning of January 28, Schleicher held a cabinet meeting at which he expressed the opinion that an even greater danger than the appointment of Hitler would be a Papen-Hugenberg cabinet with the overwhelming majority of the country opposed to it. That would lead to a crisis in the state and the presidency. Konstantin von Neurath and Finance Minister Schwerin-Krosigk agreed. Krosigk said he saw the danger of a Papen-Hugenberg government as even more serious than did the chancellor, and he suggested that Schleicher propose that Hindenburg seek the objective opinion of other cabinet members—Neurath, for example.[48]

When Neurath said he'd gladly tell the president what he thought about the peril of a Papen-Hugenberg cabinet, Schleicher went off to make his last pitch to Hindenburg. He left his cabinet meeting at 12:10 for his talk with Hindenburg. Twenty-five minutes later he was back again to tell the cabinet he and they had to resign.

Only three possibilities remained, he had told the president. Hitler could be named chancellor in a cabinet based on a parliamentary majority, or he could be a minority chancellor in another presidential cabinet, or the present government could continue in office with full powers to govern and the president's promise the Reichstag would be dissolved when it next met. The last choice could be made only if Hindenburg did not abide by the letter of the law; however, he would be justified in the technical illegality, because the country was in a crisis the constitution had not foreseen. Schleicher also warned against a Papen-Hugenberg cabinet, a government, as he said, based on one party—the German Nationals—that would have nine-tenths of the population opposed to it. Whatever happened, he told Hindenburg, the post of defense minister must not go to a National Socialist; such an appointment would imperil the integrity of the Reichswehr.[49]

According to one account,* he also told the president that the Communist party, the SA, and the SS had to be dissolved and the Reich thereby secured from tyranny and destruction. Force had to be used; dangerous radicals—above all, men like Goebbels—had to be arrested;

---

* By Hans Otto Meissner, the son of Hindenburg's state secretary, who according to his publishers had been given documents and confidential information by his father. (Hans Otto Meissner and Harry Wilde, *Die Machtergreifung*.)

and if they resisted, the police and the Reichswehr had to be called in. If the president did not agree, then he, Schleicher, must put his office at Hindenburg's disposal. Hindenburg's reply was the same he had made two months before to Papen: he could not, in his old age, agree to any course that might lead to civil war and bloodshed. And then he added: "Soon, I will stand before the Eternal Judge, and He will tell me whether or not I've done the right thing. No one here can tell me that."[50] Schleicher thereupon said he would resign, and the battle was over and lost.

Meissner thought Schleicher had had one other option; he might have continued in office for another sixty days before new elections would be held had he asked the president only for the dissolution order, and Meissner asked him why he had not chosen to attempt that. In answer, Schleicher merely shrugged his shoulders. Apparently he had decided it was all or nothing. He had made up his mind to force the president to choose once and for all between him and Papen and Hitler. He remained as defense minister, but only for a day. The *Tägliche Rundschau*, the newspaper he subsidized, published an article saying a Papen cabinet with full powers would shake the position of the president and lead to a catastrophe. Hindenburg was indignant when he read the article, just after Schleicher had told him he would resign as chancellor. He was certain that Schleicher was behind the piece and was again instructing him on his duties, and he would therefore not have him in anyone's cabinet.

When Papen came to see the president, as Schleicher left, Hindenburg was at the end of his resistance. The two men went over the alternatives again, but seemingly there remained only one—Hitler as chancellor, with two cabinet seats for members of his party, though who they would be was as yet undetermined. Papen had already explained to the president how Hitler was to be kept under control: Papen would always be present—Hindenburg had insisted on that—when the president received Hitler; as vice-chancellor Papen would have a considerable influence on decisions, and he, together with Hugenberg, Neurath, and the other conservatives, would contain the National Socialists. The last weapons were struck from Hindenburg's hand. Reluctantly he asked Papen: "Then I have the unpleasant duty to name this Hitler as chancellor?" and Papen nodded.[51] It was Papen's triumph, too. "We have hired Hitler," he said; it was he and the other conservatives, he was convinced, who had the Führer in tow. "What do you want?" he asked a conservative critic, Ewald von Kleist-Schmenzin. "I have Hindenburg's confidence. In two months we'll have driven Hitler so far into a corner that he'll squeak."[52]

As the president's confidential representative, a few hours after his meeting with Hindenburg, Papen set out on his talks with party leaders to round up the members of the new cabinet. Two days before Schleicher's resignation, he had already met with Seldte and Duesterberg, the Stahlhelm leaders, to invite them to join the coming Hitler-Papen government. Duesterberg had refused, warning Papen against "the dynamism of Hitler's nature and the fanaticism of his mass movement," but Seldte accepted as did Hugenberg. Hitler was no threat, Hugenberg said, since Papen would be vice-chancellor and he himself minister of economics, with Seldte as minister of labor. "We will surround Hitler," Hugenberg told them; it was an illusion he shared with Papen.[53]

Papen met with Hugenberg again on the twenty-eighth, and the leader of the German Nationals had news for him. He said that the German Nationals also expected two seats in the cabinet and that Hitler now wanted to lead a presidential cabinet, not one based on parliamentary support, which would have made him dependent on the vote of the German Nationals in the Reichstag. An hour later, Papen received Hitler, who, convinced nothing could stop him, raised his price; he asked not only for the Ministries of Defense and Interior for the National Socialists but also for the Reichscommissariat of Prussia, the equivalent of minister-president of the *Land*, and for the Prussian Ministry of Interior. This office had under it the well-trained Prussian police. It was a post Hindenburg had expected Papen to hold again. Papen was taken aback and asked Hitler ironically if he was otherwise satisfied with Hindenburg's proposals. Hitler airily replied that he had only one last condition—that the other ministers designated by the president should consider themselves bound by no party. Papen next met with the leader of the Bavarian Volksparty, Fritz Schäffer, to ask him if he would join a Hitler-Papen cabinet. Schäffer declared himself willing to enter a Hitler government but said his party would under no circumstances support a Papen cabinet.[54]

On January 26 or 27, one or two days before Schleicher quit, Hindenburg had received two other visitors, General von dem Bussche-Ippenburg, who was accustomed to make his weekly report on troop personnel problems to the president, joined this time by the chief of the Reichswehr, Hammerstein-Equord. Precisely what was said is uncertain, because the accounts of what went on either were written after Hitler had consolidated his power and anyone in the Reich who opposed his chancellorship would have been foolhardly to admit it, or they appeared after his downfall, when witnesses were anxious to demonstrate how they had always been against him. A number of reports on the meeting have appeared, but of the three people present only two, Hammerstein and Bussche, wrote their versions of what was said, and they contradict one another. Hindenburg was silent. The other stories are based on hearsay.*

---

* Hans Otto Meissner has written that Generals von Hammerstein-Equord and Stülpnagel (not Bussche) went to see the president and told him that the officer corps and the troops were greatly disturbed over developments and that the dismissal of Schleicher as Reichschancellor and defense minister would be untenable for the

Hammerstein wrote in January 1935 that he had visited the president to oppose the possibility of a Papen-Hugenberg cabinet, above all because the National Socialists would not take part in it and the army would face a civil population overwhelmingly against such a government. Also, Hammerstein wrote, he and Schleicher were agreed that only Hitler could be the next Reichschancellor. Hindenburg had been irritated at this attempt to exert "political influence" on the part of a general, but he made clear he had no intention of appointing Hitler.[55] Hammerstein's memorandum, however, was written at a time when it would have been very dangerous to say anything very different. One German general close to Hammerstein, Kurt von Schleicher,* and his wife had just been assassinated on Hitler's orders. And Hammerstein's account is contradicted by von dem Bussche, who was well out of range of Hitler when in 1952 he described what had happened.

Von dem Bussche in his account does not mention Papen. He says Hammerstein warned Hindenburg categorically against the appointment of Hitler. Sensing what they had come for, Hindenburg received them bruskly and told them if his generals did not obey, he would dismiss them. Hammerstein had smilingly assured him of the army's devotion and obedience, whereupon Hindenburg had relaxed and listened as Hammerstein told him he had serious objections to a possible Hitler chancellorship; Hitler's extremism could lead to disintegration in the Reichswehr and crass disobedience in the troops. Hindenburg had then said, "You cannot for one moment, gentlemen, imagine that I intend to appoint that Austrian corporal Reichschancellor."[56]

There are inconsequential points of difference; Hammerstein says the meeting took place on the morning of January 26 and Bussche says it took place on the twenty-seventh. Other differences are more substantial. While Hammerstein wrote that he and Bussche warned Hindenburg against a Papen-Hugenberg cabinet, about which rumors were afloat,

---

army. Whereupon Hindenburg is said to have risen from his chair in anger and said: "I know what is tenable for the Reichswehr and I forbid any instruction on the part of you gentlemen. . . . It would really be better if you concerned yourselves less with politics and more with the training of your troops." (Hans Otto Meissner and Harry Wilde, *Die Machtergreifung*, pp. 178–79.)

Schwerin von Krosigk tells a similar story. Hammerstein, he says, went to Hindenburg to warn him against appointing Hitler, whereupon Hindenburg said, "You'd do better to concern yourself with the autumn maneuvers." (Lutz Graf Schwerin von Krosigk, *Es Geschah in Deutschland*, p. 113.)

The British Ambassador to Berlin, Sir Eric Phipps, who had good sources of information, reported to London in the same vein. He said that Hammerstein urged Hindenburg to retain Schleicher and not to appoint Hitler. Phipps also reported that Hammerstein was ready to use force to suppress the Hitler movement and restore constitutional government. (E. L. Woodward and Rohan Butler, eds., *Documents on British Foreign Policy 1919–1939*, Second Series, vol. 6, 1933–1934, p. 266.)

* Schleicher, too, who certainly had been aware of his precarious situation, wrote a letter to the *Vossische Zeitung* on January 30, 1934, saying that since the summer of 1932 he had been in favor of a National Socialist government.

Bussche said that they were concerned with the possible appointment of Hitler and that Hammerstein used strong language in stating the objections to Hitler's candidacy. What Hammerstein and Bussche agree on is that Hindenburg told them he had no intention of making Hitler chancellor.

The conflicting stories, however, are not irreconcilable if they are placed in context. Although Hammerstein earlier had favorable words for Hitler, he had become increasingly hostile to him. He was the general who had said the SA should not only be dissolved, it should be stood against the wall; who had said he could sleep at night now that he knew the army would obey his orders to shoot at the Brown Shirts if necessary. He also said he could not believe the German people would ever elect such a fool as Hitler chancellor. There is no question of Hammerstein's aversion to Hitler; years later, in 1939, he was prepared to arrest him if he visited the area of Hammerstein's command at Cologne, and the only reason he did not was that Hitler failed to appear.[57] Hitler himself was aware of Hammerstein's feelings; talking about his generals in 1942, he said Hammerstein had told him the Reichswehr would not accept him under any circumstances as chancellor.[58] Hammerstein was an enemy who had hated him and had to be dismissed, but Hitler admitted he had good political sense. It is therefore most unlikely that Hammerstein went to see Hindenburg solely to persuade him to make Hitler chancellor.*

Bussche, writing almost twenty years later, says they talked to Hindenburg about Hitler; he does not say they did not discuss Papen. The generals knew, of course, that Papen had been trying to convince Hindenburg to appoint a duumvirate of himself and Hitler, and they also knew that Hindenburg would have liked, above all, to have Papen back at his old post without Hitler. So it was not impossible that the rumors about the president's appointing a Papen-Hugenberg cabinet excluding the National Socialists had substance, and therefore Hammerstein warned Hindenburg both against taking such a dangerous step and against making Hitler chancellor. He and the Reichswehr undoubtedly wanted Hindenburg to keep Schleicher as chancellor and defense minister—above all as defense minister if the president should appoint Hitler as chancellor.

In his 1935 memorandum, Hammerstein also described a friendly visit to Hitler on January 29, 1933, to reassure himself on Hitler's prospects. He said he and Schleicher feared that the president, despite Hindenburg's continuing negotiations with Hitler, really intended to appoint Papen,

---

* J. W. Wheeler-Bennett, *The Nemesis of Power*, and Wolfgang Sauer (Karl Dietrich Bracher, Wolfgang Sauer, and Gerhard Schulz, *Die nationalsozialistische Machtergreifung*) are among those who believe that Hammerstein was acting on behalf of Schleicher, in favor of Hitler's candidacy, to prevent Papen's appointment.

which would lead to a general strike, if not civil war. Had he been in a position to write more freely, he might have said that he and Schleicher, deeply mistrustful of Hitler, and foreseeing disaster for the Reich if Papen was made chancellor in a cabinet without the National Socialists, wanted neither of them, but Papen even less than Hitler. And ironically, it was Hitler, according to Hammerstein, they turned to, to find out whether the president was conducting serious negotiations with him.

In the atmosphere of Hitler's Reich of 1935, it is not difficult to understand why Hammerstein would want to play down any anti-Hitler sentiments, but he would not have been likely to invent his visit to Hitler and their subsequent conversation. Certainly Hitler knew whether he and Hammerstein had met and what they talked about.

In the last days of January, it was another rumor that precipitated the installation of the Hitler cabinet, a rumor with some actual substance, that the Army High Command planned an action against Hindenburg himself in order to determine the choice of chancellor. The rumor of Schleicher's plan for a putsch was widespread. The story appeared in the *London Daily Express* and was picked up by the German papers that the Potsdam garrison had been placed in a state of alert by Schleicher, and that he and the generals were preparing to arrest Hindenburg and take over the government.[59]

On the face of it, the rumor seems to be the legend that German historians have called it. The notion of the chiefs of the Reichswehr calling on the troops to arrest their commander in chief and the Reich's greatest war hero seems nothing if not preposterous. How would the other generals in the Reichswehr Ministry and the field commanders react to such an order, and what could it lead to but civil war? Bussche, Hammerstein, and Schleicher all denied that anything of the kind ever happened. Hammerstein wrote in his memorandum of 1935 that Schleicher and the Reichswehr could not have attempted a coup without him and that he would never have made one. Schleicher immediately wrote a letter to the *Berliner Zeitung am Mittag* flatly denying the rumor, and Bussche said there had been no such plot.

There was, however, some color to the story. A reliable eyewitness, Colonel Ott, later told how in the Defense Ministry on January 26 or 27 a meeting took place of himself, Schleicher, Hammerstein, State Secretary Planck, General von Bredow, and Major Marcks of the Press Bureau in the Reichswehr Ministry. Hammerstein, in the course of the discussion, suggested they present Hindenburg with an ultimatum telling him he must not appoint Hitler chancellor; if Hindenburg refused they should declare a state of military emergency. The suggestion was dropped for the time when Schleicher opposed it.[60]

But that was not the end of the matter. At a meeting a few days later, on January 29, in Hammerstein's office, attended by Generals Adam, von dem Bussche, and von Hammerstein, Schleicher, certain now that Hindenburg was going to appoint Hitler, said resignedly there seemed nothing else to do but to remain loyal to the president. One of the other generals present said there was another possibility—they could take action against Hindenburg, but that suggestion was briefly discussed and then discarded. As they were leaving the room, Colonel von Reichenau met them at the door with the remark that Hindenburg should be arrested; von dem Bussche answered "Nonsense," and that was the end of it. No orders ever reached the Potsdam garrison or any other troop centers.*

Nevertheless, we have one more interesting sidelight on the state of mind of the people involved. On the evening of January 29, Erwin Planck, Schleicher's state secretary, telephoned a friend to tell him the Potsdam garrison was ready to march if Hindenburg, under the influence of Papen or Oskar von Hindenburg, should appoint Hitler chancellor. This would be done "in order to protect the president against his councillors."[61] Planck, who was devoted to Schleicher and knew a good deal of the way Schleicher's mind worked, obviously had heard the rumors and believed them. So the kernel of truth in the putsch stories seems to lie in the fact that the generals did discuss the possibility of placing Hindenburg in a kind of protective custody to seal him off from his evil councillors, in much the same way hyperpatriotic Japanese officers at the end of World War II considered kidnapping the emperor, who, on the advice of his ministers, was going to make peace.

The Potsdam garrison was never alerted, the march on Berlin never ordered, but Papen and Hitler were convinced they had been. A member of the Herren Club, Werner von Alvensleben,† who had close connections with the Nazis, had also been in touch with Hammerstein and Schleicher, who could make use of him in keeping up with events on the swift-moving political merry-go-round. In the course of a conversation with Alvensleben, either Hammerstein or Schleicher had said that Hindenburg was no longer in full possession of his faculties and that he was likely to bring about a presidential crisis. Alvensleben, thereupon drawing his own conclusions, told Hitler and a group of his followers at a meeting

---

* During the Nuremberg trial, Hermann Göring told Papen's lawyer, Egon Kubuschok, that Schleicher, in an attempt to keep the post of defense minister, had offered to call out the Potsdam troops to arrest Hindenburg if he persisted in his refusal to name Hitler chancellor. Göring was given to tall stories, and the chief of the Berlin Political Police, Rudolf Diels (whose first wife was a sister of Göring's), reported that Göring had telephoned him to find out whether the rumor was true that Schleicher had called on the Potsdam garrison to march on Berlin. Diels said he had been able to assure Göring that the story was false. The Göring story is not convincing; Schleicher, as Diels pointed out later, was one of the chief objects of Nazi hatred, as was evidenced by his assassination the next year.

† A brother of the president of the Herren Club, Bodo von Alvensleben.

in Goebbels's apartment in Berlin that army contingents were mobilizing and on their way to arrest Hindenburg and Papen, along with Hitler and the new cabinet members. It was probably Alvensleben's report, made in the late afternoon of January 29, that instigated Göring's telephone call to Police President Diels, but Diels's answer that there was nothing in the rumor reassured no one.

Papen declared that Schleicher was playing his last card, and that if the new government were not sworn in by eleven o'clock the next morning, the thirtieth, there would be a military dictatorship under Schleicher and Hammerstein. Meissner, too, was alarmed; he had been awakened by a telephone call at two in the morning with word that Schleicher planned to arrest him and Oskar von Hindenburg.[62] They were all convinced now that the rumor was true; when Duesterberg saw a sentry posted in front of Oskar von Hindenburg's door, he was unsure whether the guard was there to protect Oskar or to keep him in custody. Oskar von Hindenburg himself was certain that Schleicher was guilty of high treason; what his father thought is not known, although he took the reports of a putsch calmly.

Hindenburg, in any event, had acted on January 29. Schleicher, he had decided, could not be defense minister in the new cabinet, and after considering a list of possibilities, he chose General Werner von Blomberg, who was serving as the military representative of the Reich at the disarmament conference in Geneva. Blomberg was a curious choice if Hindenburg had in mind balancing Hitler with a strong-minded defense minister. Blomberg was one of the few pro-Nazi generals in the Reichswehr. Brüning said in 1931 he was the only one, and he had suggested to Groener that Blomberg be dismissed, because the general was suffering from a nervous disorder after a bad fall from a horse. But Hindenburg summoned Blomberg by telegram to come immediately to Berlin, and after a fourteen-hour trip he arrived at the Anhalter railroad station at 8:00 A.M. on January 30 with no notion of what was awaiting him. What was awaiting him was interesting enough. Schleicher had had word of the Hindenburg telegram, and two representatives of his superiors were awaiting Blomberg. One was the president's son Oskar, in civilian clothes; the other an adjutant of Hammerstein's, Major Adolf Kuntzen, in military uniform.

Oskar von Hindenburg had orders to bring Blomberg directly to the president so he could be sworn in before any putschists could arrest him. Major Kuntzen was to bring Blomberg directly to Hammerstein in the Defense Ministry, where he could be briefed on the dangers of a Papen-Hugenberg cabinet.[63]

But Hindenburg was commander in chief of the armed forces, and since Major Kuntzen could scarcely disobey an order of the president,

Blomberg dutifully followed Oskar. When they arrived at the Reichs-chancellory, the president briefly explained the situation and promptly swore in Blomberg as minister of defense.

Thus at 9:00 A.M., Blomberg became a member of Hitler's cabinet before Hitler became Reichschancellor. Meissner then informed Schlei-cher over the telephone that Blomberg had taken his place as defense minister, and Blomberg himself was advised not to go to the Ministry of Defense, where he ran the risk of being arrested. The situation was so confused that at this point, only two hours before the new cabinet was to be sworn in, both the foreign minister, Neurath, and the finance minister, Krosigk, still believed Hindenburg might want to appoint a Papen-Hugenberg cabinet, and they decided between them they would resist any "moral pressure" to agree to it.[64] And as the members of the new cabinet began to assemble, Duesterberg, who had come to witness the ceremonies, joined Seldte in the Chancellory gardens. There they told Blomberg that in order to keep complete authority out of Hitler's hands, he must see to it that the Prussian police should not under any circumstances come under the control of the National Socialists.

One last scene of distemper in the National front had still to be played out. As the members of the Hitler cabinet gathered in Meissner's office, it seemed that the last roadblocks had been levelled. The dispute over Göring's becoming Reichscommissar for Prussia had been compromised. Göring would be Reichsminister without portfolio, Reichscommissar for airways, and in addition minister of the interior for Prussia; Frick would be minister of the interior for the Reich; Neurath would remain as foreign minister and Krosigk as finance minister; Hugenberg would be minister of economics; and Seldte would be minister of labor. But it was not to be that easy. Hitler, irked at Göring's having to give up the post of Reichscommissar for Prussia, suddenly declared that his government had to be confirmed by a popular plebiscite. Hugenberg, who knew that in any such vote the German Nationals would suffer defeat, categorically refused. But Hitler, who now had his repertory of conciliation at the tip of his tongue, promised Hugenberg he would never separate himself from the gentlemen present; they would remain at his side, elections or no elections. Papen, with the alleged Schleicher putsch heavily on his mind, added his voice. "Who can doubt the solemn word of honor of a German man?" he demanded of Hugenberg. Also, he pointed out, new elections would be bound to lead to the consolidation of the conservative bloc; and in any event, the cabinet could safely leave the entire question of the dissolution of the Reichstag and the calling of new elections to Hinden-burg.[65]

Hugenberg was under the impression that what Papen was saying was that Hindenburg would decide whether new elections were to be held at all, but what Papen had in mind was no more than securing the president's approval of the dissolution order. The points of view were never to be reconciled.

Meanwhile, Hindenburg was waiting in an adjoining room to administer the oath of office, and Meissner, for one, was fearful that the old gentleman, who did not like to be kept waiting, might leave before the swearing-in ceremonies were held. The crisis was resolved by a bewildered Hugenberg's filing in with the others to accept his post in the belief that he was also awaiting Hindenberg's decision on the elections. Thus at 11:15 A.M., fifteen minutes late, the cabinet finally appeared before the president, and there Hitler solemnly swore to uphold the constitution he had come to destroy. When the ceremony was over, the president said: "And now, gentlemen, forward with God!"

It was Ludendorff, though, who was a good deal closer to the realities when he wrote two days later to Hindenburg, on February 1, 1933: "By naming Hitler as Reichschancellor, you have delivered up our holy Fatherland to one of the greatest demagogues of all time. I solemnly prophesy to you that this accursed man will plunge our Reich into the abyss and bring our nation into inconceivable misery. Because of what you have done, coming generations will curse you in your grave."[66]

And on the night of the thirtieth, as the delirious Nazis celebrated the historic occasion with a torchlight march past the Reichschancellory, reviewed from adjoining windows by Hitler and the president, the story was told that Hindenburg, watching the columns of Brown Shirts, said, "I didn't realize we had captured so many Russian prisoners." The tale is undoubtedly another legend, but *"si non è vero è ben' trovato."* The old gentleman had lived past his time.

CHAPTER 10

Conclusion:
The Happening

I**T HAD BEEN** a long journey from Linz and the streets of Vienna to the window next to where Hindenburg looked down on the marching Brown Shirts with their burning torches. But the pace of the latter part of the trip had been a good deal faster than that of the earlier stretches. After ten years of invective and exhortation, Hitler had persuaded only 2.6 percent of the German electorate to vote for him while over 97 percent still ignored or rejected him. Then in the space of two years, the percentage of men and women who wanted him as Reichschancellor rose to 18, and in two years more to 37, and then back to 33. Nothing had changed in the hot gospel Hitler was preaching; he was the same man who had roused the faithful to transports of rapture in the early twenties; he still said the same things and made the same promises. Nothing had changed in his style either. The hoarse voice, the bathetic poses, the mannerisms that seemed so absurd to outsiders, the flow of oratory—all were the same, except that in the early days he was talking to himself and his nondescript disciples, and now he was talking to one-third of the German people. The man who looked to jaundiced eyes like "a marriage swindler," "a stigmatized headwaiter," or a beach photographer at a seedy resort came to appear as a knight in splendid armor, the true *Führer*, as he was widely called after Landsberg,* to be painted before long astride a white charger fully accoutred for his mission of salvation of the Germanic world.

When Hitler spoke to the Industry Club at Düsseldorf in January

---

* The word was used as early as 1921 by the younger men around Hitler: Hess, Rosenberg, Esser.

1932,[1] he did not deviate by a hair from his statement of principles in *Mein Kampf*. He merely orchestrated his variety of themes for the occasion. He did not mention Jews, but he denounced the Bolsheviks and the levelling of the democratic process to where the authority of personality was degraded. He said not Versailles was responsible for the woes of the Reich but, rather, the men who were responsible for Versailles. It was an artful pitch, well designed for the occasion, but few of those present would have listened a little while back.

The emotional core of Hitler's crusade was anti-Semitism, but in 1928 Hitler had been just as anti-Semitic as he was in 1932 or a decade after that, when, in late 1941, the extermination camps began their work. Yet in 1928 only 810,000 Germans out of an electorate of over 30 million voted for the National Socialists; they elected 11 delegates out of 481. It was an achievement not much more striking than that of the anti-Semitic parties in the Wilhelminian Reich, who in 1912, after thirty years of campaigning, elected 6 deputies to the Reichstag, where they had to surrender any pretensions of forming a power bloc and were absorbed into the Conservative party.

If Hitler was the drummer whose beat served to rouse the slumbering anti-Semitism in the breasts of the German people, he should have been more of a success at the time of the Räte republics, when Jews had been well represented in the revolutionary governments and when Rosa Luxemburg and Karl Liebknecht were murdered by impassioned nationalists. But for years the anti-Semites remained a ragged fringe at the outermost edge of the German society and politics. The spontaneous outpourings of public sorrow on the death of Rathenau in 1922 were an indication of what little effect the anti-Semitic propaganda was having, an indication that was confirmed in the Reichstag election of 1924, when the National Socialists got less than two million votes, but almost three times as many as they would receive four years later.

In many ways Nazism was antithetical to what the great mass of Germans said they admired and certainly to what they paid homage. It was noisy, undisciplined, vainglorious; its leader was a half-educated posturing foreigner; and where the general staff with its spare Prussian tradition prescribed anonymity, "to be rather than to seem," the National Socialists could thrive only on what post-Stalinists would call the "cult of personality," on the omniscient leader making all the decisions. Germans had been portrayed by critics other than Price Collier as requiring the codification of everything, the spelling out of minute rules and regulations so nothing would be left to chance, the unpredictable whims of the citizenry, or some official's, judge's, or politician's interpretations. For a decade the National Socialists were regarded as hoodlums, as part of the breakdown of what had been, if anything, an excessively orderly society before, in cities like Berlin, the taboos were all broken, and a time of intellectual and anti-intellectual ferment with its license and creativity replaced the classic styles. The movement was a caricature of what many foreigners regarded as peculiarly German characteristics. The ludicrous invention of titles to distinguish any kind of position gave rise in the SS and SA to *Herr Obersturmbannführer, Herr Obergruppenführer, Herr Hauptsturmführer, Herr Hauptscharführer*, and on and on. Some of the titles could be shortened to produce military abbreviations like OSAF for the *Oberster SA Führer*; *Adj. Gaust.*, for the adjutant of a *Gausturm*; *Gruf.*, for a *Gruppenführer*. The conviction of German racial and ethnic superiority expressed in a saying like *Am deutschen Wesen soll die Welt genesen* degenerated into the encapsulated forms of *Herrenrasse* ("master race") for Aryans and *Untermenschen* ("subhumans") for Jews, Slavs, and other non-Aryans. The tests of courage and masculinity dramatized in student duels with resulting face slashes worn as lifelong badges of honor degenerated into the slugging of political opponents that was so highly esteemed by Hitler and his lieutenants.

Politically, though, after the postwar convulsions the country remained at, or near, the center. The SPD, for all its Marxist streaks, was a party of hardworking, far-from-Communist wage earners who with leaders like Ebert and Severing believed in reform, not revolution; the Center was a Christian, mainly Catholic party led by men like Brüning; the Conservatives and Nationalists were divided between the Kapps, who were sure they could restore the good old days on the bayonets of the army, and the Reinhardts, who would have used the army's bayonets against them. From 1923 to 1929 the Reich had achieved some kind of political as well a economic and psychological balance. The National Socialists were a negligible political factor. On December 17, 1929, the British ambassador to Germany, Sir Horace Rumbold, wrote: "Until a few weeks ago the German public outside Bavaria and the southern states paid not the slightest attention to Herr Hitler or his doings. It was vaguely known that he was not German at all . . . and that he was the leader of a dwindling party in Bavaria. . . ."[2]

And then what happened happened relatively quickly—in the space of three to four years. The political structure, again subjected to strains that it was not built to withstand, simply collapsed. The Reichstag could not function as a democratic parliament when, as was the case in July 1932, more than half its members were either National Socialists or Communists determined to abolish it. The German society had withstood the shock of the lost war, the exactions and arrogance of the victors, the invasion of the Ruhr and Rhineland; it had survived the inflation and recurrent economic depressions; but the accumulation of all of them was too much. Too much at least for the almost 19 million out of 36.8 million voters who in July 1932 voted for the antirepublican parties of the National Socialists and the Communists. Even that stiff-necked Prussian

General von Seeckt had come by 1930 to believe that a Hitler government was essential, and in 1932 he wrote to his sister advising her to vote National Socialist. This was the same man who had been convinced of the need for a legal, military dictatorship but who, when given dictatorial powers by President Ebert in 1923, had obediently surrendered them after the Hitler putsch was put down. And as he had made clear in his order to the troops on November 9, 1923, he would not have hesitated to use the Reichswehr against Hitler.*

From 1930 on, Hitler collected supporters in big business, banking, and industry who had long regarded him with a cold eye. The converts were men like Schröder, Schacht, Bosch, Krupp, and conservative landowners like Oldenburg-Januschau. Even Reichswehr generals like Hammerstein and Bussche, who continued to dislike and mistrust him, when forced to make hard decisions undoubtedly preferred a Hitler to a Papen cabinet with the promise of civil bloodletting. Above all this was true for Hindenburg. The final choice between appointing Hitler or someone who might be forced to use the Reichswehr against him, was a cruel one for the man who up to two days before he made the appointment had promised he would never do it. But at the end the harassed old gentleman saw no other way out. The political advisors he relied on—Papen, Meissner, and his son—told him he had none: on the one side was the possibility, even the likelihood, of insurrection, and on the other a conciliatory Hitler eager to cooperate, who promised the president quite truly that the election that would follow the dissolution of the Reichstag would be Germany's last. Any other solution seemed bound to bring on uprisings that could be dealt with only by the Reichswehr, and Hindenburg could not tolerate the thought of that. He had never commanded an army to fight against the people it was designed to defend.

More than the political superstructure of the republic had broken down. For half the German people the perception of the past had blurred and the traditional expectations of the future had faded. Hindenburg still retained his stock of copybook maxims, but in order for him to keep Neudeck, his ancestral estate, it had to be presented to him as a gift. Every stratum of the society had been affected by the succession of catastrophes. Stresemann had lamented the attrition of the middle class and its effect on the stability of the Reich, and a few years after his death, what was left of that class was threatened with the loss of the last shreds of their respectability.

In late 1932 the *Münchner Neueste Nachrichten* reminded its readers that one-third of the people of Munich could not live without their charity. What did the old saws, the folk wisdom about the duties of

* It read: "Any unauthorized encroachments on the order of the Reich and of the *Länder* will be put down by the Reichswehr under my command from whatever side they may come." (Francis L. Carsten, *Reichswehr und Politik*, p. 206.)

citizens in a good society have to tell them, or the families of children going to school barefoot in winter, or the men who could not afford a bed in a flophouse and who paid a few pennies to sleep on their feet, their upper bodies hanging over a stretched rope in a long line of misery? Other countries suffered from the black plague of unemployment too, but, as we have seen, none was as badly hit as the Reich, and in no other country did the depression follow on the series of punishing experiences that seemed to have culminated in it.

The farming and industrial societies of Europe had been rooted for centuries in a belief in futurity. Grain, even in times of short harvests, had to be saved to make the next crop, and the story of the ant's providence as against the fecklessness of the grasshopper was the peasant's own story of survival. This was true of all agrarian societies, and when the future became too unpromising, or the exactions of the overlords out of proportion to what the peasants believed they could bear, the result was migration or revolt. With industrialization, savings against a rainy day and the accumulation of capital were the hedge against the uncertainties ahead. If man worked from sun to sun, and woman's work was never done, their work was to provide not only for the day but for the day after.

But very little of this ancient wisdom rang true any longer in Germany. The sacrifices had been for nothing; the sacrifice of life in the war and the years of hunger and privation had led nowhere. The iron discipline that had brought the fighting troops home from the front in good order had been solid evidence of German virtue, but the acceptance of the promises of the distant peacemaker in Washington that the war was being fought, not against the German people, but against their militarist masters, this was eyewash. What the Germans saw after the dust of battle and oratory had settled was the militarism of a foreign power occupying their land and paid for in large part by their own labor. The Allies' solemn promises to disarm themselves, like the promises of self-determination, were no more than a ploy to disarm and carve up Germany. And the excuse for the punitive peace, its justification? That the Germans alone had been responsible for the war, a myth clung to even after the documents released in Moscow told a very different story. As for atrocities, it had not been German troops who fired on unarmed workers in the Krupp factories.

With the aid of statesmen like Stresemann and Briand, such hard fare had been digested and a fresh start made. The Reich had attained a precarious stability. If many ardent Nationalists were still restless, they were not mutinous. Army officers were united on such basic principles as the necessity for revising Versailles and ending one-sided disarmament, and in such matters, and in the belief that a restoration of the *Volk* community would cure the divisiveness of the industrial society, many of the most idealistic among them, especially in junior grades, could agree with the National Socialists.

Scheringer, Ludin, and Wendt were three such. Former members of the Free Corps, they had fought against the Separatists on the Rhine, and despite the Wehrmacht's prohibition against membership in political parties, they had joined the National Socialists because of what they saw as the built-in weakness of the army under the republic. As their trial revealed, they were confused young men much more than they were revolutionary adepts. After their conviction one of them turned Communist, and as proselytizing members of the National Socialist party they had no luck; none of their fellow officers followed them; they were on their own, as far as sentiment in the army was concerned, before and after they were arrested for high treason.

As a whole, the upper ranks of the army were repelled by the bombast, the furor of the Nazis. They had warm sympathy for its nationalism, and the human material of the SA was a cadre that could be properly trained, but they regarded its leadership as unreliable and they had no stomach for private armies. Neither the army nor the traditional nationalists wanted a Hitlerian revolution; what most of them looked forward to was a legal, national revolution, if possible a restoration of the monarchy, a recovery of the reliable past of the Reich with a more admirable kaiser than Wilhelm. Monarchy was their only experience of an orderly society; the republic was the legacy of defeat; it had produced the anarchy of the uprisings and the sterility of the Parliament.

Nevertheless in the twenties, out of the conflicts of Right and Left, the nation of thinkers and poets emerged again in the Bauhaus, the plays, the novels, the science and industry, even in the political leaders of the republic, until the seventh plague, the Great Depression, breached the weakened defenses. The Center had not held. Half the country wanted the extreme solutions it had heretofore rejected.

The Center does not hold in any country forever. Following defeat by an outside enemy or the overaccumulation of internal hostilities, it can disappear quickly and without a trace. The revolutions of the Far Right and the Far Left have not been voted into power; they have been successful either through foreign intervention or domestic collapse when not enough organized energy remains to combat them. Democracy in the twentieth century is still an exception, although the word remains in wide favor, as may be seen in the considerable numbers of Democratic People's Republics.

Communism in Russia—or China—was never established by a popular vote. Only in one country—Czechoslovakia—has it ever come to power by way of duly elected representatives of the nation. In Russia, the Bolsheviks who overthrew the provisional government were a highly motivated, organized, but small minority under a gifted leader promising peace, land, and communality amid the confusions of military defeat. In Italy, the Fascists were never elected to govern. In the Italian Parliament of 1921, there were 31 Fascist deputies out of 535, and in 1919 there had been none. Mussolini became dictator in 1922 in a country that like the Reich saw itself on the verge of collapse. The choices seemed limited to two extremes—either the acceptance of the continuing strikes and the occupation of factories by the Left, or the countermeasures of the militant Right mobilized by the ex-socialist Mussolini. The dictatorships of South America and of Africa have emerged, in similar fashion, out of fragmentation and inanition, not through the strength of majorities ranged behind a leader; the strongmen become strong in office.

Such political shifts may result from opportunistic political coups or they may be projections of deeper changes in national character, a process that seems always in progress. The mercurial Elizabethan Englishman bore little resemblance to the imperturbable, taciturn, stiff-upper-lip Phileas Foggs of the nineteenth century. The marauding Norsemen who terrorized and sometimes settled the coasts of Europe had little in common with their peaceful descendants, who established welfare states where poverty was obliterated and where, in Sweden, the standard of living was the highest and the suicide rate was among the highest in the world. The Japanese, too, in the years after the 1945 defeat were far removed from the swaggering invaders of Manchuria and the Chinese mainland. A highly militaristic country that for centuries had glorified the samurai warrior and was equally reverent toward his reincarnation in the arrogant, bemedalled generals of the Imperial Army would, in the space of a few years, grudgingly support less than the minimum forces needed to protect their own shores and would be content to take refuge under the military umbrella of her late enemy. The converse of such retreats from martial exploits could be observed in the Israelis who produced overnight what is very likely the best military organization, man for man, woman for woman, and general for general, in the world. The Nazis had declared that Jews were enjoined by the Talmud to be the last to march into battle so they could be the first to run away, but since 1948 that spurious text would be hard for anyone in the Middle East to swallow. The Germans, too, like the Japanese, have been reluctant to rearm, and in the absence of much domestic pressure, they have needed the prodding of their recent enemies to be willing to maintain armed forces that bear no more than what they could be persuaded was a reasonable share of the burden of the defense of their own borders. The causes of such changes in national character can rarely be traced to a single factor. In Britain, the retreat from empire followed great victories; in Germany and Japan it followed total defeat. The evolution of national character is constantly being stimulated by a succession of events that have little relation to conscious decisions. It seems to come about like changes in language, where not only the vocabulary but the morphology take new forms despite the protestations of any academy. Hitler's coming to power had no single cause; he was a moving part in a series of events that shook German society to its roots.*

When he was appointed chancellor, half the country was in favor of revolution, and within that half a small fraction was the true beer hall believers, the street brawlers, the political assassins, "the old fighters," as Hitler fondly called them. By 1933 they had become the advance guard of an army of mutually warring forces united only in a will to destroy the old order. What they represented may be seen in sporadic instances in every society—in the psychopaths, the fanatics, the criminals, the heroes of the counterculture. Under abnormal conditions, they and their opportunities multiply. Under extreme conditions, bizarre behavior and even ferocities long abandoned may be seen again. Cannibalism, for example, has reappeared among civilized groups, and in a guerilla war atrocities are no longer regarded with horror but as a part of the normal course of things. In peacetime, too, and in affluent societies, a numbed

---

* What can happen to the way of life of a people exposed to existential problems for which their experience has provided no solution may be seen, grossly magnified, in a primitive model. When the mountain tribe of Iks in northeast Africa were removed from their hunting preserves in parts of the Sudan, Uganda, and Kenya and forced to survive, in any way they could, as farmers and scroungers in the barren uplands outside their former territory, become a game preserve, they soon lost all semblance of what a few of them remembered as having been a humane, functioning tribe of hunters. In three generations the most elementary relationships were dissolved in their hopeless exile. Mothers, from the time of giving birth, were indifferent as to what happened to their children, who were thrust out of the parental hut at the age of three. If children lived, they survived by foraging for food in bands, and like the adults they might turn against one of their own number without a second thought if they saw an advantage in getting rid of him. No adult ever made an attempt to protect them. If a child crawled toward a fire, it roused the joyful anticipation of onlookers, who became hilarious if it stuck its hand in the blaze. Food was snatched from the mouths of those too old or too weak to swallow it quickly enough. If a man or woman killed or found anything edible, he or she did not share it with anyone in or outside the family. The tribe was, and perhaps, if there are survivors, still is, a society of everyone for himself and against everyone else. *Homo hominem lupus est.* The sentiments that had been essential in a hunting-gathering society—affection, generosity, mutuality of any kind—have disappeared, and the recording anthropologist says the tribe has become subhuman. It was not degraded to the level of an animal group; animals hunt together, care for their young, protect them, and rarely turn their fangs against their own kind instead of against their prey or their predators. The Iks turned theirs against one another, mate against mate, mother against child. The tribe as a society has disintegrated. In a rare year of good rainfall, when crops sprouted even in unweeded, overgrown fields, the Iks made no attempt to save seed for another year's planting or to store the excess food in granaries. They preferred to do no more than live off the unexpectedly abundant crops plus famine relief provided by the Kenyan government. To avoid any risk of the relief's stopping, they allowed the surplus, anything beyond their immediate needs, to rot. (Colin M. Turnbull, *The Mountain People.*)

people who have lost a sense of community can come to accept as normal a high incidence of violent crime that would once have appalled them. Forty-five percent of the people in cities of over 500,000 in the United States, a Gallup poll of July 1975 has reported, are afraid to walk on the streets of their neighborhood at night,* apparently accepting their anxiety as part of the price of living in an urban environment. They may also reach a stage of anomie where they merely watch, without attempting to interfere, or even call for help, while a woman is being murdered. Civilization, too, is a glaze on the surface of a fragile dish.

National Socialism seldom had any appeal to intellectuals. But a few of them were attracted by some part of its catch-all program. Martin Heidegger was one; another, for a short time, was Oswald Spengler; and another was the champion of the heroic, martial life, Ernst Jünger. But the entire Bauhaus went into exile, as did most of the playwrights and novelists from Brecht to Mann, not to mention anyone with a trace of Jewish blood. Academics, for the most part, could accept or tolerate National Socialism however little they may have liked it before Hitler came to power. A Nobel Prize–winning physicist, Philipp Lenard, would one day advocate the development of a German physics, and the chief of anthropology in the Kaiser Wilhelm Institute in Berlin would meet with SS leaders to discuss measures to be taken against the inferior Eastern races.

By the early 1930s, the Nazis had some appeal to all classes, including the sons of the kaiser and men like Albert Speer, who had no trace of Hitler's anti-Semitism. Speer came from a well-to-do, upper-middle-class family; he was not one of those sleeping on ropes or eating one daily meal in a soup kitchen. He saw in the party a ray of hope for a beleaguered Germany, and he also saw in it the possibility of an architectural career that would otherwise not be open to him. As for the wildnesses, he could tell himself they were children's sicknesses and would be recovered from with time, or he could ignore them, as he did later on when he saw the debris after the night of the broken glass, the *Kristallnacht*.

The men of affairs, like their opposite numbers in Italy, were seeking a political leader who would enable them to keep their enterprises and factories in operation. Most of them, and the most powerful among them, turned to Hitler only as a last alternative. They had long been put off by the party's socialism and its talk of the slavery of interest, the nefariousness of international capital, the need to confiscate ineptly used property, and such. But they came to a point where they were again threatened with the loss of their businesses, where after the successions

---

* Nineteen percent said they did not feel safe in their homes. (*New York Times*, July 28, 1975.)

of upheavals, great and small firms alike were facing bankruptcy. Schacht, a devout believer in a sound currency and prudent government expenditures, became a convert, and his break with Hitler would come only years later, when he sternly told the Führer Germany could not afford to rearm at the tempo Hitler ordered. The businessmen and bankers had lost their reliance on the gospels of the free market economists, and they became ready consumers of Hitler's political economics. As the 2,500 cartels operating in the Reich indicated, they had, in fact, long preferred agreements in restraint of trade as well as government connections to help sustain and expand them, to the competition of the market to which they also professed their devotion.*

Hitler had shrewdly adapted his tactics to conform to the opinions of those with money and influence whom he might tap. In the Industry Club speech, the attacks on the slavery of interest and loan capitalism were missing, as were the proposals in the 1920 party platform to communalize big department stores, abolish unearned income, and execute profiteers. Instead, Hitler spoke of the leadership principle, which would work as well in government as it did in business if these captains of industry helped him become Reichschancellor. He could offer a considerable variety of allurements while confirming them in their conviction of their importance to the nation; among them were the end of industrial strife, of unemployment, and of the threat of the Left. Recruiting these entrepreneurs to his cause did not deflect him for a moment from his central purposes of accreting all power unto himself including the control of their enterprises, of nazifying the Reich, and of cleansing it of the Bolshevik-international-capitalist-Jewish infiltration into its political and economic substance. There came a point in the final phase of the depression when such men, like Speer, had only to look the other way if the message of a party spokesman or the outrageous behavior of a *Sturm* of Brown Shirts seemed too objectionable.

The Weimar Constitution was a humane, scholarly document, more the product of a nation of thinkers, poets, and professors than of statesman. It was intended to be ultrademocratic, with proportional representation permitting parties with only a scattering of followers to have a voice in Parliament. At the polls a voter could choose between dozens of candidates, and while this enabled him or her to indulge in the finest distinctions among political *Weltanschauungen*, the result in practice was to leave a large bloc of the electorate without any representation in the Parliament and no party with a working majority. It was a constitution that provided not only for all the civil rights but also for laudable but

---

* Among the contributors to the NSDAP were not only some of the chief German industrialists but also foreigners like the Dutch oil magnate Henry Deterding, who aided Hitler with sizeable donations. In the United States, Henry Ford, who was markedly anti-Semitic, was an alluring prospect, but Ford would give Hitler nothing.

difficult-to-achieve objectives, among them the provision that the economic order must guarantee a worthy human life.

Nevertheless, able men were elected or appointed to office and the awkward apparatus somehow functioned. If the Reich's political genius never equalled its achievements in the arts and sciences, that is not new in industrial democracies. Men from humble backgrounds such as Ebert, Scheidemann, Gustav Bauer, Stresemann, and Severing were elected to high posts, as were scholars like Brüning and an old soldier like Hindenburg. Political interest ran high in the electorate, 80 percent of whom, on the average, voted in national elections.* The consensus in favor of a republic, however, did not run very wide or deep. Even the most stalwart among the republican chancellors, men like Stresemann and Brüning, were monarchists at heart, as was President Hindenburg, not to mention Schleicher and Papen. Few among the leaders of the Weimar Republic would have preferred the rickety republican system they had to the solid, nineteenth-century monarchy or what they believed a revived, constitutional monarchy would bring the Reich.

The republic was what was left after the kaiser abdicated. It appeared out of military defeat, and it never had its roots in the blood of martyrs fallen in battle against ancient injustices. By comparison, the symbol of German unity, the monarchy, had functioned remarkably well up to the war despite the eccentricities of the last kaiser, and its political drift was much more in the direction of a constitutional monarchy like Britain's than toward the divinely ordained empire of the tsar's Russia. Under the monarchy, the Reich had not only lived well, but it had created a free and benign climate of intellectual inquiry unsurpassed anywhere, and despite the class structure and traditional hierarchies, its most potent political force had been the Social Democratic party.

It was also a state possessed of uncommon civic virtue; few if any scandals involving the corruption of its judges or ministers or other state officials had ever occurred, in contrast to the experiences of more permissive democracies on the Continent and in America. Intellectually and politically, it was an open society with a high degree of religious toleration, where political anti-Semitism had faded away to nothing. Einstein, Ballin, the Zweigs, Rathenau, and hundreds of thousands of their coreligionists, who were mainly middle-class, merchants, doctors, dentists, lawyers, with few big landowners or indigent proletarians among them, were very likely more at home there than they would have been anywhere else in Europe, with the possible exception of Britain. One

* Comparable to 83 percent in France in 1929, and some 57 percent in the American presidential elections of 1928 and 1932. (Statistique Générale de la France. *Annuaire Statistique, 1929.* Paris, 1930; Charles Hickman Titus, *Voting Behavior in the United States,* p. 55.)

Jewish writer has written that many of his people were so in love with Germany they voted for anti-Semitic candidates.[3]

Following the war, the ideal of the German woman devoted to *Kaiser, Kirche, Kinder, Küche,* and *Kleider** had been transformed to include the emancipated women working in offices and professions, as well as factories. In the twenties, eleven million women were employed full-time, and beyond the workaday world an erotic and esthetic cult of womanhood had become a phenomenon new in Germany, where *chanteuses* like Marlene Dietrich, topless dancers like Josephine Baker, ballerinas like Anna Pavlova, and expressionist dancers like Mary Wigman conquered large audiences, male and female. In politics women were especially well represented in the extremist parties: Rosa Luxemburg and Clara Zetkin were Communists, and Hitler, "der schöne Adolf," as police reports noted, attracted a large and enthralled female following at Nazi rallies. Hitler welcomed their presence, but women's emancipation was one of the counts against the republic, one of the signs of its decadence and its resemblance to the Bolshevik pattern of free love and the destruction of the family.† The republic was thus the image of everything that was wrong for the Communists, for the Nazis, and for many in between; it had started on evil days and had never worked free of them.

Nevertheless, it had been accepted by the great majority of the population, and with better luck it might well have survived. A more generous policy on the part of the Allies with regard to the war guilt clause, reparations, and one-sided disarmament would have drained off a good deal of the poison of the antirepublican forces. Only months before Hitler's appointment as Reichschancellor were the Allies reluctantly prepared to concede in principle to the republic what they would be forced to grant Hitler as soon as he was established in office. Their moral case against the Reich was very weak from the start, and they never made any serious attempt to modify their accusations despite the mass of official documents that refuted it. But had they made such concessions, the whole network of collective security and of postwar alliances, together with the one-way interpretations of self-determination and the rejection of German claims for treaty revision, would have been shaken, and they would have been back where they started before they adopted the slogans that caused the American President to talk of "making the world safe for democracy."

Within the Reich, Hindenburg for all his remarkable qualities was no longer up to his job; his faculties were blunted, and in his weariness and confusion he was too given to find support in old homilies and friend-

---

* Kaiser, Church, Children, Kitchen, Clothes.
† The German divorce rate doubled between 1913 and 1930.

ships. His appointment of Papen, who had no party backing of any kind, effectively put an end to the parliamentary system, and Schleicher's chancellorship was more of the same.

Although Hindenburg was determined not to appoint Hitler and two-thirds of the voters rejected him, nevertheless the president and the votes of a majority of the electorate, including those who detested Hitler, were helping him on his way to the chancellorship. Papen and Schleicher were already running authoritarian governments without the Reichstag, ruling under presidential decrees instead of being responsible, as the constitution had foreseen as the political norm, to an elected parliament. And as for the Reichstag, a majority of its members wanted it demolished.

Even so, the question remains: With Hindenburg's stubborn refusal to appoint Hitler, and with two-thirds of the country against him, would it have been possible to keep him from power? What alternatives were still open to the opposition?

The Social Democratic leadership, as some of its members urged, could have collaborated with Schleicher's government. From the Socialists' point of view, he was far and away the lesser evil; a few months later, even those among them who were most anti-Schleicher would have been glad to see him in office in place of Hitler, who was putting hundreds of their number in jail and proscribing their party. In theory, after the Potempa murder, when the National Socialists lost two million votes, it should have been possible to organize an anti-Hitler coalition. A younger Hindenburg might well have done better than to appoint Papen and then Schleicher. As Monsignor Kaas told the president, Brüning was available, and with the president, the Center party, and the Reichswehr to support him, along with a coalition of other anti-Nazis, they might have forced Hitler to make far-reaching compromises or have kept him from power. He and his party were bankrupt; only the Reich's exchequer could bail them out, and that could have been denied them for months to come. And so on.

But none of this could have much effect on the shattering distress of the Reich. The series of calamities had produced a psychic malfunction of the society as a whole, not only of the parliamentary system. By 1932 it was a majority of the society, thin, but nevertheless a majority, that wanted a revolution. Of that fifty-odd percent, by far the greatest number were National Socialists, headed by a grim, fanatical, amoral leader who became an enormously gifted demagogue, only, however, after millions of his new followers were softened up for him.

The ingredients of an anti-Hitler coalition were so mixed it was impossible to make anything cohesive out of them. A far-out nationalist like Ludendorff foresaw with terrible clarity what horrors Hitler would bring to the Reich. But how could Ludendorff, Hindenburg, Schleicher,

Brüning, and Severing, that is, the anti-Hitler Right, Center, and SPD, in an alliance with the Communists, who were also anti-Hitler but believed that what they called "fascism" was a necessary prelude to their own revolution, be brought under one roof?

It is likely that 1932 was a point of no return. Millions of people were too disenchanted with their barren lot, stretching ahead as far as they could see, to be willing to plod along with it. Their lives had become too mean and too hopeless for them to turn to any catechism they had been brought up on; hatreds came easily to them; nothing was left to lean on, or believe in, or hope for. They had been radicalized out of their tradition, *Ikified** insofar as their past ceased to have any significance. No doubt Brüning, Schleicher, and Hindenburg and perhaps millions of others would have been glad to return to a monarchy, but ranged against them, despite the fairy tale Göring told to Meissner, would have been the National Socialists and the Communists, with the almost certain prospect of civil war. The republic had died long before January 30, 1933; a little man, a half-educated foreigner followed by one-third of the country, was its chief pallbearer.

* See footnote p. 371.

Notes

CHAPTER 1: AUSTRIA

1. Friedrich Percyval Reck-Malleczewen, *Tagebuch Eines Verzweifelten* (Stuttgart: Goverts, 1966), pp. 26–27.
2. *Lienzer Zeitung*, November 12, 1904.
3. Werner Maser, *Adolf Hitler* (Munich: Bechtle Verlag, 1971), p. 39.
4. Ibid., pp. 69, 70.
5. Johann Recktenwald, *Woran hat Hitler gelitten?* (Munich: Rheinhardt, 1963).
6. Maser, *Adolf Hitler*, pp. 262–63.
7. Ibid., p. 263.
8. André Banuls, "Ein Völkisches Blatt aus Hitlers Schulzeit," in *Vierteljahrshefte für Zeitgeschichte*, April 1970.
9. *Die Tiroler Post*, November 16, 1906.
10. Ibid., September 9, 1903.
11. Maser, *Adolf Hitler*, p. 79.
12. Therese Schüssel, *Das Werden Österreichs* (Vienna: Verlag für Geschichte und Politik, 1968), p. 218. Erich Zöllner, *Geschichte Österreichs* (Munich: Oldenbourg Verlag, 1966).
13. Hugo Hantsch, *Die Geschichte Österreichs* (Vienna: Verlag Styria, 1968), vol. 2, p. 420.

CHAPTER 2: GERMANY: THE PROMISED LAND

1. Golo Mann, *Deutsche Geschichte des 19. und 20. Jahrhunderts* (Frankfurt am Main: Fischer Verlag, 1962), p. 394.
2. Rudolf Absolon, *Die Wehrmacht im Dritten Reich* (Boppard am Rhein: Harald Boldt Verlag, 1969), vol. 1, p. 163.
3. Ibid., pp. 164, 165.
4. Shakespeare, *Henry IV*, part 1, act 4, scene 2.
5. Walter Görlitz, *Der deutsche Generalstab* (Frankfurt am Main: Verlag der Frankfurter Hefte, N.D.), p. 19.
6. Absolon, *Die Wehrmacht im Dritten Reich*, vol. 2, p. 2.
7. Martin Rittau, *Militärstrafgesetzbuch* (Berlin: Walter de Gruyter & Co., 1940), p. 103, para. 51.
8. Mann, *Deutsche Geschicte des 19. und 20. Jahrhunderts*, p. 401.
9. Karl Demeter, *Das Deutsche Offizierkorps in Gesellschaft und Staat 1650–1945* (Frankfurt am Main: Bernard & Graefe Verlag für Wehrwesen, 1962), p. 28.
10. Reinhard Höhn, *Die Armee als Erziehungsschule der Nation* (Bad Harzburg: Verlag für Wissenschaft, Wirtschaft und Technik, 1963), p. 506.
11. Ibid., pp. 506, 507.
12. *Handbuch zur deutschen Militärgeschichte*, vol. 5, p. 39.
13. Görlitz, *Der deutsche Generalstab*, p. 207.
14. *Münchner Neueste Nachrichten*, June 17, 1913.
15. Ibid.
16. Ibid.
17. *Münchner Neueste Nachrichten*, June 6, 1913.
18. Ibid. *Frankfurter Nachrichten*, June 6, 1913.
19. *Münchener Neueste Nachrichten*, June 7, 1913. *Frankfurter Nachrichten*, June 6, 1913.
20. *Frankfurter Nachrichten*, June 3, 1913.
21. *Münchener Neueste Nachrichten*, June 10, 1913.
22. *Frankfurter Nachrichten*, July 5, 1913.
23. Ibid., July 22, 1913.
24. Ibid., May 18, 1913.
25. Ibid., June 16, 1913.

26. Bernhard Fürst von Bülow, *Denkwürdigkeiten* (Berlin: Ullstein, 1930), vol. 1, p. 359.

27. Luigi Albertini, *The Origins of the War of 1914*, translated and edited by Isabella M. Massey (London: Oxford University Press, reprint, 1965), vol. 1, p. 319.

28. Viscount Grey of Fallodon, *Twenty-five Years* (New York: Frederick Stokes, 1925), vol. 1, p. 84.

29. Werner Maser, *Hitlers Mein Kampf* (Munich: Bechtle Verlag, 1966), p. 173. Werner Maser, *Adolf Hitler* (Munich: Bechtle Verlag, 1971), p. 126.

30. Albertini, *The Origins of the War of 1914*, vol. 2, p. 185.

31. Ibid., p. 195.

32. Ibid., p. 194.

CHAPTER 3: THE WAR AND THE CORPORAL

1. Gerhard Ritter, *The Sword and the Scepter*, translated by Heinz Norden (Coral Gables: University of Miami Press, 1969), vol. 2, p. 68.

2. Sidney B. Fay, *The Origins of the World War* (New York: The Free Press, 1966), vol. 2, pp. 538–40.

3. Ibid., p. 480.

4. Luigi Albertini, *The Origins of the War of 1914*, translated and edited by Isabella M. Massey (London: Oxford University Press, 1965), vol. 2, p. 579.

5. Quoted Fay, *The Origins of the World War*, vol. 2, p. 481. From S. Dobrorolski, *Die Mobilmachung der Russischen Armee* (Berlin, 1921), p. 9f.

6. *Schulthess' Europäischer Geschichtskalender* (Munich: C. H. Beck'sche Verlagsbuchhandlung, 1917), vol. 55, pp. 383–84.

7. Albertini, *The Origins of the World War*, vol. 3, p. 496.

8. Werner Maser, *Hitlers Briefe und Notizen* (Düsseldorf: Econ Verlag, 1973), p. 63.

9. Joachim C. Fest, *Hitler* (Frankfurt am Main: Propyläen Verlag, 1973), p. 104.

10. Werner Maser, *Adolf Hitler* (Munich: Bechtle Verlag, 1971), pp. 138–39.

11. Maser, *Hitlers Briefe und Notizen*, p. 64.

12. Gerhard Ritter, *Staatskunst und Kriegshandwerk* (Munich: Verlag Oldenbourg, 1964), vol. 3, p. 83.

13. Herbert Michaelis, et al, *Ursachen und Folgen* (Berlin: Herbert Wendler & Co., n.d.), vol. 1, pp. 349–51.

14. Ibid., vol. 1, p. 348.

15. Ibid., vol. 1, pp. 371–72.

16. Ibid., vol. 1, pp. 372–73.

17. Ritter, *Staatskunst und Kriegshandwerk*, vol. 4, p. 85.

18. John Morton Blum, *Woodrow Wilson and the Politics of Morality* (Boston: Little Brown, 1956), p. 142.

19. Michaelis, et al, *Ursachen und Folgen*, vol. 2, pp. 61–62.

20. Ibid., vol. 2, pp. 64–67.

21. Ibid., vol. 1, pp. 388–90.

22. General von Hindenburg, *Aus meinem Leben* (Leipzig: Verlag von S. Hirzel, 1920), p. 220.

23. *Schulthess' Europäischer Geschichtskalender*, 1920, vol. 58, book 1, pp. 879–80.

24. Edwin Borchard and William Potter Lage, *Neutrality for the United States* (New Haven: Yale University Press, 1940), pp. 210–11.

25. Ibid., p. 36.

26. Quoted Ibid., pp. 99–100.

27. Colin Simpson, *The Lusitania* (Boston: Little Brown, 1972), quoting *Public Papers of Woodrow Wilson*, vol. 3, p. 321.

28. Borchard and Lage, *Neutrality for the United States*, p. 150.

29. Simpson, *The Lusitania*, p. 27. Thomas A. Bailey and Paul B. Ryan, *The Lusitania Disaster* (New York: The Free Press, 1975), p. 17.

30. Simpson, *The Lusitania*, p. 27.

31. Quoted Bailey and Ryan, *The Lusitania Disaster*, p. 36.
32. Borchard and Lage, *Neutrality for the United States*, pp. 163–64.
33. Ibid., p. 221.
34. Quoted Ross Gregory, *Walter Hines Page* (Lexington, Kentucky: The University of Kentucky Press, 1970), p. 106.
35. Ibid., p. 128.
36. Charles Seymour, ed., *The Intimate Papers of Colonel House* (Boston: Houghton Mifflin Company, 1926), vol. 2, p. 91.
37. Gregory, *Walter Hines Page*, p. 143.
38. Thomas Mann, "Betrachtungen eines Unpolitischen," in *Reden und Aufsätze* (Oldenburg: Fischer, 1960), vol. 12, p. 445.
39. James Morgan Read, *Atrocity Propaganda 1914–1919* (New Haven: Yale University Press, 1941), pp. 204, 207.
40. Ibid., pp. 187, 229.
41. John W. Wheeler-Bennett, *The Forgotten Peace: Brest-Litovsk* (New York: Morrow, 1939).

CHAPTER 4: THE DESERT OF DEFEAT

1. Herbert Michaelis, et al, eds., *Ursachen und Folgen* (Berlin: Herbert Wendler & Co., n.d.) vol. 2, pp. 295, 321, 322. Cuno Horkenbach, *Das Deutsche Reich von 1918 bis heute* (Berlin: Verlag für Presse, Wirtschaft und Politik, 1930), p. 17.
2. Michaelis, et al, *Ursachen und Folgen*, vol. 2, pp. 330–31, 336.
3. Joachim C. Fest, *Hitler* (Berlin: Propyläen, 1973), p. 107.
4. Letter, *Berliner Tageblatt*, November 25, 1918.
5. Michaelis, et al, *Ursachen und Folgen*, vol. 2, p. 527.
6. Ibid., p. 529.
7. Ibid., pp. 528–29.
8. Ibid., p. 576.
9. Ibid., vol. 3, pp. 166–69.
10. Ibid., pp. 166–69.
11. Johannes Erger, *Der Kapp-Lüttwitz Putsch* (Düsseldorf: Droste Verlag, 1967), p. 200.
12. Albert Schwartz, *Die Weimarer Republik* (Konstanz: Akademische Verlagsgesellschaft Athenaion, 1958), p. 7. Michaelis, et al, *Ursachen und Folgen*, vol. 3, pp. 333, 338, 340, 341, 342.
13. *Augsburger Postzeitung*, August 29, 1919.
14. *L'Homme Libre*, February 27, 1923.
15. *Simplicissimus*, September 16, 1919; September 30, 1919; April 1, 1919.
16. *London Times*, quoted in *Münchener Neueste Nachrichten*, February 6, 1920, p. 66.
17. John Maynard Keynes, *The Economic Consequences of the Peace* (New York: Harcourt, Brace and Rowe, 1920), p. 41.
18. *Münchener Neueste Nachrichten*, January 30, 1920.
19. Robert Lansing, *The Peace Negotiations* (Port Washington, New York/London: Kennikat Press, 1969), p. 274.
20. Ibid., p. 272.
21. *Augsburger Postzeitung*, March 14, 1922.
22. Michaelis, et al, *Ursachen und Folgen*, vol. 3, p. 417.
23. David Mitchell, *1919—Red Mirage* (New York: Macmillan, 1970), p. 211.
24. *Augsburger Postzeitung*, January 17, 1920, and July 26, 1919.
25. Michaelis, et al, *Ursachen und Folgen*, vol. 4, pp. 7–8.
26. Warren E. Williams, "Die Politik der Alliierten gegenüber die Freikorps im Baltikum. 1918–1919," *Vierteljahrshefte für Zeitgeschichte*, April 1964, pp. 147–69.
27. Mitchell, *1919—Red Mirage*, pp. 176–77.
28. Ernst Niekisch, *Gewagtes Leben* (Köln: Kiepenheuer und Witsch, 1958), p. 76.

29. *Berliner Tageblatt*, April 15, 1919.
30. Ibid., April 16, 1919.
31. Ibid., April 24, 1919.
32. Horkenbach, *Das Deutsche Reich von 1918 bis heute*, p. 67.
33. Michaelis, et al, *Ursachen und Folgen*, vol. 3, p. 129.
34. Eberhard Kolb, *Die Arbeiterräte in der deutschen Innenpolitik* (Düsseldorf: Droste Verlag, 1962), p. 332.
35. Ibid., p. 352.
36. Michaelis, et al, *Ursachen und Folgen*, vol. 3, p. 130.
37. *Berliner Tageblatt*, May 5, 1919. Niekisch, *Gewagtes Leben*, p. 77.
38. Ernst Deuerlein, "Hitlers Eintritt in die Politik und die Reichswehr," *Vierteljahrshefte für Zeitgeschichte*, April 1959, pp. 177–227.
39. Ibid., p. 197.
40. Ibid., p. 200.
41. Ibid., p. 199.
42. Ibid., pp. 203–205.
43. *Augsburger Postzeitung*, August 10, 1919.
44. *Münchner Neueste Nachrichten,* January 3–4, January 28, 1920.
45. *Berliner Tageblatt*, May 6, 1919.
46. Deuerlein, "Hitlers Eintritt in die Politik und die Reichswehr," in *Vierteljahrshefte für Zeitgeschichte*, April 1959, p. 206.
47. Reginald H. Phelps, "Hitler als Parteiredner im Jahre 1920," *Vierteljahrshefte für Zeitgeschichte*, July 1963, pp. 316, 318.
48. Ibid., p. 297.
49. Ibid., pp. 302, 313, 329.
50. Ibid., p. 303.
51. Ibid., p. 303.
52. Ibid., p. 307.
53. Ibid., p. 300.
54. Ibid., p. 308.
55. Ibid., p. 309.
56. Ibid., p. 311.
57. Ibid., p. 325.
58. Ibid., p. 327.
59. Ibid., p. 327.
60. Gustav Noske, *Von Kiel bis Kapp* (Berlin: Verlag für Politik und Wirtschaft, 1920), p. 196.
61. Heinrich Brüning, *Memoiren 1918–1934* (Stuttgart: Deutsche Verlags-Anstalt, 1970), p. 62.
62. Erger, *Der Kapp-Lüttwitz Putsch*, p. 42. E. L. Woodward, Butler, Rohan, eds., *Documents on British Foreign Policy 1919–1939* (London: Her Majesty's Stationery Office, 1956), first series, vol. 6, 1919.
63. Klaus Epstein, *Matthias Erzberger* (Princeton, N.J.: Princeton University Press, 1959), p. 334.
64. Michaelis, et al, *Ursachen und Folgen*, vol. 3, p. 548.
65. Quoted Erger, *Der Kapp-Lüttwitz Putsch*, p. 55, from Josef Bischoff, *Die Letzte Front*, Berlin, 1935, p. 243.
66. Francis L. Carsten, *Reichswehr und Politik 1918–1933* (Berlin: Kiepenheuer & Witsch, 1964), p. 93.
67. Ibid., p. 97.
68. Michaelis, et al, *Ursachen und Folgen*, vol. 4, pp. 88–91, 98.
69. Ibid., p. 99.
70. Erger, *Der Kapp-Lüttwitz Putsch*, p. 211.
71. Michaelis, et al, *Ursachen und Folgen*, vol. 4, p. 7.
72. Erger, *Der Kapp-Lüttwitz Putsch*, p. 225.
73. Ibid., pp. 280, 287–91.
74. Ibid., p. 287. Otto Gessler, *Reichswehrpolitik in der Weimarer Zeit* (Stuttgart: Deutsche Verlags-Anstalt, 1958).

CHAPTER 5: "THE ENEMY IS ON THE RIGHT"

1. Herbert Michaelis, et al, *Ursachen und Folgen* (Berlin: Dokumenten-Verlag Dr. Herbert Wendler & Co., n.d.) vol. 4, pp. 111–13.
2. Carl Severing, *Mein Lebensweg* (Köln: Greven Verlag, 1950), vol. 1, p. 266.
3. Ibid., p. 297.
4. Otto Gessler, *Reichswehrpolitik in der Weimarer Zeit* (Stuttgart: Deutsche Verlags-Anstalt, 1958), p. 159.
5. Harry Graf Kessler, *Walther Rathenau* (Berlin: Verlagsanstalt Hermann Klemm, 1928), p. 15.
6. Hans Lamm, *Walther Rathenau* (Hannover: Niedersächsischen Landeszentrale, 1968), p. 15. From Emil Ludwig, *Genie und Charakter.*
7. Helmuth M. Böttcher, *Walther Rathenau* (Bonn: Athenäum-Verlag, 1958), p. 12.
8. Lamm, *Walther Rathenau*, p. 53.
9. Kessler, *Walther Rathenau*, p. 58.
10. Ibid., p. 57.
11. Lamm, *Walther Rathenau*, p. 35.
12. Böttcher, *Walther Rathenau*, p. 125.
13. Walther Rathenau, *In Brief und Bild.* (Berlin: Verlag Annedore Leber, 1967), letter to Professor Hoffmann, March 10, 1920, p. 363.
14. Erich Eyck, *Geschichte der Weimarer Republik* (Stuttgart: Eugen Rentsch Verlag, 1956), p. 259.
15. Lamm, *Walther Rathenau*, p. 41.
16. Ibid., p. 49.
17. Ibid., pp. 102–3.
18. Kessler, *Walther Rathenau*, p. 329.
19. Ibid., p. 331.
20. Wilhelm Orth, *Walther Rathenau und der Geist von Rapallo* (Berlin: Buchverlag der Morgen, 1962), p. 128.
21. Kessler, *Walther Rathenau*, pp. 347–48.
22. Böttcher, *Walther Rathenau*, pp. 288–89.
23. Orth, *Walther Rathenau und der Geist von Rapallo*, p. 142.
24. Ernst von Salomon, *Der Fragebogen* (Hamburg: Rowohlt Verlag, 1951), pp. 105–106.
25. Lamm, *Walther Rathenau*, p. 58.
26. Ibid., p. 60.
27. Ibid., p. 59.
28. Kessler, *Walther Rathenau*, p. 356.
29. Ibid., p. 354.
30. Eyck, *Geschichte der Weimarer Republik*, p. 292.
31. Lamm, *Walther Rathenau*, p. 67.
32. Eyck, *Geschichte der Weimarer Republik*, p. 256.
33. *Münchner Neueste Nachrichten*, December 5, 1923.
34. Gessler, *Reichswehrpolitik in der Weimarer Zeit*, p. 248.
35. Ibid., p. 247.
36. Ibid., p. 248.
37. *Augsburger Postzeitung*, April 17, 1923.
38. *Augsburger Postzeitung*, May 1, 1923.
39. Friedrich von Rabenau. *Seeckt, Aus Seinem Leben* (Leipzig: Hase und Koehler Verlag, 1940), p. 341.
40. Ibid., p. 359.
41. Gessler, *Reichswehrpolitik in der Weimarer Zeit*, pp. 254, 255.
42. Michaelis, et al., *Ursachen und Folgen*, vol. 5, pp. 402–4.
43. Ibid., pp. 404–7.
44. Thilo Vogelsang, "Die Reichswehr in Bayern und der Münchener Putsch 1923," *Vierteljahrshefte für Zeitgeschichte*, January 1957, pp. 91–101.
45. Michaelis, et al, *Ursachen und Folgen*, vol. 5, p. 432.

46. Ibid., p. 434.
47. Ibid., p. 440.

CHAPTER 6: SILVER STREAKS ON THE HORIZON

1. *Schulthess' Europäischer Geschichtskalender* (Munich: C. H. Beck'sche Verlags-buchhandlung, 1917–1942), vol. 65, 1924, p. 161. *Augsburger Postzeitung,* January 22, 1924.
2. Walter Görlitz, *Gustav Stresemann* (Heidelberg: Aehren Verlag, 1947), p. 183.
3. Quoted Joachim C. Fest, *Hitler* (Berlin: Propyläen Verlag, 1973), p. 275.
4. Ernst Deuerlein, *Der Aufstieg der NSDAP 1919–1933 in Augenzeugenberichten* (Düsseldorf: Karl Rauch Verlag, 1968), pp. 208–209.
5. Ibid., p. 207.
6. Ibid., p. 215.
7. Herbert Michaelis, et al, *Ursachen und Folgen* (Berlin: Herbert Wendler & Co., n.d.), vol. 5, p. 451.
8. Ibid., pp. 457–59.
9. Deuerlein, *Der Aufstieg der NSDAP*, p. 214.
10. Gustav Stresemann, *Vermächtnis* (Berlin: Verlag Ullstein, 1932), p. 324.
11. *Le Quotidien*, January 23, 1924.
12. *Le Petit Journal*, January 21, 1924.
13. Friedrich Stieve, ed., *Der Diplomatische Schriftwechsel Iswolskis 1911–1914* (Berlin: Deutsche Verlagsgesellschaft für Politik und Geschichte, 1925), vol. 2, pp. 404–405; vol. 3, p. 96.
14. Görlitz, *Gustav Stresemann*, p. 195.
15. Michaelis, et al, *Ursachen und Folgen*, vol. 6, p. 290.
16. Michaelis, et al, *Ursachen und Folgen*, vol. 6, p. 286. *Schulthess*, vol. 66, 1925, p. 59.
17. Michaelis, et al, *Ursachen und Folgen*, vol. 6, pp. 315–16.
18. Michaelis, et al, *Ursachen und Folgen*, vol. 6, pp. 310–11.
19. Edmond de Mesnil, in *La Nation*, October 5, 1926.
20. Michaelis, et al, *Ursachen und Folgen*, vol. 6, pp. 434, 445–46. Hans von Seeckt, *Aus Seinem Leben, 1918–1936* (Leipzig: von Hase und Koehler, 1940), p. 430.
21. Helm Speidel, "Reichswehr und Rote Armee," in *Vierteljahrshefte für Zeitgeschichte*, vol. 1, January 1953, pp. 9–45. "Tschunke Report," in Michaelis, et al, *Ursachen und Folgen*, vol. 7, pp. 509–12.
22. Michaelis, et al, *Ursachen und Folgen*, vol. 6, pp. 487–89.
23. Ibid., p. 495.
24. Ibid., p. 489.
25. Stresemann, *Vermächtnis*, vol. 1, p. 582 ff.
26. *Augsburger Postzeitung*, June 11, 1924.
27. *Schulthess*, vol. 68, 1927, pp. 295–96.
28. Seeckt Papers (Munich: Institut für Zeitgeschichte), Rolle 28, April 2, 1917.
29. Ibid., Rolle 27, March 26, 1917.
30. Michaelis, et al, *Ursachen und Folgen*, vol. 7, pp. 497–99.

CHAPTER 7: "OVER GRAVES—FORWARD"

1. Friedrich von Rabenau, *Seeckt, Aus seinem Leben* (Leipzig: Hase & Koehler Verlag, 1940), p. 557.
2. Ibid., pp. 571–74.
3. Kurt Pritzkoleit, *Das kommandierte Wunder* (Munich: Verlag Kurt Desch, 1959), pp. 617–19.
4. Erich Eyck, *Geschichte der Weimarer Republik* (Stuttgart: Eugen Rentsch Verlag, 1956), vol. 2, pp. 157, 180. Cuno Horkenbach, ed., *Das Deutsche Reich* (Berlin: Verlag für Presse, Wirtschaft und Politik, 1930), p. 626.
5. Gustav Stresemann, *Vermächtnis* (Berlin: Verlag Ullstein, 1932), vol. 3, p. 263.
6. Eyck, *Geschichte der Weimarer Republik*, p. 159.

7. Ibid., p. 254.
8. Walter Görlitz, *Hindenburg* (Bonn: Athenäum-Verlag, 1953), p. 78.
9. Herbert Michaelis, et al, *Ursachen und Folgen* (Berlin: Herbert Wendler & Co., n.d.), vol. 7, p. 38.
10. *Schulthess' Europäischer Geschichtskalender, 1927* (Munich: C. H. Beck'sche Verlag, 1928), pp. 303–304.
11. Robert H. Ferrell, *Peace in Their Time* (New Haven: Yale University Press, 1952), pp. 105–106.
12. Ibid., p. 180.
13. Ibid., p. 197.
14. Ibid., p. 268.
15. Ibid., p. 251.
16. Ibid., p. 198, quoting Borchard.
17. Ibid., p. 241.
18. Ibid., pp. 177–78.
19. Ibid., p. 231.
20. Eyck, *Geschichte der Weimarer Republik*, p. 172.
21. Ibid., p. 200.
22. Ernst Deuerlein, *Der Aufstieg der NSDAP 1919–1933 in Augenzeugenberichten* (Düsseldorf: Karl Rauch Verlag, 1968), pp. 256–57.
23. Ibid., p. 277.
24. Ibid., p. 248.
25. Ibid., p. 291.
26. Ibid., p. 296.
27. Michaelis, et al, *Ursachen und Folgen*, vol. 7, p. 423.
28. Görlitz, *Hindenburg*, p. 197.

CHAPTER 8: THE TIME OF THE CROOKED CROSS

1. Gustav Stresemann, *Vermächtnis* (Berlin: Verlag Ullstein, 1932), vol. 3, p. 556 ff.
2. F. A. Krummacher and Albert Wucher, eds., *Die Weimarer Republik* (Munich: Verlag Kurt Desch, 1965), p. 285.
3. Erich Eyck, *Geschichte der Weimarer Republik* (Stuttgart: Eugen Rentsch Verlag, 1956), p. 303.
4. Krummacher and Wucher, eds., *Die Weimarer Republik*, pp. 285–86.
5. Albrecht Tyrell, "Führergedanke und Gauleiterwechsel," in *Vierteljahrshefte für Zeitgeschichte*, October 1975, no. 4, pp. 341–74.
6. André François-Poncet, *Souvenirs d'une Ambassade à Berlin* (Paris: Flammarion, 1946), p. 17.
7. Krummacher and Wucher, eds., *Die Weimarer Republik*, p. 299.
8. Ibid., p. 303.
9. Eyck, *Geschichte der Weimarer Republik*, pp. 376–77.
10. Ibid., p. 358.
11. Ernst Deuerlein, *Der Aufstieg der NSDAP 1919–1933 in Augenzeugenberichten* (Düsseldorf: Karl Rauch Verlag, 1968), p. 337.
12. Ibid., p. 343.
13. Ibid., p. 347.
14. Ibid., p. 348.
15. S. Adler-Rudel, *Ost Juden in Deutschland, 1880–1940* (Tübingen: J. C. B. Mohr, 1959), pp. 156–57.
16. Krummacher and Wucher, eds., *Die Weimarer Republik*, p. 325.
17. Hans Schlange-Schoeningen, *The Morning After*, translated by Ed. Fitzgerald (London: Victor Gollancz Ltd., 1948), p. 62.
18. François-Poncet, *Souvenirs d'une Ambassade à Berlin*, p. 19.
19. Adam Buckreis, *Politik des 20. Jahrhunderts* (Nuremberg: Panorama Verlag, n.d.) p. 547.
20. Walter Görlitz, *Hindenburg* (Bonn: Athenäum, 1953), p. 347.

21. Deuerlein, *Der Aufstieg der NSDAP*, p. 355.
22. Herbert Michaelis, et al, *Ursachen und Folgen* (Berlin: Herbert Wendler & Co., n.d.), vol. 8, p. 367.
23. Heinrich Brüning, *Memoiren 1918–1934* (Stuttgart: Deutsche Verlags-Anstalt, 1970), p. 183.
24. Otto Meissner, *Staatssekretär unter Ebert-Hindenburg-Hitler* (Hamburg: Hoffmann und Campe Verlag, 1950), p. 216.

CHAPTER 9: THE SEIZURE OF POWER

1. Herbert Michaelis, et al, *Ursachen und Folgen* (Berlin: Herbert Wendler & Co., n.d.), vol. 8, p. 392.
2. Ibid., pp. 394–95.
3. Max Domarus, *Hitler: Reden und Proklamationen 1932–1945* (Neustadt: Schmidt, 1962), vol. 1, pp. 68–90.
4. Albert Wucher, *Die Fahne Hoch* (Munich: Süddeutscher Verlag, 1963), p. 16.
5. Carl Severing, *Mein Lebensweg* (Köln: Greven Verlag, 1950), vol. 2, p. 336.
6. Erich Eyck, *Geschichte der Weimarer Republik* (Stuttgart: Eugen Rentsch Verlag, 1956), vol. 2, p. 450.
7. Heinrich Brüning, *Memoiren, 1918–1934* (Stuttgart: Deutsche Verlags-Anstalt, 1970), p. 562.
8. Ibid., p. 558.
9. Ibid., pp. 90, 578.
10. Ibid., p. 595.
11. Lutz Graf Schwerin von Krosigk, *Es geschah in Deutschland* (Tübingen: Rainer Wunderlich Verlag Hermann Leins, 1951), p. 142. André François-Poncet, *Souvenirs d'une Ambassade à Berlin* (Paris: Flammarion, 1946).
12. Otto Meissner, *Staatssekretär* (Hamburg: Hoffmann und Campe Verlag, 1950), p. 231.
13. Eugene Davidson, *The Trial of the Germans* (New York: Macmillan, 1966), p. 178.
14. Ibid., p. 179.
15. "Dokumentation zum Sturz Brünings," in *Vierteljahrshefte für Zeitgeschichte*, vol. 1, no. 3, July 1953, pp. 261–88.
16. Schwerin von Krosigk, *Es Geschah in Deutschland*, p. 143.
17. E. L. Woodward and Rohan Butler, ed., *Documents on British Foreign Policy 1919–1939* (London: His Majesty's Stationery Office, 1948), vol. 3, second series, p. 274.
18. "Dokumentation zur Politik Schleichers gegenüber der NSDAP 1932," in *Vierteljahrshefte für Zeitgeschichte*, vol. 6, no. 1, January 1958, pp. 86–118.
19. Dietrich Geyer, "Sowjetrussland und die deutsche Arbeiterbewegung 1918–1932," in *Vierteljahrshefte für Zeitgeschichte*, vol. 24, no. 1, January 1976, pp. 4–37.
20. Erich Eyck, *Geschichte der Weimarer Republik*, p. 514.
21. Michaelis, et al, *Ursachen und Folgen*, vol. 8, p. 644. Ernst Deuerlein, *Der Aufstieg der NSDAP 1919–1933 in Augenzeugenberichten* (Düsseldorf: Karl Rauch Verlag, 1968), p. 401.
22. Michaelis, et al, *Ursachen und Folgen*, vol. 8, p. 645. Deuerlein, *Der Aufstieg der NSDAP 1919–1933 in Augenzeugenberichten*, p. 401.
23. Eyck, *Geschichte der Weimarer Republik*, pp. 515, 516.
24. Thilo Vogelsang, *Reichswehr, Staat und NSDAP* (Stuttgart: Deutsche Verlags-Anstalt, 1962), pp. 479–80.
25. Michaelis, et al, *Ursachen und Folgen*, vol. 8, p. 646. Woodward and Butler, Documents on British Foreign Policy, 1919–1939, Second Series: vol. 4, p. 45.
26. Michaelis, et al, *Ursachen und Folgen*, vol. 8, pp. 676–78.
27. Ibid., p. 683.
28. Ibid., pp. 684–86.
29. Eyck, *Geschichte der Weimarer Republik*, p. 541.

30. Quoted, Hans Otto Meissner and Harry Wilde, *Die Machtergreifung* (Stuttgart: J. G. Cotta'sche Buchhandlung Nachfolger, 1958), p. 147.
31. Hans Roos, "Die 'Präventivkriegspläne' Pilsudskis von 1933," in *Vierteljahrshefte für Zeitgeschichte*, October 1955, pp. 344–63.
32. Franz von Papen, *Der Wahrheit eine Gasse* (Munich: Paul List Verlag, 1952), p. 250.
33. Joseph Goebbels, *Vom Kaiserhof zur Reichskanzlei* (Munich: Franz-Eher, 1937), pp. 218, 219, 220, 225.
34. Fritz Thyssen, *I Paid Hitler* (New York: Farrar & Rinehart, 1941), p. 87.
35. Paul Löbe, *Erinnerungen eines Reichstagspräsidenten* (Berlin: Arani, 1949), p. 142.
36. Franz von Papen, *Vom Scheitern einer Demokratie 1930–1933* (Mainz: Hase & Koehler Verlag, 1968), pp. 329–33.
37. Theodor Eschenburg, "Franz von Papen," in *Vierteljahrshefte für Zeitgeschichte*, April 1953, pp. 153–70.
38. Goebbels, *Vom Kaiserhof zur Reichskanzlei*, pp. 235, 236.
39. Otto Dietrich, *Mit Hitler in die Macht* (Munich: Franz Eher, 1938), pp. 169–70. Meissner and Wilde, *Die Machtergreifung*, p. 154.
40. International Military Tribunal Nuremberg, *Nazi Conspiracy and Aggression* (Washington: U.S. Government Printing Office, 1946–1948), vol. 2, pp. 922–24.
41. Meissner Document Book #1, p. 21. Institut für Zeitgeschichte, Munich, Germany.
42. *Münchner Neueste Nachrichten*, December 5, 1932.
43. Ibid., December 8, 1932, and January 20, 1933.
44. Meissner affidavit, in *Trial of the Major War Criminals before the International Military Tribunal* (Nuremberg, 1948), vol. 32, 3309 PS, pp. 146–53.
45. Meissner and Wilde, *Die Machtergreifung*, p. 163.
46. Ibid.
47. Michaelis, et al, *Ursachen und Folgen*, vol. 8, pp. 751–52.
48. Vogelsang, *Reichswehr Staat und NSDAP*, p. 491.
49. Ibid., pp. 486, 490, 491. Meissner and Wilde, *Die Machtergreifung*, p. 172.
50. Meissner and Wilde, *Die Machtergreifung*, pp. 172, 173.
51. Ibid., p. 177.
52. Karl Dietrich Bracher, *Die deutsche Diktatur* (Berlin: Kiepenheuer & Witsch, 1969), p. 213.
53. Eyck, *Geschichte der Weimarer Republik*, p. 582. Meissner and Wilde, *Die Machtergreifung*, p. 177.
54. Meissner and Wilde, *Die Machtergreifung*, p. 178. Eyck, *Geschichte der Weimarer Republik*, pp. 583, 584.
55. Karl Dietrich Bracher, *Die Auflösung der Weimarer Republik* (Stuttgart: Ring Verlag, 1955), p. 733. Erich Freiherr von dem Bussche-Ippenburg, "Hammerstein und Hindenburg," in *Frankfurter Allgemeine Zeitung*, February 5, 1952, p. 2.
56. Vogelsang, *Reichswehr, Staat und NSDAP*, pp. 378–79.
57. J. W. Wheeler-Bennett, *The Nemesis of Power* (London: Macmillan & Co., Ltd., 1953), p. 458.
58. Henry Picker, *Hitlers Tischgespräche im Führerhauptquartier 1941–1942* (Bonn: Athenäum-Verlag, 1951), p. 430. Major Engel, *Heeresadjutant bei Hitler 1938–1943*, Hildegard von Kotze, ed. (Stuttgart: Deutsche Verlags-Anstalt, 1974), p. 107.
59. *Augsburger Postzeitung*, February 1, 1933.
60. Thilo Vogelsang, *Reichswehr Staat und NSDAP*, citing Ott, p. 388. H. R. Berndorff, *General zwischen Ost und West* (Hamburg: Hoffman und Campe Verlag, n.d.), p. 262.
61. Eyck, *Geschichte der Weimarer Republik*, p. 590.
62. Vogelsang, *Reichswehr, Staat und NSDAP*, pp. 393, 397.
63. Kunrath Freiherr von Hammerstein, "Schleicher, Hammerstein und die Machtübernahme 1933," in *Frankfurter Hefte*, no. 3, March 1956, p. 172.

64. Vogelsang, *Reichswehr, Staat und NSDAP,* p. 398.
65. Ibid., p. 399.
66. Michaelis, et al, *Ursachen und Folgen,* vol. 8, p. 766.

CHAPTER 10: CONCLUSION: THE HAPPENING

1. Max Domarus, *Hitler* (Neustadt a.d. Aisch: Verlagsdruckerei Schmidt, 1962), vol. 1, pp. 68–90.
2. W. N. Medlicott, D. Dakin, and M. E. Lambert, eds., *Documents on British Foreign Policy 1919–1939* (London: Her Majesty's Stationery Office, 1976), series 1A, vol. 7, p. 259.
3. Werner E. Mosse, with the collaboration of Arnold Pauker, *Entscheidungsjahr 1932.* (Tübingen: J. C. B. Mohr, 1965).

r

Sources Cited

BOOKS AND ARTICLES

Absolon, Rudolf. *Die Wehrmacht im Dritten Reich.* 3 Vols. Boppard am Rhein: Harald Boldt Verlag, 1969, 1971, 1975.

Adler-Rudel, S. *Ost Juden in Deutschland, 1880–1940.* Tübingen: J.C.B. Mohr, 1959.

Albertini, Luigi. *The Origins of the War of 1914.* 3 Vols. Translated and edited by Isabella M. Massey. London: Oxford University Press, 1965.

Bailey, Thomas A., and Ryan, Paul B. *The Lusitania Disaster.* New York: Free Press, 1975.

Banuls, André. "Ein völkisches Blatt aus Hitlers Schulzeit" in *Vierteljahrshefte für Zeitgeschichte,* April 1970, pp. 196–203.

Berndorff, H. R. *General zwischen Ost und West.* Hamburg: Hoffmann und Campe Verlag, n.d.

Bloch, Eduard. "My Patient Hitler" in *Collier's,* March 15 and 21, 1941.

Blum, John Morton. *Woodrow Wilson and the Politics of Morality.* Boston: Little Brown, 1956.

Borchard, Edwin, and Lage, William Potter. *Neutrality for the United States.* New Haven: Yale University Press, 1940.

Böttcher, Helmuth M. *Walther Rathenau.* Bonn: Athenäum-Verlag, 1958.

Bracher, Karl Dietrich. *Die Auflösung der Weimarer Republik.* Stuttgart: Ring Verlag, 1955.

———. *Die deutsche Diktatur.* Berlin: Studien-Bibliothek, Kiepenheuer & Witsch, 1969.

Bracher, Karl Dietrich; Sauer, Wolfgang; and Schulz, Gerhard. *Die national-sozialistische Machtergreifung.* Cologne: Westdeutscher Verlag, 1962.

Brüning, Heinrich. *Memoiren 1918–1934.* Stuttgart: Deutsche Verlags-Anstalt, 1970.

Buckreis, Adam. *Politik des 20. Jahrhunderts.* Nuremberg: Panorama-Verlag, n.d.

von Bülow, Bernhard, Fürst. *Denkwürdigkeiten.* Berlin: Verlag Ullstein, 1930.

von dem Bussche-Ippenburg, Erich Freiherr. "Hammerstein und Hindenburg" in *Frankfurter Allgemeine Zeitung,* February 5, 1952.

Carrington, C. E. "National Self Determination" in *Modern Age,* Vol. XI, No. 3, pp. 247–58.

Carsten, Francis L. *Reichswehr und Politik 1918–1933.* Köln: Kiepenheuer & Witsch, 1964.

Cecil, Lamar. *Albert Ballin.* Princeton: Princeton University Press, 1968.

Class, Heinrich. *Deutsche Geschichte von "Einhart"* (pseudonym) Leipzig: Theodor Weicher, 1923.

D'Abernon, Viscount. *Versailles to Rapallo.* Garden City, N.Y.: Doubleday, Doran & Co., 1929.

Davidson, Eugene. *The Nuremberg Fallacy.* New York: Macmillan, 1973.

———. *The Trial of the Germans.* New York: Macmillan, 1966.

[389]

Demeter, Karl. *Das Deutsche Offizierkorps in Gesellschaft und Staat 1650–1945.* Frankfurt am Main: Bernard & Graefe Verlag, 1962.

Deuerlein, Ernst, ed. *Der Aufstieg der NSDAP 1919–1933 in Augenzeugenberichten.* Düsseldorf: Karl Rauch Verlag, 1968.

———. "Hitlers Eintritt in die Politik und die Reichswehr" in *Vierteljahrshefte für Zeitgeschichte,* April 1959, pp. 177–227.

Diels, Rudolf. *Lucifer Ante Portas.* Zurich: Interverlag A.-G., n.d.

Dietrich, Otto. *Mit Hitler in die Macht.* Munich: Franz Eher, 1938.

Documents on British Foreign Policy 1919–1939. First Series, vols. 1–6; Second Series, vols. 1–7; Third Series, vols. 1–10 edited by E. L. Woodward and R. Butler. First Series, vols. 7–11; Second Series, vol. 8 edited by R. Butler and J. P. T. Bury. Series IA edited by W. N. Medlicott, D. Dakin, and M. E. Lambert. London: Her Majesty's Stationery Office, 1947–1975.

"Dokumentation zum Sturz Brünings" in *Vierteljahrshefte für Zeitgeschichte,* July 1953, pp. 261–88.

"Dokumentation zur Politik Schleichers gegenüber der NSDAP 1932" in *Vierteljahrshefte für Zeitgeschichte,* January 1958, pp. 87–118.

Domarus, Max. *Hitler.* 2 Vols. Neustadt a.d. Aisch: Schmidt, 1962.

"Eine Denkschrift Otto Hoetzschs vom 5. November 1918" in *Vierteljahrshefte für Zeitgeschichte,* July 1973, pp. 337–53.

Engel, Major. *Heeresadjutant bei Hitler 1938–1943.* Edited by Hildegard von Kotze. Stuttgart: Deutsche Verlags-Anstalt 1974.

Die Entwicklung der Reparationfrage. 2. Ausgabe, Berlin, N. A. Berlin: Zentral Verlag, 1924.

Epstein, Klaus. *Matthias Erzberger.* Princeton, N.J.: Princeton University Press, 1959.

Erfurth, Waldemar. *Die Geschichte des deutschen Generalstabes von 1918–1945.* Göttingen: Musterschmidt Verlag, 2nd edition, 1960.

Erger, Johannes. *Der Kapp-Lüttwitz Putsch.* Düsseldorf: Droste Verlag, 1967.

Eschenburg, Theodor. "Franz von Papen" in *Vierteljahrshefte für Zeitgeschichte,* April 1953, pp. 153–70.

Eyck, Erich. *Geschichte der Weimarer Republik.* Vol. 2. Stuttgart: Eugen Rentsch Verlag, 1956.

Fay, Sidney B. *The Origins of the World War.* 2 Vols. New York: Free Press, 1966.

Ferrell, Robert H. *Peace in Their Time.* New Haven: Yale University Press, 1952.

Fest, Joachim C. *Hitler.* Berlin: Propyläen, 1973.

Fiederlein, Friedrich Martin. *Der deutsche Osten und die Regierungen Brüning, Papen, Schleicher.* Typescript. Würzburg, 1966.

Foertsch, Hermann. *Schuld und Verhängnis.* Stuttgart: Deutsche Verlags-Anstalt, 1951.

François-Poncet, André. *Souvenirs d'une Ambassade à Berlin.* Paris: Flammarion, 1946.

Fuller, J. F. C., Major General. *War and Western Civilization 1832–1932.* London: Duckworth, 1932.

Gebhardt, Bruno. *Handbuch der deutschen Geschichte*. 9th edition. 4 Vols. Stuttgart: Union Verlag, 1970.

Gessler, Otto. *Reichswehrpolitik in der Weimarer Zeit*. Stuttgart: Deutsche Verlags-Anstalt, 1958.

Geyer, Dietrich. "Sowjetrussland und die deutsche Arbeiterbewegung 1918–1932" in *Vierteljahrshefte für Zeitgeschichte*, January 1976, pp. 4–37.

Goebbels, Joseph. *Vom Kaiserhof zur Reichskanzlei*. Munich: Franz Eher, 1937.

Görlitz, Walter. *Der deutsche Generalstab*. Frankfurt am Main: Verlag der Frankfurter Hefte, n.d.

————. *Gustav Stresemann*. Heidelberg: Aehren Verlag, 1947.

————. *Hindenburg*. Bonn: Athenäum, 1953.

Gregory, Ross. *Walter Hines Page*. Lexington, Ky.: The University of Kentucky Press, 1970.

Greiner, Joseph. *Das Ende des Hitler-Mythos*. Vienna: Amalthea, 1947.

Grey, Viscount of Fallodon. *Twenty Five Years*. 2 Vols. New York: Frederick Stokes, 1925.

Hale, Oron James. "Adolf Hitler: Taxpayer" in *The American Historical Review*, Vol. 60, July 1955, pp. 830–42.

von Hammerstein, Kunrath Freiherr. "Schleicher, Hammerstein und die Machtübernahme 1933" in *Frankfurter Hefte*, No. 3, March 1956, pp. 11–18.

Handbuch zur deutschen Militärgeschichte 1648–1939. Books I, II, and V edited by Hans Meier-Welcker and Wolfgang von Groote. Books IV-1 and IV-2 edited by Friedrich Forstmeier and Hans Meier-Welcker. Frankfurt am Main: Bernard & Graefe Verlag für Wehrwesen, 1964–1976.

Hanisch, Reinhold. "I Was Hitler's Buddy" in *New Republic*, April 5, 12, 19, 1939.

Hantsch, Hugo. *Die Geschichte Oesterreichs*. 2 Vols. Vienna: Verlag Styria, 1968.

Hertzmann, Lewis. *DNVP*. Lincoln, Nebraska: University of Nebraska Press, 1963.

Hindenburg, Generalfeldmarshall von. *Aus meinem Leben*. Leipzig: Verlag von S. Hirzel, 1920.

Hitler, Adolf. *Mein Kampf*. 2 Vols. Munich: Franz Eher, 1927.

"Hitlers Handschrift und Masers Leserfehler" in *Vierteljahrshefte für Zeitgeschichte*, July 1973, pp. 332–35.

Hoffmann, General Max. *Der Krieg der versäumten Gelegenheiten*. Munich: Verlag für Kulturpolitik, 1923.

Höhn, Reinhard. *Die Armee als Erziehungsschule der Nation*. Bad Harzburg: Verlag für Wissenschaft, Wirtschaft und Technik, 1963.

Horkenbach, Cuno, ed. *Das Deutsche Reich*. Berlin: Verlag für Presse, Wirtschaft und Politik, 1930.

International Military Tribunal, Nuremberg. *Nazi Conspiracy and Aggression*. 12 Vols. and supplements. Washington: United States Government Printing Office, 1946–1948.

Jasper, Gotthard. "Aus den Prozessen gegen die Erzberger-Mörder" in *Viertel-jahrshefte für Zeitgeschichte*, October 1962, pp. 430–53.

Jenks, William A. *Vienna and the Young Hitler*. New York: Columbia University Press, 1960.

Jetzinger, Franz. *Hitlers Jugend*. Vienna: Europa-Verlag, 1956.

Johnston, William M. *The Austrian Mind*. Berkeley: University of California Press, 1972.

Kater, Michael H. "Zur Soziographie der Frühen NSDAP" in *Vierteljahrshefte für Zeitgeschichte*, April 1971, pp. 124–59.

Kessler, Harry. *In the Twenties*. New York: Holt, Rinehart, Winston, 1971.

Kessler, Harry Graf. *Tagebücher 1918–1937*. Frankfurt am Main: Insel-Verlag, 1961.

———. *Walther Rathenau*. Berlin: Verlagsanstalt Hermann Klemm, 1928.

Keynes, John Maynard. *The Economic Consequences of the Peace*. New York: Harcourt, Brace and Rowe, 1920.

Knieriem, August von. *The Nuremberg Trials*. Chicago: Regnery, 1959.

Kolb, Eberhard. *Die Arbeiterräte in der deutschen Innenpolitik*. Düsseldorf: Droste Verlag, 1962.

Krummacher, F. A., and Wucher, Albert, eds. *Die Weimarer Republik*. Munich: Verlag Kurt Desch, 1965.

Kubizek, August. *Young Hitler*. London: Allan Wingate Ltd., 1954.

Lamm, Hans. *Walther Rathenau*. Hannover: Niedersächsischen Landeszentrale, 1968.

Lansing, Robert. *The Peace Negotiations*. Boston: Houghton-Mifflin, 1921.

Liebe, Werner. *Die Deutschnationale Volkspartei 1918–1924*. Düsseldorf: Droste-Verlag, 1956.

Loebe, Paul. *Erinnerungen eines Reichstagspräsidenten*. Berlin: Arani, 1949.

Mann, Golo. *Deutsche Geschichte des 19. und 20. Jahrhunderts*. Frankfurt am Main: Fischer Verlag, 1962.

Mann, Thomas. "Betrachtungen eines Unpolitischen" in *Reden und Aufsätze*. Oldenburg: Fischer, 1960.

Maser, Werner. *Adolf Hitler*. Munich: Bechtle Verlag, 1971.

———. *Hitlers Mein Kampf*. Munich: Bechtle Verlag, 1966.

———. *Hitlers Briefe und Notizen*. Düsseldorf: Econ Verlag, 1973.

Meissner, Hans Otto, and Wilde, Harry. *Die Machtergreifung*. Stuttgart: J. G. Cotta'sche Buchhandlung, 1958.

Meissner, Otto. *Staatssekretär unter Ebert-Hindenburg-Hitler*. Hamburg: Hoffmann und Campe Verlag, 1950.

———, Document Book #1. Institut für Zeitgeschichte, Munich, Germany.

Michaelis, Herbert, and Schraepler, Ernst, eds., with the assistance of Günther Scheel. *Ursachen und Folgen*. 23 vols. Berlin: Herbert Wendler & Co., n.d.

Militärgeschichtliches Forschungsamt, ed. *Die Generalstäbe in Deutschland 1871–1945*. Stuttgart: Deutsche Verlags-Anstalt, 1962.

Mitchell, David. *1919–Red Mirage*. New York: Macmillan, 1970.

Morgan, J. H. *German Atrocities—An Official Investigation*. New York: E. P. Dutton, 1916.

Mosse, Werner E., and Pauker, Arnold. *Entscheidungsjahr 1932.* Tübingen: J. C. B. Mohr, 1965.

Niekisch, Ernst. *Gewagtes Leben.* Köln: Kiepenheuer und Witsch, 1958.

Noske, Gustav. *Von Kiel bis Kapp.* Berlin: Verlag für Politik und Wirtschaft, 1920.

Nowak, Karl Friedrich. *Chaos.* Munich: Verlag für Kulturpolitik, 1923.

Orth, Wilhelm. *Walther Rathenau und Der Geist von Rapallo.* Berlin: Buchverlag der Morgen, 1962.

von Papen, Franz. *Der Wahrheit eine Gasse.* Munich: Paul List Verlag, 1952.

———. *Vom Scheitern einer Demokratie 1930–1933.* Mainz: Hase & Koehler Verlag, 1968.

Phelps, Reginald H. "Hitler als Parteiredner im Jahre 1920" in *Vierteljahrshefte für Zeitgeschichte,* July 1963, pp. 274–330.

Picker, Dr. Henry. *Hitlers Tischgespräche im Führerhauptquartier 1941–42.* Bonn: Athenäum-Verlag, 1951.

Pritzkoleit, Kurt. *Das kommandierte Wunder.* Munich: Verlag Kurt Desch, 1959.

Pryce-Jones, David. *Unity Mitford: A Quest.* London: Weidenfeld and Nicolson, 1976.

von Rabenau, Friedrich. *Seeckt—Aus seinem Leben.* Leipzig: Hase und Koehler, 1940.

Raeder, Erich. *Mein Leben.* Tübingen: Verlag Fritz Schlichtenmeyer, 1956.

Rassow, Peter. *Deutsche Geschichte im Überblick.* Stuttgart: Metzlersche Verlagsbuchhandlung, 1973.

Rathenau, Walther. *Walther Rathenau in Brief und Bild.* Berlin: Verlag Annedore Leber, 1967.

Read, James Morgan. *Atrocity Propaganda 1914–1919.* New Haven: Yale University Press, 1941.

Reck-Malleczewen, Friedrich Percyval. *Tagebuch eines Verzweifelten.* Stuttgart: Goverts, 1966. English-language edition: *Diary of a Man in Despair.* Translated by Paul Rubens. New York: Macmillan, 1970.

Recktenwald, Johann. *Woran hat Hitler gelitten?* Munich: Rheinhardt, 1963.

Remak, Joachim. *The Origins of World War I.* New York: Holt, Rinehart and Winston, 1967.

Riezler, Kurt. *Tagebücher, Aufsätze, Dokumente.* Göttingen: Vandenhoeck & Ruprecht, 1972.

Rittau, Martin. *Militärstrafgesetzbuch.* Berlin: Walter de Gruyter & Co., 1940.

Ritter, Gerhard. *Staatskunst und Kriegshandwerk.* Vols. 3 and 4. Munich: Verlag Oldenbourg, 1964.

———. *The Sword and the Scepter.* Translated by Heinz Norden. Vols. 1 and 2. Coral Gables: University of Miami Press, 1969.

Roos, Hans. "Die Präventivkriegspläne Pilsudskis von 1933" in *Vierteljahrshefte für Zeitgeschichte,* October 1955, pp. 344–63.

Rosinski, Herbert. *The German Army.* London: The Hogarth Press, 1939.

Rudin, Harry R. *Armistice 1918.* New Haven: Yale University Press, 1944.

von Salomon, Ernst. *Der Fragebogen.* Hamburg: Rowohlt Verlag, 1951.

Schlange-Schoeningen, Hans. *The Morning After.* Translated by Ed Fitzgerald. London: Victor Gollancz Ltd., 1948.

Schueddekopf, Otto-Ernst. *Das Heer und die Republik.* Hannover: Norddeutsche Verlagsanstalt O. Goedel, 1955.

Schüssel, Therese. *Das Werden Österreichs.* Vienna: Verlag für Geschichte und Politik, 1968.

Schulthess' Europäischer Geschichtskalender. Munich: C. H. Beck'sche Verlagsbuchhandlung, 1914–1942.

Schwarz, Albert. *Die Weimarer Republik.* Konstanz: Akademische Verlagsgesellschaft Athenaion, 1958.

Schwerin von Krosigk, Lutz Graf. *Es geschah in Deutschland.* Tübingen & Stuttgart: Rainer Wunderlich Verlag Hermann Leins, 1951.

Scott, James Brown. *President Wilson's Foreign Policy.* London: Oxford University Press, 1918.

von Seeckt, Hans. *Hans von Seeckt—Aus meinem Leben.* Edited by Friedrich von Rabenau. Leipzig: Hase & Koehler, 1938.

Seeckt Papers. Munich: Institut für Zeitgeschichte.

Severing, Carl. *Mein Lebensweg.* 2 Vols. Köln: Greven Verlag, 1950.

Seymour, Charles. *The Intimate Papers of Colonel House.* 2 Vols. Boston: Houghton Mifflin Company, 1926.

Simpson, Colin. *The Lusitania.* Boston: Little Brown, 1972.

Smith, Bradley F. *Adolf Hitler. His Family, Childhood and Youth.* Stanford: The Hoover Institution on War, Revolution and Peace, Stanford University, 1967.

Speidel, Helm. "Reichswehr und Rote Armee" in *Vierteljahrshefte für Zeitgeschichte,* January 1953, pp. 9–45.

Statistique générale de la France. *Annuaire Statistique, 1929.* Paris: 1930.

Stieve, Friedrich, ed. *Der Diplomatische Schriftwechsel Iswolskis 1911–1914.* Berlin: Deutsche Verlagsgesellschaft für Politik und Geschichte, 1925.

Stolper, G.; Häuser, K.; and Borchardt, K. *The German Economy, 1870 to the Present.* Translated by Toni Stolper. New York: Harcourt, Brace & World, 1967.

Stresemann, Gustav. *Vermächtnis.* 3 Vols. Berlin: Verlag Ullstein, 1932.

Taylor, Robert Lewis. *Winston Churchill.* Garden City, N.Y.: Doubleday, 1952.

Thyssen, Fritz. *I Paid Hitler.* New York: Farrar & Rinehart, Inc., 1941.

Titus, Charles Hickman. *Voting Behavior in the United States.* Berkeley: University of California, 1935.

Treviranus, Gottfried Reinhold. *Das Ende von Weimar.* Düsseldorf: Econ-Verlag, 1968.

Trial of the Major War Criminals before the International Military Tribunal, Nuremberg 14 November 1945–10 October 1946, 42 volumes. Nuremberg, 1947–49. (Official text in the English language.)

Turnbull, Colin. *The Mountain People.* New York: Simon & Schuster, 1972.

Tyrell, Albrecht. "Führergedanke und Gauleiterwechsel" in *Vierteljahrshefte für Zeitgeschichte,* October 1975, pp. 341–74.

Usadel, George. *Zeitgeschichte in Wort und Bild.* Oldenburg: Kultur und Aufbau Verlag, 1942.

Vogelsang, Thilo. "Die Reichswehr in Bayern und der Münchner Putsch 1923" in *Vierteljahrshefte für Zeitgeschichte,* January 1957, pp. 91–101.

———. *Reichswehr, Staat und NSDAP.* Stuttgart: Deutsche Verlags-Anstalt, 1962.

Wheeler-Bennett, John W. *The Forgotten Peace.* New York: Morrow, 1939.

———. *The Nemesis of Power.* London: Macmillan & Co., Ltd., 1953.

White, Lynn, Jr. "Technology from the Stance of a Medieval Historian" in *The American Historical Review,* vol. 79, no. 1, February 1974, pp. 1–13.

Williams, Warren E. "Die Politik der Alliierten gegenüber den Freikorps im Baltikum, 1918–1919" in *Vierteljahrshefte für Zeitgeschichte,* April 1964, pp. 147–69.

Wucher, Albert. *Die Fahne hoch.* Munich: Süddeutscher Verlag, 1963.

Zöllner, Erich. *Geschichte Österreichs.* Munich: Oldenbourg Verlag, 1966.

NEWSPAPERS

Augsburger Postzeitung
> July 26, 1919; August 10, 1919; August 19, 1919; August 29, 1919; September 2, 1919; September 10, 1919; January 17, 1920; March 14, 1922; April 17, 1923; May 1, 1923; August 17, 1923; January 22, 1924; June 11, 1924; February 1, 1933.

Berliner Tageblatt
> April 24, 1918; November 25, 1918; April 15, 1919; April 16, 1919; May 5, 1919; May 6, 1919.

Deutsche Tiroler Stimmen
> March 7, 1906; May 30, 1906; March 27, 1907; May 11, 1907.

Frankfurter Nachrichten
> May 18, 1913; June 3, 1913; June 6, 1913; June 16, 1913; July 5, 1913; July 22, 1913.

General Anzeiger
> January 5, 1920.

The German Tribune
> January 11, 1973.

L'Homme Libre
> February 11, 1923; February 27, 1923.

Lienzer Zeitung
> November 12, 1904; January 7, 1905.

Münchner Neueste Nachrichten
> June 6, 1913; June 7, 1913; June 10, 1913; June 15, 1913; June 17, 1913; February 6, 1919; January 3, 1920; January 4, 1920; January 28, 1920; January 30, 1920; February 6, 1920; March 6, 1920; March 7, 1920; December 5, 1923; December 5, 1932.

La Nation
> October 5, 1926.

Le Petit Journal
> January 21, 1924.

Le Quotidien
> January 23, 1924.

Salzburger Lokal Anzeiger
> July 7, 1902.

Salzburger Tagblatt
> January 13, 1915.

Der Scherer
> January 5, 1902.

Simplicissimus
> April 1, 1919; September 16, 1919; September 30, 1919.

Der Tiroler
> January 3, 1905.

Die Tiroler Post
> March 7, 1903; August 5, 1903; September 9, 1903; December 9, 1903; November 16, 1906.

Völkischer Beobachter
> January 27, 1933; January 28, 1933.

Vorarlberger Volksfreund
> February 4, 1905.

Index